LENINGRAD
SIEGE AND SYMPHONY

LENINGRAD

SIEGE
AND
SYMPHONY

Brian Moynahan

Atlantic Monthly Press

New York

First published in Great Britain in 2013 by Quercus Editions Ltd

PICTURE CREDITS

SECTION 1: p1 *Top:* Getty Images/UIG, *Bottom* RIA Novosti/Lebrecht Music & Arts; p2 *Top:* DeAgostini/Getty Images; p3 Endeavour London Ltd; p4 *Top:* © Bettmann/CORBIS, *Bottom:* Getty Images/AFP; p5 *Top:* © Bettmann/CORBIS, *Bottom:* Endeavour London Ltd.; p7 *Top:* © Rodchenko & Stepanova Archive, DACS, RAO, 2013, *Bottom:* Getty Images/UIG/Sovfoto; p8 *Top left:* Getty Images/UIG, *Bottom:* Photas/Tass/Press Association Images SECTION 2: p1 *Top:* Getty Images/UIG/Sovfoto; p2 *Top:* Courtesy of author; p3 *Top:* © Berliner Verlag/Archiv/dpa/Corbis; *Bottom:* © Berliner Verlag/Archiv/dpa/Corbis; p4 *Top:* akg-images, *Bottom* Endeavour London Ltd.; p5 *Top:* SCR PHOTO LIBRARY, *Bottom:* akg-images; p7 *Top:* Lebrecht Music & Arts, *Bottom:* Photas/Tass/Press Association Images; p8 *Top:* Photas/Tass/Press Association Images.

Printed in the United States of America
Published simultaneously in Canada

ISBN 978-0-8021-2316-9
eISBN 978-0-8021-9190-8

Atlantic Monthly Press
an imprint of Grove/Atlantic, Inc.
154 West 14th Street
New York, NY 10011

Distributed by Publishers Group West

www.groveatlantic.com

14 15 16 17   10 9 8 7 6 5 4 3 2 1

FOR
TILLY
WITH LOVE

Contents

Dramatis Personae

Akhmatova, Anna (1889–1966) Poet of genius, whose 'Requiem' is a masterpiece of the agonies of the Terror. Her first husband was shot by the secret police. Her son and her partner Nikolay Punin were sent to the camps. A friend of Shostakovich, to whom she dedicated verses.

Berggolts, Olga (1910–1975) Poet of rare power. Arrested in the Terror in 1936, beaten during interrogation and lost the child she was carrying stillborn. During the Siege, her broadcasts on Radio Leningrad stiffened morale in the darkest months.

Beria, Lavrenti (1899–1953) Head of the NKVD 1938–1953. A sadist and rapist. Suffered the same eventual fate, of torture and execution, as his predecessor.

Bogdanov-Berezovsky, Valerian (1903–71) Composer and musicologist, studied at the Conservatoire. Close friend of Shostakovich, particularly in the 1920s. Siege diarist.

Eliasberg, Karl Ilyich (1907–1978) Conductor of the Leningrad Radio Committee Orchestra. 'We'll never play this', he said, when the score of the Seventh was flown into the besieged city. He had lost more than half his players over the winter, to hunger and shell fire, and only special rations kept him alive. The premiere was a triumph. After the war, Eliasberg was cruelly ignored as the Leningrad Philharmonia, and its conductor, Yevgeny Mravinsky, returned from their evacuation in Siberia.

Glazunov, Alexander (1865–1936) Composer and head of the Conservatoire from 1906–28 (during the name changes from St Petersburg to wartime Petrograd to post-1924 Leningrad). Taught and much admired young Shostakovich, arranging special rations for him during the civil war hunger. Emigrated to Paris in 1928.

Glikman, Isaak (1911–2003) Close and trusted friend of Shosta-kovich, acting almost as a private secretary at times, with vigorous correspondence between them. Critic and professor at the Leningrad Conservatoire.

Glinka, Vladislav Mikhailovich (1903–1983) Elegant scholar, curator and archivist at the Hermitage museum in Leningrad, and survivor of a distinguished Imperial family.

Inber, Vera (1890–1972) Daughter of a publisher, partly educated in Paris. Writer of prose and poetry, and Siege diarist who broadcast her poems on Radio Leningrad.

Izvekov, Boris (1891–1942) Professor, head of Geophysics at Leningrad Technical University, and a leading climatologist. Arrested by the NKVD on 3 February 1942, interrogated on the 'conveyor', sentenced to death for counter-revolution and treason.

Kharms, Daniil (1905–1942) Surrealist, absurdist and short story writer of wit and fantasy. Arrested in 1931, and released, but in hunger and poverty thereafter, able to write only for children's magazines. Arrested again, for 'treason', in 1941 and died of starvation in prison.

Khachaturian, Aram (1903–1978) With Shostakovich and Sergei Prokofiev, one of the trio of great Soviet composers to be condemned for 'formalism'.

Krukov, Andrei (1929–) Professor and musicologist. Kept a diary as a schoolboy in Leningrad during the Siege. The leading authority on the premiere of the Seventh.

Kruzkhov, N.F. (Unknown) Interrogator at the Bolshoi Dom with Leningrad NKVD.

Mayakovsky, Vladimir (1899–1930) Futurist poet, playwright, actor. In 1929, working with the director Vsevolod Meyerhold, Shostakovich wrote the music for his play, *The Bedbug*. Mayakovsky shot himself the following year.

Meretskov, Kiril (1897–1968) General, army commander, and survivor. Arrested at the outbreak of war, tortured, 'confessed' implicating others whom Beria had shot. Released from prison to command the Fourth Army outside Leningrad. Retook Tikhvin in December 1941, but failed to prevent the slaughter of Second Shock Army on the Volkhov in the spring and summer 1942.

Meyerhold, Vsevelod (1874–1940) Actor and theatre director of immense variety and power. Plucked young Shostakovich from Leningrad in 1928, whilst they worked on his opera *The Nose*, he and his wife, the actress Zinaida Raikh, putting him up in their Moscow flat. Defended the composer from the attacks on *Lady Macbeth*. Arrested, tortured and shot. Zinaida Raikh was murdered.

Mravinsky, Yevgeny (1903–88) Conductor, inexperienced and little known before making his name after conducting the Leningrad Philharmonia in Shostakovich's tumultuously applauded Fifth Symphony. Evacuated with the Philharmonia to Siberia during the war.

Oborin, Len (1907–74) Close friend of Shostakovich in their student years. Pianist and composer.

Shostakovich, Mariya Dmitrievna (1903–1973) Composer's elder sister. 'Our whole world crumbled around us in one night', she said when the NKVD came for her husband, Vsevolod Frederiks, in 1936. An outstanding physicist, he was sent to the camps where, his health ruined, he died. Mariya herself was exiled from Leningrad. Sofiya Mikhailova Vazar, the composer's mother-in-law, was also arrested.

Shostakovich, Sofiya Vasilyevna (1878–1955) Composer's mother. Siberian born, she had danced for the tsarevich as a young girl. A pianist of quality, she started teaching her son to play on his ninth birthday.

Shostakovich, Zoya Dmitrievna (1908–1990) Composer's younger sister.

Slonim, Ilya (1906–1973) Sculptor, and friend of Shostakovich, who worked on a bust of the composer whilst he was working on the Seventh.

Sollertinsky, Ivan (1902–1944) Linguist, classicist and wit, artistic director of the Philharmonia, whose pre-concert talks often charmed audiences more than the music. A kindred spirit of the composer – 'an insane friendship', Shostakovich's younger sister said, 'laughing, joking . . .'

Tukhachevsky, Mikhail (1893–1937) Marshal, and outstanding military strategist. Himself an amateur violin-maker, and violinist, a great admirer of Shostakovich, and a warm friend. His arrest, torture and execution placed the composer in great danger.

Yagoda, Genrikh (1891–1938) Head of the NKVD 1934–36. In Leningrad with Stalin immediately after the murder of Kirov in December 1941 unleashed the Terror on the city. Supervised the show trials of the Old Bolsheviks before himself being executed after his own show trial.

Yezhov, Nikolai (1895–1940) Head of the NKVD 1936-1938. Green-eyed, five feet tall, the 'poison dwarf.' The Terror was at its worst in his years, and is still known as the *Yezhovshchina*, the Yezhov affair. As he had his predecessor tortured and shot, so he was dealt with by his successor.

Zhdanov, Andrei (1896–1948) Became the absolute Party boss in Leningrad from the Kirov murder in 1934 until after the war. Zhdanov was interested in music – the secret police chief Lavrenti Beria called him 'the Pianist' – much to Shostakovich's peril. He hounded the composer as a 'formalist', a charge that could lead to execution or the camps.

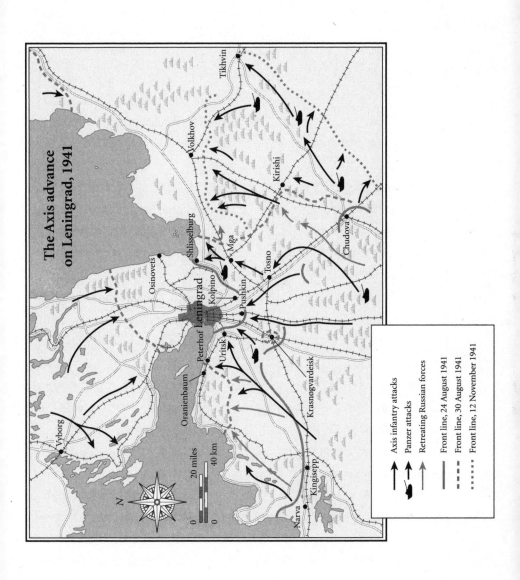

The Axis advance
on Leningrad, 1941

Tikhvin

Volkhov

Kirishi

Chudova

Shlisselburg

Mga

Osinovets

Tosno

Leningrad

Peterhof

Kolpino

Pushkin

Uritsk

Krasnogvardeisk

Oranienbaum

Vyborg

Kingisepp

Narva

20 miles

40 km

0

0

N

Axis infantry attacks

Panzer attacks

Retreating Russian forces

Front line, 24 August 1941

Front line, 30 August 1941

Front line, 12 November 1941

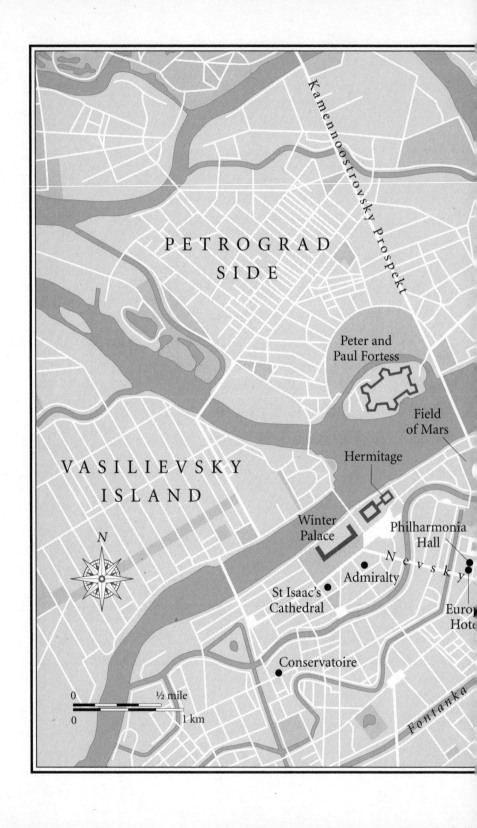

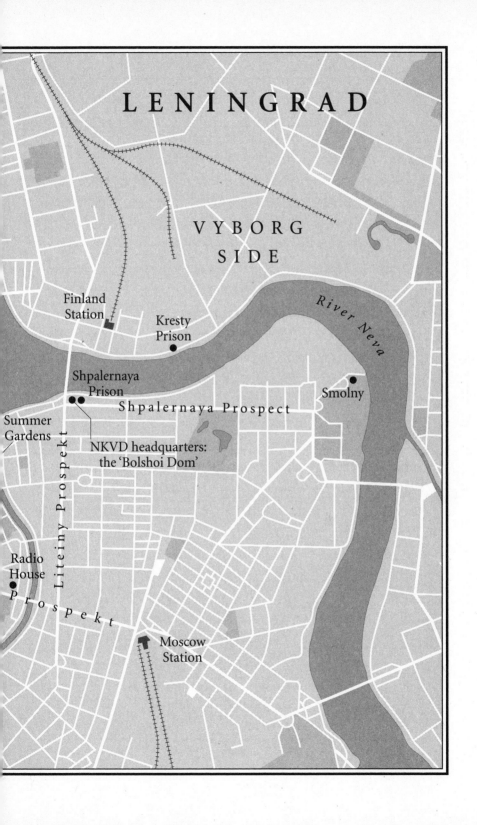

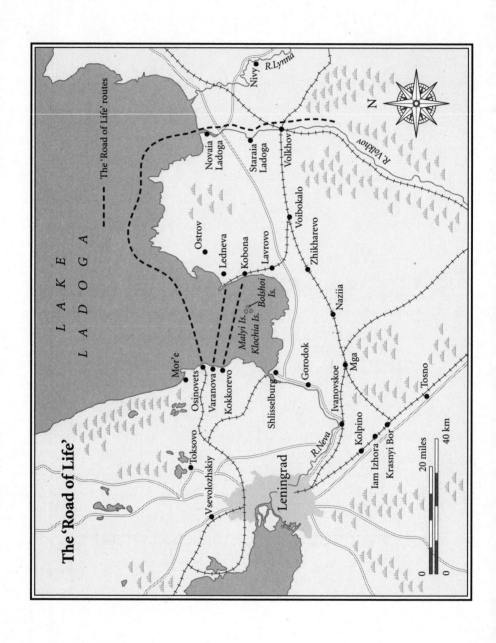

The 'Road of Life'

- - - - The 'Road of Life' routes

LAKE LADOGA

R.Lynna
Nivy
Novaia Ladoga
Staraia Ladoga
Volkhov
R.Volkhov
Voibokalo
Ostrov
Ledneva
Kobona
Lavrovo
Zhikharevo
Malyi Is.
Klochia Is.
Bolshoi Is.
Naziia
Mor'e
Osinovets
Varanova
Kokkorevo
Gorodok
Mga
Tosno
Shlisselburg
Ivanovskoe
Toksovo
Vsevolozhskiy
R.Neva
Kolpino
Krasnyi Bor
Iam Izhora
Leningrad

20 miles
40 km
0
0

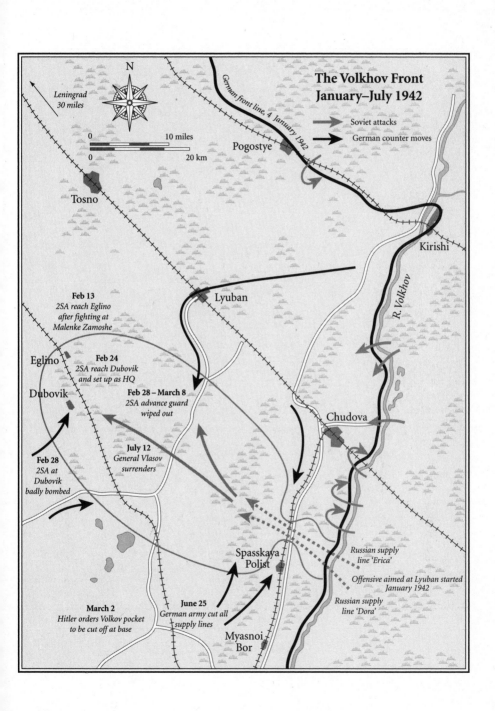

The Volkhov Front
January–July 1942

→ Soviet attacks
→ German counter moves

German front line, 4 January 1942

N

Leningrad
30 miles

0   10 miles
0   20 km

Pogostye

Tosno

Kirishi

R. Volkhov

Feb 13
*2SA reach Eglino
after fighting at
Malenke Zamoshe*

Lyuban

Eglino

Feb 24
*2SA reach Dubovik
and set up as HQ*

Dubovik

Feb 28 – March 8
*2SA advance guard
wiped out*

Feb 28
*2SA at
Dubovik
badly bombed*

July 12
*General Vlasov
surrenders*

Chudova

Spasskaya
Polist

*Russian supply
line 'Erica'*

*Offensive aimed at Lyuban started
January 1942*

March 2
*Hitler orders Volkov pocket
to be cut off at base*

June 25
*German army cut all
supply lines*

Myasnoi
Bor

*Russian supply
line 'Dora'*

Ouvertyura

Overture

There has never been a performance to match it. Pray God, there never will.

German guns were less than seven miles from the Philharmonia Hall as Dmitri Dmitrievich Shostakovich's Seventh Symphony was first played in the city to which he had dedicated it, in the late afternoon of Sunday, 9 August 1942. Leningrad had been besieged since the Germans cut the last land route out of the city on 14 September 1941.

Shostakovich had started writing his symphony in mid-July 1941, as the Germans began closing in. He was flown out of the city to Moscow at the beginning of October, with his wife, two young children and the first two movements of the symphony. From there they went east, to Kuibyshev on the Volga.

After he had completed it – and christened it the 'Leningrad Symphony' – it was played to huge acclaim in Russia, in London, and New York. At the performance in Moscow, the writer Olga Berggolts watched the slight and still boyish composer rise to a torrent of applause, and bow. 'I looked at him,' she wrote, 'a small frail man in big glasses, and I thought: "This man is more powerful than Hitler."'

The music's greatest resonance, though, its truest defiance of the Nazis – the Russians called them 'the Hitlerites' – could come only when it was played in battered and bleeding Leningrad itself. Orders were given that, 'by any means', this must take place.

The score was flown into Leningrad over German lines, the aircraft making a final dash at wavetop level over Lake Ladoga. This vast expanse of water to the east of the city was its only link with the 'mainland', as Leningraders called the rest of Russia, by truck over the ice in winter, by barge after the icemelt.

'When I saw it,' said Karl Eliasberg, who was to conduct the premiere, 'I thought, "We'll never play this." It was four thick volumes of music.' It is indeed a colossal work: 252 pages of score, 2,500 pages of orchestral parts, an hour and twenty minutes long. It demanded an orchestra of 105 musicians, battalions of strings among them. What most worried Eliasberg, though, were the demands on woodwind and brass in a starving city of ravaged lungs.

The Leningrad Philharmonia, the city's leading orchestra, was gone. It had been evacuated to safety in Novosibirsk, in Siberia, before the siege began. Its conductor Yevgeny Mravinsky, who had undertaken the premieres of Shostakovich's Fifth and Sixth, had gone with it. The city's second string, the Radio orchestra, under the Radiokomitet, the Radio Committee, and Eliasberg, was all that remained.

Over the winter of 1941–42, it had lost more than half its players. The survivors were weak and traumatized. A quarter of a million died in the city in three months, of hunger and hypothermia, with a ration of less than a slice of adulterated bread a day, and temperatures of minus 28 degrees Celsius. German shells and bombs took others. Some were dragged, on children's gaily painted sledges, to mass graves. Sappers blasted pits in the frozen earth with explosives, and the bodies were thrown in. They were the lucky ones.

With spring, the snow began to melt. It revealed the corpses of those who remained in the streets. Some were cannibalized. 'Severed legs with meat chopped off them,' said the clarinettist Viktor Kozlov. 'Bits of body with breasts cut off. They'd been buried all winter, but now they were there for all the city to see how it had stayed alive.' A neighbour pounded on the door of Ksenia Matus, an oboist, and begged her to let her in. Her husband was trying to kill and eat her.

Worse awaited her when she went to the first rehearsal of the Seventh, in the Radiokom studios. 'I nearly fell over with shock,' she says. 'Of an orchestra of a hundred people there were only the fifteen of us left. I didn't recognize them. They were like skeletons . . .' Eliasberg raised his arms to begin. No reactions. 'The musicians were trembling. The trumpeter didn't have the breath to play his solo. Silence. "Why don't you play?" Eliasberg asked. "I'm sorry, maestro. I haven't the strength in my lungs."'

Eliasberg scoured the front lines for other musicians. He found them in the remnants of regimental bands. The trombonist Mikhail Parfionov was one of them. He was given a special ID card marked 'Eliasberg's Orchestra' so that he was not shot as a deserter when he made his way through the ruined city to rehearsals. If the sirens sounded, he had to leave the rehearsal studio and return to serve his anti-aircraft gun. Nikolai Nosov, a former trumpet-player in a jazz band with no experience of classical music, was horrified to find himself playing the symphony's difficult trumpet solo. The lead trumpeter suffered a pulmonary oedema, and was too weak to play.

'We'd start rehearsing and get dizzy,' said Kozlov. 'Our heads were spinning when we blew. The symphony was too big. People were falling over. We might talk to the person sitting next to us. We spoke only of food and hunger, never music.' If a musician was late, or played badly, he lost his bread ration. A man was late one afternoon because in the morning he had buried his wife. Eliasberg said that this was no excuse, and the man went hungry.

'Some of the orchestra died,' says Parfionov. 'I recall a flautist called Karelsky. People were dying like flies, so why not the orchestra? Hunger and cold everywhere. When you are hungry, you are cold however warm it is. Sometimes people just fell over onto the floor while they were playing.'

Summer came. 'At last, leaves, blades of grass, and the will to live':
but the Germans held the city as tightly as ever. Attempts to dislodge
them failed in a welter of blood. A bridgehead the Russians had held
at desperate cost, on the east bank of the Neva river, fell after repeated
assaults so intense that, to this day, nothing grows on the pitted surface
but rank tussock grass.

An Army, the Second Shock, was meeting its Calvary in the pine
forests and peaty swamps of sphagnum moss to the south. Like the
city it was trying to relieve, the Army was surrounded, bludgeoned and
starving. A final break-out attempt was made on 28 June. None made it.
That day, the Germans took 20,000 prisoners: 'many were wounded . . .
and barely retained the semblance of human beings.' The Red Army
lost 149,000 dead in this attempt to lift the siege, for nothing. 'A giant
forest of stumps stretched out to the horizon where the dense woods
had once stood,' a German sergeant-major recorded. 'The Soviet dead,
or rather parts of their bodies, carpeted the churned-up ground. The
stench was indescribably ghastly.'

As the pale northern sun lit the July nights, Eliasberg continued
his search for musicians. A machine-gunner, M. Smolyak, had played
in a dance band in a cinema before joining up. He was astonished to
receive formal orders detaching him from his unit. 'I was put under the
Radiokomitet to perform in the Seventh Symphony by D. D. Shostakovich,' he said. 'Once again, I was "armed" with the trombone.'

The orchestra moved to the Philharmonia Hall. They began playing
small sections of the symphony. Slowly they added more. 'But we never
played the whole thing until a dress rehearsal three days before the
concert,' says Matus. 'It was the first and only time we had the strength
to practise it from beginning to end.'

The city seemed in keener peril than ever. Far to the south, after
eight months of bombardment, the ruins of Sevastopol had fallen to the
Germans. Hitler ordered five crack divisions – their victory instilling

in them 'the belief that we could accomplish almost anything' – to be transferred from the Crimea to Leningrad. Siege was no longer enough for him. He wanted the city stormed, in an operation code-named Nordlicht, Northern Light. He was confident. Leningrad, he declared, over his vegetarian lunch on 6 August, 'must disappear utterly from the face of the earth. Moscow, too. Then the Russians will retire into Siberia.'

German guns ranged across the city at will for hours each day, seeking out places where people congregated, tram stops, crossroads, factory gates when shifts changed, queues for bread rations. It seemed madness to give them a swarm of concert-goers to feast on.

But a miracle was in the making. An hour before the concert, Russian guns began laying down a ferocious barrage of counter-battery fire. It was based on an artillery fire chart as complex in its way as Shostakovich's musical score, drawn up by a brilliant Red Army gunner, Lieutenant-Colonel Sergei Selivanov,* so intimately experienced in German gun positions by now that he knew the names of some of the enemy battery commanders. The Germans took shelter in their bunkers. None of their shells hit the centre of the city for the duration of the concert.

The people who flocked to the Philharmonia wore their glad rags, perhaps for the last time. The women's stick-insect limbs were hidden beneath their pre-war concert dresses, the men in fading jackets. 'They were thin and dystrophic,' said Parfionov. 'I didn't know there could be so many people, hungry for music even as they starved. That was the moment we decided to play the best we could.'

Eliasberg wore tails. He looked a scarecrow as they flapped on his emaciated body. Members of the orchestra wore layers of clothes to stay warm. 'It was too cold to play without gloves,' says the oboist Matus. 'We wore them with the fingers cut off, like mittens.' The air temperature

---

* Selivanov was later killed by a direct hit from a German shell.

in the hall was over 75 degrees Fahrenheit, but to be cold is a classic symptom of starvation.

They began to play.

'The finale was so loud and mighty I thought we'd reached a limit and the whole thing would collapse and fall apart. Only then did I realize what we were doing and hear the grand beauty of the symphony,' says Parfionov. 'When the piece ended there was not a sound in the hall – silence. Then someone clapped at the back, and then another, and then thunder . . . Afterwards, we held each other, kissed and were happy.'

The symphony's fame circled the world. Its timing was a godsend. For the first twenty-two months of Hitler's war, as France, the Low Countries, the Balkans, were overrun, the Russians enjoyed a non-aggression pact with the Nazis. German U-boats and bombers in the Battles of Britain and the Atlantic were fuelled with Soviet oil, their crews clothed with Soviet cotton, and fed with Soviet cereals.

Together, Hitler and Stalin had dismembered Poland: the Soviets had then swallowed the Baltic states, and part of Finland. In arbitrary arrests, in the volume of executions, in the numbers slaving in labour camps, in the use of terror, the Bolsheviks – in June 1941, at least, at the moment of the German invasion – far outstripped the Nazis.

There was every reason to hold these new Soviet allies to be as godless, fanatical, and as hostile to Western values, as their erstwhile Nazi friends.

The Leningrad Symphony was the perfect antidote. The Allies wanted, badly, to believe in the Russians, in their survival, and in their decency. Their own campaigns were sagging – the United States Navy suffered its greatest ever disaster in the early hours of 9 August, losing four heavy cruisers and 1,270 men in a few minutes in the dark seas off the Pacific island of Guadalcanal, while the British were reeling from the loss of Tobruk to the German Afrika Korps – and Shostakovich's music helped to give them the reassurance they sought. Leningrad still lived, and fought, and, in drowning out the mechanical squeal and clang of the enemy's tank tracks in a creative storm of music, it seemed to the anxious watchers to confirm Russia's resilience and humanity. 'Like a great wounded snake', *Time* magazine wrote, 'dragging its slow length, it uncoils for 80 minutes . . . Its themes are exultations, agonies . . . In its last movement the triumphant brasses prophesy what Shostakovich describes as the "victory of light over darkness, of humanity over barbarism". It provided a moral redemption for Stalin and the Soviet regime.

At the heart of its first movement is an 18-bar theme with twelve accumulating repetitions. It was called the 'invasion theme', a devastating response to the Nazis that reviewers found conveyed their 'naked evil in all its stupendous arrogant inhumanity, a terrifying power overrunning Russia'. The world was spellbound by the drama.

The poet Carl Sandburg addressed Shostakovich in the *Washington Post*:

All over America . . . millions [are] listening to your music portrait of Russia in blood and shadows . . . The outside world looks on and holds its breath. And we hear about you, Dmitri Shostakovich . . . In Berlin . . . in Paris, Brussels, Amsterdam, Copenhagen, Oslo, Prague, Warsaw, wherever the Nazis have mopped up, no new symphonies . . . Your song tells us of a great singing people beyond defeat or conquest who across years to come shall pay their share and contribution to the meanings of human freedom and discipline.

The score had been copied on microfilm and flown out of Russia to Teheran. From there, it travelled by staff car to Cairo, then on to London, across Africa and round Spain and far out over the Bay of Biscay, beyond the range of German fighters based in France. In late June, to coincide with the anniversary of Hitler's onslaught on Russia, it had its Western premiere in London. Sir Henry Wood conducted at the Albert Hall.

In America, the leading conductors – Koussevitsky in Boston, Stokowski in Philadelphia, Rodzinski in Cleveland – fought for it. Arturo Toscanini in New York had NBC money behind him. He won. A thunderstorm raged as he conducted an orchestra of 110 musicians in Radio City. In its first season, the symphony was broadcast by 1,934 American radio stations, with 62 live performances.

The story of its creation – written under fire, delivered out of the besieged city – was a sensation. Shostakovich's photograph appeared on the cover of *Time*, the first time a musician had appeared there. He was wearing a fireman's helmet and uniform, looking fiercely out over the burning city. The cover line reads: 'Fireman Shostakovich. Amid bombs bursting in Leningrad, he heard the chords of victory.'

But things were not as they seemed. The famous picture of Shostakovich, for example, had been posed in a special photo-shoot before the first bombs were dropped on the city. He was too important to risk: as the siege began to bite, he had been flown out of the city.

A more crucial point escaped the world. The Russian undertones in Leningrad's symphony were as dark as the Hitlerites at the city gates. Older, too.

Even as it was being terrorized by Hitler from without, blockaded, bombed, shelled, so it was being terrorized by Stalin from within. The purges that had defined pre-war Leningrad – the arrests, interrogations, 'confessions', executions – were continuing.

Pre-war, Leningrad had been a pole of cruelty, the most defiled of all Soviet cities. Stalin had a particular hatred for the city, for the elegance of its buildings, rising in faultless lines of green and pink and blue stucco above the Neva river and the canals, for its independence of mind and its artistic genius, for its sophistication, so at odds with his own obscure origins in the stews of Tiflis, for its links with Trotsky. Leningrad was purged as no other.

With the war, the terror continued. The siege made only a technical difference: the option of exiling a prisoner to a camp in Siberia or the Arctic was no longer so easy. The Germans were in the way.

The deranged accusations, the discovery of elaborate, rambling 'plots', went on apace. The city remained in fear of its own, of fellow Russians with the purple ID cards of the secret police, the NKVD: 'You were asleep in your unheated Leningrad room, and the sharp claws of the black hand were already hovering over you.'

Informers went on informing. The interrogators were busy in the Bolshoi Dom, the NKVD's 'Big House' in the centre of the city, not fifteen minutes' walk from the Radiokom musicians and the Philharmonia Hall. One victim among many: a Lieutenant-General Ignatovsky, seen at the window of his office, overlooking the Neva, with a white handkerchief. Under torture, he 'confessed' to signalling to German agents. He gave the names of members of his 'organization'. Ignatovsky was an officer in the engineers. A score of engineers from the Technological Institute were arrested, and 'confessed'.

The cells in which they were held had been built in tsarist days to hold a single prisoner. Now each had 'ten, fourteen, even 28' awaiting execution. One of them was Konstantin Strakovich. He would survive, through a quirk, to become a post-war pioneer of turbojet engines.

The charges against him were insane: he was a ten-year-old on the date he was supposedly recruited by Ignatovsky. Strakovich's treatment was bestial. He recalled the prison doctor coming into his cell. The doctor jabbed his finger at the prisoners. 'He's a dead man! He's a dead man! He's a dead man!' It is wrong to keep them in such misery, the doctor cried to the duty gaoler: 'Better to shoot them now. Now!'

*

Shostakovich loved the city. 'An hour ago I finished scoring the second movement of my latest large orchestral composition,' he had said on radio on 17 September 1941. 'My life and work are bound up in Leningrad. It is my country, my native city and my home.'

At the heart of the Seventh was a howl at the evil washing over it. For the moment, that evil was taken to be exclusively Nazi. But Red terror had preceded it, and would outlast it. Shostakovich knew this as intimately as any. It had carried off close friends, and family, the tortured body of one dumped in a Moscow landfill, others broken in the Gulag camps. It had come, as we shall see, within the merest whisker of doing for him himself.

This difficult, complex and magnificent symphony, and the musicians who endured such horrors to play it, resisted and defied the inhumanity within Leningrad as well as without. It was Shostakovich's requiem for a noble city beset by the twin monsters of the century.

CHAPTER 1

Repressii

Terror

The Terror – to this day, the Russians speak of 'the Repression', painstakingly bland, as if the memory of their true malevolence to one another remains too much to bear – the Terror started with a murder, and a slap in the face on a railway platform.

The dead man was Sergei Kirov, the ruling Bolshevik in Leningrad. Six cities, a naval cruiser class, lakes and factories, and Leningrad's premier Ballet, were to be named in his memory. So was the great avenue where he lived, battered but aching with beauty, running from the Trinity Bridge on the Neva across the Petrogradsky district, the red granite and the soft pastels of the stucco, glowing in the cold northern light. It is back now to its tsarist name, Kamennoostrovky Prospekt, as the city itself is once more 'Peter', St Petersburg, for the Tsar who had raised it two centuries before in the marshes and frosts of the mouth of the Neva. But Kirov's apartment at No. 26–28 remains as it was when he left it on his way to work, and to his death, on 1 December 1934.

Its size alone reflected his status: eight high-ceilinged rooms, in a place where a single room, divided by sheets or curtains, housed three families. The *vertushka* telephones, linked to the Kremlin, were in banks of four in the drawing and dining rooms. The one with a direct line to Stalin was marked with a red star. In the bedroom, with twin art nouveau beds in light wood, another *vertushka* with a red star sat on the matching bedside table. Stalin liked to call him at night, Framed photographs of Lenin and Stalin enjoyed pride of place.

The rooms revealed his personal interests. He was a hunter. There was a polar bear rug (a gift), and a brown bearskin (a trophy), in the drawing room. He had two stuffed pheasants, and a large hawk, and a model of a fishing trawler named for him in recognition of his reputation as a passionate angler. His library had thousands of volumes, a globe, and the rare books that he collected. He was a gourmet in a hungry city, and the kitchen had a giant General Electric refrigerator, one of ten imported into Russia, and a deep sink in the scullery for keeping fish fresh, with stone slabs for filleting meat.

Kirov loved music. A leather-covered pass, stamped 'Number 1', entitled him to two free seats at any of the city's eight opera, ballet and dramatic theatres, at the Philharmonia concert hall, the music hall and the State circus. Despite his heavy workload, he used his pass frequently: he and his wife were childless and he had, it was said, an eye for ballerinas. His apartment had a telephone-cable link that brought him live performances of ballet and opera. He carefully kept his invitation to Box 1 in the Dress Circle at the Maly Opera for the premiere of Shostakovich's opera, *Lady Macbeth of the Mtsensk District*, on 24 January 1934. It was a treasured memento of a composer he much admired. He had a poster for the opera, too.

An aura, an affection, clung to him as it did to none other in the regime. Kirov could be cruel. As a young Red commissar in the civil war that flowed from the Revolution, he ordered the 'merciless extermination of the White Guard swine' during a rising in Astrakhan.[1] Four thousand died in the bloodletting, but it was the making of his career. He met Stalin, and, as importantly, fell out with Trotsky.

For all that, he was handsome, and open, and he made friends easily. He had run Leningrad for eight years, and his popularity was real and unforced. He was close to Stalin, closer than any other, more than a crony, bringing him a warmth and comfort after Stalin's wife Nadezhda Alliuyeva had shot herself two years before. 'My Kirich,' Stalin called him, 'my friend and brother.' On holiday, they had villas close to one another in the Crimea. They went to the *banya* (sauna baths) together – though Stalin's skin was pitted from smallpox and psoriasis, and he concealed it from most – and Stalin waited on the beach while Kirov swam.[2] On his visits to Moscow, Kirov stayed in Stalin's apartment in the Kremlin, amusing the children, who adored him, little Svetlana Stalin putting on a puppet show for him.

The two last saw each other on 28 November in Moscow. All seemed well. Stalin went personally with Kirov to his compartment on the Red Arrow express to see him off on his overnight trip back to Leningrad.

There were tensions, though. The 17th Party Congress at the start of 1934 had paid Stalin lip service as the 'ardently loved *Vozhd*', the great leader. Leon Trotsky, who had despised him, was in exile. Other senior Bolsheviks were careful to applaud him. Kirov, though, was given a standing ovation that was spontaneous and heartfelt. At the end of the Congress, Stalin's name was crossed out on at least a hundred, and perhaps as many as three hundred, of the ballot papers confirming his place on the Party's Central Committee. Just three or four of Kirov's were spoiled. The ballot papers were suppressed, but Stalin was to make his displeasure brutally clear. Of the 1,966 delegates at the Congress, 1,108 would be arrested. Two-thirds of those were to be shot, as, without exception, were those senior figures who had shown a trace of hostility or indifference to him. Leningrad suffered as no other city. All seven of its members of the Central Committee, the most powerful party organ, and the heads of all its major factories, were purged. Of 154 Leningrad delegates to the 17th Congress, only two survived to be re-elected to the 18th. Of 65 members of the city's provincial committee, just nine reappeared.

Stalin was disturbed by Kirov's popularity. He spoke of recalling him from his power base in Leningrad but Kirov resisted. Attempts were made to dislodge the head of the NKVD secret police in Leningrad, Feodor Medved, and replace him with one of Stalin's drinking cronies. Kirov liked and trusted Medved, and refused to let him go. Four NKVD men from Moscow were added unasked to Kirov's security detail, which was itself reduced.

Kirov spent the morning of 1 December at home working on a speech, before setting off for his office in the afternoon. It was in the Smolny, part convent, part school, the Institute for Noble Maidens, with a blue and gilt cathedral cascading with baroque elegance, its restrained Palladian facade picked out in white and ochre. Lenin had used it as the Bolshevik headquarters during the Revolution. The Party retained it when the government was moved to Moscow and the Kremlin.

He was with his bodyguard, Borisov, who may have been detained for a few moments by the Moscow NKVD men. Kirov walked up the main staircase, turning off into the corridor to his office when he reached the third floor. A young man, dark-haired, thin, small, let him pass and then walked behind him. Leonid Nikolayev, nervous, unstable, was a political gadfly. He had been expelled and then readmitted to the Party, blaming it for his debts and unhappy marriage. He had been found wandering in the Smolny some weeks before, with a loaded gun, but had merely been asked to leave the building.

He shot Kirov in the back of the neck with a Nagant revolver, before turning the gun on himself. An electrician close by seized him and the second bullet lodged in the ceiling. Kirov fell face down on the floor.

Three doctors were summoned. Artificial respiration failed. Stalin was informed by telephone. One of the doctors was Georgian, like Stalin, and they discussed the assassin in their mother tongue. Stalin's response was immediate. A decree was issued ordering that terrorists be executed immediately after sentencing. Later in the evening, Stalin left on a special train for Leningrad.

He arrived at about 7.30 the next morning. Medved was on the platform at the Moscow Station to meet him. Stalin struck him on the face with his gloved hand. He went on to the Smolny. The key witness, Borisov, was killed the next day, apparently in a fall from an NKVD truck. Medved and the leading NKVD men in the city were sent to the mines and labour camps of the Gulag.

Before he returned to Moscow, Stalin personally interrogated Nikolayev. It is still not clear if he ordered Kirov's murder. There were mysteries enough – the failure to arrest Nikolayev earlier, the removal of Kirov's own security men, the death of Borisov – for Valerian Kuibyshev, Stalin's principal economist, and an accomplished musician and poet, to demand an investigation. Kuibyshev was dead, officially of heart failure, within a month. His wife and brother were later shot, but, with the black humour that marked him, Stalin honoured him with burial in the Kremlin wall, as he carried Kirov's coffin at that funeral, and renamed the Volga city of Samara for him. Shostakovich was to complete the score of the Seventh Symphony in Kuibyshev.

It is certain, though, that the murder suited Stalin well. Nikolayev was tried in secret at the end of the month, and shot the same night, using the new decree. Thirteen others were also shot. A 'Leningrad centre' was identified, a nest of supporters of the exiled Leon Trotsky, to which all who displeased Stalin could be pinned. Borisov's widow was committed to an insane asylum.

Three of the small party who accompanied Stalin from Moscow were to be executed themselves. Genrikh Yagoda, the overall head of the NKVD, was shot, with his deputy, and the head of the Komsomol, (the Young Communists), Aleksander Kosarev, like Shostakovich a football fanatic, whose club, Moscow Spartak, the composer watched when he was in the capital.

A fourth man was Andrei Zhdanov. Stalin chose him to succeed Kirov in Leningrad. He was very much a survivor. For the rest of his life, he was to run the city, and to hound Shostakovich. Leningrad itself was about to be engulfed.

Dmitri Dmitrievich Shostakovich was twenty-eight. He had already composed an astonishing range of pieces: three symphonies, a brace of ballets, a piano concerto, scherzos, preludes, film scores, music for plays, orchestrations and two operas. His First Symphony, written as his graduation piece when he was nineteen, had been performed by Toscanini and Klemperer. His opera *Lady Macbeth*, which Kirov had loved so much, had brought him world renown. It played simultaneously in Leningrad and Moscow, and across Europe. Its theme, of lust and murder, was a sensation in New York, Cleveland and Philadelphia. The BBC broadcast it in London. 'The Conquest of Soviet Musical Thought', the headlines ran.

His mother had started giving him piano lessons on his ninth birthday. Sofiya Shostakovich was a fine pianist herself, a graduate of the Leningrad Conservatoire. 'We have an outstandingly gifted boy on our hands,' she said after two days. A week later, he was playing four-handed with her. He had perfect pitch, and he learned pieces instantaneously, without any need for repetition. 'The notes just stayed in my memory by themselves,' he said. 'I could also sight-read well . . . Soon after I made my first attempts at composition.'[3]

Both his parents were Siberian-born, with enough revolutionary colour in their family background to avoid easy branding as *burzhui* (bourgeois), though his mother had danced for the Tsarevich Nicholas at her school in Irkutsk. They were well-to-do now, with a dacha and a large apartment in the city – 'enormous,' his sister Mariya recalled, wistfully, of those tsarist days: 'six rooms, with another off the kitchen where the servants slept' – and his father had a car, a Russian rarity.

The young boy displayed a gift for mathematics, too, when he was sent to Maria Shidloskaya's, the school of choice of the Petrograd intelligentsia.* He was sharp and lively, and mischievous. At eleven, he went to see Glinka's *Ruslan*. The opera made 'an enormous impression on me, in a purely musical sense', independently of the drama on the stage, he said, 'most of all Ratmir's aria'.[4] He was left cold by his first symphony concert, a Beethoven cycle, a little later, but he was already set on music.

He was writing preludes for the piano at twelve. A friend remembered him playing Beethoven's C-minor sonata (No. 5) at a concert. A classmate, Irina, the daughter of Boris Kustodiev, a crippled painter of rare power and colour, recalled how he played for her father. 'A little boy with a shock of hair, he went up to my father, said hello, and handed him a long strip of paper, on which his entire repertoire was listed in a neat column,' she said. 'Then he went to the piano and played all the pieces on the list, one after the other.'[5]

At thirteen, in the autumn of 1919, he left school to enter the Conservatoire. The great grey building seemed too severe and classical for a child, an adult place that in the hungry years of the civil war that followed the Revolution was cold and damp and reeked of cabbage, the only food in enough supply. Its reputation was brilliantly lit, though, by those who had passed through: Anton Rubinstein, Rimsky-Korsakov, Tchaikovsky, Prokofiev, Diaghilev. He took to the Conservatoire, and to composing, directly.

He worked at a breakneck pace, oblivious to noise and distraction, seldom trying out a sequence at the piano. 'He wrote out his music in full score straight away,' his sister Zoya said, 'and then took his scores to lessons without even having played them.' He never needed to try

---

* His schoolmates included the sons of Leon Trotsky and Lev Kamenev. Both were his age: fortunately, perhaps, he was not close to them. Their fathers were both killed on Stalin's orders, Kamenev after a show trial in Moscow, Trotsky with an ice pick in the brain in exile in Mexico. Kamenev's boy, by then a Red Air Force pilot, was executed in July 1939. Young Lev Sedov, Trotsky's son, had died of appendicitis in Paris the year before, his bungled medical care probably contrived by Stalin's agents.

things out on the piano. He 'just sat down and wrote whatever he heard in his head, and then played it through complete on the piano'.[6] These first pieces embraced eight preludes for piano, a theme and variations for orchestra, 'Two Fables of Krylov' for mezzo-soprano, female chorus and chamber orchestra, three 'Fantastic Dances' for piano, and a suite in F-sharp minor for two pianos.

The composition of the suite, in 1922, demonstrated an obstinacy that persisted and might at any moment, if it displeased Stalin and Zhdanov, now prove lethal. It was Shostakovich's abiding misfortune that both men were fond of music, taking a personal interest in it and those who composed it. They shared a religious education, resonant in Orthodox chants, and a love of Georgian songs. They sang together. Stalin had a fine tenor voice. He liked ballet, and opera, and he went often to the Bolshoi in Moscow, where he kept a box, armoured against assassins, with a curtain that allowed him to hide his face. He enjoyed classical music on the radio, and he listened to all the new recordings, scrawling 'good . . . so-so . . . rubbish' on the sleeves. Zhdanov was a graduate of the Moscow Conservatoire. His mother was a fine pianist and taught her son to play. Lavrenti Beria, the sadist who in time became head of the NKVD, nicknamed him 'The Pianist'.

Those who did not bend to their whim, they broke. In his music, Shostakovich abandoned whole genres – ballet, opera, at grievous cost, for this was the snuffing out of a master – and he accepted that pieces, up to an entire symphony, vanished unheard for decades. But he did not bend in *how* he wrote. When his professor at the Conservatoire ordered him to rewrite the piano suite, he refused. The professor insisted, and he did so. The piece was played at a student concert. 'After the concert, I destroyed the corrected version and set about restoring the original,' he recalled later, responding to questions from Roman Gruber, the Conservatoire musicologist.[7] He thought that criticism from above, and what he called the 'dictatorship of "rules"', could wreck the creative instinct.

'It's not right to cripple people,' he said. 'Some people are more weak-willed than I am, and they can be crippled for life.'[8] Indeed they could.

His passions outside music, as a twenty-one-year-old, were for litera-ture: for Dostoevsky's *Demons*, and Gogol's *Dead Souls*, and Chekhov. 'And I adore Goethe,' he added. Next was classical ballet, then sculpture and architecture – above all Leningrad's St Isaac's Cathedral, and Fal-conet's monument to Peter the Great, the statue of the bronze horseman rearing from his plinth of stone, and gazing over the Neva.

'I love the art of theatre very much,' he said, 'and am strongly attracted to it.' Vsevolod Meyerhold was a hero. 'In general, I consider Meyerhold to be a genius as a stage director . . . I love the circus very much and often attend.' The acrobats particularly attracted him, 'and the jugglers'. He also had a lively interest in the swirl of history, of revolution and violence and social cataclysm, in which he was seized. 'Generally speaking,' he said, 'I com-pose a lot under the influence of external events.' That was not to change.

'The urge to create is constant,' he said. He was asked if this was linked to any 'externally unhealthy states of the organism'. That meant drugs or alcohol, but he replied that the one constant in his creative periods was insomnia, and that 'I smoke more than usual, take long walks . . . pace the room, jot things down while standing, and in general I can't remain at peace'[9]

This impulse to create, he said, 'is always internal. The preparatory stage lasts from several hours up to several days, no more than a week . . . The timbre always comes to me before anything else, then melody and rhythm, and afterwards the rest.' He composed with the help of a piano, by and large, 'although I can do without it, too'. When a piece was done, he was finished with it. 'I never return to a composition once it has been written out.'

His father died in early 1922, a year of acute hunger in the city, develop-ing pneumonia on a trip to scavenge the freezing countryside for food.

The family was suddenly without money and support. Shostakovich's mother gave piano lessons for payment in bread, and found temporary work as a cashier in a shop.

He suffered from tuberculosis. He became 'pale and emaciated', his godmother said, and had 'no strong footwear, no galoshes and no warm clothes'. Alexander Glazunov, the director of the Conservatoire, was so concerned that he begged for a special 'academic ration', though it was no more than a little sugar and a half-pound of pork every fortnight, to 'feed this most talented boy and to build up his strength'.

An operation in the spring of 1923 was successful. He graduated from the Conservatoire as a pianist in June, his neck still bound up with bandages. The family sold one of its pianos to fund his recovery in the southern warmth of the Crimea. The remaining piano, he complained, 'makes a sound like an old pot'. His health was back, though, and he earned money as a cinema pianist, accompanying silent films on the screen at the Piccadilly on the Nevsky, the city's grandest street, at the Barricades and the Splendid Palace. When the manager of another cinema, the Bright Reel, failed to pay him two weeks' money, he sued him – 'now I see he is only a rogue and exploiter' – and won.[10] A toughness lay below the boyishness.

The cinemas were excellent training. He learned how to improvise, across a whole range of moods, comic, tragic, light, dark, and how to jar an audience. He had fun. His fellow pianist Nathan Perelman remembered how they played funeral marches when there was dancing on the screen, and dances when there was tragedy. Sometimes he took friends with him – a violinist, a cellist – to play as a trio. His playing was 'amazing' – 'a wonderful technique, with brilliant octave passages', Perelman said; 'it was all very closely and precisely felt in his head' – and he toured as a concert pianist.[11]

His experience in the pit at the cinemas served him well in writing film scores. The first was for *New Babylon* (1929), a love story set during the Paris Commune. He used shock juxtapositions, his score giving a version of Offenbach's can-can, from *Orpheus in the Underworld*, as the communards were shot by firing squad on screen. He worked on sixteen films over the next decade. His 'Song of the Counterplan', for a film of that name made in 1932, became an international hit. It was used in American stage musicals, and in the MGM film *Thousands Cheer*. Swiss registry offices used it as a wedding march. It was a favourite with Stalin.

The city itself inspired him. As it wound down from revolution and civil war, Leningrad was awash with avant-garde artistry and wild experiment. Vladimir Mayakovsky, poet, Futurist, actor and lover, had written:

> The streets are our brushes.
> The squares are our palettes.
> Drag the pianos out on the streets.

That, exactly, had happened. Grand pianos and uprights were taken from bourgeois drawing rooms, and put on lorries, each with a driver, a pianist and a singer, and some with a cellist and a violinist. They drove round the workers' districts, and Red Army barracks, giving impromptu concerts. The musicians were often students at the Conservatoire.

FEKS (*Fabrika ekstsentricheskogo aktera*: the Factory of the Eccentric Actor) plunged headlong into the future. In their 'Eccentric Manifesto', they renamed Leningrad as Eccentropolis. In song, painting and music, they declared their devotion to 'the Torch Singer, the cry of the auctioneer, slang . . . circus posters, the jackets of pulp thrillers . . . jazz bands, black street orchestras, circus marches'. In ballet and theatre, they were for 'American song and dance routine . . . music hall, cinema, circus, cabaret, boxing'.[12] Shostakovich was no Futurist, but he loved much of what they adored, what they called '*myuzik-kholl*' among it. His first ballet, *The Golden Age*, which he wrote in 1929, had rapidly shifting sketches, and scenes set in a music hall in a 'large capitalist city', with a 'foxtrot bacchanalia', a can-can, and the captain of a Soviet football team doing down the disguised agents of fascism.[13]

Friends were vital to him in the coming dark years. The dearest was Ivan Sollertinsky, a man of enthusiasms and force, a linguist, classicist and wit, introducing the music of Mahler and Bruckner to Leningrad, and the artistic adviser to the Philharmonia, whose pre-concert talks often charmed audiences more than the performances. 'They had an insane friendship', Shostakovich's sister Zoya said. 'They spent the whole day together, laughing and joking.'

He met Vsevolod Meyerhold in 1927. The theatre director was at the height of his powers, with his own company and theatre, and no hint of the horrors to come. He was an admirer of Shostakovich's First Symphony, and he realized that the young composer's breadth of ability made him ideal for work in the theatre. The composer worked with him on the production of Mayakovsky's play *The Bedbug* in Moscow in January and February 1928. They got on well. Meyerhold called him by the affectionate diminutives 'Dima' and 'Mitenka', and put him up in his flat. Shostakovich wrote in an ironic and amused letter to Sollertinsky of the mutual praise that the 'geniuses' he was living with – Meyerhold himself, his wife, the star actress Zinaida Raikh, and her two children by her first marriage to the poet Sergei Yesenin – heaped on one another. Meyerhold and Raikh both looked to Shostakovich to confirm the children's talents: 'That's right, Dima, ah, Dima?'[14]

The painter Nikolai Sokolov remembered the director and the composer sitting together with Mayakovsky in rehearsals. Shostakovich was boyish, 'very modest and shy', his gait 'nervous and rapid', his music 'sharp, angular and unusual' – but praised by Meyerhold: 'That'll blow away the cobwebs in our brains!' Shostakovich lost the music for a passage – he was later to fear he had lost the score of the Seventh aboard a packed wartime train – and he wandered the theatre, 'distraught and upset'. Meyerhold was fatherly, and 'said to him gently, embracing him around the shoulders, "Don't you worry, my dear, your March will be found. And if the worst comes to the worst, we'll manage without it."'[15] It was found, and 'the happy composer was soon walking round the theatre, smiling'.

He also met a soldier of great distinction. 'He occupies a high position, has his own car, but like so many famous people he has a weakness,' he wrote to a friend.[16] 'He adores music and himself plays the violin a little . . . I played for him and he asked if I wanted to come to Moscow.' This was Mikhail Tukhachevsky, still young, a hereditary noble and a decorated tsarist officer who had turned to the Bolsheviks and helped ruthlessly suppress Whites, Poles, rebel sailors and peasants in the aftermath of the Revolution. He was now the Soviet chief of staff.

Three years later, he was appointed commander of the Leningrad military district. Shostakovich continued the friendship after the general was posted back to Moscow.

The composer's nature, though, and his friends, came with perils. For they were precisely the kind of qualities and companions that would leave him most brutally open to the terrors of the time and the place in which it was his fate to live.

They had already done for Mayakovsky. His enthusiasm had run dry. In April 1930, estranged from Bolshevism and its sterility, he wrote a suicide note with an unfinished poem:

> And so as they say –
> 'Incident dissolved'

the love boat smashed up
on the dreary routine.

Then he shot himself.*

Mischa Kvadri was gone, too. He was a dear friend, whose sofa Shostakovich slept on when he was in Moscow, the energetic spirit behind 'the Six', a group of Moscow composers. Shostakovich had dedicated his First Symphony to Kvadri, who returned the compliment with his own Piano Variations, and kicked up a rumpus at the sold-out premiere of the First in Moscow in 1926. He arrived without a ticket, demanding entry. 'It's *my* symphony,' he bellowed; the author himself had said so. Kvadri was too rebellious to survive for long: he was shot, as 'anti-Soviet', in 1929, and the First's dedication was removed from Russian publications.

Shostakovich's qualities were listed by his friend, the pianist Mikhail Semenovich Druskin. The composer was 'fragile and nervously agile . . . very observant, and showed curiosity for all sides of life . . . He had a keen eye for the ridiculous, often noticing the absurd when others paid no attention.' It was dangerous to question and to observe too closely in a dictatorship. Worse, he was 'gifted with an abundant sense of humour . . . He loved satirical humour.' To laugh could be lethal. He realized his personal vulnerability, Druskin thought, and this 'gave rise to his predilection for the tragic in art. It was his vocation to realize the

---

* In death, he showed how deeply Stalin's control of art and artists ran. Mayakovsky's abiding love was for Lily Brik, one of the great beauties of her age, married to a Futurist poet at fourteen, Mayakovsky's mistress at 26, painted by Chagall and Matisse. Stalin admired the tigerish way she fought to preserve his memory. She wrote to him in November 1935, complaining that Mayakovsky's books were out of print and his poems ignored. Soviet art needed a poet hero, and Mayakovsky was safely departed. Stalin's comment on her letter duly made its way into a *Pravda* editorial: 'Mayakovsky was and remains the best and most talented poet of our Soviet era, and indifference to his memory and his works is a crime.' His poems reappeared.

Among the living, though, Lily Brik had no influence. After Mayakovsky's suicide, she married a Red Army general, Vitali Primakov. He was arrested and executed in 1937.

concept of tragedy, for this was how he perceived the world . . . Without doubt, his individual destiny was not easy, to live with exposed nerves and to react acutely to everything surrounding him.' This edge of blackness gave him depth even at nineteen, when he was writing his First. 'Sometimes I just want to shout,' he wrote to a friend, the pianist Lev Oborin. 'To cry out in terror. Doubts and problems. All this darkness suffocates me.'[17] Together with these graces, which cost him dear, he had one more that saved him. 'He also had remarkable self-possession,' Druskin found, 'and however difficult the circumstances, he was always able to contain himself.'

It was as well. Stalin's reaction to, and exploitation of, the Kirov murder got under way. Leningrad was held to be specially infected with 'alien elements' and with the admirers of Trotsky and the 'oppositionist' Grigorii Zinoviev so loathed by Stalin. In a secret report on 18 January 1935, the Party central committee described Leningrad as 'the only city of its kind where, more than in any other place, there remain tsarist civil servants and their retainers, as well as gendarmes and police'. They were 'crawling around in all directions, worming their way into undermining our *apparaty*'. Its closeness to foreign borders made it easier for them to escape.[18]

It began with expulsions from the Leningrad Party of those with alleged links to Trotsky and Grigorii Zinoviev, who had opposed, and then submitted to Stalin. Factories and offices held open meetings lasting seven hours and more where workers denounced colleagues for any attitudes – 'She has an ironic attitude . . . He doesn't study politics and is always silent . . . She concealed that her husband was a White officer' – held to be anti-Bolshevik.[19]

Arrests swiftly followed. The archaeologist Boris Piotrovsky, an orientalist at the Academy of the History of Material Culture, was enjoying pancakes at a Shrove Tuesday party when armed soldiers and plainclothes NKVD agents burst into the room. He, his hostess

Marchenkova, and another archaeologist were arrested. They were taken away in *chernye vorony* ('Black Ravens': prison vans) to the Shpalernaya, an old red-brick prison conveniently close to the Bolshoi Dom (the 'Big House'), the NKVD's grandiose new headquarters in the centre of Leningrad.

His cell was awash with prisoners, lying on and under bunks. It teemed with rats. Piotrovsky found that the politicals, those connected with groups that Stalin was now turning on, behaved differently to the others. 'They were quieter and kept themselves to themselves.' The others were a mixed bag. A waiter from the dining car of a train was accused of 'wrecking', because the Gruyère-type cheese in the sandwiches he served had holes in it. An artist – Piotrovsky knew his wife – was there because his drawings of Lenin were held to be 'caricatures'. An Intourist 'sniper' – tourist officials feared lest rich foreigners who paid to hunt bear would only wound them, and then be attacked, so the snipers shot simultaneously from a concealed position – was a former tsarist officer. A young man, the son of an academician, was picked up for riding in a car with a foreign diplomat. A gravedigger was accused of hiding weapons in his cemetery, though none were found.

Like so many after him, Piotrovsky assumed his arrest had been a mistake, and that he would soon be released. 'After the third day,' he said, 'I started to understand that this was serious.' His interrogator said that Marchenkoza, his hostess at the pancake party, was the leader of a terrorist organization. He had another common reaction: 'I started to think that Marchenkova indeed wanted to get us involved.' He had the good sense, though, to remain silent. After forty days, he was released. He returned to his Academy, where the director, F. Kiparisov, received him coldly. He was told he had been dismissed. A year later, Kiparisov was arrested. He died in the camps.

Mass deportations to labour camps, and the desolate wastes of Siberia and Central Asia, broke in waves. 'Former people' – priests, tsarist officers and gendarmes, police, bourgeois, kulaks, those ex-peasants driven from the countryside by collectivization – were expelled.

Krestianskaya Pravda, a Leningrad paper, ran a series of exposés of 'hidden class enemies' it had unmasked in local schools and hospitals. It found one Troitskii, doubly damned as a former White officer and the son of a priest, working as a hospital administrator. He was well thought of at work, the newspaper complained: his superior protested that he was 'irreplaceable'. Two former nuns were found in the same hospital, and an ex-monk, Rodin, a doctor's assistant, so highly regarded that 'he even substitutes for the doctor in making house calls'. The paper reminded its readers tartly that anyone, friend or family, who was in touch with these 'lurking enemies' could themselves be charged with 'maintaining contacts with anti-Soviet elements'.[20]

The former Baron Tipolt was winkled out of the industrial canteen where he worked as a bookkeeper. The tsarist General Spasski was found selling cigarettes in a kiosk. Marginals – gipsies, tinkers, travelling tailors, women 'on the borders of prostitution', and those lumped together as 'socially degenerate elements' – were rounded up. Beggars were classified as 'Church agitators', like the *stranniks*, the religious wanderers who had roamed the tsarist empire.

Leningraders seized the chance to denounce neighbours with an eagerness that took 'even party propagandists' by surprise.[21] The reason was housing. They were crammed into *kommunalkas* (communal apartments), dormitories, corridors and passages, and each had 'its mad person, its drunkard, a trouble-maker, its informer, and so on'.[22] Every little sign of civilization – 'a radio, plumbing, the telephone, the bath, electricity' – was transformed by the tenants into a 'weapon of torture' which they used to 'torment and harry each other to death'.[23]

Packs of orphaned children, *besprizornye*, were homeless. The NKVD complained at the numbers of 'invalids, cripples, beggar women with children, and unattended minors'. They came from towns devastated in the civil war, and from villages reeling from the repression of kulaks and the other brutalities of collectivization. The city grew from 1.5 million in 1926 to 2.8 million by 1937. With its suburbs and region, it numbered almost seven million.[24]

Denouncing a neighbour meant the chance of more living space. A student at the Leningrad Technical School told how his mother had welcomed the expulsions. 'Mama says, "Damn them. Let them all be exiled. Maybe then we'll be given an apartment sooner."' Apartment hunters attended factory meetings eager to denounce those with a choice room or space. A cleaning woman at the Volodarskii factory spoke of a former gendarme with a 'portrait of one of the Tsar's family' hanging on the wall.

A Russian letter of denunciation could be a *signal*, a patriotic, loyal, responsible warning to the authorities. Or it could be a *donos*, motivated by jealousy and spite, and intended only to harm.[25] Some letters were sent to the NKVD, a few directly to Stalin or Politburo members, and many to newspapers. Every Soviet paper had a large department dealing with readers' letters. Some were published directly, under headings like '*Signaly snizu*' ('Signals from Below'), but the department passed on all those thought significant to the secret police and other government or Party bodies. One in seven of the letters sent in 1935 to the *Krestianskaia Gazeta* was successful.[26] Punishment for the person denounced ranged from the loss of a job or apartment to trial and execution.

Most were signed. The writers realized that *anonimki* (anonymous letters) would not be taken as seriously. They were also confident that there was little political risk – and much potential gain – in signing their work. The most famous of denouncers, Pavlik Morozov, had become a national hero and martyr. A thirteen-year-old peasant boy in 1932, he was said to have reported his father to the GPU/NKVD as an anti-Soviet bandit. His father was condemned to the Gulag, and Pavlik was murdered by other members of his family.

The fear that came with the expulsions, and the meetings and denunciations, had a presence, like the fogs that rose from the Neva. It rolled down the streets and into the courtyards, stairways and landings of the apartment houses, and over Lyubov Shaporina. She was the wife of the composer Yury Shaporin, and herself the director of the Leningrad Puppet Theatre. It was, she wrote in March 1935, 'like some terrible, nightmarish avalanche coming through, destroying families and homes in its path. It is all so unreal: it came, and it's still here, right before your eyes, but you still can't believe it . . .'

She had been to the room of a friend, Lida Bryullova, who ran a children's theatre, for tea a month before: 'It had been so cosy . . .' Now the room was 'in a shambles, the walls bare . . . They managed to sell the piano and the wardrobe, and they farmed out various things to acquaintances.' Bryullova had been exiled to the wastes of Kazakhstan. *Vechernaya Krasnaya Gazeta* ('The Evening Red Gazette'), noted that it was 'Bird Day'. Across the city, schoolchildren and Young Pioneers were building 'starling houses', bird boxes set in gardens and squares, 'so that when the birds come they will find shelter all ready and waiting for them!'

'Touching,' Shaporina wrote in her diary. 'Meanwhile tens of thousands of people of all ages, from newborn babies to old women in their eighties are being thrown out in the most literal sense of the word onto the street, and their nests are destroyed. And here we get *starling houses*.'[27]

The city's second-hand stores were swamped with furniture sold off by the deportees.

Lady Macbeth of Mtensk, the opera that Kirov so dearly loved, had been a triumph. It had almost simultaneous premieres, in Leningrad and two days later in Moscow. It opened in Buenos Aires, Copenhagen, Stockholm and Prague, and its lustful plot – the *New York Sun* called it 'pornophony' – made it a sensation in Cleveland and at the Met in New York.

Shostakovich was riding high, and confident. He toured Turkey, with the violinist David Oistrakh and the pianist Lev Oborin. He wrote a jazz suite, and a new ballet, *The Limpid Stream*. He returned to the concert platform. He had married a striking, dark-haired girl, Nina Varzar, an experimental physicist, while he was writing *Lady Macbeth*, and the opera was alive with sexuality. He had an affair, with Elena Konstantinovskaya, an interpreter, but he had returned to Nina when she became pregnant with Galina, their first child.

He was in his prime at the beginning of 1936: 'slender, yet supple and strong', his friend Isaak Glikman said, 'his head crowned with wonderful dark-coloured hair . . . which fell in poetic disorder with that dashing unruly lick of hair falling forward onto his forehead'.[28] *The Limpid Stream* had enthusiastic runs in Leningrad and Moscow. *Lady Macbeth* remained so popular that the Bolshoi in Moscow staged a new production. The original was still playing, and a touring company was in Moscow with another, so that three productions of the opera were running, and selling out, simultaneously in the city.

The composer himself was briefly in Moscow on 26 January 1936. He was due to leave that night on a concert tour to Archangel. In the evening, he was summoned to attend the performance at the Bolshoi. The opera, in four acts, tells a dark and passionate tale of adultery, greed and murder, set in tsarist Russia, with a score at times as abandoned as its heroine.

Stalin came to the performance, with his close henchmen Molotov, Mikoyan and Zhdanov. His last outing to a Soviet opera had only been ten days before – to *The Quiet Don* by the young Leningrad composer Ivan Dzerzhinsky – and he had enjoyed it. Now he settled behind the curtain in his armoured box, beside the orchestra pit and above the brass and percussion. Shostakovich was sitting opposite, with Meyerhold and the tenor Sergei Radamsky. He was nervous. Before curtain-up he had turned to Levon Atovmyan, a close friend and fellow composer, and told him: 'Lyova, you know I have a funny feeling about this invitation . . .'[29]

The conductor was an Armenian, Alexander Melik-Pashayev, and Shostakovich mistrusted his 'shish-kebab temperament'. The brass and woodwind seemed carried away, and played at maximum volume. Every time they struck up fortissimo with the percussion, Radamsky saw Zhdanov and Mikoyan 'shudder, then laughingly turn round to Stalin'. Shostakovich 'hid in the depths of our box' and covered his face with his hands. The audience laughed at the scene of the lovers on a straw mattress: their love-making was 'depicted with – to put it mildly – naturalistic effect'.[30]

Stalin walked out after the third act. Shostakovich went on stage to take applause. He was 'as white as a sheet', and bowed quickly. 'Feeling sick at heart, I collected my briefcase and went to the station,' he wrote to Sollertinsky. 'I am in bad spirits.'[31] On his way, he told Atovmyan: 'I have a feeling that this year, all leap years, will be bad for me.'

He was right. For himself, and for the world. In this year, 1936, the feeling hardened that the world was no longer living post-war, but pre-war to the next. Mussolini savaged Abyssinia, Hitler occupied the Rhineland, then hosted the Berlin Olympics. In Spain, the Civil War broke out: Stalin sent men and munitions to the Republicans, and Hitler and Mussolini reciprocated with support for Franco.

It was bitterly cold in Archangel. Shostakovich waited in line at a newspaper kiosk on 28 January. He bought a copy of *Pravda*. On page 3, he saw an unsigned editorial under the headline 'Muddle Instead of Music'. It was a review of *Lady Macbeth*, and it dripped with malice. The music, it said, was 'perverted', 'bourgeois', 'fidgety, screaming, neurotic': 'It quacks, grunts, pants and sighs' in the love scenes; singing gives way to 'shrieking'. It accused Shostakovich of 'formalism'. In theory, the term applied to works that strayed from 'socialist realism', failing to reflect the class struggle and the heroism of workers and peasants. The 'formalist' work, by contrast, was complex, Western-influenced, 'modernist', aimed at the elite and incomprehensible to the people. In practice, the virulence of the charge owed much to its vagueness. It could be applied at a whim to any composer, writer, film director, choreographer, architect or painter who fell into disfavour. Zhdanov was its particular zealot: he was to condemn the three greatest Soviet composers, Prokofiev and Khachaturian as well as Shostokovich, as 'formalist' and 'anti-popular'. The *Pravda* review ended in cold and clear menace. The composer was 'playing a game' that 'may end very badly'.

Stalin may not have written the piece himself – it was probably the handiwork of *Pravda*'s high-ranking writer David Zaslavasky – but it was without question that he approved of it. *Pravda* followed it ten days later with a fresh attack on *The Limpid Stream*, which is set on a collective farm at harvest festival time. It was another body blow. It was headlined 'Ballet Falsehood'. Shostakovich and the choreographer, Fyodor Lopukhov, were 'slick and high-handed' frauds, who saw Soviet farmers as 'sugary peasants' from a 'pre-revolutionary chocolate box'. They had failed to study real life and sweat on a collective, and real folk songs and dances. They were guilty of 'aesthetic formalism'.

Arrest seemed certain. The ballet's librettist was Adrian Piotrovsky, the dramatist who had suggested *Romeo and Juliet* to Prokofiev, and written the synopsis of the century's most popular ballet. He was arrested after the usual cat-and-mouse waiting game, and shot by the NKVD. Lopukhov was not taken, perhaps saved from the Gulag because his ballerina sister was married to the renowned British economist John Maynard Keynes. But his career was finished.

Shostakovich was never to write another ballet. Many of his fellow musicians denounced him at meetings, although a few backed him.

Menacingly, informers kept the NKVD abreast of what they said, in private conversations as well as in public. Isaac Babel, master of the short story, scoffed at *Pravda*: 'No one takes this seriously. The People keeps silent, and, in its soul, quietly chuckles.' The writer A. Lezhnev said: 'The horrible thing about dictatorship is that the dictator does whatever his left leg tells him to do . . . I view the incident with Shostakovich as the advent of the same "order" that burns books in Germany.' Meyerhold said of his friend: 'Shostakovich should have been rewarded . . . He is now in very bad shape.' He spoke of the 'angry, cruel headlines of the *Pravda* articles', and noted that 'Soviet subject matter is often a smokescreen to conceal mediocrity'. Lezhnev would be the first of the three to be shot.

Maxim Gorky drafted a letter to Stalin: 'All that the *Pravda* article provided was the opportunity for a pack of mediocrities and hacks to pursue Shostakovich in every possible way.' He was mysteriously dead in June 1936. Tukhachevsky, now a marshal, also wrote to Stalin to defend him. Ivan Sollertinsky stood up for his friend at a meeting of the Union of Composers. He was labelled a 'troubador of formalism' for his pains.

For the moment, Shostakovich was bruised and fearful, but still free. He had become 'frail, fragile, withdrawn', a friend, the satirical writer Mikhail Zoshchenko, said, 'an infinitely direct, pure child'. If he had been just that, though, he could not have sustained his depth and brilliance. So he was also 'hard, extremely intelligent, strong, perhaps despotic and not altogether good-natured . . . In him, there are great contradictions. In him, one quality obliterates the other. It is conflict in the highest degree. It is almost catastrophic.' [32]

He needed that strength. He worked on, and finished, the score of his Fourth Symphony in April. Its premiere was scheduled for December. Otto Klemperer, world-renowned as a conductor, was in Leningrad in May. He was an admirer of Shostakovich, and visited him on 30 May, the night that his daughter Galina was born. The composer played through the new symphony for Klemperer, who declared that the heavens had granted him the chance of conducting it. He made a small request: he asked him to reduce the number of flutes, as it was difficult to find six good flautists on tour. 'What is written with the pen cannot be scratched out with an axe,' Shostakovich replied, smiling, but as obstinate as ever.

Rehearsals began in the autumn, under Fritz Stiedry, who had fled from Austria to settle as chief conductor of the Leningrad Philharmonia.

Then, simply, the Fourth disappeared. Isaak Glikman was at the rehearsals and saw what happened. 'One fine day,' he recalled, 'Iokhel'son, the secretary of the Composers' Union, appeared at a rehearsal with a leading figure from the Smolny, Yakov Smirnov.' Shostakovich was called out of the rehearsal to go to the office of the Philharmonia director, Renzin. He told Shostakovich to withdraw the work voluntarily, to avoid the need for 'administrative measures' to be taken. Those measures, of course, could have resulted in the liquidation of Shostakovich as well as his symphony. He agreed. On 11 December 1936, he formally appealed to the Leningrad Philharmonia to withdraw his Fourth Symphony from performance, because 'it in no way corresponds to his current creative convictions and represents for him a long outdated phase'. Nothing more was heard of the Fourth until 1961.

Family members disappeared, too. On 4 June 1936, Shostakovich's piano professor at the Leningrad Conservatoire, Leonid Nikolayev, was awarded the Order of Lenin. Shostakovich thought him a man who 'trained not just pianists, but above all thinking musicians'. His mother was also an admirer, and she wrote to Nikolayev to congratulate him. She would have done so in person, she said, but 'a terrible misfortune is hanging over us, and I just can't think straight'.

This unmentionable disaster had overwhelmed her daughter, Shostakovich's elder sister Mariya Frederiks. She was married to Vsevolod Frederiks, a brilliant physicist at Leningrad University known for his research into liquid crystals. He was vulnerable to the Terror. He had studied at Göttingen university in 1914 and remained in Germany as an internee before returning to Russia in 1918.

'Our whole world crumbled around us in one night,' Mariya recalled: in the early hours, the NKVD 'came and took him away under convoy . . . I never knew why. He was a noble character, a man of science and uninterested in everything apart from scientific matters.' He was sent to the camps, and, his health ruined, died in January 1944.

Mariya herself was next. She was exiled from Leningrad. Shostakovich's mother-in-law, Sofiya Mikhailovna Varzar, was arrested. Maxim Kostrikin, his uncle, followed. One of his old lovers, the writer Galina Serebryakova, was taken, for the crime of being the wife of an enemy of the people. She vanished into the camps.

Shostakovich started writing the new, Fifth Symphony in April 1937, at a resort in Gaspra in the Crimea, where he had recovered from his early bout of tuberculosis. Nina went with him. His fellow guests were from the arts and sciences, people who, the writer Lidiya Ginzburg observed, Stalin 'nourished' for the glory they reflected on him, but who were close at hand if he wished to lash out. The pianist Lev Oborin, a friend from student days, was there. So was the film director Yakov Protazanov, close, like Shostakovich, to the theatre director Vsevolod Meyerhold. They had worked together on the 1928 film *The White Eagle*.

In the mornings, they feared lest letters came with news of the loss of 'someone near and dear to them'. Shostakovich fretted that the absence of one from Sollertinsky, his best friend, meant that he had been taken. After dark, in the hours of arrests, they froze at the ringing of a telephone, or the crunch of a car tyre on the gravel.

For now, though, they were still alive and they 'barricaded themselves with entertainment'. They went to the ballet. They played poker, which Shostakovich loved. They walked in gardens silhouetted with cypresses, and he umpired on the tennis courts. The soft luminosity of the Black Sea spread through the windows of the drawing room. He was often asked to play on the piano. He always refused, but another guest spotted him early one morning stealing into the empty room, opening the piano, playing a few notes and writing something on music paper.

He worked with tremendous speed on his new symphony. Its birth, he said, was 'preceded by a long period of inner preparation', and that helped him dash through its third movement in three days. At the beginning of June, he travelled back north.

On his way, he visited Nikolai Zhilyaev, a musicologist and teacher at the Moscow Conservatoire. Zhilyaev was a charming and brilliant man, a friend of Prokofiev and Scriabin, and an excellent pianist. At twenty, he had learned Norwegian and set off to Bergen to interview Grieg. He was almost sixty now. Shostakovich had met him at Tukhachevsky's home in 1927: the three of them had got on famously. They saw one another when they could, though the soldier had now been posted to Kuibyshev.

Zhilyaev promised one of his students, Grigori Frid, a treat if he visited him in his *kommunalka* that evening: 'Mitya Shostakovich is going to come.' Zhilyaev's room in the communal apartment on Chistiye Prudy in Moscow was crammed with books and manuscripts, spilling onto the iron bedstead where they sat, with a grand piano and a rough wooden table. A large portrait of Tukhachevsky hung on the wall. Shostakovich had brought his new Pushkin *Romances* with him, and the first two movements of the unfinished Fifth. Frid remembered that his 'thin body was always in motion', quick and angular. The manuscript of the score was written in his 'characteristic nervous hand', a testimony to the speed at which he worked. Zhilyaev was much moved by the symphony. He patted Shostakovich on the head with 'paternal tenderness', repeating, almost in a whisper, 'Mitya, Mitya . . .'

Shostakovich left hurriedly for the station to catch the overnight train for Leningrad. Frid asked Zhilyaev for his impressions. The *Romances* still had something of his 'hooliganism', Zhilyaev said. 'But the Symphony is quite wonderful. Mitya is a genius, a genius . . .'[33]

The group did not know it, but their mutual friend was not far from them, in Moscow, on Fursakovsvogo Ulitsa in cell 94 of the NKVD's Inner Prison. Mikhail Tukhachevsky had been arrested on 22 May in Kuibyshev, the Volga city where Shostakovich was later to complete the Seventh. The NKVD was no longer under Genrikh Yagoda, who had ridden with Stalin on the special night train to Leningrad on the news of the Kirov murder. He had fallen in September 1936. He was now undergoing interrogation and torture, and in ten months he would be shot. His replacement was Nikolai Yezhov, green-eyed, short, only five feet tall, a 'poison dwarf' whom the Russians thought so crammed with malice that they still refer to the crescendo of terror in 1937–38 as the *Yezhovshchina*, the Yezhov affair, though in truth he was no more than Stalin's besotted creature, who, like Yagoda, his master would turn on and destroy.

Yezhov appointed his most brutal interrogator, Ushakov, to extract confessions from the marshal and others accused with him. 'On 25 May I was given free rein to interrogate Tukhachevsky,' Ushakov stated before himself being shot after Yezhov's fall the following year. 'He confessed on 26 May.' The confessions were found later to be smeared and stained with blood in the shape of exclamation marks. Such bloodstains usually 'emanate [from] a subject that is in motion',[34] indicating that Ushakov beat Tukhachevsky with such force as he read through the confession that he jerked his head as he bled. The trial was set for 11 June.

The interrogator said that he continued to 'labour unceasingly' to drag out 'a few more facts, a few more conspirators': 'Even early in the morning of the day of the trial, I succeeded in obtaining supplementary evidence from Tukhachevsky.'[35] Ushakov and Yezhov – the NKVD chief had personally joined in the interrogations – extracted confessions of an 'anti-Soviet Trotskyist-Rightist conspiratorial bloc', and 'espionage for fascist Germany'.

Sharp at 10 a.m. on 11 June, the cream of the Red Army met in a drab three-storey building on 25 October Street, not far from the Kremlin. The command was there: marshals, Army, Air Force and military district commanders, naval flag officers, deputy defence commissars. Only Stalin's close crony, Kliment Voroshilov, the defence commissar, was absent. A military jurist with experience of show trials presided. The other seven judges were senior officers with no legal training.

The group of eight officers facing them were stripped of their insignia, and the medals, Orders of the Red Banner, Orders of Lenin, they had won. Two of them had been taken on the personal trains available to them as commanders: the Terror lapped everywhere, even – indeed, often – on the railways. Iona Yakir had been ordered to Moscow by Voroshilov. During the night, his private sleeping car was uncoupled, and he was seized in his berth by NKVD officers. Vitaly Primakov's personal guards drove off NKVD officers who tried to arrest him on his train. He telephoned Voroshilov, who told him there had been a misunderstanding. 'Some people are coming who will explain everything.'[36] A reinforced detachment of NKVD arrived. Primakov was taken.

This was the flower of the Red Army. Tukhachevsky and Yakir were developing the theory and practice of deep operations, with tanks and aircraft, the key to mechanized warfare. At the manoeuvres they held in Kiev in 1935, they used 1,800 paratroops, 1,200 tanks and 600 aircraft in a combined operation. The British observer, Archibald Wavell, a future field marshal, reported that 'If I had not witnessed it myself, I would never have believed it.' The German military attachés were equally impressed. It was *Blitzkrieg* in action. Vitaly Primakov had been a Red Cossack, and civil war hero, and was now the deputy commander of the Leningrad military district, once married to Lilya Brik, Mayakovsky's muse. August Kork, another of the accused, was the head of the Frunze, the main military academy.

The 'stamp of death', so Ivan Belov, one of their judges, said, 'already lay on all their faces. They had a sallow look about them.' Tukhachevsky, he added, 'attempted to maintain his "aristocratic bearing" and his superiority over the others'. None pleaded guilty, although in the surviving typed report of the trial their 'noes' were altered in ink to 'yeses', with the exception of Tukhachevsky, who refused to answer questions.[37] The trial was over by 2 p.m. The accused were condemned without right of appeal. Yakir was shot the same day. Tukhachevsky and the others were shot at dawn on 12 June. Their bodies were taken to a construction site near the airfield at Khodynka, thrown into a trench, and quickly covered with soil.

Those closest to them were also taken. The arrest of wives and 'ChS' (members of families of enemies of the people) was ordered in a Politburo resolution, 'On Family Members of the Traitors', on 5 July. Wives were to serve at least five to eight years in the camps. Their children were taken from them and put in 'special orphanages'. Shostakovich knew Nina Tukhachevsky well, and had played with her children on his knee. She, and the widow of another victim, General Ieronim Uborevich, were to be shot in 1941 as the Germans advanced on Moscow.

The vilification of the dead – the tone was set by Stalin who, when Yakir sent him a letter proclaiming his innocence, scrawled 'rascal and prostitute' on it – was pursued in radio broadcasts and the press, where it mingled with more ordinary fare: the visit of a Basque football team, athletics, the first flight by Soviet pilots over the North Pole to America. 'The news had an enormous impact on me,' said G. I. Naan, of the Leningrad Institute of Red Professors. 'I couldn't concentrate on my work for the rest of the day, I've been so worried about all the secrets those bastards divulged.'[38] 'Their destruction is our sacred duty,' said Joseph Orbeli, the normally cultivated director of the Hermitage museum.

German military attachés took particular note. Stalin, it seemed, was hell-bent on destroying the best of the officer corps – 'we have in our army unlimited reserves of talent,' he said of the deaths, almost nonchalantly – and the Russian bear to be losing its brains, if not its brawn. They noted it, too, when five of the military judges, two of them marshals, were themselves shot. Thus far, Hitler had done no more than reoccupy the Rhineland. Going further – the Sudetenland, the Danzig Corridor – might be less dangerous than thought.

All who knew Tukhachevsky were now in immediate danger, Shostakovich more than most. Stalin knew of their friendship, from the letter the dead marshal had sent to him, defending the composer after *Lady Macbeth*.

Frid went back to see Zhilyaev in his room a few days later. The musicologist had taken Tukhachevsky's portrait off the wall, but he could not bear to be parted from it. It was propped against the bed, so that the marshal's head appeared between the bars of the bedhead. Zhilyaev was arrested in November, and shot in January 1938. Tukhachevsky and the generals were dealt with in secret. The politicians who had led the Party, Stalin's old Bolshevik rivals, were displayed in public at show trials in Moscow. Three main trials were held: of the 'Sixteen', of the Anti-Soviet Trotskyist Centre, and of the 'Twenty-One'. They consumed Zinoviev, Kamenev, Bukharin, Radek, Rykov, men who had ruled with Lenin, former premiers, heads of the Communist International, commissars for finance and agriculture, ambassadors, and Genrikh Yagoda, who had run the NKVD.

The air buzzed with talk of spies and traitors. People felt battered by them. For fifteen years, it seems, an endless process of decay, treachery and betrayal had been going on, 'and all of it in full sight of the Chekists'. (The Cheka was the forerunner of the NKVD, but its name stuck – still sticks – to secret policemen in Russia). Shaporina's hairdresser whispered to her: 'I can't make any sense of it . . . the whole leadership!'

The worst of it was the openness of the defendants, their pleas of guilty, their admission of fantasy conspiracies. 'Even La Fontaine's lambs tried to justify themselves before the wolf,' Shaporina wrote. 'But our wolves and foxes – people like Radek, Zinoviev, old hands at this business – lay their heads down on the block like lambs, say "mea culpa" and tell everything; they might as well be at confession . . .' She thought that the accused confessed in their eerie and emotionless way because they were hypnotized.

In Leningrad, Shostakovich completed the short score of the Fifth on 20 July 1937. It was not until the end of August, though, that any announcement was made. He remained tainted and the Union of Composers was suspicious of his 'formalistic' habits. He did not play the work for his colleagues until 8 October, the orchestration by now complete, although the first performance by the Leningrad Philharmonia was already scheduled for November. It was a clear break from the doomed Fourth – more conventional, less 'modern' in its construction – and it passed initial muster.

He chose Yevgeny Mravinsky, another Conservatoire graduate, young and not much known, as conductor. Mravinsky had great technical control of the orchestra, which the composer admired, and he was simple and clear in his gestures. He had, too, an ability to heighten effects, particularly with the brass section, and took pride in capturing the composer's intended atmosphere.

The pace of killings picked up as the Fifth went into rehearsals. On a single day, 129 families from the city were exiled and deported to the camps. Shaporina felt herself in a nightmare. 'I keep thinking I'm inside the Bryullov painting of Pompeii's Last Day. Columns falling around me, one after another, endlessly. Women run past me, fleeing with terror in their eyes.' On 10 October, she wrote of nausea rising in her throat 'when I hear how calmly people can say it: "He was shot, someone else was shot, shot, shot."' The word was always in the air, she reflected, but said without emotion: 'People said "He was shot" as if they were saying "He went to the theatre".'

It was very rare for those shots to be heard. The only noises of the Terror were the cars that drove by for night arrests, the rap on the door – 'sharp, unbearably explicit', said Nadezhda Mandelstam, whose husband, the poet Osip,* was taken – and an occasional voice crying out.[39] Sounds did not carry from the execution cellars. Shaporina heard them only once, in the early hours of 22 October. 'I woke up at about three and couldn't get back to sleep until after five,' she wrote:

> There were no trams, it was completely quiet outside, except for an occasional car passing by. Suddenly I heard a burst of gunfire. And then another, ten minutes later. The shooting continued in bursts every ten, fifteen or twenty minutes until just after five. Then the trains started running, the street resumed its usual morning noise. I opened the window and listened, trying to figure out where the shots were coming from . . . The Peter and Paul Fortress is nearby. That was the only place where they could be shooting. Were people being executed? After all, between three and five in the morning it couldn't be a drill. Who were they shooting? And why?

---

* 'Only in Russia is poetry respected,' Osip Mandelstam wrote, his wit as sharp as his verse. 'It gets people killed.' Indeed, it did, and he himself was one of its most brilliant victims. He died in a Siberian transit camp in December 1938. His fellow *zeks* called him 'Poet.' This deference did not save him. He became weak and unable to get off the boards of his bunk. Typhus broke out. The prisoners were taken out to be deloused during one of the snowstorms that swept the coast just before the New Year. Mandelstam was no more, another *zek* said, than 'a skeleton with a wrinkled hide.' They waited forty minutes to get their clothes, reeking of sulphur, which 'drifted into our eyes until we cried.' Mandelstam took two or three steps, 'raised his head proudly', drew a long breath and collapsed. A wooden board with his prison number was fastened to one of his legs, and his body was tossed in a cart with others, and thrown into a common grave. [Vitaly Shentalinsky, *Arrested Voices: Resurrecting the Disappeared Writers of the Soviet Regime* (Free Press: New York, 1996), p.196]

She heard the names of people she knew. 'Vitelko, a singer who had just recently sung in competition . . . Natalia Sats, the director of the Theatre of the Young Spectator . . .' As for Shostakovich's fellow film composer Malakhovsky, the rumours Shaporina heard of him were 'so horrible that you have to cover your ears – but his wife is in Alma-Ata already, and from there they are sent out to the "regions", i.e. into the bare desert . . .'

Anna Akhmatova was in the lines outside the prisons in Leningrad where she spent seventeen months when someone called her by name. The woman behind her, with lips blue from cold, recognized it as belonging to the famous poet. She asked in a whisper – everyone whispered – 'Can you describe this?' Akhmatova replied, 'I can.' And then 'something like a smile passed fleetingly over what had once been her face'. She kept her word, in her poem 'Requiem':

> I have learned how faces fall,
> How terror can escape from lowered eyes,
> How suffering can etch cruel pages
> Of cuneiform-like marks upon the cheeks.
> I know how dark or ash-blond strands of hair
> Can suddenly turn white. I've learned to recognize
> The fading smiles upon submissive lips,
> The trembling fear inside a hollow laugh.
> That's why I pray not for myself
> But all of you who stood there with me
> Through fiercest cold and scorching July heat
> Under a towering, completely blind red wall.

All the Leningrad prisons had walls of crumbling soft red brick. This one was the Kresty, on the Neva embankment by the Finland Station, where Akhmatova's husband, the art scholar Nikolai Punin, had been sent:

You were taken away at dawn. I followed you
As one does when a corpse is being removed.
Children were crying in the darkened house.
A candle flared, illuminating the Mother of God . . .
The cold of an icon was on your lips, a death-cold sweat
On your brow – I will never forget this.

The slaughter in the Red Army reached fever pitch. All those command-ing military districts in May, at the time of Tukhachevsky's arrest, were shot or disappeared within a year. They were joined by 57 of the 85 corps commanders. More than half the 406 brigade commanders were gone. The general staffs of the regions, and of armies, corps and divisions, were 'cleaned out'. The commander of the Red Artillery, traditionally the finest of Russian arms, was shot. Five of the 80 members of the higher military survived. The Navy lost even more senior officers than the Army. The Red Air Force was savaged. Nor was it only the most senior who were purged. The victims included aircraft designers, tank commanders, a keeper of cavalry horses in Central Asia, an ex-cook who was the head of army catering on the Pacific coast, and the conductor of an army band.

A colonel, Ilya Starinov, was aboard a freighter that docked in Len-ingrad homeward bound from Barcelona in mid-October. He was back from a year instructing Spanish Republicans in mine warfare. He checked into a hotel and 'saddled' the telephone to ring his army friends. Every number was answered by a stranger. One cackled with laughter: 'Oh, your friend's at a health resort now.' Then he first heard the 'short terrible words' that made it clear: 'They took him.' Starinov roamed Leningrad until late, and then took a train to Moscow. He rang the doorbell of a friend from his regiment. His friend was nervous. 'Why are you wearing foreign clothes?' he asked. 'Because I was abroad. I haven't had time to change yet.' It was dangerous to speak to someone who had been abroad, 'Pardon me, Ilya . . . but you know, at a time like this . . . By the way, Lukov and Lermentov were taken. And they didn't belong to any opposition groups . . .' The man bent his head so far that his chin touched his chest.

A graduate from the Frunze academy, whose director had died with Tukhachevsky, S. S. Biriuzov, arrived to take up a new staff appointment with the 30th Red Banner Division. He was told that, 'strictly speaking', it had no leadership at all. The commanding officer, the political officers, the chief of staff and the service chiefs had all been arrested. The driver who picked him up at the station said: 'In corps headquarters, every last chief from the lowest to the highest was swept out. What bastards these enemies of the people are! They had everything in their control.' In 'a cold sweat', Biriuzov asked him: 'Who commands the division, then?' 'Nobody,' the driver answered. 'Except the chief of the first section. Major Etsov is still kicking.'[40] An entire rifle division had been purged down to the rank of major.

The Germans remained watchful. In Hitler's own purge of the army, in early 1938, the defence minister, Werner von Blomberg, and the commander-in-chief, Werner von Fritsch, were dismissed, along with fourteen other generals. They were neither imprisoned nor shot. The bloodletting in Russia negated the respect earned by the war games in Kiev. It smacked of a sickness in the Red Army that, when the time came, the Wehrmacht could exploit.

The premiere of the Fifth was held on 21 November 1937 in the Philharmonia Hall, where the Seventh was to create the same rapture and catharsis in its audience. It is a building of severe and restrained elegance, on Mikhailovskaya Street. It had been built exactly a century before for the entertainments of the nobility – balls, concerts, masquerades. The floor was originally flat, for dancing, but it was given a rake down to a new orchestra platform in 1904, with rows of red plush seats in white wood, and benches along the sides. The upper galleries had standing room. The

hall had eleven columns, and classical friezes, and eight crystal chandeliers were suspended above it. The Tsar had sat in Box B, second along
from the orchestra, now the preserve of Party bigwigs. The acoustics were
among the best in Europe, and its soaring whiteness had a fine simplicity.

Shostakovich had written his new symphony in classic, four-movement
form, clear and open to all, moving from tragic minor to a triumphant
major finale, like Beethoven's Fifth. It was varied, tender at times, then
harsh, almost raucous, with hints of folk songs, waltzes, and the Habanera
from *Carmen*, and climaxes that ran to the edge of hysteria before falling
back. The third movement, the largo, was its heart. First the oboe, then
clarinet, and then flute play long and haunting melodies, which resonate
with all the lonely sadness of a *panikhida*, the Orthodox requiem, to the
tremolo of the strings. This builds to a fortissimo of grief where the farewell is taken up by the cellos, and the basses add searing pains. The final
movement, allegro non troppo, re-establishes a sense of hope and survival.

The first rehearsals had been frustrating for Mravinsky. He was
inexperienced – 'my youth . . . my ignorance' – and he badly needed
help from the composer in his interpretation. He did not get it. 'However many questions I put to him,' he said, 'I didn't succeed in eliciting
anything from him.' The doomed Fourth had bred extreme reticence in
Shostakovich; Mravinsky had to rely on cunning. He sat at the piano as
they worked and deliberately took incorrect tempi. 'Dmitri Dmitrievich
got angry and stopped me, and showed me the required tempo.'[41] After
five days, Shostakovich, who had resented an 'interrogation on every
bar, on my every idea', accepted that Mravinsky was right to question
him: 'A conductor should not just sing like a nightingale.' One of music's
great moments was in the making.

It swept through its first audience with a 'sort of electrical force'. It
was like 'walking round a slaughterhouse' in the streets outside, the 'air
saturated with the smell of blood and carrion'. Now, in this colonnaded
sanctuary, they wept openly during the largo, as it released their tensions

and fears. During the finale, they leapt to their feet one after another, and began an applause that rolled in wild thunderclaps. Only once, a veteran told Shostakovich's friend Isaak Glikman, had he witnessed such emotion and triumph, and that had been in this same hall, at the premiere of Tchaikovsky's Sixth. At the end, Mravinsky held the score high above his head, to make it clear that the moment belonged not to him, or to his players, but to the composer.

No overt demonstration was possible in Russia. But the Leningraders gathered in the auditorium expressed their love for Shostakovich's music, their horror at the extension of terror to art, and their pity for him as a victim, in a standing ovation that lasted half an hour. Mikhail Chulaki, the Philharmonia's artistic director, was no blind admirer of Shostakovich – he had criticized him for formalism – but he caught the audience's need: it understood that a young man's future was at stake, and it had 'come to love the composer, not just as a musician, but as a man of crystal purity'.

It demanded him on stage, and he went, white, 'pale as pale can be, biting his lips'. The applause and the demands for him cascaded on, but his friends sensed that it might be seen as a provocation – an 'outraged response to the dreadful hounding Mitya has been through' – and he withdrew. It was as well. Music officials realized the implications, too, and did not like them.

The ovation drowned the 'healthy sentiments' of 'doubt and negative criticism' that had attached to Shostakovich, complained Isaak Dunayevsky, chairman of the Leningrad Union of Composers. The Fifth, he added ominously, did 'not bode well for the future of Soviet symphonic music'.[42] Two senior officials were sent from Moscow to investigate. They were at the second performance, and let fly a stream of acid remarks: the audience was 'all hand-picked . . . they are not normal concert-goers . . . its success has been scandalously fabricated'. It was in vain to assure them that tickets had been sold in the box office in the normal way. They were 'implacable'.

It survived, though. The symphony passed the acid test of a review Alexei Tolstoy wrote for *Izvestia*. He found it to connect with the proletarian experience, 'optimistic in essence', and to be heroic, in a mass and not individual way.[43] Tolstoy, the 'comrade count', was an aristocrat, a White officer and Paris émigré who had returned to Russia, and his survival depended on his skill in sniffing shifts in the political winds, as well as on luck and flattery. Shostakovich was sufficiently rehabilitated to earn praise from Mikhail Gromov. This aviator-hero had become an all-purpose Party mouthpiece after breaking the world distance record on a non-stop flight from Moscow to San Jacinto in California over the North Pole. The composer had grown in stature, the flyer said, a growth 'abetted by stern, just criticism'.

This was a line that Shostakovich himself followed. A front-page piece under his name was run in *Verchernyaya Moskva* on 25 January 1938, as he prepared for the Moscow premiere. The headline was 'My Creative Response'. He said that *Pravda* and his other critics had hit the mark. He would be happy if the 'demanding listener' could now 'detect in my music a turn towards greater clarity and simplicity'. It was said, he wrote, that the Fifth was 'the practical creative answer of a Soviet artist to just criticism'. That had given him special pleasure.

The emotions let loose in Leningrad were not misplaced. Shostakovich affirmed that it was 'Man, with all his sufferings, that I saw at the centre of this work'. He was careful, though, to add that the finale resolved the tragedy into a 'life-affirming, optimistic plan'.[44] Soviet tragedy had every right to exist, he said, but 'its content must be suffused with a positive idea'. This was a convenient nonsense, and he knew it. A little later, he discussed the Fifth with the conductor Boris Khaikin. 'I finished the symphony fortissimo and in the major,' he said. 'Everyone is saying that it's an optimistic and life-affirming symphony. I wonder, what would they be saying if I had finished it pianissimo and in the minor?' Khaikin had never heard the banned Fourth, and its pianissimo-and-minor ending. Years later, when he did, he realized the exquisite cynicism of Shostakovich's remark.[45]

He worked now on the music for *The Great Citizen*, a two-part film on the life and murder of Kirov. The *Yezhovshchina*, the consequence of the murder, raged on about him.

So many were taken, Anna Akhmatova wrote, that 'the city of Leningrad dangled like a useless appendage from its prisons'.[46] Alexander Solzhenitsyn, pouring his time in the camps into *The Gulag Archipelago*, recognized that Leningrad suffered a 'frontal assault': 'Only in certain places, Leningrad particularly, were wives and ChS – "members of families" – also arrested on a mass scale.'[47]

The smallest groups were vulnerable. Stamp collectors were 'wiped clean'. All the outside world was hostile – the Soviet Union remained the world's only communist state – and so it surely stood to reason that none but an enemy agent would possess a German or a British stamp. At the Hermitage museum, 'German spies' were found in the Department of Coins and Antiquities, and an elderly curator, who collected antique arms and armour, was condemned for storing weapons for 'use in an armed uprising'.

The city's orientalists were destroyed. Andrei Vostrikov was only thirty-five in 1937, but he had already earned an international reputation in the history and philosophy of Tibet and Mongolia. The NKVD came calling on him on the night of 8–9 April 1937. By 26 September, they had got what they wanted from him – the names of his fellow 'double-dealers' – and they shot him. Then they set about liquidating the others.

Vostrikov had studied under F. I. Stcherbatsky in a department at Leningrad University that prided itself on the 'Bibliotheca Buddhica' series. Publication was halted. Stcherbatasky was arrested for propagating 'Indian *Popovshchina*' – the Russian word denoting the forbidden retention of the services of priests – and died in exile in Kazakhstan.

Boris Vasiliev was an expert on the influence of Confucianism on Chinese literature. When students returned after the summer break in September, his name had vanished from the university lists.

Yulian Shutskiy was a poet and painter whose doctorate on Chinese philosophy was accepted in June 1937. He was arrested on 3 August, and not heard of again. Nikolai Nevsky was the most brilliant student of Japanese literature, religion and ethnography of his generation. He wrote his research papers in Japanese. They are studied in Japan to this day. The author was arrested on 3 October 1937, and disappeared.[48] 'Masters of Buddhist philosophy' living in the city – Buryats, Kalmyks – were taken. The entire staff of the Institute of the North was arrested, leaving only its NKVD informers.

The city had a long tradition in astronomy. Its great observatory at Pulkovo was about to celebrate its centenary. Twenty-seven leading astronomers disappeared between 1936 and 1938. The biggest wave followed the arrest of B. V. Numerov, the head of the Leningrad Astronomical Institute, in November 1936. He was accused of wrecking, espionage and terrorism on behalf of fascist Germany. Under interrogation, he confessed to this fairy tale of charges, and implicated almost all his Leningrad associates as co-conspirators.[49] Numerov was given ten years; those he named were executed. The Pulkovo director, the brilliant Boris Gerasimovich (for whom a crater of the moon is named), was shot in June 1937. As to Numerov, imprisoned in Orel, he was shot on 13 September 1941, during the German advance on the city.

The death of the leading architect Mikhail Okhitovich had worrying implications for Shostakovich. Like the composer, Okhitovich was one of the great stars of his profession, subject to the malice and spite of less talented men. He, too, ran foul of *Pravda*, which attacked him on 20 February 1936. In a chilling reprise of the *Lady Macbeth* piece, it was headlined 'Cacophony in Architecture'. This was the handiwork of Karo Alabian, who led VOPRA, an association of Proletarian Architects. He resented the lack of respect shown to him by Okhitovich's OSA, a group of modernist architects.

He accused Okhitovich and the modernists of 'Trotskyite deviationism', 'bourgeois nationalism' and 'great power chauvinism'. 'Within Okhitovich,' it was said, 'there lives the spirit of the old Trotskyite.' A letter of denunciation was sent by the Architects' Union to the NKVD. The union pledged to rid itself of 'Trotskyites and other counter-revolutionary anti-Soviet elements . . . and all excess baggage and dead souls'. Alabian also cultivated Lazar Kaganovich, a Politburo member known as 'Iron Lazar' for his ferocity, and whose signature is found on many execution lists. He became a personal informer for Kaganovich, denouncing his colleagues while a 'purge frenzy' overwhelmed architecture. The modernists were destroyed, in favour of Stalinist brutalism. Okhitovich was shot in the camps in 1937.

Musicians were repressed, too. Nikolai Chelyapov, chairman of the Moscow Union of Composers, was made a scapegoat for its 'deficiencies'. He edited the journal *Sovyetskaya Muzika*, where he favoured the 'monumentality of symphonies . . . and oratorios'.[50] He was removed from his post after severe criticism at the December 1936 meeting of the union. Critical articles were published in *Izvestia* and *Pravda* in June 1937, the latter denouncing his 'huge responsibility' for the disintegration of union affairs. He was named as an 'enemy of the people' in a list circulated by the Arts Committee in the autumn of 1937. He disappeared.

Sergei Rimsky-Korsakov, a music enthusiast, though himself an economist, was descended from the great composer's aristocratic family, and was Tchaikovsky's great-grandnephew. His noble origins saw him exiled in 1935 from Leningrad to Orenburg, where he was rearrested and shot in August 1937.[51] The Dean of the Moscow Conservatoire, Kseniya Dorlyak, was denounced and dismissed. Her crime, too, was to be descended from a family of hereditary nobles and thus have connections to enemies of the people.

It was dangerous not to denounce formalism. The composer Genrikh Litinsky, then head of the department of composition at the Moscow Conservatoire, had been linked with Shostakovich in the 1936 denunciations of *Lady Macbeth*. It was now ominously said that he 'offered no genuine self-criticism'. He was mauled in the press as an 'unrepentant and persistent formalist', an 'untalented composer' and someone who could not be trusted to teach young composers. One of Litinsky's students, Mikhail Dushky, had written a symphony about bandits in the Ukraine, which was held to be 'politically harmful' and 'counter-revolutionary'. He was expelled.

The Gulag had its own cultural education wing, the KVCh. Musicians, singers and actors among the prisoners were drafted into singing and dancing ensembles, performing 'The Ballad of Stalin', 'The Cossack Meditations on Stalin', 'The Song of the NKVD'. The violinist Georgi Feldgun, plucked from the concert halls of Leningrad, found himself playing for a few criminals in a small transit camp in Vanino, a Pacific coal port where prisoners waited to be shipped to the mines of Magadan. 'Here we are on the edge of world,' he said, 'and we are playing eternal music written more than two hundred years ago, we are playing Vivaldi for fifty gorillas.'

Camp bosses competed with each other for the best orchestras, and kept the musicians in relative luxury. A *zek* – with a certain pride, the prisoners called themselves *zeks*, an abbreviation of 'incarcerated'; the guards, with brutal indifference, called them *pyl'*, 'dust' – was astonished to see their barracks in a Magadan camp. 'Bunks neatly covered in blankets,' he said, 'mattresses and pillowcases. On the wall, a tuba, a French horn, a trombone, trumpet . . . The musicians have soft jobs.' Not always, though.

The composer Vsevolod Zaderatskiy was an extraordinary survivor of the camps.[52] During the war, he had taught music to Alexei, the Tsar's son and heir. After his young pupil, with his parents and sisters, was murdered by the Bolsheviks, Zaderatskiy joined the White armies.

He was captured in the Ukraine at the end of the civil war in 1920. A grand piano was in the room where he and other officers were being held before being shot. He played it, beautifully. He was heard by Felix Dzerzhinsky, the founder of the Cheka secret police, the forerunner of the NKVD. In the morning, at, so he said, Dzerzhinsky's prompting, Zaderatskiy was the only prisoner not to be shot.

Eking out a living six years later, he was arrested and sentenced to two years as an ex-officer. On his release, he began composing again, avant-garde and innovative pieces. He joined the ACM, the Association for Contemporary Music, which was open to modernism and Western styles. Shostakovich was also close to the ACM, which ran foul of RAPM, the Russian Association of Proletarian Musicians. The RAPM-dominated Union of Composers was formed in 1932. Zaderastkiy was obliged to join it, and to compose a sample piece. He wrote a sinfonietta for strings. It was damned and he was expelled from Moscow to Yaroslavl. Here, he taught and formed an orchestra. In 1937, after his orchestra had played pieces by Wagner and Richard Strauss, he was arrested again, accused of promoting fascist music. He was sent to Magadan, the transit point on the Sea of Okhotsk for *zeks* sent on to slave in the gold, silver, tin and coal mines of Kolyma. Zaderatsky escaped the mines, and laboured in a logging camp. Here, in a place where temperatures dropped to minus 50 degrees Celsius, and the bodies of prisoners who fell unseen in the stands of timber froze solid, in pencil on a sheaf of telegraph forms, the only paper he had, Zaderatsky wrote a cycle of 24 Preludes and Fugues for piano. In 1939, still in Magadan, he wrote a piano sonata in E-flat minor. He survived, to make his way to Lvov after his release. He worked in the Lvov Conservatoire, still composing – two piano concertos for children – until some Moscow musicologists visited the Ukrainian Union of Composers in 1950. They recognized him as a former enemy of the people, and denounced him. He died, of heart failure, a few days before Stalin.

Other ACM composers, close to Shostakovich, suffered. Alexander Mosolov, known for his early Futurist piano pieces, wrote to Stalin complaining that the 'permanent badgering . . . by the proletarian musicians' made it impossible for him to work. Stalin was unmoved. Mosolov was expelled from the Union of Composers in 1936. He was arrested in November 1937, accused under the catch-all Article 58.10, anti-Soviet agitation and propaganda. He was sentenced to ten years in the camps.

The denunciators in RAPM made a string of accusations – 'counter-revolutionary . . . alien to the proletariat . . . class enemy . . . Trotsky-ite . . . saboteur' – against Nikolai Roslavets, composer, violinist and modernist. His work, and his livelihood, disappeared. A severe heart attack intervened before he was tried.

The victims in Leningrad were drawn from every group. Terror struck in every cranny. None were exempt, including the NKVD. When first Yagoda and then Yezhov fell, swathes of officers and agents went to execution with them. The *Leningradskii martirolog* lists 16,062 who were executed between August and the end of December in 1937. The complete figure probably exceeds this by 'several thousands' as not all details have been found.[53] All of them were 'politicals'. Almost all were sentenced under Article 58; most were condemned by the three-man troikas under the Leningrad NKVD board, or by two-man dvoikas from the regional NKVD committee and the procuracy.

Yezhov's Order 00447 of 31 July 1937 set out a four-month plan for the 'repression of former kulaks, criminals and other anti-Soviet elements', with 75,000 to be shot, and 193,000 to be sent to the Gulag. The operation was extended several times, and the executions were to swell close to the half-million mark. Even Yezhov's original minimum target for Leningrad – 4,000 'Category 1', to be shot immediately, with another 10,000 to be sent to the camps – exceeded the NKVD's capacity to bury its victims in municipal cemeteries and on the Rzhevka artillery ranges.

A new site was found in the forest near Levashovo, off the main road running north towards Finland, a dozen miles from the centre of the city. It was a place of thin soil and dripping pines. The NKVD surrounded it with a high wooden fence. They began concealing bodies there in August 1937.*

The *martirolog* shows that though all were at risk, some were more so, sometimes much more so, than others. This was true of non-Russians, and above all Poles. Proportionately as many Poles were shot as Russians, just over a third of the total in each case, but where Russians made up 86 per cent of the city's population, Poles accounted for a fraction over 1 per cent. Ethnic Germans suffered badly, too, with an execution rate six times higher than their proportion of the population. Finns, Latvians and Belorussians were also at high risk. Jews were much less so, with 10.5 per cent of total deaths from 6.7 per cent of the people.[54] If the Soviets were less anti-Semitic than the Nazis, they pursued the Poles and other ethnic minorities with similar ferocity.

Most victims were middle-aged, the average forty-six years old, with very few under twenty. They came from every occupation, with low-skilled blue-collar workers the most numerous. The *intelligentsiya* suffered too, as well as white-collar managers and senior engineers: their profile made them stand out above the greater numbers of the other victims.

Of most of their ordinary lives and extraordinary deaths, we know nothing but a name, a place of birth, an occupation, and the sub-section of Article 58 under which death was imposed. Of the last days of Alfons Alfonovich Felten, thirty, engineer, motorbike enthusiast, and father, though, we know a great deal, for the file of his interrogation is preserved.[55]

---

* The villagers made no mention of the truck traffic, nor of the shots they sometimes heard. It was used until 1954. By then, it is believed that it concealed the bodies of 46,711 people, 40,485 of them 'politicals.' Its existence was first made public in the summer of 1989. It has become a memorial for those who lie there.

Alfons Felten's last glimpses of the city of his birth were soaked in its magnificence. Three NKVD men – only the identity of the arresting officer, Agent N69R, was logged – came for him a little before midnight on 31 October 1937. He lived at No. 43 on the 4th Line on Vasilievsky Island, a sturdy block of granite and rendered brick with pedimented windows, facing a small children's park on a broad and tree-lined avenue that ran down to the Neva.

Its fine tsarist apartments had been divided up into *kommunalkas*.* Felten lived on the top floor. It was a tiring climb. There was no lift, and a broad staircase with a handrail of wrought iron and wood led up to it, thirty steps to the floor, five floors in all. A fire escape went to the roof from the landing outside Felten's door. He had no opportunity to use it.

The NKVD men searched his room, and took him down to their waiting car. They drove him down the avenue, turning left onto the University embankment, past the pale ochre Menchikov Palace, with the dome of St Isaac's and the spire of the Admiralty high against the sky on the other side of the dark river, the severe blue and white and gold facades of the Hermitage and Winter Palace reflected in the waters.

They passed the dark red rostral columns at the tip of Vasilievsky Island, once lit as beacons for shipping, and crossed to the Petrograd Side. The embankment ran by the slim and audacious golden spire of the Peter and Paul cathedral, raised four hundred feet above its surrounding fortress, the symbol of the city's aching beauty. They passed the cottage where Peter the Great had begun to plan it, in 1703, finally to cross the Neva by the Liteiny Bridge. A left turn took them onto Shpalernaya Street. Here was the Bolshoi Dom (the 'Big House'), the NKVD headquarters: their destination.

They arrived in the small hours. The arrest form was dated 1 November.

---

* It is, ironically, now a training facility for future police officers.

Agent N69R filled it in as he questioned Felten.[56] His date of birth was given as *2 July 1907*, the place as *Vasilievsky Island*. He was a native-born Leningrader.

Occupation: *Head of testing, Red October Factory technical staff.*

Possessions in land and property at time of arrest: *None.*

Possessions before 1927, before 1917: *None.* [This was a dangerous question. It was designed to catch the pre-revolution bourgeoisie, and 'NEPmen' – those who had prospered as traders during the brief interlude of the New Economic Policy up to 1927. Felten safely passed that test.]

Social status at time of arrest: *Factory worker.* [A saving grace in 1935, when 'former persons' were falling into the maw. Now all were at risk.]

Underline education: *higher middle lower illiterate.* Specify: *Finished 6th Grade* [high school].

Served in Tsar's army?: *No.* [A 'yes' was not fatal, but compromising.]

Served in White Army?: *No.* [A 'yes' was highly dangerous.]

Served in the Red Army?: *1919–1923.*

Nationality: *Russian.*

Citizenship: *USSR.*

Party: from when? Party number?: *Non-Party.* [Safer to have no Party links.]

Previous court trials – convictions – where served term: *No previous trial or conviction.*

Health: *Healthy.* Family status: Mother: *Felten Sof.* [Sofiya] Age: *65, housewife.*

Daughter *Felten T.* Age: *15, student.* Identifying features: *None.*

When arrested and by whom: *31 October 1937. Agent N69R.*

Where held: *Leningrad.*

Reason for arrest: *59-12.*

Felten signed the form and dated it 1 November.

He was charged at first under Article 59 of the Penal Code. This dealt with 'dangerous crimes without counter-revolutionary purposes'. It usually involved a spell in the camps, but not execution. 59-12 was for violation of foreign-exchange rules. It was convenient for picking up Felten, since the NKVD knew that his sister and her husband were living in Berlin.

It was soon clear that something much worse than a 59 was going to be pinned on him. His position as a senior technician at the Red October plant opened him to charges of wrecking. The factory was a major producer of aircraft, tank and armoured-car engines. Its testing department was responsible for quality control. Any defects or production shortfalls were easy to blame on its staff. These crimes came under Article 58 of the Penal Code, the section that dealt with counter-revolutionary crimes. In most cases, a 58 charge was a death sentence.

He was interrogated by a police lieutenant from NKVD section 3 who signed himself with his initials, GV. The lieutenant dealt briefly with Felten's relatives in Berlin. His real interest was in his acquaintances in Leningrad: 'Tell me about them.'

They were friends who shared his interest in motor sport. Three of them – he named Pavel Petrovich Voroshalkin, Pavel Petrovich Dolgopolov and Georgiy Konstantinovich Skrobaskin – worked at the big Dynamo sports club. It was best known for its football club, which Shostakovich followed, but it also had tennis courts, swimming pools and athletic-tracks. Its position on the banks of the Neva made it ideal for rowing.

Voroshalkin was the secretary of its flourishing motor club, Dolgopolov worked in the garage, and Skrobaskin was a driving inspector. Another two friends, Feodor Karlovich Schwarz and Alexei Afansebich, both worked in the garage of a State taxi service. All were keen motorbike riders.

GV then asked Felten to list his acquaintances at work in the Red October plant. He said that he had 'good friendly relations' with just three colleagues. Semeon Ilyich Kromy and Aaron Akinovich Garkovy were in the plant's Unit 9, the first as its director, the second as his deputy. There was also Kuzhelev – no first name or patronymic given – who was the head of the construction bureau.

For the next month, Felten was on the 'conveyor', interrogated continuously by a junior lieutenant, G. B. Horsun, with two other NKVD officers, Popov and Nerelnut. We do not know if he suffered torture as well as sleep deprivation. Yezhov's appetite for victims was at its height in the late autumn of 1937. Interrogators had a vast caseload to get through, and confessions had to be extracted at speed.

Among the friends Felten mentioned in his initial interrogation, Semeon Kromy had also been arrested. It may be that Felten was told that Kromy had confessed, and incriminated him, and vice versa. This was a standard ploy. At any event, at some time before the end of November, Felten was broken. He admitted knowing Wilhelm Augustovich Zamermayer, an engineer also of German extraction, and a fellow motorcycle enthusiast. Zamermayer had already been found guilty of spying for Germany. He had been shot.

Felten's 'confession' was word-perfect, as Horsun wrote it out in the last interrogation session on 1 December.

'Do you know Zamermayer?' A 'yes' would indicate the end of Felten.

'Yes. Zamermayer, Wilhelm Augustovich. I knew him from meeting him in the German Cultural House in 1932.' The Russian patronymic shows the dead 'spy' to have been Russian born. The date – before Hitler came to power – also shows that he was not a German communist refugee.

'What was your friendship based on?'

'The main reason we got closer was our interest in motorcycle sport. When he found out I was a biker, we talked about different motorbikes, and that's why we got along. We met in the German Cultural House until it was closed in 1933. Later we met at my club.' The cultural associations of Soviet minorities had been suppressed as foreigner psychosis grew in the Thirties. Felten had joined the Dynamo motor sport club.

'Do you consider yourself guilty because you kept in touch with Zamermayer?'

'Yes. I admit that I am guilty. In 1935 he recruited me as a spy-agent for Germany . . .'

'What kind of assignments did he give you?' 'I got an assignment from Zamermayer to <u>carry out wrecking</u> at the Red October factory, to <u>cancel or slow down production</u> at the factory, and to <u>recruit a group</u> of workers in the plant to work with me.' Part of this paragraph was underlined on the page.

'What did you do?'

'Between 1935 and March 1937, I met Zamermayer seven or eight times. I gave him written reports of production at Red October. In this way, I gave him evidence of the production of tank parts, including gearboxes, cylinders for T-26 and T-46 tanks, and about Liberty engines which also go into tanks. Also about L-300 motorbikes, especially about ones that went to the army. All this evidence I gave to him in my flat.'

'Was the spy group organized in the factory as Zamermayer suggested?'

'I have just formed this group in Red October factory. It consists of the director of Unit 7 Kromy and the manager Jaroslav Sergeivich Dmitrazh.' Kromy was described as head of Unit 9 in the first interrogation: it made no difference.

'In what way did you recruit them?'

'After I received instructions from the German spy-agent Zamermayer for creating the wrecking group in the Red October factory, I thought about the people I knew best. I recruited Kromy and Dmitrazh because they were the most reliable and closest to me. After some interaction with these people in my flat and in the factory, I raised the question of their participation in my assignment and received positive answers.' How dreary and monotonous and repetitive – the 'German spy-agent', time and again, the 'interaction', the 'positive answers' – were these secret police files.

'What kind of work did your people do in the Red October factory?'

'We worked on damaging Red October production, particularly motorcycle L-300 and tank parts for T-26 and T-46 and Liberty engines. I myself as director of the testing unit was undertaking damaging actions – wrecking – in the testing of L-300 motorcycles. Dmitrazh, being head of production in the part of the factory producing parts for Red Army motorcycles and tanks, was responsible for wrecking by making damaged parts that wore out quickly. Kromy, working in Unit 7 of manufacturing, knowingly produced damaged parts, especially for L-300 motorcycles, and disorganized this part of the factory by producing unneeded parts, and taking needed parts out of production. He assigned people to different areas and took people off the tank production line.'

'Had you planned to carry on these activities if there was a war?'

'Yes, together with Kromy and Dmitrazh, we thought up a plan for wrecking production of Red Army vehicles. We planned using dynamite to create explosions in the factory. The instructions to do this would come from Zamermayer.'

The final line of typescript read: 'This is written correctly and I have read it.'

Felten signed it. A note below his signature read: 'Interrogator – Junior Lieutenant G.B. Horsun'. Horsun signed it too.

He had done his work well. The pages that he had laboriously typed out provided three men to satisfy Yezhov's hunger for Category 1 victims, five motorbike enthusiasts for future interrogations, and a rationale for shoddy Red Army equipment and the shortage of spare parts. These were not caused by impossible production targets, poor-quality metals, workers who had gone onto the production line straight from peasant villages, or sloppy driving by badly trained tank crews. They were the fault of three obscure men, Felten, Kromy and Dmitrazh, and the dead German agent-spy Zamermayer. And Adolf Hitler.

The end was close. Horsun reported that the case, NKVD No. 36256, was 'considered closed'. Felten had been recruited to spy 'by the German spy-agent Zamermayer, who has been sentenced to the 1st category . . . He fully admits his guilt.'

By now, he had picked up a string of 58s: 58-6, -7, -9 and -11. 58-6 was espionage, which carried the same penalty as 'armed uprising' (58-2), namely death with confiscation of property, and formal recognition as an 'enemy of the people'. 58-7 was for undermining state industry, transport and financial system, with the title of 'wrecker'. 58-9 was for damaging transport, communications, the water supply and state buildings and property, with the same penalties – death, 'enemy of the people' – as 58-2. Finally, 58-11 was the catch-all crime of supplying 'any kind of organization or support actions' for the other counter-revolutionary crimes in Article 58.

The papers were forwarded to 'the NKVD of the USSR for 1st category'. Sentence was passed on 26 December 1937. Felten and the other two were shot, probably the following day.

Discretion, for Shostakovich, was the better part of valour. He put it out that he was working on the safest of subjects, a new symphony based on Mayakovsky's eulogy, *Vladimir Ilyich Lenin*, a poem learned by rote by every Soviet child. It was to be grandiose, for soloists, chorus and orchestra. The Sixth was a long time coming, and when it did, it bore no relation to this.

His son Maxim was born on 10 May 1938. He was an excellent father, close to his children, delighting in their games and amusements, encouraging them, playing the piano for them – Max became a fine musician and conductor – and ever wary of their welfare. A few months later, he wrote the music for a children's cartoon film, the *Tale of the Silly Little Mouse*, with a lullaby sung by the different animals.

For now, he wrote a string quartet, in C major. It was his first venture into what he found was 'one of the most difficult' of genres. 'You know, it's hard to compose well,' he wrote to Sollertinsky in July, but he was captivated. It had images from his childhood, fresh, clear springtime days, gentle and lyrical, and it charmed the audience at the Leningrad premiere by the Glazunov Quartet in October. In Moscow, they had to repeat the whole piece for an encore.

Life still had its pleasures. 'Life has become better, life has become more cheerful': Stalin's slogan hung on giant banners in parks and sports halls. Shostakovich took it for the black humour that it was – at New Year, he would toast the hope that life 'does not get better' – but he had his passions. He went to every football game he could, getting tickets from a friend who was a sports journalist, taking other friends, eating out together after matches. He loved the circus, and 'American mountains', the roller-coaster rides in amusement parks. Leningrad was well supplied with these. In Moscow, where he made many trips, was the best of them all.

Gorky Park had dance floors, Ferris wheels, cinemas, bowling alleys, a parachute-jump tower. It had its American mountains, and its director was a young American, Betty Glan. 'This garden where sausages and würst grow on trees,' the press wrote of May Day in the Gorky, 'foaming beer with Poltava sausages, pink ham, melting Swiss cheese and marble white bacon . . .'[57] The girls dabbed themselves with Red Moscow perfume, and drank Georgian champagne with their young men, and the children tucked into chocolate Eskimo ice cream. It served propaganda as well as pleasure. It had 'agitational corners', and satirists staged parades of caricature figures from the past – God, Romanovs, monks, and capitalists, followed by ostriches and donkeys and bears, who stood for generals and counts and so on.[58] Betty Glan's revived park had opened in 1933, and was widely copied in other cities. In 1937, though, she was beginning sixteen years in prison and the camps.

Jazz, too, was one of his pleasures. It was in fashion. Leningrad Radio had jazz evenings, with recordings by Whiteman, Hilton, Ellington. The finest jazzmen, including Alexander Tsfasman, and Antonin Ziegler and his Czech group, played in the restaurants at the best hotels. Stalin's favourite was Leonid Utesov, who played the lead in the hit film *The Happy-Go-Lucky Boys*.[59] He mixed stand-up comedy with jazz, tango, Russian folk and French chansons at his 'Thea-Jazz' evenings in the Kirov Palace of Culture in Leningrad.

A new State Jazz Orchestra was formed. Shostakovich was commissioned to write a piece for it in 1938. His second Suite for Jazz Orchestra had three movements, scherzo, lullaby and serenade. The radio premiere was on 28 November 1938.

Flying was immensely popular. A crowd of a million had come to Tushino airfield outside Moscow on Aviation Day in August 1937 to hail Mikhail Gromov and his fellow 'Stalin's falcons'. Stalin and the Politburo had watched, too, as dozens of aircraft overhead formed a five-pointed Red Star, and spelled out 'Stalin', and a balloon with a giant canvas portrait of the dictator was lifted almost to the stratosphere. Shostakovich had personal reason to be grateful to Gromov. The Polar pilot – 'we didn't feel the cold, wrapped in the glowing words . . . of comrade Stalin' – had reviewed and praised his Fifth.

On 16 May 1939, at 5 a.m., a car passed through the deserted streets of Moscow from the Lubyanka to the apartment of Isaak Babel. He was a playwright, translator, and a writer of short stories – *Red Cavalry*, *Tales of Odessa* – of enduring brilliance. He had also had an affair with Yevgeniya Yezhova, the promiscuous wife of the now fallen but still living head of the NKVD. The caretaker told the NKVD men that Babel was in his dacha. They drove out of the city along the Minsk highway for half an hour to Peredelkino, the village where writers had a colony of handsome wooden cottages. Babel was still asleep when they rapped on his door. They piled his manuscripts, notebooks and letters into the back of the car, and took him to the Lubyanka.

No certain word of what happened to him was heard for fifteen years. It was as well for Shostakovich that he did not know that his name cropped up several times in Babel's 'confessions'.

The interrogators, Lev Schwartzmann and Boris Rodos, were hand-picked by Lavrenti Beria, now head of the NKVD. The Yezhov connection gave them special zeal. Nikolai Yezhov had been dismissed on 7 December 1938. Their ex-master was still alive, giving himself to hysterical drinking bouts and bisexual orgies before his arrest on 10 April. Yevgeniya, his wife, had died of an overdose of luminal in a Moscow sanatorium in October 1938. 'A woman of 34, medium height, well developed', the autopsy said of her charms.

Babel was broken by long bouts on the 'conveyor', the constant sleep deprivation and interrogation accompanied by physical torture. He told of meeting Yevgeniya in Berlin in 1927, when she was a typist in the Soviet commercial mission. They drank heavily together, and she 'agreed enthusiastically' when he suggested driving round the city in a taxi. 'I persuaded her to come back to the hotel with me . . . We were intimate.'[60] When she returned to Moscow, the affair continued.

He went on to spin an extraordinary tale, of a plot devised by Yezhov to assassinate Stalin – in the Caucasus, in Yezhov's apartment in the Kremlin, or at a dacha outside Moscow. He said that André Malraux, world-renowned as the writer of *La Condition humaine*, and as a Republican volunteer in Spain, had 'recruited me to spy for France'. In his letters to Malraux, they had discussed the campaign against the Formalists, and 'in particular' against Shostakovich and Pasternak. He confessed that he was part of an 'anti-Soviet group'. Mayakovsky's suicide in 1930 was taken as proof that creativity was snuffed out under Soviet conditions. More, 'we declared that the articles opposing Shostakovich were a campaign against a genius.'[61] It was 'common ground' for himself and others to 'proclaim the genius of Shostakovich and to sympathize with Meyerhold.'[62]

Babel had once been asked, by the poet Osip Mandelstam, why he had lingered with Yezhov. Did he actually want to touch death? 'No,' Babel replied. 'I just like to have a sniff to see what it smells like.'[63] Bravely, he retracted his confessions at his trial, on 26 January 1940. He was shot the next day.

Death brushed closer still with Vsevolod Meyerhold. Shostakovich had stayed in touch, though Meyerhold's theatre was shut at the beginning of 1938, and the threat was clear. Konstantin Stanislavsky, the man who had brilliantly transformed theatrical theory into practice in so-called 'method' acting, was happy to give Meyerhold the run of his own company of actors. The three of them discussed ways that Shostakovich could compose a new opera. Meyerhold said he was planning to write an opera libretto for the composer, based on Lermontov's *A Hero of Our Time*. Meyerhold spoke passionately to Stanislavsky's actors, among them, without doubt, an informer or two, on the need for the best composers – 'Shostakovich, Prokofiev' – to write operas for the company.

He sensed a menace. He began to talk of 'past errors' and his gratitude for being forgiven them by Stalin, 'our leader, our teacher, the friend of toilers'. He had taken to the long grass, a fellow director and admirer said, and it might be that he would come out of it, not as 'as a mighty lion' but as a 'bedraggled cat'.[64]

In the early evening of 19 June 1939, Shostakovich met Meyerhold by chance on his way back from a football match. They drank tea. Meyerhold went on to the Leningrad home of an actor friend. Former students of his were there, and the evening moved merrily on into the night. It was 7 a.m. when Meyerhold left to return to his flat on the Karpovka embankment, to change before going to a rehearsal. At 9 a.m., he was there with his sister-in-law and her husband – his wife, Zinaida Raikh, an actress of force and beauty, was staying at their apartment in Moscow – when two NKVD officers arrived. They had with them a warrant for his arrest. It had been signed by Beria in Moscow the day before. The signature was in blue pencil, indicating that the suspect was liable to execution.[65]

He was taken under escort from Leningrad on the 2 a.m. Moscow train on 22 June. His first confessions – he had used leading Trotskyists as actors, he had been involved with Bukharin, Kamenev, Radek and other oppositionists – were found inadequate. He suffered his first 'conveyor' interrogation on 8 July. It lasted for eighteen hours. His second, on 14 July, lasted another fourteen.

His wife was in their flat that night. At about 1 a.m., two men broke in by climbing up to the rear balcony. They stabbed her repeatedly, several times in the eyes. Her elderly housemaid was woken by the screams. She was then beaten unconscious. She called an ambulance but Zinaida Raikh was dead on arrival. She was buried in the black velvet gown she had worn in *Camille*, the last performance at the Meyerhold theatre before its closure. The press was silent, despite her fame. Her son and daughter were expelled from the comfortable apartment on Bryusov Lane. Beria's chauffeur took half of it, and a girl from his staff the other.

A fresh insanity – the outside world – was now at work. As it pursued a still brilliant but elderly theatre director, the Soviet regime was entering into partnership with the fascists to its West. On 23 August, Hitler's foreign minister, Joachim von Ribbentrop, arrived in Moscow to negotiate a Nazi–Soviet pact. He was welcomed with swastika banners hastily purloined from the set of an anti-Nazi film. A British cartoon caught the cynicism. 'The scum of the earth, I believe?' says Hitler. Stalin beams in reply: 'The bloody assassin of the workers, I presume?'

The pact freed Hitler to attack in the West. In return for its neutrality, under the secret protocols of the pact, the Russians were rewarded with eastern Poland. As the Germans overran Warsaw and western Poland, the Red Army attacked the Poles from the east on 17 September. They reached the demarcation line with the Wehrmacht four days later. The Russians quickly pauperized their territory, taking carpets, pictures, furniture, china, the soldiers' short jackets bulging with clothes, meat, shoes and sugar. They stripped it of 'former people', too, as Polish officers, priests, landowners, teachers were deported to the east.*

The interrogations continued. Meyerhold became so ill – 'lack of food (I was incapable of eating), lack of sleep (for three months) . . . heart attacks . . . trembling as though from fever . . . I became bowed and sunken . . . my face was lined and aged by ten years' – that his interrogators became 'apprehensive'. He was given intensive medical treatment, and then they began again. They 'threatened me constantly: "If you refuse to write (meaning 'compose'?!) we shall beat you again, leaving your head and right hand untouched but turning the rest of you into a shapeless, bloody mass . . ."'

On 9 November, Meyerhold 'lost control of myself . . . I began to tremble hysterically . . . In this state I should not have been asked to sign the statement.'[65]

Before his trial, he formally repudiated every statement he had made that might have endangered others, a list that included Boris Pasternak, the film director Sergei Eisenstein and Dmitri Shostakovich.

He wrote to Molotov, as the head of the Soviet government, to show how his 'confession' had been wrung from him, 'a sick, sixty-five-year-old man'. They had laid him face down and beat him on the soles of his

---

* Some 22,000 of the deportees were massacred by the NKVD in April 1940, in the forests of Katyn, and in prisons in Kharkov and Kalinin. Thus perished half the Polish officer corps. The chief executioner, Vasili Blokhin, of the NKVD, in butcher's apron, cap, and shoulder length leather gloves, using a suitcase full of German Walther pistols, was awarded the Order of the Red Banner by Stalin. It went with the Badge of Honour he had already won for the executions he had carried out in 1937.

feet and spine with a rubber strap. Then they sat him on a chair and beat his feet from above. His legs were now covered with extensive internal haemorrhaging. For the following few days, they 'again beat the red-blue-and-yellow bruises with the strap . . . I howled and wept from the pain.' The mental pain was as bad as the physical. It 'aroused such an appalling terror in me that I was left quite naked and defence-less . . . Lying face down on the floor, I discovered that I could wriggle, twist and squeal like a dog when its master whips it.' His body shook so uncontrollably that a guard escorting him back to his cell from the interrogation chamber asked if he had malaria. The bouts of interroga-tion lasted up to eighteen hours. The hour's rest he was allowed in his cell was of little use. 'I was woken up by my own groaning and because I was jerking about like a patient in the last stages of typhoid fever.'

Fright arouses terror, he found, and 'terror forces us to find some means of self-defence'. Hence the 'confession'.

'"Death, oh most certainly, death is easier than this!" the interrogated person says to himself. I began to incriminate myself in the hope that this, at least, would lead quickly to the scaffold.'

His trial was held on 1 February 1940. He pleaded not guilty, and again denied the testimony beaten from him. He was sentenced to death, and shot the next day.

The premiere of the long-delayed Sixth Symphony took place on 5 November 1939, as Meyerhold underwent his Calvary. It was played by the Philharmonia under Mravinsky. It was a success, and the finale was encored, but it had none of the resonance of the Fifth. Shostakovich admitted as much himself. It differed in mood and emotional tone, he told the press before the performance, with none of the moments of tragedy and tension. It was contemplative and lyrical. 'I wanted to convey in it the moods of spring, joy, youth.' It was also shorter, at thirty minutes, with three movements: largo, allegro and presto.

No such zest and lightness were on display elsewhere. On 26 November, a 'provocation' was created. Finnish artillery was said to have fired on Russian villages: Hitler had used the same trick to invade Poland. Stalin wanted slices of Finnish territory to put Leningrad beyond Finnish artillery range. Four days later, the Red Army attacked with overwhelming force, preparation and timing.

This was offset by the deficiencies of Stalin's civil war crony, Marshal Kliment Voroshilov, as commander. The Finns should not have lasted a fortnight. The snow was four feet deep, and the temperature fell to minus 40 degrees Celsius. The Red Army penetrated thirty miles over the frontier. The Finns held them, and counter-attacked on 27 December. On New Year's Eve, the Soviet survivors were retreating back across the frontier in disorder. A fresh division was ordered to their aid. Its Ukrainians had no experience of the northern forests and such cold. They froze to death in snow-holes and lean-tos made with branches in ditches. Finnish patrols destroyed their field kitchens. The division was trapped in snowdrifts. On 7 January 1940 the Finns overran its last bunkers. Vinogradov, the divisional commander, escaped over the border in a tank: Stalin ordered him shot. Snow shrouded the Russian dead and dying. The Finns estimated Russian losses at 22,500 men, their own at 2,700.

A second assault began in February. The British and French considered sending an expeditionary force to help the Finns. They had no time to dispatch it. The Russians came back with 1.2 million men, five Armies' worth, supported by 3,000 aircraft and more than a thousand tanks. The Finns were outnumbered six to one. They were slowly forced back. On 3 March 1940 they sued for peace.

Zhdanov organized a great victory parade through Leningrad. Only reserve units took part in it. Care was taken to isolate the city from front-line troops, and the wounded.

The 'Winter War' encouraged the watchful Germans. The General Staff used it to evaluate the Red Army: 'In quantity, a gigantic military instrument ... Organization, equipment and means of leadership, unsatisfactory ... Communications system bad, transportation system bad, no personalities.' It concluded: 'Fighting qualities of the troops in a *heavy* fight, dubious. The Russian "mass" is *no* match for an army with modern equipment and superior leadership.'

To others, to the poet Olga Berggolts, it was the 'unnatural silence' that was the most terrible aspect of the war, the unspoken suffering and loss of life:

> It is so quiet, so quiet that the thought of war
> is like a wail, like sobbing in the darkness.
> Here people, snarling, writhing, crawled,
> here blood foamed an inch deep on the ground.
> Here it's quiet, so quiet that it seems
> never again will anyone come here ...
> It is so quiet, so mute – neither life nor death.
> O, it is more severe than any reproach.
> Neither life nor death – muteness, muteness –
> Despair which constricts the lips.
> The dead take measureless revenge on the living
> they know everything, remember everything

Film work kept Shostakovich busy. His score for the comic *Adventures of Korzinkina* was bright, breezy and catchy, like its heroine, a railway ticket inspector with a heart of gold and an eye for romance.

He was in Luga for his summer holiday in 1940. In June, the day after France fell to the Germans, the Red Army moved into the Baltic states. So did Zhdanov, as he set up the Estonian Soviet Socialist Republic, in his brutal fashion. On the night of 14 June, the NKVD rounded up ten thousand Estonians. Word soon reached Leningrad. The first freight trains crammed with 'enemies of the people' – the better-off farmers, hoteliers, bank clerks, teachers, officers, factory owners, people who had family in America, who spoke Esperanto – rattled through the city's marshalling yards on their way to the Arctic and Siberian camps.

Shostakovich thought of orchestrating Offenbach's *La belle Hélène* – he 'loved it madly' – but he dropped it, and did Mussorgsky's *Boris Godunov* instead. He also began writing his piano quintet in G minor. It was completed on 14 September, and he was at the piano with the Beethoven quartet at the premiere on 23 November. It was charming, bright, melodic. It was nominated for a Stalin Prize by the Union of Composers. *Pravda* said that it was 'unquestionably the best composition of 1940'.

His rehabilitation, though, was far from complete. Ominously, Moisey Grinberg, music administrator and future artistic director of the Moscow Philharmonia, denounced it in a letter to Stalin. He said that it had 'aroused unhealthy passions' and, worse, was of 'profoundly Western orientation. This is music that does not connect with the life of the people.'[66] The prize, though, was awarded.

It gave the composer a little life insurance. His technical brilliance still gleamed. The conductor Boris Khaikin telephoned him in desperation one evening. He wanted an extra piece, a polka, in a production of Johann Strauss II's *Gipsy Baron* that he was doing, and he could find no material. Overnight, Shostakovich orchestrated the Vergnügungszug polka with such zest and fun that it was encored at every performance after the premiere in February 1941.

His depth, though, was inspired in part by the passion for 'external events' he had as a student. He could not write of the terror, at home or in the fresh territories on the Baltic, nor of the bloodlust of the Kremlin's German friends. Do so, and both he and the music would be as dead as Meyerhold. A new cataclysm was building, however, on which he could spill all his genius.

He had not long to wait.

CHAPTER 2

Voyna

War

Shostakovich spent March 1941 in Leningrad, finishing the incidental music for Grigori Kozintsev's staging of *King Lear*. It had its premiere in the city's Bolshoi Dramatic Theatre on 24 March. The terror had brushed close to both men when it took Meyerhold, their mutual acquaintance. Kozintsev's background – a founder of the Factory of Eccentric Actors, the director of radical films said to smack of expressionism – was as high-risk as Shostakovich's. The pair were on safer ground with *Lear*. The music so exactly captured the play, Kozintsev said, that to listen to it was 'to hear Shakespeare's verse'. Shostakovich was intrigued by the character of the Fool. He found 'his wit . . . prickly and sarcastic, his humour clever and black'[1] – much like, he might have added, his own – and he caught this in his *Ten Songs for the Fool*.* In the middle of the month, he was awarded the Stalin Prize for his piano quintet. It reduced the odds of arrest, for the moment at least.

Ice-blue winter skies gave way to sodden grey in April. He hoped to start work on *Katyusha Maslova*, an opera based on the heroine of Tolstoy's *Resurrection*. The libretto, written by the poet and novelist Anatoli Mariengof, was completed early in March. Shostakovich agreed to compose the opera, and the Kirov to produce it. Mariengof, though,

---

* Kozintsev and Shostakovich returned to *King Lear* with a magnificent film version in 1971. The director said that Shostakovich's music brought with it 'a ferocious hatred of cruelty, the cult of power, and the oppression of justice' and 'a fearless goodness which has a threatening quality'.

was tainted. He had been the closest friend of Sergei Yesenin, the brilliant and haunted poet, briefly married to Isadora Duncan, and then to Tolstoy's granddaughter, dead at thirty hanging from the ceiling pipes in his room at the Hotel Angleterre in Leningrad in 1925. Mariengof had written *The Novel without Lies*, a work about their friendship that dealt with the Revolution with unacceptable clarity and power. Mariengof had become a non-person in print, no longer published, and his name removed from the dedication pages Yesenin had placed in his collections of poems. He worked when he could for theatre and radio. The libretto was sent to Glavrepertkom, the State repertoire committee, for approval. Its cable in response was brutally brief: 'The libretto for the opera *Katyusha Maslova* has been banned.'[2]

So Shostakovich escaped to the south. He visited Rostov-on-Don, and then took a month's holiday with his wife Nina. They returned to Gastra, a spa on the Black Sea, where they had been in 1937. Tolstoy had lived here for a year or so at the turn of the century, exchanging visits with Chekhov, who, slowly dying of tuberculosis, had come to ease his ravaged lungs with soft sea breezes. A fine coastal path ran high above the sea to the great Romanov palace at Livadia, rebuilt in Italian marble by Nicholas and Alexandra. Felix Yusupov, the young prince who murdered their friend, Grigory Rasputin, had built his own colossal Moorish extravaganza close by at Koreiz. It was less than twenty-five years since the prince had dumped Rasputin's body into the ice-choked Neva. The Bolsheviks had obliterated the imperial memories as best they could – the Tsar's Path to the Livadia was renamed Solnechnaya Tropa, the Sunny Path, and the palace did humble duty as a mental asylum* – but they lingered on.

---

* Towards the end of the coming war, the victors' Yalta Conference was held at Livadia, where President Roosevelt and Winston Churchill were lodged, though Stalin himself preferred to stay in the Yusupov palace. Such a future, of course, and such allies, would have seemed quite as lunatic to Shostakovich and his fellow vacationers in 1941 as the Livadia's unfortunate patients.

It still had elegance. Geraniums tumbled steeply from stone balustrades to the sea. The composer's soul unwound, playing tennis, refereeing volleyball games, and lacing vodka with berries. His fellow composer and close friend, Vissarion Shebalin, was staying in the spa with his wife Alisa and their son. The weather turned cold, Nina went off walking with some artist friends, and Shostakovich told Alisa that they needed some *vodochka* to warm themselves up. 'I've just seen some juniper bushes in the park,' he said. 'Let's go and collect some berries and marinate them in vodka.' There was an empty water carafe on the piano in his room. He put some fistfuls of berries into it and emptied a bottle of local vodka over them. They waited a while, and he poured some into a large tea glass. 'Mitya took a gulp, and the next moment I saw him clutch his throat, while his eyes stood out on stalks,' Alisa recalled. She asked what was wrong with him. 'Try it and you'll see.' She sniffed: 'It was pure turps.' 'Never mind,' he said. 'I'll invite those artist friends of Nina's for a drink. That'll teach them.'[3]

As he amused himself, climbing up on the referee's chair to umpire volleyball games between holidaymakers, Europe fell deeper into the abyss. The Germans invaded and overran Yugoslavia and Greece, and pounded the British in North Africa. In Moscow, a non-aggression pact was signed with Japan on 13 April. In celebration, Stalin, Molotov and Yosuke Matsuoka, the Japanese foreign minister, got blind drunk.

Shostakovich travelled home by train via Moscow. He and Nina were travelling in 'international', first class, and they invited the Shebalins to join them from second class. The violinist Miron Poliakin was travelling in the next compartment. Shostakovich knew him well. Both men had studied and then gone on to teach at the Leningrad Conservatoire. Poliakin spent eight years there as a professor before moving to the Moscow Conservatoire in 1936. He was on his way back to Moscow after a concert tour. He appeared with a large box of chocolates, and handed them round. Then he and Shostakovich started playing cards.

Alisa Shebalina recalled that Shostakovich was on a winning streak. Poliakin was in 'a terrible state', so much so that she turned to Shostakovich and begged him: 'Don't torture him any more, stop playing.' The party broke up, and they returned to their compartments. When the train pulled into Moscow the next morning, Alisa saw Shostakovich rushing up and down the platform 'like a wounded animal', his face as white as a sheet. She asked him what was wrong. Poliakin could not be aroused when the train arrived. 'He is dead,' Shostakovich told her. The militia were called. Shostakovich was the last person to have seen the violinist alive. He was interrogated for an hour and a half before Shebalina convinced the militia that he was 'the People's Artist, our most famous composer', and not a criminal gambler. He was shocked – by the death, and the suspicion that he had played some part in it – and she insisted that he stay at her Moscow flat for a few days. Her husband took him to a football match to get his mind off it, before he continued his journey to Leningrad.[4]

It seemed an ill omen.

Spring in the city was cold and damp. Fogs drifted in from the Gulf of Finland over the sullen grey surface of the Neva. Sour fumes from chemical plants mixed with the sweet and acrid smoke from peat fires and clung to clothing. Snow fell on May Day. The marchers in the parades kicked up sprays of slush. Lovers traced their initials in the moisture that gave a damp sheen to the pink granite embankments along the river.

Shostakovich drove Nina and the children out to their green-painted wooden dacha in Komarovo, a resort on the Gulf twenty-five miles from Leningrad. The cottage was calm and homely, with a piano for composing, and a summer colony of artists and other musicians to visit. He spent his weekends here, though chilling rains still fell, returning to work at the Conservatoire during the week. It was a relaxing place, with a beach of smooth grey pebbles and a pale-washed clarity to the sky, though the terror lapped even here. Half seen through the birch and pines, like the sea, Shostakovich could glimpse a nearby sign, on a fine old house with intricate fretwork eaves. 'Rest House for Justice Workers and Procurators', it read. This was the dacha of lower-ranking NKVD officers.[5]

As the weather, so the times were melancholy and out of sorts. The constant rumours of war passed Stalin by. He loosed fresh purges on the senior military officers who would wage it if – when – it broke out. Most at risk were those who might have seemed indispensable, with first-hand combat experience, gained against the fascists and their German allies in Spain, and against the Japanese in the Far East.

Beria's men in their cornflower blue NKVD caps, came calling on Ernst Shakht on 31 May; for good measure, they soon arrested his wife as well. He was the Red Air Force commander in the Orel Military District, a major-general at thirty-six, Swiss-born, an idealist who had arrived in the Soviet Union after teenage years as a young communist in Berlin. Shakht had commanded a bomber squadron in Spain.

The catch-all used against him – 'member of an anti-Soviet conspiracy' – covered others who were being picked up. Yakov Smushkevich, the general inspector of the Red Air Force, had a few days' grace. Under the name 'General Douglas' he had led the air defence of Madrid. He was the leading Soviet air ace in Spain, brave, twice a Hero of the Soviet Union, with two Orders of Lenin, but he was only thirty-nine, and his lack of experience had been shown up as aviation commander during the Winter War. He had survived that debacle, but his luck now ran out.

In the early hours of 7 June, a flashlight awoke his teenage daughter Roza as she slept with her mother in the family apartment in the Dom na Naberezhnoi, a block of flats on the Moscow Embankment where the elite were housed. The NKVD men who roused her were wearing doctor's white smocks. 'The reason,' she recollected, 'was that they had just arrested Father in the hospital.' Smushkevich had been recovering from an aircraft accident. They had carried him from his sick-bed on a stretcher. They searched the flat for thirty-six hours. 'We had about 4,000 books. They went through every book and then threw it onto a pile. They took away all our mattresses and pillows, so we had to sleep on the floor . . .'[6]

Her father was already in the Lubyanka, undergoing interrogation as a preliminary to torture. He would be dead by autumn, shot – though neither man knew it – only a mile or two from where Shostakovich was to find himself working on the Seventh. Roza and her mother were left alone for eighteen months. Then, 'the Lubyanka remembered about our existence. They came for us.' Mother and daughter were sent to a transit prison in Kazakhstan, and then to a labour camp.

The same day, Colonel-General Grigory Shtern was arrested. He had been the senior Soviet adviser in Spain before commanding the Far East Front, where the Red Army had beaten the Japanese. He was a Hero of the Soviet Union, with two Orders of Lenin and three Red Banners, and he had been a member of the party's Central Committee. Boris Vannikov was also picked up on 7 June. He was the armaments commissar, a vital figure, and a convenient scapegoat for mechanical breakdowns in new tanks and aircraft coming into service, and for bottlenecks in supply.

It was folly to traumatize the officer corps at such a time. Madness, too, lay behind the NKVD squads who were sent from Leningrad into the former Baltic states on 16 May. They began mass arrests of 'former people', the usual mix of officers, landowners, teachers, civil servants, traders. Galina Vishnevskaya was a witness. Later Russia's finest soprano, and, with her husband Mstislav Rostropovich, a close friend of Shostakovich,* she was then a fourteen-year-old schoolgirl, from Kronstadt, the island fortress that guards the sea approaches to Leningrad. Her father was a violent alcoholic, with a record in Bolshevik

---

* She and Rostropovich made perhaps the most brilliant recordings of *Lady Macbeth of Mtsensk*.

repression dating back to his teenage years, so that his 'hands were spattered with the blood of his brothers . . . Not even vodka could quiet the voice of his conscience.' He was posted to Tartu in Estonia after the Soviet takeover. She went to spend her summer holidays with him.

Galina was amazed at living standards in Estonia – 'the people so well dressed, so well fed, the streets so clean' – but she had been brought up to know why. 'Of course, all this was a capitalist plot! They wanted to entice "Soviet man", stupefy him, and then . . . But you can't fool us! Every day on the radio we're warned of this, even children know better. Besides, my daddy's job is to indoctrinate you Estonians.' In his cups, her father roared at the Balts: 'We'll soon put an end to these bastards! Parasitic gluttons!'[7]

One light summer night, as she came home from a friend's house, she saw a truck in a deserted street. It was crammed with people, who were silent, 'ghostlike'. A girl suddenly sprang from the truck and started to run. First came the clacking of her high heels echoing from the cobblestones, then the pounding of jackboots as soldiers took off after her. 'And then . . . silence. They had caught her, of course, but she hadn't cried out.' That was the way 'Soviet brothers' rounded up the 'voluntary joiners' from the Baltic states, and 'took them into exile, or to be shot'. It went on in front of Galina's eyes – during the Terror, she had watched the mother of her Estonian neighbours in Kronstadt being deported, a woman she had known all her life, 'old Fenya, her feet swollen, leaning on her grown children as she inched along' – but it did not affect her deeply. It was what the leader decreed, and she had won her first encores as a nine-year-old singing on Lenin's birthday:

> In the cities, in the country,
> The great billow seethes.
> Sing it louder – this is our banner!
> Hear it, Lenin? The earth is trembling!

If the leader was now Stalin, it made no difference: 'Stalin is Lenin today!'[8]

The NKVD reported on 17 June that 14,467 people – the stocktaking was as exact as ever – were filling the local prisons to overflowing. Another 27,511 had been torn from their homes, and were on the cattle-trucks that shunting engines were making up into Siberia-bound trains in the Leningrad marshalling yards.

The American diplomat Harold Eeman saw the new exiles as he travelled home from Moscow to Los Angeles. His trans-Siberian express passed a long train of wagons on a siding where slower trains waited. Out of the tiny square windows, the heads and shoulders of children appeared, as their fathers lifted them clear of the foul air inside.[9]

The places from which they had been torn – Lithuania, Latvia, Estonia – lay on the invasion route from German-occupied Poland to Leningrad. NKVD brutality made sure that their peoples were alienated from the Soviet cause, and would welcome the Germans with pealing church bells and garlands of flowers as liberators.

A vision of Europe's cultural apocalypse tormented a Pole held in a Russian camp. 'I think with horror and shame of a Europe divided into two parts by the line of the Bug,' he said. The Bug was the river dividing Poland into its Soviet- and German- occupied halves. 'On one side millions of Soviet slaves pray for their liberation by the armies of Hitler, and on the other millions of victims of German concentration camps await deliverance by the Red Army as their last hope.'

Summer rode in behind violent thunderstorms to bring clear and brilliant skies on Saturday, 21 June. The Neva sparkled in a fresh breeze. On Yelagin Island, an elegant isle in the river, Leningraders sunbathed on the fresh green grass, playing chess and volleyball, and hired rowing boats to drift on the current. The limes were in flower on the Champs de Mars. Yellow blooms of forsythia hung in the Summer Garden. University exams were over, and the students were free to join the Gulyaniye, the promenade that marked the city's summer festival of 'White Nights' (the period of near-constant daylight), walking arm-in-arm along the university embankment and crossing the Palace Bridge. They met up at the Café Ice Cream and the Green Frog. The elite dined at the Astoria and the Europe, or danced the foxtrot to the trumpet of Eddie Rozner* and his jazz band.

Many artists and writers welcomed the weekend warmth in their dachas on the Gulf. Journalists from *Leningradskaya Pravda* were relaxing at the newspaper's dacha near Komorovo. That morning's edition had the headline 'Tamerlane and the Timurids at the Hermitage'. The museum was preparing an exhibition of Mongol treasures. The paper had been carrying regular reports on a scientific expedition to Samarkand that was examining the mausoleum where the Mongol emperor was buried. On Friday, it reported how the coffin had been opened and the skeleton had been found to have one leg shorter than the other: he had indeed been Timur the Lame. No credence was given to the legend that beneath the slab of green nephrite on the sarcophagus 'lies the source of terrible war'.[10] No mention was made either of Hitler's legions massing along the Bug.

Shostakovich did not join the weekend exodus. He had work to do in the city. The work of students at the Conservatoire was still being assessed. He was chairman of the piano commission, and a member of the composition jury. He was also awarding stipends for the next academic year. He had tickets for the Spartak Leningrad football match on

---

*Adolph 'Eddie' Rozner was Europe's finest jazz trumpeter. Berlin-born, he played on transatlantic liners between Hamburg and New York. By 1939, he found Germany no place to be 'a Jew playing Negro music, even if your name is Adolph'. He left for Poland, fleeing to Soviet-controlled territory after the Nazi invasion. His band was highly popular, and he became leader of the Soviet State Jazz Orchestra during the war. He was one of the first victims of the post-war purges in 1946, and spent eight years in Gulag camps in Kolyma in the far east of Siberia.

Sunday afternoon. They were languishing in twelfth place in the 15-team Group A league, five places adrift of Spartak Moscow, their opponents for Sunday. Shostakovich planned to go to the game with his friend Isaak Glikman, followed by supper in a restaurant.[11] His favourite team was Dynamo Leningrad. He was a passionate fan, who had once invited the whole team home for dinner.[12] They were only a point behind the Group A leaders, Dynamo Moscow, but they had a tough away game against Tbilisi Dynamo to play on Tuesday.

Weekends increased the tempo of musical life in the city. Karl Eliasberg, the director of the Leningrad Radio Symphony Orchestra, was busy all Saturday afternoon with rehearsals. Eliasberg was late home to his apartment on Vasilievsky Island. He saw in the paper that an exhibition was being held in the Catherine Palace on Sunday to mark the centenary of the death of the poet Mikhail Lermentov. He decided to go.[13]

The city's premier orchestra, the Leningrad Philharmonic, was preparing its autumn programme. Its conductor was Yevgeny Mravinsky, by now a personal friend of Shostakovich, tall, dominating his fiery orchestra with cool and precise control. He was already considered the finest conductor in Russia, and he and his musicians had the experience of performing Shostakovich's Fifth and Sixth behind them. An elite, conscious of their superiority over the humdrum Eliasberg and his second-fiddle Radio players, they had every reason to expect that they would be the first play the Seventh.

On Alexandrinsky Square, the State Ballet School spent all day rehearsing for a programme to be danced on Monday at the Marinsky. It was to celebrate the jubilee of Elena Lyukom. Her ethereal grace had made her one of Fokine's finest ballerinas. She had danced with Diaghilev, and memorably as Stravinsky's Firebird. The graduation performance of Madame Vaganova's 1941 class was to be held on Wednesday. Agrippina Vaganova was the most renowned ballet teacher of her age, and her Vaganova Method of training retains its brilliance. She was sixty-three, but was as strict as ever as her class prepared the ballet *Bela*.[14]

At the Lenfilm studios on the Petrograd Side, they were about to start shooting a film on the composer Glinka. A new opera, *Alexander Nevsky*, composed by Gavriil Popov, was on the rehearsal schedule at the Mariinsky. It was due for an autumn premiere. That evening, Popov and his wife were playing a Scriabin sonata at two grand pianos in a part of the Catherine Palace in Pushkin, as the wondrous summer retreat of the Romanovs at Tsarskoye Selo had been renamed. The music floated over the avenues of linden trees in the park. Popov was an exact contemporary of Shostakovich, whose talent he had been thought to share. He, too, had come close to destruction. His first symphony had its premiere in 1935. It was banned immediately, and was never played again in his lifetime. He, like Shostakovich, was suspected of betraying Socialist realism and lapsing into formalism, and from 1936 he drowned much of his genius for melodic grandeur in alcohol and trite propaganda cantatas, *Honour to our Party, Heroic Poem for Lenin*.

In the border fortress town of Brest, where Soviet and German troops faced each other in dismembered Poland, the Russians spent the afternoon drilling to the music of a military band. The sound of tank engines drifted on the air from the German positions on the other side of the Bug. A packed house at the officers' club watched an evening performance of the romantic comedy *A Wedding in Malinovka*. Officers of the Eleventh Soviet Army planned fishing trips for Sunday. No extra guards were posted. To avoid any accidental 'provocations', for which they would be severely punished, they had their troops deposit their ammunition in the armouries.[15]

As troops moved up to their start lines, German officers watched as 'oil tank trains rolled continuously westward, past us, from oilfields on the Soviet side', part of the million tons of oil the Russians shipped with other war materiel to the Germans. Soviet frontier guards passed the Berlin–Moscow express through Brest shortly after midnight.

Stalin had repeated warnings of what was coming. Operation Barbarossa, Hitler's invasion of the Soviet Union, was the greatest military offensive in history. It had sucked in troops, tanks, heavy guns and aircraft from across Nazi-occupied Europe. Evidence of their intentions poured in from Soviet agents.

Bridging equipment had been brought up close to the frontier. Reconnaissance aircraft were violating Soviet airspace daily. Rolling stock and locomotives were being modified in Warsaw workshops to run on broader Russian-gauge track. Instructions to German agents in Russia were intercepted, ordering them to get samples of Soviet fuel and lubricants.

Messages became more specific. In April, the Soviet agent Richard Sorge, who had access to the secrets of the German embassy in Tokyo, had warned of a surprise attack. On 15 May, he gave 21 or 22 June as the start date. The British added their own warning to Moscow on 13 June. Stalin dismissed it as a 'provocation'. Hitler explained the massive troop build-up, the constant noise of tank engines, the aircraft activity, in terms of training exercises for the invasion of Britain, which were being held beyond the range of British aircraft. Stalin accepted it.

Another agent, Harro Schulze Boysen, an Oberleutnant on the Luftwaffe staff in Berlin, reported to Moscow on 17 June: 'All military measures fully complete, attack may be expected at any moment.' The report reached the Kremlin, where Stalin scrawled in green pencil across it: 'You can tell your "source" from the German air force HQ that he can go and f--- his mother. This is not a "source" but a disinformant.'[16] Harbourmasters in Soviet Baltic ports noted that German ships were leaving without unloading. In the Baltic Shipyards in Leningrad, German technical experts had been working for a year on an unfinished cruiser that had been sold to the Red Navy. They started leaving, on one pretext or another, in May. They had all gone by mid-June.

In Moscow, where an invasion was the staple of diplomatic chatter, thirty-four staff at the German diplomatic community left abruptly for home. The Fire Brigade in Moscow reported that those who were left were burning documents. On 19 June, a Soviet reconnaissance pilot, Colonel G. N. Zakharov, flew the length of the border. He found that the Germans were getting ready to attack 'in the very near future'.[17] The report went to his superiors, Dmitry Pavlov and Ivan Kopets, who commanded Soviet forces in the west. They did not send it on to Moscow: they feared Stalin's wrath, rightly so, as the manner of their deaths would show soon enough.

In the early evening of 21 June, a German deserter, Alfred Liskow of the 22nd Engineer Regiment, crossed to Soviet lines at Brest. Details of his interrogation were forwarded to Moscow at 9 p.m. He said that the Germans would cross the river Bug and attack in the pre-dawn next morning. Stalin dismissed the report: 'the Germans might have sent him over to provoke us.'[18] At 1.45 a.m. on 22 June, the Kremlin issued a half-hearted warning. A surprise German attack was possible and the Red Army should be 'alert', but it added a rider: 'the task of our troops is not to respond to any provocative actions that might result in serious provocation.'[19]

Hitler had by now massed 3,200,000 men along the thousand miles of frontier, in 148 divisions, with 3,350 tanks and two thousand aircraft. They were divided into three army groups, each under a field marshal. Army Group North under Wilhelm von Leeb was tasked to smash the Eleventh Army and its would-be anglers, opening the way to Riga and driving on from the Baltic states for Leningrad. That the city was named for the founder of Bolshevism increased Hitler's lust to destroy it. The Centre group was to attack along the Moscow highway to Minsk and

Smolensk. Army Group South was to fight its way into the Ukraine and the Caucasus with Kiev and the Dnieper as early targets.

The seventeen panzer divisions and their armour were split from the infantry, as they had been in Poland and France. They were concentrated into four independent groups, under brilliant, driving commanders: Kleist with 1st Panzer in the South, and Guderian and Hoth with 2nd and 3rd in the Centre; 4th Panzer, under Hoepner, was to make for Leningrad in the North, with help on its southern flank from Guderian.

Hitler's Directive said: 'The mass of the Russian army in western Russia is to be destroyed in daring operations by driving four deep wedges with tanks, and the retreat of the enemy's battle-ready forces into the wide spaces of Russia is to be prevented.' The panzer groups were to penetrate the flanks of Russian forces marked down for liquidation and then wheel inwards to cut them off from their supply routes and paralyse their commands.

German *Landsers* – the infantry – would thrust in on the enemy flanks to achieve an inner and more intimate encirclement. Horses powered most of their transport, as they had for Napoleon's Grande Armée. The supply wagons of the infantry battalions were pulled by two horses. The *Protzes* were combinations of two-wheel gun carriages, the first carrying ammunition and the gun crew, with the howitzer towed behind. A 75mm gun needed four horses, a 150mm took six horses to shift it. The Germans had more than a million horses, and they requisitioned more as they advanced.

Facing them, Stalin had 174 divisions in the frontier zone and in reserve, a little over half the strength of the Red Army. The first echelon had 56 divisions and two brigades, deployed to a depth of 34 miles from the border. The second echelon was held at a depth of 30 to 60 miles, with reserves at up to 236 miles. The Germans had roughly the same strength in infantry. They were numerically inferior by seven to one in tanks, and four to one in aircraft. Surprise alone could not offset this weakness. They depended on experience, skill, leadership, initiative and élan. These qualities they had in profusion.

The final touch was put in place. At midday on Saturday, the Berlin composer Norbert Schultze was relaxing at home after an exhausting week when the director of Berlin Radio called him urgently to the studios. German radio chose a new piece of music for each major campaign. Schultze was told that Joseph Goebbels, the propaganda minister, wanted to produce a 'Russian fanfare' for Barbarossa. Schultze and his colleague Herms Niel were shown into a studio, with a grand piano. Each was to produce a tune, with Goebbels choosing the winner. They were given two hours. Both composers were Nazi party members, and had worked for Goebbels before. Niel had written popular marches, and the Luftwaffe song, 'Stuka über Afrika'. Schultze, writer of 'Bomben auf England', had written the haunting music for 'Lili Marlene', originally for a radio toothpaste commercial. Set to words, and sung by Lale Andersen, it was perhaps the song most loved by soldiers on all fronts. Goebbels declared Schultze the winner. His piece was to provide a fanfare before the music that Goebbels had chosen as the signature tune for Barbarossa. This tune was to be played before all major radio announcements, and a special recording had already been made.

The Germans were to invade Russia to Liszt's *Preludes*.

It began, in pre-dawn darkness, at 3.15 a.m. on Sunday, 22 June. 'The first salvo!' wrote Helmut Pabst, a German NCO in the Brest sector. 'At the same moment everything sprang to life. Firing along the whole front . . . The Russian watch towers vanished in a flash. In file and in line, the infantry swarmed forward. Bog, ditches, boots full of water and mud. Flame-throwers advanced against the strong points. The fire of machine guns, and the high-pitched whip of rifle bullets.'[20]

As dawn broke, the sky filled for a time with waves of Heinkel and Junkers bombers, Stuka dive-bombers and fighters flying into the rising sun. The leading tanks were across the Bug by 4.45 a.m. The clatter of their tracks faded as they raced eastward.

Army Group North, with its three panzer divisions and 600 tanks, was aimed like a dagger for Leningrad. It attacked on a narrow, 25-mile front, chopping up the Russian rifle division on the frontier piecemeal. Its radio operators picked up repeated Russian appeals for orders from Moscow. 'We are being fired on, what shall we do?' One reply was: 'You must be insane. And why is your signal not in code?'[21] The purges had destroyed any sense of initiative in the Red Army. Its commanders waited for commands from the Kremlin. None came.

Colonel Starinov, the Spanish veteran, was at an army headquarters near Brest. It was bombed. 'Thick black pillars of smoke billowed up,' he said. 'A newly felled tree lay across the street. Part of the HQ building was in ruins. Somewhere a high-pitched, hysterical female voice was crying out a desperate, inconsolable "Aaaaaaa!"' Moscow Radio was broadcasting keep-fit exercises. The news mentioned German bombing raids, on cities in Scotland. General Boldin in Minsk spoke to Marshal Timoshenko, the Defence Commissar, in Moscow. He told him that 'Our troops are in full retreat. Whole towns are in flames, people are being killed all over the place.' Timoshenko told him that no action was to be taken against the Germans without specific orders. 'Comrade Stalin has forbidden to open fire against the Germans.'

Another officer from Spain, where he had fought as 'General Pavlovich', was aboard the Red Arrow express on its way from Moscow to Leningrad. Kiril Meretskov had fought in the defence of Madrid and he had played a major role in the rare Republican victory at Guadalajara. On his return, he commanded the Leningrad Military District. He was now a major figure in the Stavka, the High Command, and he was on an urgent mission to check on the readiness of the armies in the north. The Red Arrow pulled in to the October Station in Leningrad at 11.45 a.m. Meretskov already knew that he and the other Spanish veterans were vulnerable to Stalin and Beria. He learned that they were at war with Hitler, too.

It was not until midday that Molotov went on radio to break the news of the war in a halting voice. The Red Air Force had already lost 1,200 aircraft, 900 on the ground and 300 in the air. Returning Luftwaffe pilots half apologized for the 'infanticide' they had wrought on ill-trained men in obsolete aircraft. Resistance was so slight that they were able to fly deep into the rear so low that the 'spiders of their swastikas' were clearly visible from the ground. The Red air commander on the Western Front was Major General Ilya Kopets, another Spanish veteran. His promotion had been dizzy – three years before, he had been a mere captain – and the slaughter of his aircrews overwhelmed him. He shot himself on the first evening of the war.

Shostakovich was getting ready to go to the Spartak stadium with Glikman when Molotov came on the radio. The game was cancelled. He kept his unused tickets as a memento. He was worried for his family at the dacha. Komorovo was dangerously close to the Finnish border, and the Finns could be expected to avenge the Winter War. He planned to move the children, small and vulnerable, back into the city.

The Kirov ballerina Alla Shelest, ironically enough, had danced the Peace Angel in Shostakovich's ballet *Golden Age*. She heard Molotov speak, and then headed straight off to the Kirov rehearsal hall to exercise. She was due to dance in the benefit performance for Lyukom on Monday. 'We didn't know if there would be a performance or not.' She was young, just twenty-two, a 'very rare dancer, sensitive and delicate with a physical grace and allure that was utterly captivating'. In her 1937 graduation performance, she had taken the title role in Lavrovsky's ballet *Katerina* with stunning success. The Kirov immediately engaged her as a leading soloist. She danced the whole repertoire, brilliant as the Lilac Fairy in *Sleeping Beauty*, as Giselle, as Nikia in *La Bayadère*, Street Dancer in *Don Quixote*, Siumbike in Leonid Jacobson's *Shurali*, and in Boris Aifman's *Guyana*.

For Liubov Shaporina, the brilliant stage designer who ran Leningrad's Puppet Theatre, it was the 'war of the two Herods', Hitler and Stalin. She felt that the war and the coming siege flowed seamlessly out of the great Terror that had preceded them. The horrors of both were a punishment that the *intelligentsiya* deserved. 'They have eliminated the Church. There is no God. He, our Father, has great patience, yet punishes severely . . .' She prayed to Him for mercy.

Another reaction came from the poet Olga Berggolts. She had suffered as much as any during the Terror. Her husband was shot in 1938, and she herself was arrested, pregnant, losing the child still-born when she was beaten during interrogations. She sat down with her typewriter – it was German, ironically, a Naumann Erika with Cyrillic script – at her small round table with a green velvet cloth.[22] Here she was to script many of her famous broadcasts. She wrote of how her love of her country was revived by the shock of war.

> I did not on this day forget
> The bitter years of oppression and of evil.
> But in a blinding flash I understood:
> It was not I but you who suffered and waited.
> No, I have forgotten nothing,
> But even the dead and the victims
> Will rise from the grave at your call;
> We will all rise, and not I alone.

I love you with a new love
Bitter, all-forgiving, bright –
My Motherland with the wreath of thorns
And the dark rainbow over your head . . .
I love you – I cannot otherwise –
And you and I are one again, as before.

This unforced patriotism flooded through millions of other Russians whom Bolshevism had grievously abused. Without it, the country would surely have foundered. Volunteers came forward in masses from the outset, Shostakovich among them. Ten-year-old Svetlana Magayeva was hoping to spend the day with her mother on Yelagin Island. An open-air concert was planned. Her mother insisted that they first clean their winter coats and bedding in the courtyard of their apartment block. The weather remained fine and brilliant, and she quoted a line from Mayakovsky:

The blue silken sky is above me
I feel well and it has never been so good.

But Mayakovsky had committed suicide in disillusion, and a neighbour, Uncle Vallya, destroyed the day's promise of bliss. He told them that the 'German fascists' were invading. He handed them the keys to his apartment, and said he was off to join the army. So, dressed in his summer best, in his white shirt and linen shoes he had just whitened with tooth powder, he set off. Her mother said that the trip to the island would have to wait until after the war. Svetlana was confused. The day before she had listened to a radio report that the Soviet Union had just dispatched a trainload of butter to Germany. Why, then, should the Germans attack? In the evening, her cousin Klava came to say goodbye. She was wearing an earth-brown military shirt and a dark blue beret with a small red star. She had just graduated from medical school and she was leaving for the front. Svetlana walked her to the tram stop to say goodbye.

At the front, the German tanks and Stukas were smashing deep into Soviet-occupied Lithuania. The din of gunfire and explosions hung on the horizon, far ahead of the foot-slogging *Landsers*, marching the pale Lithuanian plain, almost without resistance, while 'a kind of hypnosis set in as you watched the steady rhythm of the man's boots in front of you'. The leading tanks of the 8th Panzer Division and their motorcycle reconnaissance units advanced more than fifty miles on the first day. They threw a bridgehead across the Dubysa river. The *Landsers* came upon their handiwork in the evening: 'in drainage ditches and in the fields that lined the road, hundreds of still warm bodies lay where they had fallen . . . the enemy tanks we passed were wrecked hulks, often still belching oily black smoke.'[23]

The music played on in Leningrad. The Lyukom benefit went ahead at the Kirov on 23 June. Eliasberg conducted Borodin's Second Symphony, on warrior-heroes, and the overture to Glinka's *Ivan Susanin* (*A Life for the Tsar*). It was hardly a farewell to peace – Leningrad had not known that since Kirov had been murdered – but the audience sensed an adieu, a watershed, in the exquisite movements on stage.

The performance was shot through with quality. First there was *Don Quixote*, danced by Cherkasov, 'remarkable in the minuet, very gracious', with Lyukom drawing a 'storm of applause' as Kitre. Dudinskaya danced Street Girl, with Vecheslova and Iordan as the girlfriends, 'every number followed by a great ovation'.

It was followed by the first act of *Giselle*. Shelest danced variations in *Paquita* with Lyukom and Shabukiane. The only concession to the war was an order that the performance end by 11.30 p.m. Shelest felt 'something in the air, everyone was in a hurry, people were upset and exhilarated at the same time.' Lyukom's room backstage was awash with flowers, and she had her 'public greeting', speeches in her honour, in her room and not on stage.

Music was given military status the same day. It was to be treated as part of the war effort. 'Soviet songs are weapons to be used in battle,' the composer Aram Khachaturian wrote. 'It is our duty to forge them with total passion, pouring into them all our talent, skill and knowledge.' Frontline concert brigades, Konsertnaya Frontovaya Brigada, were formed in a revival of the old mobile agitation units that the Bolsheviks had formed in the civil war. The Union of Art Workers, which covered musicians, actors, entertainers and writers, sent a circular to troops on 23 June. It assured them that, wherever they were, art workers would be sharing their lives. 'Now, as never before,' it proclaimed, 'art will be a mighty and warlike means of victory of communism over fascism.'[24] By October, forty-one of these brigades were entertaining troops at the front. They had radio and cinema stars, comedians, dancers, singers and musicians. Special circus brigades brought their acrobats, clowns and dancing bears as close to the fighting as they could. Literary readers gave recitals of poetry and prose, for Russians are entranced by the music of their language.

The Union of Soviet Composers already had a 'defence section' devoted to patriotic and military songs. One of the most famous, 'If war comes . . .', written by the poet Vasilii Lebedev-Kumach, dated from 1938, and seemed prescient:

> If war comes tomorrow, if an enemy attacks,
> If a dark force suddenly appears,
> As one man the whole Soviet nation
> Will rise in defence of the Motherland.

Another 1938 song became the best loved of the war. It told of the greeting a girl named Katyusha sent to her distant soldier lover, asking him to guard their native land as she guards their love:

> The apple and pear trees were in bloom.
> Mists had floated out over the river
> Katyusha came out to the river bank,
> To the high, steep bank . . .

It was so popular that the Red Army called their multiple rocket launchers 'Katyushas'. The rockets were fired in bursts from frames mounted on trucks, the best of them American Studebakers. Four launchers could saturate a large area with more than four tons of high explosives in ten seconds. The Germans, who feared them, and were chilled by the characteristic and freezing whoosh that filled the air, called them '*Stalinorgel*', Stalin's organ.

Hundreds of popular songs were written in the first week. In little more than a month, 12,000 accordions were sent to the troops with 150,000 copies of a new songbook.

The House of Radio in Leningrad was militarized on 24 June. 'Barracks' or dormitories were set up so that staff could broadcast round the clock. The House was a large and elegant building on the corner of Malaya Sadovaya and Italyanskaya Streets, with cafés and terraces running to the Nevksy Prospekt in the social and artistic heart of the city. It had been built for the Assembly of Nobles, designed, like the imperious Metropol Hotel in Moscow, by the Kosyakov brothers, with its own theatre hall for concerts, and great high-ceilinged rooms that had been turned into broadcast studios. Radio Leningrad was run by the powerful Radio Committee, which had its own symphony and folk instrumental orchestras, plus choirs. It was the Radiokom's symphony orchestra, and its conductor, Eliasberg, who were to give Shostakovich's

Seventh its immortality. House of Radio programmes were transmitted and also brought to Leningraders by wire to 460,000 speakers, in apartments, factories and shops, and by 1,700 street loudspeakers.

At Dynamo Tbilisi's football ground, the Beria stadium, the home team beat Dynamo Leningrad three-two. The season was then abandoned. Shostakovich's side was not to play another Group A match for four years.* The composer himself volunteered for the army. He was told that he would be called when he was needed.

On the same day, in news that Radio Leningrad did not carry, the Soviet Northwest Front was splintered by von Leeb's assault. The Front commander, General Fyodor Kuznetsov, had so little idea of the fate of his armies that he testily refused to speak to the Stavka when an aide managed to get a line through to Moscow. 'What's the point of talking to them?' he snapped. 'They'll ask me about the situation, and I know nothing about it. We're not in touch with the armies, we have no idea of what the troops are doing.'[25]

At the tip of the Nazi spearheads, aircraft and panzers danced in the intricate combinations perfected in France and the Balkans. Dive-bombers blasted Russian positions, sirens shrieking, scattering men and weapons in the gun pits, while a distant plume of dust to the west marked the approach of the panzers. The reconnaissance units at the head motored at up to 25 mph. The dust blew off the corrugations in the dirt roads from the four- and eight-wheeled armoured cars, their sides festooned with tow ropes and jerrycans of water, swastikas draped in front of the gun mounting for recognition by the Stukas above. Black-goggled motorcyclists with stick grenades in their belts and a machine-gunner in the sidecar hastily chalked arrows for the line of advance. A few light tanks stiffened this vanguard as it flowed round points held by the Russians in strength.

---

* They beat Dynamo Minsk four-nil on 20 May 1945 in another Beria stadium, in Minsk.

The main tank force followed, in constant radio contact with the reconnaissance troops and aircraft, ready to deploy off the roads into attack formation where serious resistance was met. The panzer commanders moved constantly between the forward divisions and their command posts. In this fast-paced fury, they sometimes outran their own men. Guderian found himself in the middle of a Red Army infantry unit. 'I ordered my driver to go full-speed ahead and we drove straight through the Russians,' he wrote. 'They were so surprised that they did not even have time to fire their guns.'[26]

There were warning signs for the Germans. The panzers snapped forward on the operations maps like lizard tongues, narrow black penetrations, long, far ahead of their infantry, and vulnerable but for their speed. Around them was the immensity of Russia, in which the German units resembled battle fleets manoeuvring in the wastes of an ocean. In European terms, the 22 June front stretched from London to the coast of Algeria; for Americans, from Minneapolis to the Gulf of Mexico. It was widening, inexorably, and it would eventually run for the equivalent of London to Timbuktu, or New York to Mexico City.

Though the Germans had already taken more than a quarter of a million prisoners, a captain found it utterly unlike the French campaign. 'There was no feeling of entry into a defeated nation,' he wrote. 'Instead there was resistance, always resistance, however hopeless. A single gun, a group of men with rifles . . .'[27] Another officer spoke of 'uncanny, unbelievable, inhuman sights' in which, after the first wave of Russians vanished under machine-gun fire, other waves advanced across their own dead without hesitation. 'The fury of the attacks exhausted us and numbed us.'[28] It took a week for the largely Austrian 45th Infantry Division to subdue the Russian garrison in the fortress at Brest. This was a veteran division that had lost 462 men over the whole of the invasion of France. On the first day at Brest, 29 officers and 290 other ranks were killed. By the end, that figure had escalated to 40 dead officers and 442 other ranks, with a thousand wounded.[29] The divisional battle report spoke of 'a courageous garrison that cost us a lot of blood. The Russians fought with exceptional stubbornness and determination . . . a splendid will to resist.'[30]

The hot breath of war did not dissipate the miasma of terror.

General Meretskov had been summoned urgently to return from Leningrad to Moscow. He was in Stalin's outer office at the Kremlin in the evening of 24 June when an NKVD officer arrested him and escorted him to an isolation cell in the interrogation section of the Lefortovo prison. The questioning and torture began at once. He was joined by General Pavel Ryachagov, the former air force chief who had flown combat missions in Spain. His wife, the famous aviatrix Maria Petrovna Nesterenko, was also arrested on the grounds that, 'being Ryachagov's beloved wife, she would not have been unaware of his traitorous activities'.[31] Three days later, the commander of air forces of the Northern Front, General Ivan Proskurov, was arrested in Leningrad. Proskurov, too, had flying experience in Spain. This savaging of senior officers with combat experience had no motive beyond Stalin's wish to be rid of men whose 'independence of spirit and sense of combat brotherhood' he could not abide.[32]

Along the Baltic coast, NKVD officers were murdering their prisoners before von Leeb's fast-moving armour reached them. On the night of 24 June, the political prisoners in Telsiai in Lithuania were loaded into trucks. They included the usual 'enemies of the people' from the old regime – landowners, businessmen, lawyers and politicians, and also students from a local craft school whose crime was to have been Boy Scouts. They were driven to the Rainiai forests, in whose summery glades, by the light of summer's white night, they were brutally tortured, burned with torches and acid, their eyes gouged out, tongues, ears and genitals cut off, skulls fractured. The mutilations were such that only 27 of the 79 bodies could be identified three days later. At the Pravieniskes prison, near Kaunas, the NKVD shot the Lithuanian warders as well as 260 political prisoners.

The Party leadership fled from the Lithuanian capital that evening, some of them taking mattresses and bed linen with them on the evacuation trains. They feared, rightly, that their fellow countrymen would give short shrift to those who had collaborated with the Soviets. In their haste they left their archives intact, the radio station functioning and the high frequency telephone to the Kremlin still open.[33] Galina Vishnevskaya was alone at Tartu in Estonia. Her father was out of town. Amid chaos and shouting, she managed to get out on a bus filled with pilots. A detachment of soldiers followed, blowing up the bridges in its wake. 'It wasn't a retreat at all; it was a flight in panic.'[34] The NKVD shot some 250 prisoners in the prison courtyard and dumped their bodies in the well before they left. Officers and men of the Estonian XXII Rifle Corps, all Soviet loyalties eroded, were to desert to the Germans en masse.*

Soon found by the Germans, the bodies served Nazi propaganda in a dual capacity, for the NKVD leadership was substantially Jewish as well as undeniably Bolshevik. Some 40 per cent of high-ranking NKVD officers, at the height of the Yezhov terror, were recorded in their identity documents as Jewish. So were more than half of the NKVD generals.[35] Anti-Semitism was stirred among the locals by strident talk of 'Jewish Bolshevik' massacres.

German aircraft had flown from Finnish airfields on the first day of the war. The Finns stayed out of the war until Soviet bombers retaliated by attacking Helsinki and other targets on 25 June. The Finns then started what they called the 'continuation war', with the aim of recovering the land they had lost in 1940, and taking a slice of east

---

* Other prison massacres, in which the NKVD murdered tens of thousands, took place across the Ukraine and Belarus, as well as in the Baltic States and Russia.

Karelia. The Germans planned to link up with the Finns on the western shore of Lake Ladoga, completely cutting Leningrad off from the rest of Russia.

The Conservatoire continued its peacetime end-of-year ceremonials – exams were marked, scholarships awarded, graduations held – but Shostakovich went to retrieve his family from the dacha. Komarovo lay on the line of a Finnish advance, and it was emptying as its summer people fled. Little Galina Shostakovich's earliest memory was of a small red car that parked at the dacha gate. She was carrying an enormous doll in her arms, and she watched as her mother and father loaded it with suitcases.[36] Then they drove back to the city.

The country's most sacred object, Lenin's mummified corpse, was also on the move. It was taken from its red granite mausoleum on the Kremlin wall and placed in a special paraffin-sealed coffin aboard an NKVD 'fast' train. A mobile laboratory and the Zabarskys, a father-and-son team of embalmers, accompanied the corpse. It was taken to Tyumen, in western Siberia, safely beyond the range of German bombers.

A strong Russian force with up to 350 tanks was surrounded and destroyed by the lighter, outnumbered and outgunned tanks of XLI Panzer Corps late in the evening, after two days of ferocious fighting. The commanders of the lead tanks of the 8th Panzer Division now had the strategically vital bridges at Griva across the Dvina in sight through their fieldglasses. They were more than sixty miles ahead of the bulk of Army Group North.

Motorized infantry from the 3rd SS-Totenkopf (Death's Head) Division followed in their wake. 'We hardly saw any enemy apart from the occasional drive-by of enemy prisoners,' an SS officer, Hauptsturmführer Klinter, recalled. 'Heat, filth and clouds of dust . . .' As they motored on, the air had 'that putrefying and pervasive burnt smell so characteristic of the battle zone, and all nerves and senses began to detect the breath of the front. Suddenly all heads switched to the right. The first dead of the Russian campaign lay before our eyes like a spectre symbolizing the destructiveness of war. A Mongolian skull smashed in combat, a torn uniform and bare abdomen slit by shell splinters. The column drew up and then accelerated ahead, the picture fell behind us.'[37]

Special raiding units blooded in the Polish and French campaigns operated in the Russian rear, wearing enemy uniforms, seizing bridges and sowing confusion for the panzers to exploit. They were known as Brandenburgers after their base in Berlin. The 8th Brandenburger Company was tasked with seizing the rail and road bridges at Griva in a *coup de main* early on 26 June. They drove in six captured Russian trucks, headlights lit in the dawn, their Wehrmacht uniforms hidden beneath the Red Army uniforms they wore. The two bridges were a mile apart round a bend in the river. As they approached them, they saw that they were protected by Russian armoured cars. The bridge guards were unsuspecting, and chatting to civilian passers-by.

The Germans drove onto the main span of the railway bridge, and began cutting the wires on the suspected demolition charges before the Russians noticed anything was amiss. Even then, the armoured cars were reluctant to open fire, for fear of hitting their own men. On the road bridge, the Germans bayoneted the sentries and their trucks were on the bridge before the Russians reacted. One of the trucks was hit by an anti-tank round and the Oberleutnant commanding the Brandenburgers was killed. The leading panzers now moved up to the bridges and fought their way across with infantry in support. All day, the Germans picked off individual Russians who climbed onto the bridge spans trying to ignite demolition fuses. Soviet aircraft made bombing runs in vain attempts to destroy the bridges. The panzers knocked out twenty Russian tanks, and almost a score of anti-tank guns, and Russian infantry fought desperately along the river embankments.

By evening, though, the Germans were across the Dvina. One of the few natural obstacles in front of Leningrad had fallen. The following day,

27 June, Leningrad was placed under martial law. The city was closed
to all who did not have residence permits, an order that was to cause
immense hardships to refugees. A curfew ran from midnight to 4 a.m.
A complete blackout was imposed, though the White Nights of summer
meant that it did not inhibit enemy bomber pilots. Minsk, the capital
of Belarus, fell next day. A third of its people were Jews. The Germans
began murdering them within a day.

On 29 June, the first of ten trains, carrying a total of 15,192 children,
left Leningrad for nearby holiday camps at Gatchina and Luga, and
further afield to the countryside round Pskov and Novgorod. This put
them in the direct line of Army Group North's advance. Other trains
followed. Svetlana Magayeva went with her mother and a group from her
mother's school to a Young Pioneers' camp in Valdai, a town famous for
its lake and monastery, and sanatoriums on the Leningrad-to-Moscow
highway near Novgorod. It was a terrible error. They soon heard the
distant rumble of artillery. As it got closer, her mother took them to the
Valdai station. It was too late. No more passenger trains were leaving
for Leningrad. Only military traffic was allowed.

A troop train was coming, but the station guards said that it would not
stop. The children saw that it was being signalled. They were frightened.
'Suddenly, Mother jumped down from the station platform onto the
tracks,' Svetlana said. 'One of her old students followed her and stood
next to her . . . They both raised their arms. The train blasted its whistle.'
The train slowed slightly. There were soldiers on it and they jumped out
of the carriages. They grabbed the children and lifted them through
the windows and doors of the moving carriages into the arms of other
soldiers who had remained on the train.' Her mother clambered aboard.
She and the officer in charge stood at an open door, smoking cigarette
after cigarette. Had the driver stopped, the officer explained, he would
have been shot because it was a military train. They steamed on for
Leningrad, 'the sound of the cannonade behind us getting less and less'.

The city's wartime hierarchy was established. Supreme power lay with the State Defence Committee, chaired by Stalin, with Vyacheslav Molotov, Marshal Kliment Voroshilov, Georgi Malenkov and, underlining the NKVD's powers, Lavrenti Beria. The Committee kept close control of the administration in Leningrad through the city's Party organs. Andrei Zhdanov remained the Party boss. Peter Popkov led the Lensoviet, the Leningrad City Soviet – he described himself as mayor in interviews with western reporters – with Alexei Kuznetsov at the regional Party.

The evacuation of the city's museums and art galleries began on Zhdanov's orders on 1 July. All through the white night, trucks passed in convoys from the complex of the Hermitage Museum and the Winter Palace with thousands of boxes, and huge packing cases and wooden crates with great oil paintings and sculptures. They were offloaded by sailors and soldiers into rail cars.

At dawn, a train of treasures slipped out of the freight yards without fuss or whistles. The city was silent. Zhdanov had decreed that no clock chimes or factory hooters were to break a silence that only air-raid sirens were permitted to disturb. The train stretched for almost 500 yards, and it needed two locomotives to haul it. It had two flatcars with anti-aircraft guns, twenty-two freight cars packed with half a million pieces from the Hermitage, two passenger carriages for museum staff, and four luxurious Pullman cars. The most precious artefacts travelled in these – the Titians, El Grecos, Rubenses, Rembrandts, Murillos and Van Dykes in their elaborate golden frames. An armoured car, that had carried the Reds into battle in the Civil War, now protected the most wondrous treasures of the tsarists they had defeated, the crown jewels, collections of diamonds, fabulous confections from Fabergé's workshops, gold icons and altarpieces, and Peter I's white marble Venus. Iosif Orbeli, the Hermitage director, felt tears run down his cheeks as he watched the train pull away. The museum was lucky to have him. He was an Armenian, one of the few senior staff not to have been purged in 1938, and he had had the foresight to start planning the evacuation more than a year before. The summer palaces outside the city were soon to be looted and destroyed by the Germans.

The train was bound for Sverdlovsk, once Ekaterinburg, on the eastern slopes of the Urals. Many objects were stored in the basement of the Ipatiev mansion. It was ironic that the treasures of the Romanovs should have been placed here for safe-keeping. This was the dynasty's death-place. Here – in what they coyly called 'the House of Special Purpose' – the Bolsheviks had kept Nicholas and Alexandra, their children, the Grand Duchesses Olga, Tatiana, Maria and Anastasia, the Tsarevich Alexei, and the family doctor, chambermaid, cook and valet. They murdered them all on 17 July 1918, in the cellar rooms that now housed the crates from the Hermitage.

Shostakovich volunteered for a second time on 2 July. He was rejected again by the regular army, and enlisted in the People's Militia. 'I am going to defend my country,' Izvestiya quoted him as declaring, 'and am prepared, sparing neither life nor strength, to carry out any mission I am assigned.'[38]

Volunteers in Leningrad were being formed into a new unit, the First Guards Division of People's Militia. They were mostly workers, from the Neva and Kuibyshev sectors of the city. Younger and less famous musicians and artists joined these militia units. Shostakovich, however, and other elite musicians, were thought too precious for front-line service. They remained with the Conservatoire's civilian volunteers, building defence lines in the suburbs.

'We were digging trenches by the Forel Hospital,' one of them, Marian Rudova, recalled. The Forel was south of the Peterhof road, once the manor house of Prince Potemkin, but now a place of secret horror, a mental asylum where the NKVD took their prisoners when they drove them mad. 'Some were digging, and the others had wheelbarrows,' Rudova said. 'My partner was Dmitri Shostakovich. He was tall, and I was much shorter, so more weight fell on me as we shifted the earth. He tried to bend his knees and arms to take the weight off me.'[39]

The pair were a privileged fraction of an immense outburst of ditch digging and barbed-wire laying. Most took place in rough country far outside the city. It absorbed hordes of civilians, many of them women and girls. The toil was as back-breaking as the gruesome excavation of canals by Gulag labourers, the *zeks*, and the scale just as gargantuan. They dug 16,000 miles of open trenches, 430 miles of anti-tank ditches, and 395 miles of barbed-wire entanglements, and hauled the concrete and timbers for 5,000 bunkers and gun pits. 'No one is excused – young girls in sundresses and sandals, boys in shorts,' wrote Elena Scriabina, a young mother, who had married into the family of the composer Alexander Scriabin. 'They are not even allowed to go home to change. What use can they really be? They don't know how to use a shovel, much less those heavy crowbars they must use to break up the dry clay soil. Conditions at the trenches are extreme. The workers must sleep wherever they can, often under the open sky. Many catch a chill, get sick, but absolutely no one is excused from duty.'[40]

Earthworks did not stop the Germans. They were overrunning whole divisions, the advancing columns stalling only when rainfall turned the roads into ribbons of mud, and moving on as the sun dried them out. By 4 July, Russian losses were so immense, on a scale never seen before, that Hitler thought that the Red Army was finished. The next day, the *Landsers* entered Riga, the Latvian capital. They were greeted with cries of '*Befreier!*' ('Liberators!'), and given flowers and chocolate. Hans Luck, a colonel with a panzer corps, was astonished to be welcomed. Time and again, women came out of their wooden cottages, holding an icon to their breast, and offering the Germans gifts of eggs and bread. 'We are still Christians,' they said. 'Free us from Stalin who destroyed our churches.'[41] The welcomes were short-lived. The Germans had not come as liberators. William Lubbeck, a young *Landser*, found the greetings his company were given 'reinforced our conviction that our cause was just', but he noted that 'some remained fearful and hid in their basements'.[42] The Jews, and communists, knew what awaited them.

On 8 July, the NKVD arrested Dmitry Pavlov, the commander of the broken Western Front, and began picking up corps commanders of the Fourth Army and their senior staff. They were accused of 'damaging the combat power of the Red Army . . . crimes under Articles 58-1b, 58-11 RSFSR Criminal Code'. Officers who survived were despairing and unnerved. 'The arrests took the ground right out from beneath people's feet,' wrote Colonel Starinov. 'No one could be sure of living to see the next day.' Starinov was himself arrested, if briefly. It was the Terror once more. 'Even strong-willed experienced officers, who had never cracked in the toughest situations, completely lost their self-control at the appearance of people in the green garrison caps of the NKVD.'[43]

German infantry reached Pskov on 12 July, and caught up with their panzers for the first time. Five days later, they had marched another forty miles and were at Gdov on the northeast shore of Lake Peipus. It was only now, on 18 July, that ration cards were introduced. They were set so high that the poor were better off than in peacetime, with 800 grams of bread a day for workers, 400 grams for dependants, and good monthly amounts of meat, butter, cereals and sugar. New 'commission shops', seventy-one of them, were opened, selling off-ration foods in unlimited quantities, if at high prices.

In Moscow, as German aircraft flew over the city for the first time, a brief trial was held for General Dmitry Pavlov, the Western Front commander, his chief of staff, and six other generals from the shattered front. Among them was the wretched Major-General A. I. Tayursky, who found himself commander of the traumatized Red Air Force in the west after Ilya Kopets committed suicide on the first day of the war. The accused asked to be sent to the front as ordinary soldiers to atone for the defeat of their armies. Instead, they were shot the same day. The bodies were buried in a landfill.*

By now it was clear that Leningrad's artists and intellectuals – members of the Radiokom orchestra and Conservatoire staff were working on the northern defence line – were of scant use as muscle power. Simeon Putyakov, a soldier in an airfield defence unit, was unimpressed. He came from a village in the Kalinin region, and he had been used to hard physical work before he was drafted. 'I saw a boastful article, "Diggers from the Intelligentsia", in *Leningradskaya Pravda*,' he wrote in a diary whose indiscretions were to come to the notice of the NKVD. 'I don't agree.' They were not up to the physical demands. 'I believe that in this tough time specialists should do what they specialize in.'[44]

Shostakovich and the others were brought back to the Conservatoire. He was fortunate to be reassigned to its firefighting brigade. Had he joined the People's Militia, he would almost certainly have been dead before Christmas. The First Guards were all but obliterated in savage fighting on the Neva†. A few of the younger musicians from the Conservatoire who were allowed to enlist survived, among them the fine cellist Daniil Shafran. Most, like Shostakovich's gifted pupil

---

*A statement a week later said they had been found guilty of cowardice, passivity, and allowing their forces to disintegrate. Stalin himself confirmed that the death sentences had already been carried out. They were useful scapegoats. 'Kopets, who was mainly to blame for the loss of [his] aircraft, obviously in a desire to avoid punishment, shot himself on the evening of 22 June,' an official reference sneered. 'The other culprits received their just rewards later.' (Rodric Braithwaite, *Moscow 1941: A City and its People at War* (London: Profile, 2007), p. 106.)

† The unit was soon redesignated the 80th Rifle Division, taking the title of a regular division that was wiped out in the great encirclement battles taking place in the Ukraine.

Veniamin Fleishmann, were killed within a few weeks. Fleishmann had been working on a one-act opera based on Chekhov's story *Rothschild's Violin*. Shostakovich retrieved the manuscript of the opera and later orchestrated it in memory of his friend.*

He did compose for the Guards, though, writing their marching anthem, 'The Fearless Guards Regiments Are on the Move'. He flung himself into work now, dashing off arrangements for voice and piano, twenty-seven of them in the three days from 12 July, for front-line concerts. The NKVD had its own Ensemble, and he composed for them, too. He set a piece by the poet-turned-war correspondent Vissarion Sayanov to stirring martial music for bass, choir and piano as 'Oath to the People's Commissar' on 14 July.† 'I want everyone to sing it,' he said, not just the Secret Police choir, and they did. It was one of the most popular songs of the first months of the war. 'The great hour has come,' its last lines ran. 'Stalin leads us to battle, his order is law! Go boldly into the dread battle.'

On 19 July, Shostakovich began composing the Seventh Symphony.‡

---

* He paid tribute to Fleishmann in radio broadcasts, 'always very modest and inconspicuous in the Conservatoire,' he said, but who 'now in these trying days proved worthy of his country'. (Victor Ilyich Serov, *Dmitri Shostakovich: The Life and Background of a Soviet Composer* (New York: A. A. Knopf, 1943), p. 237.)

† Muzgiz, (Gosudarstvennoye Muzykal'noe Izdatelstvo), the submissions commission of the State music publishers, wanted it banned, and charged him with veering from formalism to primitivism, so simply was it was written. He defended it vigorously.

‡ Shostakovich had been musing over a new symphony since finishing his Sixth. This would, of course, have classified as his Seventh. It had no connection with the Seventh that he now began composing. (Manahir Yakubov, 'Preface', in Dmitri Shostakovich, *Symphony No. 7 'Leningrad', Op. 60: Facsimile Edition of the Manuscript* (Zen-On Music Company: Tokyo, 1992), p. 7.)

CHAPTER 3

Do serediny sentyabr'

To Mid-September 1941

He worked on the first movements with fevered speed and concentration. 'I wrote my Seventh, the Leningrad, quickly. I sat behind my piano and worked, fast and intensely,' he said later. 'I couldn't not write it. War was all around. I had to be together with the people, I wanted to create the image of our embattled country, to engrave it in music.'*[1] Most scientists and artists fought with their own weapons. 'My weapon was music. From the first days of war, I sat at my piano and worked, fast and intensely. I wanted to create a piece about our lives, about these days, about the Soviet people who would go to any lengths for the sake of victory.'

His urgency flowed from the Russian realization that this was not war in any familiar guise. Defeat would not be followed by settlement between victor and vanquished. It meant extinction.

They were not of course privy to the details – to the secret briefings and high-level meetings in Berlin that had preceded the invasion – but the Russians' instincts ran true. General Franz Halder, the chief of staff of the OKH, the German Supreme Command, made notes on a speech Hitler had made to two hundred senior officers on 30 March. 'This is a war of extermination,' he wrote. 'This war will be different to the war

---

* More than most composers, Shostakovich was able to conceive pieces in considerable detail before committing them to paper with exceptional swiftness. It has been suggested that themes in the Seventh pre-date the war. Perhaps. The matter remains unresolved.

in the West.'[2] Commanders, he added, 'must make the sacrifice of over-coming their personal scruples'. A paper on 'The Treatment of Enemy Inhabitants in the Barbarossa Operational Zone', issued to German officers in May, called for the least Russian resistance 'to be eradicated promptly, severely and with maximum force'. In Hitler's 'Commissar Order' of 6 June, calling for the immediate execution of captured political commissars and all prisoners deemed to be 'thoroughly Bolshevized', the preamble advised officers that in this campaign, 'handling the enemy according to humane rules or the Principles of International Law is not applicable'.*

Lest his men be in any doubt as they closed on Leningrad, Erich Hoepner, commander of the Fourth Panzer Group, issued a directive telling them that 'the objective of this battle must be the demolition of present-day Russia and must be conducted with unprecedented severity. Every military action must be guided in planning and execution by an inner resolution to exterminate the enemy remorselessly and totally.'[3]

As to Leningrad itself, Hitler's solution came from classical antiquity: *Carthago delenda est*: Carthage, the enemy city, must be destroyed, the Romans ruled. In 146 BC, Scipio had smashed it to the ground, and sold its inhabitants into slavery. 'It is the Führer's firm decision,' Halder had noted on 8 July, 'to level Moscow and Leningrad, and make them uninhabitable, so as to relieve us of the necessity of having to feed the population through the winter. The cities will be razed by the Luftwaffe.'[4]

The treatment of prisoners made clear that this was a campaign like no other. The Germans took just under 800,000 Russian prisoners in June and July, rising to 3.3 million by the end of the year. Some of

---

* The Soviet Union had not signed the 1929 Geneva Convention on the treatment of prisoners of war. Germany had, however, and its provisions (which it applied to Western prisoners) were binding upon it regardless of whether or not the prisoners came from co-signatory states.

these – commissars, Jews, Bolsheviks – were shot out of hand. Of the rest, perhaps two million died in the first few months, of starvation, forced marches, disease and neglect. German indifference to them was as colossal as their numbers. One *Landser* saw them approach his unit as 'a broad earth-brown crocodile, slowly shuffling down the road towards us. From it came a subdued hum, like a beehive.' They gave off 'the biting stench of the lion house and the filthy odour of the monkey house at the same time'. Another wondered if they were really human beings, these 'grey-brown figures, these shadows lurching towards us, stumbling and staggering, moving shapes at their last gasp, creatures whom only some last flicker of the will to live enabled to obey the order to march'.[5]

For their part, in the first months of the war, the Russians shot 95 per cent of the Germans who fell into their hands. Some were tortured and disfigured. At the beginning of July, 180 German infantry and artillerymen from the 25th Division were captured in a Russian counter-attack. The next morning, panzer crews found 153 naked bodies, many with the eyes gouged out and genitals cut off. The men of the Soviet Fifth Army were typical: 'embittered by the fascist thieves, [they] do not take any German soldiers or officers prisoner but shoot them on the spot.' Their commander, Major-General Potapov, had to categorically forbid this. His intelligence officers, he explained, could only interrogate living Germans.

The pattern of the onslaught was clear. The Germans came as slavemakers, the destroyers of cities and villages alike. Stalin's brutalities and terrors were subsumed by a more immediate evil. To Semen Lipkin, a poetry translator who wrote secret verses for himself, the *Revolutsiya* was 'an enchantress' whose beauty in 1917 had become raddled as she 'executed, persecuted, betrayed'. Now, Lipkin, and the countless Russians like him, had to confront the 'Hitlerites', as they called them, a new, Germanic pantheon of inhumanity. They looked again at the enchantress, and found that 'hatred towards her has passed'.[6] The survival of *Rodina*, Mother Russia, was all, and, for the duration at least, that embraced the *vozhd* (the leader, Stalin) and the Party.

Nikolai Glazkov,* a young poet of irony and the absurd, had been thrown out of university as an 'enemy of the people'. The terror had done for his father in 1938. He now wrote a wry and private prayer:

> O Lord! Support the Soviets
> Preserve the country from superior races
> because all your commandments are broken
> by Hitler more frequently than by us . . .[7]

A particular horror was felt at the burned-out villages that marked the German advance. Stalin had destroyed their spirit in collectivization: Boris Pasternak had found himself silenced with horror when he visited the countryside on a trip to observe its results, for 'what I saw could not be expressed in words . . . There was such inhuman, unimaginable misery, such a terrible disaster, that it began to seem almost abstract, it would not fit within the bounds of consciousness.' But they were still seen as the repositories of the Russian soul, and the anger at the flames and smoke that consumed them now added to the sense that this was a war for the survival of all things Russian:

> Over the ground a hot gust blows,
> The sky groans, a groan passes across the sky!
> The clouds, like swans, cry out above the burned grain . . .
> Grief? No . . . what kind of grief is this? . . .
> Half a wattle fence is left of this village, half a fence on a rise.

---

* He published his poetry in the 1950s and 1960s under an imprint he called *Samsebyaizdat* ('self-publishing house'). Shortened to Samizdat, this became the generic title of dissident publishing.

The clouds cry out. They cry out all day!
And alone beneath these clouds I shake the fence in my black
hands.[8]

A second museum train left Leningrad for the Urals on 20 July. It had 1,422 crates aboard, with 700,000 pieces, and fourteen members of the Hermitage staff. Plans were being made to evacuate the city's living treasures, too, including the members of the Philharmonia orchestra and the Kirov dancers. The Conservatoire staff, and Shostakovich, would be free to leave with the other musicians. Only the lower-ranking Radio orchestra was to stay put.

NKVD surveillance groups in the city were arresting people for repeating the bitter joke, 'Our soldiers are everywhere victorious but the Germans are advancing'. Informers were reporting on the 'political-moral condition' of colleagues at work. Irina Shcherbov-Nefedovich, at the Institute of Vaccines, was denounced for telling a friend about the bombing of Sverdlovsk, which she had heard in an official Sovinform news bulletin. She was sentenced to seven years in the Gulag as a 'panicmonger'.* The head of Lenoblispolkom, the executive committee of the Leningrad province, issued an order forbidding anyone using a telephone to discuss the military situation or conditions in the city. Those who did so could be charged with 'divulging military secrets'. The penalty was death. Wild talk of German paratroopers landing in the suburbs was reported.[9]

A special photo-shoot was held on the roof of the Conservatoire on 29 July. Shostakovich struck a heroic pose, in firefighter's helmet and belted uniform jacket, holding a gushing firehose. A dozen other fire-fighters stood packed together behind him, with pickaxes and crowbars

---

* She died in a camp near Khabarovsk in 1946. Her husband and daughter were not told of her arrest. They believed she had died in a bombing raid on the city. They did not learn the truth of her death until 1994.

raised, and stirrup pumps at the ready. These pictures of the composer, his face firm and steady beneath his helmet, were those that would circle the globe and grace the cover of *Time* magazine a year later. For all the drama, no smoke or flames were visible. As yet, Leningrad had still to be bombed and shelled.

The danger, though, was closing fast. The Germans had paused on the Luga river, the outermost ring of the city's defences, a hundred miles to the southwest. Their armour was battered by constant combat, and the infantry exhausted by heavy casualties and melancholia: 'Sad-looking wooden huts, forests and marshes. Immense plains, huge woods with a few dog kennels here and there . . . There was no limit. We could not see an end and we were so disconsolate.'[10] They regrouped, and recovered their morale. On 8 August, in a downpour, Reinhardt's XLI Panzer Corps assaulted the northern sector of the Luga line near Kingisepp. They broke through in three places over the next three days, at a cost of 1,600 casualties. Kingisepp, the main city on the river, was a smoking mass of rubble when it fell soon after.

Four thousand suspected Red Army deserters were arrested as troops tried to get back to Leningrad from the front. Up to half the casualties were suspected of self-inflicted wounds. In one hospital, No. 61, 460 out of 1,000 wounded had been shot in the left forearm or left hand.[11] Stalin reacted furiously in his Order 270 on 16 August. Cowards were not to be tolerated. Those who surrendered should be 'destroyed by all means possible, from the air or ground'. Deserters were to be shot on the spot, and their families arrested. The Order was not published, so naked was the terror it threatened, but it was read out to all units, and to senior Party officials throughout the country.

The Germans were now thirty miles from the Gulf of Finland, and less than seventy from the city. They were astonished at the brutal abandon with which the Russians shed the blood of the volunteer divisions. A few haphazard artillery shells presaged an attack. From far off, the Germans heard deep hurrahs, the traditional Russian battle-cry. The volunteers advanced 'as much as twelve ranks deep'. Some had no rifles. None had heavy-weapons support. They were butchered. 'Incredibly high Russian losses,' noted Halder, the German chief of staff.[12] Fifteen hundred infantry officers were taken from advanced training courses, flung into a rent in the line with officer cadets, and slaughtered. The commander of the Luga operational group, General K. P. Pyadyshev, thought that to waste such valuable men in forlorn frontal assaults on armour was madness. For his pains, Pyadyshev, experienced, courageous, well-loved by his fellow-officers, simply 'vanished from the horizon'. The men in blue caps took him away.*

The executions that went hand-in-glove with the retreat were almost casual. The journalist Valery Grossman was at the *izba*, the peasant hut, that served as field headquarters for Major-General Mikhail Petrov. A military prosecutor arrived after dinner. They sat drinking tea with raspberry jam while the prosecutor reported on pending cases. A major was listed among the deserters and cowards, with peasants accused of pro-German sympathies. 'Petrov pushes his glass aside. In the corner of the document, he approves the death sentence in red capitals written in a small hand.' The prosecutor mentioned the case of a woman who was to be shot for urging peasants to greet the Germans with bread and salt, the traditional gift of welcome. Petrov asked who she was. 'An old maid,' the prosecutor laughed. The general laughed, too. 'Well, since she's an old maid, I'll replace it with ten years.' They drank more tea. The prosecutor left, to carry out the sentences. Petrov asked him to send his samovar up to him. 'I'm used to having it around.'

Later, Grossman was with Petrov to witness a failed attack on a village. The general had won a Gold Star in the Spanish Civil War. Sometimes

---

* Accused of 'anti-Soviet conduct', he was either shot, or died in prison before the end of the war. He was rehabilitated in 1956.

he shouted at his men in Spanish, the words strange amid the wet clay and sopping fields under an autumnal sky. He told the regimental commander that, if he failed to take the village in an hour, he would be relieved of his command and made to rejoin the attack as a private. 'Yes, Comrade Army Commander,' the officer replied. Grossman noted that his hands were shaking. Not a single man was walking upright. They were running stooping low or crawling on all fours from one hole to another. 'They are afraid of bullets,' he said, 'but there aren't any bullets.' The commissar was shouting at them: 'Bend lower, cowards, bend lower!'[13]

Simeon Putyakov, though fresh in uniform, was already the very model of the unwilling soldier, feeling hard done by, fed up, and resentful. Such men abounded in all armies, they always had: but, in the Red Army, to be one of them, and to record it in writing, was exceedingly dangerous. Putyakov found life 'a shambles'. His unit had no belts or insignia. 'You can't tell the difference between high rank and low,' he confided in his diary. 'I've received no military training in a month. On top of all this, a very foolish young lieutenant pitched up and added to the disorder.' He was worried about his family. He had had no word from them for over a month, but he had heard that the local officials in his village had fled. He was worried about his possessions and his house.

Then, aware of the risk he was running, he made a note: 'Enough of the bad side because if anyone reads my notes they'll think I'm the enemy and unpatriotic. The goal of my notes is about myself and events around me.' He wrote on in mock-heroic style: 'And now I'm a soldier of our glorious Red Army. The barefooted, undressed, hungry and badly equipped Red Army – the Army the enemy couldn't defeat in the civil war – and I'm deeply sure that it will not be defeated. I'm full of hatred for vile fascism, I'll fight to the last drop of blood.' He was right to be cautious. Two people would read his notes, his sergeant-major and an

NKVD interrogator, and they could cost him his life. It was the NKVD officer who did the underlining of these passages. It was all too obvious – 'defeatism', 'slander of Soviet power' – why he chose them.

In Leningrad, the evacuation of musicians and dancers was beginning in earnest. The first train with evacuees from the Kirov left on 19 August. A second followed. The ballerina Shelest was due to take it, but her mother had a minor heart attack. Her father was a high-ranking Red Army medical officer. Before he left for the front headquarters, he told her that there was someone important whom she should see if she and her mother were in need. 'I saved his life and he promised to save me and my family if necessary.' It was a shrewd choice. The man was in charge of an army food warehouse.

On 22 August, Shostakovich went to the Moscow Station to see his friend Ivan Sollertinsky leave the city with the orchestra and staff of the Philharmonia. He had shown Sollertinsky the first movement of his symphony, almost complete. It was a long piece, more than twenty-five minutes, in sonata form, beginning with a stirring theme by all the strings, echoed by woodwinds, and rising in pitch. A slower and more peaceful passage followed, with flutes and lower strings. This led into what the world would later call the 'invasion theme', with a march that begins softly, with the strings pizzicato, repeated a dozen times, each louder and harsher, with the brass and a snare drum giving it a cruel and ruthless edge, and echoes of Ravel's *Bolero*. This 'hurricane' of music – 'to the raging backdrop of violins struck with the bow stem', Sollertinsky found,[14] 'evoking the image of dancing skeletons' – then slows, with a bassoon solo, ending softly.

He had gone through the movement with Isaak Glikman. The invasion theme, Glikman found, was a 'magnificent, noble exposition': 'We sat on, plunged in silence, broken at last with these words (I have them written down): "I don't know what the fate of this piece will be." After a further pause, he added: "I suppose critics with nothing better to do will damn me for copying *Bolero*. Well, let them. This is how I hear war."'[15]

The Radiokom orchestra, the understudy to the Philharmonia since 1931, was ordered to stay in the city as a reserve orchestra. Their seniors in the Philharmonia were lucky to get away. The train was held up at the rail junction at Mga, because the Germans had bombed a bridge on the main line to Moscow. The train was diverted onto the secondary Pestovo line, the only one left open. Shortly after it left, German bombers flattened the Mga railway station. Sollertinsky and the Philharmonia were eventually taken across the Urals to Novosibirsk in Siberia. Isaak Glikman left, with many staff from the Conservatoire. They headed for Tashkent. For the moment, Shostakovich refused to join them.

The last direct railway link to Moscow was now cut. Tens of thousands were left milling about the Moscow Station, or were trapped on carriages in suburban stations. Many were children.

Political malevolence in the city was undimmed. At eleven minutes past ten on Saturday morning, 23 August, Daniil Kharms's luck ran out. The brilliant writer of the absurd, his sentiment close to Shostakovich's *The Nose*, had a sense of foreboding, his wife Marina Malich remembered. 'Something horrible' was about to happen.

'The bell rang,' she recalled:

Dania [Daniil] said, 'I know they've come for me.' I asked why he said that. 'I know.' We couldn't do anything. We were in our little room. I went to open the door. Three strangers were there. They said they were looking for him. I said, 'He went out to get bread.' They said, 'That's all right. We'll wait.' I came back into the room. We didn't know what to do. We looked out of the window. Their car was parked there. They had come for him. There was no doubt.

We had to open the door, and they saw him and they rushed to him and caught him very roughly and pushed him to the stairs. I said,

'Take me, take me too.' One of them said, 'OK. Let her come.' Daniil was shaking. It was terrible. They took us down the staircase and pushed him into the car, and then me. They drove us to the Bolshoi Dom. They didn't stop the car at the entrance but a little bit away. They didn't want people to see what they were up to. We had to walk a few steps. They kept a tight grip on him, but at the same time they pretended that he was walking of his own accord.

We went into the lobby, and two men pulled him away and I was left alone.[16]

The car took her back to the apartment. The NKVD men searched it. They made an inventory. Two of them, Yanyuk and Bespashnin, signed it. They brought a street sweeper, a Tartar called Ibrahim Kil'deyev, to sign as a first witness. Marina Kharms was the other. The paperwork, war or no war, was immaculate: 'Letters, 202 in opened envelopes. Notebooks with different notes, five. Different religious books, four. Book in foreign language, one. One photograph.'

It was an ordinary if rather meagre haul. The twenty-four objects found on Kharms as he was searched in the Bolshoi Dom were as whimsical as the writer himself. His silver cigarette case, his amber cigarette holder and the matchboxes inscribed with his initials made it clear that he was a 'former person'. And one of some rank, as shown by the baptismal pendant icon round his neck, in 'yellow metal', gold, inscribed 'Bless Daniil' by no less than Metropolitan Antony, the erstwhile head of the Russian Orthodox Church in exile. He had three other icons in his pockets, and a personal cross, and a brooch with eight facets and different stones, and a sign: 'Jerusalem Apocalypse Chapter XXI, St Petersburg 22 April 1907'. He had rings of white and yellow metal, silver and gold, and a silver pocket watch. He had three shot glasses and a silver cup, and a magnifying glass in a square copper frame. He had a full set of paperwork: his marriage certificate, his

Union of Writers card, a document from a TB clinic, and the document excusing him from military service. He had a notebook, six photographs, five pieces of paper with different drawings, two used train tickets and an old wallet.

The paperwork was forwarded to KRO 1, the NKVD's Leningrad Counter-Revolution Department No. 1., by an NKVD sergeant called Burmistrov, the arresting officer. He laid charges of 'counter-revolution orientation' and 'spreading slander and defeatism' against the writer.

Burmistrov quoted remarks Kharms had made to 'agents', the nicer-sounding word the NKVD used in place of 'informers'. Some were normal enough in talk between friends: 'The Soviet Union lost the war on the first day . . . Leningrad will be besieged, and die by starvation, or it will be bombed flat . . .' Others were suicidally reckless, if true, and not the invention of the informers: 'If I receive mobilization papers, I'll kick the commander. Let them shoot me, but I won't wear their uniform. I don't want to be shit. If they force me to shoot from attics during street warfare, I won't shoot at the Germans but at them. It's better by far to live in a German camp than under Soviet power.'[17] He was interrogated until past midnight on 25 August, and again for two days after that. The charges were quite enough to have him shot, of course, and his arrest was formally confirmed by the NKVD's two counter-revolutionary heavyweights, Kozhemyakin, the head of Leningrad's No. 1 KRO, and the overall KRO boss, Zanin.

Kharms played his interrogators with the brilliant other-worldliness of the natural-born surrealist. He refused to answer any questions on his alleged 'participation in crimes against Soviet power'. When he did talk, his prattle was so absurdist and rambling that it was beyond Leningrad's deputy chief interrogator, Artyemov, to record it. He tossed in the towel on 28 August. 'During interrogation, Kharms showed signs of psychological disturbance,' Artyemov wrote. 'On the basis on Articles 202 and 203 of the Criminal Code of the RSFR, he is to be sent to the psychiatric wing of the prison hospital for definition of his condition.' He was moved from the Shpalernaya, the holding prison close to the Bolshoi Dom, to the psychiatric wing of the prison hospital at the Arsenalnaya.

The NKVD had other work to do. It was ordered to deport the remaining Soviet Germans and Finns from the Leningrad region. A further twenty-seven categories – including Catholics, anarchists, Trotskyites, Zinovievites, 'White bandits, kulaks, those with connections abroad, diversionists, saboteurs, and thieves and prostitutes' – were included for good measure. They were to be deported from Leningrad to Kazakhstan by rail, each train escorted by NKVD and Red Army Guards, as part of a larger-scale deportation of Germans, Poles, Finns and Balts from the Ukraine and the Stalingrad region.*

As the Germans approached – their aircraft were machine-gunning commuter trains taking people from the suburbs into the city – the NKVD found its informers becoming less fertile. They feared that scores would be settled if the city fell. 'At many factories Communists do not unify or lead the non-party masses,' the Party Secretary monitoring political mood reported, 'nor give a rebuff to disorganizers, panickers, and anti-Soviet elements . . . Several Communists show themselves to be cowards and panickers.' Many expected the Germans to hunt down and kill Party members. Admissions to Party membership hit an absolute low: not one of the city's largest factories admitted more than three candidate members in the first three months of the war.[18]

'Dear Ivan Ivanovich,' Shostakovich wrote to Sollertinsky on 29 August, 'We'll be leaving for Alma-Ata in about two days. We are all well. I miss

---

* The Germans placed the Soviet Germans in the Ukraine and other occupied areas under the formal protection of the Wehrmacht. They were the only group in the Reichscommissariat Ukraine that was not classified as Untermenschen, sub-humans. (J. Otto Pohl, *Ethnic Cleansing in the USSR, 1937–1949* (Westport, CT: Greenwood Press, 1999), p. 45.)

you very much. I've finished the first movement of the symphony, the one I showed you before your departure.'[19] He had changed his mind. He was to leave with the Lenin Film Studios. He was too late.

The Germans took the rail junction at Mga on 30 August, and consolidated their hold on the town with the reinforced 20th Motorized Division the next day. No rail line now led out of the city. 'The last transport left during the night,' the poet Vera Inber wrote in her diary. 'Leningrad is surrounded and we are caught in a mousetrap.'

It was still possible to leave the city by road, through Shlisselburg, the historic fortress-town twenty miles to the east. It lies at the point where the Neva river debouches from Lake Ladoga in a great loop to flow through Leningrad on its way to the Gulf of Finland. The 20th Panzer Division was closing on the town. It had torn its way south of the city and was advancing towards the lake along the east bank of the river. The fighting was hard. Willy Tiedemann, a veteran of Poland and France, had started the campaign in a full-strength infantry company of 180 men. Within three days, they were in Vilnius, the old Lithuanian capital. In a month, they had reached Smolensk. 'We were told we were the unit that had penetrated the furthest into Russia,' he recalled proudly. Then, on 19 August, his division had swung north for Leningrad. Losses escalated.

On the morning of 1 September, on the banks of the Neva, his company took eleven casualties. 'We sit in wet trenches, and are constantly under heavy fire from artillery, tanks. Later this day my company loses 26 men.'[20] A Stuka attack on Russian artillery positions brought them some relief, but his company had never known anything like this. There were fewer than fifty men left, but they continued the advance.

The same day, the free, unrationed sale of food in Leningrad was banned. Rimma Neratova was a young medical student. Her father drew on his experience – he had survived 'two wars, revolution, prison and famine' – to anticipate that the city would again be blockaded, as it had been briefly by General Iudenich and the Whites in the autumn of 1919, but this time for longer. He warned Rimma and her sister that transport would break down, and the snow would not be cleared. During the winter, he said, a sledge could be used to carry firewood, 'or whatever you want – it will be worth its weight in gold.' The two girls went off to the Passazh department store and bought two children's sleds. He himself laid in a large store of tomato juice.[21] A black market was already flourishing.

Shostakovich was now working on the second movement of his Seventh. It was the shortest, less than fifteeen minutes, and he dashed through it. He originally titled it 'Memories', and he described it both as a scherzo and a lyric intermezzo. It began quietly with a theme by the strings, with an oboe solo picking up a variation of the tune, interrupted by a harsher theme by woodwinds, and then brass and strings. This was followed by another ostinato, a repeated motif, but less persistent that the *Bolero*-like invasion theme in the first movement.

His colleague Valerian Bogdanov-Berezovsky was busy with more humble music. He held an audition at the Union of Composers for military tunes for a military songbook that was being put together for the troops. He hoped to set up a small mobile orchestra and choir to entertain both men at the front and the wounded in hospitals.

The Neva Operational Group (NOG) was hastily flung together to counter the threat to Shlisselburg on 2 September. The name was grand, the reality was not. It consisted of the 115th Rifle and 1st NKVD Rifle Divisions, the latter made up of NKVD border guards, with the 4th Naval Infantry Brigade of marines. It had three rifle anti-tank units, the 1st, 4th and 5th Destroyer Battalions and the 107th Separate Tank Battalion. Its supporting artillery and engineers were weak. Most of its men were soon to be killed or wounded.

On 3 September, as a counter-attack by the NOG in division strength across the Neva near Gorodok was easily and bloodily repulsed, six-year-old Anastasia Vyaltseva watched the NKVD arrest her father. She was named for her great-aunt, the 'Russian Cinderella', much loved before dying young, a mezzo-soprano of wondrous beauty in pre-1914 St Petersburg, who sang gipsy songs and operetta with delicate phrasing. 'They searched the apartment, and my mother and father and grandfather and me,' she recollected. Pyotr Vladimirovich Vyaltsev was a PE instructor at the Fire Department, exceptionally fit, an athlete and swimmer who had been the semi-lightweight boxing champion of Leningrad in 1932. He would have been invaluable in the siege, as fireman or soldier, but they took him away. 'I never saw him again,' says Anastasia. 'My mother and grandfather never spoke about the arrest.' He was accused of spreading panic and preparing to cross the front line to join the Germans.*

Heavy guns had been heard growling in the distance for several days. It was foggy on 4 September. Sounds were muffled, but at midday the city came under shellfire from German 240mm artillery to the southeast. Freight yards and factories were hit. The casualties in the streets did not inhibit the NKVD from arresting Professor A. F. Valter, an expert in high-voltage insulation and dielectrics, and driving him to the Bolshoi Dom.

The endgame seemed close. Hitler confirmed on 5 September that he wished to avoid the casualties and street fighting that would flow from a direct assault on a city he felt was already doomed. He ordered that

---

* Twenty years later, in 1961, Anastasia received an official paper with his rehabilitation. It stated: 'arrested on suspicion of committing a crime under 58-1. Date of conviction unknown. Died during transportation to Novosibirsk 14 November 1941.' (Archive file in FSB headquarters, St Petersburg, no. P-48210.) This was untrue. There had been no trial or conviction. His file contained a single document, a denunciation by someone who worked with him. The NKVD were not sure that he was dead. He and hundreds of other prisoners disappeared, as we shall see, in gruesome circumstances. In 1946, Vyaltsev was declared a wanted fugitive, and the NKVD began searching for him to re-arrest him. 'They always hoped he was still alive, but they were afraid to ask for him,' says Anastasia. 'My grandfather did ask for him once, and the reply was – if you don't want to join him, don't ask.'

it should be encircled, in cooperation with the Finns. Much of Army Group North's mobile formations, and the 1st Air Fleet, would then be transferred to Army Group Centre. The German effort in tanks and aircraft was to concentrate on the thrust to Moscow. Halder wrote in his diary: 'Leningrad. Our objective has now been achieved. Will now become a subsidiary theatre of operations.'[22]

Dive-bombers and strafing aircraft slashed into the NKVD troops defending Shlisselburg. The Neva wharves and the wooden buildings in the old town were set on fire. German infantry went in at dawn on 8 September along the eastern bank of the river. The NKVD fell back through the ruined streets, to the wharves, where some crammed onto gunboats and launches to escape across the river to the west bank. The assault lasted less than an hour. A small Soviet garrison survived in the ancient Oreshek fortress, once a tsarist prison where Lenin's brother Alexander Ulyanov had been hanged, the island on which it stands protected by the broad waters at the point where the Neva flows from the lake. The Germans let it be. They had the town and the east bank of the river firmly in hand.

Leningrad was now completely cut off by land from the rest of Russia. This Leningraders now wistfully called 'the mainland', as if they had become islanders.

They could still reach it by water, and then rail. Ladoga is immense, studded with hundreds of islands, its yellow-brown waters stretching for 136 miles from north to south, its width averaging fifty miles. It is the largest lake in Europe, the skies above it reflecting its luminosity and storms like a sea. The shoreline runs for almost a thousand miles, craggy and broken by deep inlets in the north, lower to the south, with rocky or sandy beaches, and profusions of willows and alders giving way to pine forests and peat bogs inland. The Red Army was clinging on to two slender parts of it. One was a slice of the south-western shore, served by a light railway that ran from Leningrad to the bay of Osinovets. The new German bunkers in Shlisselburg were nine miles to the south. To the north, the Finnish lines were closer yet, just seven miles away. The small lakeside town of Osinovets was at the end of the Irinovsky railway line. It was a tsarist relic, a narrow-gauge line serving commuter villages and holiday dachas and excursionists to the lake.

The Finns controlled the northern shores of Ladoga, and the eastern shore down to the line of the Svir river. Control of the Svir cut the direct route by water to Moscow, which ran through canals and the Volga. The Russians still held the eastern and southern shore between the Svir and the German positions. The Germans held Shlisselburg, the left bank of the Neva, and a corridor along it only twelve miles across at its narrowest. This corridor – the Germans called it the 'Flaschenhals', the bottleneck – stretched along the southern shore of the lake for twenty miles. Beyond it, the Russian-held shore was linked by rail to the Murmansk-to-Moscow line. Supplies could be loaded onto barges here, and towed across the lake to Osinovets. Trains would then take the freight for 34 miles along the narrow-gauge line to Leningrad.

These were not placid waters. Violent storms brought short, steep waves that reached fifteen feet. Boats from the fishing villages on the lake, out to catch salmon, burbot, smelt and pike-perch, were lost every year. Supplies came by rail to Gastinopolye, a river port on the Volkhov river six miles south of the town of Volkhov. The cargoes were unloaded from the freight trains and put onto river barges. Thirty old barges that were laid up in the backwaters of Novaya Ladoga were towed to the harbour and fitted out to carry food.

A tug towing two barges with 800 tons of wheat made the passage to Osinovets unhindered on 12 September. It was followed three days later by five more barges carrying 3,000 tons of wheat. A German reconnaissance pilot spotted them being unloaded in Osinovets. Thirty minutes later, Stuka dive-bombers arrived overhead and sank three of them.[23]

German aircraft started regular patrols of the lake. The harbours at Osinovets and Novaya Ladoga were bombed and shelled. The crossing took sixteen hours. The tugs set out in darkness, but the Germans attacked them at dawn when they were halfway across. Only 10 per cent of the food loaded at Novaya Ladoga in the second half of September arrived in Osinovets. The rest, with the barges and crews, was at the bottom of the lake.

Die Fledermaus was playing at the Theatre of Musical Comedy on the clear and warm evening of 8 September. Vera Inber was in the audience. During the interval, the alarm sounded and a loudspeaker announced that they should stay as close as possible to the walls of the theatre, because there were no beams supporting the centre of the hall. In the distance, Inber could hear anti-aircraft fire. 'We followed the advice and stayed on about forty minutes.' The secondary arias and duets were cut.

The bombers in the first great attack on the city came in two waves from airfields in Estonia. Twenty-seven Junkers were overhead a little before 7 p.m., dropping more than 6,000 incendiaries. They came in from the south, low enough for watchers on the city roofs to make out their swastikas and the spinning discs of their propellers, and they flew straight on across the city. The composer Gavriil Popov had dropped in on Liubov Shaporina. He was playing a bravura passage by Ravel on her piano when he stopped and rushed to the window. They watched a great cloud envelop the white puffs of anti-aircraft fire. Other clouds joined it until they filled the sky, at first dyed amber and then bronze by the setting sun, an 'immense spectacle of stunning beauty'.[24]

A BBC broadcast, 'London Calling: Long Live Leningrad', had been retransmitted earlier in the day. German bombers had tried to break the people of the great city on the Thames for many months before turning to the Neva. The broadcast was a reminder that they had failed: it was, of course, not mentioned that Soviet-supplied oil had helped to power the Luftwaffe engines on their flights to London.

Food warehouses were the main target. The Badaev warehouses had been built of wood in tsarist days on a four-acre site in the southwest of the city. They were packed close together, with gaps of barely twenty-five feet between them. The great bulk of the city's grain, meat, fats, butter, sugar and confectionery was stored here. No one had thought to disperse them.

Nina Abkina was an engineer in a fat and margarine manufacturing factory. It was next to the Badaev buildings, and it caught the tail-end of the incendiaries. 'In our inexperience,' she said, 'we rushed to extinguish the ones we could see, that had fallen on the wooden roofs.' Some penetrated into the warehouses below. The huge stocks of linseed and sunflower seed were 70 per cent fat with only 2 per cent moisture. There were also two thousand tons of coconuts, still in bales, which had been bought from the Americans in the Philippines, and shipped via Vladivostok, to be processed into copra. They were as flammable as the dry and fatty seeds. No one spotted the incendiaries that fell onto the bales. When all that was set alight, Abkina recollected, such a fire began that the blaze was visible from Krestovsky Island on the other side of the city.

The two warehouses with the coconuts became infernos in a few minutes. A building with 800 tons of oil-cake lay between them. Abkina joined with the factory director, Vasili Trofimovsky, to play hoses on this storehouse. The heat was so intense that Abkina had to spray water on Trofimovsky when his coat started to smoke, but they saved the oil-cake and gave most of it to the bakery over the fence from the plant. They kept some back. 'It certainly saved us from starvation,' Abkina said. 'We ground the oil-cake up and it was our main source of food. We heated it, and by that means we stayed alive . . . That's why there was never anyone who died of starvation at our place.'[25]

They were the lucky ones. The smoke the bombers left behind them was strange and frightening. Many saw it as the city's funeral pyre. It grew thicker and thicker, fed by fats and timber, devouring three thousand tons of flour and more than two thousand tons of sugar, with a lurid glow at its base that reminded Olga Berggolts, as darkness fell, of a red eclipse of the sun.

A second wave of bombers came later in the evening. They carried high-explosive bombs, 500- and 1,000-pounders, which ripped across residential areas, and badly damaged the main pumping plant at the waterworks. Leningraders were initiated in the terror bombing already familiar to Londoners. General Nikolai Voronov compared it to Madrid. Voronov became the Red Army's senior artilleryman, and his portrait was to follow Shostakovich's on the cover of *Time* magazine. He had lived through the siege of the University City in Madrid under the shellfire and bombs of Franco's forces during the Civil War. He climbed to the cupola of St Isaac's, and looked out over the anti-aircraft guns and the firewatchers on the rooftops, and the warships moored on the Neva adding their concussive gunfire to the thunder. To the south and south-west he could see the Russian lines, and the flash of the German heavy siege pieces firing into the city. 'Again and again, my thoughts returned to Madrid and what that city had survived. There also the enemy had closed in on all sides.' The size, though, was different. 'Here it was all repeated on an even grander scale – the city itself, the intensity of the battle, the size of the forces. Here, everything was infinitely more complicated.'

Lidya Okhapina lived on Volkhov Prospekt, close to the front line. She made a dash for the bomb shelter with her children when the siren sounded, but was caught out in the open. A woman took her into her apartment. 'All the air, everything around was filled with cracking and whirling noises,' she recalled. 'Our building shuddered all over. It seemed the ground was writhing in convulsions, like an earthquake. My teeth were chattering with fear, my knees were trembling. I took refuge in a corner, clutching my children to me . . . We were all standing there like prisoners condemned to death.'

Next morning, she found she had grey hairs. Nearby buildings had been demolished in the night. The girders 'stuck up like huge crosses over the people buried there'. She found a room on Vasilievsky Island, only 86 square feet, but she felt it was safer. It wasn't. The bombers followed her a few days later. Okhapina's little son Tolya had impetigo. The chemist advised that she should wash the boy in the hottest water he could stand before rubbing methylene blue in. 'He was standing naked in the round washbasin and I was washing him with water so hot I could hardly put my hands in it,' she said.

> He was yelling. Suddenly there was an air-raid warning. There and then a burst of flame seemed to fly in through the window. The old carpet that was serving as a curtain fell down. The window smashed into smithereens. Out in the street I could hear deafening explosions. I grabbed little Tolya first, naked and wet as he was, and almost flung him to the floor in the corridor. Then I ran for my daughter. I clasped them to me in a corner of the corridor. 'Monsters! Swine!' I cursed the Germans.

She went out in the morning to collect the bread ration. Half the building opposite had been blown away. She could see the wallpapers in the half-rooms that still stood, pink, blue, green, some with flower patterns and some with stripes. 'And what seemed really strange,' she added. 'On one square of wall there was a clock hanging and it was still going.'[26]

The bombers were back next day. The audience at the Musical Comedy were permitted to keep their coats on during the performance. Leningrad theatres were sticklers for etiquette – everyone checked their coats and hats into the cloakrooms – but the Muzkom had no bomb shelter. When the siren sounded, the audience were ushered as quickly as possible into the Philharmonia Hall shelter. Some of the bombs fell on the zoo. Betty, the much-loved elephant, was mortally wounded and her bellows of pain drifted on the night air, piercing those who heard her with pity and alarm. Sables, frantic with fear, escaped into the streets. The dogs kept for research at the Pavlov Institute 'screeched like banshees'. The fat outlines of three hundred barrage balloons were suspended in the air from their tethers, while the posts of more than 3,000 fire-watchers peppered the rooftops. Shostakovich manned Post No. 5 on the roof of the Conservatoire. It was not hit, but the watchers atop the Hermitage and the Winter Palace listened to shrapnel 'falling like rain' onto the paving stones of the Palace Square, while the noise of six hundred anti-aircraft guns added to the cacophony of aero-engines, bombs and sirens.

Radio Leningrad began broadcasting the sound of a metronome in the gaps between programmes, to show that the city's heart was still beating. It was run by the city's anti-aircraft command, from its head-quarters on Lononosov Square. The rhythm quickened when air raids were imminent or taking place. The radio station could be picked up as far as Moscow.

Aerial photographs of the city found on German prisoners were divided into squares. Architectural landmarks were numbered – the Hermitage was No. 9 – and arrows gave distances in kilometres and metres to other targets. An architect, Natasha Ustvolskaya, created a small camouflage group with four climbers to carry out her designs to hide or change the distinctive outline of spires and domes and palaces. Three of the climbers were girls. Olga Firsova was the conductor of the children's choir at the Kirov Palace of Culture, and a graduate of the Conservatoire. She recruited two girls who were also experienced rock climbers: Alexandra Prigozheva, who was the office manager of a sports club, and Aloize Zemba, a young lighting technician at the Lenfilm studios. Mikhail Bobrov was the youngest, a seventeen-year-old climber who was also the national junior downhill skiing champion. Two other climber-musicians, the cellists M. I. Shestakon and Andrei Safonov, helped the team. The golden spires of the Admiralty building were painted a dull warship grey, and the shapes of the great cathedrals were changed by draping them in black sail-cloth. The work was to go on for months.

A third trainload of museum treasures was still being packed when the Germans cut the rail link. The crates were moved to the Hermitage cellars. Trenches were dug under the linden trees in the Summer Garden. In them were buried the eighteenth-century marbles of Greek gods and goddesses that had added such elegance to an evening's stroll. The four bronze horsemen that stood on the Anichkov Bridge were lifted from their pedestals and buried in the gardens of the Young Pioneers' Palace.

It was not so easy to protect Falconet's magnificent statue of Peter the Great, who had ridden his rearing horse in the Senate Square since Catherine the Great had put him there on an immense stone pedestal in 1782. The 'Thunder Stone' itself was said to be the largest ever moved by man – 1,250 tons, dragged by a team of four hundred men by capstan on a track of brass globes like ball-bearings across four miles of frozen ground to the Gulf of Finland. The great rock was then carried on by sea.

Legend, as well as practical difficulty, argued against hiding it. The city might now be Leningrad, but to its people it remained instinctively 'Piter', Peter's city, and the statue was its symbol. Pushkin had immortalized it a century before in his long narrative poem *The Bronze Horseman*. It was believed that the city would never fall while its Horseman remained to guard it from his mighty plinth. The statue remained in place, heavily sandbagged, its outline broken up by a wooden camouflage frame to confuse German bomb-aimers.

The bombers returned, again and again. They smashed the huge Red Star creamery, destroying tons of butter. The Zhdanov shipyards were badly damaged. An aircraft flew low over the Kirov steel and engineering works. A parachute was seen falling from the plane. A fire-watcher reported that Nazi parachutists were landing. As he rushed towards the parachute, he was knocked flat by a shattering blast. It was not a paratrooper, but a one-ton delayed-action bomb. Seven hundred were killed or wounded. The street where Shaporina lived was clogged with personal possessions from bombed buildings. The corner was sliced off one of them, and she saw an orange lampshade dangling from the ceiling and swaying in the wind, and a peg with a man's and a woman's coat hanging from it on the only wall that was left. A house on Bolshaya Pushkarskaya Street was set alight by an incendiary. Its glow lit Shostakovich's apartment all night.

Refugees who had fled the Germans and the Finns were housed in railway freight cars. Temporary hospitals for wounded soldiers were opened in university buildings, the Palace of Labour, the Herzen Institute and some of the large hotels.

The city was divided into six military districts. Barricades sealed the main avenues, seven feet high and twelve feet thick, made of paving blocks, timbers and railway lines. Triangular concrete blocks sprouted on the approach roads that German armour was expected to use. Machine-gun posts were set up on the ground floor of corner buildings. Underground routes for men and supplies ran through the sewers.[27] Each night, almost every rooftop had its fire-watchers, equipped with sand buckets and metal tongs to throw incendiaries into the street or courtyard below, Shostakovich among them.

Dmitri Pavlov, an expert in food distribution from the Food Commissariat, had flown into the city on 8 September in an Li-2, a Soviet-built DC-3. He had powers to deal with all food matters. He found grain and live cattle and dead meat enough for 33 days, cereals for 30 days, fats for 46, and sugar and confectionery for two months. He set rations, in five categories. Best fed were to be troops, and priority workers, then blue-collar workers, white-collar workers, dependants and children.

The daily bread allowance was set at 500 grams (17.6 oz) for workers. White-collar workers and children up to twelve got 300 grams (8.8 oz). Dependants had 250 grams (8.8 oz). This last was a broad category that covered pensioners, housewives, the disabled, the sick and older schoolchildren.

Workers were also allotted the lion's share of the monthly rations. They were to have 1,500 grams (53 oz) each of groats and macaroni and meat products, 800 grams (28 oz) of fish products, 950 grams (33 oz) of fat, and 1,500 grams (53 oz) of sugar. Dependants were on a fraction of that, with 400 grams (14 oz) of meat and fish products and 300 grams (10 oz) of fats.

These were not hard rations. They were generous. In 1940, the average daily consumption of bread was 531 grams, only a whisker above the worker's ration. His monthly cereal rations were above the 1940 rate, marginally less in butter and fats. Only in sugar and sweets was he notably lacking.

The city was well served by Pavlov, an energetic and determined man with no time for propaganda. He swiftly realized that there was no hope of getting fresh food supplies through the siege lines. The grain that had come from Estonia and Latvia was gone. The market gardens and farms around the city that had grown its vegetables and potatoes were lost to the Germans, too. The only route was across

Lake Ladoga, and there were not enough boats, trucks, warehouses and piers to deal with the bulk cargoes needed. It would take time to organize them. Before then, brutal measures were needed to keep Leningrad alive. But the rations he first imposed were illusory, and could not be honoured.

Leningrad was in denial. White bread was still on sale. The young reporter Vsevolod Kochetov could buy luxuries like best crabmeat and caviar without ration coupons at the well-stocked lunch counter of *Leningradskaya Pravda*. He stocked up with a case of champagne at a closed store for the military. 'It's very nourishing,' the sales girl told him. 'Full of vitamins.' The dancer Olga Iordan was able to buy fresh caviar, real coffee and blackberry juice.

Bureaucracy was a minefield. Ten separate agencies were involved in food supply. Each answered to a different master in Moscow. Commercial restaurants continued to thrive, as they did in Moscow. Pavlov found that they were running through a tenth of all meat, and almost the same amount of sugar, and butter. Animal fats were stored in military dumps, vegetable fats in commercial warehouses. Cattle were not slaughtered to any plan. The Moscow Sugar Administration was still ordering its Leningrad staff to send freight cars of sugar to Vologda, along a line cut by the Germans weeks since.

The lead German units could now clearly see the city before them. The 1st Panzer Division penetrated the defences of the Dudergof heights, which climb to 525 feet six miles southwest of the city. They broke into the suburbs, Slutsk and Pushkin. Here, they wandered through the Alexander and Catherine palaces, the colonnades blue and white and gold through the trees and lawns and sculptures of their leafy parks. Daniel Granin, one of the Russians forced off the ridge under heavy air attacks, thought the city was lost. 'The rest of the soldiers in my unit scattered and I was left alone. So I boarded a tramcar and was driven back home with my machine gun and hand grenades. I had no doubts that the Germans were going to be in Leningrad in a few hours.'

Hans Mauermann, a German forward artillery observer, thought so too. 'Our company stopped a tramcar that had driven out of Leningrad and ordered the passengers to get out. We considered whether to hang on to the driver, so he could drive us into Leningrad the following day.' Men from the 58th Infantry Division reached Uritsk. William Lubbeck thought it was no more than another Russian village of wooden houses. 'Then we realized where we were. We could see the tall buildings and chimneys of central Leningrad seven or eight miles away.' His company, too, captured a red Leningrad tram. They felt 'no euphoria' – their casualties had been too high for that – but they were sure that the war was all but won.

The Pulkovo Observatory, on the heights overlooking the city's main airfield, was destroyed as the front line licked towards it. Its director, Professor Kirill Ogorodnikov, was killed with rifle in hand as the Russians held on in the grounds of its park. The destruction was a particular stain, for it had been the brainchild of the German-Russian astronomer Friedrich Georg Wilhelm von Struve. The shattered buildings, its burning library and the shell-blasted trees in its gardens were an assault on the Europe of knowledge. What the Hitlerites now savaged, Stalin had already mauled. Ogorodnikov's predecessor as director, Boris Gerasimovich, had been shot in 1937, with other leading astronomers. Some of the current staff survived. They were in distant Kazakhstan, on an expedition to study the total eclipse of the sun on 21 September.

Lieutenant J. Jewtuchewitsch, in the Russian 64th Engineering Battalion, had said goodbye to his mother in their Leningrad flat to go off to war two months before. 'She sits beside me, my old mother,' he had written in his diary, 'keeping back her concern, hardly able to keep back her tears. She made the sign of the cross over me.' He had been retreating for weeks, harassed by the panzers and aircraft, and he sensed it was almost over for him. 'We march from place to place the whole time . . . People have only rifles and a pathetic few machine guns. No medics! What is this supposed to be? We haven't any hand grenades either! In truth, this isn't a military unit. It's cannon fodder.' A few hours later, he wrote: 'We have landed in the rear of the enemy and are being hunted through the woods like animals, trying to get across the German-occupied road to break out and join the others.'

That night, he wrote his last diary entry. 'Shooting and panzers everywhere. What is going to happen? Will I be able to write again tomorrow in this book? If not, would the person who finds this diary pass it with a loving kiss and my last word, "Mama!", to Leningrad, Prospekt 25 October, House 114, Apartment 7, to Jewtuchewitsch, Anna Nikoilajewna . . .'[28] It was a German who found it.

As the city slid towards the abyss, and Voroshilov's defences crumbled, Stalin replaced him with a new military commander. Georgi Zhukov, a driving, ruthless young general who had beaten the Japanese at Khalkhin Gol on the borders of Mongolia in 1939, was summoned to the Kremlin. They spoke of Leningrad. 'Is this is a hopeless case?' Stalin asked him. Zhukov said it was not yet beyond saving. He wanted to go at once. Stalin feared he would be shot down if he went without a fighter escort. German aircraft, he said, commanded the skies above Lake Ladoga.[29] The forecast was for cool mist and poor visibility, which offered some protection. Zhukov could go. Stalin scribbled a note, ordering Voroshilov back to Moscow and appointing Zhukov in his place.

The transport carrying Zhukov, and three other generals he had hastily picked as aides, took off from Moscow's Central Airport on the morning of 13 September, protected by bad weather. It cleared suddenly as they flew over Ladoga. Two Messerschmitt fighters spotted the aircraft. Zhukov was lucky to escape as his pilot flew violent evasive patterns a few feet above the waters. He landed at an army airfield and was driven to the Smolny, the elegant school for the daughters of the aristocracy, white and yellow, its classical lines lifted by the baroque white and blue of the earlier cathedral, and now the headquarters of the Leningrad front as well as the Party. The sentries were not satisfied with Zhukov's identification, and he kicked his heels until the duty officer at last let him enter. He found Zhdanov and Voroshilov in a meeting room. He handed Stalin's note to Voroshilov, who read it, before passing it to Zhdanov without a word.

Zhukov was now front commander. His first order showed the aggression he brought to his desperate task. He discovered that Voroshilov had got Stalin's permission to scuttle the warships of the Red Banner Baltic Fleet, which lay silent in the anchorages off Kronstadt. Explosives had been laid in them in preparation for scuttling. 'I forbid the blowing up of the warships,' Zhukov told the fleet commander. 'I order the ships to be cleared of mines so that they cannot be blown up. Bring them closer to the city so that they can fire with all their artillery.' He wanted their formidable firepower to be used to break up German assaults. 'They had sixteen-inch guns! Can you imagine what a force this was?'[30]

In a warning read out to every unit under his command, in his Order 0064, he stated that anyone who abandoned his position without written permission would be shot immediately. At the front, he found discipline in the Eighth Army near collapse, with officers drunk, and men fleeing at the first shot. The commander of the Forty-Second Army, General I. I. Ivanov, was in shock, his head in his hands, unable even to point to the location of his troops. The commands of both armies were replaced.

On the night of 12 September, a small reconnaissance patrol crossed the river near the village of Nevskaya Dubrovka to the German-held east bank of the Neva. They observed the positions of the German 20th Motorized Division around Electrical Plant No. 8 and returned without loss to the right bank. Zhukov wanted to break the German stranglehold by driving them back from the east bank of the Neva and the southern shore of Lake Ladoga. The Russians still held the west or right bank of the river. The river is wide and fast-flowing, and the banks are steep except close to the village. Here, the slope on the far, German-held bank is much gentler. A light railway line ran down to it. It had been built to carry peat as fuel for power stations. A good road runs parallel to the river past the power station to Shlisselburg. The land between road and river had been cleared of the forest that stretched interminably eastward beyond it. The patrol found the surrounding area only lightly defended.

An interview with Shostakovich ran in *Izvestiya* on 13 September. He said that he had finished the first movement of a new symphony, and commenced on the second. 'He wants everyone to know that normal life is continuing in Leningrad, for scientists, writers, artists, composers, actors.' It was nonsense, of course, but it was suitably upbeat. 'He is sure that the enemy have not entered Leningrad, and never will.'

Defiant, the Muzkom staged the premiere of *Maritsa*, a 1924 operetta by Emmerich Kalman. It followed that with a performance of Kalman's *Silva*, as the Russians called his *Gipsy Princess*, all Viennese elegance and evening dress and gipsy romance. The Song and Dance ensemble of the Red Army, under the political command of the Leningrad Front, was performing for men from the bloodied Forty-Second Army. 'Only here did we understand what war really is,' the ensemble leader, A. Anisimov, wrote in his diary. 'Our songs were interrupted by sounds that have nothing in common with music.'

The first concert of the siege was held in the Philharmonia Hall on 14 September. 'Composer Shostakovich, writer E. Schwartz, artists of the Kirov Theatre O. Iordan, V. Legkov, S. Koren, V. Kastorsky and others performed with great artistic success,' *Leningradskaya Pravda* reported.

'The hall was packed out.' It was stunning and highly charged. An air raid was taking place as Shostakovich walked to the Nevsky and on to the Philharmonia. The all-clear sounded as he reached the hall. 'People came up to me, and they asked the same question: "Do you have a spare ticket?"' he recollected. 'These people were exhausted by sleepless nights, but they were striving for moral and aesthetic rest.' The sweetness of the music and the grace of the dance drowned out the ravages of the war beyond the hall. 'Never in my life did I feel so close a link to an audience as then,' Iordan wrote. 'I danced and danced and wanted to weave myself into the audience.' Shostakovich felt it, too: 'I was overwhelmed when I played in this strange atmosphere . . . the people who were gathered had risked their lives to be here and to prove that the beauty of art cannot be killed.'

The concert had an edge of the old terror to it. Evgenny Schwartz was a raconteur and wit, a much-loved impromptu entertainer, a brilliant and original man who survived the purges by writing children's stories and puppet shows. He was a soul mate of Daniil Kharms.

A medical conclusion to the NKVD case against Kharms had just been reached by Professor N. I. Ozeretsky, the chief psychiatrist at the Arselnaya prison. Kharms managed to convince the professor that he was insane by lying when he had no reason to. He insisted that his father was an archaeologist, and that he had studied mathematics at university. Neither, as the professor well knew, was true. Kharms's father, Ivan Yuvachev, had been a famous member of The People's Will, the revolutionary group that had assassinated Tsar Alexander II, and had served four years in the Shlisselburg fortress and eight years at hard labour in Sakhalin, where Chekhov had befriended him. The son was not a mathematician: he had studied at the Leningrad Electrotechnical Institute. The professor concluded that Kharms was a schizophrenic, although he was not released. He was forgotten, festering in the Arsenalnaya where he began to starve.

The war was ever closer to the musicians. 'A bombardment wrecked our apartment,' the Conservatoire professor Zoya Lodsi wrote in her diary. 'Moved to the Conservatoire. We live in a corner of a classroom. Only our everyday work saves us from the difficulties of life.' A large group of teachers moved in with her.[31] The composer L. Portov came across a 'very horrible sight' at the corner of Zhukovsky and Maykovsky Streets. A half-ton bomb had destroyed one building entirely, and five floors had collapsed in the next. Portov's fellow composer S. Bershtadsky lived in one of the ruined houses. 'He was very lucky he hadn't spent the night in his apartment. But everything he had was destroyed, including his Amati cello, his archive and his library of scores.' The cello had survived for 250 years.[32]

Shaporina felt heartsick. 'We are all on death row, we just don't know who's next. For twenty-three years, we've all been on death row in theory, but now we have reached the epoch's grand finale. An inglorious finale.' The twenty-three years referred to Stalin's time in power. The Germans had dropped leaflets threatening 'to grind us to a pulp'. They amused her. Had not Stalin been grinding them – 'the common people, a *quantité négligeable*' – to a pulp for all these years? 'He detests Leningrad,' she added. 'No one here has known him or seen him since the revolution.'[33]

Engrossed in his symphony, Shostakovich even took the score with him to the Conservatoire roof during his fire-watch duty, or so it was claimed.[34] In fact, he faced relatively little danger there: 'I was supposed to keep watch on Post 5 every day, and they said I'd become a good fireman,' he said, 'though no bombs fell in my area and I had no chance to test this.' Aron Ostrovsky, a senior Conservatoire official, later confessed to him that they made sure that he was never sent onto the roof during bombing raids or heavy shelling.[35] Shostakovich showed great coolness, nonetheless, when the city was under fire.

'Once the sirens sounded while Shostakovich played four-handed piano with Kamensky,' Shelest recalled of an impromptu performance. 'They finished the piece and the audience was asked to go down to the shelter. But a group of us, Shostakovich, Kamensky, my mother, [the dancer Yuri] Gofman and I got together in the blue drawing room and stayed there until the raid was over.'

The mezzo-soprano Nadezhda Velter lived on Gorohovaya Street. She met Shostakovich with the dancers Iordan and Vaganova hurrying across Palace (Dvortsovaya) Square as an alert sounded. Her house was close by and they went to its shelter. Afterwards they went up to her apartment and had tea and tiny pieces of bread smeared with mustard. As Velter talked with Shostakovich, she recollected, he suddenly stood up and said: 'Flying.' He listened hard and said: 'No explosions, not in our area.'

'At the time, I had no idea of the significance of this in his mind, when he was creating the Seventh, with the rumble of aircraft and the whistles of shells. But I could see how his expression changed – in his eyes, in the wrinkles on the bridge of his nose, in his frowning brow, I could feel the greatest internal tension. This is how the Seventh was created.'[36]

CHAPTER 4

Do serediny oktyabr'

To Mid-October 1941

Before Shostakovich went on radio to tell the world of the symphony, *Leningradskaya Pravda* carried a huge headline: 'The Enemy Is at Our Gates.' The Germans had seized the Alexandrovka tramcar terminus in the western suburbs. At Kolpino, to the southeast, 880 Red Army officers and men were killed in furious assaults, and hastily buried in a mass grave. Cylinders of hydrogen were set in the oil tanks in Kolpino's giant Izhorsky heavy engineering plant, founded by Peter the Great in 1722 to supply ordnance for his new navy, and the cranes and buildings were mined, ready to create a huge explosion if the factory fell. 'Not a step back!' Zhukov ordered. Those who did not obey were to be shot.[1]

Shostakovich spoke on the afternoon of 17 September. The sirens sounded as he was on his way to the House of Radio. On the reverse of the sheets of paper on which he wrote his talk, the studio director had scrawled notes for programme contents that captured the desperation of the city's plight: 'construction of barricades . . . fighting with Molotov cocktails . . . over us hangs deadly danger.'

The composer's words were relayed to Moscow and on across the country. 'I speak to you from Leningrad, at a time when there is heavy fighting with the enemy at the gates. I want you to know, comrades, that the dangers facing Leningrad have not emptied our lifeblood. Only now, we are not just citizens but defenders of our city, and we are all on combat duty.'

He told of his love of the city: 'this feeling has become more powerful and sharp . . . Leningrad is my country. It is my native city and my home. Many Leningraders know this same feeling of infinite love for our native town, for its wonderful spacious streets, its incomparably beautiful squares.' It would always stand, with its grandeur and beauty, on the banks of the Neva, a 'bastion of my country', rich with the fruits of culture.

'An hour ago I finished scoring the second movement of my latest large symphonic composition. If I manage to complete the third and fourth movements, then perhaps I'll be able to call it my Seventh Symphony. Why am I telling you this? So that the people listening to me now will know that life goes on in our city . . . Soviet musicians, my many and dear colleagues, my friends. We will defend our music. We will work with great honesty and self-sacrifice that no one may destroy it.'

At the moment, he said, 'the work is going quickly and easily. My ideas are clear and constructive. The composition is nearing completion. Then I shall come on the air again with my new work and wait anxiously for a fair and kindly appreciation of my efforts . . .'

Listeners said that 'each word rang like the note of a grand piano'.[2]

Maritsa was playing at the Musical Comedy theatre, the Muzkom. The first deaths began to hit the musical world. A Muzkom singer, I. Rozho, was killed by shellfire.

The German 58th Infantry Division was still advancing along the Gulf of Finland from Uritsk towards the heart of the city. William Lubbeck's company had fought its way two miles further into the suburbs, against 'intermittently stiff resistance' from the Red Army. They were surprised to be ordered to halt, and then to fall back into a more defensive position at Uritsk. They thought this was to regroup before resuming the advance. They learned 'with some frustration' of Hitler's Führer Directive No 1a 1601/41 (22 September) on what he called 'Petersburg': 'I have no interest in the further existence of this large population centre after the defeat of Soviet Russia . . . We propose to closely blockade the city and erase it from the earth by means of artillery fire of all calibres and continuous bombardment from the air.'[3] The city was not to be over-run, to free troops and armour for the advance on Moscow. It was to be starved and bombed to death.

The Germans could see the city's golden cupolas and warships moored in the Neva. 'In the distance the city pulsed with life,' a *Landser*, Walter Broschel, wrote. 'It was bewildering – trams ran, chimneys smoked and the maritime traffic on the Neva was busy.' He thought he knew, though, why his comrades had been halted. 'We had 28 soldiers left from nor-mally 120 in the company, and they have been gathered into so-called "combat battalions" – unsuitable to attack Leningrad.'[4]

Even so, they felt the city's surrender was 'only a matter of time'. They amused themselves with some abandoned Russian heavy guns they found on a bluff overlooking the Gulf. Russian freighters, oblivious, were still steaming to the Leningrad docks. Lubbeck sighted a gun along the barrel and fired half a dozen shells at one ship, getting close enough to splash it with water. They did not hit, but he was delighted to be able to claim that he had taken part in a naval battle.[5]

The Germans now dug themselves in for static warfare in a ring round the city. Lubbeck was certain that, with 'our high morale and the much worse state of the Red Army', a direct assault would have seen them reach the centre of the city 'within days'. Perhaps, but street fighting is a bloody business, and the 58th Infantry Division was a shadow of the unit that had swept through France seventeen months before. His own heavy weapons company of 300 men had lost only ten or so men since 22 June. The infantry companies they were sup-porting had all been reduced from 180 to between fifty and at best seventy-five men.[6]

Heinkel bombers were over the city in four separate attacks on the morning of 19 September. They were back for two raids that evening; they were the bloodiest yet.

A bomb hit the Mariinsky, home of the Kirov Opera and Ballet. It killed one of the oldest members of the company, S. Bazarov, and others were bruised and concussed. The building was badly damaged. Another bomb fell on a hospital on Suvorov Prospekt, killing many of the 600 wounded who lay in its wards. The big Gostiny Dvor shopping complex in the centre was hit, killing 98 and wounding 148. Most of the victims were women, including many workers in a clothing factory. Eight members of the editorial staff of the Sovetsky Pisatel publishers were among the dead.

A woman came into the Radio Leningrad studios after the raid. Her name was Moskovskaya and she had just lost two children under the ruins of her house in Stremyannaya Street. She spoke to Olga Berggolts. 'Let me speak on the radio . . . Please, I want to speak!' She told listeners what had happened to her children less than an hour before. Berggolts did not remember her words, but never forgot her breathing: the 'heavy, laboured breathing of a person who is all the time keeping down a scream, suppressing a fit of violent sobbing . . . the breathing of boundless grief and courage.' This breathing, amplified by the loudspeakers, was absorbed by the vast audience listening in the houses and bunkers of the city, and the wardrooms of the warships moored at Kronstadt.[7]

In the evening, at home, Shostakovich played parts of the new symphony to a few fellow composers who had remained in the city. Valerian Bogdanov-Berezovsky was there, and Yuri Kochurov, and sad Gavriil Popov. Shostakovich had just finished the first movement when the sirens sounded. He went down with Nina and the children to the air-raid shelter. As soon as he had settled them, he went back to his flat to play the scherzo and to show the others sketches from the third movement.

The thud of exploding bombs was a backdrop to the piano. Great sheets of manuscript paper lay on his desk, Bogdanov-Berezovsky recollected, witnesses to the grandiose orchestral scoring. Shostakovich played 'very nervously, but with great élan. It seemed that he aimed to draw out of the piano every nuance of orchestral colour. It made a colossal impression.' It was 'an extraordinary example of a synchronized, instant creative reaction to events as they are being lived through, transmitted in a complex, large-scale form, yet without the slightest hint of compromising the standard of the genre'.[8] The first movement cast a spell on them, like 'a gigantic shadow stretching far away'. The second was 'spectral and fleeting'.[9]

At midnight, a sacrificial force of marines, NKVD border guards and infantrymen crossed the Neva near the town of Nevskaya Dubrovka, where the reconnaissance patrol had reported on German positions a week before. Zhukov was determined to take a bridgehead on the left bank of the Neva, at any price, as the jumping-off point for an offensive to slash through the German lines, and link up with troops from the Soviet Fifty-Fourth Army advancing from the Volkhov front to the east.

The German-held strip of land between besieged Leningrad and the Fifty-Fourth Army, the *Flaschenhals*, was centred on the town of Sini-avino and the railway junction at Mga. At its narrowest, it was barely seven miles wide. Penetrate it, and the siege was broken; fail to do so, and the slaughter would become a ghastly and blood-soaked reprise to the agony of Leningrad, as insistent and continuous as the snare drum in the city's symphony.

The Russians were exhausted when they reached Nevskaya Dubrovka. The border guards, from a regiment of the NKVD's 1st Rifle Division, had marched for almost 40 miles. The river here is 600 yards wide, fast flowing and with banks thirty to forty feet high. There is one point, though, near the village of Moskovskaya Dubrovka. The 8th GRES, a huge power station with two tall chimneys and solid concrete buildings, stood over a mile upstream. It was the third largest peat-powered plant in the world. The Germans had taken it on 7 September, just before they took Shlisselburg.

They had turned it into a defensive position of immense strength. The main building was 130 feet high, massively built of masonry and concrete. It towered above, and had excellent views over, the flat countryside. Though the east bank of the Neva was twenty feet high, it had been lowered in front of the electric plant so as to draw on the waters of the river for cooling. It thus had a perfect field of fire over the closest crossing point. The plant was served by the little town of Vyborgskaya and two workers' settlements, Gorodok 1 and Gorodok 2. Nevskaya Dubrovka lay on the Russian-held right bank.

It was from here that the reconnaissance party had found that it was feasible, just, to cross. But, beyond the bank, the Germans were well dug in, and their communications were good. The highway to Shlisselburg ran parallel to the river about 500 yards from the bank. Beyond the highway was forest that the Fifty-Fourth Army would have to penetrate if it was to link up with Zhukov's men. The forest was thick and tangled, and laced with peat bogs and marsh.

No boats awaited the assault force. They had to make their own rafts, eight to a raft, with ammunition and grenades piled high. 'It was dark,' an NKVD officer, Mikhail Pavlov recalled, 'but as we approached the river German flare rockets suddenly lit up the sky and then their artillery opened up. It was absolute carnage.' The German gunners got the range as they neared the far bank. Hits caused huge explosions as the ammunition went up. 'Our guys on the rafts were sitting ducks. We lost an entire battalion during the crossing.'[10] Pavlov's raft was hit and he was thrown into the cold water. He reached the far bank and dug in.

At dawn, his men fought desperately to claw out a bridgehead. Russian observers at the top of a paper mill chimney at Nevskaya Dubrovka had a panoramic view across the river. The Russians on the far bank were pinned down in a small stretch of open land by the *Landsers* of the 122nd Infantry Division. During the day, they penetrated only 800 yards in from the river at most. In places, the bridgehead was only 500 yards wide. It stretched for barely 1,700 yards along the bank. The land was covered in coarse grass, treeless and flat. German machine-gunners and snipers took a terrible toll as the Russians slithered on their stomachs or ran bent double, or struggled in the sandy soil to dig trenches. The bridgehead was so small that the men called it the '*Nevsky pyatachok*', after the tiny five-kopeck coin.

Upstream, another force of marines and infantry crossed the river close to the village of Marjino. The power station's thick concrete walls made it a fortress that direct hits from Russian guns barely dented. The Germans at the top of the building were over 90 feet up, with unobstructed views of the Russians below. Even when the brown-clad figures tried to go to ground, they remained in the field of fire of the machine guns on the upper floors. Marjino was soon a smoking ruin that offered no cover and the Russians were annihilated by midday. Survivors who tried to swim back were exposed in the water, and were shot or drowned.

In the evening, the Muzkom staged *Die Dollarprinzessin*, a Viennese operetta with music by Leo Fahl, a cynical European take on mon-eyed Americans. Its subject – the heiress daughter of an American coal tycoon who comes to pre-1914 London, like Winston Churchill's mother, to marry a nobleman but instead falls in love with an impoverished Englishman – was a million miles from Stalin's Leningrad.

With its white ties, and tails, and its elegant 'Dollar waltzes', the oper-etta charmed a full house. To confirm its popularity, the Muzkom started matinees. 'Only one theatre is left where you can listen to music', the diarist Nikolai Kondratiev wrote.* 'Because of that, and because you want to forget at least for a short time, the Musical Comedy is usually full. The audience is mainly young. It's rare to see a middle-aged man. Mostly it's high-school girls who create the atmosphere. They receive the shows very well, and applaud often.'

No relief came for the men in the bridgehead from the Soviet Fifty-Fourth Army, nine miles to their east through the forests. Marshal Grigory Kulik, its commander, had a string of excuses for his inaction. Zhukov complained to Stalin, who furiously ordered Kulik to attack. 'In the next two days, the 21st and 22nd, you must breach the enemy's front and join up with the Leningraders or it will be too late. You have delayed too long.' Kulik mounted an attack, reluctantly. It had advanced three or four miles towards the bridgehead through thick trees and swamps when the Germans cut it off. The leading units were obliterated. Marshal Kulik was court-martialled. He was politically astute enough to avoid being shot.

The Nevsky pyatachok was an awful place to fight. Apart from the spot where the rail line reached the river, the bank was eighteen to twenty feet high. It offered the only protection, but it was so sandy that bunkers had to be intricately shored up with timbers to prevent them from collapsing. Back from the river, the soil was still so unstable that trenches caved in if they were more than three feet deep. The men had to crawl everywhere and use bomb and shell craters for cover. There was nowhere to wash, and no change of underclothes. Everyone was infested with lice and bedbugs. In places, the front lines were less than thirty yards apart, and they shouted at each other across no-man's-land. Resupply over the river was possible only at night. The boats were moored up in dug-out areas under the bank by day, and took the wounded out after dark, returning with minimum rations

---

* Not related to his namesake, the brilliant economist of the 'long wave' theory, shot in 1938.

of bread and cold gruel. The Germans ate well, with thermoses of hot food sent up from their field kitchens.

So intense was the fighting that at times the Germans were using 2,000 hand grenades a day, and the barrels of their guns became red hot, so constant was the barrage. On this small patch of land, 200,000 Russians became casualties. German losses were less than a tenth of that. Few of the Russian dead were ever identified. They had no metal identity tags. Each soldier had only a capsule, with a paper form inside he was meant to complete giving his name and unit. It was thought bad luck to fill them in, so most were left blank.

Casualties in Leningrad were a blank now, too. On 21 September, the city disappeared from national statistics. It was not to reappear until May 1943.

Silva was playing at the Muzkom on 22 September. Vera Inber was encouraged by that, and by Shostakovich. 'I was moved in these days in the besieged city under bombs,' she wrote. 'Shostakovich is writing his symphony. What is extraordinary is that *Leningradskaya Pravda* keeps us informed about it among the news from the front. It means art didn't die. It's still alive, shining, warm-hearted. Apollo is not strangled by Mars.'

Shostakovich found himself inspired, and at ease, roaming the city. 'I often went into the street for a break while I worked to get some fresh air,' he recollected. 'I often walked a long way, forgetting that I was in a besieged city that was being shelled and bombed. I looked at my dear city with pain and pride, full of fire and battle scenes, feeling the horrible hardships of war. For me, at that time, it was most beautiful in its stern greatness . . .' He added a reference to Lenin – 'How could I not love this city, created by Peter the Great and conquered for the people by Lenin – how could I not tell the whole world about its fate and the courage of its defenders?' – but the love for the city and its grandeur and artistry soars through the obligatory obeisance to the Bolsheviks.

'In this fight,' he said, 'a deep humanity was hidden'. 'With no food, no electricity, often leaving their workplace to pick up a rifle, the people of Leningrad fought for their city, for the sake of freeing Mankind from the most severe beast, of Fascism – and these people were firmly confident of eventual victory. I came back from my walks round the besieged city full of new impressions. I was full of desire to work and work and to contribute to the fight as much as possible.'

A further Russian battalion was fed into the bridgehead during the day, with some 76mm artillery. The Germans feared these field guns. They called them 'Ratsch-Bumm', 'scratch-boom', after their distinctive noise, and when they captured them they used them themselves. They disliked the Russians' big 120mm mortars, too, and the flesh-searing flamethrowers that were often used in attacks. Snipers and flamethrower operators on both sides were shot out of hand if captured.

For all the welter of Russian blood, the Germans were taking casualties, too, and they were stretched thin. 'Why can't the Soviets surrender?' Willy Tiedemann complained. 'We have been told they were almost finished! Later this day, nine Russian aircraft attack and my company has three dead. Are we all to die here in foreign soil?' Reinforcements had been rushed in to prevent the Russians breaking out of the bridgehead. Friedrich Lange, a twenty-nine-year-old infantry NCO, was among them.

He kept an oilcloth diary, in pencil. His first entry had been made on 1 May 1941. That day, he marched with his company beneath the Arc de Triomphe in Paris. He climbed the Eiffel Tower, went sightseeing in Versailles and made the acquaintance of a Madame Blanche and her two daughters. It may have been this meeting that led him to an appointment at the Clamart hospital at the end of the month. 'Thank God,' he wrote, 'they found only an inflammation of my urinary tract.' He enjoyed his time in Paris, drinking coffee on the boulevards, playing chess, eyeing the girls.

His idyll ended a week after Barbarossa began. His unit was sent by train, from France, to the Russian front. They left the train on 4 July, at Suwalki, close to the Polish border with Lithuania. From here they marched, 'in sun, sand and dust', the locals 'living like wild animals in hovels'. They marched and marched, across Lithuania and Russia, the panzers many miles ahead of them. On 11 September, they were close to Leningrad – like Hitler, Lange called it 'Petersburg' – where they were hurried into trucks and driven off towards Shlisselburg. They were set down in woods close to the town, and dug in.

The unit was rushed the few miles to the bridgehead during the Russian assault at Marjino. 'We were told the Russians had broken through near village B. It's a small town that had been almost totally burnt out an hour before,' Lange wrote.

We got out of the trucks and moved forward on foot. The Russians were firing on us. We had to bury Weltz. They killed him. We were fooling around all day. The second rifle company also got here by mistake. Lieutenant Portret was lost, and no one knows where he is. Lieutenant Agaheister went off to Division HQ to find out what we should do next. During this time, more Russians crossed the Neva. We don't have enough men in our trenches.

Lieutenant Portret appeared unexpectedly with an order to reconnoitre the woods. I and my platoon went to the right of a telephone line, and the second platoon to the left. We hadn't gone two hundred steps when Russians appeared. We went to try to cut them off. Some others followed us, and we were ordered back, but we couldn't, so we took cover where we were. Zummer was wounded and Astrid has fallen, seriously injured. I was near Zummer in order to bandage him and I asked Sikorsky to go to Division to ask what we should do.

The diary stopped there. Next day, 22 September, Red Army troops penetrated a copse to the northeast of the Dubrovska power station. Among the trees, they found the body of Friedrich Lange, with his diary in his pocket.

Tiedemann was edgy: 'The enemy fires from everywhere, who is really under siege? The Russians counter-attack at Neva.'

The city clung loyally to its soul. The Pushkin Society held readings and a concert for the wounded in the hospital at Plekhanov Street. From the Conservatoire, Zoya Lodsi wrote: 'We have started lessons, though they are often interrupted by air raids. It's very cold in the building – the windows are covered with cardboard, so it's very dark. Teachers and students are on fire duty at night.' Classes in chamber singing were held four times a week, from midday to 6 p.m. Twenty-five students worked on academic repertoire. Two hours a week were devoted to creating programmes for concerts that the students held for front-line units. Zoya Lodsi was in charge of these.

The All-Russia Theatre Society met to dedicate itself to the opening of the opera season. It found that fifty solo singers were left in the city. Some of its riches remained. Sofya Preobrazhenskaya, a mezzo-soprano of startling range and timbre, refused to leave her birthplace, where she had studied at the Conservatoire and triumphed at the Kirov. Vladimir Kastorsky's career had started with the Imperial Russian Opera, and his magnificent and lyrical bass had vied with Chaliapin in old 'Piter'. Another great bass from the Kirov and Maly, Andrey Atlantov, was still in the city, too; his wife Mariya Yelizarova was a fine lyric soprano. Their son Vladimir, who would become a famous tenor, was a little boy of two, a couple of years younger than Maxim Shostakovich, himself to be a noted conductor.

A singer's repertoire was established. It had ambition and sweep in plenty. *Eugene Onegin* was there, along with *Carmen*, Rimsky-Korsakov's

The Tsar's Bride, in which Preobrazhenskaya was a splendid Lyubasha, *The Barber of Seville*, Massenet's *Werther*, *Rigoletto* and Rachmaninov's *Aleko*, his first opera, based on Pushkin's poem *The Gipsies*.[11]

Three orchestras had been left after the Philharmonia had been evacuated to Siberia: the Radio and Muzkom orchestras, and a naval one at Kronstadt. The Muzkom survived, but most of the naval musicians had been sent to the front. The Radio musicians had dispersed. Some had joined the Guards, others were working in munitions factories. German radio was blaring that Leningrad was in desperate straits. What better way to show that life went on as normal, the propaganda experts at the Smolny suggested, than for Radio Leningrad to broadcast a live international concert?

The Radio Committee decided to revive its orchestra. Missing musicians were brought back from their barracks and bunkers and lathes. Eliasberg was asked to conduct the broadcast. It was to be dedicated to the Soviet Union's allies. There was only one of these, in pre-Pearl Harbor, pre-USA days: Great Britain and her dominions.

It was Shostakovich's thirty-fifth birthday on 25 September. A battalion of marines crossed the Neva that night.

A wondrous Leningrad day was enjoyed by Vladislav Glinka, on the 28th. 'I was invited out at 1 p.m,' he wrote. 'I still recall that it was the last sunny Sunday, with a beautifully served lunch.' Glinka was the guest of Fyodor Fyodorovich Notgaft at his apartment on Kireishny Lane (now Malaya Morskaya), its walls brilliant with paintings and drawings. Notgaft was the head of publishing at the Hermitage. Glinka had met him when he became curator in the spring of 1941. The two shared fire-watch duty together, and they talked of artists who had visited the spa at Staraya Russa, where Glinka's father had been a doctor in the old days. He was drawn to Notgaft as a rare survivor from that drowned world, a gentleman and a patron of the arts. 'At a glance,' he wrote, 'you immediately feel that this is a man of the best breeding, the best

education, a man who knows his own value and that of others.' Notgaft
was exquisitely well-mannered, with an easy and unforced elegance.
'His shirt, shoes, suit, were in pure colours, grey, ashen, white, black.
He was a free spirit, natural, intelligent, sympathetic, understanding,
and above all modest.'

Notgaft had travelled widely in Europe before 1914, bringing back
paintings and a striking French wife with him to St Petersburg. Renée
Notgaft had sat in black and lavender for a memorable portrait by Boris
Kustodiev in 1914. She did not take to the Bolsheviks, though, and in
1921 she returned to Paris. Notgaft loved Russia too dearly to follow her.
He remarried, Anastasia Sergevna Botkina, a woman both striking and
intelligent, who worked at the Russian Museum. She was cruel, too, and
'people said that Fyodor Fyodorovich couldn't bear her unkind character'. His third wife, Yelena, was in the department of drawings at the
Hermitage. She was a generous hostess and a wonderful cook, 'a tiny,
slim lady who reminded me of a fragile bird, not only in her figure, but
also in her manners and voice'.

'We looked first at the paintings. Each wall had two or three rows of
them, wonderful small canvases, by Benois, Lansere, Bakst, Kustodiev,
Sapunov, Dobuzhinsky, Somov, Serebryakova. Being so modest, Fyodor
Fyodorovich didn't tell me that for the main part these were all gifts
from the artists.' Glinka only realized this when he sneaked a look at
the back of the canvases. 'Also, a big collection of drawings – what a
collection! A little watercolour by Benoit, for example, of a lane in Paris.
Before the Revolution, he was a very wealthy man and he knew all the
museums of Europe.'

After a thorough look at the paintings – 'it was a sin to hurry' – they
had lunch. 'Fish baked in dough, dry Caucasus wine, coffee, a fine
tablecloth, table silver in art nouveau style to match the furniture . . .'
While they sat at table, Anastasia Botkina let herself into the apartment with her own key. Glinka recognized her in a portrait hanging

in the dining room. It was by Zinaida Serebryakova, a wonderfully talented painter upon whom the Bolsheviks had vented their spite. Her family estate at Neskuchnoye in the Ukraine was plundered. The collections built up by her architect and sculptor father, with many paintings by her uncle Alexandre Benois, were burned and the remnants left to the wind and rain. Her husband died in her lap of typhus in 1919, contracted in a Bolshevik prison. Her painting the same year of their four small children, *House of Cards*, fraught with fragility, is a masterpiece in watercolour. She had no money for oils. In 1924, she went to Paris on a commission for a large decorative mural. The Bolsheviks refused to let her back. She managed to get her two youngest children out to France, though it took her two years. She pined for Russia, keeping her Soviet passport, but she did not see her two elder children again until 1960.

It was a fine portrait of Botkina, Glinka thought, one of Serebryakova's last Russian paintings. 'Anastasiya Sergeyevna said she had sat for it twenty years ago. That was clear when you compared her with the original. She was still very beautiful. Only the colour of her face and a bluishness under her eyes told of her age.' He treasured the day as a last memento of the city's gentle and civilized face. 'We still didn't imagine the future of Leningrad,' he wrote. Notgaft's was unimaginable.

In the evening, Kondratiev was at the Muzkom for *Maritsa*. The Heinkels were overhead. 'Because of the alarms, the performance started half an hour late. There were many cuts in the operetta.' He added, grumpily, that 'Kalman's work can't be compared with classical operettas like *Perikola*'. At midnight, the Radio orchestra performed its concert for Great Britain. The musicians had rehearsed in the House of Radio during the day. Eliasberg conducted Tchaikovsky's Fifth Symphony. He recalled that there were severe air raids during the evening. The violinist V. Skibnevsky was injured on his way to the studio. After the performance, some of the musicians went on fire-watch duty.[12]

As the Tchaikovsky was broadcast, a second battalion of marines crossed into the Nevsky pyatachok. They came simply to replace the dead, dying and wounded. They had no air cover and little artillery support as enemy guns and aircraft worked them over. 'The German bombing and shelling was devastating,' Colonel Leonid Yakovlev, commander of a Soviet artillery regiment, confessed. 'They used flare rockets to light up our positions and dropped incendiaries to destroy the wooden buildings holding our ammunition and supplies. The Neva was literally boiling from the force of their fire.' Yakovlev had so few shells, he sighed, that his reply to the German barrages was 'laughable'.[13]

Four miles downstream from Dubrovka, at Petrushino, men from the 10th Infantry Brigade crossed the Neva. This new bridgehead was immediately attacked by the newly arrived 2nd Battalion of German paratroops. It was known as the Stenzler battalion for its commander, Major Edgar Stenzler, who had won a Knight's Cross for his actions against the British in Crete. His men moved in despite thick fog, and without special reconnaissance or heavy weapons. In hand-to-hand fighting, they took many casualties. The village at Petrushino was burned out.

During the day, the German barrage on the Nevsky pyatachok reached a new ferocity. It was lashed with some 8,600 shells and bombs. The new Petrushino bridgehead held out in mist and blood but Major Stenzler was dying of his wounds, and so was his battalion. The paratroopers lost all their officers, dead or wounded. The 1st Battalion, still at its training base in the rolling Bavarian countryside at Grafenwöhr, was ordered to relieve it. Other units arrived from the west to contain the bridgeheads: the volunteers of the Spanish 250th 'Blue' (Azul) division, the 72nd Infantry Division, torn from its soft billets in France, and more paratroops.

A fierce artillery bombardment rocked Leningrad in the afternoon. Olga Berggolts had gone out of the radio studio to record a short speech by Anna Akhmatova. They were in the House of Writers, in Mikhail Zoshchenko's room. They were 'terribly nervous', and the recording was interrupted by the crump of shellbursts. It was broadcast a few hours later. 'I preserve in my memory the deep, tragic and proud voice of the "Muse of Sobbing" as it floated over evening Leningrad, dark and gold and hushed for a short while,' Berggolts later wrote.

Akhmatova said that the city 'of Peter the Great, of Lenin, the city of Pushkin, Dostoevsky and Blok, the city of a great culture and labour is threatened with disgrace and destruction . . . I go numb.'

Bombs crashed on the city from fresh waves of aircraft in the evening. A quarter of those dying in the city were being killed in air raids. Adults did their best to shield children from fear during the raids. Svetlana Magayeva and her mother played games with neighbours – lotto was the most popular – while the glasses and china in the cabinet rattled from the bomb tremors. The girl found grief more terrifying than the explosions. A playmate called Rudi was a German whose mother had fled from Hitler with him. He was very blond, and the other children called him 'fascist' and bullied him. Svetlana did her best to protect him. His apartment block took a direct hit from a bomb. He was never found, and was presumed to be blown to pieces. His mother went day after day into the neighbouring courtyards, calling 'Rud-i-i-i! Rudi-i-i!' Her voice was loud and frightening. Each day she looked worse, and her hair more dishevelled. 'She looked at us in a strange way,' Svetlana recalled. 'She had gone mad with grief for her lost son. The look in her eyes was more frightening than the bombs which went on falling on our city.'[14]

Statistics for September were still collected, if not published. Twenty-five cinemas remained open, and the five Houses of Culture that had cinema screens were also showing films. The Muzkom had 35 per cent occupancy for matinees, and 45 per cent for evenings. Radio concerts were broadcast for an average of four hours a day.

Grimmer figures showed the civilian death rate in September to be 182 per cent above the average peacetime rate of 3,738 a month. The Red Army and the Baltic Fleet had lost 214,078 dead and missing in the defence of Leningrad, and 130,848 wounded or sick, since 10 July.

A few wounded men had a rare luxury on the last day of the month: lemons from the greenhouses of the Botanical Gardens on Aptekarsky Island. Staff sent flowers and orchids to military hospitals and units, and plants to decorate the wards of civilian hospitals. As yet, the magnificent collections started 227 years before by Peter the Great were still intact. All but 861 of 6,367 species would soon perish, lost to the cold and shellfire.

Morale was crumbling in places at the front. Joseph Finkelstein, an engineer who had joined a reserve division, was paraded in the morning to watch three deserters from his company being shot near the Polytechnical College. 'This was done as a lesson for us,' he said. They were crewmen who had abandoned their tanks and fled from the front. One was still wearing his padded tank man's helmet. All three had blank stares on their faces: 'probably they had already said goodbye to their lives.' They were undressed. A grave was being dug for them as they stood.

They were made to face the firing squad. The one in the tank helmet tried to hide his eyes as the firing squad took aim. His arms were forced down. 'Shoot the traitors to the Motherland!' the officer in charge ordered. They were shot in the face. Two of the bodies were still twitching. An NKVD man shot both of them in the head with a pistol. Finkelstein could see the Pulkovo Observatory on fire in the distance.[15]

A little before midnight, Shostakovich was telephoned by Comrade Kalinnikova of the Leningrad Party Committee. She told him he was to leave by air, with his wife and children, the next day. He had little time to get ready. 'On October 1st,' he wrote, 'my wife, the two children and

I left our beloved city.' He had to leave behind his mother, sister and nephew, and his parents-in-law.

The morning was overcast but it cleared at noon and the sun shone brilliantly in a cloudless sky. Gunfire rattled through the air from the Pulkovo heights. It got stronger from 4 p.m., and the city was heavily shelled. A tram was hit on Rastannaya Street with many casualties. The first air-raid alert came at 4.50 p.m. and the bombing lasted for fifteen minutes.

After the all-clear sounded, little Maxim remembered getting into his father's black *Emka*, a Gaz-M1 based on a 1933 Ford V-8, near their apartment on Bolshaya Pushkarskaya Street. They had only a single suitcase. Shostakovich carried with him the scores of *Lady Macbeth of Mtsensk* and the completed movements of the new symphony. The family boarded the aircraft, a PS-83 transport, at the Piskarevskoy airfield. 'It has just enough room for our family and three or four pilots,' his sister added. 'There is no seating inside, just a wooden floor and wooden boxes which we're not allowed to sit on, and we make ourselves comfortable on our suitcase. Above us is a glass turret through which one of the pilots is keeping a lookout. He warns us that if he gives a hand signal, we should all lie down on the floor.'

It was dark when they took off. A second German air raid started at 8.40 p.m. and the alert lasted for two and a half hours. In the city, N. P. Gorshkov recorded in his diary that heavy anti-aircraft fire blended with the distant explosions of bombs. 'The night was moonlit with a few rare clouds. It seems the city could be clearly seen from the sky. The firing was continuous. Explosions from ships and the front lines could be seen. This is the fight for Leningrad.'[16]

As their aircraft gained height, Maxim saw flashes on the ground below. One of the pilots told him that the Germans were firing at them. They landed close to a forest near Moscow: in the white marble, glass and gold Catherine the Great Room in the Kremlin, British and American diplomats were working their way through thirty-one toasts in vodka and champagne to celebrate the first protocol for Anglo-American aid, which they had just signed even before the US entry into the war. The pilots camouflaged the aircraft with branches and foliage. The Shostakoviches spent the rest of the night in a small hut. In the morning, they were taken to the Hotel Moskva.[17]

The flight path had taken them almost over the Nevsky bridgeheads. More troops were being fed in, under darkness, to replace the dead. It took fifteen minutes or more to cross the river, under fire the whole way. 'The ground was trembling and shuddering as if it were alive,' the deputy commander of the 339th Mortar Platoon, Mikhail Khalfin, recalled:

> There was the roar and wailing of sirens from enemy Junkers, dive-bombing our position. Everything became hopelessly muddled in the dark. I could hear the scream of bombs, the cracking of machine-gun fire from the far bank, and the terrible cries of our wounded. Suddenly, a bomb exploded close to our assembly point, leaving us half buried in the earth. Soldiers around us hurriedly dug us out. And then came the command: 'To the boats! Forward!'[18]

They paddled over the wide river with oars, rifle butts, wooden planks and bare hands, desperate to be over before they were hit. 'All this,' Khalfin said, 'to reach a dismal 500-metre strip of land, constantly erupting with explosions.' Of forty-six boats that attempted the crossing that night, forty were sunk or drifted, burnt out, downstream. When Khalfin and a few others scrambled ashore, and lay in a shallow communication trench, a voice in the darkness ordered them: 'Fix bayonets!' They went straight into close-quarters combat with advancing *Landsers*. They were willing to die to expel the enemy from their sacred land, Khalfin said, but he felt that this 'senseless slaughter' on the far riverbank had no point. 'Each one of us felt we would never return from this accursed spot.'

The fresh German paratroopers of the 1st Battalion of the Sturmregiment, flown in from their Bavarian idyll to relieve Stenzler's 2nd, had a brutal initiation to the Russian front. The 20th Motorized Division, which was pulling back from the Nevsky front, had lost 2,411 of its 7,000 men. 'Our plane was immediately reloaded with wounded men,' said Gottfried Emrich, a paratroop Oberjäger. 'The whole situation was pretty dicey. We could already hear the thunder of guns from far away.' They transferred to trucks, and were driven along mud roads and log causeways through forests. The driver pointed vaguely to the horizon. 'Leningrad is over there.'

As the light faded, they stopped and lay in a ditch. Their food was beyond the dreams of the hungry in Leningrad. They wolfed down ham, glucose tablets, cheese, pork and chocolate. They checked their weapons and sharpened the blades of the folding spades they used as entrenching tools. They made excellent weapons for hand-to-hand fighting. With darkness, they marched for several hours through the forests, stumbling and falling. They came out onto a large open plain covered with high grass that led to the Neva. They did not see any of the men of the Stenzler battalion they were relieving. They dug in and made a large bunker between four large fir trees on the edge of the forest, covered with branches and earth. They settled down to wait for dawn.

With light, on 5 October, the paratroopers could see the Russian positions a hundred yards away. It was difficult and dangerous to move. 'You kept stumbling over dead bodies,' Emrich said. 'Dressing materials and bandages were lying around all over the place.' Russian snipers were active. 'Messengers often disappeared or men fetching food were shot and wounded.'

Obergefreiter Friedrich Else set up a heavy machine-gun position in a shallow ditch. The Russians were close by, '100 metres in front of us at the most'. The 2nd Battalion of the Sturmregiment, which they had come to relieve, was 'ultimately annihilated. Dead Russians were still lying right beside our position.'

The remnants of the Stenzler Battalion and the surviving Russians were so closely intertwined that the newcomers could scarcely tell them apart. The commander, Hauptmann von der Heydte, had to establish a solid defensive front before he could regain the initiative and return to the attack. He assigned the central sector of the German ring round the bridgehead to the 2nd Company under Oberleutnant Wilhelm Knoche.

Knoche set up his command post in a length of ditch covered with telephone poles. It was 'dangerously close' to the Russians. The dead lay scattered around it. 'The Russians and Germans were just lying next to and on top of each other, right where they had been cut down by bullets or grenades,' he said. 'Recovering or burying the fallen was not possible.' But he managed to retrieve the body of his friend Alex Dick, a lieutenant who had been born to a German family in what was then Petrograd, and who died close to his birthplace.

Artillery was key to preventing von der Heydte's men from following Stenzler's battalion into oblivion. Once he had got it, he stabilized his line and set about planning the destruction of the bridgehead.

Stalin rang Zhukov during the day. Zhukov finally recognized that the Germans were on the defensive. 'For the first time in many days we could tangibly feel that the front had fulfilled its mission and halted the Nazi offensive on Leningrad,' he wrote later. In fact, of course, the Germans themselves had ended the offensive two weeks earlier, and transferred tanks, aircraft and men for the drive on Moscow. It was to halt this assault that Stalin now summoned Zhukov back to Moscow.

Zhukov was flown out the next day. Two of the generals he had brought with him to the city three weeks before were promoted. General Ivan Fedyuninsky replaced him temporarily, before taking over the Fifty-Fourth Army on the Volkhov. Lieutenant-General Mikhail S. Khozin took command of the Leningrad Front.

He left the men in the Nevsky bridgehead to their fate. Zhukov was well aware of the colossal casualties his Neva Operational Group had suffered, and that they would continue. Khozin went on to feed more troops over the river, as both the 20th NKVD Rifle Division and the 168th Rifle Division were reduced to fewer than 300 men.[19] It was to no purpose. A detailed report was made to the Front HQ by Ilya Izenstadt, a senior lieutenant with the 168th Division. He recognized that German tactics were highly effective. They shelled and bombed the reinforcements as they were gathering. Then, at the crossing points, the lower sandy shores on both sides of the river, they subjected them to a 'devastating bombardment, day and night'.

Izenstadt's critique was unflinching, almost suicidal in its accuracy. Men had been shot for saying much less. 'They held a total battle initiative,' he recognized of the Germans, 'and we could make no progress against them. Our own command system was crippled. We were unable to direct events in any meaningful way, and often completely lost contact with our troops.' The officers who organized the crossing were 'almost invariably' killed or wounded. The Germans were quick to locate HQs and communication centres, even as the Russians kept moving them, and then destroyed them and the men in them. 'Our losses were calamitous. We were unable to establish a proper pontoon bridge across the Neva and had to rely on makeshift crossing vessels that were often inadequate for the task. And on the far bank we could not provide our troops with any real protection from the enemy.'[20]

A regimental commissar, Ivan Pankov, pleaded with the front command on behalf of his men. 'The majority of our troops are fighting bravely but people are literally crawling over the dead bodies of their comrades,' he said. 'Because our artillery has failed in any way to disrupt the enemy's annihilating firing system, the heroic efforts of our soldiers are utterly wasted.' Zhukov ordered them to hold their ground regardless.

From the prisoners they took, the Germans found that that Mga had become 'a kind of *fata morgana* for all of the Russians'. The railway town was eight miles from the bridgehead. It acted as a sort of divine mirage flowing with 'bread, potatoes, tobacco and above all vodka in incredible quantities'. The commissars had hammered this dream into their starving men, and thus 'they fight as if berserk to capture the fabled land of plenty'.[21]

A rare Russian assault to the west of the city was dismissed by William Lubbeck, who helped to repel it, as an 'ill-conceived fiasco'. Infantry supported by armoured cars and tanks attacked his regiment at Uritsk on the Gulf of Finland. The Germans were well dug in on top of a cliff above the coast road with anti-tank guns and mortars and well-sited machine guns. They wiped out the Russian infantry almost to a man. Some tanks broke through and advanced towards Uritsk along the coast road. The German 88mm guns on the cliff top knocked out the lead tanks. The Russians could not elevate their barrels high enough to bring them under fire. Over the next twenty minutes, the German 88s picked off each tank on the street below them. Continuous machine-gun and small-arms fire caught the tank crews as they jumped out of the burning machines. German pioneers blew up the road behind them with explosives, so that there was no retreat for the Russian infantry. Some jumped into the sea and swam away. The rest were killed or taken prisoner. The Russians lost 35 tanks, 1,369 dead and 294 prisoners.[22]

In the best peacetime style, with crowds pulsing round the entrance looking for extra tickets, the concert season opened at the Philharmonia on 5 October. Sofia Preobrazhenskaya sang. The pianists, A. Kamensky and Vladimir Sofronitsky, had both been at the Conservatoire with Shostakovich, where Sofronitsky had met and married Alexander Scriabin's daughter Elena. The cellist was Daniil Shafran, the son of the Philharmonia's principal cellist. In 1937, under-age at fourteen, he had won a magnificent Antonio Amati cello as first prize in the All-Union cello and violin competition.

Kondratiev listened 'with the greatest pleasure, because I had longed for music for myself. It's been a long time since I listened to Tchaikovsky with such pleasure and emotion. The performance by Shafran and pieces from *The Queen of Spades* were the best in the concert. Sofronitsky and Kamensky's playing on the grand piano left a nice impression.'[23]

When a fund-raising concert was held a few days later, the hall was packed out, and the overflow spilled out into the streets. Eliasberg conducted the Radio orchestra, with arias and overtures from Mikhail Glinka's *A Life for the Tsar*, Rimsky-Korsakov, and Tchaikovsky's Fifth, St Petersburg composers all. Kondratiev was amused at the revival of Tchaikovsky, considered 'decadent' a few months before. 'Interesting that the stress is on Tchaikovsky now, in these days, outliving our country.'

Homage was paid to Ludwig Minkus and Marius Petipa, the ballet composer and the choreographer to the old Imperial Theatres, with a matinee and evening performance of *La Bayadère* at the Muzkom. The story of the temple dancer and the warrior had had its premiere in the city in 1877. Its revival was a poignant evocation of a grandeur that shellfire and bombs did not dim. That Minkus, like Hitler, was Austrian-born, did not matter. Despite the Hitlerites at their gates, Leningraders nourished themselves with the great German creatives: the composer L. Patrov found himself enthralled by a book he found in the library of the Union of Composers on how Goethe and Schiller worked. 'I couldn't put it down, even in air raids and blackouts. By candlelight, I forgot about everything except Goethe.'[24]

The city's grace and style still coursed with life. In the absence of any breakthrough from the Neva bridgeheads, though, Ladoga was its sole source of sustenance. The lifeline on the lake was being severed, at times in the most terrible manner.

On 6 October, German bombers sank four barges laden with flour and ammunition that were being towed across its waters. The same day, it was decided to evacuate all 'superfluous mouths of socially danger-ous elements' from Leningrad to Tomsk. That meant all the convicted prisoners and those awaiting trial in the city's gaols. As well as the big pre-war prisons, like the Kresty and the Shpalernaya, many were held in the transit prison on Konstantinogradskaya Street. A so-called 'under-ground prison', not mentioned in documents but in oral testimony, was opened at Ladoga for holding convicts due for transportation over the lake.[25] Like Anastasiya Vyaltseva's father, many had been arrested for 'spreading panic' and 'spying' over the past few weeks.

Two days later, the prisoners were sent to the Finland Station in closed vans. They were loaded into railway wagons and taken to Osinovets. From the station they were marched to the quays. A large barge, *Berlinka* ('the Berlin woman'), was lying in the port[26]. It had a maximum capac-ity of 1,000 people, but almost 2,500 were loaded onto it. Apart from military prisoners, including 141 captured German officers, the barge had 1,837 men aboard, and more than 400 women. The prisoners of war and the women were kept in their own groups. Political prisoners were mixed up with the criminals.

Struggles for breath and life began as a tug pulled the barge away from the quay. They had not got far when a German air strike began. The tug abandoned the barge during the bombardment and returned to port for another mission. The *Berlinka* was left drifting off the lake shore. In the late evening the German bombers returned. The prisoners in the holds began screaming for food and water and to be allowed on deck. Lieutenant Lenivtsev, the barge commander, took some bread and water to the hold but refused to let the prisoners up.

'Swearing and counter-revolutionary statements' echoed round the steel hull. Prisoners started crawling out of the holds. They attacked the guards and tried to seize their weapons. The guards beat them back with rifle butts. When the situation was getting out of control, Lenivtsev ordered his men to open fire with sub-machine guns. About forty prisoners were killed, and their bodies were thrown into the lake.

The *Berlinka* drifted on the lake for another three days. All the time, prisoners tried to get on deck. They were answered with bursts of automatic weapons fire. Lenivtsev made persistent appeals for help. Finally, a tug arrived and towed the barge across the lake and up the river to Volhov station. Eight days after leaving Osinovets, the *Berlinka* was blocked by a railway bridge. Here the survivors were transferred to a smaller river barge to be towed up the Syas river. A roll call was held, showing 500 prisoners were missing. Soldiers buried the bodies still on the barge on the shore by the village of Podryabinye, in a mass grave discovered in the 1990s. The missing were listed as 'did not arrive in Tomsk' or 'died of heart failure'. At least 200 of the survivors then perished in the cattle-trucks taking them from Tomsk to Novosibirsk.

Other than on the Neva, though, the front lines became static and permanent. The Germans settled in for the siege. The most forward bunkers were little more than covered ditches with a slit for observation. As the snow grew deeper, they piled it into a wall that ran in front of the bunkers and trenches to hide their movements. Further back, they built log bunkers with bunks, wood-burning stoves and tables. They were comfortable and almost homely. Lubbeck's gun crew were all under twenty-three, but they felt themselves veterans, because they had fought in France, and they hung a sign at the entrance: 'The Four Old Sacks'.[27]

They lived like kings compared to the famished Russians facing them. At night, troops from the *Tross* came up with mail and food. They carried insulated flasks of hot soup, generous rations of beef or pork and potatoes, brown loaves, butter and cheese. Often, they had chocolate. There was a regular ration of two small bottles of vodka. Sometimes they had a bottle of cognac apiece. Some in Lubbeck's regiment exploited their abundant supplies for sex. With a loaf under their arm, they headed off for an area two miles or so behind the front, where hungry Russian women and girls willingly exchanged their favours for food.[28]

Snipers took a toll on both sides even in the quietest stretches of the line. The Russians were particularly skilful. The Germans found Russian scoped rifles to be superior to their own, and preferred to use captured weapons than the standard Wehrmacht issue Kar-98 with a five-power scope. The accuracy of sniper fire was such that the number of killed to wounded was much higher than with other weapons. Sniper rounds easily penetrated German helmets if they hit them squarely. Russian snipers in large numbers waited patiently for targets in the high-rise buildings on the edges of the Leningrad suburbs. If he had to move outside the trenches, Lubbeck used skis to travel as fast as possible. Lubbeck's gunners extracted their revenge. 'The whole of no-man's-land between us became one large targeted killing zone,' he said. 'We established predetermined firing coordinates.' Counter-battery fire was another 'deadly game of cat and mouse'.[29]

How many were trapped inside the lines – for all the Soviet obsession with precise statistics – was unclear. A census had been held on 17 January 1939. On that day, the population of the Leningrad's fifteen urban districts was 3,015,188. This was one of the world's great cities. Its population was double that of Los Angeles, larger than Paris, and Rome.

Women outnumbered men by 55 to 45 per cent. Their life expectancy was higher: they drank less, fewer of them were shot, exiled or drafted, but they made up almost half of the city's workforce. Children and the young (under nineteen) made up more than a third. A cluster of babies born after 1937, the result of the banning of abortion in 1936, made up 5 per cent of them. Eleven men and thirty-four women were over a hundred years old.

Though the census takers counted 783,145 family units, these were strikingly small. Bolshevism had largely done for the traditional family, with several generations and many children. A third of households had just two members, another third had three, and 20 per cent had four. Only a tenth had five. What might seem a norm – a husband and wife, say, with two children and a grandparent living with them – was uncommon. Thirty nationalities were noted – each Soviet republic counted as one – but almost nine out of ten were Russians, leavened with 6.3 per cent Jews, and a smattering of Ukrainians, Tartars, Belorussians and Poles, with 10,104 Germans and 8,000 Finns.

Only 206 people were listed as 'unemployed', a category that barely existed in Bolshevik theory. But more than 1.2 million people were listed as 'dependants', well over a third of the population, be they children, pensioners, housewives or invalids. These distinctions were to become matters of life and death, for the daily food ration was based on them. Dependants were to have the smallest rations. The best fed, or least starved, were to be the blue-collar workers in industry, who made up over half the workforce, with other sizeable groups in construction and transport.

The biggest change in the city's make-up after the census had been caused by the Winter War. Almost 150,000 reservists and new recruits had been sent to army, navy and NKVD units. With the men absent, the birth rate in 1940 had fallen by a quarter. The city's proximity to the front line reversed the usual immigration into it. For the first time since the civil war, more people left than arrived. The population was estimated at 2.9 million at the start of 1940.

It was boosted by 81,000 boys and girls, thirteen-to-eighteen-year-olds, at the start of 1941. They were sent to industrial and occupational training schools, and a big railway training college. At least 50,000 of them were from outside Leningrad, and they crammed into hostels.

The total of those caught in the city, the evacuees replaced by refugees, was thus a smidgen under three million. What followed for them – as winter set in, with ice and blizzards and darkness, and the food stocks dwindled – has been described as 'the greatest demographic catastrophe ever experienced by one city in the history of mankind'.[31] Nowhere – not fire-bombed Dresden or Hamburg, not atom-bombed Hiroshima or Nagasaki, not razed Stalingrad or tortured Warsaw – has experienced death on the same scale.

Russian has only one word, *golod*, for the hunger, famine and starvation that embraced the city. As to the sound of the cataclysm, Shostakovich was trying – fitfully – to capture it, now from Moscow.

CHAPTER 5

Oktyabr'

October 1941

In Moscow, Shostakovich gave interviews. The theme, in the dark and fearful city, was irresistible: the young composer whose creative impulse was defying the Hitlerites. He said that the concept of the new symphony's later stages was well advanced. 'Currently I am completing the last, fourth movement. I have never worked so quickly as now.' He added that 'In the finale, I want to describe a beautiful future time when the enemy will have been defeated.'[1]

He and his family were staying in the Hotel Moskva, vast, new, its grey bulk looming over the centre of the city, by the Kremlin and Red Square. Its Bolshevik credentials were underscored by the mosaics and giant paintings of heroic workers in its public rooms. Stalin celebrated his birthdays here, behind dark drapes in the plush and overheated grandeur of its heavily brocaded restaurant. Its bedrooms, on corridors that seemed to stretch into infinity, were the preserve of foreign dignitaries and the Party elite. They now housed the cream of the refugees from cities lost to the Germans.

Guests sheltered in the basement when air-raid alerts sounded. The conductor Boris Khaykin, another Leningrad evacuee, and artistic director of the Maly Opera Theatre in Leningrad (the old Mikhailovsky Theatre), ran into Shostakovich during one alert. He was pacing the floor, muttering as the bombers flew over: 'Wright brothers, Wright brothers, what have you done?'[2]

His agitation would have been greater had he known that he was sharing the basement with a ton of high explosives. It had been placed there a few days before by the NKVD, packed into 58 boxes, with 40 lbs of explosive per box.* It was intended as a greeting for the Germans.

Moscow was on the edge of the abyss. The NKVD had hastily formed OMSBOM, a special operations force. They recruited outstanding athletes and games players: the only public commemoration of OMSBOM today is a small plaque on the wall of the Dynamo Moscow football stadium. The force prepared to make the city as uninhabitable for Hitler as it had been for Napoleon. Senior German officers had a habit of setting up their headquarters in the luxury hotels of conquered cities – the Crillon in Paris, the Grande Bretagne in Athens – and the Moskva was primed for destruction.

The orchestra pit of the Bolshoi, the Kremlin, the Cathedral of the Epiphany, and major government buildings were mined. Explosives were planted in the dachas of the leadership, except Stalin's country house in the forests of Kuntsevo. He was afraid they might be used to assassinate him. The power stations, the phone system and the water supply were also ready to be blown up.

Plans were being finalized to get Shostakovich and the creative elite out of the capital before it fell. His colleague Lev Knipper, however, and a handful of ballerinas, singers and circus acrobats, were to remain on the orders of the NKVD. They were issued with explosives and hand grenades, and trained how to use them to kill any high-ranking Germans whom they might be called upon to entertain.

Knipper was a prolific composer, of five operas and a score of symphonies, and his 'Polyushko Pole' was a favourite marching song of the Red Army. He was suitably compromised. He was of German stock,

---

* The men who laid it, and concealed it, are all thought to have been killed later in the war. They took their secret with them. The explosives were not found until 2005, when the hotel was being rebuilt, and workers found the boxes as they dug up the foundations. (*Guardian*, 16 July 2005.)

he had fought with the Whites, and emigrated. He was recruited by OGPU as the price of his return in 1922. It was his sister, the actress Olga Chekhova, who now interested the secret police. She had married the actor Mikhail Chekhov, the playwright's nephew, but divorced him and left Russia for Berlin in 1920. She was one of the Third Reich's leading film stars, much admired by Hitler, and the NKVD were greatly taken by a press photograph showing her sitting next to Hitler at a reception. If – when – the Germans took Moscow, they thought, Hitler would visit the city as he had Paris. It would be natural for Olga Chekhova's brother to be invited to any celebrations. The NKVD thus selected Knipper as Hitler's potential assassin.

The NKVD was also preoccupied by its bitter blood feud with the Red Army. It feared that the senior officers in the Lubyanka cells would be liberated by the Germans. Some would be evacuated to prisons in the east. Others were to be shot.[3]

Twelve thousand incendiaries were dropped on Leningrad on 13 October. The city had reason to be thankful for its imperial past. Other Russian cities were largely built of wood. The great Fire of Moscow, that started as Napoleon's vanguard entered Moscow on 14 September 1812, feasted for four days on its wooden houses. Three-quarters of the city was destroyed. But St Petersburg was the showplace and capital of the Romanov emperors. Its building materials reflected its status, granite or brick in the main, and its roofs were slate or tiles. It did not burn easily.

The bombers were back in force the next day. Alla Shelest was living with her mother. The ballerina was afraid to leave her alone, so she took her with her when she went to give performances in hospitals. It seemed to her that the *erker*, the glassed-in balcony common to Leningrad apartment blocks, was open to the sky and attracted bombs.

Left: At twenty-eight, in the creative burst that marked him and his city, Shostakovich had composed an astonishing range of pieces. His First Symphony, written at nineteen, had been conducted by Toscanini and Klemperer. A brace of ballets and operas, a piano concerto and film scores followed.

Below: In 1932, Shostakovich married Nina Varzar, seen here with him and his dearest and most vivid friend, Ivan Sollertinsky. Only the faintest murmurs of what was to come could be heard.

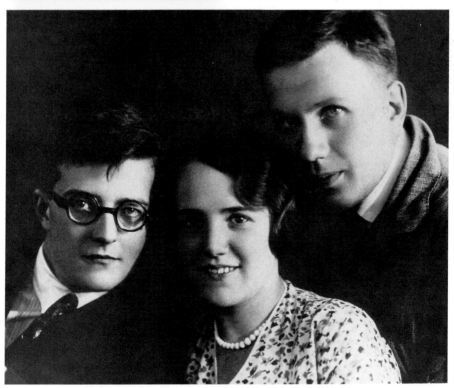

Shostakovich seemed marked down for destruction when Stalin walked out early from a performance of his opera *Lady Macbeth of Mtsensk*. The set in Moscow is seen here.

The composer's vulnerability was increased by the birth of his daughter Galina in 1936. He was an affectionate father. If he was found to be an 'enemy of the people', he would go to the camps, at best, and the little girl would go to an orphanage.

Shostakovich wrote the music for Vladimir Mayakovsky's play *The Bedbug* in 1928. Mayakovsky, poet, Futurist, actor, satirist, seen here in the Crimea with his mistress Lily Brik, was too spirited to survive the tightening Bolshevik stranglehold. He shot himself in 1930.

Stalin used the murder of Sergei Kirov, the Leningrad Party leader, to unleash the NKVD secret police and the Terror. Here (far right) he carries Kirov's coffin to be immured in the Kremlin wall. Andrei Zhdanov, who replaced Kirov in running Leningrad, much to Shostakovich's peril, is fifth from right in the light coat.

The *Yezhovshchina*, the great wave of terror in 1937–8, was named for Nikolai Yezhov, short in stature, cram-full of malice, seen here (far right) with Stalin, Molotov and Voroshilov.

Shostakovich's friend, Marshal Mikhail Tukhachevsky (far left, front row), took the salute with Stalin and other leaders in the May Day parade in Red Square in 1937. By mid-June, after arrest, torture and execution, his body had been thrown into a trench at a construction site.

Yezhov in his turn was tortured and shot by his successor at the NKVD, the sadist Lavrenti Beria. Beria is seen here with Stalin's daughter Svetlana on his knee, whilst her father goes through papers on his desk.

Vsevolod Meyerhold was a theatre director of prodigious talent and influence. Shostakovich stayed with him and his wife, the actress Zinaida Raikh, in Moscow whilst they worked together on Mayakovsky's *The Bedbug*. Meyerhold defended his friend during the *Lady Macbeth* crisis.

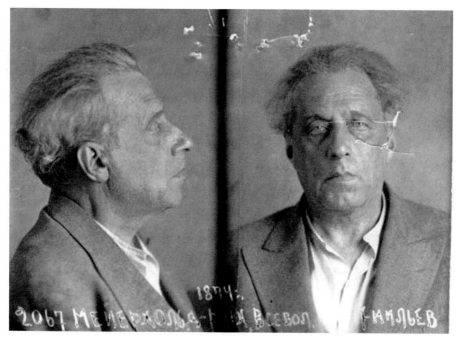

The eighteen-hour bouts of interrogation Meyerhold suffered are hinted at in this NKVD file photo. Zinaida Raikh was stabbed to death in her eyes in their apartment, which was subsequently given to Beria's chauffeur. Meyerhold was shot on 2 February 1940.

Labour camp bosses in the Gulag competed with one another to get prisoner–musicians for their orchestras. The players, huddled on the right, are serenading their fellow *zeks* as they toil at canal-building.

The three greatest Soviet composers, Prokofiev, Shostakovich and Khachaturian, denounced as 'formalists' and pursued by Zhdanov – himself a music-lover known to Beria as 'the Pianist' – were liable at any time to be liquidated or sent to the camps.

So many were arrested, the poet Anna Akhmatova wrote, that the 'city of Leningrad dangled like a useless appendage from its prisons'.

Shostakovich never wrote another ballet after the mauling *Pravda* gave to *The Limpid Stream*. Yet the city was rich in dancers, including the brilliance of the Kirov's Olga Iordan.

Shostakovich continued to write – here at the piano, though often only in his head – after the triumph of his Fifth Symphony reawakened official hostility. His Sixth ran fewer risks.

They were caught in a bombing raid as they walked to the Nevsky. 'We heard the sirens, that mean bombs, death,' she wrote, 'we heard whistles and then explosions. Even now I chill to think of it. Two bombs hit buildings next to ours. We understood that we couldn't come home. It was impossible to live there. We went to live with a friend of Mama in her tiny room.'

Impromptu concerts were held in bomb shelters in the evening. The first siege note was written in the inventory book of the Radiokom library. It recorded that a new Komsomol song had been written by Vasily Soloviev-Sedoy, the composer of 'Moscow Nights'. *Leningradskaya Pravda* reported that the Symtojazz group was giving scores of performances at the front. Its musicians were all Conservatoire graduates.

There was music, too, on the other side of the lines, in the captured Grand Palace at Peterhof. Many Germans had visited Versailles on leave in Paris. William Lubbeck and his comrades found the beauty and majesty of the Peterhof to be quite the equal of its French rival, even if its fountains were not playing. 'We strolled along panelled wood floors through elegant halls,' he recalled of his day's sightseeing. When they came across a piano, one of them, Staff Sergeant Ehlert, pulled up a bench and started to play. 'We were amazed as beautiful classical music began to echo around us in the chamber. As the afternoon sun streamed into the room through the large windows, it was almost possible for me to imagine the Tsar playing the same piano surrounded by his family.'[4]

The fresh paratroops on the Neva were now ready to annihilate the Petrushino bridgehead. Von der Heydte planned a night attack. His 2nd Company was to launch a frontal attack, while the 1st and 3rd attacked on the flanks to squeeze the Russians into a concentrated killing zone around the charred remnants of Petrushino village. German heavy weapons firing on the far bank of the Neva would stop the Russians moving up reserves and supplies.

The attack went in at 10 p.m. The ground was easy to make out in the ghostly light of signal rockets. Obergefreiter Friedrich Else was in a dugout to give covering fire with his three-man heavy-machine-gun crew. He opened fire with the German heavy guns as the first red flare went up. After five minutes, a green and red rocket followed, and the barrage stopped. The German riflemen had worked their way forward into the Russian positions. As they began their assault, Else's machine gun tipped into the sand from its carriage. The barrel was red-hot as they had fired off three belts of 300 rounds during the barrage. It could only fire single shots now. As he struggled to fix it, Else saw some Russians right in his sights coming towards him. They were yelling 'Hurrah!' He cried out to his men to get down or fire their pistols. 'We shot and shot until we'd emptied our pistols and magazines. The Russians turned aside or fell.'

The Russians counter-attacked fiercely at dawn. Their near starvation weakened them for hand-to-hand fighting, and the well-fed paratroopers broke them up, slashing and battering them with the sharpened blades of their entrenching tools. The Germans took some more ground and the men of Oberleutnant Knoche's company were within 100 yards of the river when they were stopped by Russian artillery firing from the far bank.

Men on both sides lay exhausted in their dugouts and bunkers, while artillery and snipers went about their business on the surface. Knoche had taken command of the 1st Company after its Oberleutnant, Hepke, became a casualty, Werner Krüger now taking his place at the head of the 2nd. The Germans were steeling themselves for a fresh assault in two days. At dusk, several Russian defectors crawled out of their trenches and gave themselves up. Krüger had a Feldwebel, Scholz, who spoke fluent Russian. Scholz found out that while they were defecting they had shot dead their commissar, whom they blamed for squandering lives by continuing resistance that was hopeless. Krüger sent Scholz forward with two of the defectors to urge their comrades to surrender.

Russian artillery began firing across the river onto the mass of their own men as soon as the commanders realized that they were giving themselves up. They killed some of them, and the German battalion's medical officer, Dr Petrisch, was killed by a shell fragment that penetrated his heart as he was treating a Russian casualty. Von der Heydte was also wounded. But the Russian gunners could not prevent the capitulation.

As they cleaned out the Petrushino bridgehead next morning, Gottfried Emrich, an Oberjäger, said that they discovered the reason for the 'extraordinarily good marksmanship' of the Russian artillery over the past days. A paratrooper accidentally nudged a Russian captain who had lain just in front of the German positions for several days, and whom they presumed to be dead. But he was still alive, and they found a radio set hidden under his body.

In the evening, the Russians played German marches over loudspeakers across the river. They mixed the music with propaganda about the hopelessness of the German situation and promises of safe conduct if they defected. The Germans replied with creeping artillery barrages. At night, the Russians sought to send over infiltrators on rafts and boats camouflaged to look like bits of floating islands. 'Our annihilating fire succeeded in turning them back again and again,' Emrich said. The weather was getting chilly. There was the occasional snowfall. Hauptmann von der Heydte was awarded the German Cross in Gold for his achievement and that of his men in liquidating the bridgehead.

The battalion was transferred to prevent any Russian breakout from the Nevsky pyatachok.

Shostakovich was told to go to the Kazan Station in Moscow with his wife and children at 10 a.m. on 16 October. The station square was jammed with writers, painters, musicians and dancers from the Bolshoi. 'Moscow was panicking,' recalled Clinton Olson, then a young lieutenant with the American military supply commission. He had heard a 'lot of artillery fire in the distance', and his mission had been given four hours to get ready to leave. The Americans were not yet at war. He and his general had debated whether they should stay in Moscow until the Germans arrived, and return to Washington via Berlin. They had decided it was their duty to stay with the Red Army. 'The streets were full of people, and when we got close to the station there was a mob scene,' Olson found. 'It looked exactly like you'd expect an evacuation to look: refugees from the front, a blizzard raging away, eerie lighting around, a crowd held back by bayonet.' Olson and foreign diplomats were going on the same train as the Shostakoviches. He found himself suddenly laughing. He thought he was dreaming: 'This is surely 1812 all over again.'[5]

The platforms were dark and slippery, the artist Nikolai Sokolov recalled, with 'wet and squelchy snow'. Loudspeakers blared continuously. The young composer Karen Khachaturian was there to see his famous uncle Aram off. 'I suddenly caught sight of DD [Shostakovich] on the platform,' he said. 'He looked completely bereft. He was holding a sewing machine in one hand and a child's potty in the other.' His wife was standing with the children next to a 'mountain of stuff'. Everyone pushed and shoved each other. Sokolov and Shostakovich were assigned to carriage No. 7. They were blocked: 'This carriage is only for the Bolshoi!' Whereupon Dmitri Kabalevsky, a fellow composer, a tall and impressive figure, bellowed, 'Allow Shostakovich and his children to pass!'[6]

They were all crammed into the carriage, ballerinas from the Bolshoi, set designers, sculptors, and other composers whom Shostakovich had good reason to loathe. Tikhon Khrennikov was travelling with him, a Party favourite whose 'Song of Moscow' won the 1941 Stalin Prize. He had declared his delight at the execution of the 'fascist hireling'

Tukhachevsky, and condemned *Lady Macbeth of Mtsensk*. 'The opera's entr'actes and other things,' he wrote, 'aroused complete hostility.' Dmitri Kabelevsky was another devotee of social realism. Vissarion Shebalin, though, was a welcome companion, a fine and cultured composer, and a friend to whom Shostakovich dedicated his String Quartet No. 2. The train left at 10.40 a.m.

As he went home, Karen Khachaturian heard howling dogs roaming the snowy streets, abandoned by owners who had fled the city. Flakes of ash mingled with the snow and rain falling from the low clouds that had grounded German bombers. Documents were being incinerated all over the city: Party records, membership lists, anonymous letters of denunciation, minutes of meetings, code books. The rubbish dumps in the courtyards were piled with busts and portraits of the leaders, badges, diplomas, torn Party identity cards, Marxist-Leninist books of all sorts, anything that might catch the Germans' eye.[7]

Wild rumours swept the city. It was said that Stalin had been arrested, that a coup had taken place, that the Germans had reached Fili. This was the point where the Mozhaisk highway entered Moscow, where Field Marshal Kutuzov had bivouacked after the Battle of Borodino in September 1812, and decided to save the remnants of his army by abandoning the capital to Napoleon.

Looting broke out. The roads leading east were clogged with cars, as functionaries fled from the city. A truck commandeered by a factory manager had his piano, beds, bicycles, mattresses, sideboards and his dog aboard. 'The captains were the first to abandon the ship,' the journalist Nikolai Verzhbitski heard people muttering, 'taking their valuables with them.' They were saying things that would have had them shot a day or two before. He thought that they had begun to 'count up all the humiliations, the oppression, the injustices . . . the arrogance . . . the conceit of the party bureaucrats . . . the lying and flatteries of the toadies in the newspapers. People are speaking from their hearts. Will it be possible to defend a city where such moods prevail?'[8]

The NKVD execution squads were busy. They shot more than two hundred people, the largest number to die in Moscow in a single day since 1938. Nina Tukhachevskaya, the widow of Shostakovich's great friend, was among them. She was shot with Nina Uborevich, whose husband had been executed with Tukhachevsky. The generals' wives had been arrested after their husbands' trial. Two years of interrogation and torture had driven them to accuse one another of plotting to assassinate party leaders. Their daughters had been sent to homes for the children of enemies of the people. Bliuma Gamarnik and Yekaterina Kork had already been shot, in July. The bodies of the two Ninas were thrown into an NKVD burial pit on the Kommunarka State Farm, outside the city.

Shostakovich's train crawled eastwards, swaying in the familiar slow rhythm of the Russian broad-gauge track. It was heading for Kuibyshev, on the east bank of the Volga at its confluence with the Samara river, 529 miles east of Moscow. At Ryazan, bombs were falling from a German raid. It stopped for hours to allow priority trains to pass. Arms factories were on the move to the east, their workers sharing goods wagons with their machines and tools. Trains with fresh troops from Siberia were moving west, where they would soon be fighting the Germans in front of Moscow. Tanks and ammunition stood under tarpaulins in freight yards. A wet snow, almost rain, was falling. It was difficult to sleep. They were so packed together that the men stood at night, to give some space to the women to stretch out. By morning, the snow had frozen.

Sokolov watched Shostakovich getting out at stations to collect boiling water for tea. He washed his crockery in the snow beside the carriage, a forlorn figure, in an old, worn suit, his trouser legs soaked through. He was very upset, Sokolov said, because he had lost two suitcases, 'with all his personal possessions and children's things'. He feared he had lost the score of the Seventh, too. It had been wrapped in a quilt that someone had dumped in the carriage toilet. 'DD and I did not think of this quilt for many hours,' Nina Shostakovich later told the writer Daniil Zhitomirsky. 'We were busy making the children comfortable and searching for our suitcases. In the meantime, the place where the ill-fated package was, was being visited in earnest. You can easily imagine what we saw when . . . we managed to get there. It was horrifying to touch the blanket which was in the middle of a puddle. I will spare you the details . . . It was completely by chance that it was not thrown out altogether.' The suitcases were never found. Sokolov gave the composer some new socks. Somebody else added a shirt. 'He took these things very shyly,' Sokolov said, 'and thanked everybody in a state of great agitation.'[9]

At first, he told Sokolov, when he had climbed into the dark carriage with his children, it had seemed to be 'paradise'. As the journey ground on, however, interminable, surrounded by others, 'I felt I was in hell.' At least 'Ollie' Olson and his fellow Americans were enjoying themselves. 'We had lots of booze, and that helped the morale situation a bit, if not the morals,' he said. 'We were very well acquainted with the ballerinas of the Bolshoi Ballet. They were great fun.'[10]

The same day, the fate was decided of the senior military commanders and industrial chiefs arrested in the 1941 wave of repression. Beria rushed to dispose of them lest the Germans arrived. Some joined Nina Tukhachevskaya, hastily shot in Moscow as Shostakovich boarded his train. They included Lieutenant-Generals Nikolai Klich and Robert Klyavinsh, and Major-General Sergei Chernykh.

As to the others, a convoy of 'especially dangerous state criminals' joined Shostakovich on the line from Moscow to Kiubyshev on 17 October. They included the most senior officers arrested in the Meretskov affair, and three of their wives.[11] They were not to survive for long. Two days later, Beria dispatched a trusted courier, Demian Semenikhin, to Kuibyshev NKVD with Order #2756B. It listed various prisoners, and instructed: 'Discontinue investigation, do not send to trial, shoot immediately.'[12]

The very heart of the apparatus of terror was dogging the composer. As well as the prisoners, the staff of the NKVD's central office was also on the move to Kuibyshev. The NKVD in Shostakovich's new home, under Senior Major of State Security S. I. Ogolt'sov, was second only to Moscow in the secret police hierarchy.

In Moscow, Dmitri Kedrin wrote a secret poem on the panicky escape of the high and mighty:

A train for Siberia redoubled its steam
In a compartment a painted lady sobbed . . ..
The anti-aircraft rumbled somewhere by the bridge
A heap of sacks was sliding off the benches
And, in the name of Christ, a ragged Red Army man begged for
    alms.
Up above a German aircraft droned,
The bosses ran full tilt for Kazan.[13]

In Leningrad, hunger drove a young chemist, Galina Salyamon, to scavenge for a few scraps. She walked beyond the end of the tramlines to a field with a few cabbages left and some leaves. Her thin light shoes sank in the mud. She managed to fill her bag and hitched a lift on a truck that dropped her off at the first tram stop. Plainclothes NKVD men were there, looking for looters. Snow started to fall as she waited. It covered all the vegetables still left in the fields, but the men would not let anyone scour them for last leaves of cabbage.[14]

Echoes of the civilized values and love of learning that had marked the city's pre-Terror past went hand-in-hand with the descent into the darkness. This was the 800th anniversary of the great Persian poet Nizami. A celebration was held at the Hermitage, with papers by leading academics. Pride of place was given to a talk by Captain D. M. Diakonov, who had been given special leave to attend by his unit at the front. He was a famous orientalist who had been a curator at the Hermitage before the war.

October the 22nd was the birthday of young Andrei Krukov's father. Krukov was a twelve-year-old boy, passionately fond of music, who was to become the chronicler of music in the city. It was a happy day: 'I wrote a poem for him and played Haydn's symphony four-handed with my teacher for him. Father was very pleased.' His father had been in the tsarist diplomatic service in China. He was dismissed after the Revolution. Andrei thought that had saved his life – 'he was sacked before the repressions' – but his father never talked of his former existence. He had worked for a time in the commercial department of a hairdresser's, and then as a geologist and for the waterworks.

The only survivors from those who had taken the Nevsky pocket a month before were the wounded who had got back across the river. The rest, mostly seventeen- and eighteen-year-olds, with only a few months' training, were dead. Their bodies lay in the bridgehead. A few artefacts were dug up years later: an icon, a water flask crudely engraved 'To Viktor Krovlin, on his eighteenth birthday'. It had a scratched sketch of the bridgehead, showing the shattered village of Moskovskaya Dubrovka and the pontoon bridge that linked it to the right bank. German shells had destroyed the bridge the day after young Krovlin's comrades had given him his birthday present.[14] The casualties, as fresh men were fed into the bleeding maw, exceeded 250 per cent. 'One can say,' A. V. Burov wrote in his diary on 19 October with stinging understatement, 'that it has been a month of severe and inhuman education.'[15]

At 8.10 p.m. that day, a Sunday, he recorded, two regiments of the 86th Rifle and the 330th Rifle Divisions assembled at the crossing points. The 86th were based on a People's Militia unit from Leningrad's Dzerzhinsky district, factory workers and labourers who had played at soldiers on the odd afternoon and weekend before the war. Those who survived the Stukas and shells to land on the far bank faced paratroops and infantry with skills sharpened by more than two years of combat.

The Stavka's new Siniavino offensive began on Monday, 20 October. The plan varied little from September. The Neva Operational Group was to break out of the Neva bridgehead, and link up with Fifty-Fourth Army, thus lifting the siege. During the night, more troops from the 86th and 285th infantry divisions crossed the river. At ten o'clock on Monday morning, the Russians attacked out of the bridgehead. 'Although the Hitlerites opened furious fire, our forces wedged into the enemy's foxholes and began throwing hand grenades,' Burov recorded. 'Hand-to-hand fighting began. By the end of the day, we managed to push the Germans back a bit and expanded the bridgehead somewhat.'[16] 'A bit' and 'somewhat' – a gain of 200 yards in depth and 1,000 yards in width – were little reward for a desperate attack by fresh troops, ignorant of the hostile and open terrain, upon a well-dug-in enemy, whose artillery had been zeroed in on the killing ground for weeks.

'We were losing thousands of men a day,' said Colonel Alexander Sokolov. 'The trenches were full of the dead bodies of our soldiers. The enemy bombardment was overwhelming. In all my time on the bridgehead I remember only one brief period of daytime silence, when there was no shooting, bombing or shelling. It lasted a full ten minutes. The German fire was constant – and their positions were so close that during daylight nobody was ever able to stand at full height without being immediately picked off by a sniper.'[17]

*

On the morning of 22 October, Shostakovich and his family at last saw the leaden waters of the Volga, reflecting a bruised and stormy sky. The train crossed the bridge over the two-mile-wide river, and wound its way on at a snail's pace until the scattered villages gave way to Kuibyshev. For all the elite evacuees crammed into it, Olson found it 'a mudhole'. His fellow American, Lester Raymond, agreed. It was 'slow, quiet and drab'. The old city stood on a high bluff on the east bank of the great river. It had only four paved streets, with trolleybuses on two of them. A few others had cobblestones laid down the middle. Horses and camels outnumbered the few cars and trucks. It had no more shops for its half-million people than an American country town of fifteen thousand. The water supply came from wells, and its sanitation relied on privies in the absence of main drains. The old tsarist buildings were unpainted and the stucco was crumbling. The only new ones of note were an NKVD club and a railway workers' hall of residence near the marshalling yards.

Its industry appeared to run to no more than a textile factory, a foundry, a macaroni-making plant, a grain elevator and drying sheds for the fish that abounded in the river. A modern power station was blocked off behind high walls and armed NKVD guards. A few miles from the outskirts, though, stood a second city, Bezymyanny – 'Nameless' – one of the Soviet Union's secret manufacturing cities, a place known only by a postcode. Big factories 'stood side by side like houses'. Seven of them were aircraft plants, and Raymond knew of them from American transport pilots who flew into its airfields. They told him that they had never seen so many military aircraft as here. It was a 'city of smokestacks . . . a giant conveyor belt'. Sleepy Kuibyshev was simply 'one giant dormitory for the many thousands of workers who trekked every day on foot or by ailing trolley to the Nameless factories'.[18]

None of this was visible to Shostakovich, and Soviet citizens knew better than to be inquisitive. The family was lodged in a school in the old city that was already packed with artists from the Bolshoi. They slept eighteen to a classroom, on the floor, with mattresses, their chattels piled around them. The streets outside were heavy with autumn mud, and it was tramped across the rooms. In the mornings, there were long queues for the washrooms. Sturdy men, Sokolov said, 'whistling excerpts from operatic excerpts', streamed out of the door marked 'Boys'.[19]

They had access to the Bolshoi commissariat, and a daily ration of butter, sweets, bread and salami. Shostakovich carried these treasures back to the classroom, 'a bright smile lighting up his face'. 'After three days, I was fed up,' he confided to Sokolov. 'You can't get undressed, surrounded by a mass of strangers. I again saw this as hell.' He could work on his symphony only in his head, and he was too distracted to do so.

After a week, they were moved from the school for a few days to the Grand Hotel. Chaliapin had stayed there in the hotel's palmy tsarist days, and it now housed the elite among the evacuees. A little later, the family were given a two-roomed flat at 140 Frunze Street. It had a bedroom with four iron bedsteads. The living room had a few Viennese chairs, a crudely built cupboard, a dining table, a desk – and a grand piano. This paradise, too, turned sour. 'I notice how inconvenient it is to work in a single room,' he said. 'The children are rowdy and disturb me. Yet they have every right to be noisy, they are only children. But I can't work.'[20]

He said that something had snapped inside him as he stepped onto the train. 'I can't compose just now, knowing how many people are losing their lives.' He did not lack for stimulating company. He spent his evenings playing cards with Lev Oborin, a brilliant pianist who had been playing in a trio with the violinist David Oistrakh and the cellist

Sviatoslav Knushevitsky. Sokolov sketched him in black wash and pencil as he played.

Storm-force winds whipped up breaking waves on Lake Ladoga on 23 October. Tugs tried to hold their barges bow-on to the winds, but towlines were broken and six barges were driven ashore. The same storms made it impossible for the Russians to evacuate the wounded from the Nevsky bridgehead. Resupply was also impossible. That day, Burov was noting that the Germans had counter-attacked, catching the Fifty-Fourth Army off-balance as it tried to link up with the bridge-head, and capturing Budogosh. 'Tikhvin is now directly threatened,' he added ominously.

The Siniavino offensive was a final throw of the dice to lift the block-ade before winter. The Russians had 71,200 men, 475 guns and Katyu-sha multiple rocket launchers. Their 97 tanks included 59 heavy 'KVs' (named for Marshal Kliment Voroshilov). They could call on aviation and heavy artillery from the Baltic Fleet. The 54,000 Germans they attacked had few tanks: their armour was now at the gates of Moscow. But they were well prepared and in well-sited positions, flanked by thick forest and swampy terrain, and supported by 450 guns.

The Russians lost 22,111 dead and 32,276 wounded in the small region around Siniavino over the next five days. The German paratroops had learned to distinguish between regular Red Army men and the artless and untrained Leningrad civilians who had been put in uniform and sent to the bridgehead as cannon fodder. What they had in common, the paratroops noted, was that they were all starving. Every night, Feld-webel Scholz and an Oberjäger called Canzler, who also spoke Russian, spoke to the Russians a few yards away from them. They lured a few defectors each time, most of them 'workers from Leningrad who'd just been stuck into a uniform'. The first things they always asked for was 'Germanski Brot!'

Stavka ordered Fedyuninsky's Fifty-Fourth Army to halt the barren offensive on 28 October. The forces were diverted to defend the Volkhov Front. The last hope of raising the blockade was gone. In its place was 'a deep foreboding over the prospect of the city's total isolation'.[21] Music still calmed Leningrad's nerves and fed its soul. Theatrical students gave a children's concert in the big bomb shelter on Mokhovaya Street. They acted out fairy tales and sang songs with their young audience. The 1939 operetta *The Roads to Happiness*, by Isaak Dunayevsky, the leading Soviet film composer, was alternating with *The Dollar Princess* at the Muzkom, and *Silva* and *Maritsa* were playing at the Operetta theatre. The tickets for a rehearsal by the Radiokom orchestra were sold out.

A concert was held in the Philharmonia Hall on 26 October. The conductor was Nikolai Rabinovich, who taught a generation of Leningrad conductors at the Conservatoire, with the pianist Alexander Kamensky as soloist. It impressed the diarist Kondratiev. 'The hall couldn't fit everyone who wanted to get in. Tchaikovsky's 1st Concerto was the only piece on the programme. I realized that I still don't really know this piece, and I'll be finding new things in it for a long time.' He was pleased that Tchaikovsky was no longer being written off as 'a decadent and the singer of the moods of the dying class'.[22]

He liked the soloist, too. 'Kamensky brightly demonstrated the competition between piano and orchestra . . . The chandeliers were switched on one by one, quite unexpectedly, which added to the powerful outpouring of the introduction.' The lights were on only for a few moments while a photographer took pictures of the hall for newspapers to show Russians on the mainland that Leningraders were alive and listening to fine music. Vera Inber was less enthusiastic. 'Kamensky played Tchaikovsky's piano concerto and the Prater Waltz but the concert hall is already not as gay as before. Not heated. We had to wear coats.'

The men in the Nevsky pyatachok were not forgotten. Their long Calvary was tempered by a visit from the musical comedy star Tamara Pavlotskaya, whose hit film *Anton Ivanovich serditsya* ('Anton Ivanovich Is Angry') had been released in August (in Britain as *Song of Spring*). She was now with a group of Leningrad artistes who were entertaining the troops. She had done front-line performances before, but nothing like this. Before they reached the Neva, they put on camouflage uniforms. They were given an 'emergency ration' – a few pieces of pearl barley – and crossed the river at dusk. They had to crawl on hands and knees for the final part of the journey. A makeshift stage had been built where it was hidden from the Germans in a fold of the bank. Here they changed into their costumes, to put on a short musical comedy called *Bats*.

This had the troops laughing and whistling everywhere she had played it. Here, it was met with total indifference. 'I have never seen such exhaustion,' she recollected. 'Below us, there was a sea of blackened faces. Some men had fallen fast asleep. Others, out of fatigue or shell shock, seemed absolutely numb – unable to respond to anything. Our comedy routine, with its singing, dancing and jokes, continued in absolute silence.'

Then something utterly bizarre happened. Pavlotskaya heard an odd scuffling behind her. A startled goat appeared. It had emerged from the forests, lost and disorientated, and climbed on the stage and stood there. 'For a moment our actors froze – then we decided to carry on regardless. Remarkably, all around us, we felt our audience coming back to life, as if they were all emerging from some kind of terrible trance. There was a sudden transfusion of energy. Men began laughing, smiling, and nudging their fellows.'

The goat stayed rooted to the spot for several minutes. Then it started looking around. 'The creature wandered over to the lead singer, who was performing a short aria about unrequited love. The goat stopped and began to stare at her in a most doleful, sympathetic fashion,' Pavlotskaya said. The soldiers were transfixed. Then the goat turned towards them, and started to bleat in accompaniment to the song, its 'strange sounds rising to an extraordinary falsetto'. As the duet reached its climax, the audience greeted it with a mighty roar of laughter, and rose to its feet in delighted applause. 'I have never experienced anything so moving as that moment,' the actress recalled.[23]

A convoy of five trucks in Kuibyshev on 28 October gave the briefest glimpse of the terror that had discreetly followed Shostakovich from Moscow. At about midday, the trucks left the NKVD prison bound for a settlement called Barysh on the outskirts of the city. Here they drove into a walled compound where the Kuibyshev Oblast NKVD had their summer dachas. Beria's envoy, Semenikhin, had arrived with his instructions for the 'special group' of prisoners. The senior officer responsible for them, L. F. Bashtakov, was expecting to finish their interrogations. The order to murder them immediately took him by surprise. Mariya Nesterenko was still undergoing interrogation by Ya. M. Raitses in the morning when Senior Major Rodos broke in, shouting, 'Let's go!'

The paperwork, exact as ever, was completed. Order #7/2-5017 released the prisoners from custody in order to comply with Beria's Order #2756B. The investigation was discontinued. No trial would take place. The prisoners were loaded into the trucks and driven to the dacha compound. Semenikhin had probably served in Blokhin's execution squads – a reason why he had survived the fall of Yezhov – and he was experienced in the grisly business of disposing of them. As well as the air force officers, Beria also included the last of the four members of the Ural Soviet who had organized the murder of Tsar Nicholas, and his wife, son and daughters, in Ekaterinburg in 1918. The town had long since been renamed, as Sverdlovsk, and Ezhov had had the others shot. The last living link with the massacre of the Romanovs, F. I. Goloshchekin, who had been the Party secretary in the town, was now extinguished.

The bodies were buried in a children's playground.* Bashtakov and Rodos sent signed confirmation to Beria that the executions had been carried out. It became known as the 'October massacre'. Thus were killed, in a war that was going badly, three men who had commanded the air force, the two most senior Jews in the Red Army, Shtern and Smushkevich, four Heroes of the Soviet Union, the first deputy commissar of the aircraft industry, the directors of four major factories and the director of the construction bureau. For good measure, three of their wives were also shot – Mariya Nesterenko, the dashing aviatrix, with Zinaida Rozova-Egorova and A. I. Fibikh, married to the artillery general G. K. Savchenko – and Shtern and Smushkevich's wives and children were sent to the camps.[24]

Shostakovich was less than five miles away. In the city whose symphony he was finding it so difficult to complete, *Leningradskaya Pravda* announced that a great concert was planned for the Philharmonia, with Glinka's *Long Live!*, Beethoven's Ninth and Khachaturian's cantata *Pesnya Stalina* ('Song of Stalin'). A new Theatre of Small Operetta was formed in Kronstadt to perform aboard the ships.

The strain of the aerial bombardment was telling. Shelest and her mother had moved again. 'We always went to the shelter when there was a raid, the three of us, Mama and her friend and I. But I'd had an animal instinct to move and so we went to Mama's brother. After we left, the house was hit by a bomb that also destroyed the bomb shelter, where we'd hidden, and everyone in it died.' Her Uncle Mischa found a bottle of home-made cherry brandy. 'He drank it all and ate all the cherries complete with the stones and he died.'[25]

---

* Some children heard shots in an abandoned quarry nearby, and found used cartridge shells.

There were air raids almost every evening. In the daytime, German reconnaissance aircraft flew high over the city. People thought their white contrails were part of their target-finding. If two contrails crossed, people below lived in terror waiting for the expected raid.

Dmitri Likhachev, the great scholar who had observed Soviet inhumanity as a *zek*, a Gulag labourer, toiling on the White Sea canal, now noted a Nazi variant. The Germans began their shelling in the early evening, when the streets were full of people going home from work. They had special targets: the Truda square, the Dvortsovy and other bridges, and crossroads, like the corner of Vvedenski and Bolshoi. Shells often hit trams on the Nevsky, and the broken glass caused many casualties. Likhachev and his family slept in a tiny room on the first floor. They avoided the cellars after a number of people were drowned when they were trapped in the cellars and broken mains flooded them with water. Four shells whistled over his roof before exploding on a tram crossing. The house 'danced' and the cupboards flew open. Gradually, he became used to it. Elena Martilla was an eighteen-year-old nurse in the Krupskaya hospital on Vasilievsky island. Shell shock turned her mother into a 'helpless child': 'She didn't dress herself, she feared everything, spoke in a whisper.' Elena had an inspiration. 'I informed Mama that for the time being, I would become the mother, and she my daughter.'[26]

Hunger was beginning to overwhelm musicians. Zoya Lodsi, teaching at the Conservatoire, wrote in her diary: 'When I begin the lessons, they are like the dead – empty eyes, no thoughts, only of bread. How hard, how painful, to force them to listen to music – but then such happiness, they listen, they discuss, and together with me they sing our beautiful songs.'[27]

Mass starvation was now acknowledged to be inevitable unless some radical new way was found to feed the city. The NKVD reported that the situation was now critical even in the large factories, whose workers got the lion's share of rations. The secret police put the shortfall at 70 per cent of essential foodstuffs. Canteens were serving only first courses, and then only after queues of up to two hours. Transport aircraft could carry enough food at best to keep alive less than half the troops in the front line. The others, and almost all the civilians, would be dead in a few months.

Red Army troops had a ration of 500 grams of bread and 125 grams of meat daily. In the quieter sections of the line they might also get a little fish, borscht or cabbage soup. Very often, they had half this, or none at all. The reserves behind the line had 300 grams of bread and 50 grams of meat. At times, they had shots of vodka, and an issue of *makhorka* tobacco, a mixture of hops, dry aspen, birch, oak and maple leaves, with a little tobacco dust, a concoction created by the chief tobacco manager at the Uritsky factory.

The contrast with well-fed German combat troops was brutal. They had a daily intake of 3,236 calories, adequate even in extreme cold. The bread ration was 750 grams a day, and the 250 grams of meat was supplemented by 130 grams of canned meat. Each man had 80 grams of sugar, 50 grams of fats, and 10 grams of coffee and fresh onions. Russians risked their lives crawling into no-man's-land to search dead Germans for the food in their *Brotbeutels*, the 'bread bags' on their belts where they kept emergency supplies.

In one way, though, the Russians in their white camouflage, felt boots, greatcoats and thick gloves were better off. The paratroops were still in the summer uniforms they had worn in Crete. They painted their helmets white, and improvised white smocks from sheets, and stripped the felt boots and gloves from dead Russians.

The Russians continued to mount attacks from the Nevsky bridgehead. Two or three tanks would cross during the first part of darkness and clatter up to the main Russian battle line. Obergefreiter Else saw one stop in front of his bunker, where he waited with his machine-gun crew. One of his men, Jäger Hein van Koll, had a demolition charge in his hand and was ready to jump up. The men got fourteen days' special leave for destroying a light or medium tank, and three weeks for a heavy KV. Then the tank turned and headed for a position manned by combat engineers.

'Just before it got there it stopped,' said Else. 'That was a big mistake.' In the light of signal rockets, he watched as one of the combat engineers ran up to the tank and planted a demolition charge on it. It damaged a track. The tank could only move in zigzags. It staggered up to the engineers' bunker, where it ground its track into the earth and became stuck. Else captured its crew, his first prisoners. Knocked-out tanks were used for cover by men of both sides.

Russian infantry battered the Germans with hand grenades. The blasts from their *Ratsch-Bumm* guns toppled the pine trees in the German rear with loud crashing thuds and stripped the branches and needles from the survivors. The Germans called it 'Flanders forest' in memory of the desolate stumps and remnants of the woods of Flanders in the First War.

The snow in the bridgehead was a dingy brown and black from artillery strikes. 'The distance between us and the Russians was so small that we could almost look our opponents in the eye,' said Else. He saw heaps of freshly turned earth in the Russian positions. He feared they were planning a fresh attack.

It began with a crashing artillery barrage. The Germans pressed themselves into the earth, 'each one of us alone with our thoughts'. At 3 p.m., on 30 October, the guns fell silent along the whole line. The Germans took up their weapons and waited. The Russians slowly emerged from their trenches and advanced. 'My heart almost sank to my boots,' said Else. 'Hein van Koll said calmly, "Oh, oh – they're coming and they're definitely not gentlemen. They're on their way to kill us!"All along the line, the Russians rose from their positions, and cried confidently – "Hurrah!"'

The paratroops fired burst after burst of sub-machine-gun and heavy-machine-gun fire into them. They came on steadily to within 40 yards of the German position when shells crashed into them. Nobody knew which side was firing the rounds, but the attackers took cover. Their momentum gone, they continued to creep and crawl forward. A Russian stopped just four yards in front of Else's trench. As the attack petered out, van Koll lit a cigar, and Else wondered who he had stolen it from.

CHAPTER 6

Noyabr'

November 1941

The Germans had suffered 686,000 casualties by 1 November. That was one in five of the original Barbarossa force and of all the replacements and reserves sent to Russia since June. Of these, almost 200,000 were dead, seven times as many as had been killed in the whole campaign in France and the Low Countries in 1940. Panzer divisions had lost two-thirds of their strength, sapping their once-brilliant morale. Each evening, they saw cloud building over the distant steppe and forests, and they shuddered, for they knew that 'these dark masses carried in the stratosphere the rain, the ice and snow of the coming winter'.

Outside Leningrad, Willy Tiedemann and his comrades had reached a grisly milestone. They had crossed the Polish border together at 4.45 a.m. on 1 September 1939. Their target, the town of Chojnice, had fallen to them by 8 a.m. and it was restored to its German name, Konitz. They had paraded with the Red Army at Brest-Litovsk as Poland was dismembered between them. In May 1940, they had crossed the Dutch border at Maastricht, and moved on through Belgium into France. They had fought the retreating British outside Dunkirk. Tiedemann had led a reinforced platoon on patrol one night in the Loire Atlantique. They heard horses, and opened fire. Without resistance, a hundred men with eighty horses and an anti-tank gun surrendered. They told Tiedemann more French troops were coming to attack his battalion. 'We sneaked in the direction where we heard some noise, just like Red Indians. We started firing, so much that the French would believe we were many more than we really were. It worked! We captured one colonel, nine officers, 500 men and 400 horses!' He achieved that with fifty-odd men and no casualties. Russia was not like that. 'More than half of my company are dead by now,' he recorded, before adding: 'This is hardly fun any more!'

The newly arrived paratroops on the Neva echoed him. Dead horses lay along the road to Shlisselburg where they had collapsed or been hit by shells. 'We met many Russian women looking for meat,' said Oberjäger Gottfried Emrich. 'They butchered every dead horse right there on the spot. Only the skeletons were left lying on the road.' His men were setting up a new position near Vyborgskaya. An unseen Russian threw a hand grenade among them as they were eating after a long march. 'We rushed apart, one man staggered and fell,' Emrich said. 'A fragment had slashed his carotid artery.'

They dug all night to prepare a bunker. Emrich and a young *Jäger*, Edmund Gorski, began hauling the logs to the new bunker. They had to cross a clearing that was churned up by shelling. As they did so, 'like a monster thundering and growling from far away', they heard the rush of incoming shells. Clods of earth and shrapnel flew through the clearing. They lay helpless in the snow. They had left their weapons in the bunker they were building. They could hear the Russians yelling 'Hurrah!' through the forest. 'They were coming, they were attacking!' Individual rifle shots severed the air. The cries of the Russians were getting closer, through they were still hidden by the forest. Emrich and Gorski ran back across the clearing with impacts around them. A company of engineers was brought forward for a counter-attack. Wounded men came past them, but the firing gradually stopped. The attack had failed.

Young Gorski jumped out of the dugout to collect more timbers, ignoring Emrich's pleas. He got as far as the clearing when the Russian guns opened again. Dark clouds of gunsmoke drifted above the snow, blackening the Germans' faces. They heard gurgling cries for help. Two men jumped out of the bunker and dragged Gorski back. He had been gone only a minute or two.

> With a pleading look in his eyes, Gorski whispered weakly, asking us to kill him. His body was completely shredded by shrapnel, a bull's eye had wounded him horribly. Two men were ordered to take him to the casualty station. They laid him on tent canvas and carried him away, his legs dangling loosely in his trousers. With one last look, I bade farewell to my last comrade from Meissen, Edmund Gorski, on November 3rd . . . He died on the way there. I did not even get to see his grave.[1]

The NKVD and the front command sought to deflect Stalin's rage at the failure to break out of the Nevsky bridgehead. They found their scape-goat on 2 November. He was Major Stepan Sedih, a native of Moscow, with a young daughter, nine-year-old Natalia. He had crossed the Neva with 500 men at the end of September. They were already decimated when he was wounded on 6 October. He was taken back across the river to a field hospital. His wounds were partially healed when he volun-teered to return, crossing the freezing waters under fire on the night of 22 October. Only 82 of his men were still alive. An NKVD squad came after him a week later.

Sedih was convenient prey. He was almost the only officer to have survived since the original landing on the east bank: he was still there, and with the exception of his days in hospital, he had always been there. In the blasted landscape, with its craters and explosions, the men invis-ible in their trenches and dugouts, Sedih was winkled out of his com-mand bunker and taken back to the relative safety along the riverbank.

Here, crouching by the sandy shore, an NKVD officer accused him of cowardice. The squad gathered the remnants of his men, gaunt, haggard, starving. Then they shot him in front of them.*

The 1st Shock Communist Regiment was fed into the bridgehead. It was made up of poorly trained Leningrad volunteers. Mikhail Pavlov was with a supply platoon that remained on the west bank of the river. He watched the first two battalions cross. Dawn was breaking when the third battalion followed. It was caught by German gunners and dive-bombers and annihilated. Over the next three days, Pavlov watched the rest of his regiment being destroyed by artillery, bombing and German counter-attacks. The commanding officer, Colonel Vasily Fyodorov, was killed. Pavlov's platoon was all that remained. He was now loaded into a boat in a small tributary of the Neva with seven other men. They each had a double issue of grenades and ammunition, and an ammunition box, as well as their rifles and bayonets. At twilight rockets streamed over their heads into the German positions. They paddled into the Neva as night fell.

'We had got very close to the left bank when a heavy shell exploded in the water and capsized the boat,' he recollected.

The water was icy and the current was strong, and it was pulling me out into the middle of the river. I was paddling my legs desperately. I found out later why I survived. A stream entering the river had caused a sandbank and I managed to touch the bottom with my boots. I dragged myself ashore with all my remaining strength. I had been swept below the rendezvous point. An officer shouted at me: 'Dig in!' For several days, I was recovering from my swim, lying in communications trenches and three-man foxholes.

---

* Major Sedih was rehabilitated on 14 September 2010. It is thought that his daughter Natalia emigrated from Russia before her father's innocence was so belatedly recognized by the authorities.

His unit was ordered to advance towards the power plant, the strongest German position.

> It was attack and counter-attack, a melee, close quarters, with hand grenades. We were resisting a Hitlerite attack, when the heavy machine gun that was supporting us stopped firing. I raised my head for a split second and saw that the machine crew were dead but the ammunition belt was still in the gun. They were shouting all around me: 'The machine gun! The machine gun! It's silent!' I was familiar with the weapon. I crawled to it, pushed the gunner's body away and finished the belt, firing short bursts of covering fire. The barrel became red hot, the water jacket that cooled it had shrapnel holes in it.
>
> I shouted: 'Someone help me change the belt!' An officer I didn't know crawled up to me and asked me: 'Who are you? Where's the gun crew?' I said: 'I'm from the 177th and the crew is here, all dead, and the machine gun has no water.' 'Right,' he ordered me. 'You will guard the command post of our 330th Regiment. Your division is finished. All of you who are left alive and can hold a weapon are now under our command.'

That is how Pavlov found himself in the 330th. For several days he guarded the command post with two other Red Army men. Then he joined a machine-gun crew under a sergeant positioned near the command post. On 17 November, he recorded that Vladimir Spiridonovich Putin, father of the future Russian leader Vladimir Vladimirovich Putin, was seriously wounded by shrapnel in the left ankle and foot.* Three days later, Pavlov had his eighteenth birthday: 'our sergeant on the machine gun was killed and I was wounded by a shell splinter in

---

* He was on a reconnaissance mission when he was hit by grenade fragments. After several months in hospital, he was declared unfit for further service. He worked in a tank repair shop for the rest of the war.

my right shoulder blade.' He was bandaged by a nurse, Yelena Leon-tievna Tsvetkova, and evacuated. 'I'm a hundred per cent certain that she bandaged Putin senior, too, and hundreds of others in the Nevsky bridgehead – and me.'

She was the 330th's regimental medic. She had crossed into the bridge-head with the regiment on 22 October. 'A lot of our people died during the crossing, and we landed straight into non-stop and terrifyingly bitter fighting,' Tsvetkova said. She was to spend 161 days there until she was evacuated with shell shock. She worked from a dugout cut into the bank. 'Our equipment was absolutely basic: a portable oven, dry bandages, and spirits,' she recollected. 'There were hundreds of wounded coming in every day . . . Sometimes I went out to the trenches, with just a bag of bandages hanging from the belt of my greatcoat, and carried the wounded back to the dugout on my back.'

She had a sledge for the badly wounded. If they had fallen in places the sledge could not go, she used a home-made hammock with wooden handles to get to them. 'Sometimes we fell when we were lowering the wounded down the riverbank because it was so slippery and icy.' Another nurse, Olga Budnikova, came across the ice after the ice froze and helped get the wounded back across the river. The medical post on the right bank was staffed by women, an experienced doctor, Emma Samuilovna Sheimberg, and three young medical students. From there, urgent cases were sent to a medical-sanitary battalion across eight miles of snowy tracks.

The casualties were so high that the regiment was constantly rein-forced from the right bank. 'But what sort of reinforcement! Skeletons! We were half starved ourselves, but we gave them our rations.' There were too many wounded for her to cope with them all – 'the soldiers and officers had to help each other with first aid' – or to remember their faces, 'black from powder and soot'.

*

Leningrad was battered for eight and a half hours on 4 November. Four artillery barrages were interspersed with air attacks. Naval magnetic mines, monsters with a diameter of nine feet, floated down on parachutes. The bombers were out over Lake Ladoga as well. They spotted a large transport carrying 350 evacuees that had almost reached Novaya Ladoga. A direct hit blew many of its passengers into the water, where the aircraft machined-gunned them in the water. More than two hundred were killed.

Priority in rations was given to scientists and creatives – musicians, writers, dancers, actors and artists – next day. They were put on the same basis as workers and managers in defence plants. Newspapermen qualified: in the staff canteen of *Leningradskasya Pravda*, no cereal coupons were taken for bread, and only half a coupon for a meat dish. It had been through a twisted form of respect that the Bolsheviks had persecuted intellectuals with such particular venom. The old Russian reverence for the *intelligentsiya* – the Russians had coined the word in tsarist times – was now restored. Their existence was prioritized: they were privileged, as far as was possible, to live.

The city was shelled from 11 a.m. to 6.50 p.m. on 6 November, and again from 9 p.m. That night, German aircraft attacked the Finland Station with magnetic mines. It was crowded with women and children and the elderly, who were waiting for trains to take them to Ladoga on their way to the mainland and safety. Some were already in trains in the marshalling yards. Two trains were filled with badly wounded soldiers. They were hit by a cluster of the heavy bombs, which hurled their bodies across the tracks or left them in the tangled wreckage of the carriages. Parachute flares lit up the carnage and the ghostly white faces of children, clinging to their mothers.

That night, a writer on *Leningradskaya Pravda*, Sergei Yezersky, wrote a sketch of the city: 'Midnight. The city is quiet and empty. The great streets and squares are dead. No lights. Only darkness. A cold wind whips the snow into little whirlwinds. The sound of artillery. Low clouds reflect the shelling. Nearby an explosion. The Germans are shelling . . . At the intersection and the bridges – patrols. They challenge sternly: "Halt! Who goes there?"[2]

November the 7th was the 24th anniversary of the storming of the Winter Palace, the Bolshevik *coup d'état* in Petrograd in 1917 which Party propaganda had elevated into revolution. In Moscow, Stalin addressed the troops at the traditional Red Square parade in front of the Kremlin. He spoke of their 'great ancestors', Alexander Nevsky who had beaten the Teutonic knights in 1242, Dmitri Donskoi, the victor over the Tartars in 1380, Suvorov and Kutuzov who had done for Napoleon in 1812. The nearness of the panzers heightened the impact of linking the communist regime with the old patriotism of Holy Russia. The tanks that rattled over the cobbles of Red Square were laden with combat ammunition. They moved directly on to the front. The snowstorm and the icy wind that blew off the grit and sand laid for the parade caused the first cases of severe frostbite among the approaching Germans. The winter they so dreaded was arriving.

In Leningrad, a new heroic musical comedy, *The Wide Sea*, was performed at the Philharmonia Hall. The libretto was by the dramatist Vsevolod Vishnevsky, who made a speech on radio the same day, with music by the composer Viktor Vitlin. *Leningradskaya Pravda*'s Nikolai Tikhonov gave it a stirring review:

The audience leaves in good spirits, cheerful, assured. In these severe days of siege, the performers showed true courage and firmness. Weak with hunger, in elegant theatre costumes, they played in a deep-frozen hall, where the temperature reached 8 degrees below zero. During the bombardment, a shell burst near the theatre and somebody in the audience was discomposed, and stood up. A. Orlov made a funny pirouette and said with a smile: 'Comrades, don't worry. The skylights are not falling in yet.' Burst of laughter, applause, and the performance continued . . .

The pianist Alexander Kamensky, brilliant with Schubert, Scriabin and Mussorgsky, outstanding with Liszt, gave a concert at the Pushkin. Music was played constantly on the wireless, picked up by the loudspeakers on the streets. 'For the whole day, the loudspeakers brought Leningraders their favourite songs and arias against the noise of cannonades and artillery,' Olga Berggolts noted. Vsevolod Vishnevsky's talk made a special impression. He had been a young sailor on the cruiser *Aurora* when it had opened fire on the Winter Palace in 1917. The shells had missed their huge target, and the palace defenders were no more than a motley handful of cadets and officers the worse for drink. No matter. A heroic myth surrounded the *Aurora*, which was still moored in the Neva, and its aura embraced Vishnevsky. His voice still had the devil-may-care dash of the fo'c'sle, and in that terrible autumn, Olga Berggolts thought that the city drew comfort from its fighting traditions, and from the old slogan of the civil war: 'We shall die rather than surrender our beloved Leningrad!'*

'The evening dusk has fallen over the city on the frozen Neva, which is ready for anything,' Vishnevsky said. 'The front-line city is alive and the heartbeats of the revolution are as strong in it as ever . . . The loudspeakers are broadcasting Leo Tolstoy's story, "Sevastopol, Winter 1854". The crowd listens spellbound. They recognize themselves. Tolstoy's Fourth Bastion is Leningrad today. . . A blacked-out tram goes out to the front line, to the Fourth Bastion . . . This great city is faithful to the October Revolution, it knows its destiny and itself.'[3]

---

* In fact, the city was still called Petrograd during the civil war. It was not renamed for Lenin until 26 January 1924, five days after his death.

For all that, the day was grey and grim, with no parades and few red flags. Worse was to come.

On 8 November, in a violent snowstorm, the Germans broke into the railway town of Tikhvin, 125 miles east of Leningrad. The only railway line still feeding Leningrad via Ladoga ran through the town. The Germans had started their drive eastwards from the 'bottleneck' on the Neva three weeks before. They did so 'on a shoestring' with a single motorized corps, XXXIX Corps, spearheaded by the 12th Panzer Division. The commander was General Rudolf Schmidt, a fine tactician. They slogged into the Russian Fourth Army, under Lieutenant-General V. F. Yakovlev, in the dreary swamps and forests of the Volkhov river. The panzers' progress along the narrow forest trails was halted by the *rasputitsa*, the deep mud that came with the autumn rains. It turned to sleet and snow, and then the ground froze.

The Germans were mobile once more. As they advanced, their southern flank became more and more exposed. There were vast open marshes here, with a few scattered strongpoints held by companies grossly depleted by combat, sickness and cold, with huge gaps for the Russians to pour through. The Azul (Blue) Division, fascist volunteers from Franco's Spain fighting in German uniform, were tasked to hold the southern line. They crossed the Volkhov near Sito. The ice on the river was thickening where the river slowed and widened. Planks were laid to make a pathway that supported an infantryman's weight. Someone tried to bring a horse across, but the skittish bay broke through and could not be hauled out. It froze there, half in and half out, a grotesque ice sculpture, its head a 'tragic mask of impotence and terror'.[4]

The temperatures dropped to minus 30 degrees Celsius (minus 20 Fahrenheit) as the Russians fell back. The Stavka, the Soviet High Command, shocked at the impending catastrophe, ordered two divisions to be airlifted from within Leningrad to defend the approaches to Tikhvin. Yakovlev threw them into battle piecemeal off the aircraft as they arrived. Schmidt's men cut them up, picking up enough momentum to catch the Russians unaware in their wooden bunkers among the frozen mires and copses. By 6 November, the Fourth Army had been sliced in three. Revolution Day brought them no respite. One division, the 44th, was disintegrating, its officers fleeing in chaos. That night, the Army's military council met at Berezovik, a silent wooden village a little north of Tikhvin. It concluded that the town would fall. A few senior officers made their way back in the early hours to try to get supplies and equipment out. The oil depots were already burning, and explosions echoed through the night as sappers blew up the arms dumps.

The Germans burst out of the whirling snowflakes of a blizzard next morning. They swept across the city, the fine wooden buildings in the historic centre burning fiercely, past the long white walls and grey-green onion domes of Ivan the Terrible's Monastery of the Dormition, honoured in Nikolai Rimsky-Korsakov's fugue 'In the Monastery'. They broke into the fine wooden house where the composer was born, using it as a makeshift dressing station and field kitchen, burning its panelling and banisters to keep warm. An assault group took the railway station and fanned out into the freight yards. At 5.25 p.m., Field Marshal von Leeb proclaimed triumphantly that 12th Panzer had Tikhvin *'fest in der Hand'* ('safely in its grasp'). The last railway link from Moscow to Ladoga was severed.

It was beyond the Germans to continue their planned advance northwards to link up with the Finns on the river Svir. Had they done so, Leningrad would have been cut off by water as well as land. They were too exhausted to go on. The seven divisions involved had lost 10,032 men in a month. Resupply broke down along the icy trails to Tikhvin, and they were short of food, fuel and ammunition. The woods were full of Russians cut off from their units, ambushing supply columns and laying mines along the trails. Flesh exposed for more than a few seconds became frostbitten. The Germans had entered Russia with lacquered silver shoulder straps. Now they bound their boots with rags, stripped the Russian dead of their warm quilt jackets, fur hats and felt boots, wound Russian women's scarves beneath their helmets, and slit white sheets for camouflage. The oil in their trucks became first a paste and then a glue which seized up the engines. It took two hours to start the engines of their few remaining tanks, and another hour to half thaw the gearbox. Infantry weapons froze. Only grenades and flamethrowers were reliable.

Even so, the loss of the Tikhvin rail junction was a virtual death sentence for Leningrad. Stalin gave command of the Fourth Army to Kiril Meretskov, in the knowledge that his recent treatment at Beria's hands, his torture and confession, and the narrowness of his escape from the fate that had overwhelmed his co-accused, had rendered him pliant. The Fourth's artillery commander, General Georgi Degtyarev, feared for his life when Meretskov summoned him to explain why his gunners had failed to save Tikhvin. Degtyarev, like Meretskov himself, was politically vulnerable: he had also been arrested, in 1938 as an 'enemy of the people', before being restored to the army.

He knew that Meretskov had taken part in the witch-hunt let loose a few weeks before, on another battered army, the Thirty-Fourth, by the much-loathed Lev Mekhlis, the 'secret police general' close to Beria. General Goncharov, Degtyarev's opposite number, was shot for cowardice in front of his staff; Meretskov did nothing to protect him. A Colonel Saveliev witnessed the scene in a village behind the front as Mekhlis summoned the staff officers. 'He strode rapidly along the line,' he recalled.

He stopped in front of the artillery commander, and shouted, 'Where are your guns?' Goncharov gestured vaguely in the direction where our units were surrounded by the Germans. 'I'm asking you, where are they?' shouted Mekhlis and then, after a brief pause, he began the standard phrase, 'In accordance with Order 270 . . .' He ordered an elderly major on the right of the line to carry out the sentence. Unable to overcome his emotion, and greatly daring, the major refused. A firing squad had to be summoned.[*5]

Degtyarev told Meretskov: 'I am prepared to take the responsibility for the failures which we suffered at Tikhvin.' He expected to be shot. Instead, he was astonished when Meretskov told him merely that the main thing was 'not to repeat our mistakes'.[6]

All day on 9 November, Berlin repeated a cry of triumph: '*Achtung! Achtung!* Tikhvin has fallen!' No word appeared in the Leningrad papers, but the news flew from mouth to mouth in the city. In Munich, Hitler said: 'Leningrad's hands are in the air. It falls sooner or later. No one can free it. No one can break the ring. Leningrad is doomed to die of famine.' The Germans got close enough to Gostinopolye, where Ladoga supplies were handled, to shell its warehouses. They caught fire. The transhipment chief was killed. A soldier stopped the workers fleeing, and forced them to resume loading supplies at gunpoint.[7]

A new road had to be cut through wilderness to get supplies to Ladoga. The remnant of an ancient forest trade track wound its way from Zaborye, the nearest railhead still Russian-held, for more than 120 miles to the lake at Novaya Ladoga. It skirted tamarack swamps, and peat and cranberry bogs, running along stream banks and through thick forests. A few isolated wooden hamlets lay along it, obscure places – Syasstroi,

---

* Those Soviet commanders who had fallen into German hands might have thought themselves at least safe from their own. They were not. General Pondelin was beyond the grasp of Order 270, in German hands, but his father and second wife were arrested and exiled. He fled to Paris at the end of the war, but was returned to the Soviet Union. He was held in prison for five years, and shot in 1950.

Karpino, Novinka, Veliki Dvor – that appeared on few maps. The aim was for the road to carry two thousand tons of supplies a day, and to be open in fifteen days. To achieve this in a lost and forlorn landscape in the lifeless grip of winter seemed impossible.

Thousands from peasant families and collective farms, men, women and children, were given picks and shovels, and handsaws to cut down trees. Soldiers joined them, beginning at Novaya Ladoga. A few army trucks and tractors, and a handful of tanks, helped to haul the thousands of trees that were felled and laid across the swampy stretches as a corduroy road. Most of this exhausting work fell on the famished civilians. The work continued twenty-four hours a day. They slept fitfully in makeshift shelters made from tarpaulins and branches. Blizzards lashed in from the lake, but in their absence came the calm and soul-piercing cold of northern Russia, sharp as crystal. The scene, too, was utterly Russian. Tens of thousands of them had laboured like this to raise St Petersburg above its swamps under Peter the Great. Countless thousands more had toiled – were still toiling – to build canals and nickel mines and lumber camps for Stalin. The dead were buried alongside the track. The living were crawling towards Zaborye.

In Leningrad, Dmitri Pavlov took stock of the provisions left to him. In the city, there was flour for seven days, cereals for eight, fats for fourteen, sugar for twenty-two. Meat stocks were down to less than a ton. On the far side of Ladoga were seventeen days of flour, ten days of cereals, three days of fats and nine days of meat. It was already difficult for the supply boats to batter their way through the ice on the lake. Pavlov took the desperate step of an immediate cut in military rations. Troops had been on 800 grams of bread a day, topped up with hot soup and stew. Rations for front-line troops were cut to 600 grams of bread and 125 grams of meat. Units in the rear had 400 grams of bread and 50 of meat. For a few days, Zhdanov and Pavlov held civilian rations as they were. They knew that any further cut would lead to death for many. They gambled that the ice on the lake would soon be thick enough for trucks.

That evening, the heralded concert was held in the Philharmonia. It was a spectacular, with the Radiokom choirs and orchestra, the wind orchestra of the Leningrad Military District, the Capella and vocal soloists. Eliasberg conducted: Khachaturian's 'Song of Stalin', Beethoven, the last movement of Glinka's *Ivan Susanin.* Vera Inber feared it was a last hurrah. 'Listened to Beethoven's Ninth at the Philharmonia, but it looks as though we won't have any more concerts. It's becoming too complicated and dangerous. The Philharmonia itself is dark and moody. Polar cold. Alarms very often and intense.'[8]

The Radiokom choir sang Shostakovich's 'Song of the Guards Division' next day. In Kuibyshev, the composer himself was writing notes on the first three movements of the Seventh. The exposition of the first movement, he said, 'tells of the happy, peaceful life of people sure of themselves and their future':

> This is the simple, peaceful life lived before the war by thousands of Leningrad militiamen, by the whole city, by our country. In the development, war bursts into the peaceful life of these people. I am not aiming for the naturalistic depiction of war, the clatter of arms, the explosion of shells, and so on. I am trying to convey the image of war emotionally . . . The reprise is a funeral march, or rather, a requiem for the victims of war. Simple people honour the memory of their heroes.

He had needed words for this episode, he said, and had even set out to write them himself, because he couldn't find any that were suitable. In the end, he was glad to have no words, because they would have complicated the score too much. After the requiem, there was an 'even more tragic episode'. He did not know how to characterize it. 'Maybe what is here are a mother's tears or even that feeling when grief is so great that there are no tears left.' These two lyrical fragments, he wrote, 'lead to the conclusion of the first movement, to the apotheosis of life, of the sun. At the very end, distant thunder appears again reminding us that the war continues . . .'

He wrote only a brief sketch of the second and third movements. He intended them to 'serve as a lyrical respite': 'The second movement of the symphony is a very lyrical scherzo. There is a little humour in it, but for me it is somehow connected with the scherzo of the quintet. The third movement is a passionate adagio, the dramatic centre of the work.' He was making little progress in writing the fourth.

In Leningrad, a schoolgirl in the 9th Class wrote on 13 November – the day Pavlov cut rations again – that she could not live on a dependant's ration. 'Perhaps people will start to eat cats, dogs and even their own children. I am afraid to think about the future.' She was right. Cats and dogs were already being caught and eaten. A mother was driven two nights later to suffocate her six-week-old daughter so she could feed her other three children.[9] The new ration gave workers 300 grams of bread a day. It was half that, 150 grams, for everyone else. The city's daily consumption of flour was reduced to 622 tons. Even that could not be maintained. The ice that was now forming on Ladoga made the lake unnavigable, but it was not thick enough to take trucks. The city was cut off by land and water.

An airlift began on 16 November. Cargo aircraft were loaded at the Novaya Ladoga airfield. They carried the most concentrated food possible: pressed meats, smoked fish, canned food, powdered egg, condensed milk, lard and butter. The flight was only sixty-odd miles, so aircraft could make five trips a day. The Germans soon realized what was afoot. The airfield was heavily bombed. The transports had to fly from more distant airfields and they could manage only two trips. They flew in groups of six or nine, with fighter escorts, but the Messerschmitts often got them. The German fighter unit operating over the lake, JG 54 'Grünherz', was a crack outfit led by an ace, Major Hannes Trautloft. It had destroyed 1,123 Russian aircraft since the start of the war.

Food thieves thrived. Every factory, enterprise and institution had its canteen. The first wartime arrest for stealing canteen supplies had come on the third day of the war. A cook was found to have nearly half a ton of food worth 300,000 rubles, in his rooms. The scale increased in tune with the hunger. A canteen manager in the Krasnogvardeiskii district had looted two tons of bread, 1,230 kilos of meat and 150 kilos of sugar when his racket was uncovered.[10] The pre-war penalty for food theft by officials was two to three years in prison, increased to eight years at the start of the siege. It now became death. To back that up, on 16 November General Khozin, the Leningrad Front commander, made the NKVD 23rd Division responsible for food stores. Racketeering was classified as 'banditry'. Those convicted were to be shot immediately.

Next day, the emergency services reported 20 calls for ambulances for patients incapable of reaching a clinic. A few days later, 131 calls were made, and the figure continued to climb. Almost all were too emaciated to walk. The first patient died of starvation in the Perovskaya hospital in mid-month, with a further nineteen dying by the end of the month. Men were the first to die, doctors reported, without any marked pathological change, apart from bradycardia, a slowness of the heartbeat. There were cases of workers dying just after clocking in at work. Doctors in the Frunze district noted a striking feature, the 'number of "acute" deaths, or, more correctly, deaths that seem inexplicable at first sight'. Patients came in for treatment under their own steam, and seemed reasonably well, only to be found dead in bed a few hours or days later.[11]

The ice on the lake was now thick enough to take horse-drawn sledges. The horses were weak, and many were not shod for winter. About a thousand were assembled. The sledges were loaded with flour and concentrated food, 200 to 300 pounds to the sledge. They crossed the ice, 25 yards or so apart, in a column five miles long, but the few tons they carried made little impact.

The bread ration was cut again on 20 November, for all but front-line troops, ships' crews and pilots. Workers in priority plants and engineers were reduced to 250 grams. Others – white-collar workers, dependants, children, the old – had 125 grams. This was two slices of adulterated bread. Life was unsustainable at this level. Healthy seven-to-eleven-year-old boys need 1,970 calories a day, girls 1,740, with teenagers needing 2,220 and 1,845. Healthy adult men need 2,750 and women 2,200. One hundred grams of good brown bread supply about 210 calories – with 57 grams of carbohydrate, 11 grams of protein, 2.3 grams of fat and 1.5 grams of fibre – and this bread was very far from good. Distribution was starting to break down. People began queuing from 4 a.m. or 5 a.m. Most people were reduced to an input of 500 to 600 calories a day.

An editorial in *Leningradskaya Pravda* admitted as much. 'Bolsheviks have never kept anything from the people. They always tell the truth, harsh as it may be,' it began. That, of course, was nonsense. Everyone knew that Bolsheviks very rarely told the truth – 'in *Pravda* there is no *Izvestiya*, and in *Izvestiya* there is no *Pravda*,' the old joke ran about the two great Bolshevik newspapers ('in the Truth there is no News, and in the News there is no Truth') – and that is why the next sentence was so chilling: 'So long as the blockade continues it is not possible to expect any improvement in the food situation.'

The new ration was a death sentence, and both Zhdanov and Pavlov knew it. Daily flour consumption was cut to 510 tons. That was equivalent to 30 freight wagons a day, to feed 2.5 million people. 'There is no electricity, no water, no food,' Zhdanov told Young Communist leaders. 'The fall of Tikhvin has put us into a second ring of encirclement. The task of tasks is to organize the life of the workers – to give them inspiration, courage, firmness in the face of all difficulties. This is your task.'

The dark brown ration bread had little nourishment. Its rye flour was cut with 25 per cent cellulose, as well as cottonseed-oil cake, cornflour and chaff. People were mobilized to collect edible pine and fir bark. City districts were each ordered to supply two and a half tons of sawdust a day. That, too, was considered 'edible'. Warehouses and grain elevators were swept, and flour sacks were turned inside out and beaten, and the dust and sweepings were added to the mix. Tanneries were swept and the leather dust was added to sawdust to make a paste that was used in 'patties'. Two thousand tons of sheep guts were found in the docks. They were processed into a jelly that was flavoured with aromatic herbs to disguise its vile smell. This jelly was mixed with flax seed and machine oil and given as part of the 'meat' ration. Workers in arms plants were issued with 'coffee' made from acorns, dried kelp, and fermented soy bean milk.

Most of the city's cats and dogs had been roasted or put in stews. Rats were caught, skinned and eaten. The bones of butchered animals were stewed for hours to extract the marrow. This process had already been done commercially to make carpenter's glue. Books were stripped of their covers, and the glue in the bindings was melted and used in soup. Wallpaper was stripped from walls, and the dried paste was eaten. Hair oil was used as a substitute for fat. Slabs of cattle cake were prizes beyond compare. Artists' studios were treasure troves, yielding casein, used as a form of tempera paint, and linseed oil, used to mix paints and prime canvases. Linseed, rich in fatty acids, was found in workshops, too, used to harden putty, as a lubricant, in oilcloth, and as a polish. Glycerine, from soaps, tooth powder, cough medicine and cold cream, also had some calories. Even dextrine, used for sand casting in foundries and as a textile finishing, had its price.

The city's artistic heart and its mind were still alive. Valerian Bogdanov-Berezovsky went to a recital in the Union of Composers on 20 November. Fifteen members sat in the great hall, lit by candles, with overcoats and hats to ward off the cold. Boris Asafyev, composer of the ballet *The Flames of Paris*, played attractively and with temperament, 'childishly happy at the general reaction'. A chess tournament at Grand Master level began in the People's House on Italyanskaya Street. The first edition of a news-sheet, *Theatre Leningrad*, appeared with a What's On section. Bogdanov-Berezovsky wrote a short piece for it, 'Leningrad Composers and the War', describing a new cycle of songs, *On the Defence of Leningrad*. He mentioned Shostakovich's Seventh.

A new collective started with *Eugene Onegin* at the Kirov. Kondratiev was there:

> The performance started late. It was announced that it would be done without décor but with costumes and props. And so it was. The temperature was quite low, six to eight degrees. The audience didn't disrobe. The choir and the ballet put on their best front. I have some questions of the orchestra, though. The first soloist was I. Nechayev – he played Lensky [in *Eugene Onegin*] – and he sang well and presented himself not badly.

It was the first time twelve-year-old Sasha Morozov had been to the opera: 'I liked it very much, though it was played without the theatre sets.' The audience contributed 14,000 rubles to the war effort.[12]

A jazz ensemble played twice daily at the Circus. A tribute to the young composer Minasai Leviyev by the Radiokom orchestra was played on radio. He was one of Shostakovich's most promising students at the

Conservatoire. He had joined the militia and was severely wounded. He lay now in a military hospital, so badly concussed it was feared he had become deaf.

A large concert was held at the Philharmonia on 22 November, with song and dance ensembles, operetta, instrumentalists, ballet dancers and actors. Shelest danced with Yuri Gofman. He had let his moustache grow: 'He said it was his penance not to shave until the end of the war. So that's how he danced, in his outfit and moustache.' He was weakening, though, and soon was unable to move his legs.

Shelest found herself affected by the constant shelling. She was in the big rehearsal room of the ballet school when the alarm sounded: 'Feeling of suspension, the windows shaking, fear.' She went to the shelter. Sofiya Vasilievna Shostakovich, the composer's mother, was there, with his sister Mariya Dmitrievna and her son. Shelest and her mother were now living in the Engineering Castle, where her father had worked in the military hospital as a senior medical officer before going to the Front HQ. This was the mighty castle built by Tsar Paul through fear of assassination. After he was indeed murdered, the engineering faculty of the university had moved in. 'We had a tiny room in the basement we shared with another family,' she recalled. 'But we lived comparatively well in the Castle. We had electricity and water and sewerage because it was also used as a military hospital. Paul tried to save himself in the Castle, but death still came to him, but now the walls protected us.'[13] Her father had already been through three wars, she said, the First War, the Civil War and the Winter War, and she was sure that Leningrad would survive his fourth, the Patriotic War.

She had gone to visit her fellow ballerina Agrippina Vaganova. They were walking together on Rossi Street (named for the architect). As they neared the Duma, shelling started. Weirdly, she found herself doing ballet steps. 'I had a very strange reaction. When a shell exploded, I moved my leg *battement*. I was in Papa's size 44 *valenki* [felt boots]. Vaganova was patient for a bit, then she said: "Stop it! Why are you doing *batte-ment*?" But every explosion my feet went on going up. I couldn't control it and I went on the rest of the way with moans and *battement*.'[14]

Likhachev found that the director of the Pushkin Institute, where he worked, had become 'very nervy' from hunger and shelling. He shouted at his staff and dismissed some of them. It was terrible to be left without work or ration cards, but no one could calm him down. A lot of people were in the Institute day and night. They slept in their clothes on Push-kin's and Aksakov's settees, where Gogol had sat, on Turgenev's settee, and on the bed on which Alexander Blok had died.

The sacks of rusks he had bought were keeping Likhachev's family alive. Rimma Neratova's family also had a food cache 'of inestimable value': 'Since time immemorial, Aunt Marta's light yellow cloth suitcase had been stored on a large black shelf in our front hall.' Ancient rusks were stored in it. In the early 1920s, Petrograders had stored up reserves of rusks in case of a new famine. The rusks were older than the young medical student herself, but she survived on them.[15]

A magnetic mine dropped in an air raid destroyed the greenhouses in the Botanical Gardens. Frost killed many of the plants during the night. In the morning, staff and their families moved the survivors to their apartments and to cellars. The botanist Nikolai Kornikov and his wife saved the valuable collection of 2,500 cactuses by taking them to their apartment block.

The post still operated, in terms at least of collecting letters, and NKVD agents reading correspondence reported an alarming increase in 'decadent outlooks'. Housewives were particularly prone to it in their letters to the mainland: 'We shall be glad if the bombs kill us . . . I am sick of suffering from hunger. Life has become worse than hard labour . . . Death from bombs or shells is no longer so terrible. The hunger we have is far worse.'[16]

*

The slaughter continued, implacable, on the Neva. A crisis developed for the German paratroops. Their main battle line circled the bridgehead. A deep salient shaped like a sack had developed at the seam between their 1st and 2nd Companies. The Russians had large numbers of men in this bulge and fortified it well. Oberleutnant Knoche, commanding the 2nd Company, kept it under constant fire from a 50mm mortar. The Russians suffered heavy casualties, but they dug a deep system of trenches that stretched out beyond the salient like fingers. Here they were out of sight and well protected. Knoche feared that they would burst out at a suitable moment and break through his lightly manned line. They could then attack his company from the flank and overrun it.

He had to cut off the salient, but had no reserves. Every paratrooper had been sent into endangered sectors of the main battle line. The two companies were down to between fifty and sixty men apiece. Using men from the staff and intelligence corps, the Germans were able to put together two powerful and mobile assault parties. They were to attack simultaneously at night, from the right and left of the salient, cutting it off at its base. This pocket had to be cleared out before dawn, when the Russians would realize that the Germans had stripped their battle line to provide troops for the assault. The risk of friendly fire made night attacks extremely dangerous, but there was little choice.

The attack went in before midnight, catching the Russians by surprise. Wild shooting broke out. The surprise and fear created in the salient was so great that some Russians surrendered without resistance, Knoche found, but the majority killed one another in the chaos and confusion. 'Quite a few of the prisoners confirmed that,' he said. 'Also there was no other way to explain the heaps of bodies that we found in the pocket, especially in the trenches.'

By about 3 a.m. the pocket was almost cleared. Knoche moved forward to prepare a new defence line as quickly as possible. He expected a massive Russian counter-attack at dawn. Sporadic machine-gun fire strafed the terrain, and he moved by jumping from one foxhole to another. It was almost a rule of thumb to find dead Russians in each hole. 'I jumped into another hole, and something under me moved,' Knoche said. 'In the hole a wounded Russian was crouching on top of two dead bodies and I'd jumped right on top of him.'

He was wondering what to do with the wounded Russian, who was 'just begging and moaning', when he heard the clicking of an ammunition box and saw a line of marching Russians silhouetted against the sky. He thought that the Russians must have broken through. Then he heard a German voice. It was an Oberjäger, Berndt, who had been wounded and was lying on a blanket, being carried by two Russians. Berndt had offered to take ammunition forward with seven Russian prisoners. He was shot in the leg after they set off. The Russians could have attacked him and freed themselves. Instead, they put a field dressing on his leg, laid him on a blanket and slung it from a pole. Two of them carried him forward, and the others lugged the ammunition.

But the Russians were not finished. Knoche lost one of his lieutenants, Krüger, who rushed forward from the company command post. When Knoche asked him what he was doing, he said: 'Looking for my men.' A wounded man who was still in shock had told Krüger that all his men had been killed or wounded in the assault. 'Krüger's men would go through fire and water for him,' Knoche said, 'and he would do the same for them. So he rushed into the battle sector to see for himself.' Knoche ordered him back, but he was shot in the head not far from the command post.

Another lieutenant, Karl-Heinz Enke, was killed outside the captured bunker where Knoche had just briefed him and a Feldwebel on the location of the new battle line. They thought that the bunker contained only the dead. Suddenly, a Russian came out with a machine pistol and shot the lieutenant and sergeant dead on the spot. He wounded two others before a paratrooper killed him. Knoche looked closely at the body, realizing it was a commissar.

There was no counter-attack at dawn. Instead, the Russians pounded the right wing with heavy artillery for day after day.

The paratroopers learned on 21 November that they were to be relieved. The trench strength of companies in the 1st Battalion of the 3rd Fallschirmjäger Regiment had dropped to between thirty and fifty men. The men were bitter at the use of the phrase 'trench strength', as if they were common-or-garden infantry, not the elite of the German army, trained for the most decisive and daring operations. They were 'just lying around in dugouts and letting themselves be bombed to death', Knoche said, 'instead of transforming front-line situations by daring sorties . . . When we were relieved, the Russian soil near Leningrad was blanketed with some of our best paratroopers.'[17]

They held a regimental roll call on 23 November before being withdrawn to Germany. They had dwindled to 'just a really small bunch'. The words of the regimental commander, Oberst Heydrich, were 'full of grief' and tears poured down his face. 'You are no longer my soldiers,' he concluded. 'You are my boys.' Officers and riflemen were awarded their decorations. The five battalions of paratroops who had been rushed to the Neva barely six weeks before had suffered more than 2,700 casualties.

After they had made the long journey back to Wolfenbüttel in Bavaria, the survivors assembled to march into their garrison as a homecoming regiment. There were only forty-two men left in Friedrich Else's company. As they marched to their barracks, a Wolfenbüttel innkeeper who knew many of them well was standing by the roadside. He had seen them leave two months before. He was shocked that so few had come back. 'Hey, you guys,' he called out. 'What company is this?' A Jäger snapped at him: 'Just shut up. This is our battalion.'

William Tiedemann's Panzergrenadiers, now securing the flank between Volkhov and Tikhvin, had suffered an equal mauling. 'My battalion has huge losses! 71 dead, and these were badly treated by the Russians, they took all the uniforms and left them naked in the snow. New Russian air attacks, temperature is minus 31 C.' Such losses, for armies flung as wide as the Wehrmacht, were not sustainable.

The ice on Ladoga had to be at least 200 mm thick to bear the weight of a truck. It reached that on 22 November. The convoys were under the command of Major V. Poshunov of the 389th Transport Battalion. The first ten trucks set off from Osinovets for Lednevo on the east side of the lake. Two went missing as the drivers got lost in snow squalls and went too far north. The ice was thinner here, and they disappeared. The eight surviving trucks returned to Osinovets with 33 tons of supplies. This was nothing in itself – the city had been consuming 3,000 tons of food a day in normal times – but it showed what could be done.

The ice remained dangerous for the rest of the month. It could bear only light two-ton GAZ-AA trucks, an almost exact copy of the old Ford-AA trucks, and even then half the cargo was put on sleds that they towed behind them to spread the weight.

The few ZIS-5s were better, three-tonners with six-cylinder engines that could run on low octane fuel: the designer, Evgeni Ivanovich Vazhinskii, had been shot as a 'wrecker' on 6 March 1938, but his truck remained in production for thirty years. They kept at a distance from each other, and travelled at slow speeds, but were still lost to thin ice and German bombers. At the seventh kilometre marker outbound from Osinovets, they came within German artillery range. Work parties lived on the ice to lay wooden bridges over cracks opened up by storms and shellfire. Drivers stood on the running board and steered through the open door in places where the ice was thin or fractured. Locals thought it folly. The lake was prone to violent storms all winter, and powerful and dangerous currents split the ice and piled it in pressure ridges. There were places where it never froze.

The Three Musketeers played at the Muzkom on 24 November. Two jazz concerts were held at the Circus. Extracts from *La Traviata* were staged. The Radiokom orchestra played Tchaikovsky's Sixth Symphony at the Philharmonia: the little house in Klin where he had composed it almost fifty years before was in German hands now. The Push-kin Society held a concert lecture in the hospital of the 13th Line on Vasilievsky Island. News of the trucks crossing the ice failed to lift spirits, though. The composer L. Partov wrote a single entry in his diary to cover the past week: 'Everything is the same. Starvation, cold, weakness, constant fainting. Still no change. Try to get myself busy, to write something . . .'

No change, either, in the bloodshed in the bridgehead. Fourteen tanks crossed the Neva to support fresh attacks. The Germans destroyed eight of them and disabled the remaining six. They were dug in, hull down, as stationary firing points. Ice now floated on the river in chunks heavy enough to jeopardize any new pontoon bridge. It was impossible to get heavier tanks across. The front tank commander, General Nikolai Bolotnikov, told Zhdanov that no armoured support could be given to the infantry. 'To talk about an offensive from the Nevsky bridgehead in such conditions borders on the senseless,' he said. Zhdanov, fearful of Stalin's wrath, persisted. He sent signals specialists to set up a direct link for him between the Smolny and the bridgehead. One of them was Mikhail Neishtadt. 'It was absolute hell there,' he said. 'All our attempts to break the siege from this point failed. Our positions were being smashed to pieces by the enemy's artillery. If you somehow managed to stay alive it was a total fluke.'[18]

Another 'shock group', of men from three more Soviet infantry divisions, the 10th, 80th and 281st, was sent across the Neva. The original

80th Rifle Division had been wiped out in great encirclement battles in the Ukraine in September. It was re-formed from volunteers among the workers of the Volodarsky district of Leningrad. After heavy fighting in the Oranienbaum pocket, it returned to the city. Some of its emaciated men died of exposure during its forced march to the Neva crossing point.

Its orders were to seize the two workers' settlements, Gorodok No. 1 and No. 2, which the Germans had heavily fortified. This was clearly beyond its exhausted state. The 80th's commander, Colonel I. M. Frolov, told General Gusev at front headquarters that his division was 'not ready to execute the task it was posed'. Some units had no ammunition. Zhdanov insisted that the attack go ahead at any cost. Three hours before it went in, at dawn on 26 November, Frolov repeated that he 'did not believe in the successful outcome of the operation'. A note of his remark, and of the agreement of the divisional commissar, found its way to the NKVD.

Frolov was right. His men were disorientated, flung forward with no idea of the lie of the land or the positions of the German bunkers. Many fell through the ice, as the Germans shelled it, and froze or drowned. Others, half starved, died of exhaustion. Wave after wave of those who got across were cut down. They barely reached the ruins of the outlying buildings at Gorodok No. 1 before the survivors were driven back to regroup and try again.

By now, the Germans were mocking the Russian efforts. 'They watched our movements the whole time, and knew when and where we would go on the attack,' Alexander Sokolov said. As each assault began, the Germans taunted them in broken Russian through their loudspeakers: 'It's time for you to assemble at your extermination points again. We will bury you on the banks of the Neva!' Then their shells and mortar bombs and machine guns cut the Russians down. General Halder, the German chief of staff, barely bothered to mention the assaults. 'On the Leningrad front, the usual attack was repelled,' he noted caustically.

The day was dark for Daniil Kharms, too. The case against him was reopened and he was moved back to the Shpalernaya. He was now severely dystrophic, but no one knew where he was. His wife was told that he was in Novosibirsk. On 26 November, his interrogator, Burmistrov, interviewed Antonina Oranzhereyeva, a biologist who was now working as a translator for the Military Medical Academy. It was on her sole evidence that Kharms had been arrested. Knowledge of any foreign language was suspect, and translators were highly vulnerable to arrest. Oranzhereyeva was a valued NKVD informer. She was assigned to report on Akhmatova – she had been a friend of her second husband, Vladimir Shileyko – without the poet ever suspecting that she was a stool pigeon. She had first met Kharms in the apartment of the writer Yevgeny Sno in November 1940. Sno had already been arrested and shot, but she continued to see Kharms.

Feeling himself 'among his friends,' she told Burmistrov, Kharms had raged against Soviet power. He said that a German victory was 'inevitable', that the Soviet system was rotten, and that 'order was impossible in a country without private capital'. He had told her that 'the defenders of Leningrad have no weapons, and quite soon there would only be a heap of stones where the city had stood'. He despised the workers – 'only if we get rid of the proletariat will we have a good life in this country' – and was sympathetic to enemies of the people like Tukhachevsky. 'If they were still alive', he'd told her, 'they'd save Russia from the Bolsheviks.'

The paperwork was examined by a procurator, Gribanov, the NKVD interrogator, Lieutenant Artyemov, and a Major Podchasov. They referred the case to a military troika. The three men, Gerasimov, Orlov and the military lawyer Marchuk, met in the starving city ten days later.

They found Kharms guilty of counter-revolutionary defeatist agitation, liable to lead to the decay and demoralization of the Red Army. His schizophrenia meant that he could not be held responsible, but the nature of his crime made him a danger to society. The troika ordered him to be returned to the prison psychiatric ward for treatment. This was tantamount to a death sentence. He would receive only a child's bread ration.

It was now common for people to collapse in the street or at work. Those most vulnerable were men aged between twenty-nine and fifty-nine on workers' rations. Over November, 11,085 deaths were registered, three times the pre-war rate.

'The future of Leningrad is alarming,' Vera Inber confided in her diary on 28 November. 'Not long ago Professor Z. told me: "My daughter spent the whole evening in the cellar, looking for a cat." I was ready to congratulate her on such love for a cat when Z. explained: "We eat them."' Three days later, she saw a corpse being hauled along the street on a child's sled. It was not in a coffin, but tightly wrapped in a sheet, the knees and breast clearly defined, like an Egyptian mummy. She had never seen such a sight before. It would soon be so commonplace that not a glance would be wasted on it.

The journalist Nikolai Tikhonov walked through the deserted city at night. It reminded him of Dante's *Inferno*: heavy snow, the thin light of the moon, clouds drifting on a bitter wind. At the bridge to the Summer Garden, he passed a woman in a black cloak and a black mask. She looked to be on her way to a masquerade. A man far off was carrying a heavy burden on his shoulder, which sparkled in the light. He came near, and Tikhonov saw that it was a body. When he looked again, the man and his burden had disappeared. Tikhonov shuddered, and walked on in the cold silence. He drew on the mysterious figure to write a poem, 'Kirov Is With Us', soon to be legendary and much loved, in which the assassinated leader returns to give comfort to his city:

Broken are the walls of the houses
Gaping wide are the ruined arches
In the iron nights of Leningrad
Kirov walks the city . . .
Let our soup be no more than water
Let our bread be worth more than gold
Like men of steel we will hold out.[19]

Music was faltering. Eliasberg was due to conduct Beethoven's Fifth and Tchaikovsky's *1812* Overture in the Philharmonia on 30 November. Vera Inber noted that they were 'cancelled because of heavy artillery fire'.

Far to the south, the Germans were making their final lunge towards Moscow. The panzers were moving on ground as hard as iron, only lightly dusted in snow. The sky, though, held a menace, 'neither blue, nor grey, but strangely crystalline and luminous, utterly without warmth or poetry'.[20] On 28 November, tanks from 7th Panzer, trailing plumes of powdered snow, crossed the frozen Moscow reservoirs and reached the Moscow–Volga canal.

The division had been transferred from Leningrad. The crews had seen the city's spires through their fieldglasses in September. They stretched out now for Moscow's onion domes, but their strength was failing. A woman in a village they briefly held told the war correspondent Vasily Grossman of how they had arrived:

They knocked at the door, crowded into the house, and stood by the stove like sick dogs, their teeth chattering, shaking, putting their hands right into the stove, and their hands were red like raw meat . . . Well, as soon as they got warmer, they began to scratch themselves. It was awful to watch, and funny. Like dogs, scratching themselves with their paws. Lice had started moving again on their bodies because of the warmth.[21]

The 7th Panzers had earned itself the title *Gesperterdivision*, the Ghost Division, under Rommel in France, its own high command struggling to locate it, such was its speed and dash. Its men were indeed spectres now. They had shawls over their heads, and some wore women's bonnets under their black helmets and women's knitted pantaloons. Many dragged sledges loaded with quilts, pillows and bags of food. Against them, the Russians had transferred fresh Siberian divisions from the Far East, the men in white quilted uniforms, at home in the wilds and the snow, riding on T-34 tanks or tough ponies.

The cold froze German sentries to death. It jammed their automatic weapons so that they could only fire single shots, and solidified the packing grease on their shells. They had to scrape it off with a knife to fit them into the breech. It made them huddle vulnerably together at night, burning precious petrol to keep warm in the rare buildings the Russians had not burned during their retreat. Many suffered dysentery, but it was fatal to expose their flesh in the open. 'Many men died while performing their natural functions, as a result of a congelation of the anus.' And the cold depressed them, *Landsers* and generals alike. Guderian recorded:

Only he who saw the endless expanse of Russian snow during this winter of our misery, and felt the icy wind that blew across it . . . who drove for hour after hour through that no-man's-land only at last to find too thin shelter, with insufficiently clothed half-starved men . . . who also saw the well-fed, warmly clad and fresh Siberians . . . only a man who knew all that can truly judge the events which now occurred.[22]

On 29 November, Shostakovich wrote to Sollertinsky from Kuibyshev. It was two months since he had completed the Seventh's third movement. He complained that he had hardly started the fourth movement, despite his optimistic remarks in Moscow. Next day, he admitted to Glikman that he had not even begun it yet. The main reason, he said, 'is that the strain of concentrating all my efforts on the first three movements has completely exhausted me'. Glikman had worked for a time as Shostakovich's secretary, and knew him well. 'As you have already observed,' the composer confessed, 'everything to do with composition puts me in a state of great nervous excitement.'

A change in fortunes, in front of Moscow, was at hand. Shostakovich did not know it yet, but it was to restore his inspiration.

CHAPTER 7

Dekabr'

December 1941

A pair of influential young evacuees, Flora and Tatyana Litvinova, were living in the rooms above Shostakovich in Kuibyshev. Flora was married to Tatyana's brother Misha, the son of Maxim Litvinov, the revolutionary offspring of rich Jewish bankers in Bialystok, dismissed as Soviet foreign minister by Stalin to appease Hitler's anti-Semitism, but now restored to favour as Soviet ambassador to Washington. Flora had met her husband-to-be at the Moscow premiere of Shostakovich's Fifth Symphony. She was a great admirer of the composer. She knew he had a piano in his room, and was sad he was not working and that it stayed silent.

Then, on 2 December, it changed. 'Today I heard the piano and some obviously Shostakovich-like sounds,' she noted. 'I stood next to the radiator, and then I heard Galya and Maxim singing "Three jolly soldiers in a tank" . . . What a travesty – Shostakovich's children singing *that*.'[1] No matter. Shostakovich was playing again, and working on his symphony at a furious pace. Sokolov attributed it to the news from the front: 'The fascists had been smashed outside Moscow. He sat down to compose in a burst of energy and excitement.'

That afternoon, men of the German 258th Infantry Division reached the point where the forests bleed into the western outskirts of Moscow. They were close – close enough to see the 'towers of the Kremlin reflect the setting sun' by some accounts – but with darkness they withdrew.

'We needed only another eight miles to get Moscow within artillery range,' a lieutenant said. 'We just could not make it.' It was the last exhausted push in an offensive that was in grave danger of reversing into a rout.

Fresh divisions from Siberia were spearheading a Red Army counter-offensive round Moscow. The half-frozen Germans pulled denim overalls over their standard-issue uniforms, and stuffed the loose folds with screwed-up paper for warmth. Newspapers were best, but most had to make do with pamphlets designed to be dropped on the enemy: 'Surrender is the only sane and sensible course . . .' Their formidable weaponry was disabled by the cold. An infantry division, the 112th, broke up in panic. This was the first time that such a thing had happened since the start of Barbarossa. It was a warning, a Wehrmacht report said, that 'the combat ability of our infantry was at an end'.[2]

The Russians liberated Tula from Guderian's 5th Panzers south of Moscow. The Germans had used Leo Tolstoy's estate nearby at Yasnaya Polyana as a hospital. They buried their dead next to his grave. Mozhaisk to the west was freed. A bulge developed at Klin. This was the hinge of the whole left wing of Army Group Centre. Rip it swiftly from them, and Guderian's panzers and troops would be encircled before they could withdraw to a new defence line. They fought desperately to shore up threatened strongpoints and road junctions. Russian *podvizhnaya gruppa* – mobile groups with tanks, truck-borne riflemen, ski troops and cavalry – harried them as the Cossacks had Napoleon's retreating Grande Armée. The 5th Battalion of the Grossdeutschland Regiment was destroyed when the Russians came out of the forests and fell on it at 2 a.m. on 6 December, capturing the burning town of Kolodeznaya. The regiment itself was all but annihilated. A single rifle battalion was the only remnant to pass into the new Grossdeutschland Division when it was formed the next year.

In 'the fierce blizzards of night and day', in waist-high snow and penetrating winds, the Germans fell back.[3] Soviet skiers emerged from the snows to pick off stragglers and isolated trucks. The Germans struck back at their pursuers with sudden and savage counter-attacks, their riflemen in armoured carriers screened by self-propelled guns. The temperature rose for a few hours, and arctic air gave way to rain and sleety roads on which the panzers and their wounded slithered back in a huge withdrawal from the bulge, leaving dead horses and smashed guns and trucks strewn in their wake.

The scale of the war changed dramatically, and to Soviet advantage, on 8 December. The Japanese did not turn on the Red Army, on the borders of Manchuria, where Zhukov had held them in 1939,* but on the Americans at Pearl Harbor, and the British in Malaya. It confirmed the Russian decision to withdraw the Siberian divisions from the Soviet Far East. On 11 December, Hitler acquired a new and mighty enemy. He declared war on the United States.

The Red Army broke back into Klin, fifty miles northwest of Moscow. Tchaikovsky's country house was here, a handsome wooden dacha with a summer garden of lilies of the valley and violets and bluebells, with winding paths leading to a gazebo. He had written his last great work, his Sixth Symphony, the *Pathétique*, at a desk on the second floor looking out over the lime trees. The Germans used this as a barracks, keeping their motorcycles on the ground floor. The gazebo they burned to keep warm.

The German front on the Volga was shattered. 'Discipline began to crack,' said General Schaal of the 3rd Panzer Division. 'More and more soldiers were making their own way back to the west, without any weapons, leading a calf or drawing a sledge with potatoes behind them. Men

---

* He did so with air support from General Yakov Smushkevich, whose body had rested since 28 October beneath the children's playground in Kuibyshev with Beria's other bemedalled victims, not far from Shostakovich's apartment.

killed in bombing were no longer buried. Supply units were in the grip of psychosis . . . in the past they had only known headlong advance.' They fired the villages as they left. Stove chimneys and the charred skeletons of houses were all that remained. The war correspondent Konstantin Simonov noticed gallows in liberated villages, with the bodies of hanged peasants lying by them.

Those liberated by the Red Army, though, had good reason to temper their joy. They had survived double shocks of great danger – the Russian withdrawal and German advance, and then the retreating Wehrmacht and Red Army assault – and they now faced a third. Hard on the heels of the Russian combat squads came 'Operational-Chekhist detachments', the NKVD security units. Their task was to arrest 'wreckers, traitors and provocateurs' and to set up new networks of informers and agents. The interrogators and execution squads were supported by NKVD combat companies and destroyer battalions. The latter had the additional task of shooting Red Army soldiers if they retreated. Beria signed a directive ordering NKVD front commanders to set up NKVD sections immediately in all populated areas 'liberated from enemy forces'.

They seized any radio sets and weapons that had got into local hands. They re-established prisons. All males of military age were interrogated to see if they were deserters. All documents left behind by the Germans were carefully examined for clues for collaborators and traitors. Occupation, however brief, was seen as tainting those who suffered it. The essential was 'the restoration of Soviet power', the security units were told, and all measures should be taken 'to fix the political mood of all layers of the population'.[4] They were swift and ruthless. Within days of the recapture of Tula, the front commander issued a citation commending two NKVD Junior Lieutenants of State Security, Mikhail Mokrinskiy and Vasily Grechikhin, for identifying some three hundred 'traitors to the motherland' with help from local partisans.[5]

*

Shostakovich knew nothing of this, and the victories inspired him to such an intensity of composition that Sokolov was afraid to disturb him by sketching him. For the next three weeks, he gave himself almost entirely to his symphony. He was elected chairman of the new Kuibyshev branch of the Union of Composers. Its members met on Wednesdays to listen to each other play and discuss their music. The first meeting was held on 10 December and Shostakovich played the first three movements of the Seventh.

Later in the day, he wrote a wistful letter to Ivan Sollertinsky. 'Nina, Galina and Maxim are fine, especially the children,' he noted. 'They are at a happy age. Their little bellies don't ache, they are full: they have shoes, they are warm – that's why life for them is wonderful. I'm jealous. I wish I was their age.' He said he had flown out of Leningrad 'quite light': 'I took with me only the score of Lady Macbeth, the 7th Symphony and Stravinsky's symphony, my editing [of Stravinsky] and the score.' He was living very quietly, he said, and he stayed in and worked most of the time. 'Sometimes during the day my friends come, Oborin and Rabinovich,* and we play four-hands piano, but we haven't enough music. We drink and recall friends – most often you and Shebalin. We part quite early and only sometimes stay until 1 a.m. or 2 a.m.'

He was homesick. 'We dream about returning home to our native cities, dreaming till we're half mad, and often in tears,' he wrote. 'I believe both of us will be home quite soon, and it'll be the same as it was before I left. But now I miss you and ask you, don't forget me and write more often.' He was still upset about the missing suitcases and he added a postcript. 'Did I tell you that during our journey from Moscow to Kuibyshev we lost – or they stole – two suitcases with all our clothes and underwear? It's quite a sensitive loss. Somehow I rebuilt the status quo.'[6]

---

* Nikolai Rabinovich was to repay his friendship by conducting Shostakovich operettas like *Cheryomushki*.

To stay up reminiscing and drinking into the early hours, even if only 'sometimes', was surely bliss against the blackness of Leningrad. But he did not know how desperate was its condition. No word of its horrors had yet escaped the censors and reached the mainland. That would happen only when mass evacuations began.

The artist Pavel Filonov died on 3 December. He had been at the vivid heart of the city's avant-garde, close to Mayakovsky and Khlebnikov and the Futurists, the son of a carter and a laundress, and a Red in the Revolution who had become professor at the Academy of Arts. Stalin had broken his health, but not his spirit. Filonov was forbidden to exhibit his works. He was impoverished and outcast. 'From the first days of July,' he recorded in 1935, 'I lived only on tea, sugar and a kilo of bread a day.' He continued to paint, fragile, in oil on paper, for he had no money for canvas, but wondrous. His body was already too weak to withstand Hitler's siege for long, and he succumbed to starvation. His sister guarded his works, refusing to be evacuated from the city. She then gave them to the Russian Museum, but it was forty years before the public saw any of them.

Death was stalking the theatres, too. Tamara Salnikova was the female lead in *The Three Musketeers* at the Muzkom. 'It was very difficult to get to the theatre from the Petrograd Side where I live. My hands and lips were cold. I was dizzy from starvation. Artillery started firing when I was on the Kirov Bridge.' She tried to take cover behind the snowbanks by the bridge parapets with some other women. One of them was hit by a shellburst and crawled off, leaving a thin trail of blood in the snow. Salnikova should have been in short sleeves and deep décolleté in the first act, but she wore a dressing gown beneath her costume. It was so cold that her make-up froze. 'I tried to perform with serenity,' she said. 'But I heard in the intermission that just as I was finishing the first act, the choir singer A. Abramov died.'[7]

At the Philharmonia, Eliasberg conducted the performance of Beethoven's Fifth that had been postponed the week before because of heavy shelling. Vera Inber was there: 'The Hall is dark, darker and darker. Cold as in hell. Chandeliers are lit at quarter strength. Musicians: some in sheepskin coats, some in *vatniki* [convict-type jackets]. First violinist completely unshaven, he had no water or light to shave.'[8] Young Krukov noted in his diary on 5 December: 'Today at 9 a.m. Father fainted . . . At 3.05 p.m. Father died.' He buried him three days later. 'We carried Father to the cemetery. The coffin was rough, unpainted, no handles but it was good that we had it because many people take bodies to the cemetery on sledges wrapped in cheap carpet.'

Music was creaking to a halt. Heavy snowfalls blanketed the city. A further concert planned at the Philharmonia was cancelled. Instead, the radio broadcast songs by a platoon of the Propaganda Brigade of the House of the Red Army. They included an insulting little ditty about Goebbels. The Composers' Union was hit by shellfire. 'Everything is shrunk from the cold,' the Conservatoire professor Zoya Lodsi wrote. 'This is something I cannot overcome. I sit near the stove in Class 22. Starvation is nothing compared with cold.' The composer L. Portov was struggling to work on English and American melodies. His legs were frostbitten. 'Every step is a hellish thing. After a few steps, I need a rest.'

Zhukov's successes outside Moscow, perversely, made the situation worse for Russian commanders in Leningrad. Stalin became convinced it was only timidity that prevented the siege from being lifted. He insisted that further assaults would bring breakthroughs. Fresh attacks unrolled in the Nevsky bridgehead at the beginning of December. Oberstleutnant Werner Richter, the adjutant of the German lst Infantry Division, which faced them, noted that the Russians had mounted seventy-eight assaults in the past six weeks. They had broken into German positions seventeen times, and were repulsed each time.

They were as doomed now as ever. The Germans did not know how many Russians they killed. They could see scores lying dark against the snow, in clumps in no-man's-land. Many others were concealed in the shell holes and bomb craters that honeycombed the bridgehead from the river to their own lines. The men from the 1st Infantry Division were a cohesive force of East Prussians. They were hardened and experienced, from families who had provided *Landsers* for generations. Each night, they reinforced their bunkers and dug new communications trenches. At dawn, they awaited the whining change in air pressure and the crump-crump of Russian shells and the swooping roar of rocket launchers. A few minutes later, the Russians moved forward to try to enlarge the bridgehead. They brought more tanks across the river, though the ice was too thin for them, and they were dragged on pontoons. A direct shell hit on a pontoon was often enough to capsize the tank riding on it and send it to the bottom.

Those that reached the far bank had little room for manoeuvre, and were knocked out before they reached the German foxholes. They did protect the Russian infantry following them and, even burnt out, they offered cover. Russian supply lines were short. Brand-new tanks were driven to the Neva straight from the Kirov factory in Leningrad. The *Landsers* were going through 8,000 hand grenades a day, so furious and close-range was the fighting. Their gunners needed at least 3,500 shells a day for the light 105mm guns, and 600 for the heavy 150mms. Their supplies barely kept pace.[9]

'There was so much artillery here, and the bombing was so intense that the earth was black and the snow was black too,' says Leonid Matorin, a rare Red Army survivor of the battle. 'So many explosions at a time! So many of our infantry died here.' It was ten years before the grass began to grow again, and then it gleamed in the moonlight, from the shards of metal it unearthed. Seventy years later, trees will not grow and the pitted surface has only tussock grass, and mass graves.

Zoya Vinogradova was responsible for the sanitation service of a battalion, which included evacuating the wounded. 'You could not see more than three metres in front, and the ground was trembling and groaning,' she said. 'There were so many wounded I hardly managed to take them from the battlefield.' After three days in the bridgehead, she was hit in the chest and stomach by shrapnel, and her arm was injured. She was saved when her own battalion was all but destroyed, and marines were fed across the river. 'I was unconscious till the morning,' she said. 'The naval infantry came to replace our battalion. Somebody stepped on my hand by chance and I groaned. That's how I was saved.'[10]

Stalin tore into Zhdanov over the government telegraph. 'It is strange that Comrade Zhdanov never feels the need to come to the machine,' he said, 'and ask at least one of us for reciprocal information in such a dificult moment for Leningrad. If we, the Muscovites, had not summoned you, perhaps, Comrade Zhdanov, you would have forgotten about Moscow . . . We might imagine that Leningrad under the leadership of Comrade Zhdanov is not in the USSR, but somewhere on an island in the Pacific . . .'[11]

Zhdanov needed scapegoats for the failed offensives on the Neva. The blame was shifted to the 80th Division's ex-commanders, Colonel Frolov and Commissar Ivanov. They were arrested, and brought before a military tribunal the same day. They were found guilty of 'cowardice and criminal negligence that resulted in the failure of the operation'. They were shot next day, with the executions publicized in the press at Stalin's suggestion.* The NKVD, ever forward-looking, finalized on 5 December

---

* The 80th carried the stigma until 1944, with few decorations given to its men. It was then renamed after Ljuban, a city that it had liberated. (Sergei Glezerov, *Pravda*, 1 March 2006.)

a further list of 1,514 people to be evicted from the city as soon as possible. They included 'counter-revolutionary elements', the usual mixture of former persons, kulaks and the like, 'criminal recidivists', those with passport restrictions, usually ex-prisoners, and foreigners.[12]

The following day, the labourers on the wilderness road at last broke out of the swamps and forests onto the flat farmland on the outskirts of Zaborye. A truck convoy had been waiting three days for them. It set out within the hour. Its travails began as soon as it left the fields and entered the forests. The leading truck was continuously bogged down in snowdrifts. The track was too narrow for others to get round it and it had to be dug out each time. Axles and suspension were pounded by the log surface and gave out. At night and in blizzards, drivers were almost blind and slowed to a crawl. Causeways laid across swampy ground disintegrated. The Germans bombed them. On its best day, the convoy travelled twenty miles. It took it a week to get to the lake, with less than a day's supply of food for the city.

Leningrad would not survive if this continued.

Salvation, at best – at worst, a way of prolonging the agony – was at hand at Tikhvin. As the town had fallen, Stalin had given command of Soviet forces to General Kiril Meretskov. As we have seen, he was exceptionally fortunate not to have joined the generals who lay beneath the Kuibyshev children's playground. Beria had used his 'confessions' to have them shot.

Meretskov was still in the Lubyanka awaiting execution when the crisis on the Leningrad Front prompted Stalin to have him released and returned to the war.[13] His deputy commander, Grigory Stelmakh, was also on an NKVD knife-edge. He was lucky to have survived arrest and interrogation in 1938. He owed his release to the Winter War. He was released, promoted to major-general the same day, and sent to train new commanders as a senior instructor at the Frunze military academy.

Commanders as vulnerable as these were not held back, like the doomed Colonel Frolov, by fear of casualties. Stalin telephoned Meretskov and ordered him to attack, whether he was ready or not. To make sure that the message was clear, Grigory Kulik arrived at Meretskov's headquarters – the 'murderous buffoon' whom Beria used as an enforcer, and whose sycophancy to Stalin was such that he remained dog-loyal to him, despite Stalin having ordered his wife's kidnap and execution.[14]

The Stavka planned to use Meretskov's forces to cut off the German XXXIX Corps at the Volkhov river crossing, and to annihilate the 'Tikhvin bulge', the area east of the river that the Germans held around the vital Tikhvin rail junction. If they did so, Shlisselburg might be liberated and the whole German position on the Neva unhinged. The siege would be lifted.

His men fought their way through to the outskirts of Tikhvin on 7 December. The German 18th Division had lost 5,000 men in fierce fighting in deep snow and bitter cold. It was a virtual skeleton, with a combat strength of less than a thousand. A battalion of Panzergrenadiers had lost 250 men. Most had frozen to death. General Franz Halder, the Chief of the Army Staff (OKH), had noted in his diary on the 6th: 'Enemy before Tikhvin has been reinforced. Very severe cold – 38 degrees below freezing – numerous cases of death from cold.' On the 7th, he added: 'Very tight situation at Tikhvin. Army Group North thinks it cannot hold the town.' In the early hours of the 8th, Hitler finally consented to desperate requests to withdraw. He had promised 100 tanks and 22,000 men. The 12th Panzer Division was down to regimental size with thirty tanks left when it began retreating towards the Volkhov. As the temperature fell to minus 30 degrees Celsius, the tanks could no longer rotate their turrets. Meretskov had been reinforced by 27 trainloads of troops over the past three days.

The Red Army broke into Tikhvin in a swirling blizzard on 9 December. The 51st Panzer Regiment was sacrificed as a rearguard as the Germans pulled out. The handful of armoured vehicles left to them froze up or threw their tracks. Their wounded lay on sledges pulled by little steppe ponies taken from Russian peasants. Two of the regiment's Panzergrenadier companies were killed to the last man.[15]

Leningrad was reprieved, the city having enough flour for nine or ten days. 'The oil-cake, bran, mill dust and other "reserves" had been completely consumed,' Pavlov wrote. The emergency food supplies on the ships of the Baltic Fleet had been eaten. So had the army's reserves of hard tack. 'People were so badly nourished that the death rate increased daily. Yet in order to maintain the existing ration level, nearly 1,000 tons of provisions had to be delivered to the city every 24 hours.' Pavlov could not manage that, or anywhere near it, without Tikhvin. It was impossible to bring in more than 600 or 700 tons a day on the Zaborye wilderness route, and that was a total figure, including oil, petrol, ammunition and other vital military supplies. 'It is not hard to imagine the plight of the besieged in this situation,' he wrote. 'The liberation of Tikhvin must rightfully be regarded as a turning point in the defence of the city.'[16] Tikhvin soon resembled 'a gigantic ant hill' as thousands of troops and workers unloaded trains as they arrived, and transferred the supplies to trucks. But the journey on was long: nearly 120 miles on a poor road, the trucks passing through Koskovo, Kolchanovo, Syasstroi, Novaya Ladoga and Kabona, before reaching the Ice Road. A driver did well to make one trip in two days.[17]

The immediate effect of the Tikhvin victory was a disaster for those close to death in the Leningrad. On 12 December, the evacuation effort in the city was called off for the moment – 'postponed' – by the Military Soviet of the Leningrad Front. No reason was given, and no official mention was ever made of the preceding eleven days of evacuation in November and December. Many tens of thousands were sacrificed – those who were dead or too weak to travel when the evacuation resumed forty-one days later. The weather is no explanation. The cold was fiercer, the storms as violent, and the people more emaciated and vulnerable when it restarted in late January. The decision was made in secret, and in a matter of this gravity, it was almost certainly taken by the Supreme Command. The defence of Moscow had convinced Stalin, in particular, that the Germans would be destroyed by the vigorous counter-attacks he had ordered at Tikhvin and on the Volkhov. He was confident that the siege was about to be lifted. When it was, the problems of evacuation and starvation would disappear. So trucks with food and ammunition rolled across the ice into the city. They returned empty, or lightly loaded with specialist workers and industrial plant for the new arms factories in the east.

Blood counted for nothing in Meretskov's assaults. The Spanish Blue Division, whose volunteers saw themselves as part of a crusade against Bolshevism, fought hand-to-hand on the Volkhov front with Russians who charged them across frozen snow in pre-dawn temperatures of minus 30. They broke through to the divisional chapel before the Spaniards held them, leaving a hundred dead in the shadow of the bent cross on the cupola. In a day's fighting, the Russians lost 550 killed, to the Blue Division's 130 casualties. The Spaniards wondered what ferocity had driven these men to sacrifice themselves on the very barrels of their machine guns. They examined the bodies. Beneath their white camouflage, the Russians wore uniforms from all services. Some had been pilots, some were army officers, medics even. They were fodder from a punishment battalion.[18]

The Germans had no reserves. The Red Army came close to breaking across the frozen river. Had they done so, and swung north, they would have cut the German Sixteenth Army's supply lines and trapped XXXIX Corps. The siege would have been lifted. But the Germans held. When the Russians did cross the river, it was to be a Red army that would find itself encircled and annihilated, as Leningrad festered. But for all the Russians they killed on the Volkhov and in the Neva bridgehead – 'heavy bloody enemy casualties', noted one German OKW diary of a typical attack – German losses were as grievous.

By 10 December, a battalion of the 1st Infantry Division was reduced to seventy men, and one from the 223rd Infantry Regiment to eighty-eight.[19] As recently as mid-November, the rule of thumb was 100 men for a company, 500 for a battalion, 1,000 for a regiment, 10,000 for a division. Now, *'in der Hölle von Dubrowka'*, the hellish pit of Dubrovka, only a single officer and NCO and six men were recorded as fully fit in one battalion.[20] Their comrades were dead, wounded or suffering extreme exhaustion and shock. The *Fallschirmjäger* had taken 782 casualties since the paratroopers had been rushed to the Neva at the end of September. Badly mauled, they had now to be withdrawn.

The Wehrmacht was strung out from Norway and France to North Africa and Greece. It could not long afford such attrition, and morale was low. A large sign at the start of the road to Schlisselburg proclaimed *'Hier beginnt der Arsch der Welt!'* This quotation ('You are now entering the world's arsehole') was attributed to General Wandel of the 121st Infantry Division. The men had summed up its autumnal charms as *'Tod, Strapazen, Sumpfwald, Mücken und Laüse'* (death, strain, forest-swampland, mosquitoes and lice). Now they had blizzards and ice to contend with. They whispered: *'Was wussten wir wirklich von der Sowjetunion?'* ('What did we really know about the Soviet Union?') What were they doing in Russia? What, really, did they want from it?

In the dark city, on 11 December, the coal stocks remaining in the boiler houses of apartment blocks and hospitals were taken to keep the No. 2 power station running. The district heating of buildings, factories and works was halted. Public utilities, bathhouses, laundries, hairdressers, were shut. The Gorispolkom (*Gorodskoi ispolnitel'nyi komitet*, the city executive committee) tried to introduce compulsory snow clearance with everyone putting in between three and eight hours a day. It was unenforceable. People were too weak, the snowdrifts too severe.

The trams stopped running, adding two or three hours of walking to the daily workload. 'The additional burden of walking weakened the muscular system,' Z. M. Shnitnikova noted, 'including weakening of the myocardium [the middle layer of the heart wall, the heart muscle] and frequently to a denouement, death from heart failure, cardioplegia, and fainting and freezing when out and about.'[21] The number of sudden deaths in the street was escalating. Between 6 and 13 December 841 corpses were taken from the streets to mortuaries. By the middle of the month, at least 160 people were collapsing and dying in the street each day.

It was only now that the authorities began to get to grips with the terminology of death. Starvation did not appear as a disease or cause of death in Soviet classifications.[22] Neither did dystrophy, the wasting of tissue. This in itself was revealing. Experts trained in tsarist days were not afraid of language. The eminent demographer Sergei Alexandrovich Novosel'skii was blunt in his explanation of the 19,516 deaths in Petrograd during the Civil War caused by lack of food. 'Starvation and cold are the main causes of the exceptionally high mortality, because they created a massive reduction in the vitality and viability of people,' he wrote in 1920.

By 1941, though, most doctors in Leningrad had been educated in the Soviet period. They had 'a very weak grasp of dystrophy and the diseases that it occasioned'.[23] The very word 'hunger' was inhibiting to the Party, and for good reason. Millions had died during the hunger-terror

it had imposed on the Ukraine in 1932 and 1933.* The people themselves called this the 'holodomor', the 'killing by hunger'. They did so
in whispers, but there was no doubt as to who was responsible. As
the first had been a deliberate act by Stalin, so Hitler had chosen this
second *holodomor* in Leningrad. The resonance was disturbing. It was
only on 7 December that the Leningrad health department approved
proposals by three professors on 'the Terminology and Treatment of
Nutritional Disorders'. The term 'nutritional dystrophy' was to be used
for 'malnutrition'. '*Golod*' ('hunger' or 'starvation') was not used. Two
types of dystrophy were recognized. 'Oedematous form' was used when
oedema was present, and the body puffed up with fluid in the tissue
and cavities. 'Cachetic form' was used for cases of dystrophy with acute
emaciation, and physical and mental debility. Army doctors preferred
to use the catch-all 'nutritional emaciation'. The civilians stuck with
'nutritional dystrophy'.

Science as well as the arts was part of the city's glory – seen most
neatly in Alexander Borodin, chemist, physician and composer of
Prince Igor – and, fitfully perhaps, research continued. The Institute
of Experimental Research, the LFVIEM, was to lose seventy of its
scientific workers to starvation, and four of its buildings to bombs
and shells. The sixteen surviving researchers carried on with work
on nutritional dystrophy.[24] Blood was needed in profusion for the
wounded. The supply of ampoules was exhausted. Empty vodka, wine
and milk bottles were used. Two of the Blood Transfusion Research
Institute staff invented a universal stopper when it was found that the
heat of sterilization destroyed the only rubber they had. The buildings
of the Neurosurgical Institute were destroyed in an air raid. Its clinic
moved to an empty school, where B. E. Maksimov studied mental

---

* Scholars' estimates run from 2.4 million to 7.5 million. The higher figures include the Kuban
as well as the Ukraine. Others perished during collectivization in Russia, Kazakhstan and
Belorussia.

depression. He found that the siege increased the acuteness of mental disease. The best antidote was belief in the correctness of the cause, and in its ultimate triumph. This was powerful enough to raise the individual to a 'state of high tone and vital activity'.[25]

Less reassuring were the findings of Yulia Mendeleva, the director of the Paediatric Institute, itself bombed out of its original building. She was noting a 'catastrophic' drop in the weight, length and circumference of the head and chest in new-born infants. They were two centimetres shorter and 600 grams lighter than pre-war infants.

Music offered escape. Vladimir Sofronitsky, the pianist son-in-law of Alexander Scriabin, gave a concert at the Puskhin Theatre in lieu, as it were, of rent: together with several other artists, he was living in the theatre. 'It was dark, cold, morose,' he recalled. 'The public in winter coats and felt boots. I played in gloves with the fingers cut off. But frankly I have never played so well. And what a reception from the audience! This evening was one of the happiest days of my life.'[26] Alexander Kamensky, one of the Conservatoire's finest pianists, gave a musical evening – Beethoven, Chopin, Liszt – in the Pushkin Theatre.

A special programme for the Baltic Fleet, whose warships were now trapped in the ice, was broadcast on 10 December. V. Petrova, one of the musicians, passed a freshly ruined building on her way home from the House of Radio studios. 'The largest part had collapsed. It was in semi-darkness. Big bright stars were lit one by one. The rooms and windows looked like the black parts of an abandoned beehive and from the black holes music came. It seems somewhere a radio had survived.'

Audiences at the Muzkom were whirled off to the Canadian Rockies at a matinee and evening performance of *Rose-Marie* on 14 December. An air raid took place in the evening. Some of the cast had to go up to the roof in the freezing darkness to wait for incendiaries. After the all-clear was sounded, two shots were heard. They were from the rifles of an execution party outside the theatre. 'Like oil stains on clean water,' Pavlov wrote of those who were shot, 'there appeared the egoists who would snatch bread from their own children, the thieves who stole their neighbour's rations or took a sick women's overcoat for a hundred grams of horsemeat, and all the other parasites.'

A Tchaikovsky concert was held the same day at the Philharmonia, with his Sixth and the *Romeo and Juliet* overture-fantasy. Vladimir Sofronitsky was the soloist, with the veteran Miklashevsky conducting. S. Permut wrote of his rapture in his diary:

> The same sounds of God, moving, the notes touch something intimate in the soul. But the atmosphere of the Philharmonia is not the same. The audience are in coats, many musicians in hats, fur coats and felt boots. Only the 'Grenadier' [leader] of the Philharmonia is faithful to himself. To a thunder of applause, he came out in uniform, black jacket, shining white waistcoat. Only his gloves made his outfit different from normal times. Victor Miklashevsky was also in uniform, a perfect image of a conductor. The Old Guard may be dying, but they never surrender.

Kondratiev was equally impressed. 'Who is not warmed by it?' he wrote. 'It needs real heroism to play with fingers stiff from cold. Audience in coats but the cold is so intense it paralyses hands and feet. The hall was fifty to sixty per cent full. I heard Miklashevsky conduct for the first time. He made a good impression, artistic values, smooth movements and flexible gestures . . . A little detail, listening to Tchaikovsky's Sixth,' he added nostalgically. 'I recalled how two years ago we sat at the dining table with Miklashevsky and [his wife] Natalia Nikolayevna offered us wonderful cutlets, and we ate four of them. What a wonderful time it was, to be warm and full!'

Miklashevsky was called back for an encore and played sentimental pieces from Tchaikovsky.

But this was the end of the Philharmonia's activity. The same day, 14 December, Kondratiev stopped writing up his artistic diary. The Muzkom musician A. Silin, and the Capella choir singer Abakshev, both died. The daughter of the violinist Victor Zavetnovsky, who was to become the long-standing leader of the Philharmonia orchestra, noted that the attitude of musicians had changed dramatically. 'Everyone has only one wish, to move this dam that holds us, to get away.' The temperature dropped to minus 20 degrees Celsius. Winter was early, and abnormally harsh. The cold, doctors noted, was 'somehow internalized. It went through everything. The body generated insufficient heat.'[27] Portov had felt well enough to work a little on English and American melodies, for a broadcast of Allied music. The recovery was short-lived. 'Suffering from starvation, cold, brain too paralysed for any work, impossible to go anywhere because of my legs,' he wrote now. 'Looked through books of counterpoint all evening.'

Bogdanov-Berezovsky found a way of keeping warm: 'Little bits of music – I was able to play in the freezing room because warmed up by working on Rachmaninov.' He was made director of the Leningrad Komsomol theatre. It no longer had any musicians. He himself replaced the vanished orchestra, playing music for performances on a grand piano.[28]

The American entry into the war had musical resonance. *Leningradskaya Pravda* reported that Alexander Kamensky was preparing a special programme of chamber concerts of English and American piano music. It was to be transmitted by the Radiokom at the end of December. Kamensky was a big, powerful pianist, a Conservatoire professor who had played in all the major concert halls before the war. He was a stalwart for the Radiokom, but he was losing weight rapidly. His wife A. Bushen kept him going. It was so cold in the House of Radio that people's breath steamed. 'In the studio they used, the *burzhuika* [stove] gave a little heat but the smoke was poisonous. The eyes of the people in the room were tired and full of tears. People worked in *vatniki* (convict-style jackets) and fur hats. It was impossible to warm the keys. Kamensky warmed his hands on the stove, and then he took off his coat at the last moment and started to play.'[29] He scoured the libraries before he found a few suitable pieces. He played pieces by the British composer Cyril Scott for his first radio concert, and adapted American folk songs for the piano for the second.

It was obvious by 17 December that not enough musicians still capable of making music were left to stage the traditional New Year concert at the Philharmonia. Instead it was decided that a special jazz ensemble with the singer Klavdiya Shulzhenko would perform in the Hall on 31 December. She had won the first All-Soviet competition for popular singers in 1939: her recording of 'La Paloma' was a great pre-war hit, and during the war her iconic song was 'Let's Smoke'.

Plans were still ambitious enough. The radio reported that Boris Asafyev, the 'great composer, the writer of ballets, a multi-talented man . . . has made a very interesting plan for music for *War and Peace*.' He intended turning Tolstoy's great novel into a musical. In reality, though, Asafyev had to be put on special rations on 19 December – together with Agrippina Vaganova, director of the ballet school, and the great soprano Sofia Preobrazhenskaya – to keep him alive. The writers' and composers' unions begged the Management of Artistic Affairs (*Upravleniye po delam isskustv*) for special rations for eighteen others. They were given two kilos of oil-cake each.

Almost all activity ceased at the Conservatoire and classes had terminated. 'The teachers who were still in the city had no strength to teach, and the students were too exhausted to study,' the young oboist Ksenia Matus wrote. She was serving in Shostakovich's old firefighters' brigade. 'At the sound of the alarm, we grabbed our kerosene lamps, which we called "Bats", and went to our posts, the attics, in the Grand Hall,' she said. 'The posts were scattered through the whole Conservatoire.'[30]

She also helped to make camouflage nets. They were used by the small camouflage team – the young mountaineer Mikhail Bobrov and the three girls, Olga Firsova, Alexandra Prigozheva and Eloise Zenbo – that was still working flat out. 'You can't explain in words how we climbed and camouflaged,' Bobrov said of their work, suspended in the freezing air on climbing ropes. 'Some spires we painted. Others we covered with canvas. We were thin and hungry. Our heads were spinning. We fainted. Eloise's feet swelled up. Olga could barely walk to the camouflage sites. Alexandra was dying.'[31] He did not know it, but Eloise was to die, too, in the spring. They had finished three of the most difficult landmarks – the spire of the Engineering Castle, the cupola of St Isaac's, and the model of a sailing ship that served as a golden weather vane on the Admiralty – but they were still working on the 120-foot needle spire and its golden angel atop the 360-foot Peter and Paul Cathedral. It was icy and bitterly cold, and they got what sleep they could lying by the tombs of former tsars in the dark cathedral.[32]

The evening and night of 20 December were ominous, the sky swelling with dark black clouds. Flashes from the guns lit the horizon on all sides but no noise penetrated to the centre of the city. The number of sudden deaths in the street was escalating. At least 160 bodies a day were being taken from the streets to the mortuaries. By law, autopsies had to be carried out on each of them. Hospital dissecting rooms could no longer cope. This day, the Leningrad police accepted that no autopsy need be carried out on bodies found in the street that showed no signs of violence.[33]

Nikolai Gorshkov, an accountant at the Leningrad textile institute, exchanged some cigarettes for bread and oil-cake in the market, though he knew the latter caused chronic constipation. It was getting difficult to buy for cash so everyone wanted to do deals and swaps. Next day, a colleague told him that on a 25-minute walk from the Novo-Kamenny Bridge to International Prospect (now Moscow Prospekt) he had counted 57 corpses being pulled on sledges to the Volkovskoye cemetery. The air-raid sirens sounded at 2.40 p.m. It was the first raid for a fortnight. People had been getting calmer, Gorshokov wrote in his diary, but now their nerves were back on edge as one-ton naval mines were dropped with no discernible pattern.[34]

The Three Musketeers was playing at the Musical Comedy on 22 December. Bodies lay in the snow near the theatre. Partov, the diary-keeping composer, wrote: 'People just fall on the streets from starvation and lie there. The number of dead grows and grows. Just finished rewriting the first part of my Quartet. Worked a little on the second part. Looked through the scores and tried to sketch variations. Starvation constantly reminds one of itself. Trying not to think about it.' A shell hit an apartment block on the Moika where a wake was being held for the pianist Dulov. Guests were badly injured.

Olga Berggolts helped to keep up morale with regular broadcast chats. But she despaired of the gap between what she was allowed to say on radio – defiance, courage, hope, no surrender, no defeatism – and the reality all about her. 'I am working furiously, writing "uplifting" poems and articles, and writing them from the heart, that's what's so surprising! But who will that help? Against the background of what is happening, it's just lies.' Anna Akhmatova wrote a bleak and secret verse on the starving city:

> The birds of death stand at the zenith.
> Who will come to help Leningrad?
> Make no noise around – it is still breathing,
> It is still alive, it can hear everything:

It hears, on the damp bed of the Baltic,

Its sons moan in their sleep

And from its depths, the wails 'Bread!' rising up to the seventh
  heaven.

But this firmament is without mercy.

And from all the windows, death looks out.[35]

Shelest was visiting a hospital when she noticed a figure near the main gate and its red-faced guard. An old man in a black coat was crouched there, staring in front of him with blue eyes as transparent as glass. His face was smooth and yellowish and intelligent, and utterly lifeless. 'I have him in my memory, at his life's end, his being a crouched silhouette against the whiteness.'[36] The hospital guard paid him no attention. Death, Shelest thought, was accepted quite differently than in normal times. 'Death from the sky, from starvation, from cold. Death was so fruit-ful, so everyday, so commonplace a thing.' She was passing the chapel at the Engineering Castle when she saw a five-ton truck at the door. A mountain of naked frozen corpses was inside. Two soldiers moved the corpses by their hands and feet, with a cold crisp sound made by the movement of the frozen bones, and threw them into the truck. 'I didn't have the strength to pass by, so I stood and watched. Then at last they covered the load with white sheets, and left, and I left, too.' The scene reminded her of a Breughel painting. That was how Leningraders accepted death, she thought, 'understanding that you can't help anyone, can't give them bread, or shelter, or heat'.[37]

The neighbours of Kamilla Senyikova did their best to keep her alive. She was the oldest resident in the block. Her daughter and grand-daughters had been evacuated before the blockade, and her son-in-law lived at the arms plant where he worked. Her neighbours tried to feed her, but she got weaker and weaker. She lay in bed. 'Please give me a small cup of tea with a spoon of milk,' she asked constantly. If she had that, she said, she would be happy to die. There was no milk. Just before she died, she took her china out of the cabinet, and dropped it piece by piece on the floor. Then she got down on her hands and knees on the floor, and began looking for bread crumbs among the broken dishes.[38]

A dying neighbour helped to keep Svetlana Magayeva alive. The girl had no real grandmother. A kind old teacher called Maria became her adopted granny. She was a cultured lady, who gave the girl beautiful engravings of Pushkin's *Tale of Tsar Saltan*, and a miniature tea service, with teapot, samovar, cups, and sugar bowl in a finer carved box. Svetlana was lying weakly in bed when she woke to find Maria leaning over her. She whispered that she had sold some of her things, and had bought a block of butter. She left the butter, and was gone. Svetlana did not see her again. At the end of the month, though, a young soldier called Peter came to the apartment with some millet and several pieces of sugar wrapped in paper. These, he said, were for 'Svetlana, the granddaughter of Maria'. He had been one of her students. He came back a few days later. He whispered that Maria had died, and that he had wrapped her body in a sheet he had found in her wardrobe. Svetlana's mother thought it was a piece of Dutch linen, and it pleased her. 'If Maria was to be buried in a common grave, it was important that her body be wrapped in beautiful linen.'[39] Peter promised to visit again, but he vanished.

This noble generosity was shared by Alexis Alexeevich Ukhtomsky, the professor of human and animal physiology at Leningrad State University, who was leading important research into shock and trauma. He was a near neighbour of the Magayevas, living on the 16th Line of Vasilievsky Island. When he met them on the street, he insisted on giving the girl half of his Academician's bread ration. 'Half is enough to keep an old man alive,' he said. It was not. He died in the New Year.

The post and telegrams, remarkably, continued to function, though delivering letters in the big apartment buildings was exhausting work. Natalia Petrushina recalled that it could take her two hours on dark and slippery staircases. Sometimes she went into a flat and found a body lying there. Once, she had a letter for a man she knew was waiting for a letter from his son at the front. He was sitting on the stairs. She read the letter to him. The son wrote that he was engaged in fierce fighting in an offensive. The man thanked her, and asked her to give him a hand up. 'I began to help him up and collapsed onto the stairs myself. We couldn't get up, neither he nor I. What a terrible thing! But another man appeared and he was a bit stronger and so between us we got one another up.'[40]

Mail was judged to be good for morale, and given priority. Men at the front yearned for it, though sometimes it must have broken their hearts. A thirteen-year-old girl, Tanya Bogdanova, wrote to her soldier father:

> Dear Daddy! I am writing to you . . . because I am awaiting death and because it comes most unexpectedly and very quietly. Dear Daddy, I know that it will be hard for you to hear of my death, and I most terribly don't want to die, but there is nothing to be done if that is fate. Mummy has tried very hard to keep me going and has supported me in every way she could and can. She even took bits off her bread and a little off each of the others for me, but as it was very difficult to keep it up it turns out that I have to die . . . I am writing this letter to you and crying myself, but I am very much afraid of getting upset as then my arms and legs start [to shake and tremble]. But how can I not cry when I so desperately like to live . . . I lie and every day I wait for you, and when I start dropping off to sleep you begin to appear to me . . . Well, dear Daddy, don't get very upset and take my words about death calmly. I just want to thank Mummy and my sisters and my brother for all their care and attention.[41]

From Kuibyshev, Shostakovich wrote to Isaak Glikman to say that he had moved into a separate two-roomed flat on Frunze Street. 'It has made life easier, and I am finishing the Finale of the Symphony,' he reported.

There was to have been a concert of his works, but the viola player had gone down with pneumonia so it was postponed. His work for the new branch of the Union of Soviet Composers ate into his time. He was the chairman. Semyon Chernetsky, the Red Army's chief conductor and the composer of stirring military marches, was one of his members. So, less happily, was the Czech Zdenek Nejedly, a musicologist and a Party bigot. Shostakovich was doing some four-handed playing with Lev Oborin, but he was pining in the provinces. 'I miss not only hearing orchestral music, but also just being in Moscow and Leningrad. I long to go home as soon as possible.'[42]

Home, though, had fewer and fewer people he knew. *Leningradskaya Pravda* reported the death of Lieutentant Tomilin in heavy fighting in the Nevska Debrovka area. 'Many composers knew Tomilin well,' it said. They included Shostakovich. Victor Tomilin was thirty-three, known for his children's songs and love songs set to Lermontov lyrics, 'The Circassian Woman' and 'The Sail Shows White'.* The leading Muzkomediya musicians M. Ivanov and H. Stepanov died. Shostakovich had reason to be ambivalent at the death of the composer and critic Andrei Budyakovsky the same day. Budyakovsky, who wrote a pioneering study of Tchaikovsky, had attacked Shostakovich's early works in a review of the Fifth Symphony in *Pravda* as having a 'pernicious print' of 'ostentatiousness, deliberate musical affectation and misuse of the grotesque'. He went on to praise the Fifth as 'a work of great depth, with emotional wealth and content', but he had ended with a whiff of menace. Shostakovich, he said, 'must turn boldly towards Soviet reality, he must understand it more profoundly'.

Valerian Bogdanov-Berezovsky recorded the death, and the visit he made to another composer, Malkov, who was lying ill in a tiny room.

---

* His Party hack work included the 'Song of the Hungarian Communist', on Mathias Rakosi, the singularly repellent Hungarian Stalinist.

He despaired at the impotence of the Composers' Union to help the dying. It had no money, and the Central Music Fund was exhausted. The Union had drawn three places in the *statsionar*, the feeding and medical centre at the Astoria. It was pitifully little. He had received 'many' urgent requests, he complained.

I have been especially disturbed by the call of L. Portov, who said several times in a pleading voice: 'Please arrange it for me now. If you don't, within a week it will be too late. I'll not live.' And in spite of this I could promise him only second place, together with F. Rubtsov and A. Peisin who are terribly weak, but in even worse condition is A. Rabinovich, long ill with tuberculosis, V. Deshevov, almost unable to move, and I. Miklashevsky. It is so difficult to choose.[43]

It took six weeks for Portov to die.

The staff and musicians of the Radio Committee complained bitterly that their canteen was serving only soup to staff who were on call 24 hours a day, weekends included. They were starting to fall sick. 'The canteen represents a danger for radio broadcasting,' they said. 'We don't ask for special privileges, even though we have 60 people on special rations ordered by Lensoviet. There is no reason why our canteen should not be the equivalent of the canteens at the Astoria and the Europa.' They listed other gripes. 'We have no firewood provided. Colleagues from *Leningradskaya Pravda* come to our canteen. They don't wash up, and they took all the cutlery away.'[44]

Shelling badly damaged the Muzkomediya, wrecking the building next to it. Operettas were transferred to the fine old tsarist Alexandrinsky Theatre, now known as the Pushkin. The sculptress Vera Isayeva was working by guttering oil-lamp on a statue of the 'Twentieth-century Vandal' who was shelling them. She modelled Hitler in gypsum as a slumped and ageing warrior mounted on a decrepit, broken-down donkey. At the Institute of Theatre and Music, Alexander Ossovsky, who had studied under Rimsky-Korsakov and helped Prokofiev to publish his early works, presented his research on eighteenth-century musical aesthetics. The cultured heart of the city was still beating.

An increase of 100 grams in the daily bread ration of workers, and 75 grams for others, was announced on 25 December. The effect on morale was astonishing. The streets and squares filled with those able to walk. 'Strangers embraced each other, shook hands, shouted "Hoorah!" and wept tears of the triumph of life,' Pavlov wrote. 'The light that had vanished reappeared in their eyes.'[45] This was Christmas Day for the Germans, the front lines quiet and foggy. Orthodox Russians would not celebrate it for another eleven days, and then as a festival of far less importance than Easter.

At the same time, a secret decision was made to provide privileged Party leaders and others with off-ration rusks, tea, cocoa, sugar and chocolate. The norms were life-saving: 350 grams of bread made of 50 per cent wheat, 50 grams each of meat, cereals and pasta, 31 grams of flour, 100 grams of vegetables, and a monthly allocation of 50 millilitres of grape wine, 20 grams of coffee, 18 grams of tea and fifteen eggs.

The public knew nothing of this, and their rapture with their own rations was short-lived. When, rarely, they got their full bread ration, additives now made up 60 per cent of it. Despite the Tikhvin–Ladoga route, the food situation was getting worse. The UNKVD (*Upravlenie narodnogo komissariata vnutrennikh del leningradskoi oblasti*, the city's secret police) acknowledged it. They reported to Beria that 'ration cards are not being honoured. Apart from bread [350g for workers, 200g for office staff] people are not receiving any other products.'[46] In November, adult ration cards had provided 125g (4.4oz) of tea, 150g (5.3oz) of powdered egg, 100g to 200g (3.5 to 7oz) of chocolate, and 200g (7oz) of salted tomatoes. Children's ration cards gave ten eggs,

200g (7oz) of soured cream and 100g each (3.5oz) of dried fruit, salted tomatoes and juices.

These were tiny amounts spread out over a month – the workers' chocolate ration gave less than 2 ounces a week – and there were short-falls. In December, they were gone.

Ice hung next day in intricate lacework from the trees after the fog. The big white trees in the Summer Garden seemed a set for a fairy tale. A half-moon was clear to see high in the sky at 3 p.m. For the third successive day, there was no incoming artillery fire. The Nevsky was full of people, hurrying about their errands, their coats shining with frost. An air-raid alarm sounded at 6 p.m., but no bombs fell and the all-clear followed in fifteen minutes. The moon shone brightly over the city, until the quietness was broken at 4 a.m. by the big guns of the warships on the Neva.

Deaths had now reached 2,340 a day. The registry offices in Leningrad's fifteen districts recorded 53,843 deaths for the month. Seventy-one per cent were men, and 5,671 were infants of less than twelve months. The survivors had one longed-for moment to look forward to: the New Year, traditionally the greatest celebration in the Russian calendar. The authori-ties were sensitive to that. They raided the alcohol stocks so that people might toast it. Each adult got a thimbleful of vodka, half a litre of wine and two litres of beer. Children had 200g of dried fruit and 400g of juices.

On 27 December, the day before the festivities began, the symphony orchestra gave a final concert. Eliasberg conducted Johan Svendsen's Norwegian Rhapsody No. 3 and Berlioz's Overture to *The Roman Car-nival*. The concert was broadcast to Sweden and the presenter spoke in Swedish. The orchestra was not to play again for three months, and when it was reassembled, few of its original members were still alive.

In Kuibyshev, the same day, Shostakovich finished the fourth, twenty-minute movement of his symphony.

CHAPTER 8

Noviy god

New Year

Dmitri and Nina Shostakovich gave a party in their rooms in Kuibyshev on 28 December. Flora Litvinova was there. They came up with vodka, food and even coffee – 'at that time you could still get coffee beans in Kuibyshev' – and he and Lev Oborin played the piano. They sang songs from operettas, and the Gallop from *The Bedbug*, and they danced. Shostakovich 'twirled Nina round in some sort of *pas*, and then he danced with the ballerina Mura Petrova, a lovely girl he was very fond of.' Then, suddenly, he announced in a quiet voice: 'And, d'you know, today I finally finished my Seventh.' Flora went back upstairs to her flat, and wrote in her diary: 'How happy I am! I spent the whole evening at the Shostakoviches. DD has finished his Seventh, and we will hear it soon. What a marvellous, merry evening it was.'[1]

'Ollie' Clinton and his housemates, the third secretaries from the British and American embassies, gave an epic New Year's party. They didn't think much of Kuibyshev – 'it was really just a mudhole' – so they decided to celebrate in style. They got hold of a suckling pig, a rare achievement. The party went on for a day and a half. The Bolshoi ballerinas were there, in their Sunday best, for they had lost most of their clothes. The NKVD could never be shaken off. Agents spied on the revellers. The ballerinas were all arrested when they left, and given the choice of 'contact with their American and British friends or their careers in the ballet'. The NKVD also noted that Clinton was getting front-row seats at the ballet, and put an end to it.

The strains between the 'allies' were ever present. Long columns of the Studebaker trucks that Clinton's commission was supplying passed through the streets. The Russians were told: 'Look at all the German trucks we have captured.' Clinton was arrested wearing American uniform thirteen different times. They were unimpressed by his diplomatic pass. He found one piece of paper that had a magic effect. As the NKVD started to bully him, often with drawn revolvers, he produced the menu of an official dinner he had had with Stalin. 'You better knock this off, comrades, or I'm going to have your neck,' he told them, drawing his finger across his throat. They turned pale and begged him to excuse them.

It seems no informers were present when Shostakovich greeted the New Year with the toast: 'Let's drink to this, that things don't get any better!' It had been dinned into Russians for years that life was getting better, when manifestly it was getting worse. Hence the unmistakable irony in his toast.

The weather in Leningrad on New Year's Eve was cold, minus 25 degrees Celsius, and clear. A lot of people were on the streets and ice hung from their scarves where their breath had frozen. Two or three cinemas were open unexpectedly for the holiday. They were packed. An air-raid alert sounded but the all-clear was given after twenty minutes. There was heavy shelling that night. A big glow smeared the horizon where the Second Five-Year Plan Factory in Ligovka was on fire.

In the evening, the Muzkom played *La Bayadère*. It was utterly evocative of the city's brilliant past, created in 1877 by Marius Petipa to music by Ludwig Minkus, respectively the Maître de Ballet and the Ballet Composer of the St Petersburg Imperial Theatres. It took its audience far from the dark and freezing theatre, to India, and the love triangle of the warrior Solor, his rich and loveless betrothed and his true love, Nikiya, a low-born temple dancer. The radio was claiming that the theatre was full at every performance. It was not. The matinee house was 42 per cent full, the evening 46 per cent.

There was no bravura radio performance. Small concerts were given in hospitals. The Capella choir sang in the big hospital on Fontanka 36. A diarist, N. Kotlkova, spent the day in church. 'The choir sang beautifully,' she wrote. 'This church singing slowly clears the brain of the dross of everyday life. The spirit becomes bright.' The propaganda brigade of the 389th Infantry Regiment arranged a concert with singers, guitarists and pipe players in an army club. A crowd packed into it and queued outside. German gunners dropped six shells onto them. One of them exploded inside the club. The brigade leader was among those killed. It was a sad time, too, for Zavetnoskaya, the violinist's daughter: 'Tonight Aunt Dunya died. It's very difficult to bury her. We have to move the body tomorrow on a sledge. Some women from the Philharmonia promised to do it for money.'

A party was held by the painter Ivan Bilibin in the basement shelter of the Academy of Fine Arts on the Neva Embankment. Bilibin was an elegant figure, wearing a stiff collar and bow tie with his bulky *vatnik* jacket, the man who had designed the set for Rimsky-Korsakov's *Golden Cockerel*, and whose vivid and translucent illustrations of folk tales were much loved. He was an aristocrat, and had lived in Cairo and Paris after the revolution, before the homesickness so many émigrés felt brought him home. The professors at the party were all dressed in their best. Yakov Gevirts, the dean of the architecture faculty at the Academy, was a striking figure. His friends called him 'Don Quixote' and Bilibin sketched him with his sharp black beard.

A 'speculator woman' came to trade bread. One of them was willing to give a gold bracelet for a lump of it. He deserved to be shot without trial, Gevirts said, for giving such a treasure for so little. Each had brought a bottle of wine. They had crystal glasses and Sèvres porcelain gleamed in the candlelight. As midnight approached, they all raised their glasses, and Bilibin read his 'Ode to 1942':

> During the days of wild storms
> When people are soaked with blood
> When lapis lazuli becomes black
> When thunder howls and whistles
> And overwhelms mankind
> When disasters, grief, death and weeping meet
> We greet our New Year's Eve.

In this civilized cellar, beneath a building whose glowing interiors led out to a quay on the Neva decorated with Sphinxes, there was no need to point out that Bilibin's lines were in the style of Gavrila Romanovich Drzhavin, poet and minister of Catherine the Great. They knew it. They knew, too, the irony that Catherine, who had commissioned the building, and Konstantin Thon, who so sumptuously decorated it, were German, from the same race that was now striving to obliterate both it and them. The building would survive, unlike Bilibin and Gevirts.

At the Hermitage, Glinka noticed that Fyodor and Yelena Notgaft had not been seen for several days. When they had last met, Notgaft said that he regretted not giving his paintings to the Hermitage in August or September. 'Now I don't have the strength to carry them,' he added. Glinka asked him whether he was worried about being bombed or shelled on the way. 'No, it's just not possible,' Notgaft replied. 'Look at us, look where we are going.' 'He didn't say where,' Glinka recalled. 'But it was obvious. I offered to help, but he never came back to the subject.'

He was worried enough to send someone to the Notgafts' apartment to check on them. Anastasia Botkina, Notgaft's second wife, and the curator of the Russian Museum, got there first.

The man went in, the door was open, and it was cold inside as out. Fyedor Fyedorovich and his wife lay on the sofa covered by a blanket. Botkina was hanging from the copper door handle by a rope she had taken from the curtains. It was obvious that when she came, and found them dead, she decided not to wait for her own death and killed herself. On the walls the paintings were undisturbed and there were priceless drawings in the drawers.[2]

Vera Inber saw in the New Year twice, first at the Writers' Union, where she read the first stanza of a new poem she had written. She walked home 'past the tram depot, from which no tram leaves, past the bakery which gives us so little bread, past a bus riddled with shrapnel'. German bombers were overhead in the evening. At midnight, she went to the Medical Superintendent's room. They poured out their last bottle of sour Riesling. Before they could drink it, the house telephone rang. The duty doctor reported from Casualty that he had forty bodies lying in corridors, even in the bathroom. 'So the Medical Superintendent went to Casualty, and we went to our room and bed.'[3] Elena Scriabina was in bed by 10 p.m., in a fur jacket and a large kerchief and boots. At midnight, she woke to see her husband sitting at the table in his military coat, with a tiny candle, staring into space. In front of him lay three pieces of black bread, which he had brought as a New Year's treat. Her heart burst with pity 'for him, for us, for all the others caught in this mousetrap'.[4]

Children remembered the miracles of that 31 December long after. A six-year-old embroidered a single lettuce leaf on wrapping paper and sent it to her father at the front, with her dedication: 'To Father from Galya.' But food more wonderful than a lettuce leaf was on offer. Some truckloads of mandarin oranges and cookies came in along the Ice Road. These marvels were given to children at special lunches. The Muzkom gave a special performance of *The Three Musketeers* for children, with some soup afterwards.

No such pleasures awaited a twelve-year-old girl, E. M. Gromova, and other children behind the German lines. The inhabitants of Shlisselburg were turned out of their houses early on New Year's Eve. She was separated from her mother and younger brothers and taken by train to Mga with her sister Anna. They went on by horse sled, spending the night in a barn with 35 degrees of frost. The next day they reached Tosno. Gallows stretched along Lenin Prospekt, each with bodies hanging from it. Thousands of other deportees were on the street: 'you could not see the beginning nor the end of the stream of people.' Gromova and her sister spent the night in a piggery on the outskirts. They walked on next day. 'Frost, snow, a lot of people fell from fatigue. Bodies of women and children lay on the roadside.'

The sisters were allowed to stay in a village, Barskiye Kusoni, with an old woman. SS units were billeted there. The sisters went from house to house, begging. The Germans made them clear snow from the roads, and weave straw baskets for them that they put over their boots for warmth. 'I washed the floor in their house. Usually the SS people would sit around the table, drink, behave themselves horribly.' They 'unashamedly spoiled the air'. When her sister remonstrated – 'that is not accepted in our society' – they beat her. 'One SS man tried to rape me but I jumped from a high porch and ran away.'

At the front, Simeon Putyakov was issued with a mug of beer to celebrate in his dugout. His BAO battalion was guarding the airfield at Sosnovka in the northern suburbs. The beer did little to lift his mood. 'We had a political hour. The meeting was led by the bastard Zakrutkin, that's why it was a waste of time.' It was not wise to refer to his unit's commissar as a bastard, and the remark was duly underlined. Later that day he was sent on an errand to Leningrad with a package. He went to look up a relative, Shura, at 11 Ulitsa Mira in Petrogradsky. Her room on the sixth floor had been hit by a shell, but a militiaman told him that she had survived and moved down the street to 27, though he did not find her. 'That's how I spent New Year's Day,' he confided in his diary. 'Now I'd like to go to Rachia [his home village] but the bastard Starshina didn't allow my request.' The reference to his sergeant-major was also later underlined.

On the German side of the lines, Willy Tiedemann's unit was deployed to Volkhov with an infantry division newly arrived from France. He had spent a miserable Christmas in Luga – 'the Russians are getting stronger, and have better clothes and equipment' – and now found himself back in foxholes and bunkers. 'The temperature is minus 45C,' he wrote, 'and in my company we have 50 to 60 soldiers with severe frostbite.' In September, he had started thinking about Napoleon. 'What when winter comes?' he asked. Now he knew.

More blood, much more blood, was about to be spilled at the front. Stalin sent a personal message to Kiril Meretsov. 'This is a historic order,' he wrote. 'The liberation of Leningrad, you understand yourself, is a great task. I would like the advance of the Volkhov Front not to be piecemeal in small combats. There must be a united, powerful shock on the enemy. I don't doubt that you will try to make this advance a definite, inclusive blow. I shake your hand and wish you success. Stalin.' Beneath the apparent bonhomie, the general will no doubt have detected the whiff of the executioners whom he had so narrowly avoided, and who would await him again should he use his forces – the Fourth and Fifty-Second Red Armies, and the Second Shock Army – too sparingly.

At 5 a.m. on 1 January, the first train ran on the Tikhvin–Volkhov–Voibokalo line. 'This fine New Year's present came to Leningraders from the railway reconstruction units,' Pavlov wrote.[5] They had rebuilt bridges and embankments destroyed by the Germans. From now, the truck run was short – a mere 34 miles from Voibokalo to Lake Ladoga and the Ice Road, instead of the 200 miles to Zaborye and the 120 miles to Tikhvin.

The young oboe student Ksenia Matus at the Conservatoire poured out her bitterness. The whole world was celebrating, except for Leningraders. 'Surely life should not end like this? I do not want to die like that – it's a pitiful and paltry death . . . I want to live, live and live!' She put a record of Tchaikovsky's Sixth on her gramophone. 'My heart is bleeding . . . I can hear the familiar, dear but distant sounds. I close my eyes and see the hall of the Philharmonic, the orchestra and familiar faces . . . I am slowly returning to the recent but remote past.' She heard V. I. Gensler playing the clarinet solo from the first movement. 'He is magnificent! He is standing alive in front of my eyes ... Will I ever see him play again?'*

'Do they [the evacuated Philharmonia musicians] celebrate the New Year in Novosibirsk?' she asked. 'The sounds of the waltz are fluttering. I can hear the oboe of Amosov, the flute of Trizno. The music is luring me to the light and the good but in a flash only . . . It's only the music, and besides it's being played on a record, and life is still a nightmare.'[6]

---

* Gensler survived to become a professor at the Conservatoire. The centenary of his birth was celebrated with an evening of clarinet music at the State Classical Circus on the Fontyanka in June 2012.

CHAPTER 9

Yanvar'

January 1942

Shostakovich wrote to Ivan Sollertinsky on 3 January. He expanded his notes on the symphony's second and third movements. The second 'is a scherzo, a fairly well-developed lyrical episode, recalling pleasant events and past joys. The atmosphere is of gentle sadness and reverie. Joy of life and the worship of Nature are the dominant moods of the third.' He had originally given each movement a descriptive title – 'War', 'Memories', 'The Country's Wide Expanses' and 'Victory' – but he had thought better of it. He now described the fourth movement. 'It is still much too fresh and thus I can't treat it sufficiently critically, but it seems that everything is also fine,' he told his friend. 'The first three movements, especially the first and third, have stood the test of time and still continue to please me.'[1]

A longer letter, to Glikman, followed the next day. He said he was happy in the new apartment. 'I finished my Seventh Symphony here. Apart from this landmark distinction, it boasts a bathroom, a kitchen and a lavatory.' He gave a brief history of the piece: 'The first movement lasts twenty-five minutes and was finished on 3 September 1941. The second movement lasts eight minutes and was finished on 17 September 1941. The third movement lasts seventeen minutes, finished 29 September 1941. The fourth movement lasts twenty minutes, finished 27 December 1941.' He said that those who had heard it found the first three movements 'very good'. Opinion was more divided among the few people who had seen the fourth movement.

The conductor Samuil Samosud had been drafted in by the Committee for Artistic Affairs to conduct the premiere. Shostakovich wrote again to Sollertinsky that Samosud 'thinks it is all very fine but not, in his opinion, a proper finale'. The conductor wanted to bring in a choir and soloists to sing Stalin's praises, giving it an optimistic and choral apotheosis. Shostakovich disagreed and consoled himself that Lev Oborin liked the whole work and rated it highly. He said that the symphony had already been nominated for a Stalin Prize.

It nagged him that it was to be performed in Kuibyshev, with the Bolshoi Theatre Orchestra and Samosud. 'I worry that there are not enough orchestral forces here to cope, because the symphony does call for a very large orchestra.' He said his nervous system was 'shaky': 'Sometimes at nights I don't sleep, and I weep. The tears flow thick and fast, and bitter. Nina and the children sleep in the other room, so there is nothing to prevent me giving way to my tears.' He had been to an ice-hockey match, but did not enjoy it much. The teams had no strip, and most of the time he had no idea which side a player was on. The referee failed to make things any clearer. 'You could tell who he was though,' he added, 'because he had a fur coat and felt boots and no skates on.'[2]

He fretted about conditions in Leningrad.

They were worse than he could have imagined. A letter was written in the city the same day by Olga Saharova, the sister of Alexandra Rozanova. Known as Shura, the diminutive for Alexandra, she had taught at the Conservatoire. In 1919, during the civil war, when there was no fuel to heat the building, Shura had taken young Shostakovich and his sister and her other students back to her elegant apartment at 22 Fontanka Embankment. Here, with leopardskin rugs on the floors and eighteenth-century portraits on the walls, she presided over lessons from her piano.

It was from this room, in which the family now huddled together for warmth, that Saharova wrote to family on the mainland:

Happy New Year. I hope that next year will be easier than this, and that we will meet again in easier times. But my hope is gradually fading . . . Father died on 24 December. Aunt Manya died on 19 December. Uncle Kostya died on 28 December. I was the one who had to bury them. Mother is in hospital. Aunt Shura is very sick and I'm trying my best to get her into hospital. Aunt Lyuda and Olga Grigorievna are breathing their last breaths. I'm not getting Olgushenka out of bed. She is constantly hungry and asks for food. It's very difficult to witness that. There is no electricity, no water. We can't use the toilet because the water is frozen. On 31 December, the house was hit by two shells. I don't know how we stayed alive. In this huge, cold apartment, I can feel that death is coming . . . Hugs and kisses. Olga.[3]

Twelve members of the family died, including Shura Rozanova, on 9 January, the details of whose death Shostakovich was at pains to discover. *

'The streets are full of snow up to the knees. Nobody clears it,' wrote the daughter of Rudolf Mervolf, the composer and director of instrumentation at the Conservatoire. She had just been to visit him there.

It was hard to believe I was walking on Theatre Square, Plekhanov Street or the Nevsky – moody, snowy streets, covered with snow hummocks and holes. Many people move along the streets, wrapped in many layers, exhausted, pale with grey swollen faces. Leningrad is

---

* He came up to a Leningrad acquaintance after a concert in Moscow in May 1944, 'as serious as ever, and asked me about the death of Rozanova'.

in a condition of agony. Everything is dying. Every day I see people falling on the street. Every day I see sleds with the dead covered in scraps of material. Can't find coffins. We haven't had electricity for a month. Radio hasn't worked for a few days. There's no running water almost anywhere.[4]

An eeriness was on the loose. A five-year-old, Peter Tzvetkov, lived near the city's main water treatment plant, which had taken several direct hits from bombs in October. He lived with two aunts in a large apartment building where there was only one other family left. His mother worked in a military hospital. At night, men broke into the building. Peter recalled hearing them tearing up the parquet floors and smashing furniture and doors for firewood. One day, their front door was jammed shut. His aunts could not budge it. They were trapped. If they did not get their bread ration, they would die. That evening, providentially, Peter's mother came. She found the frozen corpse of a man lying in front of the door. He was a plunderer who had died before he could force an entry.

The Muzkom was steadily losing its performers – the singer N. Zasimovich was the latest to die – but it managed a special performance of *A Wedding in Malinovka* for schoolchildren on 6 January. It was followed by games. Children who were still well enough made presents for men at the front. They embroidered handkerchiefs, made tobacco pouches from old curtains, and notebooks from wallpaper. They wrote messages on them with pieces of graphite.

The symphony orchestra diary at the Radiokom, though, recorded: 'No rehearsal. Sick people noted.' Olga Berggolts could never forget the grey mornings when Yasha Babushkin, the Radiokom art director, dictated his current reports on the state of the orchestra to his secretary. It kept dwindling. Some went away to the front, and others died. 'The first violin is dying, the drum died on his way to work, the French horn is at death's door,' he dictated, his voice hollow with despair, his face leaden and dropsical.

After a week lying in bed with his younger brother, Adick Derjugon realized that he and little Tolya would die if he did not get help. He dragged himself to his mother's factory. The manager recognized him. He gave them some soup and brought them to the children's home. He was much loved. 'Adick became a nurse to many of the children in our room,' remembered Svetlana Magayeva. He fussed over them, particularly the youngest ones, and made sure their needs were met.[5]

At least Adick had an identity, whereas some of the orphans brought to the home had no names. Their mothers had died, and their fathers were gone – to the Red Army, to the Gulag, no one knew. When they were laid on a bed, they were so far gone they could not move or make a sound. They were barely breathing. When a spoon of food touched their lips, they took into their mouths and struggled to swallow it. Not one these children survived. They died, 'soundless and nameless.'[6] A pale exhausted blonde with 'a nice warm face', Dr Lyolya, who had been sent to the children's house by the medical university, checked that they were dead. She carried a small mirror with her, and put it next to the child's nose. If it did not fog up, the child was considered dead. She and her assistant put them onto stretchers and carried them to a room where they were stored until the spring, when a detail of soldiers took them to be buried. The children knew what the room was used for, but the presence of the little corpses 'never frightened us'.[7]

Svetlana lost consciousness one morning. An assistant called Dr Lyolya. She rechecked the mirror and listened to her chest with a stethoscope. She could not find a heartbeat, but something urged her not to dispatch the girl to the room of the dead. The doctor carried her to her office. She lit a kerosene lamp to warm the air. She injected Svetlana with glucose, and continued her rounds. When she came back, Svetlana was conscious. 'I had returned from the dead,' Svetlana said. 'Dr Lyolya was so amazed and so happy that she'd check me again and again with her stethoscope to listen to my heartbeat.' The miracle did not extend to the doctor. 'She disappeared one evening. She went home and the area where she lived was shelled.' Whether she was dead or wounded, Svetlana never knew. But she never forgot the gentle doctor, and she adopted her way of dealing with stress, calming herself by drawing treble clefs on a notepad.[8]

Christmas Day fell on 7 January in the Orthodox calendar. Simeon Putyakov spent it in the guardhouse. 'I was arrested for nothing,' he wrote in his diary. 'Coming off duty, I found someone had taken my bunk. I was told to move without being told where I should go. I refused. That was all I did.' He was released at 10 p.m. He felt stronger when he washed himself with snow on his way back to his bunker. 'Nature is so good,' he wrote. 'Weather is beautiful. I enjoyed my walk. Such a pity to die, but dammit, what will be, will be . . .' Then he did something very reckless. 'I'm going to write a report for this wrongful arrest.' He was roused for reveille at six next morning. 'Immediately we went for the political hour led by the impudent creature Zakrutkin.' Then he cut timber. As he worked, he gnawed on a horse bone that soldiers from another battalion had given him. He felt the work was worthwhile – 'when I saw timber I feel I help the Motherland' – but he poured his hunger into his diary. 'I want to eat so badly. I want to eat until I'm full. I want to eat to death. They say tomorrow the ration will be increased but I don't believe it. I want to eat. The commanders promise and promise more. They say we all have equal rations. They lie. They drink beer and have better food.'

In truth, he was better off than he knew. 'Woke up with great difficulty,' the composer Portov noted. 'Rewrote only two choral preludes for the whole day.' Three days later, he wrote that he was finding it hard to continue his exercises in polyphony. 'Apathy has started to develop.

It's very bad, but there's nothing to eat. And the cold, too.' It was his last diary entry before he died.[9] Young Krukov wrote in his diary: 'Dog's life. Went to go out and found a corpse on the staircase. We live like pigs. No water. We melt snow. No light. We burn oil. Lavatory doesn't work. Nothing to eat. Recently Mama exchanged our silver-plated coffee pot for a kilo of bread and we were full for one day. We all live in the kitchen where we have a stove but we don't have wood.' His music teacher, Yekaterina Ivanova Tsesorenko, was in poor shape. A 'friend' had cut and stolen ten days' worth of food stamps from her ration book, so she was dying.

Vera Inber wrote a secret poem with a detailed description of the dying. How fast faces aged now, she wrote, the features reduced to bird-like sharpness, as if by the hand of some ominous make-up artist:

Add some ashes, mix in some lead, and a person looks like a corpse –
Teeth are revealed, the mouth stretched taut, and face waxen.
A corpse's beard (even a razor can't get rid of it)
A gait almost without a centre of gravity,
A grey hand almost without a pulse.
The onset of death. Break-up of proteins.[10]

The temperature fell to 30 below after dark on 10 January, but for Olga Berggolts this was one of the 'happiest and most sublime nights' in her life. She was with the dying Babushkin and Makogonenko, the editor of the Radiokom's literary department. They had the idea of writing a book, to be called 'This Is Radio Leningrad'. For three days now, the radio had been silent in nearly all the districts of Leningrad. The night was racked with explosions, and the literary department's hostel, where they were, seemed like a ghostly railway carriage, a big long room with the department's staff sleeping on camp-beds, sofas and armchairs. They moaned and muttered as they slept, distended or withered by hunger, in their coats and hats and felt boots.

As they toiled by the light of a bare bulb, with a newspaper for a shade, the three would-be authors were overwhelmed by a physical exhilaration that made them tremble with joy. In planning their book, they had looked back at the path their city and its people and its art had taken since the war began. They were 'full of wonder to find it so appalling and so glorious', and the joy flowed from the fact that, however ghastly the reality, the 'wonderful, natural, wise mode of human existence referred to as "peace" was bound to return'. They felt that victory and peace were only a matter of days away. And so, the three of them, hungry and weak as they were, were 'proud and happy, and felt a magic influx of strength'.

'We *are* going to live to see it, don't you think?' Yasha Babushkin said as eagerly as a child. 'I so want to live to see how it'll all be, don't you?'

He laughed shyly, with an avid, impatient pleading in his fever-bright eyes that brooked no denial.

'Of course, we'll live to see it, Yasha,' Berggolts told him. 'We *all* shall!'

She knew he wouldn't. He was bloated all over, and his skin had the greenish tinge of approaching death. He could barely climb the stairs. Yet he slept little and worked hard. She was powerless to stop him, though now, when he closed his eyes, his youth sped away from him and he looked old and tired and terribly ill. Then, without opening his eyes, he began quoting the poet Mayakovsky slowly and softly. 'We shall include broadcasts of his poems in our book,' he said. 'They mean a lot more in a situation like this. Leningrad speaks with his voice too!'

As he launched the counter-offensive by the Second Shock Army on the Volkhov, Stalin was supremely confident that the siege was about to be lifted, and the war won. It is likely that he dictated the New Year's Day editorial in *Pravda*, so masterful – and misguided – was its tone. Soviet forces had reached 'the turning point of the war', it said, and with its 'inexhaustible reserves' was on track to 'completely defeat . . . Hitlerite Germany' over the course of 1942. The secret of Soviet success lay in 'permanently operating factors'. These were 'the stability of the rear, morale', and above all, 'the quantity and quality of equipment'. All this carried far more weight than the 'temporary factors', such as surprise, on which the Germans had gambled.

The reality was bloodily different. Raw and ill-trained troops, desperately short of shells and radios and field telephones, were committed to frontal assaults against an experienced and disciplined enemy. The first objective was to storm across the frozen Volkhov, without artillery preparation, to create a bridgehead that would extend to the small towns of Myasnoi Bor and Spasskaya Polist. From there, it was planned that they would advance through the thick woods and frozen marshes to Lyuban, a small town of lumber and freight yards on the Moscow–Leningrad railway line, a little over fifty miles south-east of Leningrad. If they succeeded, they would trap a German corps in a huge encirclement, and break the siege.

They paid a terrible price to get across the river. From his observation post on the east bank, the political commissar of the 59th Independent Brigade, I. Kh. Venets, 'watched with bitterness' while the German gunners caught his men as they attacked. 'Each explosive burst left dead and wounded across the snow.' I. D. Yelokhovskiy was a platoon commander with an artillery battalion attached to the 59th. The brigade had been formed less than two months before with men drawn from towns in Saratov province. Its equipment was horse-drawn, with horses taken from local collective farms. They were unschooled, and gun-shy. The men attacked after a rail journey of nearly 750 miles, almost directly from the trains. Yelokhovskiy had been trained, scantily, on 152mm guns. The nineteen-year-old was now given command of a platoon of 45mm guns. Each gun had between 15 and 20 rounds. The standard issue for any form of attack was 200 rounds.

The infantry moved onto the river ice under continuous mortar fire. The Germans also deployed tanks. A shell exploded directly in front of the horses pulling the lead gun in Yelokhovskiy's platoon. The gun sank through the ice. 'Both the horses and all six crew went with it.' He managed to get his gun to the far bank, where he joined the surviving infantry. They were attacked by tanks. 'We managed to knock out two, but the third drove over our gun at full speed,' he wrote. 'The crew was crushed. I was sitting on the tail of the gun, which flipped over, and I flew almost six metres – which saved me. I was wounded in both hands by splinters.'

A breakthrough was achieved, but it was difficult to exploit. The forests were dense and near roadless. The ground was frozen solid to a depth of over two feet. Shovels and crowbars bounced off it. The Germans used flares to light the terrain and force the Russians constantly to seek cover lying in the snow. No twin-mounted anti-aircraft machine-gun mounts had been issued to the anti-aircraft defence platoons. 'Enemy aircraft would bomb our positions with impunity,' recollected S. I. Kochepasov, a lieutenant in the 1102nd Rifle Regiment. Resupply became steadily worse. 'Matters reached the point that only five shells were allotted for each gun. The regimental mortars generally had no shells. The commander . . . severely restricted the use of shells in case of a German attack. Indiscriminate fire from rifles and machine guns was strictly forbidden.'

Later in the month, only some seventeen men remained in the rifle companies of a battalion of the 1100th Rifle Regiment. A German tank overran a position the battalion held close to the Leningrad–Novgorod road. I. P. Ogurechnikov, a platoon commander, crawled towards a 45mm gun two hundred yards away. He hoped to use it to knock out the tank. 'The gunners had no more shells, and all around in the melting snow were piled up nothing but rifle cartridges,' he recalled. 'Over to the right, in a snowy trench, I caught sight of Sergeant Ushakov with a damaged machine gun and broken skis.' The battalion commander and Ogurechnikov's company commander had been killed.

The survivors gathered in the cellar of a hut belonging to the peacetime Forest Reserve. Next morning, the regimental commander assembled them, and organized a combat group to counter-attack. Ogurechnikov was given command. The assault group advanced 'in quick spurts': 'The Germans opened up with continuous mortar fire. I gave the order to surmount the barrage zone in one quick rush. I hadn't advanced more than two steps when I collapsed from a blow to the leg. I had been wounded by a mortar shell fragment.'

Food became as scarce as shells. 'We were saved by the fact that the artillery was horse-drawn,' the gunner Yelokhovskiy wrote: the horses were killed and eaten. Others resorted to murder and cannibalism. Vasily Yershov, a senior supply officer, recalled that regimental and battalion commanders of the 56th Rifle Division sent urgent complaints that food carriers were failing to get through to front-line units, where their men were starving. It was assumed that the men carrying the big thermos flasks of soup and hot gruel from the field kitchens were being targeted and shot by German snipers. But it was found that Russian soldiers in the front line were leaving their trenches and dugouts and ambushing the carriers, stabbing them silently to death. They gorged themselves on the contents of the thermoses before hiding the bodies and returning to their positions. Some of them went back to the murder sites later, finishing what food remained and cutting off pieces of flesh from the bodies. About twenty cases like this were found in Yershov's division over the winter.[11]

On 10 January, the Muzkomediya bowed to the inevitable. Various parts and instruments were cut from a performance of *Silva*. There were fewer and fewer performers to play them.

The next day, the last winter concert was held in Leningrad. It was a literary and artistic concert in the Capella dedicated to 'six months of the Great Patriotic War'. There were readings by poets as well as music. The musicians included the pianists Alexander Kamensky and Vladimir Sofronitsky, the composers Asafyev and Bogdanov-Berezovsky, and the Capella choir under I. Miklashevsky. Sofronitsky had studied with Shostakovich at the Conservatoire and was married to the daughter of Alexander Scriabin, whose music he played with great brilliance; he was evacuated to Moscow later in 1942.* Tickets were sold to raise funds for defence, but they didn't sell well. The audience was largely made up of sailors ordered to attend.[12] Kamensky tried to keep his hands warm with two hot bricks that he put on either side of the piano to radiate some heat.

The assistant director at the Capella, Mikhlachevsky, tried to cheer himself up by planning a list of concerts for the first quarter of the year. None took place. Bogdanov-Berezovsky had no such optimism. 'After breakfast of terrible left-over skins from a handbag maker, there was a rehearsal in the Lenin Komsomol Theatre,' he wrote. 'Physical weakness and threat of death.' On 14 January, he braved the cold and walked to a flea market. There he was offered sheet music that belonged to dead musicians. No food at all remained at Rudolf Mervolf's home. 'Our family has become very close,' his daughter felt. 'I hold my mother in special esteem. Have just read the interesting memoirs of Savina [Maria Savina, the beautiful actress at the Alexandriinsky Theatre beloved of Turgenev]. I want something light, cosy and gay to read.' Her father was less sentimental: 'The ghost of death is now present in every family. It's 5.5 degrees in my room. Tomorrow I will go again to the Conservatoire and try and get food. It's minus 30 outside and I fear I may not make it.'

---

* Some thought him the most brilliant pianist in the world, but he had only one foreign tour, to France in the 1920s, before suddenly being picked by Stalin to entertain Allied leaders at the Potsdam Conference in 1945.

It was as cold, or colder, for a further eight days in January. The mean monthly temperature for January was minus 18.7 degrees Celsius, where for many years before it had rarely fallen below minus 7.6. Drainage and piped water broke down across the city. By the end of the month, 95 per cent of standpipes were frozen. Electricity generation was at 4.3 per cent of its pre-war level. There were almost twice as many house fires as normal. The police blamed the 'careless handling of fire' by freezing people, and the lack of water to extinguish a blaze and stop it spreading.

Food was getting to Ladoga from Tikhvin, and it was crossing the lake. Responsibility for the Ice Road – it was later called 'the Road of Life', but nobody in the city yet called it that – had been given to a man equal to the task. Major-General Shilov was a logistics specialist. He saw to it that he had enough tractors, graders, wooden angle bars and logs for snow clearance and laying prefabricated wooden bridges to cross crevasses in the ice. He encouraged drivers to compete with one another to see who could make two or three round trips a day. He wrote a personal letter free of the usual verbiage. It was addressed to all 'drivers, traffic controllers, snow removers, mechanics, signallers, commanders, road workers and' – this being the Soviet Union – 'political workers'. He told them that the feeding of Leningrad 'is hanging by a hair', that its people 'have the right to demand honourable and selfless labour from you all', and that their assignment was 'of paramount national and military importance'. It inspired them.

The Ice Road was now properly monitored for patches of open water, bomb craters, and breakdowns. Each driver was made responsible for one truck, and so nursed it with care. A norm of 2.25 tons a day was fixed for each GAZ-AA truck. The road was divided into service sectors, with breakdown crews responsible for each. Four routes were established, two each way for loaded trucks, two for empties. Drivers and traffic controllers were given 50 grams of vodka a day, and enough food to work hard on, 690 grams of bread and cereals, 125 grams of meat, 40 grams of fats, 35 grams of sugar. The drivers often mixed their vodka with fats.

But the bulk of the food was not getting through to the city. It was piling up at the railhead on the western shore of the lake. Pavlov made a snapshot of food supplies on 20 January. They were desperately strained, but an improvement. Enough cereals and fat for nine days were in warehouses or in transit, sugar for thirteen, flour for twenty-one. But very little of this was in warehouses in Leningrad. Most was in the lakeside warehouses. Here were 2,202 tons of meat, with only 243 tons in the city. In flour, Leningrad had 2,106 tons and the lake warehouses 8,749 tons. The trucks were hauling 1,500 tons of supplies across the lake on days when the conditions were good. The light railway from Osinovets to Leningrad had been used by one train a day in peacetime. The need now was for seven or eight in each direction. It could not cope.

Fuel was so short that the train crews had to go into the woods to cut timber, that spluttered with damp and frost and threw off little heat. The trains could make only six or seven miles an hour with two engines hauling them. As the pressure fell after a mile or so, the engines had to stop while the crews stoked the firebox to get up more steam. The drivers, firemen and guards on the freight train were given an extra bread ration of 125 grams a day to keep them going.[13]

Thefts were another problem. Pavlov admitted that it was possible for 'certain dishonest drivers' to steal food during the trip, and to sell it on the side. Canned goods, fruit and chocolate were stolen from their boxes. Flour and cereals were poured out of sacks. The boxes were made of thin planks that broke easily. Sacks were made of patched cloth and flour often sifted out. It was difficult to pin plundering on the train crews.

Those who were caught were shot, but Pavlov thought public opinion was the best weapon. 'There were many petty thefts at first,' he wrote, 'but shame rather than fear of being shot seems to have been the factor in reducing it.'[14] Tobacco was another matter. It was considered fair game. *Makhorka*, the rough shag tobacco Russians smoked, was carried loose in sacks. In damp weather, shag absorbed moisture and became heavier, so thieves could not be caught through checking weight. No fat-proof oil-paper was available and food concentrates were wrapped in newspaper which absorbed a fifth of the fat content.

The NKVD were well aware of a slump in morale. 'We began January boldly, with joyous expectation,' a woman wrote in a typical letter that they intercepted. 'Who, whether fortune teller or prophet, could have known what terrible inhuman calamaties history had in store for us?'

It was extremely dangerous for doctors in particular to discuss starvation or to show the slightest pessimism. If the NKVD got wind of it, they could be arrested and shot for defeatism. Though medical staff themselves were starving, they were charged with keeping patients 'cheerful and believing in a better future close at hand'. They could not openly research or discuss the effects of malnutrition. All statistics on mass starvation were stamped 'SECRET' and suppressed. Doctors mentioning them could be arrested for 'divulgence'. This happened to a senior doctor early in the year. The NKVD charged him with 'being in possession of actual data on morbidity and mortality arising from starvation'. He was accused of 'using the information for anti-Soviet propaganda', a charge that carried the death penalty.[15]

Arrests were continuing apace, under the old 58-10 catch-all, by which any criticism was deemed counter-revolutionary. The scientist S. I. Voloshin was among the fresh victims. He was held in Cell 72 in the Shpalernaya Prison, the red-brick remand prison on Shpalernaya Street, where Kharms had been held, conveniently close to the interrogation chambers of the Bolshoi Dom. Lenin had also been an inmate, lodged in Cell 193 while awaiting trial in 1895. In his time, it had 317 single cells, 68 communal cells, a large and airy prison hospital and its own Church of St Alexander Nevsky. The church had been closed in 1919, the hospital no longer functioned, and cells with a single inmate were a distant dream.

Fifteen prisoners were packed into Voloshin's cell. The bunks were planks. Prisoners lay on the bunks and below them on the freezing concrete floor. At 6 a.m. each day, two guards entered to check how many had died during the night. They dragged the bodies out by their legs to the morgue. 'Some of them were still alive,' Voloshin recalled. 'They said, "Where are you dragging me? I'm alive." They were told – "Consider yourself already dead."' Three to five would survive the week. The spaces were filled up with new prisoners. 'Among them, the majority were professors, military people, historians, literary people, workers from regional committees, even people from the procurator's office.'

After he was sentenced, to twelve years, Voloshin was transferred to Cell 5. It was a large cell, where as many as a hundred people were kept after being sentenced. They were aged up to eighty, of all nationalities, 'Poles, Finns, Jews, Estonians, Russians and so on'. This was a place of horror. 'On the upper bunk lay all those who were not cannibals, and beneath them lay fifteen to twenty cannibals,' Voloshin said. 'They would crawl up during the night, and drag a person down from the upper bunk and eat him fresh. We asked the guards to take measures against the cannibals. They told us, "The more of you are eaten, the less work we have." In this cell, ten to fifteen people died every day.' He remained in Cell 5 until the end of March.[16]

Prisoners sentenced to hard labour were taken from the city across the Ice Road on their way to the distant Siberian camps. The 2nd Division of the NKVD, meticulous as ever, did some stock-taking of its prisoners on 1 January 1942. The five secret copies that were printed – one for Beria, three for his deputies,* and a file copy – recorded that 1,383,396 were being held in ITLs (*Ispravitelno-Trudovoi* Lagers: corrective labour camps). A further 353,217 were held in ITKs, labour colonies. A quarter of those held in the camps were to die of disease, hunger and overwork in 1942 – 352,560 of them. In 1941, 115,484 had died. Though Russians and Ukrainians predominated, they came from every Soviet Republic, from Poland and the former Baltic states, and from a score of foreign countries. They included five Englishmen and seventy-one Frenchmen, but no Americans: the volunteers who had come to work in Soviet industry had surrendered their passports, and were classified as Russians. The figures did not include those who were shot, and the great numbers of those deported, exiled and held in special camps.

The lack of openness engendered by the NKVD bred ignorance. Most doctors believed that dystrophy sufferers were in need of food, but not of treatment. It was only later that they learned to spot the precursors of the disease, a 'latent kind of incubation period', with symptoms that included amenorrhoea among women, the absence of menstrual periods, and a tendency to oedema and bradycardia, slowness of the heartbeat. These ravages were made worse, doctors reported to the *gorkom*, the Party's city committee, by strains that prolonged aerial and artillery bombardments put on the neurophysiological and cardiovascular systems. The NKVD knew well what was happening, and in great detail. They had produced a daily report since mid-December. It included the number of corpses in hospital mortuaries and in stacked-up cemeteries. Only

---

* Vsevolod Merkulov, a member of Beria's 'Georgian mafia', who was to be shot with his master in 1953; Vasily Chernyshov, responsible for labour; and Egorov, a survivor from Yezhov days, who had carried out mass arrests in Chechnya on the night of 31 July–1 August 1937, and the subsequent executions and deportations.

three copies of this report were made. They went daily to Zhdanov, General M. S. Khozin, the commander of the Leningrad Front, and Alexey Kuznetsov, the first secretary of the Leningrad *gorkom*. Popov had a copy on a less regular basis.

The Party bigwigs were well catered for. The *gorkom* distributed an additional two cans of preserves, 200 grams of chocolate and of butter, and two bottles of wine to the favoured in mid-January. They could not avoid seeing what was happening to others. A big concert was held for senior Party men and army officers and commissars at the Smolny. Some of the choir were near collapse during the performance, the singer P. Chekin recalled. They were held up by their elbows, and those who were fainting were steered to the back.

A concert was given in the Conservatoire director's study by students of Professor Zoya Lodsi on 16 January. They played old Russian romances. Lodsi was defiant in her diary entry: 'Death is all around but I'm not afraid of it. It's a duel, me and death, and I will not surrender.' The Writers' Union was less sanguine. It appealed for help that day to the Leningrad Front Council. It said that the situation for writers and their families was 'extraordinarily critical'. Twelve writers had starved to death in recent days, fifteen were in hospital and many more were awaiting places. The Writers' House had starving people who 'cannot walk and whom we do not have the strength to help'. The death toll was heavy and growing. 'Suffice it to say that in the family of the major Soviet poet Nikolai Tikhonov . . . six persons have died.'[17]

Some of the leading lights at the House of Radio were now so weak that the chairman of the Radiokom made an urgent plea to the city health department to save them. He asked for the urgent admission to 'the hotel hospital at the Astoria' of the leading newsreaders, N. A. Khodza, the head of children's broadcasting, Yusha Babushkin, the artistic director, and the conductor Karl Eliasberg and the pianist Nina Bronnikova, whom the conductor was to marry. Boris Asafyev was invigorated enough by the favoured rations he received to complete both his Cycle of Ten Sacred Choirs, and his memoir, *About Myself*. He signed it off: '19.1.1942. Leningrad in former Alexandrinsky Theatre, Make-up room No. 26.' The old theatre was now the Pushkin, and the elegant composer was lodging in one of the make-up rooms.

The Muzkomediya struggled through *Rose-Marie* on 17 January. The night before the company had lost the musician Vozhdeva Alymova. It gave another performance of the piece the following evening. The singer E. Voroviev was missing from the choir. He had died that day. Young Krukov noted in his diary: 'Yekaterina Ivanovna died.' She was his music teacher. Bogdanov-Berezovsky visited the composer M. Fradkin, who had been writing lyrical music for songs about the Red Army. He found him dead.

The eighteenth anniversary of Lenin's death fell on 21 January. The radio transmitted the 'Anthem of the Bolsheviks' and the 'Song of the Oath'. A performance of *A Wedding in Malinovka* was given for crews from the Baltic Fleet in the Kronstadt fortress.

The evacuations restarted, and en masse. The Military Soviet of the Leningrad decreed that 500,000 would leave the city. Priority was given to children, women, and the sick who were fit enough to travel. People went by train from the Finland Station along the little branch line to the lake shore. The trip had taken 45 minutes for the happy summer excursionists and dacha dwellers. Now the line was often blocked by snow and the ancient steam engines broke down. It sometimes took 24 hours and the dead were dumped from the train at wayside halts. A particular effort was made to get Leningrad's children out. There were 400,000 of them at the start of the war. They had suffered terribly. Of the city's hundreds of schools, only 39 stayed open throughout the siege.

The ink froze in the ink pots, the meals were a thin soup and hot water infused with pine needles, and the children's heads were 'like shrunken skulls'. But those who were at school were lucky. Their morale was kept higher by the reassuring normality of lessons and the use of their minds to learn and not mope.

On 23 January, the water supply for the big bakery on the Petrograd Side failed. A human chain passed buckets of water from the Neva to the factory. When peat supplies at the 5th hydroelectric plant ran out, only the Smolny and the bakeries had power.

Next day, the bread ration was increased to 400 grams for workers, 300 grams for office staff and 250 grams for dependants and children. The NKVD soon reported that it had made no impact: 'Except for flour, no food products reached Leningrad in the first half of January. Deliveries that began on 16 January are insufficient to meet amounts due on ration cards. The increase in the bread ration from 24 January and the limited delivery of other rationed foodstuffs did not improve the situation of the people.'[18]

The young diarist Krukov noted the effect of the Ice Road. 'Today they increased the bread ration and it looks as though more food is coming into the city. We received 1 kilo 700 grams of flour, 175 grams of butter, 600 grams of meat and 100 grams of chocolate.' But it was no cornucopia. 'This is for two people for 20 days,' he added. It meant just 42.5 grams of flour a day each for himself and his mother, and the merest morsel of meat, 15 grams. The chocolate – 2.5 grams a day – was no more than a lick. 'The radio worked a few days ago,' he said, 'but now it's dead again.'

The Radiokom chairman begged for forty litres of kerosene for heating and lighting the broadcasting studios and editorial rooms. He also put in a request to *Prodtorg*, the city supply agency, for five washstands and ten zinc washbasins, and to the director of *Soyuzplodoovoshch*, the fruit and vegetable authority, for three barrels to store drinking water. Form-filling was as onerous in war as in peace, and just as fruitless.

In Kuibyshev, Shostakovich played the piano score of the Seventh in the rooms of the harpist Vera Dulova and her husband, the singer Alexander Baturin. Lev Oborin was there, with the Armenian conductor Alexander Melik-Pashayev, who hoped he would be able to perform the symphony. The telephone rang while Shostakovich was playing. It was the Bolshoi's conductor, the former cellist Samuil Samosud. He was ringing from the flat below, and asked if he could come up to join them. Shostakovich knew him well. He had conducted the premieres of *Lady Macbeth of Mtsensk* and *The Nose*.

Samosud came up. He found the music 'shattering', and he asked if he could take the score away with him. He said he wanted to start rehearsals right away. Shostakovich thought him to be a 'supreme interpreter' of opera, who had brought a special brilliance to *Lady Macbeth*, but he also said he 'didn't have great faith in Samosud as a symphonic conductor'.[18] He preferred Yevgeny Mravinsky, the principal conductor of the Leningrad Philharmonia. But Mravinsky and his musicians were far distant in Siberia. Samosud was at hand, and he had his Bolshoi musicians with him.[19]

Flora Litvinova was present when he played the score again at home. She was overwhelmed by the theme in the first movement. At the start, it was just playful and primitive, she found, but it was gradually transformed into 'something terrifying' with a 'force capable of obliterating everything in its path'. It was mechanical and relentless, possessing unlimited and inexorable strength. Someone else found it 'ratlike'. There was great excitement when he finished playing – 'exhausted and highly agitated' – and everyone spoke at once about its theme: 'fascism, the war and victory'.

Later, after she had put her four-year-old son Pavlik to bed, she popped back downstairs to the Shostakoviches. She was alone with them.

They drank tea, and they chatted about what lay behind the symphony. 'Of course, fascism,' Shostakovich said. 'But music, real music, can never be literally tied to a theme. National Socialism is not the only form of fascism. This music is about all forms of terror, slavery, the bondage of the spirit.' Did that mean Stalinism? The self-inflicted Terror that had savaged Leningrad before the Nazi siege? Litvinova said that it did. 'Later on, when DD got used to me, and started to trust me,' she claimed, 'he told me straight out that the Seventh Symphony, and for that matter the Fifth as well, were not just about fascism, but about our system, or any form of totalitarian regime.'[20]

Did he say this? It was a prodigous risk to tell anyone that the Soviet system was comparable to the fascist one. To confide in the daughter-in-law of Stalin's former foreign minister was doubly dangerous. It was wholly out of character. Shostakovich guarded his tongue meticulously. When the regime demanded praise, he gave it. He was at pains never to criticize. It was the price of staying alive and continuing to compose. It was dangerous for the lowliest Soviet subject to speak his or her mind. For one as lofty as Shostakovich, it was suicidal. But, if he did not say what Litvinova claimed, there is little doubt that he thought it. Only a fool or a fanatic who had lived through 1930s Leningrad could think otherwise, and he was neither.

Just how dangerous the slightest indiscretion remained was clear from a young man who attached himself to the Shostakoviches. Soso Begiashvili had studied music at the Leningrad Conservatoire, but he had gone on to make a career in the administration. He was very use-ful to the family. He had contacts in food distribution, and got them extra rations. Nina Shostakovich suspected that he was an informer. Shostakovich shared her doubts. He wrote to Isaak Glikman on 4 January. He said that the young man had criticized the symphony's fourth movement – 'it does not manifest enough optimism' – and added a telling remark. 'My friend Soso Begiashvili is a marvellous person,' he wrote, 'but he can't boast of much intelligence, so one should regard his comments critically.' Glikman knew that when his friend described a 'marvellous person', he meant the exact opposite. Soso was dangerous.

Nina was able to get rid of him. She was good at that. She was a considerable character in her own right, her father an old school St Petersburg engineer, her mother an astronomer. She herself had been to ballet school, and then studied maths and physics at the Leningrad School of Physics, with fellow physicists as brilliant as the cosmologist Georgi Gamov and Lev Landau, a Nobel laureate for his theory of superfluidity. A little later, Shostakovich was plagued by a playwright who dabbled in operatic librettos. He kept pestering Shostakovich to write the music for one of them. When the composer departed briefly for Moscow, he left Nina a list of things to do. It included the request: 'Tell the librettist to f--- off.' This, rather more tactfully, Nina did.[21]

In Leningrad, the Shostakoviches had a large apartment and servants. Now, the composer crossed the courtyard with kettles to get boiling water from the boiler room. Nina cooked in a tiny communal kitchen, on a small stove that was lit only at lunchtime. But there were pleasures. They took the children for long walks along the banks of the Volga. They entertained the neighbours: 'Today, DD played *The Nose* for us. How lucky I am! What good fortune!' He read as voraciously as ever, and he amused himself by setting favourite passages to music in his head. He could quote pages – of Gogol, Pushkin, Chekhov, Zoschenko – verbatim. He cited Gogol's *Dead Souls* to Flora Litvinova. It was a passage where Chichikov changes into evening dress for a party, and as he recited it, he told her: 'Here I would use a bassoon, trumpet and drum. Then when he puts on his shirt front, having plucked two hairs from his nose, I'd use the piccolo.'[22]

He sat for Ilya Slonim most days. The room had a desk with an ink pot and chair, and a grand piano. Slonim used to store the bust under the piano when he finished for the day, until the children took some of the clay. They stuck little bits on the ends of pencils and threw them at the walls to see if they would stick. The sculptor was astonished at the composer's powers of concentration. 'He'd be working at his desk, with children running all over the room playing – and they were the sort of children you can not only see but also hear. They'd say "Papa, Papa!" "What?" "What are you doing?" "I'm writing." Long silence. "Papa, what are you writing?" "Music."[23] Slonim never saw him sit at the piano when he was working. 'He'd pace up and down, composing the music in his head.' Then he wrote it straight down at his desk. 'He liked order on his desk,' his daughter Galina recalled. 'He always had paper, ink and his ruler ready.'

He had a habit of practising five-finger exercises on his cheek as Slonim sculpted him. If they talked of books, he would illustrate a point by quoting long passages from an author. When the conversation turned to music, he dashed to the piano for emphasis. Slonim remembered him playing most of *Boris Godunov* when the talk turned to Mussorgsky, and *Petrushka* when they touched on Stravinsky.[24]

The temperature in Leningrad dropped to minus 35 degrees Celsius on 24 January, and remained there on the 25th. On these two days, 5,369 death certificates were issued by the registry offices in the city's fifteen districts. The NKVD sent the figures to Beria in Moscow, but it is impossible to know how many deaths went unregistered. Whole families, and the inhabitants of entire apartment blocks, disappeared, leaving no one to register their passing. People lost contact with relatives, friends and neighbours. The lists of the dead of 1941 and 1942 continued to grow for years afterwards, as evacuees returned and reported missing relatives and friends.[25]

There was another, dark reason why Leningrad death lists were not what they seemed. Since the mid-1930s, deaths in custody, in prison, in the camps and penal colonies, were recorded not where they happened but where the deceased had lived before arrest. So those Leningraders who died or were executed in the Gulag in 1941 and 1942 were recorded as 'Dead in Leningrad'.

Galina Salyamon had worked at the research institute of organic products and paint. The young chemist worked mainly on pharmaceuticals for the army, but also on camouflage paint. The institute closed, and she was assigned to the registry office on Zagorodny Prospekt. 'Usually they registered births, marriages, divorces and deaths,' she said. 'Now it was all deaths. But I remember one couple in their forties. They had been living together for twenty years, but they came in to register their marriage. We gave them witnesses from the staff, and from people waiting to register deaths, and we married them.'

The office was open only in daylight hours. The floor was a mottled purple. The ink pots iced up so the staff kept them on the stove, and when they cracked the official purple ink they used on the register leaked onto the floorboards. Long lines of people waited to report their dead. Galina wrote the details down in her ledger: name, family name, patronymic, year of birth, address. The 'cause of death' was always the same: 'Dystrophy, 2nd stage.' She issued them with death certificates and gave them coupons for funerals. These were now useless. Individual burials had become very rare. It was expensive to have a grave dug, and most gravediggers demanded bread, not money.

'We didn't demand the food stamps of the dead,' she said. 'They kept them. That way the dead helped those who were still alive, for a few days at least, until the stamps went out of date.' Eliza Greinert's husband died in mid-January. She described the aftermath in a letter to her children on the mainland. For a day, she sat at home in shock. Then she queued for five and a half hours to register the death. 'I went to get a coffin, but I couldn't,' she wrote. 'There were fist fights over them.' She found someone in her building who made her one for 400 grams of bread and 50 rubles.[26]

Every section of the city had a morgue. Most people would take the corpse there, show the death certificate and leave it to be taken by truck to a common grave. But, as the living grew weaker, and unable to haul sledges, more and more bodies were left where they died or dumped on the street.[27] The mortuaries of the big hospitals were taking a daily average of 566 corpses, of patients, those who died in the waiting rooms and those brought in from the streets.

Death had many harbingers as the body ran down: nausea, heart and lung disease, dropsy, scurvy, eyes that protruded from their sockets, lips that shrank back from the teeth, paper-thin skin. Children's stomachs protruded, and their heads were abnormally large above their matchstick limbs. Pubescent girls stopped menstruating. The breasts and the sex drive of adult women shrivelled.

Electricity was cut off from the Pushkin Theatre on 25 January. Israel Nazimov, a senior doctor in the 23rd Polyclinic, was told some 'scary stories' by N. N. Yumskov, the head of the local firefighting division. He had just put out a fire in the dormitories of a workers' hostel. Two of the rooms were being used as a makeshift morgue. Many dead craftsmen were in it, 'frozen in the weirdest poses, just thrown in, lots of them'. The same rooms were used by the living as a toilet. 'Excrement was everywhere,' Nazimov wrote. 'Blasphemy! But how can you blame the living, people still clinging to life, fighting for their existence?'

Hunger and a raging sense of injustice were unhinging Putyakov. The dangerous passages in his diary had grown:

I decided to do a crime and then through the revolutionary tribunal I could leave this soul-killing BAO [his airfield service battalion]. There is no other way. I may die here. If I die, these are the people responsible for my death, Sergeant-Major Arlov, assistant platoon commander Yefromov and sub-lieutenant Zakrutkin. They are not humans. They are animals in human skin . . . How soon will this vermin leave us in peace, us, so hungry, and give us a chance to eat! Bandits! They know it's so hard here and they do their best to kill us with hunger.

In his fitful sleep in his bunker in the early hours of the 25th, Putyakov's wife appeared. 'I saw Mother in my dream, slept with her, but she didn't talk to me. I didn't see the children. Life . . . life . . . let it be more beautiful soon.' It was not. At 4.35 p.m. that afternoon, he was arrested again, and for the same reason. He returned from cutting wood and found someone else in his bunk. He was told to move. He refused.

They gave me 2 days' arrest, and it was done by this bastard Zakrutkin at the request of Yefromov. Tomorrow I'll be released and I'll write a report on their wrongful action. Bastards. Soul-killers. So many people died in this company because of Sergeant-Major Arlov, Lieutenant Zakrutkin and others. They keep a prison regime.

I have to do something or I'll die. Today my face is swollen. I feel awful hunger. Half my bread ration was stolen. Bastards. God, God, when will this suffering be over? I've become not human. Before this unit 38 BAO I looked like a human being. Now it's over . . . The life of the arrested man doesn't differ from the others, but I don't want the have the title of 'arrested'. I will complain to higher authority. They are not commanders in this BAO. They are soul-killers. It would be good to eliminate these reptiles . . . They are straight-up enemies of the people. These vipers eat our rations. They take our crumbs, they don't let us wash, they keep us in a stuffy dugout and not a house. It's a wasp's nest.

Putyakov wrote his last entry on the 26th. His face was still swelling. His rations were short, but he managed to buy a ration of butter for 30 rubles. At 7 p.m., he wrote: 'I will be released at 10 p.m. In front of me, Ruvilov, the son-of-a-bitch, doesn't want to give me a little food.' He thought of his wife and children. 'In a dream I saw my Mummy, she was not tender to me and it was in an unknown place. Is she alive? I hope they don't suffer like me. OK, I'll wait for better.'[28]

He was not released at 10 p.m. At some time after 7 p.m., his diary was found, probably by Ruvilov, the sergeant in charge of the guardhouse. He was done for. Complaints, at rations, at NCOs, at living conditions, are a universal part of army life. In the Red Army, though, it was fatal to record them. The diary was handed to the NKVD, and attached to the file that was opened on him. An NKVD officer read through it, underlining passages. Putyakov was charged with 'anti-Soviet activity' and 'slander on the food supply of the Red Army' under 58-10. The diary entries were held to be sufficient evidence in themselves. The process – his arrest, interrogation in the Bolshoi Dom, death sentence, and his execution – took a little under five weeks.

The first trainload of evacuees reached Vologda on 26 January. The flow of people was steadily increasing. About 650 a day were crossing the Ice Road now. That would reach 4,283 by the end of February, and hit 7,734 in mid-March. It began to snow on the lake. The Germans used it as cover to send two companies of troops on skis across the ice from Shlisselburg to attack the road. They reached it and shot up several trucks before retreating. A special unit had to be formed to guard the road. Machine-gun positions were established along the lake by the southern shore. They were protected by blocks of ice and snow. The soldiers lay on straw mats with chemical heaters in their pockets, the freezing winds piercing them to the bone. No further raids were mounted. The Germans still bombed and shelled the road regularly, and fighters strafed the trucks with machine-gun and cannon fire. The days of their total air superiority were over, though, and Soviet fighters took a toll on them. The road service crews, too, had become adept at marking craters in the ice. They raised poles topped with fir branches next to them, which drivers could see from a distance.

The numbers leaving were not great enough to increase the rations of those who were left. As many people were dying each day in January as had died in a month before the war. A total of 126,898 deaths was registered for the month.[29] Seventy per cent were male. The city was losing its young at a terrifying rate. A fifth of those dying were under the age of twenty. The 4,365 births in January were eclipsed by the deaths of 7,267 infants of less than one year. The snowbound streets yielded 2,734 bodies.

The NKVD noted how far food deliveries in January fell below the amounts necessary to honour ration cards. Leningraders were entitled to 1,362 tons of fat over the month. The shortfall was 899 tons. They got less than half the meat ration. Only 837 tons of meat arrived, instead of the specified 1,932 tons. It was the same with confectionery, where 996 tons came over the ice in place of the 2,369 tons called for. An increase in flour deliveries, and a reduction in additives, was the only ray of hope. In Oranienbaum, the refugees who had fled there from Peterhof were dying apace as the bread ration collapsed to 100 grams.

A poem by Konstantin Simonov caught the mood with brilliant wistfulness. Published in *Pravda*, it was almost at once picked up in front newspapers. Troops clipped it out and sent it to wives and girlfriends at home. Many memorized it, and at least ten composers, notably Matvei Blanter, set it to music that echoed in dugouts and bunkers:

> Wait for me, and I'll return,
> But really wait for me.
> Wait for me when the yellow rains

Bring on melancholy;
Wait for me when the snow is driving;
Wait for me in the heat.
Wait for me when they forget about yesterday
And stop waiting for others . . .[30]

January was the worst month. Dmitri Likhachev, the tough literary scholar, had no doubt of that. 'I can't remember whether there was any bombing or shelling in January,' he wrote. 'We couldn't have cared less.' No one went to the air-raid shelter. It had been turned into a mortuary. His friends and relations were dying one after another. His wife Zina's father had a hard death all alone. Zina used to visit him and barter his belongings for food. 'He didn't want to eat, and when the desire for food is gone, it's the end.' He died with food in the sideboard. Likhachev bartered a samovar and some dresses for a few hundred grams of peas. It helped to keep them alive, though he was walking with a stick and his legs were shaky. There was a corpse on the stairs and another outside the house. 'We couldn't sleep for lack of food. One's whole body ached and itched – that was the system consuming its nerves. A mouse ran about our room in the dark, couldn't find any crumbs and died of hunger.'

In Kuibyshev, 'open' shops and restaurants for the public and 'closed' ones for the elite still existed. Shostakovich's sense of irony was tickled by a sign he saw stuck on a door. It read, he told his children with delight: 'From 1st February, the open restaurant will be closed. A closed restaurant will be opening here.'[31] In Leningrad, there was no bread at all on some days. Bogdanov-Berezovsky wrote: 'In the evening, Tamara [his wife] stood in line for eleven hours to get bread for the first time in four days.' 'For the first time we were without bread,' Krukov noted. 'Today we ate a jelly made of carpenter's glue for the first time. Mama soaked the glue in water for two days, cooked it for four hours and cooled it. Not bad with vinegar and mustard.' The Radiokom orchestra lost two more violinists, I. Lipin and M. Sergeev.[32]

Music limped on, though the Muzkomediya closed temporarily. *Leningradskaya Pravda* ran an article, 'New Works of Leningrad Composers', claiming that more than 200 songs had been written in the city since the start of the war. It mentioned Shostakovich's 'Anthem to a Leader', and the songs of Victor Tomilin, killed in the Nevsky bridgehead. Several other composers had written chamber pieces, auteur pieces on themes of liberation and war, and symphonies: Boris Asafyev's *Motherland*, G. Popov's *Alexander Nevsky*, Bogdanov-Berezovsky's *Power of War*. The piece finished with a reference to Shostakovich's Seventh.

A concert was given in late January for senior Party figures in the Regional Committee building. They sat with blank faces and expressionless eyes, glum and stony. The singer Z. Gabrielyante broke into the popular song, 'Please Smile, Sweetie', and addressed it to the front row, singing on until at last one or two smiled.[33]

CHAPTER 10

Fevral'

February 1942

The bodies of the last prisoners at the Kresty were carried by warder D. I. Sh'apov from their cells to the courtyard on 2 February, the day that Daniil Kharms died in the Shpalernaya. They had all starved.* Sh'apov had been keeping a tally of numbers all winter. By his count, 1,853 prisoners had died there since 16 October. Now there were none left.

'We had to carry out from thirty-five to forty corpses a day,' he said. 'Their clothes were a moving crust of lice. They had no name tags or numbers. All these people were off any record. We took the corpses to the yard. They were put in vans and taken somewhere. Nobody knew who these people were or where they were taken. And on 3 February I saw the doors of all the cells were left open. There was no one to lock up any more.[1]

Its emptiness was temporary. New prisoners arrived, though they, too, did not live long enough to more than half fill a wing.

It was only on 9 February that Marina Kharms went to the Shpalernaya with a piece of bread for her husband, and learned that he was dead. 'I told my friends where I was going, because I thought I might not make it, as it was a long walk,' she said.

---

* The NKVD set the bread ration for those in prison and the camps at 700 grams a day on 11 April 1942. In Leningrad, however, they frequently had no food at all. On 8 June, when the crisis was easing, the Military Council of the Leningrad Front set the ration at 400 grams a day for those within the city limits. It was 300 grams for those in the suburbs.

I walked, the sun was shining, the snow was sparkling, it had a fairy-tale beauty. I met two boys in the uniforms of cadets. One held the other, and he cried: 'Help! Help!' I kept my tiny package. I couldn't give it to them. One of the boys started to follow me, and to my horror I saw he was dying. The second cadet collapsed.

Everything was sparkling. The beauty was inhuman, with these two boys. I was very tired. I'd walked for hours. I reached the prison. In '37 and '38 there was always a great crowd near the little window where they receive packages. Now there was no one. I knocked at the window and it opened. I gave the name Yuvachiev Kharms and handed in the package. The man in the window said, 'Wait, citizen.' He closed the window. After five minutes, the window opened again, and the man said: 'Passed away, second of February.' He threw the package back at me. I was empty of feeling. I thought it would be best to give the bread to the two boys. But it was not possible to save them.[2]

Nikolai Gorshkov was keeping a diary in handmade notebooks, a particular risk given his capitalist past. He had owned a mustard factory in old St Petersburg, and the NKVD had picked him up for currency offences in 1932, but let him go. He was now the chief accountant of the Leningrad Textile Institute. He was normally careful to restrict himself to accounts of air raids and shelling and the weather. On 4 February, after the usual entry – 'northeast wind, rare foggy patches, minus 11 in evening' – he included an account of a visit by his colleague Roman Vasilievich Christoforovich to the local police station. Christoforovich was looking for a broken-down car that had vanished from the street.

Twelve women were being held at the station, all accused of cannibalism. None of them denied their guilt when Christoforovich spoke to them: 'because of hunger, they could not fight even their disgust.'

One shrunken woman told him that when her dying husband lost consciousness, she cut part of his leg off to make a stew. She fed it to her children, who were also dying, and to herself. Another said that she had been cutting up a corpse on the street when she was seen and caught. Khristoforov described them as 'middle-aged women', though they were only 'about thirty years old'. They 'are rude and uncultured, understanding that they are guilty, they cry and plead for mercy and are sure that they will be shot.'

'Everything is so awful . . . Cold and hunger everywhere, and the bodies of the dead', Gorshkov continued with reckless indiscretion. 'Today they talk a lot about robbery of food stamps and bread, from women and especially from children sent by mothers to get bread. They steal from pockets and purses, but mainly they just take by mugging them. Very often part of the ration card is left in the victim's hand . . . They talk already in the city about cannibalism and banditry openly and without shyness.' He concluded with his normal account of shelling – the Oktyabrsky district had the worst of it – but the damage was done. He was to survive the siege, but the NKVD were to find his diaries, and judge them to be 'anti-Soviet'. They did for him.*

The same day, 4 February, the Maly Operny theatre was damaged by shellfire. The big mirrors in the rehearsal room were shattered. The symphony orchestra viola player M. Dorfman died. So did the clarinetist A. Kozlov. He had always seemed one of life's survivors: a prisoner of the Germans in the First War, he had organized and directed an orchestra in the camp.

---

*The NKVD unearthed his siege diaries during a search of his apartment on 26 December 1946. They were said to show 'hostility to Soviet power'. He was sentenced to ten years in the camps under 58-10. He appealed to the Chief Prosecutor on the grounds that the diaries were personal. 'I wrote them for myself and that is clear from their style and content. I've never been an anti-Soviet person and it's obvious from my diaries.' It did not save him. He died on 8 November 1951 in a camp near Ribinsk. (*Blokadnie dnevniki i dokumenti Arkhive Bolshova Doma* (St Petersburg, 2004), pp. 14–15.)

Little Mikhail Kurayev's grandmother and his baby brother Boris also died on 4 February. Mikhail was evacuated over the ice with his mother and surviving brother later in the month. His mother remained traumatized by two sights she could never drive from her mind: a child of four or five wandering through the snowdrifts of the Maly Prospekt in December, whom she could not help, for she could barely keep her own three children alive; and a middle-aged 'woman of the intelligentsia' she had seen, motionless but alive, loaded onto a truck full of bodies.[3]

Shostakovich's status was reflected in a telephone call he made from Kuibyshev. Isaak Glikman was astonished to be summoned to the post office in Tashkent, the 'far-off, unfamiliar and mysterious city' to which the Leningrad Conservatoire had been evacuated. He waited for three hours in a musty, dimly lit room. 'Then I heard in my ear the dear familiar voice of Dmitri Dmitrievich speaking on the telephone.' Conversation was almost impossible, the words lost in the hissing and crackling of the wires. It did not matter that he could not make them out. The 'familiar, lively and inimitable intonations' of his friend's voice were enough, Glikman wrote, 'to arouse the strongest feelings in me'. It was a 'small miracle'.[4] Private long-distance telephone calls were all but unknown.

Life itself was the reward of such standing in Leningrad. Karl Eliasberg owed his to being the only man in the city who could conduct a symphony orchestra. He could not be allowed to die. The 5th of February was his red-letter day. He was brought to the *statsionar* at the Astoria, already so weak that he was pulled to the hotel on a sled. 'The temperature in the hotel is no more than 6 or 7 degrees,' he wrote. 'No running water or sewerage. The complete darkness in the corridors and rooms is oppressive. Rare oil lamps don't help. But they give food here!' The hotel had its own little musical scene. The pianist Vladimir

Sofronitsky played in its drawing room.* He had run out of tobacco, and he was happy to perform for *papiroska* cigarettes. Agrippina Vaganova, once a star of the Imperial Ballet, and creator of the 'Vaganova Method', was there with her most brilliant pupil, Olga Iordan, a dancer of fine strength and temperament. Iordan recalled the wild behaviour of some in the hotel: they stole bread, licked plates, and howled as if driven out of their minds.

Less privileged musicians shared the fate of the city. As Eliasberg and his wife moved into the Astoria, the violinist Viktor Zavetnovsky wrote to his wife on the mainland. He had no thought for the censors. 'Leningrad looks like a sterilized city of the dead,' he told her.

> Trams don't work. No light, no running water, no lavatories. Artillery shelling almost every day. Yesterday two shells hit our building. They say lots of people were killed on Zhelyabov Street and the Nevsky. Concert activity has almost stopped. It's colder than hell in the Philharmonia, but the main problem is no electricity. Rehearsals at the Radiokom are cancelled, because of the cold or no electricity. Instead of seventy musicians, only thirty turn up. Somebody's dead, somebody's sick.

His daughter, N. Zavetnovskaya, was still with him. She was also a musician. 'We didn't receive even the rations printed on our food stamps,' she added. 'Many people have yellow, swollen faces. I was a young woman, and in two weeks I look an old hag, and my mouth is puckered.' She complained angrily that the newspapers were hiding the truth and saying that all was fine in the city. They wanted to take press

---

* Sofronitsky was married to Alexander Scriabin's daughter, and taught at the Conservatoire. Stalin chose him to play for Churchill and Truman at the Potsdam Conference at the end of the war. As with Shostakovich and the Seventh, Sofronitsky supplied a cultured veneer to Soviet brutality.

photographs of the Radio Orchestra, she said, as if it were playing a normal concert. But they couldn't, because there was no electricity and few musicians. Fifteen or seventeen people – she wasn't sure which – had died in the Andreev Folk Instruments orchestra, once much admired by the balalaika-loving Tsar Nicholas II. She worried for her father. He came back once 'in a terrible state' when his bread was stolen from him at the bakery.

It was strictly forbidden for any worker who ate in a canteen, like the Radio staff, to take rations home to their families. Staff were searched when they left the workplace, though some factory directors turned a blind eye. No leave was granted to soldiers serving at the front to visit their families a few miles away. Margaret Markova was eleven. Her mother's abdomen had become so distended that she could not sit up to feed her one-year-old son. His eyes were closed and he was silent. Her father was in a division stationed on the other side of the Neva. Margaret was too weak to walk as far as a bridge, so she crossed the river on the ice. She found some soldiers who took her to her father. He and his comrades gave her bread and salted fish, and her father carried her in his arms to the Neva. It was against orders for him to cross it. The little girl went back alone, and fed her mother and baby brother.[5]

A little before midnight on 3 February, two secret police officers, one from the regular Leningrad NKVD, and the other from the NKVD 3rd Special Unit, had climbed 150 stairs up to the fifth floor of House 44. It was a granite tsarist block of solid bourgeois respectability and classical facade on the 11th Line on Vasilievsky Island. The staircase was broad, with a wrought iron and wood handrail, useful to cling to on the long ascent to the top of the building. They knocked on the door of apartment 14. It was opened by Boris Izvekov, the professor of geophysics at Leningrad Technical University. He was a strikingly handsome and intelligent man in his early fifties.

Unknown to him, a mathematics professor, V. S. Ignatovich, had been picked up earlier. In a 'confession' he made under interrogation, he had named Izvekov as an 'active participant' in a German spy group. He added that Izvekov, 'having ancestors of higher social status', had created an attitude of poisonous mistrust of the Party and Soviet government among his scientific colleagues.

Terror was breaking over the city afresh.

The officers arrested Izvekov and searched the apartment, taking the usual haul of letters, notebooks and photographs. Then they drove him through the dark and ghostly beauty of the city. The NKVD never lacked for petrol and cars. They passed the elegant facades and colour-washed stucco of the Academy of Sciences, the University, and Pushkin House, places where the finest minds had roamed, and across the Dvortsovaya Bridge to turn left onto the Neva embankment. The pedimented windows of the Winter Palace faced the river in long columns as faultless as the regiments of the departed tsars, giving way at last to the soft and open spaces of the Summer Garden. Here they turned right, away from the river, for the Liteiny Prospekt and the Bolshoi Dom. It was past midnight when they arrived. The arrest document was dated 4 February.

It was filled in by Lieutenant Kruzkhov, who signed himself 'Senior Investigator, NKVD Leningrad District'[6]. It was identical to the pre-war forms. NKVD methods did not change just because the Germans were a few miles away on the Pulkovo road. It recorded that Izvekov, Boris Ivanovich, was born in Kaluga in 1891. He was an ethnic Russian. His internal passport, 5PS 631481, confirmed his right to live in the city. His occupation: 'Professor of Leningrad Technical University, head of the geophysics department.' His social origins: 'Son of a priest.' That was not good: it backed up Professor Ignatovich's denunciation of him as a class enemy. He was married, to Olga Alexandrovna, and had a twelve-year-old daughter, Tatiana. His education rated as 'highest'. He had graduated in 1914 from St Petersburg University (though this was entered as 'Leningrad State University'). He had received his doctorate of geophysical science in 1930–31. He had not been arrested previously. He had been conscripted into the tsarist army, as an engineer, but he was otherwise militarily clean: 'No service in White Army.' At least for the moment, he was politically clean, too. Party: 'Non-Party.' Participation in opposition groups and movements: 'None.'

What the form ignored, of course, was the type of man he was. His daughter was in Anufriyevka, a village in Vologodskaya, where he had sent her with her mother before the siege. She remembers him still[7]. He named her Tatiana after the Pushkin heroine, and his pet name for her was Malik. He loved to recite Pushkin, Lermontov, Tyutchev. He liked poetry and history. He worked at the observatory in Pulkovo – he had met his wife there – and he spent every moment he was free with Tatiana. He took her to the theatre, and every Sunday to a museum. On their last summer together, in 1940, at their dacha in Anufriyevka, he bought her a little boat. 'We went swimming and sailing, we picked mushrooms and berries . . . Before I fell asleep, he'd come to my room and ask: "Malik, are you cosy in your little nest?" And we prayed every night.'[8] He had stayed in the city to safeguard his fine collection of mainly Russian artists. He was, in his manners and his blending of science with artistry, a *beau idéal* of the city's long tradition.

This, then, was the man Lieutenant Kruzkhov set out to break. The first interrogation began at 10.00 p.m. on 6 February. It lasted until 11.15. Kruzkhov got nowhere. His account of 75 minutes of repetitive and ill-tempered questions and stonewall answers was brief:

Kruzkhov: Tell us about your counter-revolutionary activities.

Izvekov: I am not engaged in counter-revolutionary activities.

Kruzkhov: You are hiding facts about your counter-revolutionary activities and your colleagues' names in front of your interrogator. We advise you to give us the evidence.

Izvekov: I am telling you again. I'm not engaged in counter-revolutionary activities. Moreover, I have no information about any such activity or of people engaged in it.

In Kuibyshev, Shostakovich calmed his nerves with drink and chain-smoking. He always broke for a beer at 1 p.m. when he was sitting for Ilya Slonim. It didn't take much to make him drunk. After his second drink he would start looking round for an empty bed. Tanya Litvinova once saw him very drunk. He was trying to mend a clock on the top of the piano with a hammer.[9] She found his humour 'deadpan and cruel' when he was in his cups. He parodied the sullen and long-winded Soviet-speak of bureaucrats with brilliance. This was given an edge by his fear of them. He conquered this now by going to the State Committee for the Arts on Slonim's behalf. He persuaded them not to draft the sculptor into the army, arguing that he should be exempt because he was working on his bust.

He fretted in a letter to Glikman on 6 February. 'Things are not good with me. Day and night I think of my family and loved ones, whom I had to leave behind.' He worried that money he was sending to his mother was not getting through. He seldom had news of them, but he had some idea of how bad things were, and he knew that his wife's niece Allochka was ill with malnutrition. 'There are no cats and dogs left,' he wrote, whereas in Kuibyshev he had acquired a gingery-coloured dog that wandered in off the street. 'We hadn't the heart to shoo him away, so now he lives with us. The children call him Ginger. He seems to like his name.' As to his symphony, 'the saga continues'. Rehearsals were in full swing in the Philharmonia Hall, close to his rooms on Frunze Street. It was a handsome art deco building that had started life as a theatre-circus in 1907.

The first two movements had their first full run-through on 5 February. Shostakovich and Samosud had their differences. The conductor tried to persuade Shostakovich to rewrite the finale to include soloists and a chorus singing the praises of Stalin. 'There are a whole host of other valuable remarks about the fourth movement', Shostakovich wrote to Glikman, knowing that his friend would see the sarcasm in 'valuable'. 'I take them into consideration, but not into practice, because as far as I am concerned there is no need for a choir and soloists in this movement, and the optimism is entirely sufficient.' For now, though, the composer felt the Bolshoi was rehearsing it 'outstandingly well'. The orchestral play-through 'made a great impression on me and for half a day I rejoiced over my baby'.[10]

The musicians were aware of the political and emotional significance of creating a symphony in the midst of war. It gave the lie to the old axiom: 'When cannons fire, the Muses remain silent.' Flora Litvinova watched from the stalls as they worked their way through the piece. Shostakovich took time to talk to a flautist, and a flock of Bolshoi ballerinas in tricots came running out of a rehearsal room and fluttered through the hall like birds.[11] The conductor Alexander Gauk described how Shostakovich sat calmly in the hall during rehearsals, never shouting or making a display, and careful to make any points in a delicate way. Only when he found a mistake in the written music would he come up onto the podium, and quietly wait for a pause to point out the mistake.

'He was always extremely modest,' Gaul found. Many composers could learn from him, notably 'those who demand from the first rehearsal that the conductor and orchestra play the work as if at a concert'. He realized that a rehearsal was not a performance. It was a way to learn a new work. He also had an 'incredible musical ear'. Gaul recollected once seeing a pained expression on his face during a rehearsal. 'Alexander Vasilievich,' Shostakovich told Gaul when he asked what was wrong, 'the second violinist on the third podium of first violinists played a black note instead of a white.' In a full-scale symphony orchestra, he could detect a single violinist playing a half-note higher.[12]

Shostakovich went to every rehearsal. Nina and the children were sometimes in the director's box. Samosud asked them what they had come to hear. 'Our symphony,' they said proudly. During the first movement, little Maxim once suddenly started waving his arms and conducting with 'such desperate energy' that Nina had to take him home.[13] The children loved the first movement. 'They often beg their father to play it for them,' Nina wrote, 'and they climb onto the lid of the grand piano and sit as quiet as mice.'

The intensity of the silence in Leningrad was broken only by the rhythm of the metronome. 'A magnificent tragic silence . . . as if you have been lowered deep into a well, and the shaft filled up with earth,' young Elena Martilla wrote in her diary. 'And like a simple distant and weak but living pulsation: tick! . . . tick! . . . like the pulse of a fatally ill patient in the silence of a ward, the radio reverberates in the heart of those awaiting a miracle – recovery – no, death. Hopes. Valia Emolaeva is dead. The neighbours in apartment 74 are dead. Fima Efimov's son and many more are dead. Especially men and boys.'[14]

On 6 February, the Radio Committee sent a report to the Party City Committee about the critical condition of the symphony orchestra and the choir. The Germans dropped leaflets addressed 'To the Russian People'. They quoted the city's 'genius prophet and great writer', Dostoevsky: 'What has moved the Jews down the ages? Pitilessness and their thirst for sweat and blood.' The leaflets asked ordinary Russians what would happen if the Jews took control. 'Would they let you pray openly among them? You would be their slaves, and they would flay you alive until the final extermination, as they did in their ancient history.' As to the war, the Jews had started it. 'It's their war, for their own ends. Mountains of Russian corpses, rivers of Russian blood. Anything to protect themselves . . . Why has their lying propaganda made you blind and drugged? Look around you. How many Jews do you see who are suffering like you, giving up their lives like you . . . ? Why do they sit in the rear?'

The greatest numbers of deaths of the siege were registered on 6 and 7 February – 4,719 and 4,720. The severe frosts continued, with a mean air temperature of minus 12.4 degrees Celsius. The norm was minus 7.7. Coal stocks were completely exhausted early in the month. Power generation was down to 2.4 per cent of the pre-war level.

The rector of St Nicholas Cathedral, Nikolai Lomakin, went to his church for the first time for a month on 7 February. Hunger had left him too spent to make the long walk from his home, but he made a special effort for this Remembrance Day, set aside for the remembrance of the dead before the beginning of Lent. 'I was astounded,' he was to tell the Nuremberg tribunal. 'The church was surrounded by dead bodies, some of them blocking the entrance. These piles each contained thirty to a hundred bodies . . . I witnessed people, exhausted from starvation who in their desire to bring the bodies of their relatives to the cemetery, would fall down and die on the spot beside the bodies.'[15]

Seven members of the orchestra had died over the past few days. Sixteen more were seriously ill and exhausted. A further dozen were at least temporarily very weak. Four members of the choir had died. Fifteen were sick and exhausted, and five were very weak. The orchestra was unable to work properly. It still had 25 to 30 musicians who could perform, but 'this group too is beginning to melt'. The Committee wanted to evacuate them from the city to the mainland. Any performances they were able to give from there, it suggested, could be transmitted back to Leningrad. There was a crisis, too, with the Radio's repertoire of recorded music. All its gramophone records and film clips had been sent for safekeeping to the Lenfilm studios in Pushkin in the summer. They were lost to the Germans. An urgent plea went out to VKPD Broadcasting, the All-Soviet Party organ for radio in Moscow: 'We need recordings of all new works, all operas and symphonies, and soundtracks from musical films . . . If it is difficult to deliver them, please send them to Tikhvin.'[16]

The composer L. Portov died on 7 February, as he had foreseen when he had begged Bogdanov-Berezovsky for a place at the Astoria in December. The journalist Nikolai Markevich, who was staying at the hotel, shuddered at its atmosphere – 'cold, dark, inhabited by ghosts . . . in the dark corridors rarely appears a figure, lighting his way with a "bat", a hand-generator flashlight or a simple match' – but its food might have saved Portov. The Muzkomedia choir singer A. Voronina died the same day; so did Ivan Bilibin. Yakov Gevirts, who had partied with Bilibin from crystal glasses in the basement of the Academy of Fine Arts on New Year's Eve, lasted a little longer.

Professor Mervolf's son did not think his father would last much longer. 'Papa looks like a living corpse, lying all day in bed in his suit and coat thinking only about food. He has become very bad in the last few days.' He added a little later: 'For the third day we had only a scrap of bread. Yesterday Papa played the piano, Chopin, Glinka. It became so sad.'

Alla Shelest and her mother set off to find the man whose life her father had saved, to see if he would honour his promise and help them. They crossed the Liteiny and found him in an army warehouse on Ryleev Street. 'He was well-fed, his figure was full, which was very unusual to see, and very polite. He gave us half a kilo of cranberries. It was like having wings.' When they got back to their basement in the Engineers' Castle, they counted the hours before they saw him again. 'It was so important that before we went, we opened a volume of Pushkin,' she later remembered, 'and I put my finger on a sentence at random. It was a sort of prophecy. And I read: "He may run away." In spite of our tragic situation, Mama and I laughed and laughed. But when we went back, he wasn't there. We spotted him on the Liteiny on our way back. He recognized us and crossed the street to the other side. Maybe he thought, "I've already saved their lives once." . . .'[17]

February the 10th was the 105th anniversary of Pushkin's death. The Party had claimed the great poet as a pre-Bolshevik pioneer of social realism, and the Radio transmitted readings of his lyrics as a tribute.

Snipers were active as the Second Shock Army, exhausted, but now within twenty-five miles of troops from the Leningrad Front, struggled on to break the siege. The Russians made exceptional snipers. The ace on the Leningrad front, Theodore Smolyachkov, had 125 kills before he was himself killed in mid-January. A number of snipers were women. Olga Kolnitskaya, who had completed a sniper's course in 1934, had already killed thirty Germans in the southern suburbs.

A Russian rifle battalion south of Lyuban was tormented by a German sniper 500 yards away across open ground. The brigade commissar, I. Kh. Venets, lost one of the officers from his political section to the sniper. He found a young Siberian in a ski battalion whose father had taken him hunting for squirrels from childhood, teaching him to aim directly for the eyes, so as not to damage the pelts. He agreed to hunt for the German, and selected a partner for himself. Snipers often worked in pairs, with one using the breadth of vision provided by field-glasses to spot for the rifleman with his telescopic sight, and diverting attention away from him. The lad was supplied with a Mosin-Nugent rifle, an old but highly accurate weapon dating from tsarist days, with a four-power scope.

His first kill was a 'girl-traitor', who had been given a megaphone by the Germans to appeal to the Russians to cross over to the enemy. Both snipers used dummies and other tricks of the trade – using a mirror to reflect a glint of sunlight, disturbing the snow to suggest movement, having their partner reveal himself for a moment – to try to get their target to fire and so betray his position. After an 'exhausting hunt', Venets said, 'our modest Siberian killed the German'.[18]

Over the first ten days (or 'dekada') of February, 37,296 deaths were recorded in Leningrad. There was then an improvement in logistics, however, on the far side of the lake. A new branch line was built, in snow and ice and under constant shellfire, from Voibokalo to Kabona. Freight trains now ran right up to the lake. The first of these made the twenty-mile trip on 10 February. Kabona, a quiet lakeside village, now echoed to locomotive whistles, and its fishermen's cabins were lost among warehouses, sheds, dumps, and mountains of sacks of cereals, flour and grain. Trucks left the railhead to cross the ice in a stream.[19]

The bread ration was increased next day. Workers were to have 500 grams, office staff 400 grams, and children and dependants 300 grams. Canteens were allowed to provide cereal dishes for half a ration coupon, instead of one. The increase looked better on paper than on the plate. This was still a starvation level. An inquisitive academic took the portion of soup served to him in the canteen of the Scientists' Club to his laboratory. He found it had 8.1 grams of cereal instead of the 25 grams laid down. Bread apart, other rations had minimal increases or fell. The flour per head actually supplied fell from 11 grams (a little over a third of an ounce) in January to 4 grams (a little over a tenth of an ounce).

Those with remaining valuables traded them to live. 'Mama exchanged our crystal decanters and glasses and shot glasses, everything valued at 300 rubles, with Mariya Abramova,' young Krukov wrote, 'for 1½ kilos of carpenter's glue.' Bogdanov-Berezovsky, queuing up before dawn to stand a chance of getting bread, also got a new supply of glue. 'Dreamed of my violin concerto, which is now the symbol of my new life. Hope to come back to it in the spring.' He started work on a new opera, *Leningradtsi*.

Georgi Kniazev, the historian and archivist of the Academy of Sciences, was crippled. He depended on his wife to push his wheelchair. She was weakening, but took a dress to barter on the market. He was frightened when she went. It was windy, and he doubted that she could withstand the cold. 'I have taken off my belt, held in readiness for a long time,' he wrote in his diary. There was a stout hook in the ceiling of his room. 'Will it ever be put to use? If anything happens to my wife, it might well be.' He had measured the drop. She came back, though, with a hundred grams of bread. She was happy. Her eyes regained their sparkle. He was glad she felt better, but sad that he knew what their relationship, their mood, their hopes depended on. 'Upon 100 grams of bread!'

He liked to escape into the distant past, into Hittite culture, but he was also a sharp observer of the present. He noted the odd plump person, like a neighbour who had access to bread, cereals and pork skins through her husband, and who would sell a handful of millet and a few pieces of sugar for a well-kept carpet or an antique lamp. 'She is not feeling the pinch,' he wrote. 'Amongst us who are starving in Leningrad, there are some well-fed people too!'[20] Now that individual graves were no longer dug, people had taken to warning each other: 'Look out, or you'll end up in a trench.' In the streets, he saw how some women still struggled to look chic. They allowed baggy oriental trousers in vivid reds, browns and light blue to peep out from under their skirts. Many, though, 'simply go around without skirts, with just thick knickers as their lower garment'.

Air raids were rare, but Alla Shelest was caught out by the constant artillery fire on 12 February. She had left her room in the Engineering Castle to get food stamps from the Kirov theatre when the shelling caught her on the corner of Engineernaya and Sadovaya Streets. Few people were out on the street, and they kept close to the houses on the safe side of the street and lay down on the pavement. 'I looked at them, and thought, "My God! To lie there until they kill you!" I turned and started to walk back towards the Castle. They shouted at me: "Get down! Get down, you crazy!" I thought, it's better to be crazy than to lie down and wait to be killed. If a shell finds me, it's meant to. If not, not.' She had just reached the front gate of the Castle when a shell exploded next to her. 'I was blown onto a pile of logs and fainted. I don't know how long I stayed there. When I came to, I understood what had happened. I started to shake and ran home to Mama. From then on, I could hardly step outside the Castle in daylight. It was too much shock.'

Far, far away in Siberia, Tamara Petkevich's father Vladislav died. The scores of thousands of Leningrad *zeks* in the camps were dying in wartime as they had in peace. The cause of death was given as 'liver abscess'. The section of the form giving the place of death – the city, village or settlement – was left blank. The certificate itself, with its official number, PB293408, was not sent to his daughter Tamara until 1956.*

Shostakovich wrote an article for *Izvestiya* that was published in Moscow on 13 February. It was the first time that he mentioned his desire for his new symphony to be played in Leningrad. 'My dream is that my Seventh Symphony will be performed before long in the beloved city that inspired me to create it.' Three days later *Pravda* published a piece by Aleksei Tolstoy, 'At a Rehearsal of Shostakovich's Seventh Symphony'. It was vivid, capturing the colour and power of the opening movement. He called Shostakovich 'the new Dante', and stressed that the symphony was a deeply patriotic work that was studded with the 'raging Russian conscience' of the composer. 'Hitler did not scare Shostakovich,' Tolstoy thundered. 'Shostakovich is a Russian man, and that means an

---

* Even then, the site of his camp and of the mass grave into which he was flung remained a state secret. (Tamara Petkevich, *Memoir of a Gulag Actress* (DeKalb, IL: Northern Illinois University Press, 2010), p. 50.)

angry man, and if you get him really angry, he is capable of fantastic feats.' Stalin will have read this – he scrutinized *Pravda* with care – and Tolstoy's description of the Seventh made a precise fit with his use of Motherland and Russian nationalism as the ideological foundations of the war effort. The symphony and its composer had the makings of a propaganda coup within them.

Reading the *Pravda* piece in Tashkent, Isaak Glikman recalled Shostakovich playing the piano version of the movement. In his mind's eye, he saw the splendour of the orchestral colours and the invasion theme, and imagined Shostakovich himself, 'sitting unobstrusively in his usual place in the fifth or sixth row of the stalls, listening intently to the rehearsal but not intefering in the work of the conductor . . . I seemed to see his face standing out in sharp relief from all around him, deep in reflection at the music he was hearing.'[21]

Pieces in *Time* and the *New York Times* showed the immense value the symphony might have with Americans, long so wary of the Soviets. *Time* despised Bolshevism, but it warmed to Leningraders. They, the magazine said, knew 'solemn, youthful Dmitri Shostakovich' as 'a firefighter, a trench digger, an embattled citizen like themselves'. The rest of the world thought of him as the only living composer, 'aside from Finland's Jean Sibelius', who could make history writing a new symphony. And now, it said, 'history was again on the make [with] Shostakovich's long-heralded Symphony Number Seven'. The *New York Times* man in Moscow, Ralph Parker, interviewed the composer 'in a shabby Kuibyshev bedroom'. Shostakovich sat pulling cigarettes to pieces, and nervously stirring a cup of tea, slight and 'extraordinarily youthful-looking'. He spoke passionately of the work 'to which he was then adding the final bars'. He said he had written it to illustrate how war affects 'ordinary, good, quiet people'.

He sketched the movements. The first, marked allegro moderato, was a calm, lyrical exposition intended to show their simple, happy existence. Then, the main theme, 'inspired by the transformation of these ordinary people into heroes' by the war. 'This builds into a requiem for those who are perishing in the performance of their duty . . . I introduce something very intimate, like a mother's tears over her lost children. It is tragic but it finally becomes transparently clear.'

In the scherzo and adagio movements, he told the American, 'I am moved by the idea that war doesn't necessarily mean destruction of cultural values. The fourth movement can be described by one word – victory. My idea of victory isn't something brutal . . . It's the victory of light over darkness, of humanity over barbarism, of reason over reaction.'

This cleansed the image of the Soviets – the secret police, the slave labour camps, the execution cellars, the butchery and the Terror – in the most brilliant fashion. It spoke not of tortured thinkers and artists, but of the preservation of cultural values. Russians and Americans were the forces of light and humanity. The symphony swept them together, true Allies in the struggle against blackness and barbarity. The *Times*'s headline was irresistible: 'Shostakovich, Composer, Explains His Symphony of Plain Man in War'. The strapline gave the story romance and vigour: 'People's Heroism and Victory of "Light Over Darkness" Among Concepts in Work, Written in Siege and Now in Rehearsal.'

The piece confirmed its title, too. In his 'Domestic Symphony', Shostakovich said, Richard Strauss satirized people, taking negative types and poking bitter fun at them. He didn't want to laugh at silly or commonplace people. 'I always try to make myself as widely understood as possible,' he added. He had written it for, and dedicated it to, 'the ordinary citizen of Leningrad'.

Leningrad, though, was in no position to stage its symphony. The Radio Committee was struggling to get eighteen ailing members of its orchestra, and twenty from the choir, into feeding stations before they died. The wife of the violinist Zavetnovsky had written to her daughter on the mainland: 'Many in the orchestra are dead or weak and very exhausted and still dying. Father is very weak.' Now she had better news. He was given an Academician's ration. That included, at least in principle, 2 kilos of meat, 2 kilos of flour, a kilo each of buckwheat, wheat grain, beans and sugar, and half a kilo of butter. Such of these life-savers as in practice existed were given to him in the elegant Style Moderne surrounds of the famous old Yeliseyevski delicatessen on the Nevsky.

For many, like the choir singer P. Shokorov, who died on the 13th, it was too late. That day, soldiers from anti-aircraft units were drafted in to deal with the accumulation of corpses. They collected 6,537 bodies and buried them in the Serafimovskoe, Bogoslovskoye and Preobraz-henskoye cemeteries, and on Decembrist Island. Dmitri Likhachov, the great scholar of Old Russian language, made his children use the back stairs when they went out of their apartment. Dead bodies lay on the main stairs. He thought the children were 'heroes'. They never talked about food, and were never naughty, but he was saddened that they were prematurely adult, so slow-moving and serious, sitting close to the *burzhuika* warming their hands. Real adults, or at least his colleagues at Pushkin House, the Literary Institute, disgusted him. At their canteen, they 'ate in the dark and snatched one another's bread, potatoes, coupons'.[22]

The Volkhova cemetery was 'awash with corpses', and it was clear the others could no longer cope. The director of the Funeral Trust, Koshman, was a convenient scapegoat. He was charged with criminal negligence in burials and sentenced under 16-58 paragraph 14 of the RSFSR criminal code. It was decided to bury the bodies in a single cemetery at Piskarevskoye in the north of the city. Mass graves were blasted from the frozen soil with explosives and then dug out by soldiers. On one day, 20 February, 10,000 bodies were buried there. The gravediggers had a grim sense of humour, fuelled by their vodka ration. On the paths leading to fresh communal graves, they stood a tall corpse with a cigarette sticking out of his mouth. His frozen arm pointed the way.[23]

The Germans were dying, too, if in smaller numbers. On 14 February, the Russians overran a bunker near Pushkin held by men from the SS Police Division. Albert Hassdenteufel was among the dead, and the Russians found a diary on his body. He had written the SS motto on the title page, '*Meine Ehre heißt Treue*' ('My Honour is called Loyalty'), in painstaking Gothic script. Like so many, Hassdenteufel's journey to oblivion on the Neva had begun in Paris. His unit had sung as the men marched to the train that took them back over the German border to Osnabrück and Hanover and on to Berlin. They had a 'rousing reception' in Berlin, he wrote, and washed and had coffee and a meal before leaving for the east early in the morning of 2 January. The winter landscape, he said, began at Kustrin and it stayed with them as they passed though Elbing and Königsberg. They halted at Insterburg. 'We got acquainted with East Prussian beer here,' he noted, in this ancient bastion of the Teutonic knights.*

Hassdentenfel's luck was in. He was transferred to a hospital train, with clean beds and even some pretty nurses to flirt with. The countryside was forbidding when they scraped the frost from the carriage windows to look out – 'a bleak and cheerless picture of snowbound forests and fields' with a village huddled with cold every ten miles or so – but it was warm and cosy on the train and they anticipated the bliss of comfortable beds. 'We sang our throats sore. 10 p.m. lights out.

---

* Insterburg was to lose its name and its Germanic people, and re-emerge as Soviet Chernyakhovsk. Elbing is likewise now the Polish city of Eblag, and Königsberg now Kaliningrad in Russia.

Sleep.' The luxury was over when they reached Pskov as it grew dark on 9 January. The cold was terrible. They were ordered to march to a new train at 2 a.m. 'We couldn't stand. We started bellowing and jumping to get warm.' It took another three days in trains and trucks to get to their new position.

He found he had drawn a relatively quiet sector, in the line near Pushkin (the old Tsarskoye Selo, the Tsar's Village, where the Romanovs had their summer palaces). Lice, wood smoke and the shortage of cigarettes were his main gripes in his ten-man bunker. The Russians were 500 yards away. For the moment, they were quiet. The small stove produced more smoke than heat. He had one hour on, and two hours off, guard duty, watching for enemy movement while machine-gun fire flickered back and forth. A shot whistled past his head as he ate breakfast on 15 January. 'The culprit was a comrade. He shot off his finger by mistake.' Self-inflicted wounds were a German as well as a Russian problem. Later in the day the Russians attacked but were driven off by heavy artillery fire. On 24 January, the unit marched in 42 degrees of frost to one of the Pushkin palaces. Their uniforms went into an oven at 120 degrees, and the lice were killed off. 'Then we went to the bath-house. Hot water!' A red-letter day followed on the 25th: 'Today we had warm winter clothes, a whole fur coat, really warm.'

The next day, he loaded his sledge, wrapped himself in his new clothes, and moved to a new dugout. 'It's better than the last one, the stove is better. We sleep on old mattresses. As a reward for this comfort, we have the enemy close by and bullets whistle past our ears. But our guns are firing back, and they aren't shooting peas.' Snow and blizzards gave way to a hard frost on 31 January and a brilliant moon that lit the night like day. 'Not enough to eat, to sleep, to smoke' – the soldier's eternal gripes – but Hassdenteufel wrote of growing fear on 3 February. 'Worried at a coming Russian attack . . . A Russian probe of 20 skiers . . . A machine-gun duel between the forward trenches. Impossible to put your head above the trench.' A blizzard came in on 4 February. 'Bitter cold. Slept little. By day, had to clear snowdrifts. Otherwise quiet. The nights are worst – greatest stress at 2 a.m. waiting for an attack.' On some days, the sun shone so brilliantly that it hurt his eyes. At night, he could hardly move his arms and legs for the cold, despite a roaring fire.

A storm broke over the trenches on 8 February, as he waited to be relieved by his battalion's 4th Company. 'Lice torment me more each passing hour.' Next night, Russian artillery 'opened a murderous fire on our position at 0029.' It was over in half an hour. The guns were back on 10 February, hitting four dugouts. No one was killed. His company stayed in the line. Russian sub-machine-gunners fired at him as he went to get food from the field kitchen. They had worked their way forward in their white camouflage onto the German side of no-man's-land. Hassdenteufel was tensed for a Russian attack on 11 February. A 'killer snowstorm' raged for two hours. The day brought no offensive, but the Russian machine-gunners were unusually active at night. Hassdenteufel was on night watch and he slept in until midday next day. At 12.40 p.m. Russian heavy artillery opened up. The logs on top of his bunker were opened up by the explosions, and the trenches filled up with earth. He and his comrades pulled back from the front line, ready to go forward again if a ground attack came in. 'We sat in a freezing hut, as it is impossible to build a fire, and warmed ourselves with a flask of brandy. Who knows what tonight will bring us! The Russians are resolute, and so hard, and spread wide. They attacked four times over five hours – it's almost a major offensive. Only in the evening does the fire slacken.'

The weather changed, and it presaged Hassdenteufel's death. He wrote his last entry on the evening of 13 February. 'Foggy and chilly night. Passed without the arrival of Russians, but every hour strained the nerves. You can only see for 2 metres in the fog. The fog hung around for three hours in the day. Around 6 p.m, a strong wind and a storm got up. Awful cold, but no one appeared.' They did, though, at about midnight, coming out of the storm in their camouflage whites with their sub-machine guns, and they made a clean sweep on the men in Hassdenteufel's bunker. They searched their uniforms for papers to give to their intelligence officer. They found souvenirs that the Germans had kept from their earlier campaign in France, so lyrical and gentle by comparison: leave passes for entry into Paris, restaurant advertising cards, street maps of the city, photographs of 'mistresses and prostitutes'. On the body of Hans Forster, they found a photograph of Jacqueline Lebzen of Brabant, whom he would never now marry, and a portrait of Forster himself, on which was written 'Hans Forster geb [*geboren*: born] den 5/4/1920'; beneath that, the Soviet intelligence officer now wrote: 'severe lower jaw, cold, cruel face, Iron Cross 2nd Class ribbon on his uniform.' There were Happy New Year cards from SS Polizeipräsident Zurndorf, in Berlin, to the SS Polizei infantrymen: 'Dear Comrades, the past year has brought us incomparable success, for which the Fatherland thanks you . . . I wish you continued success, Happy Christmas and a healthy New Year.' Hassdenteufel's body yielded his diary.

To the south, on the Volkhov, the Russians broke through the German defence line across frozen swamps and forests and reached Eglino, halfway to Leningrad from their start line. Venets, the commissar with the 59th Independent Rifle Brigade, recalled that his ski battalions came out of the woods in the rear of the German positions. 'The enemy faltered and fled in panic,' he said. 'They left a mound of corpses stacked with German efficiency into piles in cellars or outside in the courtyards. They did not have time to bury them or ship them back to Germany.' A group of SS troops and *Landsers* from the 426th Regiment were cut off in the little town of Malenkoye Zamoshie. The Spaniards of the Blue Division reinforced German infantry in the attempt to relieve them. They set off at 6.00 a.m. on 12 February, in snow flurries and 10 degrees of frost. The snowdrifts were waist-deep in the swamps, and chest-high in places in the forests. They reached the town in pitch darkness. The evacuation to Bolshoye Zamoshe began at once. Music awaited the wounded as they were evacuated westward on the hospital train *Lili Marlene* to Riga. *Aïda* was playing at the opera, with live elephants appearing on stage, while girls in short skirts skated on the frozen Duna river. They found Riga 'a happy town, oblivious to its burned-out synagogue and the emaciated Jews sweeping the streets'.[24]

When he had left Leningrad, Shostakovich told Flora Litvinova, he was promised that his mother would be put on the next flight out. 'He was obsessed with the idea of chartering a plane to go and get her,' Flora said. His parents-in-law, and his sister and nephew were trapped, too. 'How will they be?' he kept muttering. 'What state will they be in?' The Soviet press and radio were well aware of what was happening in the city – Nikolai Markevich, working for *Komsomolskaya Pravda* from his room at the Astoria, was recording 'sleds carrying corpses in plain coffins, covered with rags or half clothes . . . daily six to eight thousand die . . . the city is dying as it has lived for the last half-year, clenching its teeth' – but no word of this appeared. They spoke only the city's 'heroism' and 'determination'. Evacuees were widely spread by now, though, and Russians on the mainland had a growing idea of the horrors. Flora found Shostakovich was 'churned up' by the deaths of friends and stories of cold and hunger.

He was at a rehearsal on 13 February when he was told that his family was to be evacuated without the usual long wait in the queue. 'This news gave me the greatest joy, and I spent the next two to three hours in the best of spirits,' he wrote next day to Isaak Glikman. He had been made Chairman of the State Committee of Piano Studies, and he said he hoped to get to Tashkent to examine students and see

Glikman. 'I very much want to come, but if I cannot make the journey by air then I am nervous of coming by train.' His tip, he added, was 'to wear an amulet of garlic round the neck and wrists. Girls don't like the smell much, of course, but neither do all kinds of bugs. So it is probably sensible to sacrifice the girls, for the time being . . .' Shostakovich had a notoriously wandering eye. 'Actually, I am not very interested in them [girls] at the moment. Wretched nerves playing up,' he confided to Glikman. But he added: 'All the same, there is a certain Yelena Pavlovna, and the possibility of finding her here was one of the reasons I settled on Kuibyshev to come to. But my quest has been unsuccessful, a circumstance which strikes me as mysterious in the highest degree.'[25]

The interrogators were back at Izvekov on 14 February. The professor had been held close by in the Shpalernaya, lodged with cannibals and men like himself in the crumbling red brick prison, and fed on a child's rations. Kruzkhov, with Sergeant Kozlov, got less than a page of questions and answers from him. It was vital for the accused to say as little as possible. Thus far, Izvekov was sticking to it.

They started at 6.30 p.m. 'Please': that is what they wrote in the protocol of interrogation, though such politeness surely existed only on paper. 'Please give truthful answers about your counter-revolutionary activities for this investigation.'

'I am not engaged in any counter-revolutionary activities. Please believe me. I am telling the truth.' The plea to be believed suggests a fear that had not been there on the 6th.

'You are lying. You are trying to hide your counter-revolutionary activities against the Soviet government.'

'I am not lying. I am telling the truth.'

'Does that mean you've decided to continue to hide the truth from the Soviet government?'

'I never fought the Soviet government. This hasn't been proved and it will never be proved by anybody.'

Kruzhkov and Kozlov continued for hour after hour. 'The investigation has concluded that you engaged in activities against the Soviet Union. Please give us your evidence.'

'Please believe me. I never have and never will fight against the Soviet government.' Izvekov had courage and fortitude.

'Interrogation concluded at 0000,' Kruzkhov wrote. Midnight. They had questioned a starving man for five and a half hours and got nowhere. This time there was to be no long gap for Izvekov to recover.

They were back in the interrogation chamber at 6.30 p.m the next day, 15 February. Izvekov was to be posthumously rehabilitated, like so many of Stalin's victims, in 1955. This was on the grounds that, in the absence of any material facts, the only evidence against him were 'confessions' that had been obtained illegally. It was established that 'investigator N. F. Kruzkhov used beatings, fraud, threats and other means of investigation forbidden by law.'[26] Izvekov's fellow academic at the University, Professor Roze, died under questioning by Kruzhkov. Whether Izvekov had been tortured in the Shpalernaya, or Kruzkhov beat him as he questioned him now, we do not know. But from now, Izvekov began to give longer answers, a response that was almost invariably fatal.

'How many times have you been abroad?' Abroad: fascists, capitalists, spies.

'Twice, on scientific trips. The first time in 1925 to Switzerland and Norway. The second, to Germany in 1928.'

Germany. Here was an opening.

'How long were you away on these trips?'

'Both times in summer, in July and August.'

'What kind of connections did you have with scientific institutions abroad?'

'During my visit to Switzerland, I met the following people – Berkins, Wilhelm, professor at Bergen University. Solberg, professor at Oslo. Stürmer, Karl, professor at Oslo. Gesselberg, professor of the Meteorology Institute in Oslo. Angstrem, head of the observatory in Stockholm.'

Names were the raw material with which interrogators spun their web, and foreign names were the finest of all.

'And in Germany?'

'On my trip in 1928 I went to Berlin and Frankfurt-am-Main. I met these scientific colleagues: Linke, Franz, professor at Frankfurt. Ficker, professor of meteorology at Berlin. Mügge, professor at Frankfurt. Stüve, at Berlin.'

'Have you had any correspondence with international professors?' So simple and so dangerous a question: correspondence, letters, papers, the physical evidence of crime committed in the mind.

'Yes, I did. I corresponded with German professors for four or five years.' German professors! How evil it seemed. Yet these were Europe's leading meteorologists. Mügge and Stüve were experts on boundary layers. Heinrich von Ficker was the most civilized of men, the son of a historian known for his writings on the Holy Roman Empire, and himself an expert on cold fronts, heat waves and the *Föhn* winds of his native Alps.

'And what kind of correspondence was that?'

'It was purely scientific.'

'Which German scientific colleagues who have been to the USSR have you met?'

'Professor Ficker came from Germany to Leningrad in 1930. In 1933, a professor from Sweden, Tureer-Zheron, and in 1936, Koschmieder, a professor from Danzig. These are the ones I had contact with.'

It was perhaps as well that the interrogators were too ignorant of science to pick up on Harald Koschmieder. He was currently the director of the Aeronautical Observatory at Lindenberg. It was a pioneer of aviation meteorology. It had begun aeronautical weather services in 1910 – the year that Kaiser Wilhelm II had inaugurated it outside Berlin – and it was still supplying them to the Lutwaffe. Koschmieder specialized in visual range theory and other meteorological applications relevant to bomber and fighter pilots. Men he had trained were attached to all the Luftwaffe's air fleets, including Luftflotte I on the Leningrad front.

Izvekov was still giving blanket denials of political involvement: it was, of course, the truth, and he was a truthful man. Too truthful.

'What kind of conversations did you have with them on political topics?'

'I never had any political conversations with scientific colleagues, either abroad or in Leningrad. I had contact with them for purely scientific reasons.'

'Please tell us about your political beliefs.'

Izvekov, hours into the interrogation, weak with cold and hunger, in a half-lit chamber, now made a fatal error. He allowed himself to enter into conversation with Kruzkhov.

'To answer that,' he said, 'please let me tell you of the way I was brought up. Then I will answer.'

'Yes, please do.' Establish a relationship, an intimacy with the accused, Kruzkhov knew, and a confession would surely follow.

'I was born into a noble family.' That in itself was an admission, of sorts. 'My father was the priest in the convent at Kaluga. I had a very comfortable upbringing. I studied at the Gymnasium [the best school in the town]. I finished in 1909 with a gold medal. Because my father was involved in religious activities, religion obviously played a part in my childhood. I then went to St Petersburg University, and studied for five years. I graduated in 1914. I then went to serve in the Tsar's army until

1918 [*sic*]. I was always far away from political activities. The Revolution wasn't interesting for me.'

He felt that honesty was his best policy – he had, after all, not the slightest interest in politics – but it was not. His answers were too elaborate, and too truthful.

'While serving in the Tsar's army I had to accept the tsarist system, and protect the interests of the monarchy. During the February democratic bourgeois Revolution I was in Latvia, in Riga. With the Provisional Government, I remained an officer and I served the government. During that time, a big revolutionary movement was growing. Our artillery division was ordered by the Provisional Government to start an offensive against the Germans. The revolutionary soldiers in the division, perhaps they were Communists, they started a movement against the offensive. About seven of them were arrested and given prison sentences.'

'What part did you play in the trial?'

'I didn't attend the trial and I wasn't involved in it. I heard about it from other officers in our division.'

Kruzkhov and Kozlov were anxious not to stop the flow of reminiscence. 'Please continue with your story.'

'I met the October Revolution with some fear. I was afraid of revenge from the Soviet government. I tried to find the strength in myself to serve the proletarian revolution and find my place in life. On the other hand, I wanted to fulfil the promise of my education and turn to scientific work, where I always try to achieve benefit and progress.' Such fatal frankness.

'I wasn't always happy with the Soviet government and sometimes I thought their actions were strict and severe.' Izvekov was giving the interrogator access to his thoughts, too exhausted, perhaps, to realize the extremity of the danger: for thought crimes were the easiest of all for Kruzkhov to pin on him. No physical proof or evidence was needed.

'For example,' the professor went on, 'I never agreed with – and spoke against – repression, and particularly the repression of people of noble origins. Moreover, I believe that Soviet law lacks democratic rights and that there are many restrictions in comparison, let's say, with England.' Ah, Boris Ivanovich! Now you're hurtling to your unmarked grave. 'I believe that there, in England, the law is broader and brings benefit to the people, not like here in the Soviet Union.'

He had held out so well, but now he was swept into the vortex of confession that had ruined so many before him.

'According to the problems experienced in the country, I concluded that the Soviet system of government is not stable. It cannot compete with the capitalist countries that oppose it. In the end, the Soviet Union will be over.' This intelligent man, trained in the dispassionate examination of scientific data, had done for himself.

'I didn't believe in socialism in one country, and I was against collectivization and industrialization. During the civil war –' and here we have the first confession of a crime – '*following my anti-Soviet beliefs* [the phrase was underlined in the protocol of the interrogation], I was for the restoration of capitalism in Russia and for a bourgeois democratic republic. I didn't support the German attack on the Soviet Union. But I claimed that the Germans are able to take over Leningrad and that, in the end, I doubt that the Soviet Union can win over Germany.'

The interrogators had their breakthrough.

'What kind of other anti-Soviet propaganda have you been involved in?'

'I had a few anti-Soviet beliefs. I'd like to talk about them in our next interrogation.'

It was past midnight. They were not letting him go now, sensing the kill. 'You've said you'll talk in detail of what you have done. Please tell us now. Right away.'

Starvation, exhaustion and fear had done their work: so, too, may investigator Kruzkhov's fists and belt. Izvekov was thinking in their terms. It was a small step for his private doubts to move on from being 'anti-Soviet' to full-blown 'counter-revolutionary'. And he had a deep vulnerability: his wife. She had been in the camps.

We do not know whether they told him that she, too, was now under arrest. It was common for interrogators to do that: so they had told Osip Mandelstam in 1934, and Nadezhda had found that it was a part of their technique.

It had a particularly chilling resonance for the professor. 'On what grounds,' they asked, though they must have known full well from her file, 'was your wife, Izvekova, Olga Alexandrovna, arrested?'

'She was arrested in 1935 for counter-revolutionary crime.' It dated her to the post-Kirov purge in the city. 'She was sentenced under 58-10 for anti-Soviet agitation and in addition she was accused of wrecking in the geophysical observatory where she was working as chief scientific assistant. She was sent for five years to Saratov. Later she was arrested in Saratov and she was sent to the camps for ten years.'

'How long was your wife in the camps?'

'From 1937 to 1940, and then she was freed. She wasn't allowed to be registered in Leningrad. She appealed against that and she was registered in Leningrad.'

The interrogators had clearly seen her file.

'Did your wife really have the Izvekov surname when she was arrested?'

'No. She had her first husband's name: Kostareva. When she was allowed to register and live in Leningrad she had my last name: Izvekova. We started living together in 1923 but she still had her first husband's name. In 1927 we separated but we got back together again after a year. But we didn't register our marriage. We lived together until her arrest in 1935. And then we got married in 1940.' They must have thought that at last they were safe.

'Please tell us about your wife's social background.'

'She is the daughter of a famous lawyer in Petersburg, Vassver, from before the Revolution.' So that was why – as the child of a 'former person' – she went down in 1935.

'In what way was your wife condemned?'

'She was tried by a troika of the NKVD, and sentenced to ten years in the camps, but she was released early.'

'What's your wife's opinion of the Soviet government?'

At that, Izvekov fell victim to the strange incontinence of confession that undermined so many.

'My wife's beliefs are the same as mine. She often openly talked about her counter-revolutionary beliefs and criticized the Party and the Soviet government. Many times she reminded me of her wrecking activities. As an example of her beliefs –' interrogators always made a point of extracting an actual example – 'she said that the best system for Russia is bourgeois democratic, and not socialism.'

They were in the small hours now, but sleep would wait until they had begun the snaring of Izvekov's colleagues. They wanted names, and they got them, six of them, the cream of the city's mathematicians and geophysicists. Each was listed as 'Professor', and, under the list, it said: 'All have given opinions against the Soviet government.'

The most significant name was Professor N. V. Roze, who had been lecturing in analytical mechanics at Leningrad State University for twenty years. Kruzkhov was Roze's investigator, too, and Roze died in custody. Confessions naming colleagues were extracted from Roze, most probably under torture, before his death.

Kruzkhov and Kozlov stopped now. They had broken him and had a good haul of names. They made him sign: 'The protocol is written correctly in my words.' It was counter-signed 'NKVD interrogator, Sergeant of Government Security Kozlov.'[27]

Shostakovich's fellow composer Boris Asafyev left his lodgings in a make-up room at the Pushkin theatre on 16 February. His family pulled him on a sled to a more comfortable billet at the House of the Institute of Theatre and Music. Nikolai Markevich described him: 'An extremely exhausted old man laid on the bed. It was a big surprise how lively he was in conversation.' This vigour of mind kept him alive. His room was not heated, but he sat on the end of his bed with a white scarf round his neck, and he wrote in a copy book perched on his knee, blowing on his hands when his fingers were too cold to hold the pen. He was a prolific composer, with operas and five symphonies to his name. His ballets included *The Flames of Paris*, a stirring evocation of the city in revolution.

Paris was much on the mind of Alexandra Pavlovna Lyubovskaya, a staff librarian in a factory on the Petrograd Side. She was a graduate of the Philological faculty of the Sorbonne in Paris, and, as well as having lived abroad, she was an expert in a dozen languages. She was lucky to have escaped the purges. She and her son were reading *Paris Assiégé*, the diary that Jules Claretie had kept during the siege of 1870–71. On 16 February, she drew up a two-page table in her diary comparing the two sieges. She found that Parisians had it easier in every aspect. Paris had been shelled for only two weeks. In Leningrad, the shells and bombs fell month in, month out. 'They had hardship, we have – torture! They had malnutrition, we have – starvation!' She held that Parisians, much weaker in her opinion than Leningraders, were responsible for the fall of their city. 'Unlike Paris,' she wrote, 'Leningrad, although facing anguish and huge loss of life, will never surrender. We – the heroic defenders to life and death.'[28]

Leningraders still had the freedom to walk, she said, and she used it to escape from the feeling of being 'inside the ring'. On her walks, she mentally left the city and carried on a dialogue with her Parisian counterpart. She observed people carefully as she went about. Many of those in the streets were driven by rumours that there was kerosene to be had, or a little grain, 'or other fantasies'. As a trained philologist, she noted how little they spoke. 'We use spoken language to the full only when we are fed and our basic needs are satisfied,' she wrote. 'For hungry people, all talk is idle. There is no news. Newspapers are not stuck up in the streets: either there is not enough paper, or no glue and nobody to stick them up. We have no radio. And those who may have some news simply do not wish to share it, because they do not talk.'

She found a particular horror on the Nevsky, once so fine a promenade, a place to see and be seen on, but now a spectral landscape of crumbling buildings and shuffling skeletons. 'Oh, our once handsome Nevsky! The sidewalks littered with frozen snow, clumps of filth and broken boards . . . exhausted, dirty, grimy people in rags . . . only the white snow in the light of a bright winter sun lifts the overall gloom a little.' The contrasts were pitiful, of the grand and majestic city landscape and its ruined residents, the sparkling snow and the fire-darkened buildings and stationary trams and tumbled factory walls. A glance was enough to tell her a person's degree of exhaustion. 'The posture of the besieged man, the look on his face, whether he was a "man-skeleton" or swollen with hunger', these were the signs. The emaciated looked more terrible, but she knew it was the 'puffed-up people' who were dying.

At times, she suffered what she called 'psychological bombardment', the feeling that shells and bombs, whatever their actual trajectory, were hunting all over the city to find her. There was 'starving psychosis', too, recurrent attacks of insatiable hunger. Walking in February, she recorded how colourful pre-war shop signs – 'sausage', 'dumplings', 'snacks', 'vegetarian dining' – caught her eye and tortured her stomach. The familiar street signs, the old newspapers from November and

December that still hung on walls and the sudden shellfire forced her constantly to compare past and present with the unknown future. But the worst, she found, were the hours of pitch darkness, and the lack of news, which oppressed the mind and so lowered the body's resistance to hunger and disease.

Two paths to life were open to those on the downward slope to oblivion. Alla Shelest saw the effect of the feeding stations, the *statsionari*, on 18 February. 'Went with Mama to the Astoria to see Iordan and Vaganova. They look and feel themselves to be better. It was foggy in the morning, the sun shining through the day, the ice a little melted. By 6 p.m. the sun had already set behind the Mikhail Garden and it was burning red in strict outline, without beams/rays, but shining.' Her ballet partner Yuri Gofman, with his flamboyant moustache, was brought into the Astoria during the day. 'He is thin, pale, crouched from stomach pains. My God! He's so spineless!'

Only the elite, and a handful of them at that, were chosen for the feeding stations.* Evacuation over the ice was the only way for the rest. On 20 February, the Radio Committee warned the Artistic Management Committee (*Upravleniye po delam Iskusstv*) that live music would die unless twenty more of its singers and musicians were put on special rations at *statsionari*.[29] The same day, an 'almighty exodus' from the city was under way. 'They are arriving in droves at the Finland Station, young and old, men and women, dragging their goods and chattels on little sleds,' Kniazev observed. 'They are turning their backs on Leningrad, and they are leaving behind their loved ones who are too weak to die.'

Others leaving the city did so secretly in convoys of trucks guarded by NKVD troops. They were destined for the camps in central Asia.

---

* The number of *statsionari* eventually reached 109, helping 56,000 people, but most were opened later in the year.

The target for this deportation embraced the 'social-foreign element' as a whole – former nobles and White officers, passport violators, Poles, kulaks. Most were Soviet Germans and Finns who had escaped deportation to Kazakhstan at the beginning of September when the rail links were cut. The Finns still living in the Vsevolozhskiy region, for example, just north of the city, were expelled to Siberia and Yakutia. They were joined by the 'criminal recidivists' and others on the December list who were still alive. Hilma Stepanova's husband had been editor of a Karelo-Finnish newspaper. He had been executed at the time of the Winter War. His wife, who had worked every day in the vast Leningrad Public Library, was now expelled with her five-year-old son.[30] The NKVD meticulously recorded the total number at 58,210. The Ice Road now sealed their fate.

It was clear to Valentina Petrova what was afoot. She was from a musical family, and a Conservatoire student, living on the Griboedov canal. She noticed that people with foreign names in their apartment block were beginning to disappear. Her German teacher lived in the building, the widow of the famous tenor Karav'ia: 'He was liquidated even before the war.' She was one of the first to vanish. 'They say she perished on the Ice Road.' Others followed. 'Some were taken away, others were given a 24-hour notice of eviction.' Several former tsarist officers with German names lived in the block. They went, one by one. 'Someone would come from the police to deliver a summons to report to the police station,' she said. 'They were given an order to leave within 24 hours. That was it. And the next day they had to clear out. They went by convoy.'[31]

On the Nevsky, a neighbour recalled the fate of the Triberg family. They lived at number 11, a grand and ancient building, where Hector Berlioz had stayed on his first visit to Russia almost a hundred years before. Their ancestor Aleksandr Triberg had owned the building and opened the famous 'Aleksandr' shoe store there before the Revolution. The family had three children, two boys of sixteen and twelve, and their aunt's little girl of three. The neighbour had taken German lessons from their mother and their aunt, 'such beautiful, elegant and intelligent women'. She was particularly struck by the elder son, who seemed to have inherited his mother's kindness, and the skills of his father, an engineer who spoke several foreign languages. She was certain that the country 'lost a future scholar' when the boy died.

'More precisely, it lost them all,' she said. 'This is how it happened: In 1938 they arrested the father. In 1941 they arrested the mother.' The children were left with nothing. All their parents' possessions were confiscated. They had nothing to trade for food. The elder boy died of starvation. The younger son remained with his aunt and her little daughter. 'They were living shadows: a woman dying from starvation and two dystrophic children'. In this condition they were to be 'deported from Leningrad – over the ice of Lake Ladoga'. As deportees, they were now in the hands of the NKVD. The aunt died while they were waiting for the crossing. The two children were each other's only remaining relatives. They were now separated. The little girl was torn by force from the boy's arms, 'and the crying boy left for who knows where'. Such was the fate, the neighbour said with acid accuracy, of a family 'who perished during the last war with the Germans, but not, strictly speaking, at the hands of the Germans'.[32]

Olga Berggolts's father, Fedor, a medical doctor who had spent his career practising in the city, paid for his German name and his refusal to inform on patients with exile to Siberia. His other daughter, Maria, had no illusions about what was happening. 'During the war, we had two enemies: German fascists outside the country, and Russian within,' she recollected. 'The NKVD slipped out of control.' Olga also lost her husband, the literary critic Nokolai Malchanov, and three aunts and her

As the Germans broke through the Red armies defending the city, Shostakovich became a firewatcher on the roof of the Conservatoire. This propaganda picture – German aircraft had yet to bomb or drop incendiaries – was taken on 29 July 1941. A year later, the composer's helmeted profile (he is on the right) circled the world with the fame of the Seventh, appearing on the cover of *TIME* magazine, the first time a musician had been thus honoured.

Russian divisions, cut off by German panzers, dive-bombed by Stukas, suffered immediate and catastrophic losses. The Germans took 800,000 prisoners in the first seven weeks of the war, and 3.3 million by the end of the year. They gave off, a German said, 'a subdued hum, like a beehive', and perhaps two million died of neglect, disease and forced marches in the first few months.

Above: The Bolshoi Dom, the NKVD's Big House, broods above the Neva beyond the battleship *Aurora*. The war did not interrupt – indeed, it spurred on – its daily round of arrests, interrogations and 'confessions'. Despite the siege, mass deportations and exiles continued.

Right: The elegant Fyodor Notgaft, 'a free spirit, natural, intelligent, sympathetic', was a collector of exquisite taste. He and his third wife starved to death in December. When she found them, his second wife hanged herself. On the wall, the paintings were undisturbed, and there were priceless drawings in the drawers.

The shelling of the city was not indiscriminate. The Germans concentrated on the richest targets, the busiest streets, tram stops, factory gates at the change of shift, cinemas and theatres, anywhere with queues. 'Leningrad is in a condition of agony. Everything is dying. Every day I see people falling on the street . . .'

The 'feeding of Leningrad is hanging by a hair . . .' The hair was the Ice Road across Lake Ladoga. Twenty thousand worked on the ice, drivers, guides, mechanics, anti-aircraft crews, medics. The drivers, fortified by a ration of fats and vodka, made two round trips a day.

Bombs and shells sliced through the city as Hitler sought its destruction as well as starvation. On the worst days, it suffered multiple air raids and continuous shelling.

A wounded man is carried back from the desperate winter fighting in temperatures that fell below minus 30°C. Both sides reached the outer limit of their strength, but the Germans were able – just – to hold their siege lines.

Above: A compulsory clean-up of ice and snow in the spring brought some horror – 'severed legs with meat chopped off . . . bits of bodies in bins . . .' – but did much for morale. The courtyards, cellars and staircases of 16,000 buildings were cleared, the foulness was reduced – and those who took part were rewarded with a visit to the public bath. After the unwashed winter, they, too, were clean.

Left: The German siege lines were close, so close that some of the city's tram network was in their hands. No trams ran in winter for lack of power. When some power was restored, and trams ran again on 15 April, people wept with joy, stroked them and asked if they could ring the bells. The sight of moving tramcars depressed the watching Germans. It was a sign that the city was enduring.

As the Seventh was being rehearsed, a Red Army, Second Shock, was dying in the marshes and forests of the Volkhov pocket southeast of the city. Its aim was to break the siege, but it found itself surrounded and starving. After the snow and ice came the mud of spring, a desperate business even for these well-fed, well-equipped Germans, but a calamity for the Russians.

The Russian commander, General Andrei Vlasov, who had been flown into the Volkhov pocket, was one of the last to surrender, on 12 July. He met his opposite number, General Lindemann (right), who much admired Second Shock's courage. Disillusioned, Vlasov was soon suggesting that anti-Stalinist prisoners of war should collaborate with the Germans. He was shot in Moscow after the war.

Right: Shostakovich was sketched by Nikolai Sokolov as he worked on the Seventh in Kuibyshev. The sculptor Ilya Slonim was astonished at his powers of concentration. 'He'd be working at his desk, with children running all over the place playing . . . He'd pace up and down, composing the music in his head.' Then he wrote it straight down at his desk.

Below: The conductor Karl Eliasberg rehearses the Seventh. The score was flown in over the German lines in July. 'When I saw it,' Eliasberg said, 'I thought "We'll never play this".' It was indeed a colossal work, eighty minutes long, demanding an orchestra of over a hundred, barely a fifth of whom had survived the winter.

The Leningrad Symphony was at last performed in the city to which it was dedicated. At the premiere, ferocious Russian counter-battery fire – 'symphonic artillery' – silenced the German guns as it was played in the early evening of 9 August. The poet Olga Berggolts was in the Philharmonia Hall. 'These people deserved to perform the symphony of their city, and the music was worthy of them', she said, 'because it conveyed all they had survived'.

In the end, the gardens of crosses where the Germans buried their young men became too large for them to sustain. Leningrad was much more than a symbol of their coming defeat. In the sweep of their victories across Europe, it was the first great city to resist, and then to overcome, them.

grandmother, to starvation. She continued to stiffen the city's resolve with her broadcasts.

Cannibalism was inevitable in so large a city.* Some Leningraders even found a fierce joy in the flesh-eaters' instinct to live. Israel Nazimov did: 'Cannibalism can stop a person starving. If he wants to live, the cannibal will survive. The strong win, the weak die. Those are the rules.' He was proud of his fellow survivors. 'How do people adapt?' he wrote in his diary in mid-February.

The enemy drops landmines, and the person hides in a bomb shelter. Artillery opens up. The person throws himself to the ground. Electricity stops. He uses candles, improvises lamps, burns vegetable oil. There is no water. He melts snow. There is no heating. He uses little *burzhuikas*. When there is no food, he eats skins, glue, casein, cellulose, cotton, gut, horses, cats, dogs, mustard seed. Local bathhouses are turned into toilets. Hairdressers – people cut their own with razors. No trams or buses. Use a sledge. No entertainment. Work.

Nevertheless, fear of cannibals was adding to the city's other horrors. There were now 866 cases under investigation and December had seen

---

* Leningraders, with their talk of the rest of Russia as the 'mainland', thought of themselves as cast adrift. The law in sea-going nations had long recognized that shipwrecked crews may eat one another. In Britain, it was not an offence for sailors *in extremis* to eat human flesh. The death sentence was formally imposed on those who killed shipmates for food, but the guilty served only a short prison sentence. The test case was in 1884. The yacht *Mignonette* foundered 1,600 miles off the Cape of Good Hope on a voyage from England to Australia. The four-man crew took to the ship's boat with two tins of turnips. After nineteen days, two of them killed and ate the semi-conscious seventeen-year-old cabin boy. They were rescued three days later. The death sentence was commuted to six months' imprisonment. The highly disciplined Royal Navy crews of HMS *Erebus* and HMS *Terror* ate at least forty of their shipmates when they were trapped in the Arctic ice in 1848.

the first 26 arrests, with a special squad of NKVD detectives formed
to combat it. The pace had picked up to 366 in January and accelerated in the first two weeks of February, with the arrests of 494 alleged
cannibals.[33] Most were women in the last stages of emaciation. In one
typical case, a citizen Hazova was found in the cemetery in Gorskoe
north-east of the city with pieces of meat she had cut from bodies.
Commercial cannibalism began with chopping off parts from corpses
lying in their homes or in the street. Olga Trapitsina-Matveenko helped
to carry the body of her grandmother downstairs to the courtyard on
the night that she died. When she went back at first light to take it for
burial, the cadaver had already been cannibalized.

The cuts were sold as meat pies in the alleys round the Haymarket,
the Sennoy Rynok where Dostoevesky's Raskolnikov had roamed in
Crime and Punishment, the centre of the city's black-marketeering. They
were sold as horse meat, or dog, or cat. Bones were broken, and the
nutritious marrow extracted to sell for soup. There were cases of people
being murdered for their meat. Soldiers had the best-fed physiques in
the city because although rats had disappeared from the city, they were
still plentiful at the front where rations were also higher. There were
persistent rumours that isolated soldiers were killed on their way to and
from the front, until they began to move in groups, with their weapons
to hand.[34] The largest group of cannibals were refugees, who had come
into the city without permission. They had no ration cards; the trade in
human flesh was a lifeline for those with the stomach for it.

'Circles' or fraternities of cannibals, in rumour at least, assembled
for special feasts to sate themselves on human flesh. The most depraved
were those who demanded their meat 'fresh', from a still warm victim,
and not a cut from a frozen corpse. The NKVD made special reports
on a group who lived in the railway station at Razliv, on abandoned
children who had become 'murderer-cannibals', and on another group
in the town of Oranienbaum. Anatoly Darov recounted the escape of

Dmitri, a young friend of his who had gone with his girl friend Tamara to the Haymarket to buy her a pair of *valenki*. They saw nothing but large and cumbersome men's working boots. A very tall man, smartly turned out in a fur hat and sheepskin coat, powerfully built and healthy, was holding a single woman's boot of the right kind. They haggled, and the man agreed to take 600 grams of bread for the pair. Dmitri set off with him through the alleys to collect the other boot. They reached the top of the staircase in the giant's building. He turned to Dmitri and told him to wait. He knocked on an apartment door. 'It's me,' he said. 'I've brought a live one.' Dmitri froze. The door opened. He saw 'a hairy red hand and a muglike face . . . a strange, warm, heavy smell.' A gust caught the door. The guttering candlelight shone on hunks of white meat, swinging from hooks on the ceiling. One was still attached to a human hand, with long fingers and blue veins. Dmitri ran down the staircase as the men lunged for him. He alerted passing soldiers: 'Cannibals!' They raced into the building. Dmitri heard two shots, and the soldiers reappeared with a greatcoat, and the loaf of bread he had paid for the *valenki*. He thanked them for his life.[35]

People were killed for their ration cards. In the first half of the year, 1,216 arrests were made for murder and incitement to murder for ration cards, sometimes by people who also cut up the bodies. Sofia Buriakova felt that her brother's end fitted the pattern. He had died unexpectedly on the last day of January. His neighbours refused point-blank to let her into his room to see his body. They had his body removed and handed the key over to the *zhakt*, the house-management office. She was convinced they had killed him for his card.[36] The accused were usually neighbours of the dead, or were from the *zhakt*, concierges and gatekeepers, who had easy access to their apartments. Others were victims of the bandits and traffickers now operating in the city in small, two-to-six-man gangs. They were armed and desperate. Many were deserters and escaped criminals. Orphaned children joined them.

They hijacked bread trucks so often that the police had to escort them on their delivery runs.

Police resources were strained beyond breaking point. The Leningrad force lost 378 dead to dystrophy in January and February. Policemen were collapsing and dying of starvation on duty. The NKVD's well-fed anti-bandit department, the OBB, dated back to the civil war. Its campaign now was war-like, its shoot-outs with the desperadoes marked by automatic weapons fire and grenades. Patrols roamed the streets. They searched anyone they found suspicious, and if they discovered stolen ration cards or unexplained food, they shot them on the spot.[37] The Military Court sentenced 2,104 bandits over the siege, more than the combat strength of many a division at the front, and 435 of them were executed.

The young musician Ksenia Matus, who was to play the oboe in the Seventh, was well aware of the criminals. 'A lot of people in my apartment block died, and some became bandits,' she said. 'A neighbour's room was searched and they found bowls and plates of human flesh. I had to be present while they were searching. I went to court as a witness. I thought I'd feel bad for a long time, with this odour of meat that clung to me.'

At the lowest street level, thieves waited for vulnerable-looking people to get their ration, and grabbed it from them. Sofia Buriakova saw an incident that had become commonplace. A teenager tore a piece of bread from the hands of a weakened old woman, and quickly shoved it in his mouth. He dropped down with his face to the ground and chewed feverishly. 'No matter how much they hit and kicked him, he chewed and swallowed it all.'

Thefts on a much grander scale, from warehouses and in transit on the Ice Road and railway freight cars, continued despite the efforts of the NKVD 23rd Division. Its troops were guarding sixteen major food warehouses, and two fuel depots. They travelled on the freight trains carrying supplies to Ladoga, and from the lake on to Leningrad. The theft of Red Army supplies was also rampant. A decree at the beginning of March confirmed that those guilty of the 'theft and squandering' of military supplies would be sentenced as enemies of the people: they would be shot, and their property confiscated.[38]

The racketeers were not intimidated. The chief inspector of the City Industrial Trading Board was responsible for verifying and destroying used food coupons. He and several of his staff were stealing coupons, disposing of them to accomplices in food shops, who used them to plunder supplies. In the three months from March, they took over a ton of butter, cereals, meat and sugar.[39] The manager of a bread store in the Smolninsky district, and her assistant, short-weighed the bread and stole four or five grams from each customer. They bartered the bread for furs, antiques and gold. They were both shot. 'The air was cleared of something foul,' Pavlov noted with satisfaction. The deputy manager, the deputy chief engineer and the Party secretary in the Lenenergo power station stole meat, butter, sugar and tinned food, a huge haul weighing over a ton. The City Fire Brigade was not exempt. Managers were claiming to feed 247 more staff than they had. At Hospital 109, staff fed themselves the patients' food, without surrendering their own coupons. They kept back half of deliveries of potato flour and tea, and 91 per cent of vegetables, for their own use.[40]

Vladislav Mikhailovich Glinka was a writer and curator at the Hermitage.[41] He met an old classmate who told him of a racket run by the head of the convoy that delivered bread and flour to the shops. The man sold bread and horsemeat for cash and valuables, gold, silver, and fabrics. The friend was on his way to see the man, with silver spoons and crystal glasses in his pockets. Glinka collected some valuables from his room, and and went with him. They went to the gate of the docks on the Obvodny canal. The friend told the guard: 'Oleinikov.' They were allowed in. They crossed a courtyard surrounded by stables and barns full of carts. They knocked on the door of a wooden house in the courtyard. It was answered by Roman Artemivich Oleinikov. He was about fifty, not very fat but round and broad-shouldered. He was in good shape with some belly, a round face, dark eyes, self-confident and sharp. His movements were unfussy, but hard. He was well turned out, in a camouflage jacket, military trousers and a corps commander's fine boots. He bargained with Glinka's friend. They agreed on three kilos of horsemeat and two kilos of bread.

He asked what Glinka had brought. Glinka showed him his grandmother's gold clock, old and delicate, but still working and with the key. He also had some fine wool textile he had bought before the war with the money he had made from *Borodino*, his first book. Oleinikov looked at them carefully. 'Two kilos of bread and two kilos of horsemeat,' he said. 'I didn't bargain,' Glinka wrote. 'This was treasure.' Oleinikov gave him the bread, and rang a bell. Immediately a bearded man in a white apron appeared. 'Evseich – weigh two kilos of horsemeat, wrap it up and bring it.' He checked carefully where Glinka worked and lived, and told him that he could come back for more if he wanted.

On their way back, Glinka asked how Oleinikov could get his hands on so much food. 'It's easy, stupid,' his friend told him. 'He's the head of food delivery. Every cart driver, and there are about thirty of them, gives him a kilo of bread off their load every day. Once a week, they kill a horse, and report that it died of starvation, and they get another horse from the army.'

Glinka paid a second visit, with a gold pencil case decorated with precious stones, and a small watercolour by Mykola Azovsky. The artist was well known for his fine use of watercolour, gouache and ink, and his work had hung in the Soviet pavilion at the 1937 World Fair in Paris. Oleinikov took the painting to the window, bringing it close to his eye, and looking at it with a connoisseur's intensity. He gave Glinka an extra kilo of bread along with his horsemeat, well pleased with his watercolour, which he at once put on his table, surrounded by rare books with gold-blocked titles.

Vera Inber crossed Ladoga on 22 February on a truck with a delegation to the front from her district committee. They carried presents with them for the troops, camouflage clothes, shaving gear, guitars and mandolins, handkerchiefs, and five automatic rifles with inscriptions carefully carved on the stocks: 'To the best exterminators of German occupiers.' The truck reeked of petrol. They had to drive fast. The ice was riddled with bomb craters, and after noon, when it was further weakened by the sun, heavy trucks had to stop. They were across the lake in ninety minutes. On the far side, Inber heard people singing, and saw a live goat, a dog and a chicken. She was stunned by these miracles, and astonished by the people, so different to the pale ghosts of Leningrad with their shallow breath. Here, 'the people have rosy cheeks, they talk fast, they take deep breaths, and thick clouds of steam come out of their mouths.'[42]

They drove on towards Gorokhovetz, looking for the political department of Fedyuninsky's army. The road was 'worn-out, bombed, tormented', wrecked machines lying in potholes and bomb craters, the snow turned to sand. At sunset, the German aircraft bombed a supply train carrying paraffin and petrol in the railway yard at Zhikarevo. Never in her life had she seen such flames, 'purple, thick as a feather bed with black smoke twisted round'. The aircraft turned, and machine-gunned the station and her convoy of trucks. The others took cover in the snow, but she stayed on the truck, saved, she was told, because the German pilots must have thought it was abandoned. When the aircraft circled for another run, she got down and ran for a ditch.

The cold on her return trip across the lake was as sharp as a knife blade. She sat with the driver in his cab – they put her there from pity – and he told her to pray to God that he had no trouble with the truck.

'If I stop the engine, it will put paid to you.' Its heat, and the drink of vodka, fat and sugar she shared with him, nourished her. Dawn came up over the forest, with a pale green sky like an apple that turned red on one side. Then they were on the ice. Everything on it was made of snow, windbreaks of snow bricks, igloos for the anti-aircraft crews, ice-blocks for the gun positions. Everything that was not white came as a shock. She could see the poppy-red flag of a traffic controller from over half a mile away. Scarlet signs on shields asked: 'Driver, have you done two runs today?' She was long-sighted and she could see to the horizon. Trucks were moving like multi-coloured dots. Pink meant they were loaded with mutton carcasses, black for coal, smooth and white for flour sacks.

Inber's description suggested that, German aircraft apart, the evacuees had reached the Promised Land when the trucks dropped them at the Zhikarevo railhead. This was not so. From here, they were packed onto special trains that took most of them on through Vologda. The first evacuation train arrived there on 26 January. By 25 April, and the ice melt on the lake, 215 special trains carrying 486,287 people had passed through Vologda. No train arrived without bodies, sometimes many bodies. 'Not only people, but dozens of bodies were taken off the train,' eyewitnesses said of the first arrival. 'It had not been realized that things were so bad in Leningrad.' Two piles of corpses were found at the station.

Vologda was 'neither materially nor morally ready' to take in people who were on the point of death. The emergency 'hospitals' were 'more like railway stations', the head of the Vologda Hospitals Management Board, R. V. Turkestanskaya, wrote in a report.[43] Several families were crammed into each room. There were no kitchens, no duty doctors, no drugs, no clean sheets, no disinfectants, few nurses. The food was scanty and arrived stone cold, with nowhere to heat it. Four-fifths of patients had severe gastrointestinal complaints, but there were no toilet blocks and nowhere to wash. 'There were no operating theatres, though many patients had frost-bitten limbs and gangrene,' Turkestanskaya wrote angrily. 'The procedure for taking the sick to hospital was to put them on a bus and take them round hospitals, making them get off at each one, until one took pity on them and accepted them.'

It was no better in Yaroslavl, the alternative destination. A medical orderly saw 'indescribable scenes'.[44] 'Hundreds of people already beyond the limits of exhaustion lay before us. Their dystrophy was absolute and irreversible . . . Skeletons in which departing life still flickered lay on beds in hospital rooms.' In February, more than a hundred bodies were dumped from trains in Yaroslavl. Others were found lying by the track deeper into Russia.

The 23rd of February was Red Army Day. Stalin and Beria celebrated it by having forty-six military men executed, seventeen of them army and air force generals. Some were shot in Kuibyshev, where the rehearsals for the Seventh were continuing, their bodies buried in the children's playground next to those killed in October. The others were shot in Saratov, another Volga town.

Their names were in a list that Beria had sent to Stalin on 29 January. Stalin had signed it: 'Shoot all named in the list. J. St.' They were sentenced to death by the Special Council of the NKVD. Beria had successfully lobbied Stalin for the right of the NKVD to impose extra-judicial death sentences without the prior permission of the Military Collegium of the Supreme Court. The condemned included scapegoats for the early disasters at the front. General Ivan Selivanov had had the misfortune to command XXX Rifle Corps in June. Ivan Sergeyev had been the People's Commissar of Ammunition. Several had links to the Frunze military academy. There is a poignancy to the fate of the Frunze's Komdiv, A. A. Talkovskii. He was arrested during the *Yezhovshchina*, the purges of 1937–38, but escaped with his life and was released in May 1940, only to be rearrested at the end of June 1941. The military historian

Major-General A. N. de-Lazari was a victim of his own name. He was accused of spying for Italy.

Men who had fought together in Spain were the core group, as they had been in October. One was Shakht, the bomber commander who had been arrested in hospital in June as he recovered from a flying accident. The Latvian P. I. Pumpur, a Lieutenant-General of Aviation, had flown in Spain under the pseudonym 'Colonel Julio'. He had commanded the fighter group on the Madrid front, a Hero of the Soviet Union who had shot down five Italian and German aircraft. He had gone on to lead a group of 'volunteer' fighter pilots who flew with Chinese forces against the Japanese in the Far East. He had also been head of combat training. His experience did not save him from arrest as an 'architect of an anti-Soviet plot'. He was tortured and admitted his guilt, but retracted his 'confession' before he was shot.[45] Yevgeny Ptukhin was also an air ace, a Hero of the Soviet Union and a lieutenant-general. He was to become a legend in the Gulag. Solzhenitsyn recorded Ptukhin's defiant words after his arrest: 'If I'd known, I'd first have bombed our Dear Father [Stalin] and then have gone off to prison.'

No hint of these killings broke surface in Stalin's traditional Red Army Day order, of course. Nor did he mention Allied aid, though ten convoys with aircraft, armour and supplies had arrived in Murmansk and Archangel by now, at a heavy cost to British and American merchant sailors running the gauntlet of German U-boats and bombers in the Arctic winter seas. His only oblique reference to his new allies was to speak of 'the rout of the foreign interventionist invaders during the Civil War', a reminder of the days when, in Churchill's phrase, the British and Americans had tried to 'stifle Bolshevism at birth'.

He remained over-confident, still convinced that the Lyuban offensive would lift the siege. He flattered the military, predicting that 'the day is not far off when the Red Army, by a powerful drive, will hurl the brutal enemy back . . . and Soviet flags will again wave victoriously over all Soviet soil'.

Radio Leningrad marked the day with its first live concert of the year. It was performed by the Ensemble of Song and Dance of the Political Management of the Leningrad Front, and the Theatre Collective of the Baltic Fleet. The musicians were on military rations and played with some gusto. Two singers from the Kirov, who had refused to be evacuated, added sparkle to the concert. The baritone Ivan Nechayev had sung at the first performance of Shostakovich's opera *The Nose*. The fine mezzo-soprano Sofiya Preobrazhenskaya had been a soloist with the Kirov, famous for her Joan of Arc in Tchaikovsky's *The Maid of Orleans* and as Maria in Mussorgsky's *Boris Godunov*. Her reluctance to leave the city with the Kirov had been noticed by the NKVD in August. She was asked, a diarist recorded, why she did not go. She said she was 'sure that Leningrad won't be surrendered'. At this, 'the administration thought to themselves, "We know you. It's already certain that Leningrad will have to be abandoned, and you want to go over to the Fascists! We'd better interrogate you, so as to see exactly what kind of Soviet people you really are."'[46] Her presence brought the city opera in its darkness. Muzkomediya players went to Ladoga to entertain the troops with hit songs like 'Please Smile, Sweetie'.

Instincts from old Russia were resurfacing in children brought up to be godless proletarians. A little boy dying of dysentery kissed his teacher's hand when she changed his sheets in the children's house. He was an eleven-year-old with dark serious eyes, Dima, with a 'graceful air about him'. The teacher said he was not to kiss her hand – it was bourgeois affectation – but he insisted. He said that he had seen his father kiss his mother's hand like this while she cared for him as he was dying. He died one night. The teacher stood motionless by his bed for a long time. Then she took his body and washed it and wrapped it in a clean blanket. She paid a cemetery worker several pieces of bread to bury him immediately. She told Svetlana Magayeva that she did not want him to join the pile of corpses waiting for a team of soldiers to dump them in a mass grave.

The teacher said that she had planned to adopt Dima after the war. 'She added that if I should ever choose to marry someone like Dima,' Svetlana recalled, 'then no one would ever have to be concerned about my well-being.' Svetlana was too young to know what she meant until later. Then she understood that good manners revealed goodness of heart.[47]

No child was taught to pray. Another teacher, Varvara Alexandrovna, was careful to do so in secret. Her son Georgy was missing in the militia. She never wept in front of the children, but they saw traces of tears in her 'kind eyes'. She slept in Svetlana's room. There was no one waiting for her at home, and her presence through the night calmed the children. Svetlana woke one night and saw Alexandrovna kneeling. 'Her eyes were open . . . I could see her lips move.' She realized that she had been seen. She whispered to Svetlana that she had prayed to God to protect her son at war and bring him back to her. 'She did not want anyone to know she'd been praying, and she asked me to promise not to tell anyone that I had seen her pray.'

After that, Svetlana started to pray as well. She had no idea of how to go about it. 'I decided just to talk to God. I started by saying "Dear and dearest God! Please do what is needed to end the war quickly and bring Varvara's son Georgy home". Georgy never did come home – in her grief, Alexandrovna said he must have been killed before she began her prayers – but Svetlana continued to pray.[48]

Lidiya Okhapina turned to God when she and her children faced five days without bread. A woman had befriended her, and she had moved into her apartment, because it was warmer than her own. Lidiya's bread started disappearing, and then the woman's daughter 'lost' or more likely stole her ration cards. She moved back into her own room in a desperate mood. 'I got out of bed and threw myself to my knees . . . There was no icon and, besides, I didn't know a single prayer. My children had never been baptized and I didn't really believe in God myself . . . "I am at the end of my tether. Lord, I beg, send us death, but make it so that we all die together . . . Lord, take pity on these blameless children." The next day, there was a rap on the door. It was a lieutenant from her husband's unit at the front. He gave her a letter, and a kilo of rice and a kilo of semolina and two packets of biscuits.[49]

On the eve of the Revolution, the eparchy of St Petersburg and Ladoga had 790 churches and sixteen monasteries, with 1,700 clergy and 1,629 monks. The Bolsheviks had done for most of them. The last monastery, the Alexander Nevsky Lavra, was closed in 1933. By the outbreak of war, the eparchy was reduced to twenty-one churches. Only eight were within the city limits.

Stalin's atheist credentials were impeccable. He was at particular pains to ensure that the country's children, its Svetlanas, remained godless. His Law of Religious Associations in 1929 banned churches – they were renamed 'prayer buildings' – from all work with children and young people. Children between eight and fourteen were enrolled in Groups of Godless Youth. At least five million adults enrolled in the League of the Militant Godless. Yet, as the League's chairman, Yemelian Yaroslavsky, admitted wearily, 'Religion is like a nail. The harder you strike it, the deeper it goes.' Stalin, himself a former seminarian, retained an instinctive grasp of the uses of liturgy and faith. It was he who had urged the preparation of Lenin's tomb on Red Square, knowing it would become a place of secular pilgrimage. He had composed the Communist pledge: 'In leaving us, Comrade Lenin ordained us to hold high and keep pure the great title of Member of the Party. We vow to thee, Comrade Lenin, that we shall honourably fulfil this thy commandment . . . In leaving us, Comrade Lenin ordained us to guard and strengthen the dictatorship of the proletariat. We vow to thee . . .'

He recognized that, as a lay religion, Marxism-Leninism lacked the compelling power of appeals to the Motherland and to old-fashioned patriotism. It was why he had evoked Alexander Nevsky, who had defeated the Germans and Swedes, and Suvarov and Kutusov, the scourges of Napoleon, in his dramatic address to the troops in Red Square in November. He revived links with the old army, restoring tsarist decorations, ranks and Guards units. The traditional bluish-grey officers' greatcoats returned, embroidered in red for staff officers, and grey-blue trousers with the red *lampa* stripe. The tsarist army had been intensely religious, too. On its battlefields, its dying soldiers 'almost to a man clutched at the image of the patron saint he wore about his neck, and pressed it to his lips'. Religious ceremonial consumed an amount of time Western attachés found 'almost incredible'. Its Lenin rooms and political commissars did not bring the same solace as its departed icons and priests.

For the moment, he conceded, it was useful for God to be tolerated. He made a particular point of praising Dmitri Donskoi, the warrior-saint who had defeated the Moslem Tartars of the Golden Horde on the Don in 1380. The Orthodox Church responded with wholehearted support of the war effort. Stalin had Patriarch Sergei taken from his sick-bed in Moscow and deported to Ulyanovsk in November, but he was then returned, and given the grand buildings of the German embassy for his patriarchate, in place of his former log cabin on the outskirts. The church was to raise 150 million rubles for the war effort, equipping an armoured division.

Leningrad retained its Metropolitan, Alexei, who was active throughout the siege. He was based at the St Nicholas cathedral, narrowly escaping when his spartan cell was hit by artillery fire. His fiery sermons helped to raise several million rubles for the war effort. Services were held in the few remaining churches. Solace was given to the relatives of the dead on an escalating scale. Father Lomakin, Alexei's dean, recalled that the demand for funeral masses was so great that long rows of coffins and boxes stood outside the cathedral. Each day, the priests chanted the funeral service over them. They also said requiems in memory of the ever-increasing number of dead whose bodies could not be brought to the church, because their relatives and friends were too weak, or because they were buried under rubble.[50]

This toleration was restricted to the Orthodox. Others were not so fortunate. A single synagogue remained open for the city's many Jews. Moslems and Buddhists prayed in private, though many of them were serving in the Red Army, and the city boasted a Buddhist temple, and a vast and ornate mosque, its azure dome a landmark beyond the Trinity Bridge, both opened in 1913. The mosque was now a warehouse, and the temple was used as a youth physical training centre, and a radio studio, with a barrage balloon tethered to it to carry the aerials. Old Believers, Baptists and Jehovah's Witnesses lay low. The NKVD picked up the members of one small sect, whose believers included *kulaks*, former nuns and other social undesirables. Its leader, Archimandrite Klavdi, confessed under interrogation to hostility to Soviet power.[51] The group was reported to have been liquidated.

The lead elements of the Red Army's 327th Division in the Volkhov salient had now reached the Bolshoye Mkhi, the Large Mosses, a tract of swamps and forests within ten miles of the railway station at Lyuban. Fighting in the salient was a desperate business. The horse-drawn guns were swallowed up in the snow, I. D. Yelokhovskiy, the artillery platoon commander, recalled. His crew cut down trees and put wedges under the wheels as the horses strained to pull them out. In action, they dug a shallow hole in the snow for the gun, but they were still so exposed that his crew had christened the gun 'Farewell, Motherland!' They were short of ammunition and the food issue for ten men was a single pot of pea-soup mash. They were saved by their horses. 'We could not feed them,' he said. 'How many horses can survive on birch branches alone? The horses died and we ate them.'[52]

Another gunner, P. P. Dmitriev, had grown so fond of his horse, 'my beloved Terazka', that he could not bring himself to shoot her when she became too exhausted to pull the howitzer. He let her go, hoping against hope that someone would find her and provide her with fodder. The companies in his battalion had taken 70 per cent casualties. They moved forward on a compass course through the forests and bogs. Surveyors went ahead to establish a route. The snow was deep and thick, but the swampy land beneath it was unfrozen. When the wheels of the 5,000-pound howitzers sank into it, the men, both gunners and staff, put on straps and helped the remaining horses to pull them out. The speed of the advance was 'measured in metres . . . All along the line we encountered large numbers of dead horses, left behind by the 80th Cavalry Corps.'[53]

A twelve-man patrol led by Lieutenant S. I. Kochepasov of the 1102nd Rifle Regiment reconnoitred the swamps that ran up to the Moscow–Lyuban-Leningrad railway line. They found no sign of the enemy. On 24 February, General Meretskov, under continuing pressure from Stalin to relieve Leningrad, ordered the division to capture Lyuban. The advance was to be led by the 1100th Rifle Regiment and the 80th Cavalry Corps under General Gusov.

It worried the commander of the 327th Division, Major-General I. M. Antyufeev. 'To carry out this order, the division had to accomplish a 25-kilometre march, including ten kilometres through a trackless snow-bound forest,' he recollected. 'It moved at a pace of two kilometres an hour.' Kochepasov's regiment was typical. It had suffered terrible casualties when it had attacked across the frozen Volkhov in the initial assault in January. It was under-strength, and short of ammunition and food. The further it penetrated towards Lyuban, the worse its resupply through the roadless forests had become. Each gun was allocated a maximum of five shells. No rounds were left for the mortars. Indiscriminate fire from rifles and machine guns was strictly forbidden.

German reconnaissance aircraft spotted the forward detachments almost immediately. They came under heavy air attack. 'Many horses were killed in the cavalry corps and in our division,' Antyufeev wrote. 'The guns and carts were unhitched. Anti-aircraft defence was woefully deficient. Enemy aircraft literally hung over our heads from dawn to dusk and continually bombed and strafed our positions. Even the smallest group of men were incapable of moving.' During the night, the main force failed to break through the German defences.

Marshal Voroshilov visited the headquarters at Dubovik, a large village southwest of Lyuban, on 25 February. German Stukas dive-bombed it shortly after he left. A headquarters clerk, V. N. Sokolov, thought that 'even the most dreadful nightmare' could not surpass the horror. The windows were blown in, and wood, thatch and clumps of earth flew everywhere. Then he saw the rest of the village. It was reduced to 'blood-stained snow, arms, legs, heads, scraps of clothing and shapeless pieces of human flesh . . . We lost over a hundred men.' The log huts were blazing, and the street was strewn with smashed carts and trucks, the bodies of men and horses, and household debris.

The interrogators had Izvekov brought to them at 6.15 p.m. on 26 February. They were hungry for more names, more details. They were oblivious to the siege: this was old-style Bolshevik Terror, self-contained and feeding on itself.

Who was the leader of the conspiracy at LGU, Leningrad State University?

'Roze was the leader in the maths faculty.'

'Why do you claim that Roze led the group only in the maths faculty? Explain who was the general leader at the university.'

'I don't know, but I am inclined to think it was not Roze. He's only a little figure. The university has ten faculties and a hundred professors. The leader would have to be a professor of worldwide significance.'

He was told to list all members of the group in the maths faculty.

He added three names to the ones he had listed on 14 February: Zhuravsky, Andrei Mitrofanovich, professor; Stroganov, Vasily Georgevich, *dozent* [lecturer]; Milinsky, Vladimir Ivanovich, *dozent*.

How did he know they were in the group?

'I had conversations with them with counter-revolutionary views.'

Who recruited him?

'Roze recruited me because he knew my anti-Soviet views . . . He said he was going to stay in Leningrad, and I said I would too. Then Roze explained that there was a counter-revolutionary group among professors who were waiting for the arrival of the Germans. We had to prepare for a meeting with the Germans at LGU and this meant that we had to prepare a political-scientific declaration in the name of professors and express our wish to cooperate with the Germans and fight against the Soviet Union. After explaining this, Roze asked me to join the group. I agreed.'

The interrogators now struck a mother lode of fantastic invention. 'What tasks did your group set itself?'

Izvekov listed two. 'First, the overthrow of the Soviet Government. Second, the rebuilding of capitalist Russia with a bourgeois democratic system.' An ambitious programme indeed for a small band of professors and lecturers, some evacuated, the others half starved or dying. Kozlov solemnly wrote it down: perhaps Izvekov made it up, but as we have seen, prisoners were often reduced to semi-insanity.

He was told to give the names of other counter-revolutionary groups at LGU. He came up with five new people who were 'engaged in similar activities' to himself: Tikhomirov, Yevgeny Ivanovich, professor at the Arctic Institute; Sverdlov, Alexander Vasilievich, professor at the

Electrotechnical Institute; Zhongalovich, Ivan Danielovich, professor of the Astronomical Institute and Academician; Molchanov, Pavel Alexandrovich, professor of geophysics and Academician; Kedrolivansky, Viktor Nikolaievich, professor at the Leningrad observatory. 'I have interacted with the above on many occasions when they told me their anti-Soviet views. These people, even though they are not members of our anti-revolutionary group, are obviously members of similar groups as they speak in the same way as us.'

This was not enough for them. 'You haven't named all the counter-revolutionary people you know. Continue your listing.'

It was the small hours now, 1.25 a.m. The interrogation had lasted for seven hours and ten minutes. We may presume that, exhausted, he had run out of names. He needed time to dream up fresh ones.

'Please let me list them in our next interrogation.'

Izvekov had time to reflect in his cell in the Shpalernaya, lying on the shelf of planks with the other politicals, the cannibals and criminals crouched beneath them on the floor. He was back in the interrogation chamber at 1.25 p.m. on 28 February.

He had dredged up two fresh names.

'I forgot to name the following persons engaged in counter-revolutionary activities': Hudiakov, Nikolai Nikolayevich, *dozent* [lecturer] of the Electrotechnical Institute; Verigo, Alexander Bronislavovich, professor of the Radium Institute and Academician. 'They are enemies of the Soviet Union. I came to this conclusion after numerous meetings when we discussed political affairs.'

The interrogators were not after Verigo. He was a popular hero, a member of the three-man crew of the balloon USSR1-bis which had reached a height of 16,000 metres in June 1935, breaking the world record. The NKVD let him be during the war, working on radon baths to treat wounded soldiers and making luminous paint for the lightless city.

The interrogators changed tack.

'Didn't Friedmann and his wife contribute to your counter-revolutionary views?'

Laboriously the interrogators took down his details, though he had been dead for sixteen years. 'Friedmann, professor of Leningrad State University and head of the geophysical observatory, and his wife, opposed the Soviet government and they talked to me personally about their counter-revolutionary views when I visited them at home. I should note that Professor Friedmann died in 1925. I visited his wife up to 1940. She hasn't changed her counter-revolutionary views and still declares them today.'

'Please give examples of Elena Friedmann's thoughts.'

'She is opposing Soviet government and believes it should be overthrown by internal pressure. She supports the rebuilding of the bourgeois system in Russia. She says all Soviet affairs are lies.'

'What other professors have visited Friedmann at her house?'

'Besides me, Roze, Tihomirov, Viziukovich and –' another new name here – 'Golzman visited her in her house where they openly discussed views against the Soviet union.'

'This means that visits to Friedmann's house –' she, too, was now in mortal danger – 'had a political motive.'

'Yes. I must confess that's the truth.'

'What kind of agenda did your organization –' it had moved up from a 'group' to something even more sinister – 'have during the Blockade?'

'The main agenda was to provide help to the fascists in their fight against the Soviet Union.'

In the world outside the prison, Galya Plisova and her mother had a routine. They went to the river to get water. Galya pulled a small sled and her mother carried a pail. It was safer for two of them to go. The ice round the hole for water was wet and slippery. Some women on their own slipped, and crawled to the hole on their knees to ladle up water.

Then they found they were unable to get up and as night approached they froze to death on the ice. Galya found a dead woman lying in the snow. She was in a sheepskin coat but her boots had gone. The coat soon disappeared, and then the stockings and clothes and underclothes until the corpse was naked. Finally, Galya saw that chunks of flesh had been taken from the corpse. She knew that it had not been done by dogs. There *were* no dogs, and no cats, either. Galya's grandmother used to take the family cat Pushock to the bread queues under her coat to keep her warm. Pushock slipped out one day, and was not seen again.

Remarkably, though, the staff of the Leningrad Zoo were keeping some animals alive. The Lensoviet gave the zoo a special allocation of hay and vegetables. The keepers added their own ingenuity to this. They found that carnivores – fox, ermine, vultures – would eat minced vegetables if it was mixed with a little meal. Tigers and eagles, fussier, would still devour it if it was sewn into rabbitskin.[54] When the zoo reopened in the summer, it made stars of the survivors, Grishka the bear, and the hippopotamus Krasavitsa ('Beauty').

Three more musicians from the symphony orchestra died. The Union of Composers had now lost 21 members to starvation since November.[55] Kondratiev recalled 'How we looked, we dystrophics, in December, January, February. Pale, thin, skin and bone, elongated faces, especially noses. Our eyes move slowly, expressionless, we speak quietly without intonation, our voices low and slow, and we pull our legs along the floor.' Deaths in this shortest month had reached 122,680. In itself, though, this brought relief to the living. It combined with the flow of evacuees – 117,000 against only 11,000 in January – to mean that there was more food per head for those who remained. The number of male deaths had fallen to 55 per cent, not through any physiological improvement, but because they made up a dwindling part of the total population. Fewer were falling dead in the streets. In the first ten days of the month, 1,060 bodies were found lying in the drifts and ice. That fell to 679 in the second ten days, and 366 in the shorter third period of February. 'Death looked straight into our eyes, and stared long, without faltering. It wanted to hypnotize us, as a boa constrictor hypnotizes its intended victim, stripping him of his will and subjugating him,' Berggolts wrote. 'But those who sent us so much death miscalculated. They underestimated our voracious hunger for life.'

There was a glimmer of gladness for musicians on 28 February. It was decided to restore electricity to the Muzkomediya. The military situation was, however, getting worse. The 30th Cavalry Corps and the 1100th Rifle Regiment were dying. Though the Germans had sliced through their rear, they had continued the advance, reaching the southwest outskirts of Lyuban, the railway yards visible through fieldglasses. The Germans counter-attacked with tanks, forcing them back into the swamps and forests. There, over the next ten days, they were annihilated.

Leningrad was not to be relieved through Lyuban.

CHAPTER 11

Mart

March 1942

The conductor Karl Eliasberg was called to talks with Boris Zagorsky, the head of MMA, the Management of Artistic Affairs, on 1 March. They discussed resuming symphony orchestra performances. Eliasberg made a careful tally of the orchestra with Babushkin, the artistic director of the *Radiokomitet*. They counted twenty-seven musicians who had died in the past month alone. Of the survivors, only sixteen were fully fit to work. Shostakovich's Seventh needed at least eighty. The Leningrad Gorkom Party organization, agreed to give the woodwind players additional rations. Eliasberg and Babushkin pleaded that members of the Radio choir and stringed instrument players should also be put on first-category rations.

A radio appeal was made: 'We ask that all musicians remaining in Leningrad report to the *Radiokomitet* for registration. The symphony orchestra is going to start performing again.'

Galina Lelyuhina heard the radio loudspeakers 'hissing' as she walked home to Litovskaya Street, 'starving and exhausted', from work in the Molotov automobile plant in Petrogradskaya Side. Before the war, she was taking flute classes at the Mussorgsky music academy. 'They said all musicians who were still alive must come to the House of Radio and register. Without any rest, I took my flute and plodded at a snail's pace.' When she got there, she was enrolled for the orchestra, though she had severe scurvy, and found it extremely difficult to play. 'My arms would not bend.'[1]

The oboist Ksenia Mikhaylovna Matus was another young recruit. 'I bumped into the oboist Kukleva on Theatre Square. She had just buried her husband and was due to be evacuated,' she recollected. 'She asked me to go to the House of Radio studio.' A little later her friend Vera Petrovna Chernetskaya 'came creeping' – 'we didn't walk any more' – to see her. She confirmed the 'thrilling news' that the orchestra might play again.[2] Matus found that her oboe had turned green with neglect. 'The valves were green, the pads were coming off.' She walked to an instrument maker on the far side of the city. He was sitting wrapped in a rug. An armchair was in a corner with various pelts – 'like ruffs or collars' – lying on it. She knew what they were. He agreed to repair the oboe. She asked him the cost. 'Bring me a little cat!' he said. 'I've eaten five cats already.' She said that no cat, or bird or dog, remained alive. 'I can pay only with money.' He fixed it anyway.[3] It took her fifty minutes to walk the short distance from Gertsen Street to the House of Radio. She barely recognized Alexander Romanovich Presser, the orchestra's supervisor, but he was 'still full of energy' and signed her up as a staff member of the orchestra.[4]

The violinist V. Petrova was on duty with the local air defence division at the House of Radio. After the orchestra stopped playing at the end of December, all its members who had enough strength were billeted in the building and served in different squads. Eliasberg came to the House. Petrova was delighted when he said that the orchestra would be resuming its work soon. 'The city must listen to our voice,' he told her. 'The voice of music.'[5]

The city added to its long musical lustre the same day. The musicologist Roman Ilyich Gruber saw through the publication of the first volume of his *Istoriia muzykal'noi kulture*. This majestic history of musical culture was a work of courage and selflessness. Gruber had left the safety of the Conservatoire in Moscow, where he was teaching, to fly into Leningrad to work with the printers. He fell sick. He agreed to go to a feeding station next to the publishing house, where he insisted on sharing his ration with the printers. His grand obsession inspired them to complete the printing. He collapsed the moment he achieved his goal.

It seemed, too, that the orchestra was too weak to go on. When Matus went to the House of Radio studio to meet them, she 'nearly fell over' with shock. 'Of the orchestra of a hundred people, there were only fifteen left,' she recalled.

> I didn't recognize the musicians I knew from before, they were like skeletons. I don't think Eliasberg called the first rehearsal to look for musicians. It was evident we couldn't play anything, we could hardly stand on our feet! Nevertheless he said, 'Dear friends, we are weak but we must force ourselves to start work,' and raised his arms to begin. There was no reaction. The musicians were trembling. Finally, those who were able to play a bit helped the weaker musicians, and thus our small group began to play the opening bars. And that was the beginning of the first rehearsal.[6]

It was scheduled to last three hours. It broke up after only fifteen minutes.

Whatever the musical glimmers, the regime's blackness remained inviolate. Boris Izvekov was brought back to the interrogation chamber at 5 p.m. on 1 March.

The interest now was in Postoyeva, Natalia Ivanovna. Was he familiar with her?

'Yes, I know her from 1936–37, from when she started working at the Electrotechnical Institute.'

What did he know about her?

'I'm not familiar with her personal beliefs, or her attitude to the Soviet government. We met rarely and never discussed politics.'

She and her friends were not going to escape so lightly.

'Please describe persons closely related to Postoyeva.'

'Postoyeva is the friend of Professor Smirnov's wife and she visits her often. She also has a close relationship with a professor in the mathematics department at LGU, Professor Petraim, and with Koshliakov, whose wife she visits a lot.'

What did he know of Smirnov?

'He is quite a religious person. His father served in the church in Leningrad. He is a supporter of the bourgeois democratic system.'

'How do you know Smirnov has these sorts of beliefs?'

'While Friedmann was alive, Smirnov supported his beliefs. And I know Friedmann was opposed to the Soviet government, and I conclude Smirnov was too, taking his background into account. One of his brothers was repressed and sent away. Taking all this into account, I'm led to believe that Smirnov is not a hard-working Soviet citizen.'

Had he met Smirnov or Postoyeva at their homes? No. Where then? At Friedmann's. And Koshliakov? Had he visited Postoyeva?

'Yes. I know that Koshliakov went to her place with birthday greetings in 1938 or 1939. And I know that Postoyeva was an assistant of Koshliakov at the Electrotechnical Institute, and that she had been Smirnov's *dozent* at LGU.'

What did he know of Smirnov's ties with the Whites?

'I know that Smirnov lived in the south during the civil war, and he served as a professor in Simferopol University, when it was occupied by the Whites.'

Vladimir Smirnov had indeed been in Simferopol between 1919 and 1922, before returning to Leningrad, where he became head of the Institute of Mathematics and Mechanics. He was, too, a man of 'exceptional nobility, benevolence and culture', according to the biographers of his friend Alexander Friedmann, *burzhui* qualities that will not have endeared him to the NKVD.[7] His forte, conjugate functions in multidimensional Euclidean space, was no doubt beyond them.

'How long have you known Koshliakov?' And so it went.

It was 2 a.m. on 2 March. They had been at him for nine hours, for five fresh names. Perhaps they were as exhausted as he. They stopped.

A few hours later, Hitler ordered Army Group North to cut off the Volkhov pocket at its base. The mouth of the pocket was only six miles wide. At the centre, about a mile apart, were two hundred-foot-wide supply lanes linking the Second Shock Army to the Russian forces on the east bank of the Volkhov river. The trees and brushwood were cut, and compacted snow had raised the surface of the lanes above the tree stumps. The Germans gave them girls' names: Erika for the northern route, Dora for the southern. They were the lifelines for the 100,000 Russians inside the pocket.

The operation was named Raubtier ('Predator'), and its pincers were to snap shut close to Myasnoi Bor, the small town at the base of the pocket. Leningrad's would-be saviours would then find themselves besieged in twenty square miles of forest and swamp. Once that was achieved, General Halder wrote the same day, 'no blood is to be wasted on reducing the enemy in the marshes. He can be left to starve to death.'[8]

Stalin, though, was still confident that his Fifty-Fourth Army, driving southeast, could link up with the Second Shock pushing north to Lyuban. Three days earlier, the Stavka (the Russian High Command) ordered Meretskov to continue the Second Shock's stalled attack on Lyuban without pausing to regroup. General Khozin, commander of the Leningrad Front, was ordered to set the Fifty-Fourth Army driving down on the railway town immediately. If they succeeded in linking up – Stalin promised generous air support, as Hitler did for Operation Raubtier – the Germans would be trapped, and the siege lifted.

The German position was precarious. To the south of Lake Ilmen, one German corps, and half of another, were pinned into a pocket at Demyansk. The Red Army counter-offensive had trapped them there since January. They were utterly dependent on each day's supply flights, by aircraft and gliders, the II Corps commander, General von Brockdorff, told Hitler at the 2 March meeting at the Führerhauptquartier. Half the 5,500 men of the garrison trapped since January in Kholm, another of the winter 'hedgehogs', were already dead or wounded. General Scherer feared that the next determined Red Army assault would finish off his ad hoc unit, Kampfgrüppe Scherer.

The Volkhov pocket was a desperate place to fight. Only the brick chimneys of Myasnoi Bor were left standing. Its name meant 'Meat Wood', in memory of the cattle that had drowned in the bogs and forests on the old drover's trail to the market in St Petersburg. The terrain was lying beneath several feet of ice and snow that would give way to mud and water when the thaw came. In places, the birch trees and reed beds and stands of peaty water gave it a misty beauty in summer, but it had no food or berries for men, and no fodder for their horses.

While the ground was frozen, horse-drawn *panje* wagons and sleds took Russian supplies to the front. When it thawed, the only roads running from east to west were corduroy, made of trees cut from the gloomy forests, stripped of their branches, and laid side by side. The Red Army men who built them laboured like *zeks* in the Gulag. They were exhausted and they had only their entrenching tools. 'We even lacked files for sharpening the saws,' P. P. Dmitriev recollected of his platoon, 'and how much wood can be sawed with a blunt instrument? Yet, we worked day and night.' Only the commander and the gun operator in each battery remained at his gun. The others were all building the road or collecting supplies and shells from the stores more than 30 miles in the rear. 'It took five or six days to go there and back. One can imagine how much one man could bring, if a single shell with fuse weighed thirty kilos.' When the road was finished, the supply trucks often fell through the surface, and the logs sank into the swampy ground. Road workers were posted along the road to pull out trucks that got stuck. 'This was truly hellish work.'[9] The surface was difficult for marching men, and dangerous and leg-breaking for horses. Both sides laid narrow-gauge railway tracks on log sleepers. The Germans called theirs the 'Volkhov Express'. Locomotives on the Russian line were vulnerable to shelling and air strikes. The supply wagons had often to be pulled along the track by horse and hand.

The desperate attempts to break through to the Russians trapped in the forests outside Lyuban foundered under mortar and artillery fire. Dmitriev lost his battery commander. 'We carried him to the firing position and buried him with full military honours, swearing revenge upon the invaders.' German mortar shells burst in the tree tops, scattering a mass of lethal splinters. Dmitriev was in the battery's forward observation post, in the combat positions of a battalion of the 1098th Rifle Regiment. Visibility was poor through the solid mass of birch trees and bushes and it was difficult to get targets for the two howitzer batteries. Shells began to run out, and 'our fire became weaker and weaker'. On 8 March, Antyufeev himself visited the combat positions. He called out Dmitriev by name, and ordered him to lead a combined force to attack towards the trapped units.

Dmitriev put together sixteen men – signallers, cooks, drivers and eight soldiers. He examined their weapons and ammunition. They took up their starting positions. 'The machine guns went to work and with a cry of "Hurrah!" we rose to the attack,' he wrote. 'At this moment for me, time stood still . . . I regained consciousness when, through a dull mist, I caught sight of people in white smocks and heard the sound of someone moaning.' He was in a field hospital.

The encircled cavalry and riflemen met their end. The few aircraft that attempted to resupply them were shot down. Their radio sets broke down and communications were lost. Food and ammunition ran out. At the last, they destroyed their vehicles and heavy weapons – 'right down to the machine guns', Antyufeev noted – and they tried to fight their way out at night with their personal weapons. Only eighteen men of the 1100th Rifle Regiment succeeded.[10]

The offensive strength of the 327th Rifle Division was exhausted, Antyufeev admitted. 'It went over to the defensive.' It was the Germans who were preparing to go on the offensive. Wilhelm Lubbeck's 154th Infantry Regiment was moved from outside Leningrad to the Volkhov Front. They were replaced by an SS division manned by Swedes, Norwegians and Danes. He noted that the tall and inexperienced Scandinavians took a dozen casualties from snipers on the day of the handover.[11] Stuka pilots from Luftflotte I, and the men of the 58th Infantry Division and the SS Police Division, were being briefed on Raubtier. It was the sort of operation at which the Germans excelled.

Boris Izvekov was back in the interrogation chamber on 3 March, a day of cold so exceptional that Dmitri Likhachev's father died 'in fearful torment.' Dmitri took him to the mortuary in the garden of the Narodny Dom on a child's sled. The memory of leaving him among the dead never left him.[12] The young composer Boris Golts was killed serving with a rifle company at the front, where forlorn attacks to break through to the Volhov salient were continuing. He was twenty-eight, and he had been one of the most promising students in the Conservatoire, admired by Shostakovich.

The surreal questioning of Izvekov continued through the day. He had edited *Climate Through the Ages*, a classic account of climate change by C. E. P. Brooks, the distinguished British climatologist.

'What political crimes did you commit while editing this book?' We do not know what preliminaries – fear, exhaustion, hunger, fists, eagerness to please – produced this admission: 'I allowed anti-Soviet statements to be published . . . that a person's development is not related only to economic development but to the climate of the environment.' This, he agreed, was 'anti-Marxist' and a 'bourgeois theory.'

The session finished at 5.30 p.m.

The Muzkomediya celebrated its revival after weeks of silence with a matinee and an evening performance of *Silva* at the Pushkin Theatre on 4 March. The operetta had triumphed on Broadway and London as *The Gipsy Princess*,* and it was fine escapist fare. 'Rossi's magnificent creation [the theatre] on empty Ostrovsky Square, covered with high snow hills. In the dusk of the day, about 2 p.m., the square came to life,' T. Karskaya recollected in her memoirs:

> By the narrow pathways through the mounds of snow, human figures crawled, one by one, dark against the snow. The theatre's many doors were closed. The windows were covered with plywood panels against shell blasts. People came in through a single door into the cold vestibule. No carpet, no paintings, the chandeliers gone, people in coats, uniforms, in hats, in shawls, coming into the hall.
>
> People taking their seats – many military people, and teenagers and the young. Near the orchestra in the central aisle is a big box with sand and shovels, against incendiaries. There are the same boxes in the tiers. The conductor appears. Not in tails or tuxedo. Like the audience and the musicians, he is in a fur coat and hat. His hands are frozen, but one movement of his baton, and tender sounds fly through the silent hall.[13]

---

* Ironically, Kalman, a Hungarian Jew, was one of Hitler's favourite composers. He was offered honorary Aryan status after the Anschluss. He refused it, and went to Paris and then America. His work, well-loved in Leningrad, was now banned in Germany.

There was shelling in the evening. A musician on fire duty at the House of Radio left his post to relieve himself during the bombardment. His name was pinned prominently on the noticeboard for all to see his shame: Isaac Yasenovsky, one of the best viola players of his day. The cellist K. Ananyan wrote to his sister in Armenia: 'I was in hospital for 2½ months. Outlived very severe diseases. Only one pressure on us at present – lack of food. That's why we wait for your parcels like manna from heaven. Let it be just black dry bread or a crust, a potato, cheap flour, or fat – anything like that for us is happiness, a dream. I have to confess that in all my life I have never known such terrible days.'[14] Simeon Putyakov, the diarist and disillusioned soldier from Sosnovka in the northern suburbs, was shot for anti-Soviet propaganda under 58-10. The sentences underlined in his diary were held to 'slander the Red Army food supply'.

Alla Shelest determined that day to leave the city. Her mother had suffered a heart attack. She knew she would lose her if they stayed. She told Agrippina Vaganova that she was going, and the old dancer had asked her, 'Alla, take me with you.' She began to pack for evacuation. 'I took underwear and civilian clothes for Father. If he survives the war, he'll need them. I packed all our clothes, and the family silver dinner service, a tea set, jewellery and bronzes to sell for food.' But the ice in the streets was half a yard thick. Her father had promised to send a staff car from the Front HQ. None came. 'I was in a terrible condition and Mother couldn't move. After I was caught by the shell blast, I didn't go out by day, but it was spooky after dusk.'

A three-year-old, Lidya Karasyova, was evacuated on 4 March. She was an exceptional survivor. She had almost died in December. She lived in a single room with her mother, aunt and grandmother – who had bought a pigeon shortly before they disappeared. She made a bouillon broth from the meat, and fed it to the feverish little girl cup by cup. Her mother and aunt gave up their bread rations for her. Slowly little

Lidochka came back to life. By 4 March she was well enough to leave with her mother. The Germans bombed the convoy on Ladoga. The shock waves hurled the girl across the truck and split her head open. She was given first aid at one of the posts on the ice. Surgeons operated on her when they reached the far shore. She was put in a cattle car with her mother, with a paltry wood-burning stove against the cold. At least one person in the car died each day on the long journey, their bodies removed at stops along the line. Lidochka was alive when they reached sanctuary in Moscow.[15]

The world premiere of the Seventh took place in Kuibyshev on 5 March. Shostakovich was always in high spirits during rehearsals, but he found the first performance a terrible ordeal. 'He was in and out of our rooms all day,' Slonim recalled, 'never staying longer than ten minutes, looking even paler than usual and, almost stammering, imploring us not to go to the concert, hoping we would all stay away. The next moment, he was calling the theatre and begging for "just one more ticket" for a girl in the post office who had asked him to get her in.' He took this state of 'feverish agitation and tension' with him to the theatre, running from room to room, mumbling greetings as he passed. He was pale and clenching his fists.

Nina told Flora Litvinova that he was always like this for a premiere. 'He gets terribly wound up. He's frightened it will be a flop,' Flora observed. 'DD himself acknowledged that he felt physically ill to the point of nausea before a premiere.' He still made a point of signing a programme for every musician in the orchestra: it might 'make them try a little harder'.[16] The audience called him on stage before the beginning of the concert. 'He was very tense and unsmiling,' Slonim observed, 'in front of a merciless crowd of admirers.'[17]

The symphony made huge demands on conductor and musicians. It was sprawling, lasting 80 minutes, and Samosud played it with an interval after the first movement. This was music on a vast scale, scored for an abnormally large orchestra. Eight French horns, six trumpets and six trombones made up the brass. The woodwind needed three flutes, two oboes, a cor anglais, three clarinets, a bass clarinet, two bassoons and a contrabassoon. The strings soaked up sixteen first violins, fourteen second violins, a dozen violas, ten cellos, eight double basses and two harps.* It made no compromises. In half-starved, half-overrun, bleeding Russia, its lavish use of surviving musical talent was startling and defiant. This was a symphony as giant as the city it portrayed.

It was a triumph, the applause cascading on and on through the packed hall. The audience cheered and clamoured for the composer. Tanya Litvinova was struck by his nervousness when he went onto the platform to take his bows. It went together with 'a Leningrader's reserve and a eunuch's youthfulness'. Nobody who saw him could forget his 'crooked figure, his grimace of misery, and the fingers that never stopped drumming on his cheek'. It was torture just to watch him. 'He minced his steps and bowed like a circus pony,' Ilya Slonim agreed with his wife. The audience, he said, was 'in raptures' by the end of the Seventh, but the 'severe young man mounted the stage as if going to the scaffold'.[18]

From this moment, the symphony lodged itself in the emotional landscape of the war. It was the sound of Leningrad, the defiance and courage of the besieged city set to music. It laid a blanket of decency and humanity over the men in the blue caps, the execution squads, the interrogators: it hid the continuing vileness of the regime from its allies beneath a veneer of culture. Tchaikovsky had touched a powerful chord of war with his *1812*, the overture commemorating Russian resistance to Napoleon, which Radio Leningrad was playing again and again. But he had written it sixty years after the event. The Seventh was instantaneous.

---

* Even percussion demanded a dozen musicians: five timpani, a bass drum, snare drum, cymbals, tam-tam, triangle, tambourine and xylophone. Add the single keyboard player, the pianist, and the total is 109.

It was conceived during the air raids and artillery barrages that were still falling on Leningrad. It came from the heart of the war, and millions, in Russia and far beyond, took it to their own hearts.

The premiere was broadcast on radio stations across Russia. The violinist David Oistrakh, listening in Moscow, wrote of his 'enormous pride' that Russia had produced an artist 'capable of responding to the terrible events of war with such convincing strength and inspiration'. The music 'resounded like a prophetic affirmation of victory over fascism, a poetic statement of the patriotic feelings of the people, and of their faith in the eventual triumph of humanism and light'.[19] Glikman was huddled round a decrepit, tinny little set in Tashkent with the director of the Leningrad Conservatoire, Pavel Serebryakov, and other professors. Though many 'precious details' were lost in the awful reception, Glikman said, they were all overwhelmed by the power of the music. 'We could hear the fateful, tragic music of the first movement, the searing lyricism of the scherzo, the savagely triumphant beauty of the adagio, the heroic spirit of the finale.'[20]

The composer gave his own judgement in a letter to Sollertinsky. 'It was a big enough success,' he said. The orchestra played 'remarkably' but he was less impressed by the conductor. 'Samosud was quite good in the first 3 parts, but he's got a little bit tired by the 4th. He's 58. But in any case the 4th part sounded quite convincing.' His son Maxim forgot the rehearsals, but he remembered the premiere. 'The theme of invasion in the 1st part, the coming of something horrible, entered my soul,' he recalled. 'Galya and I had a religious nanny called Pasha. I heard this music in my dreams – the drums sound in the distance and get closer and closer, louder and louder. I awoke from this nightmare and ran to Pasha. She crossed me and said a prayer.' He also remembered the chocolate praline he was given after the performance. 'I never had such candies again.'[21]

*

As the Seventh was playing, the war correspondent Pavel Luknitsky returned home to Leningrad from a visit to Fifty-Fourth Army. A woman walked towards him in the dusk, chanting 'Death! Death! Death!' She stared straight through him as she passed him 'like a terrified spirit', continuing to howl. 'Death by starvation will take us all. The soldiers will live a while longer. But we will die. We will die. We will die.' When he climbed the staircase to his apartment, he found the roof had been blown off.[22]

On March 6 at 7.40 p.m., the endgame was played out for Boris Izvekov.

Kruzkhov began: 'You haven't named all the counter-revolutionaries.'

'I admit I forgot the following members of our organization . . . Obrazov, archivist . . . Ainovsky, professor of the Hydrophysics Institute . . . Budkov, professor in the physics faculty . . . Izakson, dozent at LSU. He comes from a bourgeois family and his beliefs and mine are the same . . .'

Kruzkhov was finished with him at 9 p.m. He had enough names now.

Iszvekov was returned to his cell in the Shpalernaya, to await sentence, should the cannibals and the child's bread ration allow him to live that long. Lidiya Okhapkina was on the Ladoga ice. She had been almost too weak that morning to reach the assembly point on Tchaikovsky Street with her two children. A snowstorm was whipped up by a fierce wind. She was wearing clean linen and two woollen dresses with her husband's suit on top for 'warmth and safekeeping'.

She feared she was too late. 'One last effort, one more step, one more . . .' Her truck was still there. As it started towards Ladoga, she made her farewell: 'Goodbye, my long-suffering city.' It was still snowing when they began to cross the lake. The truck slowed to a crawl. A man on skis went ahead, looking for shell holes that had weakened the ice. The truck was boarded over with plywood and exhaust fumes built up. She vomited several times. She was running a high temperature and she drifted in and out of consciousness. 'When I came to, I asked where I was, where the children were. They told me that I was in the lorry, that my children were still alive. Someone had given them something to eat.'

At the first stop, after the lake, 'good, kind-hearted people' helped her down and laid her on a bench. They fed the children on semolina and condensed milk. She was given some meat broth. 'My whole mouth and throat were furred . . . I couldn't swallow.'[23]

She went on to Cherepovets, where her husband was stationed. He leapt on to the truck, looked around and jumped off. The children did not recognize him in uniform. The emotion of seeing him again had left Lidiya speechless. He was told that his family were indeed on the lorry, and climbed back. At last he saw them. 'Is it you? Is it you?' When she undressed that evening, she stood naked in front of her husband. '"See what I have become," I said. I was nothing but skin and bone. My chest was especially awful – just ribs. And I was a nursing mother when the war began . . . Vasili looked at me and started to blink his eyes again. "Never mind," he said. "Since the bones are in good shape, the body will follow."'

The fame of the Seventh was reaching out beyond Russia. *The Times* in London ran an article on the premiere on 7 March, next to stories on the Japanese advances in Java and Burma, and the 'great battle now raging on the Volkhov River for the relief of Leningrad'. It described it as 'a work of great eloquence and urgency in which the composer's usual tense, uneasy style is broadened'. It was 'partly in the character of a requiem', but it closed optimistically 'in what the composer describes as "the victory of light over darkness, of humanity over barbarism"'.

That, of course, is how the Allies saw their own cause, and the symphony seemed evidence that the Russsians embraced the same values. From Imperial Japan and Nazi Germany came barbarity; from Soviet Russia came music. The ground for the symphony's travels abroad was already being prepared. 'It is to be hoped that it will soon be given a performance in England,' *The Times* correspondent concluded, 'for it is a composition of great character.'[24]

It was acquiring wings in Russia, too. Serebryakov was determined that the Leningrad Conservatoire players in Tashkent should perform a work by a composer who had been so illustrious a student and professor. He proposed that his deputy should make the long trip to Kuibyshev to get a copy of the score. He was miffed when Shostakovich sent him a telegram asking that Glikman should go. He doubted that Shostakovich's obscure friend would cope with getting hold of manuscript paper and making an accurate copy of the score. Shostakovich insisted.

The composer was 'absolutely overwhelmed' to receive a telegram from his mother from Cherepovets on the evacuation route: 'Got away safely from Leningrad longing to see you love to all Babka.' He had moved from the rooms on Frunze Street to a separate four-room flat at 2a Vilonovskaya Street. He needed the space. 'If only they can get here to us safely,' he wrote to Glikman. 'We are expecting eight people altogether: Mama, Marusya, Mitya, Sof. Mikh., Vas. Vas., Irina, G. G. Efros and Allochka. Somehow or other we'll all manage to squash in.'

He added that he was flying to Moscow in a few days. 'Samosud has already left to fix up an orchestra there for my symphony.'[25]

A reminder of the old elegance of the city's *grandes dames* remained in a fashion atelier at Nevsky Prospekt 12. It was particularly busy on 8 March. This was Women's Day, a time for presenting gifts to wives and girlfriends, and it had a special resonance, for it was on this day in 1917 that the women working in the city's textile factories had come out on strike, and precipitated the Revolution.* The workshop had been a

---

* The Bolsheviks played no part on this day, from which the revolution flowed over the next three weeks. They preferred to celebrate 'Red October', the *coup d'état* eight months later when, the Tsar long gone, they had seized power.

boutique before the war, called Smert Muzhyam ('Death to Husbands'). It was run by the designer 'F', who created magnificent ballgowns and evening dresses and exotic underwear, which were modelled by his wife, Maria Yelizarovna F. They were still busy making these heady concoctions, which were flown out of the city to Moscow in suitcases, destined for Kremlin wives and the mistresses of army generals.

The Muzkomediya celebrated the day with a performance in the House of the Red Army. Everyone in the audience was given a little bag of food. The women living in the Conservatoire were given a festival breakfast, lunch and dinner. Women at the Kirov theatre were asked to lead a blitz on hygiene, and make sure everyone washed their hands and faces.

The head of the MAA, the Arts Committee, reported to the city Party. He said that the reopening of the Muzkomediya was 'a great event'. The theatre was always full. 'They are in fur coats and felt boots but for some time they forget the world outside and are swept up in the show.' He asked for the Philharmonia Hall to be opened for a wide range of performances, Red Army and Red Navy ensembles, chamber concerts, symphonies, ballet evenings. 'The hall is in good condition – it's only necessary to give an order to Lenenergo to turn on the lights.' Electricity was restored to the hall five days later.

Directors as well as musicians were dying now. Igor Mikhlachevsky was gone on 8 March. He was the artistic director and conductor of the Capella, the oldest choir in Russia, which had once accompanied the Tsar on military campaigns, and had graced St Petersburg from its elegant building on the Moika embankment since 1703. He was followed next day by V. Maratov, the artistic director of the Radio Choir. The place the Radiokom had got him at the Astoria feeding station came too late.

Elena Martilla reached her low point: 'In a bread line, someone called me "grandmother". I'm eighteen. I'm walking with a cane.' She walked across the city to the School of Art. She had ambitions to be a set designer. She went along alleys to the university, and across the ice of the Neva to the Champ de Mars. She crossed the field to Swan Bridge, the beauty of the city laid out around her. On the Liteiny, she passed the Bolshoi Dom. 'Along the way I met more dead than living – ten dead for every five alive, some felled by hunger, some by shells and bombs,' she recorded. She realized that if she were to lie down, she would never get up again. She was having fainting spells two to four times a day.[26] She saved herself, as others did, by clinging to an interest. She started painting again, sketching her own face in a mirror with blue paint on her brush. She became exhilarated that she was defying Hitler's order that Leningraders should be exterminated. 'I realized that I will not die – this I felt with every cell of my dystrophic organism and it infused me with strength. Now I had caught my second wind, no, my tenth. I even became happy and . . . calm.'[27]

The theatre also revived spirits. The Muzkomediya staged a premiere of Benatzky and Friml's *Sailor's Love* on 14 March. Valerian Bogdanov-Berezovsky went with his wife. 'It was a good performance,' he noted, 'but our mood was very stern.' L. Vasten, a singer in the choir, recalled that she wore a winter coat beneath her costume, a geisha's kimono. No one noticed. She was proud of the way they hid their exhaustion and dystrophy.[28] Plans were discussed on radio. A new comedy was to be staged, *The Broken Walls*, with music by N. Timofeyev and a libretto based on the adventures of the partisans. Concerts of one sort or another were held almost every day at the front or in hospitals. Twenty singers were transferred from the Capella to boost the Radio Choir. The other Capella survivors were evacuated over the ice.

The Radiokom asked *Gorzdravodel* (the city health department) for four more places at the Astoria on 16 March. It also asked the energy department to give them a wooden house or wrecked apartment block that they could dismantle for firewood. It was back a week later begging for another five places for members of the orchestra and choir.

The singer Zoya Lodsi was less fortunate. She failed to be awarded an academician's ration at the Conservatoire. She wrote to the MAA's Boris Zagorsky. He was a good man, who had been wounded at the front, and she appealed to him: 'I try to be merry and vivacious. I believe you will save me. I ask you to give me the ration on medical grounds. If not, then all my art will be in vain. I created it despite the difficulties of my disease. Boris Ivanovich, please understand, I am dying. It's the first time in my life that I am so afraid.'

Operation Raubtier opened at 7.30 a.m. on 15 March with waves of Stukas dive-bombing Russian positions at the mouth of the pocket. By nightfall, 263 missions had been flown. The pilots had to judge their bomb release exactly. Too close to the ground fighting, and they killed their own men; too far, and the Russians had time to recover before the advancing infantry and SS Police got at them. By the end of the first day, only four miles separated the leading troops.

A young nurse, T. I. Obukhova, was ordered to join the 111th Rifle Division in the forests in the west of the pocket. She was with other nurses and three doctors in the 120th Medical Battalion. Near Myasnoi Bor, they had to pass through the middle of a half-frozen swamp. One of the nurses fell and cried out. The Germans heard her and she was wounded by automatic weapon fire. It was evening by the time they reached the medical station. It had tents and small huts with plank bunks. They gathered moss to insulate the huts.

The wounded lay where they could, in their hundreds. 'Operations went on day and night, and so did bandaging and dressing wounds,' she recollected. 'Blood and groans were continual . . . constantly looking on bloodied and helpless men, squeezing their fingers as they grew cold, looking into their fading eyes and trying to reassure them: "Hang on, just a little longer. You will get better!" And to hear the response: "No, nurse, I'm not long for this world . . . Here, take this address, my son is there . . ."' When a soldier died, she wept for a few moments in a corner, and then return to the wounded. 'They arrived in a never-ending stream, carried, dragged . . . You forced yourself to smile, roll cigarettes for them with trembling hands, soothe and reassure them, while sensing their anguish.'[29]

Women served in combat at the front, as partisan fighters, snipers and pilots, but it was as field nurses that they had most impact on morale. It was said that 'every front-line soldier without exception' knew the song 'Nurse Anyiuta' ('*Medestra Anyuta*'), though it was never recorded or played on radio. It was written by the composer Iurii Slonov, and it told of a wounded soldier who was saved by a nurse:

> I can never forget
> Our meeting and that winter night.
> A cold, gusty wind was blowing
> And the water froze in my canteen.[30]

Route Erika, bomb-blasted, strewn with destroyed wagons and the dead, fell to the Germans on 18 March. Then they reached Dora. Late that afternoon, on 19 March, their spearheads made contact. The life-lines were severed. The Red Army cavalry had their dead horses to eat. A telephonist set out every morning with an axe, Sokolov recalled, in search of horsemeat. 'We cooked it without salt. It was loathsome, but we ate it all the same.' The surviving horses fed on the thatch from roofs and steamed birch branches. The infantry began to starve. As the weather became warmer, the stench of decay became all the more palpable. Burial teams were organized. One night, returning to headquarters, Sokolov stumbled on a strange scene. 'On a snow-covered clearing, I saw corpses standing under the moonlight. The burial crews had placed the corpses upright in the snow so they could find them when they returned.'[31] As the dead horses thawed out, the bodies bloated and became inedible and infested with maggots.

On 21 March, Lieutenant-General Andrei Vlasov was flown into the pocket. He did not formally take command of the Second Shock Army for almost a month, but the commander he replaced, General Krukov, was already sick. Vlasov was a tall and charismatic man, his height increased by the tall astrakhan hat he wore. He was only forty, but he had made his name with his skilful handling of the Twentieth Army during the November battles in front of Moscow. Stalin and his High Command, the Stavka, trusted him enough to show him off to the British and American press. His vigour and his aura of success made him the ideal man to break the deadlock in the frozen bogs. The position was critical, but not hopeless. Even though now surrounded, the Second Shock continued its efforts to break through to Lyuban. They were within five miles of it. Travelling south-west towards the town, the Fifty-Fourth Army had driven a deep wedge into the German line at Pogostye and were ten miles from it and still advancing. It needed only the slightest German blunder for their hold on the Volkhov Front to be unhinged, and Leningrad relieved. The commander of the German Eighteenth Army, General Georg Lindemann, warned his corps commander, von Chappuis, that 'the situation demands hard decisions and inspired leadership or else the army is lost'. After Vlasov's tanks reopened the Erica supply line, Lindemann relieved von Chappuis of his command, a disgrace that saw him commit suicide in the summer.

It was the weather, and their continuing tactical brilliance, that came to the Germans' aid. The start of *rasputitsa* was put at 23 March, a little later than usual. The spring thaw turned unsurfaced tracks into rivers of mud and every entrenchment and dip into a mudhole. In winter, the ground freezes to eight or nine feet – at least that in the severe cold of 1941–42 – and locks within it the autumnal rains and the winter snowfall.

In spring, it takes five to six weeks to thaw from the top down, the mud ever deeper. Snow still fell, heavy and wet, before it melted. Every gully and shellhole filled with water. The mud was more than three feet deep on the roads. The only reliable transport were the *panje* peasant carts. With their high wheels, light weight and wooden frame, they surged through like boats. Pack-horses were used by both sides. Some became mired in the mud and drowned.

The Russians, of course, were used to the thaw, but it left them at a disadvantage. On 27 March, using tanks supported by infantry, they managed to drive the Germans from Erika and reopened the supply lane. It was constantly shelled, deep in mud and craters, and usable only at night and without lights. The *rasputitsa* made it a torment to distribute the supplies that did get through. Messerschmitts were constantly overhead, Sokolov said, hunting down 'every vehicle, every wagon, every person on foot'.

Like Leningrad, the Second Shock Army was besieged. It was starting to starve, too.

Shostakovich's mother Sofiya, sister Mariya and nephew arrived in Kuibyshev on 19 March. They were emaciated. 'My mother is nothing but skin and bone,' he wrote to Glikman. 'Vasily Vasilyevich looked absolutely terrible and his wits seemed to be wandering.' The sculptor Slonim, though, was much taken by Sofiya's 'brilliant blue Russian eyes': 'The son is strikingly like his mother, and they share many interests.' She was astonished at seeing the many dogs that roamed the streets. She hadn't seen a live dog in Leningrad for weeks. Mariya shocked them by saying casually, 'You know, once we ate a cat. Of course, I didn't tell mother and little Mitya.' They were in a much better state than Nina's parents, who arrived at the end of the month. 'My father-in-law looks awful,' he wrote. 'Mama looks pretty grim too. The others are in a passable state. Now I have the task of feeding and restoring them to health.'[32]

He was flown to Moscow on 20 March with the principals of the Bolshoi orchestra. They were preparing to play the Seventh in the capital. It seemed less and less likely that enough musicians would survive to play it in Leningrad. Two more, A. Budishev and A. Nomerovsky, and the music critic N. Malkov, died that day. Malkov's widow, wishing to bury him decently, had a grand mahogany wardrobe converted into a coffin.

The MAA begged for a privileged canteen to be set up where 300 of the city's most creative people could be fed with extra rations. It said that 538 such 'artistic people' had died over the winter.[33] Later in the month, the canteen at the Bolshoi Drama Theatre on Fontanka was opened up to 'artistic people reviving the cultural life of the city'. In exchange, the Radiokom was required to broadcast more music, and to include live transmissions by ensembles and others.

Eliasberg was going from apartment to apartment where he knew musicians had taken to their beds. 'He bribed them,' the oboist Matus recalled. 'He said: "Come to work, and there'll be food." He arranged for us to be fed in the Bolshoi theatre canteen.' Those who came to the auditions were often too weak to play properly. This was true of most of the trombonists, trumpeters and tuba players. The strings made fewer demands. 'They had no wind instrument players, so they turned to the army, and asked if they could use us,' the clarinettist Viktor Kozlov recalled. He was serving as a military clarinettist at Leningrad Military Headquarters. 'That's how I came to be in the orchestra.' 'First violin dies and the drummer dies on his way to work,' Olga Berggolts wrote of this time. The drummer was Dzhaudat Iaydarov, and he did not die. Eliasberg found him lying with others who had been given up for dead. He saw his fingers move slightly, and he shouted, 'He's alive!' Iaydarov was revived and given special rations. He would survive to play the Seventh.

All those who played at auditions were paid. Kryukov saw a note that the orchestra director made for the Radio commercial department on one musician: 'I want him paid right away, as he'll be too weak to come back.'[34] It was a slow process, but eleven new musicians were accepted into the orchestra after auditions in March.

The conductor himself was still weak. The Radiokom asked that he should continue to be nourished at the Astoria, though this was no guarantee of survival, and the Radio's double-bass player, N. Trakan, died at the feeding station. 'Comrade Eliasberg works very hard to revive a big symphony orchestra,' the committee said. 'He is the only prominent conductor left in Leningrad.'[35]

A volunteer, a maths teacher called Olga Symanovskaya, had been raising morale in Svetlana Magayeva's children's home for the past five weeks. She wore coloured dresses and a bright white beret, and she came in the morning and pulled back the blackout curtains to let the pale winter light flood in. Then she said: 'Come on, let's all do our morning exercises.' She meant mental exercises – the children were too weak for PE – and she made them repeat a little stanza she had written for them:

> We have survived the month of January
> We will survive the month of February
> When March comes, we will sing songs of happiness and joy.

Often, a fresh death was found when she arrived in the mornings, but she made them do their exercises and stopped them from 'nodding off and thinking of hunger and death'. They looked forward to her visits, and the sparkling colour of her clothes. One day in March, she stopped coming. The children were told she had fallen while walking home. They still did her exercises, and the new arrivals who replaced the dead learned her stanza. By now, they were promising themselves that they would sing of happiness and joy in April.[36]

Some of them would not see the spring. 'Death had been standing next to the body of Olya,' Svetlana recalled. 'But it was unable to take her because her brother Seryozha was still alive.' Olya was twelve. She shared a bed with her five-year-old brother Seryozha, tiny for his age, thin and blond. The boy slept almost all the time. He sat up only when a spoon of food touched his lips. He never opened his eyes. He ate his ration of food, and then Olya gave him hers, and he lay back and slept again. The doctor and nurses tried to persuade her to eat, but she refused, giving it to her brother. She got thinner and weaker. Despite his extra ration, the boy died. Olya kissed his cold face and would not let the doctor or nurse take him away for some time. When finally they took his body, Olya 'just sighed and died'.[37]

The will to live abandoned Sasha, too, another orphan. He was eleven or twelve when he was brought in. His mother and brother had starved to death. He had wrapped their bodies in bed sheets and pulled them on a sledge, one at a time, to the mortuary. He went home, and the apartment block where he lived was hit by shellfire. One tore off the lower part of his left arm and badly mutilated the lower part of his leg. Neighbours got him to hospital. Surgeons amputated his left arm up to the elbow and his leg up to the knee. At night, in their room, Svetlana saw him silently crying. When his bandages were changed, and his crusted blood was torn away with them, he grimaced with pain but remained silent. One day, Sasha said out loud that he did not want to live any more. He turned his face to the wall. In the morning, his bed was empty. His crutches were still propped up next to it. Svetlana composed a poem, and whispered it to Lena, the girl in the next bed, who wrote it down:

> In our children's house
> Now only the crutches
> Stand
> Gathering dust near his bed.
> He could not walk
> And yesterday he said

That he did not want to live.

He became silent forever.

Sasha, Sasha, please live.

I have two arms

I have two legs,

I will help you.[38]

His death made the children realize that they had to become more involved with one another if they were to live. They pulled back the blackout curtains. It was snowy outside, but the sun was visible beyond the winter clouds, and its dim rays still illuminated the room. 'For us the light represented life, and as it entered the room, it chased away the darkness of death.'[39]

Easter Saturday fell on 22 March.* In Moscow, the churches were allowed to hold candlelit processions as the curfew was raised for a night. The writer Ilya Ehrenburg, who had been in Kuibyshev with Shostakovich, recalled going to a midnight service. 'After the darkness of the night the candles looked unbearably bright, and the choir sang, "Vanquishing death with death".'[40] Radio Leningrad broadcast a recording of

---

* Easter in the Western churches was a fortnight later than the Orthodox. Unlike the Wehrmacht, the Spanish volunteers of the Blue Division who were suffering grievously on the Volkhov made much of Holy Week. On Holy Thursday, the division's 2nd Battalion was partly overrun when Russian T-34 tanks broke through their positions in a snowstorm. Only the lead tank had a radio. The others communicated by ringing bells, and they became disorientated, thrashing round and firing and clanging fiercely. A mixed German force of telephonists and couriers with some sappers and a single 150mm gun held them overnight. On Good Friday, the remnants of the battalion counter-attacked and restored the line. The *segunda* had lost eleven dead, four of them officers, and seventy-one wounded, in two days. It was reduced to a hundred men. High mass was held at a field altar, the men kneeling in the snow and slush: 'A chill wind blew burning incense towards swaying trees which served as a rustic reredos.' On Easter Sunday, the remnants of the 2nd Battalion were withdrawn to Novgorod, to be reformed for a third time. (Gerald R Kleinfeld and Lewis A. Tambs, *Hitler's Spanish Legion: The Blue Division in Russia* (Philmont, VA: Southern Illinois University Press, 1979), p. 182.)

Tchaikovsky's Fifth. 'With such sounds, you can die in happiness,' the librarian V. Lyublinsky wrote in his diary. German bombers appeared over the city a little later, at 5 p.m. Two bombs fell on the southwest part of St Vladimir's Cathedral. Father Lomakin had been transferred to it a few weeks before. 'The faithful were standing in line at that moment, waiting to approach the tomb our our Lord,' he was to tell the Nuremberg tribunal. 'I saw some thirty persons lying wounded near the altar. Other people were lying about the church. They lay helpless . . . the concussion of the bombs was so heavy that for some time there was a constant fall of shattered glass, mortar and pieces of stone.'

He was stunned by what he saw – the wounded, others huddled against the walls in terror. 'People flocked around me. "Father, are you alive? Father, how can we understand this? We heard that the Germans believed in God, that they love Christ . . . Where is their faith then, if they can act like this on Easter Eve?"' The raid continued into the darkness. 'This night of love, this night of joy for all Christians, the Resurrection night, was turned by the Germans into a night of blood.'[41] Lomakin was convinced that the Luftwaffe and the German artillery timed their bombardments not only to demolish churches, but so that worshippers who sought refuge in them would be killed as well. Next day, in the shattered cathedral, they sang the Easter hymn, 'Christ is Risen'.

It was not, though, only Germans who pursued Russians. They continued to persecute their own. Ivan Zhilinsky's wife died in her sleep during Easter Week. He was arrested a few days later. Zhilinsky was a railway clerk, less exotic and more typical prey for the NKVD than Izvekov and the *intelligentsiya*. He had not worked since the trams stopped running, and he had tried to keep body and soul togther by taking photographs of evacuees for one hundred grams of bread a picture. His dead mother lay in the room he used as a studio, hidden behind a cupboard and a piano. Despite his efforts, he had not been able to save his wife. He may have been denounced by neighbours as a defeatist. His diary was found when he was arrested. His undoing was his all too accurate vision of post-war life. The Allies, he thought, would put pressure on the Soviets to allow freedom of speech and religion. 'Our lot will wriggle about just enough so that America and England back off and leave us to stew in our own juice,' he wrote.[42] It was enough to get him a death sentence for 'slandering Soviet reality'. It was commuted to ten years in prison, where it is likely that he died.

The scale of the deportations of undesirables and ethnic minorities was noticed by N. Mervolf. He noted in his diary that his father 'is weaker and weaker every day, swollen, abnormal'. Then he added: 'They are moving all Poles, Estonians, Latvians, Finns and Germans out of Leningrad. They give them 24 hours to get ready, and then deliver them to the *zvanka* [city limits] and they are on their own.' The Radio orchestra lost its violinist, V. Skibnyevsky, like this. His name gave him away to the NKVD as a Pole. Exhaustion and starvation carried off another two of its musicians, P. Konev and G. Shreyder.

The commissar of the 59th Independent Rifle Brigade, Colonel I. Kh. Venets, reported a rare intelligence success in the Volkhov pocket. The staff of the Second Shock Army wanted prisoners taken to interrogate on German intentions. 'This we did,' said Venets, 'and what a success we had – a liaison officer of the German General Staff!' Venets organized a search party – 'from among the best communists and *komsomol* members' of a sapper company, he said – and sent it into the German rear. Amid these waterlogged forests and reed beds, there was no front line in a continuous sense, only strongpoints built of logs on the higher ground, with firing slits and raised platforms for mortars. The art of a search party lay not so much in infiltrating as in retaining a sense of position and direction to find a way back.

By day, the Russians found a German trail through the woods. They lay in wait as night fell. Two figures came down the path, one of them merrily bawling out a song. Their uniforms identified them as an officer being escorted by a soldier. The Russians killed the soldier, silently, with a knife, and gagged the officer. They led him back to their own lines, and to the commissar's dugout. 'They looked tired but happy,' said Venets, 'bringing with them a German *Oberleutnant* wearing the splendid uniform of a general staff officer.' Lieutenant Lindemann was carrying decorations, documents and orders, and had decided to drop in on a friend. That explained the singing. Their meeting involved a fair number of drinks, Venets found, thus leading to the visitor's 'rather ignominious end'.

Venets and his brigade commander, I. F. Glazunov, began questioning the prisoner. Their rank insignia were hidden under their coats, and the lieutenant was 'insolent' at first. He lounged back in his chair, and said that Germany was winning the war. Venets ordered him to stand up, and pointed at Glazunov, telling him that he was in the presence of a colonel. Lindemann 'immediately stood at attention, transformed'. Glazunov then pointed at Venets and said, 'And this is a commissar.' The German turned pale, and asked in a trembling voice, 'Are you going to shoot me?' Venets reassured him – 'We do not shoot prisoners.' This, as we have seen, was untrue. The Russians did shoot prisoners, and the Germans, as Venets well knew, were under orders to shoot any commissar who fell into their hands. Both sides, however, recognized that it was against their interests to shoot any prisoner who might have valuable intelligence. The young staff officer certainly fell into that category, and Venets told him that he would even be sent to Moscow.

He relaxed, particularly when Venets returned his photographs to him, which included his wife and 'two chubby little children'. One photograph showed a general standing beside a magnicent staff car, with a number of officers and the Oberleutnant. Asked who this general was, he replied, 'My father.' Both corps and army headquarters were demanding that the prisoner be sent to them immediately. Venets had little time to interrogate him. What he found was not reassuring. The German asked for a piece of paper and drew 'the precise boundaries' of the Second Shock. He marked 59th Brigade's exact position in red, and said that he was carrying orders for it to be surrounded. He produced them from his jacket, and added that the brigade was '*kaput*' – finished, destroyed.

'I notified corps commissar Tkachenko about the enemy's intentions by telephone', Venets said, 'and he responded, "Don't worry ... we'll be able to deal with Germans!"'[43]

He was wrong. The Second Shock was slowly being annihilated. The Oberleutnant had reason to be confident. A German sergeant-major, A. Gütte of the 20th Infantry Division, put it succinctly. The salient was 'too narrow and the flanks much too long . . . all attempts to widen the corridor led to heavy losses. Thousands of Red Army soldiers were left lying in the woods and forests of the Volkhov.'[44]

With warmer weather, a *Landser* noted, the Germans' 'courage and vitality are returning'. They knew they could not sustain the casualties for long: the 'gardens of crosses' where they buried their dead were spilling over. Those who went home on leave found their families looking at them 'with a certain look in their eyes, that animal curiosity when you gaze on something condemned . . . And deep down so many of us believed it . . . Some slit-eyed Mongol sniper was waiting for each one of us.' In terms of strategy and morale, the Germans had to get done with Russia in 1942. That knowledge ran right through the ranks, and it gave a desperate edge to their campaigning.

The Muzkomediya was doing fine business in Leningrad. 'To escape from the prison of starvation and the awful smell of death, I dragged myself to the theatre', N. Mashkova wrote in her diary on 23 March. 'The theatre was besieged and sold out. There was vivid speculation for tickets.' She stayed in a long queue and her patience was rewarded with tickets for all four current shows, *Silva, A Wedding in Malinovka*, an operetta by Boris Alexandrov, *La Bayadère* and *Sailor's Love*. The performances were at 10.30 a.m. and 4 p.m. 'If you go to the 4 p.m. show, it helps you forget the hungry evening,' she noted.[45]

She saw *La Bayadère* first. This tale of the love of an Indian prince for a French diva, set in his palace and a Paris bar, transported its audience far from their own pitiless plight. The lead actress, L. Kolesnikova, recalled that she was very nervous during the performance. 'It was bitterly cold in the theatre, but without costume *Bayadère* makes no sense. So I had to wear a chiffon blouse and little shoes on the bare stage.' The operetta, which had played on Broadway as *The Yankee Princess*, was by Emmerich Kalman.

Musicians' rations were not enough to save the symphony orchestra's Aleksandra Mayger, who died on 24 March, but there were fresh signs of life. The pianist Alexander Kamensky held a meeting of composers in his room at the Pushkin theatre. He played new piano pieces, and Valerian Bogdanov-Berezovsky presented parts of his piano concerto.

A seven-year-old girl, Alevtina Ivanova, entranced the wounded in the wards of the military hospital where her mother worked. She had seen *Swan Lake* at the Mariinsky before the war, and ballet had captivated her. She was determined to dance for the soldiers. Her mother made her a ballerina's costume and created a headdress from the rolls of cotton used for bandages. She wore white gym shoes. A little girl with matchstick legs, she hummed the music to herself as she danced in the wards. After a while, she felt dizzy and had to stop. The soldiers clapped and cheered, and her mother scooped her up and took her home. The soldiers made a certificate of honour for her, with a picture of T-34 tanks, and the inscription: 'For Motherland, for Stalin!'[46] It was her proudest possession.

The Seventh had its Moscow premiere on 29 March. *Pravda* reported Shostakovich's words on his new symphony: 'To our fight against fascism.

To our coming victory over the enemy. To my native city Leningrad. To these I dedicate my Seventh Symphony.'[47] Ilya Ehrenburg was driven through the blacked-out capital and its dark streets, empty but for the occasional patrol, a scattering of stars adding to the sense of mystery. 'Sometimes the sky becomes alive with the fire of explosions,' he wrote. 'In the houses the window-panes rattle with the roar of the anti-aircraft batteries . . . Even the sparrows are battle-hardened. Only the rooks are excited, they did not live through the Moscow autumn, they have just returned, so to them the Junkers are new.'[48]

The premiere was held in the Hall of Columns in the House of Unions. This had been the clubhouse of the Moscow Assembly of the Nobility, a monumental palace where aristocratic Moscow met for the most brilliant balls. Pushkin described one in his poem *Yevgeny Onegin*, and Tolstoy wrote of it in *War and Peace*. The acoustics were as perfect as the colonnaded setting. Memorable concerts by Tchaikovsky, Rimsky-Korsakov and Liszt had preceded Shostakovich. It served grimmer purposes under the Bolsheviks. Lenin had lain in state in the hall before his entombment in Red Square. In time, Stalin would follow him. It was here, too, that Bukharin, Kamenev and Zinoviev had been tried and sentenced to death in 1936.

Samosud again conducted. The Bolshoi players joined forces with the All-Union Radio Orchestra. Ehrenburg was there. The audience was 'greatly moved. On the streets the sirens screamed,' he wrote. 'The screams did not penetratre into the hall. The audience was informed about the alarm when the concert was over, and the people did not hurry to the shelters, they stood applauding Shostakovich. They were still in the power of the music.'[49] Olga Berggolts had been flown out to Moscow, her aircraft pursued by Messerschmitts, and she saw Shostakovich rise and take a bow. This fragile, bespectacled man struck her in that moment as being stronger than Hitler himself.[50]

The appeal of the music and its setting were immense – a defiant premiere held as swastikas cruised overhead on the tails of Ju-88s – and the message was easily grasped. Shostakovich put it himself in a radio address he made to the All-Slav Congress, which was meeting in Moscow. 'We are happy in the certainty that our children and grand-children will one day say: "In those memorable days Russian culture, Russian science and Russian art rose to their full height." They produced wonderful inventions which helped the Red Army to fulfil its historic mission. They also produced wonderful inventions of art, memorials of the great struggle against fascism.' This, he said, 'displayed the inherent qualities of the Slav people, their age-old striving to support all mankind in the struggle against the dark forces of the oppressors.'[51]

Some of those producing 'wonderful inventions' for the Red Army were doing so in *sharashkas*, the NKVD's laboratory-labour camps where scientists were held. These had been called NKVD Special Technical Bureaus. Lest that give away their purpose, in 1941 Beria had renamed them the 4th Special Department. Not far from Shostakovich as he spoke, in the *sharashka* for aircraft designers in Bolshevo near Moscow, Andrei Tupolev and his team of prisoner-engineers were designing bombers for the Red Air Force. No hint of that in his speech, of course, and none of the Terror that had for so long stalked the composer himself. But his symphony drew the eye and ear away from such unpleasant-nesses. It was awarded the Stalin Prize, First Class, to coincide with the Moscow premiere.

Berggolts knew well the cynicism behind such apparent rewards. Her broadcasts had made her famous enough to be summoned to Moscow for a round of poetry readings and receptions. She used one at the NKVD headquarters – 'I suppose there were some humans among them. But what oafs, what louts they are' – to petition for her father. He was still being transported east. 'In his wagon six people have already died, and several more await their turn.' It filled her with horror. 'My God, what are we fighting for? . . . For a system in which a wonderful person, a distinguished military doctor and a genuine Russian patriot is insulted, crushed, sentenced to death.' The secretary of the NKVD Party committee promised to look into his case. She knew nothing would be done. She found that nobody in Moscow had the faintest idea of what was happening in her city, only that Leningraders were 'heroes'. 'They didn't know that we were starving, that people were dying of hunger, that there was no electricity or water.' She couldn't open her mouth about it on her radio talks, she said. 'I was told: "You can talk about anything . . . courage, heroism . . . but not a word about hunger."'[52]

There were heavy air raids that evening in Leningrad, too. Marshkova went to *A Wedding in Malinovka*, and noted that the performance started late because bombers had been overhead.

At one o'clock the next night, the city was shelled. It seemed to Vera Inber that it was bombing. 'In the strange atmosphere, listening to those far-off explosions, I felt a fear as I have never experienced in my life before.' She could not sleep. The night was as clear as day, with the moon and snow, and in the fluffy spring snow the trees looked like apple trees, covered in blossom. She read a French novel to calm her nerves, but it seemed too unreal – 'this life, those loves, somewhere on the Riviera, in Nice' – like a dream within a dream. 'I am distressed and very much afraid. I wrote about it without false shame. I AM AFRAID. Today Marietta told us that the Germans are very close to the city. Evidently I sensed this, although I didn't know it. They have brought up a powerful battery on a railway truck and shelled the city.'[53]

It seemed ever more doubtful that the Seventh would be heard in the city. Lengorsovet had organized privileged feeding for 150 arts workers, but the effects were not yet felt. Dmitri Likhachev went into the Pushkin Institute for ration cards. He was no longer being paid, as there were no wages clerks – they were all dead. The building was terribly empty, with only the elderly porter, dying, and warming himself by the boiler. People left the Institute, and died without trace, never reaching their homes. Likhachev fell in the street once himself and scarcely got home.

He was taken into a 'dystrophy clinic' in the Dom Uchenykh. They gave him rather more to eat there, but it merely increased his desire for food. He never stopped thinking of it in his time there. He slept in his clothes and ate in the canteen in temperatures of minus 30 degrees Celsius. Looking out of the window onto the Neva, he could see the explosions of renewed shelling.

The violinist Viktor Zavetnovsky's daughter wrote to her mother on the mainland: 'He is giving up . . . He's become weak though he is eating in the privileged canteen at the Bolshoi.' Aleksandra Mayger's death was followed in less than a week by two more orchestra stalwarts, P. Konev and G. Shreyder.

Others, too. Shostakovich wrote to Glikman from Moscow on 31 March. Valerian Bogdanov-Berezovsky's mother had brought a letter from him. 'He told me that Golts, Kalafati, Fradkin, Budykovsky and several other composers had all died.' Golts and Kalafati were in the March crop of fatalities. Golts was a mirror image of Shostakovich in many ways. He had played piano in silent movie houses as a fifteen-year-old to help to feed his family. He completed his exams at the Leningrad Conservatoire with a public performance of his own piano concerto. He left only the slightest of traces. The concerto was lost. A scherzo and the twenty-five preludes that Vladimir Sofronitsky recorded, each an evocative miniature, weaving genre into genre, 'crystalline and perfect', showed what talent was snuffed out when he was killed at the front at twenty-eight.[54] Vasily Kalafati's death was not so shocking. He was a veteran, who had studied under Rimsky-Korsakov. He is only fitfully remembered now, for his opera *Cygany*, a polonaise for orchestra, a Symphony in A. Then, though, he was one of the pillars of the Conservatoire, his music widely known, and his death of starvation on 20 March was a shock.

It had been a dreadful month. The Leningrad Funeral Trust was the state enterprise that handled individual and mass burials. It kept no records for January and February. The Trust recorded 89,968 burials in March. The number of registered deaths was ten thousand above that, and the total will have been higher still.

For the first time, more women than men were now dying. The imbalance had persisted through February, with 57,990 men dying to 38,025 women. But the number of men in the city was now so much reduced that it was inevitable that female mortality would overtake that of men. This happened in the second ten days of March, with 15,084 women registered as dying against 13,175 men. By April, women's deaths were a fifth higher than men's, and in May, almost twice as many women died as men.

And yet. Music was breathing morale back into the city. The Muzko-mediya was packed. People queued for tickets from 6 a.m. The Machine Construction Company rewarded 500 of its workers with a block booking for a special performance of *Sailor's Love*. *The Three Musketeers*, Louis Varney's classic musical comedy, played again for the first time since November.

The revived symphony orchestra held its first rehearsal at the House of Radio on 30 March. 'I was frightened,' the young oboist Ksenia Matus recalled. 'The old orchestra was a distant memory. Just a few of the same people were around. They were black from wick lamps, wearing God knows what, short and stooped . . . Lice were crawling on some of their collars. Maybe they were on me too and I didn't even see them.'[55] Eliasberg was still being treated at the Astoria *statsionar*. 'How on earth he could wave the baton with his arms flying . . . It was a miracle!!!'[56]

It was difficult for him. Some musicians coming from the front had forgotten the feel of intsruments in their hands. Others from army musical groups had developed non-orchestral styles and habits. 'They were good musicians but we had to start with the elementary,' Eliasberg said.[57] He was even short of tuning forks. 'We tried the introduction and the big waltz from *Swan Lake*,' he recalled. 'But I let them go after forty minutes. We couldn't do any more.' He was a hard taskmaster. He used the threat of taking the special rations away from any player he thought was malingering. The first trumpet was once silent when his solo arrived. 'I'm sorry. I just don't have the strength in my lungs,' he said. Eliasberg was insistent: 'I think that you do.' The trumpeter acknowledged the conductor's glower, and played. The clarinettist Viktor Kozlov remembered rehearsals lasting only twelve minutes, and producing little enough real music. 'Those of us playing wind instruments couldn't play properly,' he said. 'We were unable to hold our lips, we couldn't strain and our lips were weak.' The cellist Nikolay Kramov had to be pulled to rehearsals on a sledge clasping his instrument.[58] Even so, Boris Zagorsky, the head of MAA, wrote in his diary: 'It's impossible to describe the overwhelming feeling of hearing the orchestra again after so long a break.'

CHAPTER 12

Aprel'–Maj

April–May 1942

The month started badly. Musicians continued to die apace. Starvation claimed the Muzkom's choir member V. Chelnokov and the string player B. Tarasov on 3 April. Zavetnovsky's wife wrote to her daughter: 'A day when I was shaky. I fell and broke my shoulder when I went to get water. I got nothing in hospital – no splint, no bandages.' She had not long to live. Shell splinters from a heavy air raid the same day killed the Conservatoire professor Mikhail Chernogorov. A concert for the Baltic Fleet had to be abandoned when the bombers moved on to attack the base at Kronstadt. The all-clear did not sound until after dark.

April the 5th was a red-letter day. The concert season opened at the Pushkin. It was eerie, the oboist Ksenia Matus recollected, the famished entertaining the half-dead in a hall as gloomy as a dungeon. 'I'll tell you, in the hall there were only the ghosts of listeners, and on the stage the ghosts of performers.' It was too cold for the brass players to hold their instruments in their bare hands. They would have frozen. So they cut the fingers off their gloves and played like that. They had quilted jackets under their tailcoats. Eliasberg came out 'all starched, in tails . . . But when he started to conduct, his hands shook. And I had the feeling that he was a bird that had been shot, and any moment he would plummet.' They played Glazunov's *Ouverture solenelle*, arias from Tchaikovsky's *The Maid of Orleans* and scenes from *Swan Lake*, and the overture to the opera *Ruslan and Ludmilla*. Vladimir Kastorsky, who had rivalled Chaliapin, his bass still rich and vibrant at seventy, sang the echoing and redolent aria of Ivan Susanin from Glinka's opera. The mezzo-soprano Nadezhda Velter sang a piece from *The Maid of Orleans*.

The hall was packed. The audience applauded each piece. 'But there was no sound, because everyone was wearing mittens,' Matus said. 'And if you looked round, you couldn't tell who was a man and who was a woman. The women were all wrapped up, and the men were covered in scarves and shawls. Some were wearing women's fur coats. But after we played this concert we were all inspired, because we knew we had done our job and that our work would continue.'[1]

Plans to play the Seventh were slowly progressing. The Radiokom drafted a letter to Shostakovich asking him for help in getting the score of the symphony to the city. *Leningradskaya Pravda* reported that an orchestral cycle of symphony concerts was being prepared. Zavetnovsky was mentioned as a solo violinist.

A second concert was held in the Philharmonia on 12 April. Eliasberg conducted. The soloists were the tenor Ivan Nechayev and the wonderful mezzo-soprano Sofya Preobrazhenskaya. They got through a full card. Tchaikovsky's polonaise from *Yevgeny Onegin* flowed with his waltz from *The Nutcracker*. The pure notes of Lyubasha's aria from Rimsky-Korsakov were followed by pieces from his opera *The Golden Cockerel*. Eliasberg revived the Varangian ballad from Alexander Serov's opera *Rogneda*. The musicians had enough energy for the overture from Rossini's *William Tell* and Charles Gounod's *Faust*. Liszt's Hungarian Rhapsody No. 14 wrapped up a memorable evening.

The hall was smoky. The chandeliers had gone. Large boxes of sand with shovels and barrels of water and tarpaulins were in the aisles. It was very cold, Zinoviy Lifhits wrote in his diary. 'I recognized some of the musicians. But their faces were very thin and tired and they moved with the help of walking sticks. Eliasberg conducted, as elegant as ever in tails.' Valerian Bogdanov-Berezovsky was there, and he wrote on his calendar: 'Enjoyed really listening to a symphony orchestra after such a long time.' The music inspired Kondratiev to restart his diary. 'Tickets sold out for 12 April concert. I bought a ticket from someone at the entrance – many people were looking for tickets. The hall wasn't heated. You had to have a coat. The musicians performed without coats but were obviously cold. I didn't meet any of the regulars in the audience from before the war. They were mainly military types and girls from seventeen to twenty. Sofiya Preobrazhenskaya had the biggest success.' After the performance, the singer wrote to her friend the ballerina Tatyana Vecheslova: 'Hello from the symphony orchestra. I just sang the *Rogneda* aria [from Serov's opera] with them. We live life to the full as never before.'

Music was a political priority now. Bogdanov-Berezovsky, the pianist Zamensky, and a handful of other musicians and composers were awarded academician's rations. The trumpeter Dmitri Chudnenko had his food stamps stolen from his room. This was a death sentence for most, but he was too valuable to the orchestra to be let go, and the Radiokom had them replaced. The pianist Vladimir Sofronitsky was flown out to Moscow. A friend who met him and others off the flight was surprised. 'He didn't look bad. Yes, they'd all lost weight but we'd thought it was even worse.' The Muscovite did not realize that all those on the aircraft had been on special rations.

For the rest, the new emphasis was often too late. The Muzkom orchestra member V. Simonova died. Mervolf wrote that he did not think his father would survive the week. 'He lies in bed all day, his head covered, and only comes alive when he sees food.' Shelling destroyed the house of Evgeniya Bronskaya, once the leading coloratura of the Imperial Mariinsky, famous for her recordings of *La Traviata* in New York in 1909, and now a professor at the Conservatoire. The huge building on the corner of Dekabristov Street and Maklina burned like a torch for three days after it was hit, while she watched from the courtyard. 'The most awful thing is that during the darkness, people came and stole everything we'd saved that that they could carry off. I was swamped with horror and sadness. I thought it was the end of everything.'[2]

Elena Martilla went to see her friend Koze. 'You can't imagine a more terrible picture,' she wrote. 'Roza Markovna sat at the table in a cold dark room, and with her arms and clenched fists on the table, she howled! Like an animal – people don't shout like that. She howled. Marik and Izia, both dead, are lying right there, so long and skinny (they're fifteen) but there's no Koze . . . What happened to her, it's terrible to say . . . arrested for non-appearance at the Tenants Cooperative Association clean-up post.' Zhdanov had decreed that those who failed to put in their full work quota in the clean-up would be treated as 'parasites' or, more chilling, as 'helping the enemy', and arrested or shot. The quota had been set at two hours a day for those working full day shifts, with six hours for housewives and students, and eight hours for everybody else. All had to carry papers certifying that they had fulfilled their hours. The arrest of a mother, like Koze, led to the death of her dependants.

Sometimes a mother, driven mad by hunger, killed a child. Galina Salyamon was working on the clean-up of snow and sewage in the courtyard of her block at Bolshaya Moskovskaya Street, near the Admiralty, where she had a room on the fourth floor. Two women pulling a sledge with another woman on it came into the courtyard. The two women were nurses. They helped the woman get up from the sledge. She had a package at her breast covered with a coat. It was her new-born baby. One of the nurses asked Salyamon to help her. Salyamon asked if the woman had ration stamps for the baby. The nurse said she had, and left. Salyamon gave the woman tea. She thought she might be able to get more food from the 'children's kitchens' which cooked them the gruel known as *kasha*. Two of her neighbours said they would look after mother and baby.

Next morning, a neighbour came, crying: 'She's killed the baby!' Salyamon told her to make certain. She could not believe it. The neighbour came back and said that the woman had killed her baby and admitted it. 'Girl or boy?' Salyamon asked. 'Girl,' the neighbour said. 'The mother said, "I gave birth to her, so I cut her up and ate her."' It was 'impossible, horrible', Salyamon said, 'but it was fact. A tragedy worthy of Shakespeare.'[3] She was a local representative of the Raikom, the regional Party committee. She did not go to the militia, afraid that they would arrest the mother as a murderer. 'Her punishment will come when she realizes what she did. She must be insane – no mother could do that otherwise.' So she did not report her. The next day, the neighbour found the woman dead. A militiaman came twice a week to check on the clear-up. Salyamon told him that both mother and child had died, and gave no cause.

The compulsory clean-up was a moral and physical necessity. 'We only really saw what winter did when the snow began to melt,' recalled the clarinettist Viktor Kozlov. '"Look, here comes spring!" But what did it bring? Decomposing, dismembered corpses in the streets that had been hidden under the ice. Severed legs with meat chopped off them. Bits of bodies in bins. Women's bodies with breasts cut off, which people had taken to eat. They had been buried all winter but there they were for all the city to see how it had remained alive.'

Some musicians avoided physical labour by entertaining the cleaners. 'The city is being cleaned of ice and snow,' the boy diarist Krukov noted. 'Musicians support the working people by playing music . . . Leading musicians and singers perform on the streets and in courtyards, giving a festive air.' The popular singer I. Kedrov stood on the Anichkov Bridge, singing from one of the plinths where Klodt's magnificent equestrian statues had stood before they were moved to shelter from German shells.

The public support for the hygiene campaign was spontaneous, a part of the city's will to live. The Germans celebrated the thaw by bringing up more artillery. Up to 800 heavy guns were brought to bear in fresh barrages, targeting tram stops, large apartment blocks and the busiest streets. They made little dent in morale. Leningraders remained defiant, and 300,000 of them took to cleaning their city with pride, with brooms and shovels, piling the dirt on sleds to which three or four adults might harness themselves, pulling until their strength was gone. Zhdanov had less need than he thought to resort to the NKVD and police to enforce his orders.

That did not mean that the NKVD was inactive. Hilma Stepanovna Hannalainen had worked all through the winter in the Leningrad Public Library, despite being deafened in a bomb blast. The reading room was packed with people, wrapped up in layers of clothes against the cold, their minds escaping from the siege into the books they read by the light of little oil lamps and candles made by the staff. Hannalainen's five-year-old son Edik was always there, sitting on a stool as his mother worked among the shelves. His father had been the editor of a Karelo-Finnish newspaper. The NKVD had picked him up and executed him during the Winter War. Hannalainen and the other librarians had toiled to clear the filth and rubbish in Stremyanny Lane close by. Edik stood motionless in the cold, his eyes never leaving his mother as she worked. The librarians found the perfectly preserved and deep-frozen body of a young man at the bottom of a heap of rubbish, but they cleaned the street thoroughly. A few days later, Hilma and Edik disappeared. They had been arrested by the NKVD as the widow and child of an enemy of the people. For all her hard work and loyalty, she and her son were exiled to Siberia.[4]

Musicians were as supportive in public of cleanliness as the librarians, but were less house-proud at home. There was an official complaint that they were leaving chamber pots of sewage on the main staircase of the Radiokom. They were warned that those who continued to do this would be punished. The threat had little effect. 'In spite of many warnings, many colleagues behave as hooligans and criminally pollute the premises of the Radio Committee,' the vice-chairman thundered. 'They throw sewage out of the window, they defecate on staircases, in buckets of sand, etc. Loafers and idlers don't clean the toilets. Those who live in the Radiokom have forgotten that they have electricity and other conveniences that other Leningraders do not have. Warning: this disorder will be got rid of!'

The city was breathing more easily, though: the foulness was reduced. It was calculated that the courtyards, cellars and staircases of sixteen thousand buildings were cleared. Including streets and alleys, the city rid itself of a million tons of snow, ice, refuse and human waste. The reward for clean-up work was a visit to a public bath. These had previously been open only to those medically certified as dangerously dirty.[5]

Vladislav Mikhailovich Glinka, the curator at the Hermitage, went to one near the Smolny. All of the bathers were green and emaciated, except for a pink fat man with a bar of pink soap. They crowded around him, jabbing at his fat, asking him how he had it. He was frightened. 'I'm a chef in a Party kitchen,' he said. They screamed at him. He managed to run away. He left a piece of pink soap on the bench. No one touched it. Glinka knew of others whose Party privileges had kept them sleek and well-covered. He met Natalya Vasilyevna Krandiyevskaya Tolstoya, the ex-wife of the 'Red Count' Alexei Tolstoy. She had once lived on the same staircase as Kirov. He chatted to her about the Hermitage, and asked where she lived now, and who were her neighbours.

She said that one of them was Petr Sergeevich Popkov, the chairman of the Leningrad City Soviet, a big party wheel who had been prominent as the chairman of the *raion* (district) Soviet in the purge years.

Throughout the winter, she said, Popkov had fed his cat with 200 grams of fresh meat a day. The pet was one of a handful to survive the siege. As to Zhdanov, whose greatcoat could not wholly conceal his gut, it was said that he had fresh fruit flown in daily, and had a regular pedicure and manicure for good measure.[6]

Popkov was unabashed by his belly. He blamed doctors for the scale of the famine deaths. He said that only Zhdanov and himself had done anything practical. 'We wanted to halt deaths from starvation as quickly as possible. We raised this several times, asking what would be best, but we never got any answer,' he claimed. 'Only after we ourselves discussed it were special canteens opened on the initiative of Comrade Zhdanov. It was not done because of the doctors.' A scapegoat was found. V. S. Nikitsii was sacked as head of the city Health Department. Popkov called for doctors to reduce mortality 'by approximately eight times, if not more'.[7]

The chaotic state of the cemeteries and burial grounds was blamed on the 'criminal negligence' of those nominally responsible for them. The director of the Koshman funeral trust and the administrative head of commercial enterprises, an unfortunate called Korpushenko, were prosecuted and found guilty under 58-14. This covered 'counter-revolutionary sabotage', or the deliberately careless execution of 'defined duties'. They were shot and their property confiscated.

The ice on Lake Ladoga was yellowing with melt water. The trucks threw up fountains of spray that froze solid on the windscreens. The ballerinas Vaganova and Shelest, two of the finest dancers of their generation, were among the last to be evacuated early in the month. The Neva ice was still hard enough for Glinka to cross on his way to the Piskaryevsky Prospekt.[8] He was responsible for the collections of Pushkin House, and the archives of literature of the Academy of Sciences. He was going to the Mechnikov Hospital to get some papers his mother-in-law needed for her evacuation. On the way back, the thaw had progressed and he crossed by the Liteiny Bridge on his way to her apartment on Tchaikovsky Street.

He became a witness of 'unforgettable horror' at the great house at 46–48 Tchaikovsky Street. It had been the palace of the Grand Duchess Olga Alexandrovna, the younger sister of Tsar Nicholas II. As he walked, he was going through the architects of the art nouveau style – Georgi Bosse, Gavril Baranovsky – in his head. He saw a big truck standing at the palace doors. A man was doing something in the truck.

> When I got closer, I felt I would fall to the ground. There were two red-faced men, in good windbreakers and trousers. They were throwing naked corpses into the truck and stacking them one on one like logs. I looked through the vastness of the vestibule and it was full of corpses lying in layers. There were men there in the same windbreakers and they were passing corpses to one another like a conveyor belt.
>
> They started to cover the horrible cargo with pink blankets. Soon another truck arrived and two soldiers got out and started to smoke, waiting. The first truck left. I hardly remember the rest of my journey. I saw shadows of walking people. But on my way along Pokrovsky Prospekt some army trucks passed me and I could see pink blankets in them being blown by the wind. There were so many of them.

He met a friend who told him that the bodies were being taken to the Piskarevskoye cemetery. It was vital to move them now because the thaw had started and there was a danger of epidemics. 'The trucks were sent from the mainland. Those who worked on them were well fed and they say they had half a litre of vodka every day.' A fresh horror awaited him. He saw the corpse of a man in a black coat and fur collar on the ice on the Neva near the Smolny. 'It was nothing special. I was used to it. But something nearby was sparkling in the sun, and I regret that I approached to look at it. The coat was thrown open on the body, but the body had no legs and a saw was glinting next to one of the severed limbs. It looked as though the one who had cut off the legs didn't have the strength to carry both of them away.' He went on home, too shocked to tell his wife.

A little later Glinka met a lawyer friend of his, Alexander Arvan, who was assigned to work in the prosecutor's office on the Volkhov Front. Arvan told him of the unfolding tragedy on the Volkhov, as Leningrad's would-be rescuers fought desperately to save themselves. Glinka mentioned the body without legs he had seen on the Neva ice in April.

'You say you cannot forget it, but we see it all the time,' Arvan said. 'Eating corpses isn't the worst. We have cases where the cannibals killed living people, boiled their meat and ate it. But we found most of those arrested to be insane.'

Glinka asked him: 'What about others? Those who are normal?'

'Those are shot, they aren't people,' Arvan replied. 'It's dangerous to leave them even among criminals. We have cases where the managers of houses killed their tenants. Why? To get their food stamps, for fur coats, for gold.'

Glinka was immediately reminded of the concierge of his house, Bechova, 'this awful woman with the manners and vocabulary of a low tavern'. She had not lost weight, even in February, and 'her bossy voice had become a yell'. He had seen her carrying big bags from apartments where everyone had died. 'She told me: "I'm carrying it to storage." But later there was nothing in the storage.'

She was ruthless. A little later, she adopted a boy called Lyeva, an eight-year-old whose parents and grandmother had died in their apartment. Using the adoption papers, Bechova cleared the apartment of porcelain, paintings, furniture and suitcases. 'I'll never forget this thin boy with huge black eyes,' Glinka wrote. Bechova sent him to an orphanage.

*

The thaw was a fresh devastation for the Second Shock Army. Its objective – the relief of Leningrad – slipped further from its grasp. Its wooden bunkers had filled with water at the beginning of April. The guns started to sink and the men laid logs under them. Horses were mired in the mud. 'Shells had to be dragged by hand for five kilometres from the supply depot,' said Igor Yelokhovskiy, a platoon commander in a 76mm artillery battalion. 'And how many could a hungry man carry? Two shells at most.'

Rations were cut by half, and then to a quarter. On some days, there was no food at all. 'We were almost continuously encircled,' Yelokhovskiy wrote. 'By my own calculation, the Germans closed the corridor at Myasnoi Bor about eight times.' The Russians managed to reopen it each time, at heavy cost. Kukuruzniks, Polikarpov crop dusters,* dropped sacks of dry rations. The biplanes were so slow and flew so low that the German fighters found it difficult to shoot them down, but the sacks often fell into a swamp or hit a tree stump and broke into a dusty cloud of grain that was soaked up by the mud.

The men began feeding themselves on the food they found on the belts of dead Germans. During heavy combat, or when on the move, the *Landsers* carried *Brotbeutels*, food bags, on their webbing with emergency supplies – 'canned food', Wilhelm Lubbeck wrote of the supplies in his unit, 'like tuna, sardines, herring or sausage with canned crackers or bread'. A dead German was a potential feast for a starving Russian. 'Defensive fighting was a daily occurrence,' Yelokhovskiy wrote. 'The Germans attacked and we repelled them. There were

---

* More of these aircraft, 40,000 of them, were produced than of any other biplane. Nikolai Polikarpov, the designer, had worked for the great Igor Sikorski in tsarist days. He designed the U-2 Kukuruznik in 1928: he was arrested a year later, accused of sabotage and counter-revolutionary activity, and sentenced to death. After waiting for two months to be executed, he was transferred to the OGPU design bureau in the Butyrka prison in Moscow. A crop duster in peacetime, the biplane was used as a light bomber and for reconnaissance as well as a supply aircraft during the war.

mountains of dead. At night, we would crawl into no-man's-land and grope through the dead Germans to find something to live on.' The Germans became wise to this. They started going into combat without their *Brotbeutels*. They also sent flares up into the ever-briefer night, their guns pre-registered on the positions where their dead comrades lay, ready to fire on scavengers.

A battery commissar with the 327th Rifle Division, P. V. Rukhlenko, stumbled on a 'frightful scene' as he scavenged for nettles and wood sorrel in the forests. German aircraft had bombed and machine-gunned the sector. A horse in the care of a sergeant was killed. A wild group of men attacked the sergeant, slashing his hands, butchering the horse and making off into the trees. 'All that remained of the horse was its head, legs and innards.' Rukhlenko paid the sergeant 300 rubles for a part of the leg. 'I left very pleased.' He noted that quartermasters had to send men to guard the sacks of dry rations dropped by aircraft from soldiers distraught with hunger. The sergeants and men who protected these 'paltry rations' were heavily armed, Rukhlenko said, 'so that they could fight off the robbers'.

He came across a field hospital in the dense forest. The wounded lay where they could, on pine boughs, flatcars from the narrow-gauge railway, and wooden boards. The many dead were 'buried right there in the swamp. Holes were dug for them using bayonets and they were laid side by side in their uniforms.' There were large piles of felt boots taken from the dead. Men hid themselves under them during shelling and bombardment: 'shell splinters could not pass through the thick felt, thus many felt it safe to hide themselves here.'[9]

Rukhlenko also witnessed the killing of a captured *Landser*. 'The Fascist conducted himself in a provocative manner, and would respond to us with "Russians – *kaput*!" and "Heil Hitler!" His *kaput* remark, however, led to his demise, since no one felt any reason to put up with him.'

The NKVD, prowling behind the Russian lines, also dealt in instant executions as they searched for prey. They found one in Yelokhovskiy's unit. 'The Germans scattered leaflets all over, promising a comfortable life in captivity,' he recollected. 'But here is the interesting thing – no matter how desperate things got, none of the lads thought about captivity. Every one of them believed that we were certain to make it out of the ring. Since we had no paper and newspapers rarely reached us, we started using leaflets to roll cigarettes. No *makhorka* was supplied in the spring and we took to smoking moss and dead leaves.'

He had a gun-aimer named Lukin, a simple-hearted fellow from Novgorod. 'Not being very clever, he had torn a leaflet and put the paper in his pocket to use later. Unfortunately, part of it stuck out and he was arrested.' Lukin was very lucky. Before he could be shot, Yelokhovskiy went to the battalion commander, Captain Belov, a brave officer who had been chairman of a collective farm. He told him that Lukin had been arrested, and that he was good soldier although irresponsible. Belov spoke with the NKVD. They told him that it was none of his business.

Belov would have none of it: 'he was afraid of no one. As battalion commander, he ordered that Lukin be released and that was that!' The NKVD officer wrote a report on him. Belov, though, was the well-loved leader of a unit fighting for survival, and the NKVD was despised by the combat troops. 'No one paid the fool any attention.'

Isaak Glikman was travelling from Tashkent to visit Shostakovich and copy the Seventh's score. The journey took ten days, the harsh brilliance of the skies of Central Asia giving way to snow-covered fields, cranes on the wing, and the familiar Russian scent of aspens on the breeze.

The Conservatoire supplied him with twenty rock-hard pies for the trip. When he broke one open, with considerable difficulty, he found it was alive with little Tashkent ants, like poppy seeds. His companion in his sleeper, a most respectable gentleman with the Order of Lenin in his lapel, saw Glikman's distress. Without a word, he took a piece of the pie, and with 'a courage worthy of Pasteur risking his life in the service of humanity', put it in his mouth and ate it. 'Speaking as a doctor,' he said, 'I can assure you this pie is perfectly edible.' The two dined together each day, demolishing all the pies with the relish of connoisseurs of Central Asian ants. The pies made an important point, Glikman thought: 'no material hardship could stifle the voice of the Muses, nor could the guns.' The fire of the spirit burned as fiercely as ever. There was no lessening of the passion for music, and for the new symphony in particular. 'Everywhere there was a burning desire to hear this work played.'[10]

He arrived at Kuibyshev on 15 April. Shostakovich was waiting for him on the platform, shyly hiding his joy at greeting him by snatching a cigarette packet from his pocket and lighting up, 'an incorrigible smoker'. Glikman noticed that his friend was wearing a smart new hat, overcoat and shoes. He had been given them to compensate for the clothes he had lost on his way out from Moscow. They walked to town. Shostakovich said that an epidemic made it unsafe to travel by tram. The composer's new lodgings were four rooms and a bathroom on Vilonovsky Street. They were the 'height of luxury' in wartime Kuibyshev. The largest room Shostakovich used as a study, with a grand piano, a desk and several armchairs. Glikman slept there on a divan.

After a few days, Glikman persuaded him to play through the whole of the Seventh on the piano. He did so 'wonderfully', bringing out subtle nuances in the second and third movements. At the end of the finale, Shostakovich heaved a little sigh, and got up from the piano stool. 'On the whole, I think I'm happy with the symphony,' he said. 'But you know, when I was writing the finale, the place was full of rumours and I got a great deal of advice from people here, some of which I asked for and some I didn't.' He had problems with copies of the score. 'It seems to have become a very fashionable piece just now,' he said. It was an understatement. It was already legendary. 'Couriers arrive from all over the place, asking me to help them get hold of a copy . . . Of course, there is nothing I can do, and I just have to get rid of them.' He quoted Khlestakov, from Gogol's *Government Inspector* – 'Couriers, couriers, couriers . . . nothing but couriers, thirty-five thousand of them!' – and burst out laughing.

The British and Americans realized the immense potential the symphony had for audiences in London and New York. It would show their Soviet allies to be cultured and humane – a great and complex work of art conceived in a city with the Hunnish barbarian at its gate – and quieten the abiding echoes of past terror and atrocity. Moscow had sensed this from the start. The Soviet ambassador in Washington, Maxim Litvinov, Flora Litvinova's father-in-law, was doing all he could to promote the symphony and its composer. The embassy was translating dramatic pieces by Russian writers to run in its Information Bulletin, where they were seized on by the American press, eager for stories from Russia.

The writing was irresistible. Alexei Tolstoy said that, as he listened to the rehearsals in Kuibyshev, he had realized that Shostakovich had 'laid his ear to his country's heart and played its triumphal tune'. This was more than music. It denied death. It defied Hitler: 'The accursed rat-catcher and his rats are weltering in blood.' It was not granted to him to 'turn the Russian people back to the gnawed bones of the caveman state'. In Leningrad, he said, 'the Red Army is writing its own awe-inspiring symphony of victory.' In reality, one Red army, the Second Shock, was entering its death throes. But, if that meant that Leningrad was as tightly besieged as ever, Tolstoy's passionate words reminded Americans that one fiery beacon illuminated the darkness of continued defeats. The city still stood.

Most poignant was a piece by Yevgeny Petrov, the satirist whose witty account of the American road trip he had made with Ilia Ilf in 1935 had greatly charmed Shostakovich. Petrov was now a war correspondent, and an account of the Seventh was one of the last pieces he wrote. He had seen Shostakovich at rehearsals, a 'pale and very slender man with a sharp nose', sitting quietly in the tenth or eleventh row of the empty hall, 'his auburn bristling hair cut student fashion'.

He described the first movement and its 'invasion theme' with brilliant vigour:

> The melody is repeated again and then again . . . It is an integument of iron and blood. It shakes the hall. It shakes the world. An iron machine runs over human bones and you hear them crack. You clench your fists. You want to shoot at this monster with a zinc snout that is marching down on you . . . When it seems nothing more can save you, when the limit of might of this monster is reached . . . behold, a musical miracle takes place without parallel in the world's symphonic literature . . . a few bars, and in the middle of its career, when the orchestra is at its full pitch of intensity, the idiotically simple, yet intricate and jocular, yet terrifying theme of fascism triumphant breaks up and is replaced by a theme, direct and serene and overwhelming, the theme of resistance.[11]

The impact that Petrov's words had on American readers was increased by news of his death. He was killed in the summer while returning from another great Soviet city under siege, Sevastapol on the Black Sea, which had been cut off by land from the rest of the Crimea since November. It was burning from incessant air attacks and artillery barrages as the Germans tightened their stranglehold on the city before launching a summer offensive to overrun it.

Copies of the score of the Seventh were microfilmed on 35mm film, and flown on a transport aircraft to Teheran. There, they were put on a British armoured car, which took them on the long overland journey across Iraq and Jordan to the Canal Zone in Egypt, and on to Cairo. The air route on to London crossed the Mediterranean to Gibraltar, and then swung west of the Bay of Biscay to avoid German fighters, before making landfall in Cornwall. New York was a more intimidating destination, the transatlantic leg from North Africa routing first to Brazil. While this great journey got under way, Shostakovich entertained Glikman with further piano recitals. He played several pieces from Verdi's *Otello*: Iago's Credo, Desdemona's Prayer, the Willow Song. It was one of the operas he loved best in the world. He talked of composing another opera, with the libretto taken word for word from Gogol. It was fourteen years since he had written *The Nose*, treating Gogol's text with great freedom. He was now thinking of *The Gamblers*: 'I shall keep in every word of every line.' He had loved playing cards when he was younger, 'though I always lost', and Glikman suggested that Shostakovich's *The Gamblers* could join Tchaikovsky's *Queen of Spades* (after Pushkin) and Prokofiev's *The Gambler* (after Dostoevsky) as a trio on the eternal theme of cards. He was to write forty minutes of music – Glikman found it 'magnificent, corruscatingly witty' – before abandoning it.*

The triumph of the Seventh had not dissipated his dread of Stalinism and its minions. He had to go to the local Soviet of People's Commissars to ask permission for his friend to eat with him in the restaurant of the National Hotel. He was in a fearful state as he set off. When he came back, clutching the treasured pass, his 'face was aglow with pleasure'.

---

* His decision to be faithful to the Gogol text meant that the opera would have to be four hours long. It was also unthinkable that Stalin would allow a piece on card sharks to be performed when every composer was expected to inspire the war effort. The abbreviated Act I was eventually played at the Leningrad Philharmonia under Gennady Rozhdestvensky in 1978.

Glikman found this 'strangely touching . . . even after the world-shaking first performance of the Seventh, Shostakovich had no conception of the power and influence which was in reality his to command.' He never asked for anything for himself, Glikman observed. 'It was so much against his nature that he was actually incapable of doing so.'

When Glikman left, Shostakovich walked with him out to the station, at night, carrying a heavy rucksack. He could have had his own car, such was now the fame and reputation the Seventh had brought him, but it would have meant speaking to the authorities again, and attracting their attention. The train took them to the local airfield. Glikman flew back to Tashkent, with a score of the Seventh in the rucksack. Five weeks later, under Ilya Musin, it was played there.[12]

The Ice Road was closing as the thaw advanced on Lake Ladoga. The last of the 20,000 who worked on it, the drivers, guides, guards, mechanics, anti-aircraft crews, the medics and the teams of divers who tried to recover trucks and their loads, sloshed ashore through the deepening surface water. More than 300 trucks had sunk through the ice over the 160 days the road was open. Barges and pontoons had been built in the Leningrad shipyards over the winter to replace them. More than 700 huge petrol tanks had also been made. They were to be towed across the lake by tugs. The divers also laid a fuel pipeline, and a cable to the Volkhov power station to bring in electricity.

The city was totally cut off from the mainland for some days. The lake was too choked with ice to navigate by boat. The thaw flooded the airfields, grounding all aircraft. Vera Inber was due to fly to Moscow. The cultural heritage that so marked Leningrad was reflected even in the pilots of the DC-3s who flew the dangerous route over the German guns to Moscow. The most experienced was Nikolai Kekushev, the son of the great art nouveau architect Lev Kekushev, who flew 53 round trips to the besieged city.* Inber's trip had to be postponed. When she did arrive, she was instantly homesick. 'Only when I'm here can I feel how dear Leningrad is to me, how close,' she wrote. 'I want to be there, to share its fate.'[13] When she returned, her aircraft landed at the Smolny aerodrome, 'and then – silence, the special indescribable silence of a besieged city hit us.'

Then, on 15 April, as Shostakovich had greeted Glikman's arrival in Kuibyshev, half-forgotten sounds – the clang of bells and the crackle of electric sparks – broke the Leningrad silence. Power Station 5 was back in operation. At 6 a.m., 116 tramcars left their depots and rattled off through the city. People wept with joy to see them. They touched them in admiration, and patted and stroked them, and asked the drivers if they could ring the bells. Vsevolod Vishnevsky wrote: 'The city again is lively. A Red Army unit, probably convalescent, came by with a band. So surprising, so strange, after Leningrad's quiet. Streetcars are moving, jammed with passengers.'[14] Two of the routes that were reopened went out almost to the front. The sight of the tramcars moving depressed the Germans, prisoners later recalled, as a sign that the city was enduring. Tram stops were now pre-targeted by German artillery.

The electricity, and the peat needed to generate it, came at a price. Girls were drafted into the peat pits to replace the prisoners who had worked and died in them. Valentina Bushueva, a teenager, was mobilized and assessed as a labour conscript. 'They looked at me, saw I was tall and, at first glance, healthy, and said "This one – to the quarry".' This was a deep pit in the peat bogs. Powerful pumps produced peat liquid, which was piped to the power stations. Bushueva worked alone at the bottom of the pit, driving pieces of floating wood and ice away from the pumps, up to her waist in the peat liquid, in canvas trousers and thigh

---

* Kekushev was a veteran of Polar flights, who was on the first aircraft to land at the Pole on 5 May 1937. He survived the war but his bourgeois background caught up with him in 1948, when he was sentenced to eight years in the camps.

boots. She was brought out on a rope. 'Just imagine, twelve hours in a pit,' she said. 'When they brought us some gruel, they had to pull me out. But we were given five hundred grams of bread there.'[15]

Sailor's Love was playing at the Muzkom on 16 April. The radio broadcast a talk on 'The Symphony of a Heroic Fight for Victory'. It detailed the attention that the world was beginning to give to the Seventh. The music was a perfect fit with its time. The war was going badly, in both Europe and the Pacific. The Germans, the early summer warmth restoring their vitality and mobility, knew they must be done with the Red Army over the coming months before the autumnal mud and winter cold robbed them again of their mobility. Army Group South was preparing Operation Blau, which would hurl them deep into the Caucasus and across the open steppe to the great industrial city of Stalingrad on the banks of the Volga. On the Black Sea, Sevastapol was in its death agonies, a fate shared with the Second Shock Army on the Volkhov, the German guns almost within earshot of Leningrad. In the Pacific, the American troops on Bataan in the Philippines had surrendered on 9 April. Next day, 12,000 of them began a forced march to POW camps during which 5,000 of them died without food or water. The British had lost Singapore, and were about to face the German Afrika Korps in Egypt.

The Seventh was a great beacon of faith and hope. War might inspire fine canvases from artists. No composer had ever written anything as complex and sophisticated as a symphony while his people were fighting for their existence. The musical Muses were speaking through Shostakovich, and despite the desperate condition of the city to which he had dedicated it, his symphony described with power and conviction a future victory. In London and New York, it was beginning to become a front page story.

Three days later, the symphony orchestra gave a major concert for the navy at the House of the Fleet. They managed to end their performance by getting through an energetic Strauss polka – the 'Thunder and Lightning' – but Zavetnoskaya, the wife of the first violinist, wrote to her daughter that her father was unhappy with his performance. 'He had pains in his hands and weak muscles, so he overplayed,' she wrote. 'Father complains that he cannot raise his legs enough to climb onto a tram. That is how weak he is.'

As dusk fell on 24 April, and the Radio Orchestra was playing Tchaikovsky in the Alexandrinsky theatre, the Nevsky bridgehead was being snuffed out. The nurses and all non-essential personnel had been evacuated at the end of March. One of the nurses, Olga Budnikova, had fallen in love with an officer, Boris Agrachev. She had given him her pistol as a keepsake. 'It's good to kill Germans with,' she said. 'It's good to commit suicide with,' he replied bleakly. Agrachev was still there, with 1,400 men of the 330th Rifle Regiment of the 86th Rifle Division. They had watched with foreboding as the ice on the river broke up in floes and drifted away on the current. Resupply was at its most dangerous. Boats had to be used, but they were easily picked off as they bumped between the great lumps of yellowing ice. The wounded piled up in the bunkers in the river bank. Food and ammunition ran short. No armour could cross to replace their brewed-up tanks.

Five German assault groups came for them at 8.20 p.m. The men were from the 1st Company of the 43rd Regiment, and the 6th Company of the 2nd, drawn from the 1st Infantry Division. They were led by Oberst Louis von Pröck. They attacked the 2nd company of the 330th Rifle Regiment holding the line in its central part. Before Eliasberg had reached *Swan Lake*, the company had been overwhelmed in hand-to-hand fighting, von Pröck's men running through the Russian foxholes tossing grenades. They used satchel charges to destroy the forward bunkers, the earth and splinters of logs showering in the deepening dusk.

The rest of the 330th launched six separate and desperate counter-attacks. They failed to dislodge the Germans from the bulge they had driven into the bridgehead. They took heavy casualties from German grenades and machine-gun fire. German artillery went all but unanswered. The Russian gunners had exhausted their ammunition. They tried to get KV-1 heavy tanks across the ice-clogged river that night. It was a disaster. They weighed sixty tons, and they sank into the gunmetal grey waters, and their crews drowned. The 330th was down to less than six hundred men, desperately clinging to two and a half miles of river bank.

On 26 April, the Germans 'walked' their artillery through the Nevsky pocket all day and into the night. The two senior men there, Major A. Ya. Kozlov, the divisional Chief of Staff, and Senior Commissar A. V. Shchurov, were killed. Even though the ice was now drifting fast with the current, the Russians managed to send 500 men across the river that night. They were lambs to the slaughter. At 10.40 next morning, the Germans slammed into the northern and southern ends of the bridgehead. They had two battalions of the 1st Infantry Regiment, a pioneer battalion to build bunkers and saps if needed, and the 1st Artillery Regiment. In fierce fighting, they quickly overran two-thirds of the bridgehead. The Russians were forced into a shallow semicircle, with their backs to the river. Many were wounded. Towards the end, they ran out of ammunition. They fought with shovels, bayonets and rocks until they were cut down by volleys of grenades. The last defenders held out in the 330th's command post on the river bank for ten hours. They were overrun in the gloaming at 9 p.m. on 27 April. Only a few were taken prisoner. Among them was Major Blohin, the commander, so badly wounded that both his legs were amputated in prison camp by Russian surgeons.* Fewer than a hundred men managed to swim back across 350 yards of river to the Russian lines on the west bank. A single officer, Major Alexander Sokolov, was among them.

---

* The major survived the operation and captivity to be freed in April 1945. He was immediately investigated by the NKVD, but he managed to convince them that he had been too badly wounded when the bridgehead fell to be a coward or a spy.

The bridgehead had been held for 222 days. A hundred thousand Russians had died or been wounded in this tiny place. The Germans took 115 prisoners. The rest of the 330th were dead. Govorov resisted all attempts by Zhdanov to win back the bridgehead. 'Nothing can be expected from that except a bloodbath,' he said.[16]

At the end of the month, E. M. Gromova and the other children transported from Shlisselburg by the Germans on New Year's Eve were loaded onto freight cars and taken to Tosno. Here, they were put into a camp surrounded by barbed wire, twenty-five to a room, sleeping on plank beds infested with bedbugs and lice. They were fed a liquid broth of swedes to which a little tripe was sometimes added. They spent the summer unloading wagons of sand. A typhus epidemic broke out. 'The Germans were more afraid of typhus than of partisans,' she found. They were told they would be shot if they left the camp. Gromova was infected and lay in a typhus barrack.

When she recovered, she escaped from the camp by day to run to the town and beg for food. 'The citizens of Tosno were in a bad position themselves but they always helped.' She was caught by a patrol once and badly beaten. The commandant was not in the camp, and this saved her from being shot: prisoners recorded the deaths of nine by hanging, twenty-four who were shot, and 'the Jew Tseplakov was tortured to death'.[17] A boy and a young woman called Lyuba were caught smuggling beet greens into the camp. They were beaten to death. 'Lyuba was hit so severely with sticks that I recall this terrible scene every time I see beets.' In the evenings, they made campfires and boiled up what anyone had found in the day. 'I remember one man boiling potato peelings in a pot. It was said he was a professor. I do not think he survived.' The Germans had a special way of getting rid of lice. They forced everyone to strip naked and throw their clothes onto red-hot bricks. 'The lice made such a noise as they popped it was like machine-gun fire.'

*

April was the cruellest month, in terms of the official record of burials. The Leningrad Funeral Trust recorded the burial of 102,497 bodies.[18] It did for Izvekov and his eleven fellow accused, too.

The Military Tribunal of the NKVD forces of the Leningrad Front passed judgement on them on 25 April. All were sentenced to the supreme punishment. All, that is, except Professor Roze, who had died under interrogation. Their crimes included sabotage, spreading false rumours and ideas, preparing to meet German troops, establishing communications with the German army command, and identifying and recruiting 'anti-Soviet determined individuals'. Izvekov was specifically found to 'have conducted his scientific work in a way that contradicted Marxist-Lenin theories' – those bourgeois references to the influence of the enviroment – and of aiming 'to disband the Soviet government'. They were found guilty under Articles 58-3, 58-10 and 58-11. 'They are sentenced to the highest criminal sentence, SHOOTING, and their personal belongings to be confiscated.' The sentence, the verdict concluded, 'is final and not liable to appeal'.[19]

Shostakovich made a special May Day greeting to Leningrad, which was transmitted on Radio Moscow. Olga Berggolts was just back from Moscow, glad to find the city transformed while she was away, the streets clean, the corpses and snow hills gone. She spoke on radio about the reception the Seventh had had in Moscow.

'It's about us, about September days in Leningrad full of rage and challenge,' she said. 'It's our sorrow, without the tears, about our families and loved ones, about the defenders of Leningrad killed in combat outside the city, and those who fell on its streets and died in its half-blind houses.' She told how the audiences in Moscow had got to their feet to applaud the people of Leningrad and Shostakovich – 'I looked at him, a small frail man in big glasses, and I thought: "This man is more powerful than Hitler."'[20]

The composer himself continued to work on his operatic version of *The Gamblers*. He realized that he was unlikely to complete it, though he was to use themes from it in the second movement of his final composition, Op. 147, the sonata for viola and piano. He was also frustrated that he could not work on the score of *Rothschild's Violin*, an opera based on a Chekhov story that his pupil Veniamin Fleishmann had been writing at the start of the war. Shostakovich knew that Fleishmann was missing at the front – in fact he had been killed at Krasnoye Selo on 14 September – and he regretted that he had not taken the score with him on the aircraft out to Moscow. 'I could have completed its orchestration,' he wrote from Kuibyshev to another of his pupils. 'Dear friend, if the opera is still at the Leningrad Composers' Union, please take care of it, and still better make a copy of it and if possible send it to me in Kuibyshev . . . I like the opera very much and am worried it may get lost.'*[21]

He was also composing for the NKVD. Beria had put together an NKVD Song and Dance Ensemble of artists who had been released from military service to entertain the troops. It boasted a symphony orchestra, folk and jazz orchestras, a choir and a dance company. Shostakovich was asked to collaborate. 'He was too scared to refuse,' the theatre director Yuri Lyubimov said. 'So he wrote songs like "Burn, Burn, Burn". It was also known as 'The Torches', about the torches used in the blackout. 'It became incredibly popular and everybody hummed it,' Lyubimov said. 'As our boss Beria used to say, "We need a song to set the people singing. Both words and tune should sink easily into the ears."'[22]

It is small wonder that he felt obliged to compose for the monster's musicians. His susceptibility, honed under Yezhov, was as sharp as ever under Beria. 'I think Stalin's Terror had an especially painful effect on Shostakovich, more than on the rest of us,' Lyubimov said. 'He was a man

---

* The score was later sent to Shostakovich, who completed orchestrating it in February 1944. Largely at his prompting, it had its first performance on 20 June 1960 in Moscow by the Moscow Philharmonic Society.

with exposed nerves and a keen perception. The fact that he was more vulnerable and receptive than other people was no doubt an important feature of his genius.'[23]

Perhaps the NKVD's presence in Kuibyshev, their numbers swollen by the transfer of staff from Moscow, preyed on him in his celebration of little Maxim's fourth birthday, which fell early in May. He started writing a setting for bass and piano for Sir Walter Raleigh's 'Letter to my Son', with the words from Boris Pasternak's recent translation. In this, at least, Elizabethan England had a grim resonance with the Russia of Stalin and Hitler and their executioners:

> Three things there be that prosper up apace,
> And flourish whilst they grow asunder far;
> And on a day, they meet all in a place,
> And when they meet, they one another mar.
> And they be these: the Wood, the Weed, the Wag;
> The Wood is that which makes the gallow tree;
> The Weed is that which strings the hangman's bag;
> The Wag, my pretty knave, betokeneth thee.
>
> Mark well, dear boy – whilst these assemble not,
> Green springs the tree, hemp grows, the wag is wild;
> But when they meet, it makes the timber rot,
> It frets the halter, and it chokes the child.

In Leningrad, *A Wedding in Malinka* played at the Muzkom on May Day, without the orchestra's talented violinist N. Zil'berg, who died that day. Big crowds swarmed round the entrance trying to get tickets. Bombers were over Kronstadt in the afternoon, but the operetta ensemble paid them no attention and carried on with a performance of *Silva*, for the Fleet.

The sports season started the next day. Bicycle races were held, and oarsmen were out on the Neva in eights and coxless fours. Other races had people running in gas masks and carrying stretchers. A marathon was held on the streets. Football kicked off with a match between an NKVD team and a factory side in the Dynamo stadium. The competitions were as visible as possible – hurdling, sprint races, long-jumps and boxing bouts were held in parks – and they helped to reassure people that all was not nightmare. Mariya Minina was a touchstone for many. They had seen her out skating and skiing in the winter, and now she was a champion bicycle racer and an athletics star.

'We had circus teams in the city, and military bands, and operettas and cinema,' recalled the young diarist Krukov. 'A person will always try to amuse himself, even if he is close to death. I played chess and read a lot. I played on a neighbour's old piano, and then my mother found a grand piano on a rubbish dump whose owners were dead. It took up the whole room.'[24]

Eliasberg gave a concert in Hospital No. 70 on 5 May, a major performance, with Sofya Preobrazhensky singing the arietta from Rimsky-Korsakov's *Snegurochka* (*The Snow Maiden*). He was worked hard. Two days later, he conducted a radio broadcast of Solveig's lullaby from Grieg's *Peer Gynt*, and 'Last Spring' from the elegiac melodies. He was back in the Philharmonia Hall on the 10th, with Tchaikovsky's Fifth Symphony and his symphonic poem *Francesca da Rimini*. He was in the House of Radio four days later, conducting the March from Meyerbeer's *The Prophet* and the overture from Rossini's *Thieving Magpie*. Liszt's *Venice and Naples* was also played. On 23 May, he was conducting Glinka's overture from *Ruslan and Ludmilla* and Antonida's Romance from *A Life for the Tsar*, and Rimsky-Korsakov's *Scheherazade*. Four days after that, he made a Mozart broadcast, of the 'Jupiter' Symphony and the overture from *Don Giovanni*.

The radio was transmitting music with a vengeance. A dozen concert recordings were broadcast on 6 May alone. Yakov Babushkin, the artistic director of the Radio Committee, explained why in an interview with the novelist Alexander Fadeyev. He said the city had drifted beyond imagination in the winter:

> A city of ice. The Germans at the gates. Shelling every day. Trams don't work. We thought music inappropriate at such a severe time. There were whole hours when only the metronome sounded . . . tuc . . . tuc . . . tuc. Can you imagine that for the entire night and day? Suddenly, they said: 'Why do you keep this mood? Play something.' They say it was Zhdanov. I started to look for musicians in the city. We could employ them and pay them a salary. But we couldn't feed them. We had nothing.
>
> Then we went to the Management Committee of Arts. They had their own canteen, and we said, 'We have an orchestra which can play not only on the radio but also in the Philharmonia Hall. Let's do it this way. We provide the orchestra. You provide the *kasha* [gruel].' This is it.

Another increase in the number of musicians on special rations – recorded in a so-called 'Belly Book' from 1 May, which listed all those receiving them – accompanied the greater volume of music played. Mervolf found it was too late for his father. 'Papa is very bad,' he wrote on 6 May. 'There is no light in his eyes. He is swollen and cannot walk at all. He went to the *ambullatoria* [feeding station] for food and fell in the street.'

But the revival of concerts was bringing Zavetnovsky back to life. He was up at 5 a.m. to fulfil all his home errands, to bring water, get food and feed his sick wife with her broken shoulder. At 8.30 a.m. he was in rehearsal with the pianist Kamensky. At 10.15 a.m. he went on to the rehearsal at the Philharmonia. At 1 p.m. he played in hospital wards. At 3 p.m. he was performing in military unions. At 7 p.m. he played in the Philharmonia concert. A car took him there, but he walked to all the other engagements. He had a difficult violin solo to play in *Swan Lake*, but he did it beautifully. His wife was listening on radio. 'The sound was good,' she wrote to her daughter. 'Musicians are now fed during the day and he is eating well.'

The music came at a price. 'It was a hard victory that the musicians had to win over themselves,' recollected the bassoonist Grigorii Zakharovich Yeryomkin. 'We had to overcome the pain of sitting on our bones, because our muscles had wasted away. We tried putting soft things under us, but the pain did not go away. It was a real pain.'[25] Eliasberg could be savage with them at rehearsals. It led to great tensions but most of them accepted it. 'He was the only one who with his will and courage, and at times his cruelty, was able to make us famished musicians square our shoulders, grab our instruments and, most importantly, play,' Ksenia Matus admitted.[26]

The summer evacuation by boat and barge across Lake Ladoga was under way. The purpose by now was not so much to save the dying, as to make Leningrad a military city. Those who left now were mainly unfit for work, women with children, orphans from homes, pensioners.

The surviving prisoners in the Kresty were assembled and searched by guards after dark. Those who could still walk were marched along Komsomol Street near the Finland Station to Nizhegorodskaya Prison. There were about 800 in all. A few days later they were taken on to the Finland Station. The guards had dogs, the imprisoned scientist Voloshin recalled, the first live dogs to be seen in the city since winter. At the Ladoga station, they were locked below deck on a barge for the journey across the lake, where they were herded into freight trucks for their long journey to the Gulag. Only 200 survived to arrive at the salt mines of the Solikamsk camp.[27]

People had to be able to walk unaided to qualify for evacuation. This applied to children, too, and those in the orphanage spent hours practising. The weaker ones walked from bed to bed through their rooms, holding on to the bed legs to support themselves. When they were a little fitter, they went out into the long corridor outside, staying close to the wall in case their strength gave out. If a child could walk the length of the corridor three or four times, as Svetlana Magayeva could, he or she was passed fit for evacuation. They were nervous. They knew that the Germans bombed the boats. They had heard a story of how a boat carrying children had been sunk, and their little white straw hats had floated on the surface of the lake like the white lilies that people dropped into the water as funeral flowers.

They were sleepless in the week before the evacuation. They got out of bed and stared out of the windows into the night sky and shivered at the perils to come. One night they heard a heart-rending cry from the corridor outside. An orphan called Aristotle was lying on the floor with blood coming out of his mouth. The locked door to the storeroom where food was kept had been forced open. Food was missing. It seemed the boy had gone into the corridor and had seen food being stolen from the storeroom. The thief had murdered him as the only witness to his crime. The other children suspected another boy they knew as 'Bismarck'. Some of them beat him up badly, and he was removed from the home. They thought he had gone to prison, but Svetlana overheard a doctor and nurse discussing the case. They said that the murderer was far too physically strong to have been Bismarck. Svetlana was left with the frightening thought that the thief and murderer was an adult member of staff, and still among them, or a stranger who could come back for more food.[38]

Vladislav Glinka, the curator, was waiting for his nine-year-old daughter to be evacuated. She was too weak to qualify for a place on a truck convoy to the boats at Osinovets. He hoped to get a car to take her. His heart was now warmed by the humanity of strangers. 'In this horrible time, surrounded by robbery, cheating and death', two completely unknown men showed him 'the pure light of their sincerity and sorrow. Their appearance for our family was like fresh water for the thirsty, a warming light.'

He was taking a walk every day. 'I'd noticed how those who lay down thinking they were saving their strength were in fact already close to the end. Passiveness and ignoring reality led to the decay of the spirit, and that is the end. Those who suffer from dystrophy, they should sleep only at night. So I forced myself to walk.'

He found himself one day by a kiosk selling old books. It was kept by an old man with the green face and blue lips of dystrophy. He dealt in Russian translations of novels, and told Glinka that he paid cash for them. A military car drew up. Two marine officers in black sheepskin coats and belts with revolvers and black caps got out. They were marine captains; one was the commander of a battery. They started flicking through the books. One of them asked for *The Three Musketeers*. The old man had *Twenty Years Later*, the sequel, but the marine did not want it. He asked for something about love. The old man offered him *Anna Karenina*. He said no. The other marine bought a fine edition of Pushkin with illustrations by Bilibin.

'I dared to say, "I have some novels translated from French and English at home",' Glinka recalled. 'The marine said, "Do you live close by?" "Yes, Nekrasov Street." "Let's go."' In the car, they asked him what he was doing. He told them he was a curator at the Hermitage. He explained that some of the collections had not been moved out, but were in the basement, where there were two floors of brick vaults that were safe from bombs.

They got to Glinka's 'half-starved room'. His daughter and mother-in-law were lying on their beds, covered with blankets and shawls, and his wife was heating some water on the stove. A little square of bread was drying near the pan. Glinka asked the marines to sit at the table. He got books down for them, novels by Jack London and H. G. Wells.

They didn't look at the books, but took in the room, amazed.

'Why didn't you evacuate your daughter?' one of them asked roughly.

'We're waiting for a car to take her, if we're still alive,' Glinka's wife said.

'How old is the girl?'

'Nine,' the girl herself said, showing her wan face.

The marines looked at one another. One was carrying a bag, and he started emptying it, loaves of bread, two or three cans of preserved meat, and a full pack of sugar.

'Feed your daughter until your car arrives,' they said. Glinka pressed them to take the books. They told him that in truth they had little time for reading at the battery. He insisted. The commander looked at the bookshelf and chose a book on Cossack regiments before the Revolution. He said, 'We're both Don Cossacks,' and he put the book in his empty bag. 'Be well,' they said. 'And leave as soon as possible.'

Glinka's mother-in-law, still lying under her blanket, asked, 'Please at least tell us your names.'

'Pray for us both, Mama, as my grandmother prays, who is a believer,' the battery commander said. He gave his name: 'Vesnyankin.'

They cried when the marines had gone. Glinka's daughter counted out the pieces of sugar.*

On 28 May, the radio asked Leningraders to pay attention to their clothes and appearance, a sign of revival. It reminded them that summer was

---

* Glinka's daughter survived. Twenty years after the war, in a book called *Warriors of the Baltic*, Glinka found a reference to Battery Commander Vesnyakin. He, too, had survived the war, but then the trail went cold.

coming. People began to scour the parks and open spaces for chervil, orach, dandelions and nettles. They made nettle and sorrel purée, rissoles of beet-tops and goosefoot, and picked daisies and field roses to brighten their rooms.

The book trade flourished as minds that had focused inward, on survival, began to reach outward. People sat reading in gardens and parks and on the avenues. They brought chairs out of shattered buildings and into the sun on pavements. Leningrad had been a treasure house of rare first editions and beautifully bound books with valuable hand-finished illustrations. Many had been looted from apartments that had been shelled or whose inhabitants were dead or evacuated. They found their way to the Haymarket.

The Radiokom orchestra picked up a badly needed new recruit. A. Zatsarny had started the war as a viola player in a quartet that played in a concert brigade, with puppeteers, folk singers and actors, at forward air bases and hospitals. The brigade was evacuated from Leningrad in August, but he was enlisted as a machine-gunner. He was badly wounded in the thigh in heavy fighting in the Tosno forests south of the city in late November. He was lucky. Two medics from a nearby cavalry regiment brought him to a field hospital at the Pontonnaya railhead. He was transferred to hospital in Leningrad. As he convalesced, he gave viola recitals to his fellow wounded. He was found unfit for military service on 5 May – he was lame – and discharged from hospital. He 'bumped into' some Radiokom musicians on their way to give a performance in hospital by chance three weeks later. They told him about the Seventh, and the need for more musicians. He went to the House of Radio and played for Eliasberg in the studios. He was signed up as a violinist.[29] Two military conductors, Genshaft and Sopov, were drafted in to work with the soldier-musicians on symphonic music and to help Eliasberg in rehearsals.[30]

The Germans had brought in SS Police divisions and the 2nd SS Infantry Brigade to close the ring round the wastes of Miasnoi Bor where Vlasov's Second Shock Army was dying. It had lost two-thirds of its strength. It had few tanks, its artillery lacked shells, and its food supplies were running out. Stavka, the High Command, wanted to continue its offensive, but its only realistic task was to try to save itself. As the few roads and trails dried out, some cavalry and Guards' rifle units got out of the pocket through a narrow and treacherous corridor. Most of XIII Cavalry Corps had got back to the east bank of the Volkhov. On 17 May, V. N. Sokolov, the headquarters clerk, one of the few who remained in the pocket, was ordered to get all the corps' documents out in a ZIS-5 truck. He headed for the Volkhov but found himself stuck at the tail of a seven-mile column of ambulances, trucks, guns and horses.

A 'swarm of humanity' had assembled near the bridge over the Kerest river, a tributary he had to cross to get to the Volkhov. The forest was full of abandoned saddles, fur coats, felt boots, horse blankets, barrels and crates. Vehicles and carts crawled slowly over the bridge, carrying the sick and wounded, soldiers streaming past on foot. The path of German bombers overhead was traced by the fragments of vehicles, carts, personal belongings and bodies they left behind them. Once across the river, a corduroy road led to the Volkhov. It had no cover for the solid mass of men and vehicles moving along it. The trees in the surrounding forests had been stripped of their branches bare to their trunks. A 'shroud of bluish-grey smoke hung over the earth'. The narrowest section of the corridor came when the road turned towards Myasnoi Bor. The rumble of aircraft, the explosions from bombs and shells, and the muffled bursts of machine-gun fire produced a 'fear of remaining forever in some putrid hole in the ground' that crept involuntarily into Sokolov's soul. 'Five hundred metres remained, three hundred, one hundred . . . and then, there it was: the Volkhov.'

He and his cargo had covered nineteen miles and remained alive. It had taken him a week.[31]

On 30 May, as Eliasberg conducted the overture from *Fingal's Cave* and Svendsen's Norwegian Rhapsody No. 3 in a Leningrad Radio concert, two German corps began to pinch off the pocket. Some units suffered 30 per cent casualties in bitter fighting, but at 1.30 a.m. on 31 May, they linked up. By midday they had established a continuous front. Route Erika, the vital escape corridor Sokolov had taken, was severed. Commissar Venets and his unit, the 59th Independent Rifle Brigade, were too late to get out. They fought their way down into the corridor under heavy machine-gun and automatic weapons fire. A meeting of commissars and commanders was held. Venets hoped that later that night they would get through the narrowest and most dangerous part of the corridor. Major-General Petr Alferev, the deputy commander of the Second Shock Army, told them that the Germans had cut the corridor. Several of the officers present suggested that they attack immediately and break through to the Volkhov. They pointed out that their men were ready, and that with safety beckoning from the east bank of the river, they had every incentive to fight fiercely.

The general told them that a detailed breakthrough operation was being planned. They were ordered to withdraw to a less exposed position deep in the swamps and await orders. Regrouping, Venets said, was 'just a waste of time'.* It gave the advantage to the Germans, who now increased pressure on the trapped army along the entire front. Repeated attempts to break out were overwhelmed by heavy fire. As well as hunger, the Russians were tormented by persistent air attacks. They cursed the bright nights that allowed the Germans to seek out targets with impunity round the clock. 'Our salvation lay in

---

* The commissar could afford to be critical of the general. Alferev was last seen alive wandering in swamps near Myasnoi Bor on 25 June.

the swamp,' Venets said. 'Many bombs exploded within the depths of the sodden ground.'

More than 600 miles to the south, two Red armies, the Sixth and the Fifty-Seventh, were trapped and dying. A violent Russian offensive with 640,000 men had opened around Kharkov on 12 May. They bit deep into positions held by General Paulus and his Sixth Army. Five days later, General von Kleist's First Panzer Army slashed into the Russians and cut a forty-mile rent in the Soviet front. Against urgent advice, Stalin refused to allow his forces to go over to the defensive. With blind optimism, he ordered that the Kharkov offensive continue. The Germans trapped them in a bloody pocket, ringed with tanks and dive-bombed with Stukas. The death agonies lasted for more than a week, as Russian infantry charged gun pits and tanks by day and by the light of flares by night. Shortly before the end, General Gortodnyansky, the commander of the Sixth Army, committed suicide. The Russians lost 240,000 men captured, and 1,249 tanks.

In the Crimea, 1,200 miles south of Leningrad, the Russians were being overrun by General von Manstein's Eleventh Army. The Stavka's representative at the Crimean Front was Lev Mekhlis, propagandist, commissar, former editor-in-chief of *Pravda*, and militarily incompetent. It took Manstein a week to seize the Kerch peninsula on the Black Sea. Mekhlis lost control of units that were panicked into reckless retreat. He escaped with his life and a demotion, but 176,000 men and 350 tanks were lost. It freed Manstein to move on Sevastopol. Once he had dealt with that, he was to progress to the other great besieged city: Leningrad.

The optimism that had lifted spirits in the city in the early spring dissipated. Even Kuibyshev, Shostakovich's refuge, watered by the mighty Volga, was not as remote from the front as it seemed. In a few weeks, downstream, the Germans were to appear on its banks.

CHAPTER 13

Iyun'

June 1942

'The symphony orchestra has started to rehearse Shostakovich's Seventh Symphony,' Olga Berggolts announced on Leningrad Radio on 3 June. It was not true. 'It was agreed that the Seventh *had* to be played in Leningrad,' Ksenia Matus said. 'But there was no score, there were no people to play it.'

The *Radiokomitet* chairman, V. A. Khodorenko, said that the idea was 'wonderful indeed', but 'everything was difficult'.* He ticked off the problems: 'The re-manning of the orchestra to replace the many who have died of starvation . . . negotiations with the command of the Leningrad Front about the release of mobilized musicians . . . flying in the score . . .'[1]

The symphony seemed beyond the city's grasp, but music continued at a pace. Eliasberg conducted a radio concert – Mozart, Tchaikovsky, Schubert, Glazunov and Mily Balakirev – on 3 June. At a concert in the Philharmonic three days later, the orchestra played Bizet's *L'Arlésienne* suite, Liszt's *Tarantella* and the overture to Mendelssohn's *Ruy Blas*.

---

* He said that it was the composer Mikhail Chulaki 'who gave me the idea of staging the Seventh in Leningrad'. This is doubtful. The impact of a performance in the besieged city had been obvious to all since the triumphant premiere in Kuibyshev. Chulaki was an unlikely supporter of Shostakovich, whom he had spoken out against on formalism and *Lady Macbeth of Mtsensk*. He was a politicized former director of the Conservatoire. He later taught composition in Moscow, where he encouraged his student, Mstislav Rostropovich.

Musical propaganda groups were performing at the front and in hospitals. The United Collectives of Agitation Brigades and Ensembles under A. Anisimov played at one of the largest concerts of the war at the House of the Red Army on 7 June. The diet was largely propaganda: the opening number was 'Anthem to the Bolshevik Party', followed by 'The Song of Fighter Aircraft', 'Song to Leningrad', 'Popular Songs of the Cooks', and 'The March of the Women's Brigades', performed by the Youth Ensemble. They also tackled 'The Meeting of Budenny and the Cossacks', a piece on a Bolshevik legend from the civil war written by the Leningrad composer Vasily Soloviev-Sedoi.

Before the interval, the famous blues singer Klaudia Shul'zhenko sang her much-loved song 'Blue Scarf' ('*Sinii Platochek*'), with a jazz ensemble. Jugglers took to the stage. The comedy ensemble Merry Fighters opened after the interval with a satirical duet on the Finnish and Rumanian leaders, 'Mannerheim and Antonescu'. The famous balalaika song '*Kamarinskaya*' was played. The mood then turned serious. Asimov performed the 'Cantata on Stalin' with the Red Army Song and Dance Ensemble. Alexandrov's 'Everything for the Motherland' followed. Finally, there was Khrennikov's 'Song of the Kuban Cossacks'.

The same day, though, the Radio choir singer V. Korchazhnikov died. So did N. Mervolf's father. 'I had my Papa on 5 June,' she wrote. 'On the 7th, he became Corpse No 685.'[2] She wrapped him in a blanket and paid her neighbour 600 grams of bread to take him to the morgue. The head of the Arts Committee (the MAA), Boris Zagorsky, did not hide the continuing mortality in a letter to the mainland. 'Death is a constant guest in Leningrad. He walks freely about the streets. He sits at the table with you. Every day the city is shelled. Lots of damage and victims.'

The city was getting noticeably emptier. A check on hostels and apartment blocks was completed by police, also on 7 June. They reported that 241,687 former residents of these properties had gone. Of these, 123,757 had been evacuated, 81,305 had died, 33,029 had been drafted into the Red Army, 11,637 had moved address for various reasons – and 2,959 had been arrested.

Food racketeering was still rife. It was big money. More than 23 million rubles in cash was seized from racketeers during the siege, with 4 million in bonds, 73,420 gold ruble coins, 4,628 carats of diamonds, 78 kilos of silver, and 40,628 US dollars.[3] Workers in Factory No. 211 knew how this dirty money was amassed. They complained bitterly in a letter to Zhdanov: 'Look at the staff of the canteen – you could harness them up and plough with them. They are taking all these grams from us, and converting them into kilograms, and they are getting things for themselves with them and speculating.'[4]

Summer, though, was stirring. 'At last, blades of grass and the will to live,' young Krukov noted. 'People were different, of course, but not broken. Their stomachs were empty but the streets were full.' The lime trees in the Botanical Gardens were beginning to bloom. Their scent drowned out the smell of decay. The radio played Tchaikovsky's operas *Mazepa* and *Iolanthe*. 'In the blue sky are the beautiful sounds of Tchaikovsky melodies,' the schoolgirl M. Bubovna wrote. Vera Inber heard gramophone records playing, while young militia girls hung out of windows listening. The sky was pale pink and the silver barrage balloons seemed to dissolve into it. *Kholopka* was playing at the Musical Comedy: it was a historic choice, for the theatre had first opened its doors in 1929 with a performance of Nikolai Strelnikov's operetta.

Posters urged people to collect maple leaves – a target of 35 tons was given – and to use them in place of tobacco. People who smoked maple cigarettes called them 'my grandmother's mattress' or 'fairy tales of the forest'. Krukov did his bit, planting lettuce and dill on his balcony, and his mother scavenged nettles, and made a 'very tasty' soup from them.

Musicians, though, were lackadaisical about preparing and planting the plots assigned to them in the suburbs. 'Comrades who are assigned to the vegetable garden campaign do not pay it serious attention,' the director of the Theatre and Music Institute, A. Mashirov, complained, 'though it is part of the struggle against the Nazis.'

In the other, primeval struggle, in the Volkhov pocket, the trapped Russians were caught by artillery as they grouped to try to break out to the east bank of the river. Wilhelm Lubbeck, acting as a forward observer for the German guns, called in half a dozen 75mm shells wherever he thought the Russians were massing. Infantry then swept the area with machine-gun fire for any survivors.

German units were being re-equipped with MG-42 machine guns, a formidable weapon with a rate of fire so high that the sound of individual bullets was lost in a continuous noise that sounded like cloth being ripped, or a circular saw. It could fire 1,500 rounds a minute, though the gunners were trained to fire no more than 250 rounds in a single burst, or 300 rounds a minute in sustained fire. It took only five to seven seconds to change the barrel, giving the enemy only the briefest window of time to close in on it. Lubbeck saw one at work as the Russians attacked through dense brush. Lubbeck called in 75mm shells in a curtain 25 yards in front of his position. The machine-gunner fired continuously until the barrel overheated. He yanked it off, and tossed it into a puddle, where it gave off a cloud of steam. He locked a fresh barrel into the gun and resumed firing, surrounded by a mound of empty shell cases. Lubbeck ducked behind the log palisade protecting their position to change the clip on his sub-machine gun. As he did so, the machine gun fell silent. The gunner slumped over it, and Lubbeck saw blood running from a hole in his temple just under the rim of his helmet. A Russian sniper, patient and accurate as ever, had got him.

The attack, though, was beaten off.[5] Lubbeck found the Russians 'increasingly suicidal'. They were so short of rifles that they took them from the dead as they went forward. Once, he said, 'I watched with amazement as an enemy soldier ran directly towards my position without a weapon.'[6] Prisoners told German intelligence that special NKVD units with automatic weapons were deployed behind these 'hopeless attacks' to make sure that the orders to advance were obeyed. 'A couple of the larger assaults briefly penetrated our front, but they produced only terrible losses among their troops without accomplishing any purpose,' Lubbeck said. 'Afterwards their bloated and decaying bodies lay scattered in the open ground just in front of us.'[7] In many places, only 50 yards separated the two sides.

Dmitriev's battered artillery regiment was ordered to withdraw to a final defence line around the ruins of Finev Lug, a village within the cauldron seventy miles southeast of Leningrad. The Germans opened fire with all weapons as the young platoon commander abandoned his forward observation post and the gun pits. 'We were incapable of replying,' he wrote. 'We had one shell remaining for each gun, and that was set aside for blowing them up.' The Germans pursued them. Their tanks reached the heights outside the village and opened fire on Dmitriev's men at close range. 'A German soldier drove me out of my trench and destroyed the rangefinder. I barely managed to flee to the edge of the forest.' The guns were hidden in the woods. The gunners and their officers were given carbines and cartridges and transferred into the rifle units. 'The wounded, bandaged with scraps of linen, did not depart for the rear, but fought to the last cartridge,' Dmitriev wrote. 'I do not remember a single instance of voluntary surrender, despite the German leaflets promising good treatment.'[8]

The shattered remnants of Vlasov's men made another attempt to break out eastwards in the early hours of 5 June. The shock units – the

Germans said that they were 'all drunk' – tore into the surrounding enemy at 2 a.m. The Germans held them and then counter-attacked deep into the Russian positions. By the evening of 6 June they had severed all possible escape routes. Seven rifle divisions, and six rifle brigades, were trapped.

The heavy shelling of Leningrad city continued, traumatizing some of the already deeply disturbed children in the orphans' home. Alik was a four-year-old who had been brought in by an army officer wrapped up in a blanket when his mother died. At first he was so weak that he slept most of the time. He was silent. In June, fresh eggs were airlifted into the city. Each child had half an egg a day. The smell comforted them and reminded them of 'peace and life before the war'. After Alik finished eating his first half-egg, he suddenly began to speak again. His first words were of the joy the egg gave him. Now, he spoke from morning until night, chattering happily, the girls fussing after him.

Shells from a fierce artillery barrage began falling close by. Alik hid under his bed. Svetlana Magayeva took him by the hand and started leading him down the stairs to the shelters. The next building was hit. The windows of the children's home shattered, the doors were blown open and the air became red with brick dust. 'It seemed as if my eyes were covered with blood,' Svetlana recalled. 'The force of the explosions pushed me against Alik who was sandwiched between me and the wall. His body was trembling, but he was not hurt.' He began to stutter: 'Ah-give Alik ah-a piece of ah-bread.' He repeated this sentence over and over for days. Then he stopped saying anything except the sound 'Ah'. That is the only noise he made for the next two years, when his father came back to collect him. He began to cry, and suddenly he uttered: 'Ah-give Alik ah-a piece of ah-bread.'[9]

When the writer and journalist Alexander Fadeyev* visited an orphanage, he found that the children's faces and eyes 'told me more than could be gathered from all the stories of the horrors of famine'. At lunch, he noticed that one little girl kept putting pieces of bread aside. 'I wanted to remember Mummy,' she explained. 'We always used to eat bread together late at night in bed . . . and I wanted to do the same. I love my mummy and I want to remember her.' Another told him about her mother. 'I remember how she died at home,' she said. 'When she came in, she fell down on the floor . . . I put her on the bed, she was very heavy, and then the neighbours said she was dead.'[10]

There were happier stories, of children who found inner strength. One of them was a teenager, Denis Davidov, a shy, polite and timid boy. At the least confrontation, he covered his face with his hands and cried for pity: 'Please do not hurt me!' He was terribly bullied by a much younger little thug called Leonid Smirnov. Someone had stolen Davidov's belt, so that he had to keep his trousers up with a hand. Smirnov delighted in pinching him or hitting him, so that he lost his grip and his trousers fell down. The staff were aware of this. One of them tried to help by saying that the boy was a descendant of Denis Vasilyevich Davidov, the hussar-poet, a hero of Napoleon's invasion much admired by Pushkin for his verse and his courage. Smirnov sneered that the Davidov bloodline could never have produced this trouserless weakling. Then the bullied boy appeared in a real leather soldier's belt and buckle. He had saved his daily sugar cube until he had enough to exchange for this mighty belt. It gave him a fierce self-confidence. Smirnov left him well alone.

---

* Fadeyev's own life was tragic. He was a co-founder and chairman of the Union of Soviet Writers, and suborned his own undoubted talents as a novelist to serving Stalin, whom he described as 'the greatest humanist the world has ever seen'. After the war, he was a prime mover in the repression of writers and composers, including Shostakovich, in the 'Zhdanovshchina', the persecutions in Leningrad in the late 1940s. He died an alcoholic in 1956, after Stalin's death, unhinged by his denunciations of fellow writers, 'floundering in oozy, putrid mud', a colleague said, 'and drowning his conscience in wine'.

Music helped to keep adult morale alive, though at a price. Vera Inber went to the Philharmonia concert on 14 June: 'Many new faces in the orchestra, for many did not survive the winter.' The trombonist Viktor Orlovsky found it difficult to walk to the hall. His feet were so swollen that he had to cut open the edges of his *valenki*. But he loved the importance of what he was doing. He had heard that even German prisoners looked forward to their broadcasts. 'They admitted they couldn't wait to listen to us. They needed music as much as Russians.'

Valerian Bogdanov-Berezovsky was also at the concert – Eliasberg conducted Tchaikovsky's Italian Capriccio and arias from *Yevgeny Onegin* – and he noted how much weight the singer Pleshakov had lost. He considered his work plan for 1942. 'If I am still alive, which doesn't look possible, I have to finish a piano sonata, finish the score of a violin concerto, and finish my second opera. That's if I can survive.'

On 19 June, the Musical Comedy staged a new operetta, *Lesnaya By'l* (*What Happened in the Forest*). The music and libretto were written by actors and musicians from the theatre. Fadeyev wrote in *Leningradskaya Pravda*: 'At a time when the furious enemy threatens Leningraders with bombs and shells, we have the White Nights of June, the poplars and the blossom, and in the crowded Philharmonia Hall, the powerful sounds of Tchaikovsky's Sixth Symphony are heard calling out to the whole world as a symbol of the strength of the human spirit.' He was, in fact, writing in Moscow but his copy was sent to Leningrad.

On 22 June, Andrei Krukov's mother gave him an 'anniversary present' after a year of war. It was sheet music for piano by Schumann and Liszt. 'To my little son: thank you for your help. You have survived this very severe year.'[11] The radio news was grim. 'Tobruk has fallen, and the Germans have driven a wedge into the defences of Sevastapol,' Vera Inber noted.

Von Manstein's Eleventh Army had overwhelmed the Red armies in the Crimea a fortnight before, as German infantry began its final advance on the besieged city on the Black Sea. Sevastopol's fortifications had been blasted by 42,000 shells in the four days before the assault. Luftwaffe bombers mounted 1,200 sorties, the crews staying in their cockpits while their aircraft were rearmed and refuelled, flying three or four missions without rest. They had dropped 954 tons of bombs on the burning city on 11 June. The Russians held out in the ruins and redoubts among the rubble. They exacted a heavy toll as the *Landsers* were drawn into hand-to-hand fighting in the trenches and scrapes that honeycombed the fallen masonry, but they were finished. Within a week, Stalin would have the top Party officials taken out of the city by submarine. Three days later, the last Soviet defence line was breached.

On the Volkhov, the tragedy was reaching the endgame. The Russians in the pocket – the Germans called it a *Kessel*, a cauldron – were fighting on rations of 50 grams of dried bread a day at best. One rifleman, A. Bazyuk, recorded: 'We ate everything that could be eaten . . . leaves and fir cones. We boiled old horse bones and gnawed on them. To say nothing about bark – all the trees around us were stripped. Any insects, worms and frogs were eaten.'[12] Birch sap had been a help, but it had disappeared by the end of May. The groves of birch were pale and slender ghosts, stripped of bark by men who chewed it for its nutrients.* 'Many are disabled by emaciation,' the divisional commissar I. Zuyev recorded. 'Aviation failed to deliver foodstuffs today. As of 19 June 1942, there is not a single gram of food left.' Despite this, he said, 'the men's mood is sound. The units are fighting heroically.'

---

* Ironically, for the men who harvested it were starving, modern research shows that birch bark has a powerful compound, betulin, that helps to prevent obesity and diabetes. The inner bark contains xylitol, a type of sugar.

That afternoon, in pouring rain, Vlasov's men made brief contact with the Fifty-Ninth Army. Stalin had summoned to Moscow the man who had retaken Tikhvin, General Meretskov. He personally sent him to the Volkhov front, held by the Fifty-Second and Fifty-Ninth Armies, with orders to 'take the Second [Shock] Army out of encirclement even if you have to abandon the heavy artillery and equipment'. Meretskov had flown to the front, and he scraped together what troops he had to reopen a narrow escape corridor to Vlasov's trapped men.

A dozen T-34 tanks from the Fifty-Ninth went through the 150-yard-wide corridor into the pocket that night, while 6,000 men escaped in the opposite direction. Next morning, the tanks were trapped and destroyed. The Germans resealed the pocket by nightfall.

Vlasov and his surviving officers were still functioning. On 21 June, he and Commissar Zuyev signed orders awarding thirty-one men medals 'For Valour' and 'For Combat Merit'. That same day, Zuyev reported: 'During the past three days we have had no food at all . . . The personnel are famished to excess. There is no ammunition.'[13]

Dmitriev's men were ordered to blow up their guns and head to an assembly point near Myasnoi Bor. A mass of men had collected here under continuous bombardment. 'Hunger left them without any strength. Several of us commanders took up positions around a thick aspen. Each of us had a foxhole between the roots, our heads below the tree. Every day someone was killed.' The Fifty-Ninth Army opened a gap 500 yards wide on the morning of the 21st. Dmitriev and N. F. Ushakov, the divisional communications officer, were authorized to try to make their own way out along it, little more than a path that had been forced through next to the narrow-gauge railway line. The gunners of the German XXXVIII Corps kept it under constant artillery and machine-gun fire. Dmitriev had severe dystrophy and Ushakov had tuberculosis. 'My legs were swollen and refused to move. Ushakov could walk and promised to help me.'

They walked and crawled to the path. A knocked out T-34 tank sat at the entrance. The Germans were on both sides for the full two-and-half-mile length of the corridor. The only favourable factor for Dmitriev was that the Germans had to be at pains to avoid killing their own men. 'Taking our time, we would choose the next shell crater. Ushakov would run, and I would roll across the ground towards it.' They had got halfway when Ushakov was cut down by a burst of machine-gun fire. 'I tried to crawl up to him, but was fired upon. The bullets grazed my clothes, but I remained unharmed and continued to crawl my way out.' He reached the river Polist. It was 'filled with corpses right up to the bank. The living crawled over the bodies of the dead.' The 'corridor' was called 'the Valley of Death', he said, 'but no words can express what took place there'. Fate took pity on him: Dmitriev collapsed after he had reached the end of the corridor, and medics attended to him.[14] 'No one can recreate what was happening in the valley of Death,' the infantryman Bazyuk, who was among them, wrote. 'A continuous wall of fire, unceasing howling and roaring, and a stupefying stench of burnt human flesh . . . and thousands of people rushing into this fiery corridor. We all thought it would be better to die in the fire than be captured by the Germans. But only those who could move tried to escape. Many collapsed through starvation or could not move because of wounds, and all of them still lie there.'[15]

Another desperate attack was made in the late evening of 23 June. By the early dawn of the White Nights, a narrow corridor was opened. Igor Yelokhovskiy, the artillery platoon commander, began his breakout attempt with the remnants of the 59th Independent Rifle Brigade. He tried to help a friend with severe leg wounds, Valya Fomchenko, a fellow gunner from Leningrad. Yelokhovskiy supported him as he hopped on one leg in a mass of men surging down the track of one of the narrow-gauge supply railways. 'He stumbled and fell but I was pushed forward by the mass of men,' Yelokhovskiy recalled. 'I heard only his fading cry: "Igorek . . . help . . . help me . . ." I still hear this faint cry for help at night . . . and I awake in a cold sweat . . . not having helped him.' He crossed two small rivers that lay on the escape path, the Glushitsa and the Polist. 'I do not remember the water, however, as a slippery train of human bodies lay under our feet.' He went through the whole war, but 'I never witnessed such carnage anywhere. There was no open "corridor". The Germans were everywhere . . . on all sides. One could run, but there was no place to hide from the shooting.'

Only thirty-two men from the 59th Brigade escaped that day. They were covered in mud, in scorched winter jackets and torn felt boots or barefoot. 'Some were skeletons while others were so swollen their eyes were not visible.' The survivors were rested for ten days, and then they were flung back into the line to hold a German thrust. 'From our thirty-two men,' Yelokhovskiy wrote, 'only six would return.' He managed to avoid the attention of the NKVD. Those stragglers who escaped later, singly, were less fortunate. They were suspected of having bargained with the Germans. They were harshly interrogated. 'Many were released,' Yelokhovskiy noted, 'but others . . . The screening was vigilant.'[16]

The dismounted 100th Cavalry Regiment was fighting with the Fifty-Ninth Army to protect the escape route from the Volkhov side of the ring. Its commissar, P. I. Sotnik, was shocked at the condition of the survivors, though his own regiment was reduced to eleven men at the end of the fighting. 'They were half dead and barely moving,' he wrote. 'Their escape took place under heavy bombing and continuous artillery and mortar fire. So many men perished here, that there was nowhere to stand. The whole earth was strewn with corpses and no one could tell who was killed and where they were buried.'[17]

The Germans attacked those still trapped throughout the day on 24 June. Attempts to organize another break-out party were impeded by large numbers of service troops from rear units, who milled around, leaderless. Venets and others withdrew deeper into the Zamoshskoe swamp. They made final radio contact with Colonel-General A. M. Yakovlev, the commander of the Fifty-Second Army. He ordered them to cease organized resistance and fight their way out in small groups. The ring was tightening, Venets said: 'We could hear the barking of German dogs in the forest.' There was only one way of escape, through the minefields they had sown in the January offensive in the Zamosh-skoe swamp.

They left a rearguard of wounded machine-gunners from the 305th Rifle Division to cover their retreat into the swamp. For an hour, hiding in the swamp, waiting for nightfall, they heard the sounds of the unequal battle by these men, lying in open positions, 'whose names remain unknown but whose heroism cannot be forgotten'. Only a few, already seriously wounded, escaped. At night, as Venets's little group moved out of the swamp, they ran into a company of Germans combing the ground. They lost more men in the firefight. Only seven survived to get through to Russian lines, with 'all our documents, weapons and insignia'. As well as the brigade commander, they included two commissars and the ranking NKVD officer, Sinev, and his security platoon commander.

They were immediately subjected, as Venets delicately put it, to 'the formalities at the Special Section'. This meant that they were interrogated by the NKVD. They were fortunate that it was the missing Vlasov, rather than themselves, who would be scapegoated. They had hoped to meet senior military officers, and waited eagerly for interviews and questions, feeling their experiences to be valuable. They met only the deputy chief of the Front's political administration.

General Meretskov was told by some officers who had got out that they had seen Vlasov. He sent a tank regiment and some infantry to penetrate the area where Vlasov had been spotted. They failed in that mission, but they saved the life of P. V. Rukhlenko. The battery commissar was with his assistant, a medic and an orderly on a small group breakout. They moved in short dashes, going to ground behind tussocks or in shell holes, when the Germans opened up on them with machine guns. They plunged across a small river, their wet clothes becoming unbearably heavy, and they drained their waterlogged boots while tracer bullets whistled above them, sighting shots as the German gunners tried to find the correct range. Rukhlenko gave the hand signal: 'Forward!' His assistant, Sobolev – his friend, 'the man I had looked after especially' – lay still a yard away from him. The medic crawled over to him, checked his pulse, and said, 'He's dead.'

Rukhlenko crawled on. 'I was growing weaker with every step ... The thought constantly rang in my head – "You must not fall behind" . . . An enemy battery opened up from the right flank. One of the shells landed among us. A cloud of smoke, dust and dirt swirled around and men lay prostrate. The shell had hit near by, in front of me. It was a testament to the right of existence, that, although being thrown back and deafened, I nevertheless crawled away . . . Ahead the corridor grew wider and wider – we had passed through. We ran into four T-34s and cheered.' He learned that 'Meretskov had sent the tanks to bring General Vlasov out of the pocket'.

But of Vlasov, there was no trace.

Mosquitoes swarmed over the swamps and neither gloves nor netting gave the well-equipped Germans relief. 'With this plague,' Sergeant-Major Gütte noted, 'came the almost unbearable nausea caused by the decaying flesh of the fallen, lying in the swamps and woods.' He described the Russians emerging from their hiding places to surrender in the hundreds and thousands. 'Many were wounded. Most of them were half starving and barely retained the semblance of human beings.' Stukas beat back the attempts at breakouts, until the pocket was split in four and the end came.

No more escapes were recorded after 9.35 a.m. on 25 June. Several hundred officers and commissars made a final attempt on the 28th. None got out. Their men were not fighting any more. The Germans took more than 20,000 prisoners that day. Two days later, the headlines in the Army Group North newspaper recorded: 'The Leningrad relief attempt has failed. The Volkhov battle has ended. 33,000 prisoners have been taken, 649 guns and 171 tanks have been captured or destroyed.'[18]

'A giant forest of stumps stretched out to the horizon where the dense woods had once stood,' Gütte wrote. 'The Soviet dead, or rather parts of their bodies, carpeted the churned-up ground. The stench was indescribably ghastly.'[19]

It was at this low moment that the Seventh had its first great foreign triumph, in London. The original plan was to play it in a BBC concert at the Albert Hall on 4 June, accompanied by Elgar's Cockaigne Overture Op. 40, and Tchaikovsky's First Concerto in B flat. *The Times* reported a 'hitch over the proposed first performance'. The orchestral parts had not yet arrived. Shostakovich's Fifth was played instead. A later date, 22 June, slipped past before Sir Henry Wood conducted the first performance with the London Philharmonic on the 29th.

The Albert Hall was sold out. The audience, both in the hall and on BBC Radio, was enthralled. 'It was listened to with profound attention by an immense audience,' *The Times* reported. 'It is a wonderful thing that a young man of service age, taking his part in the defence of his country, should be able to construct this prodigious score.' The critics saw Shostakovich as the heroic fireman who, the newspaper said, was inspired by ideas that came to him as he was 'waiting for the next moment of action . . . in his duties as an air-raid warden, watching for incendiaries on the roof of the Leningrad Conservatoroire'.

They were less sure of the quality of the music.* *The Times* described the 'invasion' passage in the first movement, with its repetitive theme and ever-increasing drumming, as 'a deliberately dull tune'. But to the audience and the popular press, this was the march of the aggressor, the brutal and mechanical sound of the Nazis, the noise of their panzer armies and their tanks and half-tracks, transformed into music. The critics agreed that the audience, seeing the big battalions of the orchestra assemble – 'six trombones, eight horns, &c.' – expected an 'exciting, battle piece of the *1812* kind only more so and lasting for over an hour'. That was not, *The Times* said, what they got. 'Certainly through most of its long length there is nothing to suggest action of any kind . . .' The *Sunday Times* was more cruel still. To find the Seventh's place on the musical map, its critic wrote, one 'should look along the seventieth degree of lassitude and the last degree of platitude'.

The critics mattered little. To the British, the music was thick with the blood and heroism of their Russian allies, proof of their humanity, and an elegy to the defiant city on the Neva. A yet more ecstatic welcome waited the piece across the dark and U-boat-haunted expanses of the North Atlantic.

*

---

* *The Times* review was headlined 'Unsorted Thoughts' – close indeed to the 'Muddle instead of Music' that had so nearly cost Shostakovich his head in 1936 – and it spoke of the composer putting down the first thing that came into his head. 'It is a palimpsest of ideas that occur in the intervals of duty: what he might have said to a fellow fire-watcher if he had had a full orchestra to say it with.' Though it preserved the traditions of a four-movement symphony, the material showed 'little deliberate contrast.' Was it a 'magnificent work', as so many listeners thought? 'It may not even be a great work judged by the principles of selection, balance and shapeliness which apply generally to the symphonic form,' the critic went on. 'But if one can have the patience to hear it out, it becomes an absorbingly interesting one, just what a musician thinks when he has little time to sort and sift, and the moments when patience is severely tried are compensated for by others of spontaneous eloquence.' (*The Times*, 3 July 1942.)

The score arrived in New York on 25 June. It was famous already. *Time* put Shostakovich on its cover. 'Not since the first Manhattan performance of *Parsifal* in 1903,' the magazine proclaimed, 'has there been such a buzz of American anticipation over a piece of music.' A torrent of other stories, ten in the *New York Times* alone, preceded the symphony. *Time*'s cover set the tone, with a portrait of Shostakovich painted by Boris Artzybasheff. There was an irony here, for Artzybasheff was a Russian émigré who had arrived in New York with 14 cents in his pocket after fighting in the ranks of the White armies. Had they not fled, he and his father, a well-known anti-Bolshevik writer, would surely have been devoured in a camp or an execution cellar.

No matter, now. Artzybasheff did Shostakovich proud – and a few months later he was to paint Stalin's cover portrait, as *Time*'s 'Man of the Year' for 1942. Shostakovich was resplendent and fiercely martial in fireman's helmet and uniform, in a striking pose from the set of propaganda pictures taken on the roof of the Conservatoire in September 1941. The bold-type caption read: 'Fireman Shostakovich – Amid bombs bursting in Leningrad he heard the chords of victory.'

This was the composer from the besieged city, a man who had dug trenches and fire-watched as the Nazi bombers came in, and yet still found the passion and will to write a vast and cascading piece of music to snub Hitler. The theme was compelling. It fed the growing American fascination with their Soviet allies, with their culture and the way they were fighting. The *New York Times* gave a graphic description of the microfilm of the score – on a 100-foot-long roll of 35mm film, with each page of the score and instrumental parts on one of 450 separate frames of film – and an account of its arrival on a US Navy aircraft from Brazil.[20]

It got its dates wrong. It said that the North American premiere would take place in August, under Serge Koussevitzky at the Berkshire Music Center. Arturo Toscanini was to give the New York premiere with the New York Philharmonic in October. The NBC Symphony

Orchestra was 'almost certain' to include the Seventh early in its season, under Toscanini or Leopold Stokowski. Rus-Am Music, which
had a monopoly on the American market in Soviet music, was confident that 'many of the country's major orchestras will play the work,
preferably in October'.

The errors were understandable. No piece of music had ever been so
bitterly fought over by elite conductors. A 'battle royal' for 'the glory of
conducting the premiere', *Time* said, broke out between 'sleek, platinum-
haired Leopold Stokowski, the Cleveland Orchestra's Artur Rodzinski,
and Boston's Serge Koussevitzky'. It looked as though Koussevitzky had
won for an August 14th premiere at Tanglewood. But then Toscanini,
the 'old fire-and-ice Maestro', beat him with a special broadcast for 19
July from Studio 8-H in New York's Radio City.

Toscanini was not a natural choice. He had shown little or no interest
in modern Russian music; indeed, as *Time* noted, he had declined to
give the premiere of Shostakovich's Fifth Symphony four years earlier.
Koussevitzky and Stokowski were both known champions of Shostakovich. Toscanini had, however, the immense clout of NBC behind
him. NBC had started bidding for first American performance rights
in Kuibyshev in January.

It had won them by April, and it now chose Toscanini to conduct
the NBC orchestra. It was touch-and-go, though, or so *Time* recounted,
whether Toscanini's disdain for Shostakovich would cause him to refuse.
The photostat pages of the score were rushed to him. 'NBC held its
breath. He looked, and said: "Very interesting and most effective." He
looked again, said "Magnificent!"' The date of the premiere was brought
forward, to a radio concert on 19 July. Night after night, 'nearsighted
Maestro Toscanini, who conducts from memory, never from notes, sat
up with eyes buried in the score . . .'

Stokowski complained bitterly, and said that his Slav blood and his
regard for Shostakovich should have won him the honour. It cut no ice.

Toscanini ignored him, and the consolation prize, the concert premiere, went to Koussevitsky.

Shostakovich himself wrote a piece for the *New York Times* that ran on 21 June. It was headlined 'Stating the Case for Slavonic Culture'. Its subject was the dignity and beauty of Slavonic music in a world at war. He praised the courage of Slav composers in the struggle against the fascists, the 'dirty robber gang . . . the lowest, dirtiest and vilest specimens'.[21] Art, he said, was a weapon of beauty against the ugliness of fascism. He quoted Pushkin's remark from *Mozart and Salieri*: 'Genius and villainy, the two are incompatible.' In another piece, for the American Marxist weekly *New Masses*, Shostakovich wrote of 'Art . . . becoming a new type of armament, striking the enemy'.

The *New Yorker* had a long preview of the premiere in the 18 July edition. At least one American, NBC's Thomas Belviso, the head of the music department, was heartily sick of the whole project. 'I don't think I'll even go to the broadcast,' he said. 'I wouldn't care if I never heard another word about Shostakovich's Seventh. It's been one vast headache.' The microfilm of the score had arrived in a small tin can, 'about the size of a guest-room ashtray'. With Toscanini 'clawing the air and demanding to be let at it', Belviso had to dig up a firm of photographers to blow up to normal size the parts for the conductor and a hundred and ten instruments. It needed 2,038 separate prints in all.

The printers had to go on a three-shift schedule, and 'earned their dough'. To make matters worse, it was found that the microfilm had been under-exposed, making enlarging more difficult. Belviso then discovered that wartime priorities prevented the purchase of enough dull-finish paper for the final prints. 'As it stands now, the parts are printed on glossy paper, and the orchestra will just have to take its chance in being able to read them under lights.' He showed the *New Yorker* reporters a copy of an extra score of the first violin part he happened to have in his office. It struck them as straightforward enough. 'We opened its green covers with due reverence, noting that it was thirty-five pages long and seemed to be CXMPOHNR No. 7. Anyway, it was Op. 60, and the tempo markings of the four movements were in orthodox Italian; allegretto, moderato poco allegretto, adagio and allegro non troppo.'

The business of the score shows the gulf between New York and Leningrad. Belviso's complaint, of the shortage of matt paper, is almost comically frivolous in terms of the Russian city, where the score was copied out by hand, and where the only items in ready supply were death and terror. It shows, too, scant understanding of the circumstances that had inspired the Seventh, and that gave nobility to its music and to the people and the place it commemorated.

The NBC and the Radiokom orchestras nonetheless had one shortage in common. Both lacked enough musicians. NBC found itself short of four French horns, three trumpets, three trombones, five woodwinds, and five assorted percussion instruments. The circumstances were different, of course. Radiokom players were still succumbing to the ravages of the siege. On 23 June, for example, two days before the score arrived in New York, Radiokom's Ya. Savich was evacuated. The violinist's frostbitten toes had been amputated during the winter. He had tried to play on in rehearsals but he became so infirm that he was given permission to leave. Radiokom searched for a replacement at the front. NBC made up its shortfall by recalling some players from vacation. Others, who had not expected to go to work again until the autumn, were immediately sent for, and 'a few were hired just for this one chore'.[22]

Toscanini, the *New Yorker* reported, had retired for three days with the score, and 'came forth with the whole thing committed to memory, as well as with a critical verdict: "Inspired". Leopold Spitalny, the Director of Orchestra Personnel who had drummed up the extra musicians, also described it. 'Well,' he said, 'it starts with deceptive softness – a roll of a single snare drum. But it ends, ninety minutes later, with hell breaking loose.' 'We can,' the magazine concluded, 'hardly wait.'

Only *Time* reminded its readers of the Russia of the terror. Its description of the symphony was compelling. 'Like a great wounded snake, dragging its slow length, it uncoils for 80 minutes . . . Its themes are exultations, agonies . . . In its last movement the triumphant brasses prophesy what Shostakovich describes as the "victory of light over darkness, of humanity over barbarism".' But it also spoke of the darkness in the soul of the Soviet state that had, in 1936, come so close to wrapping itself round the composer himself. At the height of the Purge, it said, when 'people were plopping into prison like turtles in a pond', Stalin had decided to hear *Lady Macbeth of Mtsensk*. 'He did not like it, [and] walked out before it was over.'[23]

From its first note, American audiences received the Seventh with rapture. Millions listened to the broadcast from Radio City between 4.15 and 6.00 p.m. EST on 19 July. Toscanini stirred the patriotic blood by opening the concert with 'The Star-Spangled Banner'. At the end of the Seventh, after his long and furious stint of non-stop conducting, he looked 'as if he had just come through the siege of Leningrad. The studio audience jumped up and cheered as if it had heard news of a Nazi defeat.' An unidentified voice read out a radiogram from Shostakovich to Toscanini, praising his ability and regretting that he could not be in New York for the performance. There was an appeal to buy war bonds.

It was a triumph. Audiences and radio listeners thrilled to the music. There was a ten-minute standing ovation at the first concert performance on 14 August. Serge Koussevitzky conducted the Berkshire Music Center Orchestra at the Berkshire Symphonic Festival. Five thousand attended, a high turn-out for rural Massachusetts with petrol now rationed to three to four gallons a week. Ambassador Litvinov was there, and 'The Internationale' was played with 'The Star-Spangled Banner' as a curtain-raiser. Koussevitzky was renowned for his dislike of unruly audiences. When the audience burst into spontaneous clapping after the first movement, astonished reporters noted that the pernickety conductor 'sanctioned the breach of custom'.

The Chicago Symphony Orchestra attracted an audience of five thousand for the first Midwestern performance at its summer home in Ravinia Park on 22 August. They stood and cheered wildly for ten minutes.

Nina Shostakovich gave American readers an intimate and human picture of her husband in a widely syndicated interview. He was a great sports fan. 'Heat or cold, rain or snow, not one soccer, ice hockey or boxing match would he miss.' He was an enthusiastic volleyball player. He loved going to the circus. For all his fame, he was unusually modest. 'Putting it mildly, he doesn't like performing at concerts . . . His greatest bane is having to be filmed. He can't stand being photographed either. The result is a scowling face.'

She described his working day. He did not demand special conditions: 'He just sits down at his writing desk and writes, morning, noon, evenings. At night he sleeps. If it isn't singing or shouting, noises don't affect him at all.' He kept his door open, and 'often the children romp around in his room. Sometimes Galya climbs on his knee while he is composing, but she sits quietly . . . He composes swiftly, writing the score straight through, usually without changes or deletions.'

Her sketch was a charming insight into genius. She finished it with his courage. It was accurate enough, as far as it went. He seldom stopped working, she said, even during the Leningrad air raids. 'If things began looking too hot, he calmly finished the bar he was writing, waited until the page dried, neatly arranged what he had written, and took it down to the bomb shelter.'[24] But he was not in the city, of course, in the starvation winter; he was not on the Nevsky pyatachok or on the Volkhov, spilling his blood in forlorn attempts to lift its siege: he could not know, and his Western admirers could not conceive of, the true horror.

No matter, as his Leningrad Symphony swept all before it. By the end of the year, more than a dozen orchestras had tackled it. New York had performances by Stokowski in an NBC broadcast, by the Philharmonic under Rodzinski in Carnegie Hall, and by the Boston Symphony Orchestra within a few months. The great and good conducted: Dmitri Mitropoulos in Minneapolis, Hans Kindler and the National Symphony Orchestra, Eugene Goossens in Cincinnati, Stokowski again, with the San Francisco Symphony Orchestra, this time to a wildly enthusiastic audience of more than nine thousand.

It was a rare audience that disliked it. In November, Stokowski conducted it in front of 14,000 soldiers at an army camp in southern California. The troops were bored stiff. Stokowski had cut its length, but even so they 'shuffled and groaned impatiently . . . and a bad time was had by all.' By now, though, *Life* noted, it 'is almost unpatriotic not to like Dmitri Shostakovich's Seventh . . . This work has become a symbol of Russia's heroic resistance.' People who were less than fulsome in their praise 'are looked on as musical fifth columnists who are running down our brave Russian allies'.

Shostakovich was made an honorary member of the American Academy of Arts and Letters, and so, warming to the new Soviet musical theme, was Prokofiev. Toscanini sent long cables to Shostakovich in Kuibyshev begging him to come to New York to conduct the Seventh himself. 'Your visit would have great political as well as musical value, and would help dramatize the close ties between the US and the Soviet Union.' Shostakovich replied: 'Regretfully admit that I do not master the art of conducting thus unable avail myself opportunity conduct before American audience.'

The New York Philharmonic's Ruth Pratt upped the ante by inviting him 'to conduct our beloved Orchestra or to appear as piano soloist'. She cabled Wendell Willkie, Roosevelt's ambassador-at-large, who was at the American embassy in Kuibyshev. She asked him to use his 'utmost efforts' to get Shostakovich to agree.[25] It was said that his coming would 'exercise such commotion as not even Tchaikovsky or Dvorak did in the Gay Nineties'. Ambassador Litvinov did his best – 'I myself have many times invited Shostakovich to come to this country,' he told the Philharmonic, 'but so far without results'[26] – but Shostakovich would not budge.

American critics, on the whole, liked the Seventh much less than audiences and conductors. 'Uneven in interest, originality, ideas and inspiration . . . in short, an overblown bore,' wrote the *Philadelphia Inquirer*.[27] B. H. Hagan in *The Nation* found it 'an excessively long piece of bad music . . . feeble, inane, banal . . . unresourceful, crude, blatant'.[28] The *Christian Science Monitor* found it 'brilliant and dull, individual and imitative, terse and repetitious'.

The *Minneapolis Morning Tribune* caught the contrast in reactions. To the detached critic, it said, the music might seem an 'overlong and uneven tour de force'. But listeners would rob themselves of 'an experience they have never had before' if they thought in those terms. No, this was Russia's greatest composer translating into music his first-hand impression of the attack by the 'modern Genghis Khan'. They should see it as a message from 'a gallant fighting ally', a cry from an agonized country 'rising by sheer force of will to one of the supreme feats of resistance of all time'. Take it in that spirit, and 'it's impossible that it could leave you cold'.[29]

The terrors that *Time* alone mentioned – the innocents 'plopping into prison' – were continuing, secretly, in Leningrad. The writer Vsevolod Vishnevsky, working as a journalist for the navy, noted that 'A certain

B—k somewhere in an after-dinner conversation openly defended Fascist conceptions . . . He was removed from the ship and taken into custody. Where do such types come from?' This referred to S. Abramovich-Blek, once a tsarist naval officer, who was also a navy journalist and the director of a fleet newspaper. Vishnevsky had encouraged Blek's ambitions to write and had sponsored his literary debut. 'B—k', Vishnevsky now claimed, was secretly hoping for Hitler to win. He may have believed that Blek was a traitor.[30] It is as likely that he was covering his own back.

The NKVD had their claws into other writers in the city. Two had already been shot. Blek now joined those who were being interrogated in the Bolshoi Dom, as a prelude to their deaths. The Writers' House on Ulitsa Voinovo had only a few members to lunch on the good barley soup, borscht and glucose bars it served in its dining room. Thirty-three members had died of starvation over the winter. Eleven had been killed on the front. Most of the others had been evacuated or were serving in the army.

It was left to the NKVD, too, to add the final touches to the blame game on the Volkhov. Those still at large in the pocket floundered in the swamps and forests as the Germans mopped up. The grave of Commissar Zuyev was found many years later near the 105th kilometre of the Chudovo railway. He had come out of the woods, wounded and weak, to beg some bread from the workers repairing the line. They ran to tell their German guards. Zuyev shot himself with his revolver before he could be taken. Commissars knew what would happen to them if they fell into German hands. Two of them, S. Bulanov and F. Chornyi, were killed making hopeless charges against dug-in machine guns. The head of the Second Shock's Special Section also shot himself.

The commander of the 327th Rifle Division, General I. M. Antyufeev, tried to break out to the west, in the German rear, which was more lightly defended than the front along the Volkhov to the east. He gathered several dozen officers and men from various units. 'We succeeded in breaking through the chain of German machine guns into the enemy's rear,' he wrote, 'but few managed to escape. The majority of the men perished, while some were taken prisoner. This latter fate was one I also failed to avoid – on 5 July 1942.'[31]

General Andrei Vlasov was at large for another week. He had been seen, with Commissar Zuyev and four sub-machine-gunners, on the banks of the Polnyet' river. V. N. Ivanov, the secretary of the Leningrad Young Communists, parachuted behind German lines to try to contact him. The pilot dropped him by a small village that was occupied by an SS unit. Ivanov was wounded but sought sanctuary in the forest. Here he met Vlasov, in uniform, still defiant. They got separated. No further trace was found.

The general gave himself up to the Germans on 12 July. He was brought to General Lindemann, his opposite number, who much admired the courage of the Second Shock, and was well treated.

Stalin needed scapegoats. He had already relieved Lieutenant-General Mikhail Khozin of his command of the Leningrad Front, 'for his failure to fulfil Stavka's orders on the timely and rapid withdrawal of the Second Shock Army'. For good measure, the wretched general was also damned in a special report drawn up by a high-ranking NKVD officer, Ivan Moskalenko, the assistant head of the Osobii Otdel, the Special Section dealing with military counter-intelligence. Khozin was savaged 'for his bureaucratic control, and for isolating himself from the forces'. Moskalenko accused him of 'deceiving' the Stavka, the High Command, by falsely claiming that the withdrawal was under way. The general was lucky to escape with his life.

Moskalenko reported that Vlasov had last been seen, with Zuyev, directing the breakout from a knocked-out tank. He criticized Vlasov for ordering 'all radio sets to be destroyed by setting them on fire, which led to a loss of control over the forces'. What he did not yet know was that Vlasov had begun to collaborate with the Germans after his capture. Vlasov told his captors that, in the ten days when he was hiding from them in the swamps, he had concluded that his men had been destroyed by Stalin and the subservient Stavka, which had abandoned them to starve, unable to defend themselves for lack of ammunition.*

It is possible that his treachery followed a coded order to arrest him sent by Kiril Meretskov after the ring was finally closed on 25 June. Meretskov, as we have seen, was utterly vulnerable to the NKVD, which had obtained confessions from him before being released from their cells to fight at Tikhvin. He had recommended Vlasov to be appointed to the Second Shock Army. He may have been searching for a scapegoat. Had Vlasov got wind of this, he would have understood that both his honour and his life might be taken from him. There is no evidence that Meretskov was seeking to betray him, but Vlasov was soon suggesting that anti-Stalinist prisoners of war should collaborate with the Germany army. The Germans allowed him to form a Russian Liberation Committee, and he wrote an anti-Bolshevik leaflet, the 'Smolensk Proclamation'. Hundreds of thousands of the leaflets were dropped over Russian lines, urging the troops to defect to the Germans.

Vlasov's name became synonymous with treason, and with the Volkhov catastrophe.† Between 7 January and 10 July 1942, the abortive attempt to break through to the city had cost 149,328 dead and 253,280 wounded. Leningrad was not to be relieved, and the siege went on.

*

---

* Moskalenko's report confirmed that, at best, Russian aircraft were dropping 7 tons of food a day to the trapped army, instead of the required minimum of 17 tons, and 2,000 shells instead of the needed 40,000. Only 300,000 cartridges were airdropped, roughly 5 cartridges per man.
† Hitler mistrusted him, and it was only in September 1944 that he was allowed to raise a Russian Liberation Army from prisoners of war. Vlasov was taken prisoner by the Americans at the end of the war. He was forcibly seized by Soviet troops in Austria on 12 May 1945, then held in the Lubyanka for more than a year. Vlasov was hanged with eleven officers from the Liberation Army on 1 August 1946.

There were signs, though, of musical resilience at the end of the month. On 27 June, a new ballet collective formed at the Kirov gave its first performance. It was led by Olga Iordan, as strong and individual a ballerina and teacher as ever. She prepared the dancers. 'I scaled my demands to their weakened abilities, and I didn't give them difficult exercises,' she wrote. 'But in what they did, I demanded perfection and didn't allow any excuses about health.' The Arts Committee had provided extra rations to help get them into better shape.

The food helped to inspire them. They danced *The Little Humpbacked Horse*, by Pugni, the ballet composer from the Mariinsky, and scenes from *Don Quixote* and *Le Corsaire*. Scenes from *Bayaderka* were a reminder of tsarist days: *La Bayadère*, by the ballet master Marius Petipa to the music of Ludwig Minkus, had first been performed at the Imperial Bolshei Kammeny Theatre in 1877. There were dances, too, by Delibes, Rubinstein, Strauss and Alyabiev. The brilliance of Iordan, and the Forty-Second Army's dancer R. Gerbek, shone out, but the whole performance by weakened dancers was thought amazing and a great boost for morale.

A major piece of siege composition was performed three days later. The 'Heroic Aria' for mezzo-soprano and symphony orchestra was composed by Yuri Kochurov. He dedicated it to the great mezzo-soprano Sofya Preobrazhenskaya. The first al fresco concert was held in the Summer Garden of the Anichkov Palace. Eliasberg conducted a programme of Bizet, Mesmer, Johann Strauss, Zuppe and Liszt. A poster in the Garden was a reminder of a grimmer presence in the city. It advertised daily concerts by the Wind Orchestra of NKVD Troops.

CHAPTER 14

Iyul'

July 1942

An aircraft carrying the score of the Seventh touched down in Leningrad towards the beginning of July. The exact date and time is not known – details of blockade-breaking flights were a military secret – but it was flown by a pilot called Litvinov. German fighters were active as he crossed their lines and he skimmed the surface of Lake Ladoga to escape them. *Leningradskaya Pravda* announced the arrival on 2 July.

The story, under the headline 'The Public Performance of Shostakovich's 7th Symphony', recorded that: 'The score has been delivered to Leningrad by aircraft. It is one of the greatest of all symphonies inspired by the heroic fight of Leningraders. The composer was a participant and witness of this fight. The performance is planned for mid-July to be conducted by Karl Eliasberg.'

In fact, from the moment he first looked through the score, Eliasberg doubted that it was possible to play the symphony in Leningrad. It needed too many musicians. It seemed too demanding – physically and technically – for many of those he did have. The orchestra was not keen on it, either.

'We didn't understand the music,' said a flautist, Galina Fedorovna Yershova. It was a typical reaction. She was a teenager in 1942. She had no diploma or qualifications. The war had come before she had finished her studies in the city's Mussorgsky College of Music. 'I was working in the Kirov factory making shells,' she said. 'The radio was on in the factory, and they said that all the musicians who were still alive should report to the Radio Committee. So I went. I took my flute and I could hardly walk straight. I had dystrophy and scurvy. But I was registered and they asked me to come back when the scores for individual instruments were ready.'[1] The Seventh frightened her. 'It was very difficult. It was too complex. We didn't really want to play it.'

The foreboding was justified. The Leningrad is exceptionally long, eighty minutes with no interval. Each of its four movements requires the conductor and orchestra to deal in emotions that change, constantly and brutally, and that involve the whole range of instruments. Each has its own structure, but the symphony remains a piece that must be played as a whole. It is physically demanding to sustain for an orchestra in the pink of health. Fail in one part, as seemed inevitable for the Radiokom's raddled musicians, and the performance slides readily into an overblown triteness. The concentration the piece demands is intense and unyielding. The conductor has to maintain this high pitch of attention throughout its many moods and half-hidden subtleties.

Shostakovich was a born theatre composer – the fine British conductor Sir Mark Elder is sure he would have been the century's greatest opera composer, had *Lady Macbeth of Mtsensk* not fallen foul of Stalin – and the symphony is full of musical drama. At first, it is song-like and pastoral as Shostakovich sketches the beauty of life at peace – Alexei Tolstoy, listening in Kuibyshev, called it the 'flawless small happiness' of peacetime – becoming sweeter and rising higher and higher until, low down, it is destroyed by snare drumming and the 'invasion' passage crashes into it. This was to become its most famous part, audiences hearing in it the squealing metallic sounds and clatter of Nazi tank tracks, vulgar, coarse music, violating the sensibilities, a chilling portrait of brute force – 'this monster with a zinc snout' that Yevgeny Petrov described, 'marching down you'.*

The extra brass that the composer demanded is there to give it grotesque exaggeration. Shostakovich scored it officially for 'four horns' but in fact it needed eight: he concealed the extra players since they had been judged to be 'decadent' by his critics when he had used them in his withdrawn Fourth Symphony.

The passage is insensitive, and clamorous, though it is music that the brass players drafted from the military bands at the front were well placed to create. To Tolstoy, it resembled 'a dance of trained rats to the rat-catcher's tune', the drums triumphant, the violins howling 'with pain and despair'. But it requires poise and delicacy from the snare drummer, despite seeming crude and repetitive, for it lasts three times longer than anyone could imagine. The conductor must control the snare with great care, so that it slowly builds a sense of the sinister. And, after this battering of the senses, the orchestra must at once sustain a passage of passionate sadness until the music winds down.

The second movement seems lighter emotionally. Tolstoy described it as 'a renaissance – beauty reborn out of dust and ashes. It is like the vision of a modern Dante . . . the threat of death to great art, to great goodness, is revoked by the face of austere and lyrical contemplation.' Look at the music on the page, conductors say, and the movement looks transparent and easy. Play it, though, and it demands poise and subtlety. The solo oboist and clarinettist bear a heavy responsibility, for the oboe solo is hard and testing, and the clarinettist is very exposed. The movement is bittersweet, washed with the enigmatic nature of much

---

* Perhaps this was in deliberate contrast to Prokofiev's score for the 1938 film *Alexander Nevsky*. The Germans here crashed into Russia not in panzers but as Teutonic knights on horseback. The music written for the German crusaders was more powerful than the Russian passages, so that, some thought, evil was glorified and made brilliant. Certainly, in the Seventh Shostakovich did not waver from the ugliness of evil.

of Shostakovich's work, and the influence of klezmer, the music of East European Jews, full of ecstasy and despair, that he much admired. The bassoon, for Shostakovich, also has a very important personality in the orchestra, plangent, emotional and melancholy at times, satirical and clown-like at others.

After the intimacy and delicacy of the second movement, the third is inspired by the vast landscapes of Russia, described in great passages whose physical demands test the endurance of the string players. They must give it grandeur and majesty, and maintain a difficult control of the bow. A broad slow passage in the middle of the movement requires brilliance in the flautist, for the flute plays a touching song, rather beautiful, pure and consoling. The movement is difficult for the audience – it is meditative but it has moments of distress and despair – and the strings, and the piano in its fiercest fortissimo, must articulate it with enough fluency to keep their interest.

The fourth movement, where one expects the crashing drums and fireworks of victory, is the hardest of all for the conductor to get the pacing right. The body of it should have the feeling of an elegy – 'as if the orchestra is keening for lost souls' – and it should build up little by little to the final moments. Superficially, the finale lights up and celebrates victory in a blaze of C major. But that C major is so hard-won, and the victory within it is so hollow that, Mark Elder says, 'to me it suggests the Russian people, tears streaming down their faces, pushed to the last borders of survival and sanity'. The conductor has to make sure that the end is not exhilarating, but moving, 'so that the whole orchestra seems to speak for the whole people', and for Leningrad. 'No symphony mattered as much to a people, to a cause, as the Leningrad Symphony', Elder says, 'and no symphony may ever again carry the same gigantic emotional and political power.'

The drain on Eliasberg's energy was immense. This is a heroic work, aspiration on a large scale, written in big arcs of music, strong, singing and confident music. It needs a ferocity from the conductor, to inspire the orchestra to sustain its deep humanity, that seemed beyond his emaciated grasp. The adrenalin of playing in public would help to sustain the musicians during the premiere. But the Seventh was hell to rehearse. Working on mere fragments of music is taxing and exhausting, and the emotional temperature so vital to the piece is speedily ruined by the stop-start nature of rehearsals.

A major difficulty was that the conductor and orchestra had no contact with Shostakovich himself. 'We could not consult the composer and we had no idea how the other orchestras had built their performances', said the leader S. A. Arkin.* 'The character of the great composition and its pace were to a great extent a mystery. For young Eliasberg to get down and create an interpretation of a totally unknown and difficult piece of music was a great feat.' Arkin said that Eliasberg 'hungered to penetrate into the world of the composer' through the smallest traces and signs that had been left in the score.

He managed, too, to depict the 'inexorability in the fight of our people': and it was, of course, this persistence that German soldiers had come to know and to fear. 'Fierce discontent of the members of the orchestra, the harsh war conditions, the terrible ordeal that Leningrad was exposed to' – none of that was allowed to undermine his drive for his exhausted musicians to achieve the 'flawless'. And, in the most desperate moments, Eliasberg would tell his leader in ringing tones: 'You will remember this as the happiest moment of your life.'[2]

First, the score had to be copied. This was not New York. It had to be done by hand. The copyists – and Khodorenko, the Radiokom chairman, was specific – were 'elderly people who had not succumbed . . .

---

* Arkin was one of the heroes of the siege. He was credited with returning ration cards he found in the street to the owners, though his own children were starving at home.

Theirs was a feat, too.'* They worked until the light failed with pen and ink that they scrounged or made for themselves. The violinist Grigorii Fesechko was a copyist of parts for strings, working after performances and rehearsals. He made his own device for writing the note heads on paper with a thin copper tube. He sharpened the end of the tube at a special angle to make the note heads match printed ones as closely as possible. He put a small pipette on the top of the tube and a stopper made of cork. He used the pipette to fill the tube with ink enough to apply more than ten note heads. Treble clefs, accidentals, tails and some others he drew himself, and he used a ruling pen to draw staves, note stems and links. There is a completeness to his travails, for he copied the music, and he played it.†³

The Radiokom had realized in mid-June that its forty or so musicians were not enough. Eliasberg would need at least eighty to play the Shostakovich. The army agreed to release musicians serving at the front and with military bands. They were given special passes to get them past checkpoints and patrols searching for deserters: 'Permission to enter Leningrad to perform the 7th Symphony with Eliasberg.'

A wind ensemble was poached from a military orchestra. The regular musicians called the servicemen 'the Crew'. The French horn player M. T. Parfyonov was with the Lenfront orchestra. His military duties had been grim. 'I was ordered to report with a crowbar and a spade to dig out the mass graves at Piskariovskaya,' he recollected. 'It was a terrible spectacle.' He suffered pains in his legs when a collapsed roof caught

---

* Khodorenko singled out others for particular praise. The orchestra supervisor, A. R. Presser, took as much of the load off Eliasberg as he could. Concertmaster Arkin, the viola player Yasenyavsky, the trumpeter Safonov and the flautist Telyatnik made an experienced Old Guard. Political cover, equally essential, came from the secretary of the Party city committee, Makhanov, who worked closely with the Arts Committee's B. Y. Zagursky. The head of the Lenfront ensemble, A. Y. Anisimov, also did 'an enormous job for us'.
† Fesechko, a scholarly man, survived to write brilliantly on Ivan Khandoshkin, St Petersburg's great eighteenth-century violinist and composer.

him during a bombing raid. He found his music, though, to be a saving grace and he was an enthusiastic army bandsman. 'It is in people's nature to remember facts connected to life and creation. And, for all the tragedies we had in the war, I could never forget how I brought sixteen musicians to the Seventh.'[4]

Another French horn player, Y. Pavlov, recalled how he was on his way to the Radiokom from his military band when he saw an old lady with a walking stick. She was leaning against the wall of a building. He asked her: 'May I help you, Granny?' She replied faintly: 'Granny? I'm only nineteen.'[5] The flautist S. Karelsky was serving with the Lenfront brass band. He had been on burial duties, too.

The crisis in wind instruments eased when the band of the Leningrad military district supplied thirteen brass and woodwind players. Others were scrounged from elsewhere. Captain Parfionov was the senior officer in the 45th Division's orchestra. He had studied at the Mussorgsky College in the city, and he was frustrated that 'all we ever got to play were short concerts during pauses between fighting'. His delight at being ordered to play with the Radiokom was short-lived. 'Rehearsals were from ten to one o'clock. No time for fun or to ask anyone who they were. We came, did our job and left,' he recollected. 'People were in a terrible condition. Often Eliasberg would have to repeat instructions two or three times before people could understand. We went over the same passage of music over and over, simply to get strong enough. To be honest, no one was very enthusiastic.'[6]

Those manning anti-aircraft guns left rehearsals when the sirens sounded. Others were called out for fire-fighting emergencies. Some died. 'Three, as I recall, including a flautist called Karelsky,' said Parfionov. 'People were dying like flies, so why not the orchestra? Hunger and cold everywhere. When you are hungry, you are cold however warm it is. Sometimes, people just fell over on the floor while they were playing.'[7]

A smattering of aged musicians insisted on playing. Zavetnovsky, the old first violinist of the Philharmonic Society, was emaciated but 'as trim and collected as ever'. The city's oldest musician, Nagornyuk, was in his seventies. He had played the French horn in orchestras conducted by Rimsky-Korsakov. His son had been demobilized with severe wounds, and pleaded with his father to be evacuated with him, but the old man refused. He had to play the Seventh. But the orchestra was still under-manned. On 21 July the Radio Committee instructed the director of the Astoria to provide a room for seven musicians who 'were assigned by the Political Management of the Leningrad Front to perform in the premiere of the 7th Symphony'. The seven were taken straight out of the front line.

One of them was a trombonist, M. Smolyak. Before the war, he played in a dance band at the Rot Front cinema in Dnepropetrovsk. He joined an NKVD division as a machine-gunner and was wounded in mid-August fighting at Narva, the nearest Estonian city to Leningrad. He was transferred to a construction brigade after he recovered. In late July, he was astonished to receive a formal duty order certificate. 'I was detached from the army and put under the orders of the chairman of the Radiokomitet to perform in the Seventh Symphony by D. D. Shostakovich. Once again, I was "armed" with the trombone.'[8]

Music was the only sliver of sunlight in a darkness that was welling again. A performance of *Carmen* in the Philharmonia on 1 July sold out. The Radiokom choir was accompanied by the symphony orchestra. The Spanish Dance was performed by the inexhaustible Olga Iordan. But singers with dystrophy and swollen feet who could hardly move lined the side of the stage.

The same day, police began re-registering identity cards. It would take them three weeks. Their report revealed – to the few who were permitted to read it – a catastrophe in the hero city. The population had collapsed. There were 775,364 people left in the fifteen districts of Leningrad proper, 134,614 of them children of sixteen or less. Kronstadt was reduced to 7,633 adults and 1,913 children, and Kolpino to 4,417, of whom 272 were children. The total number of people receiving rations in greater Leningrad was 836,788.

The figure in October had been 2,371,000. The city had shrunk by more than a million and a half. Over the ten months, 100,000 had been drafted into the Red Army, and 813,000 had been evacuated. There had been 573,325 registered deaths, with perhaps 80,000 passing unrecorded. Since the siege had begun, some 653,000 Leningraders had died. This does not include the hundreds of thousands of military casualties, nor those who died outside the city limits.

Three of every four in the 1939 census had disappeared. One in three women, and one in seven men, remained. The balance between the sexes had gone haywire. There were 291 women for every hundred men. At prime child-producing age, matters were worse still. In late July 1942, there were 4,247 civilian men between 20 and 25 in the great city. The number of children in the first year of life was 30 times less than in 1939, and the decline among one-to-four-year-olds was 4½ times. Of the 180,000 children born in the abortion-banned baby boom of 1937 to 1938, only 32,000 remained in the city.[9]

The birth rate was 67 times down on pre-war. Only 62 babies were born in one month that autumn (October 1942), and that included two sets of twins. Marriages, 3,238 over the year, and divorces, down to 652, were respectively 12 and 17 times lower than in peacetime. That, too, showed how profoundly natural population patterns were disturbed.[10] A memo to the re-registration figures noted that 72,922 mothers had one child, 14,963 had two, and only 3,096 had three or more. The purges had started the decline in family life. The siege continued it at a gallop.

The official statistics of deaths in 1942 made no mention of dystrophy or war wounds. They were lumped together with avitaminosis, vitamin

SIEGE AND SYMPHONY | 467

deficiency, under 'others causes of deaths'. Heart disease, gastroenteritis, pneumonia and other pulmonary diseases and tuberculosis were listed, as were 587 murders and 318 suicides: combined, they accounted for less than half of those who died of 'other causes'.[11]

People were still dying in large numbers. In July, 15,716 died. It was an improvement on June's figure of 24, 672. It fell to 7,612 in August. By October it was down to pre-war levels at 3,518. But the dead were drawn from an ever-declining pool of the living: if women now made up more than two-thirds of deaths, it was because there were so few men left to die.

Evacuations reached a new pitch as fears of an imminent German offensive grew. The fall of Sevastopol was a body blow. Leningrad, home of the Baltic Fleet, had a fellow feeling for it as the home port of the Black Sea fleet. Young Krukov wrote on 9 July, the day that all resistance ceased: 'Exam in music school. I played very well. The events at the front are terrible. One town after another falls – recently we gave up Sevastopol. They say that they will start evacuating women with one child. At present it's a woman with two children.' He was an only child: he might be evacuated.

By now, German combat teams were assaulting the western suburbs of Voronezh in Operation Blau, the great summer advance by Army Group South on Stalingrad and the Caucasus. Already, the panzers had reached the Don. No cold, no snow or forests came to the Russian aid in the rolling steppeland and cornfields of the south. Tracked by German aircraft in the clear heat of high summer, Russian units, losing contact with each other, wandered until their fuel or strength ran out, and they clustered round a farm building or a stream bed to await the end. Sevastopol was a warning, to the German Sixth Army as it drove towards Stalingrad, of the nemesis that awaited them among the scorched bricks and ruined buildings of the great city on the Volga. But that was with hindsight. To the watching world, Sevastopol was a German triumph.

Hitler thought so. 'The Russian is finished,' he told his Chief of Staff, General Franz Halder, on 20 July. 'I must admit, it looks like it,' the cautious general replied.

There were ominous signs of a fresh German build-up in men and artillery around Leningrad. Hitler issued directive No. 45 to Field Marshal von Kücher, newly in command of Army Group North, and the Eighteenth Army's General Lindemann.* They were to prepare to capture Leningrad by early September. German reconnaissance aircraft were overhead most days, a sure sign of trouble to come. General von Manstein's Eleventh Army was ordered to move north from the Crimea for Leningrad. Four of his divisions were given priority on the rail network, and appeared on the Leningrad Front. They were followed by a mountain division. The fall of the great Black Sea port freed the German siege guns to batter Leningrad. Schwerer Gustav and Dora, the huge siege guns that had pounded Sevastopol, 1,350-ton monsters that hurled seven-ton shells over twenty miles, were mounted on railway flatcars and joined the traffic moving north. By the end of July, the Germans had amassed 21 infantry divisions, a tank division and an infantry brigade round the city.

City officials were rattled, and fearful, though they arranged a parade of German prisoners through the city to reinforce civilian morale. The Germans were marched down the Nevsky, 'unshaven, dirty, lousy, wearing jackets of ersatz wool', and vengeful women shouted: 'Give them to us! Give them to us!' Police and troops held them back.

---

* By contrast, Stalin's Order No. 227 seemed that of a beaten man, flailing round for scapegoats for the mounting disasters in the south. It blamed the defeats on 'panic-mongers and cowards'. He ordered that 'the commanders of companies, regiments, divisions and corresponding commissars and political workers abandoning combat positions without a senior commander's orders are traitors of the Homeland, and therefore such commanders and political workers should be treated as traitors of the Homeland.' That meant, of course, that they were to be shot. (David M. Glantz, *The Battle for Leningrad 1941–1944* (Lawrence, KS: University Press of Kansas, 2002), p. 211.)

Valerian Bogdanov-Berezovsky wrote of the new fear that the city would soon be stormed. A month before, he was working on a new opera, and confident. 'I thought about Fate,' he mused, and concluded that 'in spite of irreplaceable losses, the war has given me a lot in terms of shaping my character and personality.'[12] Now, he reported: 'Even those who were certain they would stay in Leningrad until the end have started to leave. I accept the idea of death. All my hopes are broken. There is no goal for creativity, no need for it, in this kingdom of hatred and callousness which now possesses the world.'[13]

More and more people were trying to sell their possessions in the streets. There were few buyers, except for gramophone records, snapped up by officers visiting from the front.

Those whose loyalty the NKVD suspected, because of their ethnicity or bourgeois background, were removed to further reduce the population. Bogdanov-Berezovsky noted on 4 July: 'Tonight evacuation by emergency and by force of Lipatov. Tomorrow the same for Gan.' Both were composers. Vasily Lipatov had made the mistake of setting poems by Sergei Yesenin to music: Yesenin, who had been married to Isadora Duncan, had committed suicide in Leningrad in 1925, and his poems were banned.

The persecution of Finns and ethnic Germans continued. Many of the Finns who congregated near the Irinovskaya railway station had already been dispatched to Yakutia in the northern Siberian wastes. More than 80,000 remained, and they were accused of being a security risk. It was said that the Red Army men stationed around Irinovskaya had become too familiar with them. A good number of ethnic Germans were also still in the city. The Military Council resolved that they should undergo 'obligatory evacuation', to the arctic tundras of the Komi republic and to Archangel.

During document checks, the internal passports of 241,684 people were found to be flawed. Most were people with registrations that had expired or that were not valid for Leningrad. Others were evading conscription. The precision of this vast number was typical of the Soviet obsession with human stock-taking: its actual accuracy mattered much less than the semblance of it.

Another and more modest figure is no doubt close to the mark. NKVD statistics were brought up to date. Since the first days of the war, they had uncovered 1,246 'spies and saboteurs sent by the enemy'. They claimed to have unmasked 625 'counter-revolutionary groups', and in them they had found further 169 'spy-traitors'.

A total of 9,574 people had been arrested and 'repressed' – shot, sent to the camps, or deported – by special units of the NKVD. They included 31 'terrorists', 34 'rebels', 226 'nationalists', mainly Finns, Balts and Poles, and seven members from 'church sects'. The haul of scientists, professors and teachers from Leningrad institutions – embracing Izvekov and his 'circle', and also the Polytechnic Institute's Professors N. P. Vinogradov, L. V. Klimenko and V. S. Verzhbitsky, a distinguished physicist and academician – was put at a little less than one hundred.[14] All were found guilty of 'aiding the invaders'.

More mundane criminals were listed separately. There were 192,832 prosecutions for administrative violations in the first eight months of 1942. These ran the gamut from food speculation, muggings, thefts from stores and depots, and stealing ration cards to breaking sanitary rules.

Eliasberg and his orchestra were worked hard. They played the Fifth symphonies of Beethoven and Tchaikovsky in a concert broadcast from the Philharmonia on 4 July. A few days later, they performed a glorious medley of Mendelssohn, Strauss, Massenet, Verdi and Berlioz in the

Garden of Rest. That was followed by a radio concert of Mendelssohn's Italian Symphony.

The musicians resented the rehearsals for the Seventh. They complained that they were overloaded. Eliasberg demanded perfection, and they feared it was beyond them. He set a tone from the outset. Clear intonation, accuracy of rhythm, the intertwining and interrelating of timbres, unity of strokes in stringed instruments and breath in wind instruments were his constant concerns. He relied heavily on the experience of the few musicians he had – the cellist I. O. Bric, the oboist E. A. Yelizarov – who knew the peculiarities and traditions of symphonic composition and performance. Arkin agreed that he was a hard taskmaster, and that he was faced by 'serious annoyance and grumbling' over the way he instilled discipline.

The clarinet player Viktor Kozlov shared the fear that the Seventh was too long and too complex for them to cope with. 'We would start rehearsing and get dizzy with our heads spinning when we blew. The symphony was too big. People were falling over at rehearsals. We might talk to the person sitting next to us, but the only subjects were hunger and food. Not music.'[15]

Pavel Orekhov was a serving soldier as well as a French horn player. He felt himself close to collapse. 'The whole orchestra was strained,' he recollected. 'As well as our obligations as musicians, we had to search for saboteurs and looters, and arrest deserters. We knew that in an emergency, bridges and factories would be blown up, and we guarded them.' He was on liaison duties with Lenfront. He delivered top secret orders by hand to the most dangerous parts of the front, and guided troops into new positions. He had to gather up the propaganda leaflets dropped by German aircraft, and guard radio sets confiscated from the public. He found Eliasberg a persistent taskmaster. 'My lips could scarcely touch the horn, it was so cold, and Eliasberg himself was wrapped up in woollens,' he said. 'But he'd wait for me to blow.'[16]

They rehearsed every day except Sunday, sometimes twice a day, in the cold studios of the House of Radio. 'They gave us a little extra food in the canteen at the Pushkin Theatre,' the young oboist Ksenia Matus said. 'Not really soup, more water with a few beans in it, and a teaspoon of wheatgerm. We began playing small sections, slowly adding more. But we never played the whole thing until a dress rehearsal three days before the concert – the first and only time we had the strength to perform it from beginning to end.' Eliasberg was unyielding. She recollected the first trumpeter sitting with his instrument across his knees, too exhausted to play. 'You're not playing,' the conductor snapped. 'Karl Ilyich, I don't have the strength.' 'What do you mean, *you* don't have the strength? You think *we* have the strength?'[17]

Eliasberg attributed one brutal incident to his nervous state. He asked a musician why he was late for rehearsal. The man replied that he had been burying his wife. 'Make sure it's the last time,' the conductor snapped. Was this ruthlessness, he was asked? Or was it because death was too commonplace to use as an excuse, or because musicians were the soldiers of music and must obey and fight?

'I was excited and nervous,' he explained. 'Three of them were late. He was the last. By then, I could think of only one thing – that the people in the orchestra were not ready for the concert, and they had to be.' When he waved his baton, he felt, there were no bombs or shells, just music. He was giving back to the people something that had been taken from them. To him, moral dystrophy was worse than physical, because it was the death of the spirit, and it included unpunctuality.

But he had to keep within limits. The rehearsals were short. 'We rested more than we played', Matus said. Where he could, he worked a group, especially the violins. 'But with the wind instruments, flutes, oboes, and percussion, he worked on each musician's part separately.'

He was precise in all things. He knew the exact time it took to walk from the music store between Nevsky and Sadovaya to the Philharmonia. A musician recalled that he agreed to meet him there at 2.17 p.m. 'I was just a few seconds late, and I saw his back as he got on a tram and the doors closed. I was a bit sad and I mentioned it to Tatyana Vasilyeva, who ran the store. She just said, "Well, Eliasberg is Eliasberg."' He was at pains to be well turned out in public, the shirt front starched, the tails cleaned, the trousers pressed. With this elegance and the punctuality – people learned to be two or three minutes early for a meeting, and waited for the exact moment hidden round a corner – he became a reassuring legend. 'Is Eliasberg in bow tie and tails?' people asked. 'Yes.' 'Then all's well,' they said.[18]

Tensions grew so acute that the Arts Committee – the MAA – and the Radiokom prepared an order on 'the successful work of the symphony orchestra'. The musicians were told that they should be grateful to Eliasberg 'for his efforts for their artistic performance'. Leader Arkin and lead violinist Zavatnovsky were owed a debt of gratitude, too. There was a final warning: 'The MAA and the Radiokom trust that the orchestra will have a responsible attitude towards preparation for the 7th Symphony.'

That was a grim threat indeed, for the city's political masters were ruthless in their desire to see the symphony triumph.

Slowly, the musicians came round. 'We were weak and tired,' said Galina Yershova, the teenage flautist. 'It was difficult. Shostakovich's music is very complicated. I don't like it that much. But the Seventh was different. It came at exactly the right moment. It reflected what was happening. It showed the awfulness of the time, but the hope that was now alive was reflected in the music. We were very determined to play it well.'

They were aware of the rapturous reception the symphony was getting elsewhere. *Leningradskaya Pravda* reported on the 'deep impression' it had made on the big audience in London. They knew that Shostakovich had travelled to Novosibirsk to hear the Leningrad Philharmonia – of whom they were the poor relations – play it under his favourite conductor, Mravinsky. The paper reported: 'Success of Shostakovich's 7th Symphony in the USA.' The poet Carl Sandburg addressed the composer directly in a review in the *Washington Post* that had the Soviet propagandists purring with pleasure:

All over America last Sunday afternoon goes your Symphony No. 7, millions listening to your music portrait of Russia in blood and shadows . . . On a long battlefront sagging towards Moscow the Red Army fights against the greatest war machine that ever marched into any country . . . The outside world looks on and holds its breath. And we hear about you, Dmitri Shostakovich – we hear you sit there day after day doing music that will tell the story. In Berlin . . . in Paris, Brussels, Amsterdam, Copenhagen, Oslo, Prague, Warsaw, wherever the Nazis have mopped up . . . no new symphonies . . . Your song tells us of a great singing people beyond defeat or conquest who across years to come shall pay their share and contribution to the meanings of human freedom and discipline.

The music succeeded perfectly. It hid the camps and the interrogation chambers. The Soviets were not only civilized and cultured: they were also upholders of human freedom.

The regime made its satisfaction clear. The Military Soviet was preparing the city for the expected German onslaught. New pillboxes, machine-gun positions and tank traps were being built. The civilian population was being reduced as far as possible. But musicians were specifically forbidden to leave. The staff limits for the city's surviving musical institutions were exceptionally generous. The Musical Comedy was allowed to keep 270 staff, the Opera and Ballet Theatre 234. The Conservatoire retained 85 staff, the Philharmonia Hall 50, the eight children's music schools 37, and the Union of Composers 15.[19]

Orchestra members were excused the compulsory weeding that others had to do on allotments on the outskirts, where they were vulnerable to German shelling. They were, however, expected to collect fifty bricks apiece to help build the new defences.

Eliasberg conducted a brief radio concert – some Haydn, Mozart's *Eine kleine Nachtmusik* – on 25 July. After that, he and the orchestra concentrated entirely on the Seventh. On 2 August, he sent a cable to the head of the MAA in Moscow: 'The premiere of Shostakovich's Seventh will be on 9 August. Please assure your attendance and that of the composer if possible.'

The air link was still too dangerous for Shostakovich to be allowed to fly in. Eliasberg went ahead anyway. He gave a press interview, published on 7 August: 'All the preparatory work is over. The orchestra is busy now polishing the symphony. Shostakovich's work is specially precious to us Leningraders. Not just because he wrote it under bombardment and shelling, but perhaps it is because of that that he was able to express so deeply the vulnerable feelings of freedom, culture and happiness of the Soviet people.'[20]

A general rehearsal of the symphony was held at 8 a.m. on 8 August. A sell-out was assured. 'The event was unmissable,' said Tamara Korolevich. 'This music had been dedicated to us and to our city. Can you imagine the power of that?'

The die was cast.

CHAPTER 15

Simfonya Nr. 7

Symphony No. 7

It dawned chilly on 9 August, a Sunday. Nikolai Gorshkov recorded that it was 10 degrees at 6 a.m. with a clear sky. Artillery began firing at 9 a.m. After midday, thunder clouds appeared and it poured with rain at intervals. For him, it was a normal day: 'Nothing special happened.' A teacher, Zinkorov, was hoping to avoid military service. He was summoned to the military commissariat. He passed the medical, but was delighted to be considered of 'limited suitability'. 'They let me go in peace,' he confided to his diary. Foolishly, he added: 'How can it be explained? Maybe shortage of weapons. In town, you can often meet commanders who have revolver holsters filled up with cloth – and have no revolvers.' An NKVD interrogator was to come across that remark, and underline it, as 'defeatist'.[1]

Isfir Levin, an architect responsible for the camouflage of a sector of the front, noted that the Seventh Symphony of 'Shestakovich' was due to be played later in the day. He was briefly reflective. 'Life before the war is a different epoch, like childhood remembered without problems. Life after war – dream of incredible beauty – everyone has their own vision of it.' As for now, he found that dystrophy was still 'something very deep' in the soul of the city. People 'talk of nothing else'. A friend, Tatyana, 'speculates in food stamps' – a dangerous remark to commit to paper if the diary, as it did, was to fall into the hands of the NKVD – at a rate of 20 rubles for a grain stamp. She used them to get vegetables and to upgrade to workers' stamps. It was doing her little good. 'She's getting thinner and thinner.'[2]

The city camouflage team were having a rare day off. Eliasberg had personally invited Olga Firsova and Tatyana Vizel to the performance, in admiration of their courage. They managed to borrow two evening dresses – they were determined to be elegant as a mark of their defiance and femininity – and they spent the morning tuning their make-up. The team's Mikhail Shestakov and Andrei Safonov would be seated in the orchestra, their cellos adding lustre to the symphony. Next day, the four would be back on their ropes, clinging to another steeple and sewing on its protective cover.[3]

Half a world away, in rain storms and darkness, the Japanese sank four American heavy cruisers off Guadalcanal as US Marines clung on within their perimeter on the Pacific island. The monsoon had reduced the few roads and tracks in the wild and steep borderlands between Burma and India to quagmires. British troops waited, wasted with malaria and dysentery, for the Japanese onslaught to continue. At daybreak on the 9th, garrison troops in Bombay began to arrest Mahatma Gandhi and other nationalist leaders of the 'Quit India' movement. In North Africa, where Tobruk had fallen to the Germans, Lieutenant-General 'Strafer' Gott had been killed two days earlier when his aircraft was shot down. His successor as commander of the British Eighth Army, General Montgomery, had yet to arrive in the desert. Erwin Rommel, the brilliant Afrika Korps commander, was planning a new German offensive to drive towards the Suez canal.

Thirteen hundred miles south of Leningrad, units of von Kleist's First Panzer Army were smashing their way into the burning outskirts of Maykop in the southern Soviet oilfields. Manstein and five divisions of his men – morale superb after their victory at Sevastopol, 'extraordinary leadership skills, combined with personal bravery' instilling in them 'the belief that we could accomplish almost anything' – were en route for Leningrad with their heavy guns.

The city seemed in keener peril than ever. Hitler now wanted it stormed, in an operation code-named Nordlicht, 'Northern Light'. He was confident. The city, he declared over lunch on 6 August, 'must disappear utterly from the face of the earth. Moscow, too. Then the Russians will retire into Siberia.'[4] Manstein planned to break the Russian front lines to the south of the city with massed artillery and air strikes. Part of his force would then swing east, to cut off and destroy the Red Army units who were keeping the supply line from Lake Ladoga open. 'Thereafter,' the German field marshal added caustically, 'it should be possible to bring about the rapid fall of the city.'

The symphony was a flash of radiance in the gloom. To keep the German artillery at bay during the performance, the Russian guns were to lay down ferocious counter-battery fire. The Lenfront command, realizing the impact that the music would have on the world, protected it with 'symphonic artillery'. The planning, General of Artillery M. S. Mikhalkin said, was 'painstakingly hard'. Reconnaissance parties pinpointed the ammunition dumps for German guns within range of Arts Square. 'We even knew the surnames of some of the battery commanders.' In the morning, recalled M. S. Olshansky, the intelligence officer with the 14th Artillery Regiment, his gunners received 'an exceptional bulk of ammunition – three sets!' Olshansky's guns had been in action throughout the long retreat from the Polish border. He felt that for them now to roar in defence of the concert fulfilled some ancient myth.[5]

The artillery-fire chart for 9 August was drawn up by Lieutenant-Colonel Sergey Nikolaievich Selivanov. He came from Izmail, from an old noble family with a long military tradition. He was lucky to have survived the Terror: as, indeed, was his brother Vasily, a painter who had also danced over his aristocratic roots, and was now the chief TASS artist in the city, creating the giant posters that covered the facades of ruined buildings and empty storefronts. Selivanov, to be killed two years later by a direct hit from a heavy shell, was a Leningrader by adoption. He had graduated from the Artillery Institute in the city, with a particular brilliance in mathematics. His plan to suppress German artillery was meticulous. The Russian barrage was to commence at 5.30 p.m., half an hour before the start of the symphony.

Crowds began flooding towards Arts Square in the early afternoon. Soldiers came on foot from the front at Pulkovo. A group of women from the Sverdlovsky plant walked to the hall straight after work. A party propaganda worker – Nina Mikhailovna Zarubinskaya, whom they nicknamed 'Dolores Ibarruri' after the fiery communist orator in the Spanish Civil War – urged them to smarten themselves up before they set off. 'She said that some adjustments to our clothes wouldn't be amiss,' Eliza Petropavlovskaya recollected. 'We looked at each other. Indeed, we were a pathetic procession.' Hair brushed, blouses and skirts smoothed, they set off. It was a long way. Some lagged behind. A theatrical student, Ylyusha Olshvanger, kept up their spirits. She made sudden little jumps as she walked to make them laugh. She explained her theory of long-distance walking, cutting it up into stages. 'Are you walking far, walkers?' 'Yes. You bet.' 'First goal: walk to the crossroads. Close enough? Off you go then . . . Next is the lane . . . then – the grey building. You reached it!'

They arrived at the familiar entrance of the Philharmonia, jostled by people begging a spare ticket. The sky was a brilliant blue, the white columns were shining, and 'only this hall could have this peculiar philharmonic audience – people with dignity and restrained enthusiasm,' Eliza Petropavlovskaya thought. 'Indeed, you are special in this concert hall. It was a miracle, this 335th day of the siege. What is a miracle? A miracle is just the most sublime truth.'[6]

The crystal had long been removed from the eight great chandeliers in the hall. The bulbs in the chandelier frames were dimly lit, and a floodlight shone on the stage to give the orchestra a little extra warmth. The trombonist Viktor Orlovsky remembered people in the audience screwing up their eyes. 'They weren't used to electric light. But everyone was dressed up and some had even had their hair done. The atmosphere was so festive and optimistic.'

With half an hour to go, the Russian guns opened up. Vasily Gordeev, the chief of staff of the Krasnoselsky 14th Artillery Regiment, recalled it as a 'hailstorm of fire': 'We targeted the German batteries first, then their observation posts, and then their communications centres. In a nutshell, we targeted the enemy's fire management remorselessly. Then we targeted their headquarters and held them under continuous fire for a total of two hours and 30 minutes . . . The result? Not a single shell fell on the streets of Leningrad. The hailstorm covered the whole front. We ensured the performance of the Seventh.'[7] In fact, one German artillery unit continued to shell the city from a position between Pushkin and the Gulf of Finland. Artillerymen from a Guards regiment revealed their own position by using tracer shells to tempt the German unit into an artillery duel. Arts Square and the rest of the city were spared.

It was as well, because the square was overflowing. 'It seemed that the whole city had come,' Bogdanov-Berezovsky said. 'Many of them were an unusual sight at the Philharmonia, top military and Party men.' The commander of air defence mingled with powerful city committee members. Suddenly, the audience started to whisper: 'Marshal Govorov . . .' Everyone stared at the entrance door on the right. Officers stood up, and everyone else followed. The marshal walked in with his pretty wife. She 'looked as if she was at a ball in her pink satin dress covered with white lace.'[8] The grandees were seated in Box B, next but one to the orchestra, the Tsar's old box. Zhdanov was the only senior figure who was absent. He was said to be afraid of German shelling. 'In fact, if Zhdanov and his people wanted a concert, the orchestra had to go to the Smolny,' Krukov recollected. 'And they had to have detailed information on every member of the orchestra before they were allowed into the building.'[9]

The chairs in the upper floor had been taken away to make more room. The audience stood packed together. 'We were stunned by the number who had turned out,' the trombonist Mikhail Parfionov recollected. 'Some were in suits, some had come straight from the front. Most were haggard and emaciated. And we realized that these people were not just starving for food, but for music. We resolved to play the very best we could.' As she walked to the hall with her oboe, Ksenia Matus remembered 'feeling strangely happy for the first time since the blockade'. They were told to wear something dark. Women in the audience were in their best dresses, but 'they looked as if they were on hangers', everyone was so thin. As she got to the Philharmonia, she saw jeeps in front, with soldiers in boots and sheepskin jackets climbing out of them with machine guns.

'We couldn't wear concert outfits because we were so thin,' said the flautist Galina Yershova. 'We knew that Govorov had given this order to keep the Germans quiet. But then I heard the chandeliers shaking, and I was frightened. But it was our artillery. The doors of the hall were flung open, and we could see many people listening outside. Some were in infantry and naval uniform, with wound stripes and medal ribbons.'

The programme named 80 musicians, conductor Eliasberg, assistant to conductor Arkin, heads of wind orchestra A. Genshaft and M. Masolov, inspector of orchestra A. Presser and librarian O. Shemyakina. Lynd was to find ten errors when he fine-combed the programme after the war. Most were substitutions due to illness and death. In all, he found 27 musicians who had played in rehearsals but did not appear in the premiere. Twenty-five of them died of starvation. Two were military musicians, named Kats and Kutik, who were killed at the front.[10]

The notes quoted Tolstoy's February piece in *Pravda*: 'The symphony comes from the conscience of the Russian people who entered without hesitation into the battle against the forces of darkness, and in Leningrad it became world art which can be understood on every latitude and meridian, because it tells the truth about Man in years of great hardship and trial.'[11] It gave Shostakovich's dedication of his work: 'To our fight against Fascism, our forthcoming victory over the enemy, to my city, the city of my birth, Leningrad, I dedicate this symphony.'[12]

Olga Berggolts made out the nucleus of the orchestra on the huge platform of the Philharmonia. She saw the stalwarts of the Radio Orchestra: I. Yasinarsky, who had put out the first incendiary on the studio roof, the violinist A. Presser, commander of the fire-watching squad, A. Safonov and Y. Shakh, who had helped dig trenches near Pulkovo. Some musicians were in army tunics and naval pea jackets.

Karl Eliasberg mounted the rostrum, wearing a tailcoat that hung from his emaciated frame. He had preserved his conducting clothes carefully: his wardrobe was otherwise so bare that an appeal was made to the Lensoviet to supply him with a suit and a wool jumper, and a coat for Bronnikova.[13]

'Everyone stood up and applauded when Karl Ilyich came on,' Matus said. 'He had us stand up, and all this went on for a long time. And the symphony itself takes fifty minutes without a break. There's no time to catch your breath.' She wondered if they would get through it, and when the bombers would come. She waited for the air-raid sirens. She heard people say: 'Here they come, they're flying overhead.' She thought, 'Now it'll begin!' But it didn't.[14]

At 6 p.m., Eliasberg introduced the work in a speech that went out over the radio: 'Comrades, this is a great event in the cultural life of our city. It is the first time you will hear, in a few moments, the Seventh Symphony of our compatriot Dmitri Shostakovich. His symphony calls for strength in combat and belief in victory. The performance of the Seventh in the besieged city itself is the result of the unconquerable patriotic spirit of Leningraders. Their strength, their belief in victory, their willingness to fight to the last drop of blood and to achieve victory over their enemies. Listen, Comrades.'

He made no mention of Stalin, nor the Party.

After a few moments of silence, the Symphony began. 'It made the heart bleed – once again the pictures of the beginning of the war became alive. The faces of the musicians were unrecognizable. They resembled the images on ancient icons, parchment skin, stretched cheekbones but shining eyes set alight by inner creativity,' wrote V. A. Khodorenko. Then he asked: 'What gave us the strength, dear comrades? An additional portion of yeast soup? No! The spiritual victory of the music showed the world clearly and unconditionally that the strength of people who believe in a just cause is inexhaustible.'[15]

From the very first bars, Berggolts found, 'we recognized ourselves and the path we had trodden, the epic of Leningrad which had already become legendary: the ruthless enemy bearing down on us, our defiant resistance, our grief, our dream of a bright world . . . The orchestra was worthy to play this music, and the music was worthy of them, because it expressed all they have overcome.' She could hear through the wonderful music the 'subdued, calm and wise voice of its creator', and she remembered Shostakovich's words in September 1941: 'I assure you, comrades, in the name of all Leningraders, that we are invincible and that we are ever at our posts.'[16]

Listening in from the radio control room, the sound supervisor N. Belyaev was certain that this was a much greater event than just the premiere and a musical feast.* Thousands of Leningraders were also listening in on radio, and he felt that it bound them together in the hope of victory. He was later to re-broadcast the symphony, and to hear it performed by the best orchestras and conducted by the most prominent conductors. 'I have never again experienced the incomparable impression left by the performance on 9 August 1942, with Eliasberg at the conductor's stand and performed by the starving people who were my comrades at work, and with whom I kept vigil during the shellings and bombings that engulfed our dear city.'[17]

The writer V. Vishnezitsky noted: 'People were captivated, tears of deep feeling welled up in their eyes.' They had not cried over the dead bodies of their loved ones in winter, but now the tears came, 'bitter and relieving' and unashamed. It was a moment of catharsis, mingled with the sheer joy of being in the Philharmonia. The audience sensed a magnificence in the tattered job lot of musicians on stage. Olga Berggolts thought that 'Those people deserved to perform the symphony of their city, and the music was worthy of them because it conveyed all that they had lived through.' Vera Inber observed that 'The musicians were moved, and the conductor, too. As I listened to it, for me, it was all about Leningrad. The rumbling approach of the German tanks – there they were.'[18] To Nikolai Tikhonov, the symphony was 'quivering with excitement': 'Perhaps it was not so grandiose as in Moscow or New York. But in Leningrad it had something authentic, something that joined the storm of music with the storm of combat

---

* No recording survives of the 9 August performance. A later recording was made with Eliasberg conducting. The sound technician L. Spector recalled Shostakovich himself coming to the Radio House with Eliasberg to listen to it. 'I was startled by Shostakovich's modesty, his bashfulness. He looked as if he tried to occupy as little space as he could in the studio. And then I played the recording. When the first signs began to fill the room, I saw a totally different man in front of me. There he was, the great musician listening to the musical composition irrespective of who had composed it. The expression on his face hinted to me that the recording had been successful.'

around the city. It was born in the city, and perhaps only in this city could it have been born.'[19]

An artilleryman at the front listened to the loudspeakers that relayed the radio broadcast as the first movement built to a crescendo: 'My unit were now listening to the symphony with their eyes closed. It seemed as if a cloudless sky above us had become a storm, bursting with music.'[20] It was relayed live to the Germans, too, through Russian propaganda loudspeakers. Dzhaudat Iaydarov, the drummer whom Eliasberg had rescued from the morgue in March, drummed with such rage during the invasion theme that it seemed he 'held a fascist's horned helmet instead of a musical instrument'. His drumming was 'frightful in its stupidity – ruthless and senseless'. Zhaudat looked at the serious and attentive faces of the audience, and was happy that the spiteful invasion music failed to raise their fears. Instead, 'the listeners' eyes reflected hatred and determination to fight on'.[21]

Five minutes into the symphony, the trombonist M. Smolyak heard sounds of shelling. He had plenty of combat experience, and realized it was outgoing. 'I figured out: "That must be us." The cannonade increased as if in response to the orchestra's intensified forte. We understood that Russian artillery was protecting us. It gave us more strength.'[22] There was, the bassoonist Y. Y. Karpets said, 'a grandeur to the time, terrible but beautiful in its peculiar sense.'[23]

Eliza Petropavlovskaya was transfixed by the woman sitting in front and slightly to one side of her. She wore an austere dress and her greying hair was up in a tight plait with her fringe falling on her forehead. She mistook her for Anna Akhmatova, not knowing that the poet had been evacuated to Tashkent. Her companion whispered that she was mistaken, but she was still inspired by the resemblance: 'Looking at her profile and her face helped me understand the music better, which was full of jubilation, triumph and peace.'

Galina Yershova was elated as she played. 'We knew it was a historic moment. We were weak, exhausted, the Germans were very close. But it was a real sign of hope, this concert. We knew now that we could manage.'

The most nervous musician was the trumpeter Nikolai Nosov. He had survived great danger at the front. 'I remember taking a package to Forty-Second Army under heavy shellfire, jumping from ravine to ravine. It was a miracle that I lived,' he recollected. He had no background in classical music. 'When I found out that I, a former trumpet player in Utyesov's jazz band, was to play in the Seventh, I realized how difficult it was going to be.' He was relieved that Dmitri Chudnenko, an experienced musician who had been with the Muzkomediya orchestra, was playing the symphony's difficult trumpet solo. Then, to Nosov's horror, Chudnenko suffered a pulmonary oedema and was unable to play. The solo part was given to him, though the programme still credited Chudnenko.

At rehearsals, he found that 'I could not pull myself together for a very difficult part'. The solo trumpet depicted the invasion theme in pianissimo. 'I somehow played an extraneous note in the last phrase – the octave "re–re" – during every single rehearsal.' This had come to be normal. During the premiere, Eliasberg indicated the start of the prelude without even looking at Nosov. 'And then something unusual happened – the octave was played immaculately clean. Karl Ilyich turned to me and blew me a kiss,' the trumpeter said. 'Those were some incredibly happy moments in my life.'[24]

As the symphony neared its end, some musicians had given their all and started to falter. 'It was so loud and powerful I thought I was going to collapse,' the trombonist Mikhail Parfionov said. The audience spontaneously rose to its feet as if willing the orchestra on and revived them.

At the end, there was a moment of silence. It was broken by clapping at the back, and the ovation swelled into a thunder. A little girl brought Eliasberg a bouquet of flowers.* A note was pinned to them: 'With eternal thanks for preserving and performing symphony music in blockaded Leningrad. The Shnitnikov family.' The girl was an orphan, Lyubov Zhakova, who had been adopted by a family of that name.

'People just stood and cried and cried,' Eliasberg said. 'They knew that this was not a passing episode but the beginning of something. We heard it in the music. The concert hall, the people in their apartments, the soldiers at the front – the whole city had found its humanity. And in that moment we triumphed over the soulless Nazi war machine.'

'We were asked to leave immediately the applause ended. The Germans started a counter-barrage,' said Galina Yershova. But the audience lingered. The sisters Sofia and Ruzanna Lalayan, military surgeons taking a short break from an operating theatre at the front, were chatting in Armenian when the cellist Koiryun Ananyan overheard them. He told them how homesick he was, how he visualized the peak of Mount Ararat shining in the August sun with the valley at its foot drowned in vineyards. They arranged to send him a pack of tobacco, which he lacked, but he was dying. He had played with the very last of his strength.[25]

'The Seventh might have been performed better in some places but never has it been performed the way we played,' S. A. Arkin, the Leader, said. 'For the symphony was about us, the people of Leningrad, during the terrible ordeal, washed clean by our blood.'[26] The enthusiasm and rapture were 'universal' after the performance. 'The enemy was still close, but nothing could undermine the belief in the full and inevitable victory over him.'

---

* The flowers were grown by her grandfather, Zakhar Frenkel, a demographer and gerontologist, at the Svetlana factory in Leningrad. He survived to live to 100, clearly having followed the advice in his book *The Prolongation of Life and Active Old Age*, which he wrote during the Blockade and published in 1945.

The sentiment was far from universal. Many feared that Leningrad was about to fall. The Radiokom was given a bombed-out house on Gogol Street, and its able-bodied musicians were ordered to collect fifty bricks each from its ruins within three days, to build new defences for the expected assault. Within a few days, von Manstein, newly created a field marshal for his triumph in the Crimea, arrived and treated himself to a grandstand view of the city from a forward artillery position. He could make out 'the silhouettes of St Isaac's Cathedral, the pointed tower of the Admiralty, and the fortress of Peter and Paul'.[27] Soon enough, he thought, the city would be his.

Neither, it must be said, was there much truth in Bogdanov-Berezovsky's claim in his review in the next edition of *Leningradskaya Pravda* that this 'anti-fascist symphony' was a 'remarkable musical manifesto' made possible by a Soviet system that 'reflects human progress, a victory for culture, thought and freedom of character'. The system remained as inhuman as ever, as the dying wretches in the Kresty and the other red-brick prisons bore witness, and when the war was over, it would turn its terror once more onto Leningrad, and onto Shostakovich.

Yet the performance in the martyred city is perhaps the most magnificent, and certainly the most moving, moment ever to be found in music. Through it, the great city on the Neva retained its artistic soul, in the face of its attempted annihilation by Stalin and Hitler. Those who played showed a courage that gave comfort and confidence to an audience that, like themselves, had already passed far beyond what we might suppose to be their breaking point.

All that is best in humanity was seen, in those eighty minutes in the Philharmonia, to have survived all that the lowest and most cruel had flung at it.

Do svidaniya

Farewell

The siege was broken five months after the symphony was played. It was the Germans who were now besieged and bleeding, in the ruins of Stalingrad, and outside Leningrad the Russians were strong enough by winter to challenge them. The Russian front commander, Leonid Govorov, compared his men to the musicians of the Seventh. By the beginnning of January 1943, he said, 'all the men in our artillery orchestra knew their scores'. Four and a half thousand guns and mortars were drawn up on either side of the German-held corridor on the east bank of the Neva.

They opened fire on the morning of 12 January. At noon, Russian infantry began crossing the frozen river, retaking the Nevsky pyatachok, where so much blood had been spilled in failed assaults in the past. Eight miles to their east, the Red armies of the Volkhov front began their advance towards them.

The Russians were fighting in the streets of Shlisselburg by 15 January. They were within a mile of linking up. The town fell to them the next day. The distance between them was down to less than half a mile. The two Russian forces met on the morning of 18 January. The *Flaschenhals*, the German bottleneck, was smashed. That night, everyone was out on the streets of Leningrad. They were no longer an island people. They had rejoined the mainland. 'The cursed circle is broken,' said Olga Berggolts.

Though their stranglehold was gone – food and supplies could now reach the city along a land corridor – the Germans were not. They held their positions to the south and west of the city, and they continued to shell it for a year. A Red Army force of more than a million men, rich in heavy guns and rocket launchers, was gathered finally to expel them. The Germans could not withstand the fury of their assault. They retreated. The evening sky over the city on 27 January 1944 was lit with celebratory flares – greens, reds, yellows, magnesium whites – and searchlight beams from moored warships, and it echoed with the thunder of victory salvoes.

Govorov declared at 8 p.m.: 'The city of Leningrad has been entirely liberated.'

But it was not, of course. Zhdanov had not gone. Stalin's malevolence was aroused, not dimmed, by the city's heroic status. The Bolshoi Dom, and its apparatus, its interrogators and their chambers, remained.

Indeed, though the NKVD became the KGB, and in turn the FSB, and though Leningrad has returned to its origins as St Petersburg, the Bolshoi Dom still harbours the state security police, and dominates Liteiny Prospekt, to this day. Its most famous graduate, the ex-Leningrad KGB officer Vladimir Putin, is himself an echo from the violent past. Putin, President of what is once more Russia, owes his existence to the wound his father suffered in the Nevsky pyatachok, so serious that he was dragged back over the ice from the bridgehead, and thus survived the slaughter of his comrades.

As to Zhdanov, he laid out a doctrine of Soviet culture in 1946. The world, he said, was divided into two camps: the 'imperialist' one, led by the Americans, and the 'democratic' one, led by the Soviets. The arts must reflect this: nothing nuanced, nothing individual, nothing modern would be tolerated.

He attacked the literary magazine *Leningrad* for being, like the city itself, a fount of poison, citing two of its contributors for particular blame. Mikhail Zoshchenko, a writer of exquisite wit and irony, and a friend of Shostakovich, he described as a 'living corpse'; Anna Akhmatova, who dedicated poems to the composer, he dismissed as a 'whore and a nun', 'a slimy literary rogue'.

Music was next: Zhdanov, the man known as Beria's 'Pianist', had retained his interest in it. A decree in February 1948 attacked Formalism. It was 'bourgeois', Western, 'imperialist'. Shostakovich, Prokofiev and Khachaturian were singled out as practitioners. On 14 February, a long list of Shostakovich's works was removed from the repertoire by Glavrepertkom, the State Committee for Repertoire. The composer Marian Koval, editor of *Sovetskaya Muzyka*, denounced Shostakovich as 'Formalist vermin', oozing 'decadence' and 'cacophony'. In September, Shostakovich was driven out from his composition classes at the Moscow and Leningrad Conservatoires. He never taught again.

Stalin was nevertheless anxious to exploit Shostakovich's propaganda value, as the composer of the Seventh, at a cultural and scientific peace conference in New York in April 1949. When the composer pointed out to him that his symphonies were played in America but not at home, Stalin declared the ban 'illegal'. Shostakovich was duly dispatched across the Atlantic, to be greeted by Norman Mailer and Aaron Copland at the Waldorf Astoria.

He was no longer the magnificent fireman who had graced *Time*'s 1942 cover. The magazine now found him 'painfully ill at ease . . . he cringed visibly from the photographers' flashbulbs, mopped his brow'[1] He reminded the Russian émigré Nicolas Nabakov of 'dirty laundry washed, ironed out and sent to America'.

Zhdanov was dead by now, but the composer, and his city, remained vulnerable to terror. A new 'Leningrad centre' was uncovered by Beria, a 'nest' of 'anti-Soviet traitors', allegedly plotting to restore the city's old pre-eminence over Moscow, and their own over Stalin. Six city leaders, including the mayor, were accused of embezzlement and treason on 30 September 1950. They were shot the next day.

Two thousand members of the city and regional authorities were arrested, and hundreds shot, exiled or sent to the camps. Nikolai Punin, Anna Akhmatova's partner, art scholar, preserver of icons, had declared some portraits of Lenin to be tasteless. For that, he was sent to a freezing barracks amid the coal-mines of Vortuka, north of the Arctic Circle, where, after four years, he died.

The city's proud Museum of the Siege was closed. The fragments that remain – giant canvases, battle reconstructions, sculptures – illustrate the magnificence of what was destroyed. The heroism of the siege itself was written off as a myth designed to denigrate the grandeur of Stalin.

Stalin died in March 1953. Beria was arrested in June. He was interrogated in the Lubyanka, the place that, along with Leningrad's Bolshoi Dom, he had ruled for so long. He was shot, with a rag in his mouth to stop his screechings, on 23 December.

The daily prospect of arrest and oblivion eased a little for Dmitri Shostakovich. The strains imposed on him, though, and on countless others, were still obvious to a visiting American conductor in 1962. '[He] chews not merely his nails but his fingers . . . twitches . . . chain smokes . . . wriggles his nose . . . There is no betrayal of thought behind those frightened, very intelligent eyes.'[2]

He continued to work, his music as intense and broad-ranging as ever, until his death in 1975. Some see in the public appearances he made – like his New York trip, they were of undeniable propaganda value to the Soviets – a convinced defender of the regime. Others feel that the depths of his loathing for it are expressed in his compositions themselves.

A book, *Testimony*, by the Russian musicologist Solomon Volkov, emerged in New York in 1979. Volkov claimed it to be Shostakovich's memoirs, which he had transcribed and edited on his behalf. The composer, Volkov said, had not wanted it published in his lifetime. Small wonder. Shostakovich is revealed there as viscerally anti-Soviet, apparently acknowledging that many passages and allusions in his music directly reflect his revulsion at that regime.It may, or may not be, a genuine memoir. Argument and counter-argument still rage. Would a man with those eyes – with 'no betrayal of thought' in them – have spilled out his most intimate and dangerous feelings to a young man he did not know well? We may think not. Even if it is, in the literary sense, a 'fake', could it not also be that Shostakovich indeed felt this revulsion? We may think that he did.

In the end, perhaps, it does not matter. His music survives. So does the sense of his love for his city, his country, and his friends. For the rest – for what the Russians call '*intonatsiya*', a reading between the lines, in music and literature – let us leave him the last word, expressed to his Soviet biographer not long before his death:

'A lot has been written and is still being written about me. They write good things and they write bad things. But I have learned not to pay attention. Neither to the praise nor to the criticism. I have learned not to pay any attention whatsoever.'[3]

Notes

Chapter 1: *Repressii* Terror

1. John Biggar, 'The Astrakhan Rebellion', *Slavonic and Eastern European Review* 54, No. 2 (April 1976), p.240.
2. Simon Sebag Montefiore, *Stalin: The Court of the Red Tsar* (Phoenix: London 2004), p.115.
3. Elizabeth Wilson, *Shostakovich: A Life Remembered* (Faber: London, 1994), p.10.
4. Responses of Shostakovich to a Questionnaire on the Psychology of the Creative Process', prepared by Roman Ilich Gruber, trans. Malcolm Hamrick Brown, in Laurel E. Fay (ed.), *Shostakovich and his World* (Princeton University Press: Oxford, 2004) p.28 *et seq*.
5. Dmitri and Ludmilla Sollertinsky, *Pages from the Life of Dmitri Shostakovich*, trans. Graham Hobbs and Charles Midgley (Hale: London, 1981).
6. Wilson, *Shostakovich*, pp.11–12.
7. 'Responses of Shostakovich to a Questionnaire'.
8. Ibid.
9. Ibid.
10. Wilson, *Shostakovich*, p.70.
11. Ibid., p.67.
12. Neil Edmunds, *The Baton and the Sickle: Soviet Music and Society under Lenin and Stalin* (RoutledgeCurzon: London and New York, 2004), p.35.
13. Ibid., p.36.
14. Letter to Sollertinsky, 10 January 1928, in Wilson, *Shostakovich*, p.88.
15. Wilson, *Shostakovich*, pp.89–90.
16. 16 April 1925, in ibid., p.44.
17. Shostakovich to Lev Oborin April 1925.

18. Lesley A. Rimmel, 'A Microcosm of Terror, or Class Warfare in Leningrad: The Exile of "Alien Elements", March-April 1935', *Jahrbücher für Geschichte Osteuropas* 48 (2000), pp.528–51.

19. Fond 24 5 1963, Central Archive of Historical and Political Documents St Petersburg.

20. Sheila Fitzpatrick, *Everyday Stalinism: Ordinary Life in Extraordinary Times: Soviet Russia in the 1930s* (Oxford University Press: London and New York, 1999), p.125.

21. Rimmel, 'A Microcosm of Terror', p.528.

22. Fitzpatrick, *Everyday Stalinism*, p.48.

23. Rimmel, 'A Microcosm of Terror', p 546, fn 4 (citing the novelist 'I. Ivanov').

24. Ibid., p.528.

25. Sheila Fitzpatrick, 'Signals from Below: Soviet Letters of Denunciation of the 1930s', *Journal of Modern History* 68 (1996), pp.831–66.

26. Ibid., p.859.

27. Véronique Garros, Natalia Korenevskaya and Thomas Lahusen (eds.), *Intimacy and Terror: Soviet Diaries of the 1930s*, trans. Carol A. Flath (New Press: New York, 1995), pp.336–7.

28. Wilson, *Shostakovich*, pp.124–5.

29. Ibid., p.128.

30. Ibid.

31. Letter from Archangel January 28 1936.

32. Laurel E. Fay, *Shostakovich: A Life* (Oxford University Press: Oxford, 2000), p.121.

33. Wilson, *Shostakovich*, p.147.

34. Conclusions of the Main Judicial-Medical Laboratory of the Military Medical Administration attached to the Ministry of Defence, 28 June 1956. Skoblin .blogspot.com.

35. Skoblin Shvernik Report on the trial against Tukhachevsky and other members of the RKKA II, 28 April 2009. Skoblin.blogspot.com.

36. Vitaly Rapoport and Yuri Alexeev, *High Treason: Essays on the History of the Red Army, 1918–1938*, ed. Vladimir G. Treml, translated and co-edited by Bruce Adams (Duke University Press: Durham, NC, 1985), p.242.

37. Ibid., p.11.

38. Igal Halfin, *Stalinist Confessions: Messianism and Terror at the Leningrad Communist University* (University of Pittsburgh Press: Pittsburgh, PA, 2009), p.213.

39. Nadezhda Mandelstam, *Hope Against Hope: A Memoir*, trans. Max Hayward (Athenaeum: New York, 1970), p.4.

40. Brian Moynahan, *Claws of the Bear* (Houghton Mifflin: Boston 1989), p.77.
41. Wilson, *Shostakovich*, p.155.
42. Laurel E. Fay, *Shostakovich: A Life*, p.158.
43. *Izvestia*, 28 December 1938.
44. Laurel E. Fay, *Shostakovich: A Life*, p.102.
45. Ibid., p.103.
46. Katherine Bliss Eaton (ed.), *Enemies of the People: The Destruction of Soviet Literary, Theatre and Film Arts in the 1930s* (Northwestern University Press: Evanston, IL, 2002), p.22 n.
47. Alexander Solzhenitzyn, *The Gulag Archipelago* (Collins: London 1974) p.3 *et seq.*
48. MEMORIAL Historical, Educational, Human Rights and Charitable Society. St Petersburg Files.
49. R. A. McCutcheon, 'The 1936–37 Purge of Soviet Astronomers: An Emerging Soviet Perspective', *Bulletin of the American Astronomical Association* 20 (1988), p.985.
50. Francis Maes, *A History of Russian Music: From Kamarinskaya to Babi Yar*, trans. Arnold J. Pomerans and Erica Pomerans (University of California Press: Berkeley, CA and London, 2002), p.258.
51. Fitzpatrick, *Everyday Stalinism*, p.204.
52. Vsevolod Zaderatsky Jr., 'Vsevolod Petrovich Zaderatsky (1891–1953): A Lost Soviet composer', trans. Anthony Phillips, *International Centre for Suppressed Music* (online journal, posted 23 May 2006).
53. Denis Kozlov, 'The Leningrad Martyrology: A Statistical Note on the 1937 Executions in Leningrad City and Region', *Canadian Slavonic Papers* 44 (September–December 2002), pp.175–208.
54. Ibid., p.189.
55. MEMORIAL Historical, Educational, Human Rights And Charitable Society, St Petersburg. Felten file.
56. Ibid.
57. Fitzpatrick, *Everyday Stalinism*, p.94.
58. Ibid., p.95.
59. Timothy Johnston, *Being Soviet: Identity, Rumour, and Everyday Life under Stalin, 1939–1953* (Oxford University Press: Oxford, 2011).
60. Vitaly Shentalinsky, *Arrested Voices: Resurrecting the Disappeared Writers of the Soviet Regime*, trans. John Crowfoot (Free Press: New York, 1996), p.43.
61. Ibid., p.48.
62. Ibid., p.36.

63. Efraim Sicher, 'The Three Deaths of Isaac Emmanuilovich Babel', in Eaton, *Enemies of the People*, pp.179–204.
64. Edward Braun, 'Vsevolod Meyerhold: The Final Act', in ibid., pp.145–162 .
65. Ibid., p.157.
66. Laurel E. Fay, *Shostakovich: A Life*, p.117.

Chapter 2: *Voyna* War

1. Laurel E. Fay, *Shostakovich: A Life*, p.121.
2. Ibid., p.118.
3. Wilson, *Shostakovich* p.168.
4. Ibid., p.170.
5. Mikhail Ardov, *Memories of Shostakovich: Interviews with the Composer's Children and Friends*, trans. Rosanna Kelly and Michael Meylac (Short: London, 2004), p.68.
6. *Moscow Times*, interview with Roza Smushkevich, 16 March 2007. Although she gave 7 June as the date of her father's arrest, some accounts date it twenty-four hours later.
7. Galina Vishnevskaya, *Galina: A Russian Story*, trans. Guy Daniels (Hodder & Stoughton: London, 1984), pp.36–7.
8. Ibid., p.35.
9. Harold Eeman, *Inside Stalin's Russia: Memories of a Diplomat 1936–1941* (Triton Books: London, 1977), p.199.
10. Harrison E. Salisbury, *The 900 Days: The Siege of Leningrad* (Pan: London, 2000), p.5.
11. Isaak Glikman, *Story of a Friendship: The Letters of Dmitry Shostakovich to Isaak Glikman, 1941–1975*, trans. Anthony Phillips (Faber: London, 2001), p.xxxiii.
12. Dmitri and Ludmilla Sollertinsky, *Pages from the Life of Dmitri Shostakovich*, trans. Graham Hobbs and Charles Midgley (Hale: London, 1981), p.93.
13. Salisbury, *The 900 Days*, p.8.
14. Ibid., p.8.
15. Constantine Pleshakov, *Stalin's Folly: The Secret History of the German Invasion of Russia, June 1941* (Cassell Military: London, 2006), p.148.
16. Chris Bellamy, *Absolute War: Soviet Russia in the Second World War* (Macmillan: London, 2007), p.147.
17. David E. Murphy, *What Stalin Knew: The Enigma of Barbarossa* (Yale University Press: New Haven, CT and London, 2005), p.205.

18. Ibid., p.214.
19. Ibid.
20. Helmut Pabst, *The Outermost Frontier: A German Soldier in the Russian Campaign* (Kimber: London, 1957; reprinted 1986), p.11.
21. Alan Clark, *Barbarossa: The Russian-German Conflict, 1941–1945* (Hutchinson: London, 1965), p.36.
22. Salisbury, *The 900 Days*, p.121.
23. William Lubbeck and David Hurt, *At Leningrad's Gates: The Story of a Soldier with Army Group North* (Casemate: Drexel Hill, PA, 2006), p.85.
24. Richard Stites (ed.), *Culture and Entertainment in Wartime Russia* (Indiana University Press: Bloomington, IL, 1995), p.127.
25. Pleshakov, *Stalin's Folly*, p.151.
26. Brian Moynahan *Claws of the Bear, op. cit.* p.505.
27. Clark, *Barbarossa*, p.48.
28. James Lucas, *War on the Eastern Front 1941–1945: The German Soldier in Russia* (Bonanza: New York, 1982), p.35.
29. Bellamy, *Absolute War*, p.187.
30. Ibid.
31. Murphy, *What Stalin Knew*, p.225.
32. Ibid., p.226.
33. Pleshakov, *Stalin's Folly*, p.149.
34. Vishnevskaya, *Galina*, p.37.
35. Timothy Snyder, *Bloodlands: Europe between Hitler and Stalin* (Basic Books: New York, 2010), p.93.
36. Ardov, *Memories of Shostakovich*, p.15.
37. Karl Ullrich, *Wie ein Fels im Meer: 3. SS-Panzerdivision 'Totenkopf' im Bild* (Munin-Verlag: Osnabrück, 1987) p.100, quoted in Robert Kershaw, *War Without Garlands: Operation Barbarossa, 1941–42* (Ian Allen: Shepperton, 2000).
38. 'Idu zashchishchar' svoyu Rodinu' ("I am Going to Defend my Country"), *Izvestiya*, 4 July 1941.
39. Evgenny Lynd *Sedmaya, The Seventh* (St. Petersburg, 2005) p.20.
40. Elena Skrjabina, *Siege and Survival: The Odyssey of a Leningrader*, ed. and trans. Norman Luxenburg (Southern Illinois University Press: Carbondale, IL, 1971), p.12.
41. Hans von Luck, *Panzer Commander: The Memoirs of Colonel Hans von Luck* (Praeger: London, 1989), p.70.
42. Lubbeck and Hurt, *At Leningrad's Gates*, p.86.

43. Seweryn Bialer *Stalin and his Generals* (Westview Press: Boulder 1984), p.187 *et. seq.*
44. Simeon Putyakov diary.

Chapter 3: *Do serediny sentyabr'* To Mid-September 1941

1. Dmitri Shostakovich, 'Kak rozhdayetsya muzyka', *Literaturnaya Gazeta*, 21 December 1965.
2. Franz Halder, *The Halder War Diary 1939–1942*, ed. Charles Burdick and Hans-Adolf Jacobsen (Greenhill: London, 1988), p.346.
3. Williamson Murray, quoted in Bellamy, *Absolute War*, p.8.
4. Halder, *The Halder War Diary*, p.458.
5. Bellamy, *Absolute War*.
6. Katharine Hodgson, *Written with the Bayonet: Soviet Russian Poetry of World War Two* (Liverpool University Press: Liverpool, 1996), p.60.
7. Ibid.
8. Ibid., p.63.
9. Central State Archive of Historical and Political Documents, St. Petersburg. Fond (File) 7179, list 53, file 416, page 139.
10. Bellamy, *Absolute War*, p.294.
11. David M. Glantz, *The Battle for Leningrad 1941–1944* (University Press of Kansas, Lawrence, KS: 2002) p.58.
12. Anna Reid, *Leningrad: Tragedy of a City Under Siege, 1941–44* (Bloomsbury: London, 2011), p.83.
13. Vasily Grossman, *A Writer at War: Vasily Grossman with the Red Army, 1941–1945*, ed. and trans. Antony Beevor and Luba Vinogradova (Harvill Press: London, 2005), pp.33–4.
14. Ivan Sollertinsky, Munich Philharmonic programme notes, 15 December 2009, p.16, quoted in Verena Nees, 'The enigma of Shostakovich's Leningrad Symphony', World Socialist Web Site, 12 September 2012: www.wsws.org/en/articles/2012/09/shos-sl2.html.
15. Glikman, *Story of a Friendship*, p.xxxiv.
16. Marina Durnovo, *Moy Muzh Danill Kharms*, My Husband Daniil Kharms (Ima Press: St. Petersburg, 2005) pp.107–18.
17. Valeri Shubinsky *Danill Kharms: Life of the Man in the Wind* (Vita Nova: St. Petersburg, 2001.
18. Richard Bidlack, 'The Political Mood in Leningrad during the First Year of the Soviet-German War', *Russian Review* 59, issue 1 (January 2000), pp.96–111.

19. Sollertinsky, *Pages from the Life*, p.100.
20. Björn Jervas, 'Memoirs of a Panzergrenadier Veteran' www.feldgrau.com/articles.
21. Lisa A. Kirschenbaum, *The Legacy of the Siege of Leningrad, 1941–1995* (Cambridge University Press: Cambridge, 2006), p.25.
22. Glantz, *The Battle for Leningrad*, p.57.
23. Svetlana Magayeva and Albert Pleysier, *Surviving the Blockade of Leningrad*, trans. Alexey Vinogradov (University Press of America: Lanham, MD, 2006) p.14.
24. Cynthia Simmons, with Nina Perlina, *Writing the Siege of Leningrad: Women's Diaries, Memoirs, and Documentary Prose* (University of Pittsburgh Press: Pittsburgh, PA, 2002), p.23.
25. Ales Adamovich and Daniil Granin, *Leningrad under Siege: First-Hand Accounts of the Ordeal*, trans. Clare Burstall and Dr Vladimir Kisselnikov (Pen & Sword Military: Barnsley, 2007), p.55.
26. Ibid., pp.57–8.
27. Magayeva and Pleysier, *Surviving the Blockade of Leningrad*, p.10.
28. Bellamy, *Absolute War*, p.271.
29. Otto Preston Chaney, *Zhukov* (rev. ed., University of Oklahoma Press: Norman, OK, 1996), p.145.
30. Ibid., p.147.
31. A.N. Krukov *Muzyka v Dni Blokady*, ('Music in the Days of the Blockade'), (St. Petersburg, 2002).
32. Ibid., pp.11–15.
33. Simmons, *Writing the Siege*, p.23.
34. I. Rudenko, 'Razgovor s kompozitorom' ('conversation with the composer'), *Komsomol'skaya Pravda*, 26 June 1973 (p.4).
35. A. Ostrovskiy, 'V godinu ispïtaniy' ('In the Hour or Trial'), (Leningrad, 1962), p.392, quoted in Fay, *Shostakovich*, p.123.
36. Lynd, *Sedmaya, The Seventh*, pp.20–21.

Chapter 4: *Do serediny oktyabr'* To Mid-October 1941

1. Glantz, *The Battle for Leningrad*, p.75.
2. Salisbury, *The 900 Days*, p.284.
3. Glantz, *The Battle of Leningrad*, p.86.
4. Bellamy, *Absolute War*, p.276.
5. Lubbeck and Hurt, *At Leningrad's Gates*, p.101.
6. Ibid., p.102.

7. Olga Berggolts, '*This is Radio Leningrad': Password Victory 1941-42* (Moscow, 1985), p.346.

8. Valerian Bogdanov-Berezovsky, War Diary fragments (1941), quoted in Wilson, *Shostakovich: A Life Remembered*, p.172.

9. Sollertinsky, *Pages from the Life of Dmitri Shostakovich*, p.103.

10. Michael Jones, *Leningrad: State of Siege* (John Murray: London, 2008), p.119.

11. Krukov, *Muzyka v Dni Blokady, op. cit.*, p.27.

12. Ibid., p.24.

13. Jones, *Leningrad*, p.122.

14. Magayeva and Pleysier, *Surviving the Blockade*, p.43.

15. Josef Finkelshteyn (Finkelstein) Diary.

16. Stanislav Bernev and Sergei Chernov *Blokadnyje Dvevniki i Dokumenti Bolshoi Dom Arkhiv Bolshogo Doma* (St Petersburg, 2007), p.23.

17. Ardov, *Memories of Shostakovich*, pp.16–17.

18. Jones, *Leningrad*, p.122.

19. Glantz, *The Battle for Leningrad*, p.39.

20. Jones, *Leningrad*, p.123.

21. Edgar Alcidi, *Along the Neva: German Paratroops of the 1st Battalion*, 3rd *Fallschirm-jäger Regiment on the Russian Front: September–November 1941* (Schiffer: Atglen, PA, 2010), p.39.

22. Lubbeck and Hurt, *At Leningrad's Gates*, p.104.

23. Krukov, *Muzyka v Dni Blokady, op. cit.*, pp.28–9.

24. Ibid., p.37.

25. Irina Reznikova(Flige), *Repressii v period blokadi Leningrada*, (Repression during the period of the Leningrad Blockade), (St Petersburg, 2010).

26. Berlinka's file. Memorial Society, St. Petersburg.

27. Lubbeck and Hurt, *At Leningrad's Gates*, p.106.

28. Ibid., p.113.

29. Ibid.

30. John Barber and Andrei Dzeniskevich (eds.), *Life and Death in Besieged Leningrad, 1941–44* (Palgrave Macmillan: Basingstoke, 2005), p.1.

Chapter 5: *Oktyabr'* October 1941

1. Dmitri Shostakovich, 'Moya Sed'maya simfoniya' ('My Seventh Symphony'), *Vechernyaya Moskva*, 8 October 1941.

2. Boris Khaykin, *Discourses on Conducting* (Moscow, 1984), p.98.

3. V. S. Khristoforov *et al.*, *Lubyanka in the Days of the Battle of Moscow* (Moscow, 2002).

4. Lubbeck and Hurt, *At Leningrad's Gates*.

5. Helene Keyssar and Vladimir Pozner (eds.), *Remembering War: A U.S.-Soviet Dialogue* (Oxford University Press: New York, 1990), p.171.

6. Wilson, *Shostakovich: A Life Remembered*, p.17.

7. Rodric Braithwaite, *Moscow 1941: A City and its People at War* (rev. ed., Profile: London, 2007) pp.245–6.

8. Ibid., p.250.

9. Wilson, *Shostakovich: A Life Remembered*, p.151.

10. Keyssar and Pozner, *Remembering War*, p.172.

11. Murphy, *What Stalin Knew*, p.236.

12. Ibid.

13. Hodgson, *Written with the Bayonet*, p.65.

14. Jones, *Leningrad*, p.121.

15. A. V. Burov, *Blokade den'za dnem: 22 iunia 1941 goda 27 ianvaria 1944* (The Blockade: 22 June 1941–27 January 1944), (Leningrad, 1979).

16. Glantz, *The Battle for Leningrad*, p.93.

17. Jones, *Leningrad*, p.136.

18. Bellamy, *Absolute War*, p.297.

19. Wilson, *Shostakovich: A Life Remembered*, p.152.

20. Nikolai Sokolov, *Nabroski po pamyati (Sketches from Memory)* (Moscow, 1987), pp.54–7, quoted in Wilson, *Shostakovich: A Life Remembered*, pp.150–54.

21. Glantz, *The Battle for Leningrad* p.44.

22. Krukov, *Muzyka v Dni Blokady, op. cit.*, p.44.

23. Jones, *Leningrad*, pp.137–8.

24. Michael Parrish, *The Lesser Terror: Soviet State Security, 1939–1953* (Praeger: Westport, CT, 1996), p.72.

25. Alla Shelest, *Articles, Interviews, Diaries, Thought*, (St Petersburg, 2007), p.26.

26. Simmons, *Writing the Siege*, p.177.

27. Krukov, *Muzyka v Dni Blokady, op. cit.*, p.45.

Chapter 6: *Noyabr'* November 1941

1. Alcidi, *Along the Neva*, p.66.

2. Salisbury, *The 900 Days*, pp.385–6.

3. Berggolts, Password Victory, *op. cit.*, p.348.

4. Gerald R. Kleinfeld and Lewis A. Tambs, *Hitler's Spanish Legion: The Blue Division in Russia* (Eastern Front/Warfield Books: Philmont, VA, 1979), p.11.

5. Parrish, *The Lesser Terror*.

6. Salisbury, *The 900 Days*, p.398.

7. Ibid., p.397.

8. Krukov, *Muzyka v Dni Blokady*, *op. cit.*, p.56.

9. Barber and Dzeniskevich, *Life and Death*, p.38.

10. Ibid., p.217.

11. Ibid., p.38.

12. Krukov, *Muzyka v Dni Blokady*, *op. cit.*, p.62.

13. Shelest, *op. cit.*, p.28.

14. Ibid., p.26.

15. Kirschenbaum, *The Legacy of the Siege*, p.26.

16. Barber and Dzeniskevich, *Life and Death*, p.38.

17. Alcidi, *Along the Neva*, p.88.

18. Jones, *Leningrad*, p.139.

19. Albert Pleysier, *Frozen Tears: The Blockade and Battle of Leningrad* (University Press of America: Lanham, MD, 2008), p.133.

20. Clark, *Barbarossa*, p.151.

21. Grossman, *A Writer at War*, p.64.

22. Clark, *Barbarossa*, p.154.

Chapter 7: *Dekabr'* December 1941

1. Wilson, *Shostakovich*, p.156.

2. Clark, *Barbarossa*, p.153.

3 John Erickson, *The Road to Stalingrad* (Weidenfeld & Nicolson: London, 1983), p.275.

4. Bellamy, *Absolute War*, p.336.

5. Ibid., p.339.

6. Mikhail Ardov, *Velika Dusha: Vospominaniya o Dmitri Shostakovich [Great Soul: Memoirs of Dimitri Shostakovich]* (B.S.G.-Press: Russian Federation, 2008), pp.15–16.

7. Ibid., p.71.

8. Ibid.

9. Hasso G. Stachow, *Tragödie an der Newa: Der Kampf um Leningrad 1941–1944* (Herbig: Munich, 2003), p.43.

10. *Russia Today*, 10 May 2010.

11. Barber and Dzeniskevich, *Russia Today*.

12. *See* Irina Reznikova, *Repressii v Period Blokady Leningrada*, (Repression During the Leningrad Blockade) (Memoriala, 1995) pp.4–5.

13. Earl F. Ziemke, *The Red Army 1918–1941: From Vanguard of World Revolution to US Ally* (Frank Cass: London, 2004), p.290.

14. Kleinfeld and Tambs, *Hitler's Spanish Legion*, p.131.

15. Glantz, *The Battle for Leningrad*, p.109.

16. Dmitri V. Pavlov, *Leningrad 1941: The Blockade*, trans. J. C. Adams (University of Chicago Press: Chicago, 1965), p.140.

17. Ibid., p.151.

18. Kleinfeld and Tambs, *Hitler's Spanish Legion*, p.132.

19. Hasso, *Tragödie an der Newa*, p.44.

20. Ibid., p.45.

21. Barber and Dzeniskevich, *Life and Death*, p.42.

22. Classifications of the People's Commissariat and the Central Statistical Office of the USSR State Planning System.

23. Barber and Dzeniskevich, *Life and Death*, p.40.

24. Ibid., p.94.

25. Ibid., p.105.

26. Pleysier, *Frozen Tears*, p.91.

27. Barber and Dzeniskevich, *Life and Death*, p.42.

28. A. N. Krukov, *Muzyka v Aephire Voyennogo*, Leningrada (St. Petersburg, 2005), p.60.

29. Lynd, *Sedmaya*, *op. cit.*, p.99.

30. *Honourable Citizens of St Petersburg 1941–45* (St Petersburg, 2010), p.113.

31. M. M. Bobrov, *Khraniteli angela: Zapiski blokadnogo al'pinista Guardian Angel: Notes of a Blockade Mountaineer* (Izdatel'stvo universiteta prosoiuzov: St Petersburg, 1998).

32. TsGA SPb 9156/4/311,13; Barber and Dzeniskevich, *Life and Death*, p.41.

33. Hodgson, *Written with the Bayonet*, p.66.

34. Shelest, *op. cit.*, p.27.

35. Ibid., p.28.

36. Magayeva and Pleysier, *Surviving the Blockade*, p.61.

37. Ibid., p.54.

38. Pleysier, *Frozen Tears*, p.87.

39. Ibid., p.88.

40. Glikman, *Story of a Friendship*, pp.5–6.

41. Salisbury, *The 900 Days*, p.418.
42. Krukov, *Muzyka v Aephire Voyennogo*, p.357.
43. Pavlov, *Leningrad 1941*, p.148.
44. Barber and Dzeniskevich, *Life and Death*, p.42.

Chapter 8: *Noviy god* New Year

1. Wilson, *Shostakovich*, p.158.
2. Glinka, Chapter 17 p.126 *et seq.*
3. Vera Inber, *Leningrad Diary* (Hutchinson: London, 1971), pp 38–9.
4. Pleysier, *Frozen Tears*, p.92, quoted in Skrjabina, *Siege Survival*, pp.65–6.
5. Pavlov, *Leningrad 1941*, p.151.
6. Seventh pp.101–2.

Chapter 9: *Yanvar'* January 1942

1. Shostakovich, letter to Sollertinsky dated 4 January 1942, quoted in Fay, *Shostakovich*, p.129.
2. Glikman, *Story of a Friendship*, pp.7–8.
3. Lynd, *Sedmaya, op. cit.* pp.11–12.
4. p.93.
5. Magayeva and Plesier, *Surviving the Blockade*, p.77.
6. Ibid., p.78.
7. Ibid.
8. Ibid., p.80.
9. Lynd, *op. cit.* p.80.
10. Hodgson, *Written with the Bayonet*, p.79.
11. Reid, *Leningrad*, pp.319–20.
12. Lynd, *op. cit.* p.97.
13. Pavlov, *Leningrad 1941*, p.156.
14. Ibid., p.158.
15. A UFSB 12/2/19,164. Qu Cherepenina Barber p.48 and fn 96 p.69.
16. S. I. Voloshin from Zven'ya edited Ohotin and Roginsky (Moscow, 1991), pp. 45–46.
17. Salisbury, *The 900 Days*, p.493.
18. Glikman, *Story of a Friendship*, p.7.
19. Wilson, *Shostakovich*, p.158n.
20. Laurel E. Fay, Shostakovich, p.128.

21. Wilson, *Shostakovich*, p.162.
22. Ibid., p.166.
23. Ardov, *Memories of Shostakovich*, pp.21–2.
24. Wilson, *Shostakovich*, p.179.
25. Barber and Dzeniskevich, *Life and Death*, p.32.
26. Simmons, *Writing the Siege*, p.55.
27. Ostrovki Pamyati *Memoirs* (Galina Salyamon: St Petersburg, 2008) pp.41–2.
28. Blokadnie dnevniki I dokumenti Arkhive Bolshoi Dom, (Siege diaries and documents from the Big House), pp.339–94.
29. This statistic includes Leningrad's fifteen districts, and Kronstadt and Kolpino.
30. Stites, *Culture and Entertainment*, p.84.
31. Ardov, *Memories of Shostakovich*, p.23.
32. Ibid., p.109.
33. Ibid., p.108.

Chapter 10: *Fevral'* February 1942

1. D.I. Sh'apov, oral message, 23 May 1994: Archive of St Petersburg Science-Research Centre 'Memorial'.
2. Valery Shubinsky *Daniil Kharms*, p.502.
3. Kirschenbaum, *The Legacy*, p.295.
4. Glikman, *Story of a Friendship*, p.xxxv.
5. Magayeva and Pleysier, *Surviving the Blockade*, p.63.
6. Izvekov file. Memorial, St. Petersburg, trans. Konstantinos Konovovas.
7. Interview with author, Tatiana Izvekova, November 2010.
8. Ibid.
9. Wilson, *Shostakovich*, p.170.
10. Glikman, *Story of a Friendship*, p.8.
11. Wilson, *Shostakovich*, p.159.
12. Ardov, *Memories of Shostakovich*, p.34.
13. Victor Ilyich Seroff, *Dmitri Shostakovich: The Life and Background of a Soviet Composer* (Knopf: New York, 1943), p.240.
14. Simmons, *Writing the Siege*, p.178.
15. The Very Reverend Nikolai Ivanovich Lomakin, evidence to the Nuremberg Tribunal, 69th day (27 February 1946), (Nuremberg Trial Proceedings vol. 8, Yale Law School) p.24.
16. Krukov *op. cit.* p.363.
17. Shelest p.32.

18. Colonel I. Kh. Venets, former Commissar, 59th Independent Rifle Brigade www. volkhovfront.blogspot.com.
19. Pavlov, *Leningrad 1941*, p.163.
20. Ales Adamovich and Daniil Granin, *Leningrad under Siege* (Pen & Sword: Barnsley, 2007), p.168.
21. Glikman, *Story of a Friendship*, p.xxxvi.
22. Dmitry S. Likhachev, *Reflections on the Russian Soul: A Memoir*, trans. Bernard Adams (Akadémiai Nyomda: Budapest, 2000), p.266.
23. Simmons, *Writing the Siege*, p.101.
24. Kleinfeld and Tambs, *Hitler's Spanish Legion*, p.174.
25. Glikman, Story of a *Friendship*, p.9.
26. Conclusion to Izvekov File: Rehabilitation, 1955
27. NKVD Interrogation 15 February 1942. Boris Izvekov File, Memorial Society Archive, St. Petersburg. The NKVD file on Professor Izvekov includes his interrogations, trial convictions, sentence and eventual rehabilitation. The Memorial Society preserves documentation on political repression and its victims in the Soviet Union.
28. Diary of A P. Lyubovskaya. Comment by Alexis Pep.
29. Krukov, *op. cit.* p.365.
30. Salisbury, *The 900 Days*, p.509.
31. Simmons, *Writing the Siege*, p.123.
32. Ibid., pp.57–8.
33. Barber and Dzeniskevich, *Life and Death*, pp.223–4.
34. Magayeva and Pleysier, *Surviving the Blockade*, p.18.
35. Salisbury, *The 900 Days*, p.480.
36. Simmons, *Writing the Siege*, p.99.
37. Salisbury, *The 900 Days*, p.478.
38. Barber and Dzeniskevich, *Life and Death*, p.219.
39. Ibid.
40. Ibid., p.218.
41. Vospanimaia o Blokade St Petersburg 2010.
42. Inber, *Leningrad Diary, op. cit.* p.62.
43. Dated 5 March 1942: Barber and Dzeniskevich, *Life and Death*, p.76.
44. Ibid., p.78.
45. Michael Parrish, *Sacrifice of the Generals: Soviet Senior Officer Losses, 1939–1953* (Scarecrow: Lanham, MD, 2004), p.312.
46. Reid, *Leningrad*, pp.103–4.
47. Magayeva and Pleysier, *Surviving the Blockade*, pp.93–4.

48. Ibid., p.99.
49. Adamovich and Granin, *Leningrad under Siege*, p.125.
50. Nuremberg Trial Proceedings, *op. cit.* p.23.
51. Reid, *Leningrad*, p.249.
52. I. D. Yeolokhovsky, Independent 76mm Artillery Battalion, 59th Independent Rifle Brigade www.volkhovfront.blogspot.com.
53. Lieutenant-Colonel P.P. Dmitriev, former Platoon Commander, 6th Battery, 2nd Battalion, 894th Regiment, 327th Rifle Division. www.volkhovfront.blogspot.com
54. Reid, *Leningrad*, p.226.
55. Krukov, *Muzyka v Dni Blokady*, *op. cit.* p.125.

Chapter 11: *Mart* March 1942

1. Lynd *op. cit.*, p.109.
2. Ibid., p.99.
3. Simmons, *Writing the Siege*, p.148.
4. Lynd *op. cit.*, p.99.
5. Ibid., p.108.
6. Ed Vulliamy, 'Orchestral Manoeuvres', *Observer*, 25 November 2001.
7. See Eduard A. Tropp, Viktor Ya. Frenkel, and Arthur D. Chernin, *Alexander A. Friedmann: The Man Who Made the Universe Expand* (Cambridge University Press: Cambridge, 1993).
8. Halder, *The Halder War Diary*, p.608.
9. P.P. Dmitriev, former Platoon Commander, 6th Battery, 2nd Battalion, 894th Regiment, 327th Rifle Division www.volkhovfront.blogspot.com
10. Ibid.
11. Lubbeck and Hurt, *At Leningrad's Gates*, p.113.
12. Likhachev, *Reflections on the Russian Soul*, p.266.
13. p.127.
14. Ibid., p.128.
15. Magayeva and Pleysier, *Surviving the Blockade*, p.107.
16. Wilson, *Shostakovich*, pp.159–60.
17. Ardov, *Memories of Shostakovich*, p.18.
18. Ibid.
19. Richard Stites, *Culture and Entertainment in Wartime Russia* (Indiana University Press: Bloomington, 1995) p.69.
20. Glikman, *Story of a Friendship*, p.xxxxvii.
21. Ardov, *Memories of Shostakovich*, pp.18–19.

22. Salisbury, *The 900 Days*, p.506.
23. Adamovich and Granin, *Leningrad under Siege*, p.183.
24. *The Times* 7 March 1942 (dateline Moscow, 6 March).
25. Grossman, *Story of a Friendship*, p.10.
26. Simmons, *Writing the Siege*, p.179.
27. Ibid., p.80.
28. Krukov, *Muzyka v Dni Blokady, op. cit.* p.132.
29. Nurse T. I. Obukhova, 120th Medical Battalion, 112th Rifle Division www .volkhovblogspot.com.
30. Stites, *Culture and Entertainment*, p.85.
31. V. N. Sokolov, clerk, Personnel Section, HQ, XIII Cavalry Corps www.volkhovfront .blogspot.com.
32. Wilson, *Shostakovtch*, p.167.
33. Krukov, *Muzyka v Dni Blokady, op. cit.*, p.135.
34. Krukov, interview with the author, November, 2010.
35. Krukov, *op. cit.* p.367.
36. Magayeva and Pleysier, *Surviving the Blockade*, p.83.
37. Ibid., p.84.
38. Ibid., p.90.
39. Ibid.
40. Ilya Ehrenburg, *The Tempering of Russia*, trans. Alexander Kaun (Alfred A. Knopf: New York, 1944), p.189.
41. Lomakin, Nuremberg Tribunal, 69th day (27 February 1946), *op. cit.* pp 24–5.
42. Reid, *Leningrad*, p.306.
43. I. Kh. Venets, Commissar, 59th Independent Rifle Brigade www.volkhovfront .blogspot.com.
44. Sergeant-Major A. Gütte, 5th Company, 90th Motorized Regiment, 20th (Motorized) Infantry Division www.volkhovfront.blogspot.com.
45. Krukov, *Muzyka v Dni Blokady, op. cit.*, p.135.
46. Magayeva and Pleysier, *Surviving the Blockade*, p.113.
47. Krukov, *Muzyka v Dni Blokady, op. cit.*, p.138.
48. Ehrenburg, *The Tempering of Russia*, p.189.
49. Ibid., p.189.
50. W. Bruce Lincoln, *Sunlight at Midnight: St Petersburg and the Rise of Modern Russia* (Boulder, CO, 2001), p.289.
51. Ivan Martynov, *Shostakovich: The Man and His Work*, trans. T. Guyralsky (Philosophical Library: New York, 1947), p.105.
52. Reid, *Leningrad*, p.336.

53. Inber, *op. cit.* p.75.
54. Boris Goltz, *Complete Works for Solo Piano:* Sergei Podobedov, piano (Music & Arts, B0017RUBVS).
55. Lynd, *op. cit.* p.99.
56. Ibid., p.100.
57. Ibid., p.69.
58. Ibid., p.130.

Chapter 12: *Aprel'–Maj* April–May 1942

1. Simmons, *Writing the Siege*, p.149.
2. Ibid., p.144.
3. Ostrovki Pamyati Galina Salyamon St Petersburg 2008 p.54.
4. Salisbury, *The 900 Days*, pp.508–9.
5. Magayeva and Pleysier, *Surviving the Blockade*, p.24.
6. Vladislav Glinka, *Vospanimaia o Blokada* (Memoirs of the Blockade), (St Petersburg, 2010), p.220.
7. Barber and Dzeniskevich, *Life and Death*, p.51.
8. Glinka's diary was found by his heirs after his death. It was published unedited.
9. P.V. Rukhlenko, Battery Commissar, 1102nd Rifle Regiment, 327th Rifle Division www.volkhovfront.blogspot.com.
10. Grossman, *Story of a Friendship*, p.xxxix.
11. Information Bulletin, Embassy of the USSR, Washington DC, May 1942.
12. Glikman, *Story of a Friendship*, pp.xxxix–xlii.
13. Inber, *op. cit.* p.85.
14. Salisbury, *The 900 Days*, p.510.
15. Simmons, *Writing the Siege*, p.136.
16. Jones, *Leningrad*, p.265.
17. Commission of Investigation of Atrocities of the Nazi Invaders: Oredezhskiy Region, 9 March 1994 TsGAIPD SPb
18. Glantz, *The Battle for Leningrad*, p.148.
19. Boris Izvekov file. Memorial *op. cit.*
20. Lincoln, *Sunlight at Midnight*, p.157.
21. Allan B. Ho and Dmitry Feofanov, *Shostakovich Reconsidered* (Toccata: London, 1998), p.130.
22. Wilson, *Shostakovich*, p.182.
23. Ibid., p.183.
24. A. N. Krukov, interview with the author, November 2010.

25. Lynd, *op. cit.* p.44.

26. Ibid., p.100.

27. S.I.Voloshin Zven'ya 'Links' ed. Ohotin and Roginsky (Moscow, 1991) p.46.

28. Magayeva and Pleysier, *Surviving the Blockade*, p.95.

29. Lynd, *op. cit.* p.131.

30. Ibid., p.134.

31. V. N. Sokolov, clerk, XIII Cavalry Corps, Personnel Section, HQ www.volkhovfront .blogspot.com.

Chapter 13: *Iyun'* June 1942

1. Lynd, *op. cit.*, p.140.

2. Ibid., p.173.

3. Barber and Dzeniskevich, *Life and Death*, p.224.

4. Ibid., p.224.

5. Lubbeck and Hurt, *At Leningrad's Gates*, p.127.

6. Ibid., p.125.

7. Ibid., p.126.

8. Lieutenant-Colonel P.P. Dmitriev, former Platoon Commander, 6th Battery, 2nd Battalion, 894th Regiment, 327th Rifle Division. www.volkhovfront.blogspot.com.

9. Magayeva and Pleysier, *Surviving the Blockade*, p.88.

10. Lincoln, *Sunlight at Midnight*, p.292.

11. Ibid., p.181.

12. Glantz, *The Battle for Leningrad*, p.204.

13. Ibid.

14. He fought to the end of the war and reached the rank of Lieutenant-Colonel. www.volkhovfront.blogspot.com.

15. Glantz, *The Battle for Leningrad*, p.204.

16. I. D. Yelokhovskiy, Platoon Commander, Independent 76mm Artillery Battalion, 59th Independent Rifle Brigade. www.volkhovfront.blogspot.com.

17. P. I. Sotnik, Commissar, 100th Cavalry Regiment, 25th Cavalry Division. www .volkhovfront.blogspot.com.

18. Sergeant-Major A. Gütte, 5th Company, 90th Motorized Regiment, 20th (Motorized) Infantry Division (Der Landser, Nr. 1073). www.volkhovfront.blogspot.com.

19. Lubbeck and Hurt, *At Leningrad's Gates*, p.128.

20. *New York Times*, 21 June 1942.

21. Ibid.

22. *New Yorker*, 18 July 1942 (p.9).

23. Christopher H. Gibbs, in Fay (ed.), *Shostakovich and his World*, p.70.
24. Information Bulletin, Embassy of the USSR, Washington, Summer 1942.
25. NY Philharmonic archives 18 September 1942.
26. Ibid., 9 September 1942.
27. Linton Martin, *Philadelphia Inquirer*, 28 November 1942.
28. Fay, *Shostakovich and his World*, p.77.
29. *Minneapolis Morning Tribune*, 27 November 1942.
30. Salisbury, *The 900 Days*, p.536.
31. Major-General I. M. Antyufeev, Commander, 327th Rifle Division. www .volkhovfront.blogspot.com.

Chapter 14: *Iyul'* July 1942

1.   Galina Eschove, interview with the author, November 2010.
2.   Lynd, *op. cit.* pp.79–82.
3.   Ibid., p.140.
4.   Lynd, *op. cit.*
5.   Ibid. p.118.
6.   Ed Vulliamy, 'Orchestral Manoeuvres', *Observer*, 25 November 2001.
7.   Ibid.
8.   Lynd, *op. cit.* p.111.
9.   Barber and Dzeniskevich, p.59.
10. Ibid., p.61.
11. ibid., p.64.
12. Krukov, *Muzyka v Dni Blokady*, *op. cit.*, p.182.
13. Ibid., p.190.
14. Reznikova (Flige).
15. Vulliamy, 'Orchestral Manoeuvres'.
16. Lynd, *op. cit.*, pp.44–6.
17. Simmons, *Writing the Siege*, p.150.
18. Lynd, *op. cit.*
19. Krukov, *Muzyka v Dni Blokady*, *op. cit.*, p.l98.
20. Ibid., p.202.

Chapter 15: *Simfonya No. 7* Symphony No.7

1.   Dokumenty Bolshoi Dom Gorshkov Diary, *op. cit.* p.24.
2.   Ibid.

3. Lynd, *op. cit.* p.38.
4. *Hitler's Table Talk, 1941–1944*, trans. Norman Cameron and R. H. Stevens, with an introductory essay by H. R. Trevor-Roper (Weidenfeld and Nicolson: London, 1953), p.617.
5. Lynd, *op. cit.* p.61.
6. Ibid., pp.152–7.
7. Ibid., p.143.
8. Ibid., p.157.
9. A. N. Krukov, interview with author November 2010.
10. Seventh, pp.35–6 (translation by AS).
11. *Pravda*, Issue 47 (23 February 1942).
12. *Pravda*, Issue 88 [misprint for '48'] (26 February 1942).
13. Krukov, *Muzyka v aephire, op. cit.*, p.376.
14. Simmons, *Writing the Siege*, p.150.
15. Lynd, *op. cit.* p.98.
16. *Password Victory*, p.351.
17. Lynd, *op. cit.* p.l21.
18. Inber, *op. cit.* p.102.
19. Ibid., pp.203–4.
20. Jones, *Leningrad*, p.260.
21. Lynd, *op. cit.* p.129.
22. Ibid., p.112.
23. Ibid., p.133.
24. Ibid., p.117.
25. Ibid., p.161.
26. Ibid., p.82.
27. Jones, *Leningrad*, p.266.

Do svidaniya Farewell

1. *Time* magazine (4 April 1949).
2. Robert Craft (Stravinsky's artistic partner), quoted in Wilson, *Shostakovich*, p.376.
3. Shostakovich to his biographer Sofiya Khentova, *DSCH Journal* 13 (July 2000), pp.27–33 (p.28).

Bibliography

Adamovich, Ales, and Daniil Granin, *Leningrad under Siege: First-Hand Accounts of the Ordeal*, translated by Clare Burstall and Dr Vladimir Kisselnikov (Pen & Sword Military: Barnsley, 2007)

Akhmatova, Annav *The Complete Poems* (Zephyr Press: Boston 1992)

Alcidi, Edgar, *Along the Neva: German Paratroops of the 1st Battalion, 3rd Fallschirmjäger Regiment on the Russian Front: September–November 1941* (Schiffer: Atglen, PA, 2010)

Applebaum, Anne, *Gulag: A History of the Soviet Camps* (Penguin: London, 2003)

Ardov, Michael, *Memories of Shostakovich: Interviews with the Composer's Children and Friends*, translated by Rosanna Kelly and Michael Meylac (Short: London, 2004)

———, *Velika Dusha: Vospominaniya o Dmitri Shostakovich* [*Great Soul: Memoirs of Dimitri Shostakovich*] (B.S.G.-Press: Russian Federation, 2008)

Barber, John, and Andrei Dzeniskevich (eds.), *Life and Death in Besieged Leningrad, 1941–44* (Palgrave Macmillan: Basingstoke, 2005)

Bellamy, Chris, *Absolute War: Soviet Russia in the Second World War* (Macmillan: London, 2007)

Berggolts, Olga, '*This is Radio Leningrad*': *Password Victory 1941–42* (Moscow, 1985)

Bernev, Stanislas and Chernov, Serge, *Blokadnie dveniki i dokumenti Arkhiv Bolshogo Doma* (European House: St Petersburg, 2007)

Bialer, Seweryn, *Stalin and his Generals* (Westview: Boulder, 1984)

Bidlack, Richard, 'The Political Mood in Leningrad during the First Year of the Soviet-German War', *Russian Review* 59, Issue 1 (January 2000

Biggar, John, 'The Astrakhan Rebellion', *Slavonic and Eastern European Review* 54, No. 2 (April 1976)

Bobrov, M. M., *Khranitelli angela: Zapiski blokadnogo al'pinista* (St Petersburg 1998)

Boterbloem, Kees, *Andrei Zhdanov: The Life and Times 1896–1948* (McGill-Queen's: Montreal, 2004)

Braithwaite, Rodric, *Moscow 1941: A City and its People at War*, revised edition (Profile: London, 2007)

Burov, A. V., *Blokade denza dnem* (Leningrad, 1979)

Chaney, Otto Preston, *Zhukov* (rev. ed., University of Oklahoma Press: Norman, OK, 1996)

Clark, Alan, *Barbarossa: The Russian-German Conflict, 1941–1945* (Hutchinson: London, 1965)

Conquest, Robert, *The Great Terror: A Reassessment* (Pimlico: London, 2008)

Durnovo, Marina, *Moy Muzh Daniil Kharms* (IMA: St Petersburg, 2005)

Eaton, Katherine Bliss (ed.), *Enemies of the People: The Destruction of Soviet Literary, Theatre and Film Arts in the 1930s* (Northwestern University Press: Evanston, IL, 2002)

Edmunds, Neil, *The Baton and the Sickle: Soviet Music and Society under Lenin and Stalin* (RoutledgeCurzon: London and New York, 2004)

Eeman, Harold, *Inside Stalin's Russia: Memories of a Diplomat 1936–1941* (Triton Books: London, 1977)

Ehrenburg, Ilya, *The Tempering of Russia*, translated by Alexander Kaun (Alfred A. Knopf: New York, 1944)

Erickson, John, *The Road to Stalingrad* (Weidenfeld & Nicolson: London, 1983)

Fay, Laurel E., *Shostakovich: A Life* (Oxford University Press: Oxford, 2000)

———, (ed.), *Shostakovich and his World* (Princeton University Press: Oxford, 2004)

Figes, Orlando, *The Whisperers: Private Life in Stalin's Russia* (Allen Lane: London, 2007)

Fitzpatrick, Sheila, *Everyday Stalinism: Ordinary Life in Extraordinary Times: Soviet Russia in the 1930s* (Oxford University Press: London and New York, 1999)

Garros, Véronique, Natalia Korenevskaya and Thomas Lahusen (eds.), *Intimacy and Terror: Soviet Diaries of the 1930s*, translated by Carol A. Flath (New Press: New York, 1995)

Ginzburg, Lidiya, *Blockade Diary*, (London, 1995)

Glantz, David M., *The Battle for Leningrad 1941–1944* (University Press of Kansas: Lawrence, KS, 2002)

Glikman, Isaak, *Story of a Friendship: The Letters of Dmitry Shostakovich to Isaak Glikman, 1941–1975*, translated by Anthony Phillips (Faber: London, 2001)

Glinka, Vladislav, *Vospanimaia o Blokada* (St Petersburg, 2010)

Goure, Leon, *The Siege of Leningrad* (London, 1962)

Grossman, Vasily, *A Writer at War: Vasily Grossman with the Red Army, 1941–1945*, edited and translated by Antony Beevor and Luba Vinogradova (Harvill Press: London, 2005)

Halder, Franz, *The Halder War Diary 1939–1942*, ed. Charles Burdick and Hans-Adolf Jacobsen (Greenhill: London, 1988)

Halfin, Igal, *Stalinist Confessions: Messianism and Terror at the Leningrad Communist University* (University of Pittsburgh Press: Pittsburgh, PA, 2009)

Ho, Allan B., and Dmitry Feofanov, *Shostakovich Reconsidered* (Toccata: London, 1998)

Hodgson, Katharine, *Written with the Bayonet: Soviet Russian Poetry of World War Two* (Liverpool University Press: Liverpool, 1996)

Inber, Vera, *Leningrad Diary* trans. Serge Wolff and Rachel Grieve (London, 1971)

Jansen, Marc and Petrov, *Nikita Stalin's Loyal Executioner: People's Commissar Nikolai Yezhov* (Hoover: Stanford, 2002)

Johnston, Timothy, *Being Soviet: Identity, Rumour, and Everyday Life under Stalin, 1939–1953* (Oxford University Press: Oxford, 2011)

Jones, Michael, *Leningrad: State of Siege* (John Murray: London, 2008)

Kershaw, Robert, *War without Garlands: Operation Barbarossa, 1941/42* (Ian Allen: Shepperton, 2000)

Keyssar, Helene, and Vladimir Pozner (ed.), *Remembering War: A U.S.–Soviet Dialogue* (Oxford University Press: New York, 1990)

Khentova, Sofiya, 'Sofia Khentova talks to the DSCH Journal', *DSCH Journal* 13 (July 2000)

Khristoforov, V. S., *Lubyanka and the Days of the Battle of Moscow* (Moscow, 2002)

Kirschenbaum, Lisa A., *The Legacy of the Siege of Leningrad, 1941–1995* (Cambridge University Press: Cambridge, 2006)

Kleinfeld, Gerald R., and Lewis A. Tambs, *Hitler's Spanish Legion: The Blue Division in Russia* (Eastern Front/Warfield Books: Philmont, VA, 1979)

Kozlov, Denis, 'The Leningrad Martyrology: A Statistical Note on the 1937 Executions in Leningrad City and Region', *Canadian Slavonic Papers* 44 (September–December 2002)

Krukov, Andrei, *Muzyka v Dni Blokada*, (St. Petersburg, 2002)

——, *Muzyka v aephire voyennogo leningrada* (St. Petersburg, 2005)

Likhachev, Dmitry S., *Reflections on the Russian Soul: A Memoir*, translated by Bernard Adams (Akadémiai Nyomda: Budapest, 2000)

Lincoln, W. Bruce, *Sunlight at Midnight: St Petersburg and the Rise of Modern Russia* (Boulder, CO, 2001)

Lubbeck, William, and David Hurt, *At Leningrad's Gates: The Story of a Soldier with Army Group North* (Casemate: Drexel Hill, PA, 2006)

Lucas, James, *War on the Eastern Front 1941–1945: The German Soldier in Russia* (Bonanza: New York, 1982)

Luck, Hans von, *Panzer Commander: The Memoirs of Colonel Hans von Luck* (Praeger: London, 1989)

Lynd, Evgenny, *Sedmaya, The Seventh* (St Petersburg, 2005)

McCutcheon, R. A., 'The 1936–37 Purge of Soviet Astronomers: An Emerging Soviet Perspective', *Bulletin of the American Astronomical Association* 20 (1988)

Maes, Francis, *A History of Russian Music: From Kamarinskaya to Babi Yar*, translated by Arnold J. Pomerans and Erica Pomerans (University of California Press: Berkeley CA and London, 2002)

Magayeva, Svetlana, and Albert Pleysier, *Surviving the Blockade of Leningrad*, translated by Alexey Vinogradov (University Press of America: Lanham, MD, 2006)

Mandelstam, Nadezhda, *Hope Against Hope: A Memoir*, translated by Max Hayward (Athenaeum: New York, 1970)

Martynov, Ivan, *Shostakovich: The Man and His Work*, translated by T. Guyralsky (Philosophical Library: New York, 1947)

Montefiore, Simon Sebag, *Stalin: The Court of the Red Tsar* (Weidenfeld & Nicolson: London, 2003)

Moynahan, Brian, *Claws of the Bear* (Houghton Mifflin: Boston, 1989)

Murphy, David E., *What Stalin Knew: The Enigma of Barbarossa* (Yale University Press: New Haven CT and London, 2005)

Pabst, Helmut, *The Outermost Frontier: A German Soldier in the Russian Campaign* (Kimber: London, 1957; reprinted 1986)

Parrish, Michael, *The Lesser Terror: Soviet State Security, 1939–1953* (Praeger: Westport, CT, 1996)

———, *Sacrifice of the Generals: Soviet Senior Officer Losses, 1939–1953* (Scarecrow: Lanham, MD, 2004)

Pavlov, Dmitri V., *Leningrad 1941: The Blockade*, translated by J. C. Adams (University of Chicago Press: Chicago, 1965)

Petkevich, Tamara, *Memoir of a Gulag Actress* (Northern Illinois University Press: DeKalb, IL, 2010)

Pleshakov, Constantine, *Stalin's Folly: The Secret History of the German Invasion of Russia, June 1941* (Cassell Military: London, 2006)

Pleysier, Albert, *Frozen Tears: The Blockade and Battle of Leningrad* (University Press of America: Lanham, MD, 2008)

Pleysier, Albert and Magaeva, Svetlana, *Surviving the Blockade of Leningrad* (Oxford, 2006)

Pohl, J. Otto, *Ethnic Cleansing in the USSR, 1937–1949* (Greenwood Press: Westport, CT, 1999)

Rapoport, Vitaly, and Yuri Alexeev, *High Treason: Essays on the History of the Red Army, 1918–1938*, ed. Vladimir G. Treml, translated by and co-ed. Bruce Adams (Duke University Press: Durham, NC, 1985)

Reid, Anna, *Leningrad: Tragedy of a City Under Siege, 1941–44* (Bloomsbury: London, 2011)

Reznikova (Flige), Irina, *Repressii v period Blokadi Leningrada* (Vestnik Memoralia: St Petersburg, 2010)

Rimmel, Lesley A., 'A Microcosm of Terror, or Class Warfare in Leningrad: The Exile of "Alien Elements", March–April 1935', *Jahrbücher für Geschichte Osteuropas* 48 (2000)

Ross, Alex, *The Rest is Noise: Listening to the Twentieth Century* (Fourth Estate: London, 2009)

Salisbury, Harrison E., *The 900 Days: The Siege of Leningrad* (Pan: London, 2000)

Seroff, Victor Ilyich, *Dmitri Shostakovich: The Life and Background of a Soviet Composer* (A. A. Knopf: New York, 1943)

Shapalov, Veronica (ed.), *Remembering the Darkness* (Rowman and Littlefield: Lanham, MD, 2001)

Shelest, Alla, *Articles, Interviews, Diaries, Thoughts* (St Petersburg, 2007)

Shentalinsky, Vitaly, *Arrested Voices: Resurrecting the Disappeared Writers of the Soviet Regime*, translated by John Crowfoot (Free Press: New York, 1996)

Shostakovich, Dmitri, *Symphony No. 7 'Leningrad' Op. 60 (1941): Facsimile Edition of the Manuscript, with a Commentary by Manahir Yakubov* (Zen-On Music Company: Tokyo, 1992)

Shubinsky, Valeri, *Daniil Kharms* (Vita Nova: St Petersburg, 2008)

Siegelbaum, Lewis H., *Cars for Comrades: The Life of the Soviet Automobile* (Cornell University Press: London and Ithaca, NY, 2008)

Simmons, Cynthia, with Nina Perlina, *Writing the Siege of Leningrad: Women's Diaries, Memoirs, and Documentary Prose* (University of Pittsburgh Press: Pittsburgh, PA, 2002)

Skrjabina, Elena, *Siege and Survival: The Odyssey of a Leningrader*, ed. and translated by Norman Luxenburg (Southern Illinois University Press: Carbondale, IL, 1971)

Snyder, Timothy, *Bloodlands: Europe between Hitler and Stalin* (Basic Books: New York, 2010)

Sollertinsky, Dmitri and Ludmilla, *Pages from the Life of Dmitri Shostakovich*, translated by Graham Hobbs and Charles Midgley (Hale: London, 1981)

Solzhenitsyn, Alexander, *The Gulag Archipelago: 1918–1956*, translated by Thomas P. Whitney (Collins/Harvill Press: Glasgow, 1974)

Stachow, Hasso G., *Tragödie an der Newa: Der Kampf um Leningrad 1941–1944* (Herbig: Munich, 2003)

Stites, Richard (ed.), *Culture and Entertainment in Wartime Russia* (Indiana University Press: Bloomington, IL, 1995)

Tropp, Eduard A., Viktor Ya. Frenkel, and Arthur D. Chernin, *Alexander A. Friedmann: The Man Who Made the Universe Expand* (Cambridge University Press: Cambridge, 1993)

Tzouliadis, Tim, *The Forsaken* (Little, Brown: London, 2008)

Vishnevskaya, Galina, *Galina: A Russian Story*, translated by Guy Daniels (Hodder & Stoughton: London, 1984)

Volkov, Solomon, *Testimony: the Memories of Dmitri Shostakovich* (London, 1979)

Vulliamy, Ed, 'Orchestral Manoeuvres', (*Observer*, 25 November 2001)

Werth, Alexander, *Russia at War 1941–5* (London, 1964)

Wilson, Elizabeth, *Shostakovich: A Life Remembered* (Faber: London, 1994)

Zaderatsky, Vsevolod, Jr., 'Vsevolod Petrovich Zaderatsky (1891–1953): A Lost Soviet composer', translated by Anthony Phillips, *International Centre for Suppressed Music* (online journal, posted 23 May 2006)

Ziemke, Earl F., *The Red Army 1918–1941: From Vanguard of World Revolution to US Ally* (Frank Cass: London, 2004)

Acknowledgements

Transliteration: in general follows the Library of Congress system with traditional transliterations where these are more familiar.

I am deeply grateful to Nikolay, Tanya and Dmitri Yermolayev in St Petersburg for their invaluable input during the research and writing of this book. This embraced interviews, and appointments with muse- . ums, theatres and concert halls, archives and institutions. Dmitri Yermolayev also accompanied me on trips to the scenes of major events, both within and well beyond the city limits of St Petersburg, including, as well as the landmark sites of Dmitri Shostakovich and music in the city, the topography of the Terror, and the battlefields. Their knowledge of and enthusiasm for their native city was immeasurably enriching to the book, and their help has been unstinting. Special thanks go to Andrei Krukov, musicologist, and historian of music during the siege, to Irina Flige and the Memorial Society of St Petersburg, whose preservation of documents protects the victims of the repression from oblivion, and to Tatiana Izvekova, the granddaughter of Professor Boris Izvekov. Thanks are also owed to Oleg Sukhodymtsev of the Diarama Museum in the Nevsky bridgehead, Irina Muravyeva of the Museum of the Siege, Aleksandr Kolyakin, director, State Museum of the History of St. Petersburg, Olga Prutt of the School-Museum 'The Muses were

Not Silent', Oksana Morozan of the Central Archive of Cinema and Photography TsGAKFFD SPb, Lyudmila Mihailova of the Museum of Political History, Admiral Lev Charnavin of the museum-ship *Aurora*, Alexandr Belov, artist, the staff of the Central Archive of Historical Political Documents TsGAIPD SPb, the House of Radio, the Philharmonia Hall, Konstantinos Konovovas, Aleksandra Korsakova, Annabel Merullo and Tim Binding of PFD, to Ryan McMahon for his enthusiasm, and to my wife Priscilla for her selfless and unflagging support throughout a prolonged and difficult period. Sir Mark Elder, musical director of the Hallé Orchestra, provided insights into the Seventh that could only come from a conductor who has performed it. My editor at Quercus, Richard Milner, was a model of kindness, forbearance and patience, as was David North. This book would not have been completed without the skill and dedication of Professor George Hanna, and of Professor David Cunningham and Dr Gillian Ostrowski.

Index